Marketing Management

Third Edition

Greg W. Marshall
ROLLINS COLLEGE

Mark W. Johnston
ROLLINS COLLEGE

MARKETING MANAGEMENT, THIRD EDITION

Published by McGraw-Hill Education, 2 Penn Plaza, New York, NY 10121. Copyright © 2019 by McGraw-Hill Education. All rights reserved. Printed in the United States of America. Previous editions © 2015 and 2010. No part of this publication may be reproduced or distributed in any form or by any means, or stored in a database or retrieval system, without the prior written consent of McGraw-Hill Education, including, but not limited to, in any network or other electronic storage or transmission, or broadcast for distance learning.

Some ancillaries, including electronic and print components, may not be available to customers outside the United States.

This book is printed on acid-free paper.

56789 LKV 22 21

ISBN   978-1-259-63715-5
MHID   1-259-63715-8

Executive Portfolio Manager: *Meredith Fossel*
Lead Product Developer: *Kelly Delso*
Product Developers: *Alyssa Lincoln and Lynn Huddon*
Content Project Managers: *Melissa M Leick, Danielle Clement, Karen Jozefowicz*
Senior Marketing Manager: *Nicole N. Young*
Buyer: *Sandy Ludovissy*
Design: *David Hash*
Content Licensing Specialist: *Ann Marie Jannette*
Cover Image: *©kudla/Shutterstock.com*
Compositor: *MPS Limited*
Printer: *LSC Communications*

Library of Congress Cataloging-in-Publication Data

Marshall, Greg W., author. | Johnston, Mark W., author.
   Marketing management/Greg W. Marshall, Rollins College, Mark W.
   Johnston, Rollins College.
   Third edition. | New York, NY : McGraw-Hill Education, [2019]
   LCCN 2017048393 | ISBN 9781259637155 (alk. paper)
   LCSH: Marketing–Management.
   LCC HF5415.13 .M3699 2019 | DDC 658.8–dc23 LC record
   available at https://lccn.loc.gov/2017048393

mheducation.com/highered

To Patti and Justin.

-Greg

To Susan, my love, and Grace, my joy, thank you

-Mark

Greg W. Marshall

Greg W. Marshall is the Charles Harwood Professor of Marketing and Strategy in the Roy E. Crummer Graduate School of Business at Rollins College in Winter Park, Florida, and is also the academic director of the Executive DBA program there.

For three years he served as vice president for strategic marketing for Rollins. He earned his Ph.D. from Oklahoma State University and holds a BSBA and an MBA from the University of Tulsa. Before joining Rollins, Greg was on the faculty at the University of South Florida, Texas Christian University, and Oklahoma State University. He currently also holds an appointment as professor of marketing and strategy at Aston Business School in Birmingham, United Kingdom.

Prior to returning to school for his doctorate, Greg worked in the consumer packaged goods and retailing industries with companies such as Warner-Lambert, Mennen, and Target. He also has considerable experience as a consultant and trainer for a variety of organizations and has been heavily involved in teaching marketing management at multiple universities to both MBA and advanced undergraduate students.

Greg is editor-in-chief of the *European Journal of Marketing* and is former editor of the *Journal of Marketing Theory and Practice* and the *Journal of Personal Selling & Sales Management.* His published research focuses on the areas of decision making by marketing managers, intraorganizational relationships, and sales force performance. He is a member of the board of directors of the American Marketing Association and is past president of the AMA Academic Council. He is a distinguished fellow and past president of the Academy of Marketing Science and is a distinguished fellow, past president, and member of the board of governors of the Society for Marketing Advances. Greg also serves as a fellow and member of the academic advisory council of the Direct Selling Education Foundation.

Mark W. Johnston

Mark W. Johnston is the Alan and Sandra Gerry Professor of Marketing and Ethics in the Roy E. Crummer Graduate School of Business at Rollins College in Winter Park, Florida. He earned his Ph.D. from Texas A&M University and holds a BBA and an MB from Western Illinois University. Before joining Rollins, Mark was on the faculty at Louisiana State University. Prior to his academic career, he worked in industry as a sales representative for a leading distributor of photographic equipment. His research has been published in a number of professional journals including the *Journal of Marketing Research, Journal of Applied Psychology, Journal of Business Ethics, Journal of Marketing Education, Journal of Personal Selling & Sales Management,* and many others.

Mark has been retained as a consultant for firms in a number of industries including personal health care, chemical, transportation, hospitality, and telecommunications. He has consulted on a wide range of issues involving strategic business development, sales force structure and performance, international market opportunities, and ethical decision making. Mark also works with MBA students on consulting projects around the world for companies such as Tupperware, Disney, and Johnson & Johnson. He has conducted seminars globally on a range of topics including the strategic role of selling in the organization, developing an ethical framework for decision making, improving business unit performance, and structuring an effective international marketing department.

For more than two decades Mark has taught marketing management, working with thousands of students. His hands-on, real-world approach has earned him a number of teaching awards.

PREFACE

INTRODUCTION

No doubt about it, marketing is *really changing*. Marketing today is:

- Very strategic—customer-centricity is now a core organizational value.
- Practiced virtually, digitally, and socially to a greater degree than ever before imagined.
- Enabled and informed by analytics and new technologies.
- Accountable to top management through diligent attention to metrics and measurement.
- Oriented toward service as driver of product.
- "Owned" by everybody in the firm to one degree or another.

Given the dramatic changes in the field of marketing, it is a sure bet that the job of leading and managing marketing's contributions to the organization and its customers, clients, partners, and society at large has changed at a similar level. Yet the typical marketing management book on the market today does not effectively capture and communicate to students how marketing management is really practiced in the 21st-century world of business. We hear it from colleagues all the time—the complaint that the book they are using in their marketing management course "reads like marketing was practiced a decade ago," or that it "doesn't say what I believe the students need to hear," or that it "doesn't match what my working students actually do on the job," or that it "reads like an encyclopedia of marketing," or that it "has too much about everything and not enough focus on anything." These remarks come from instructors who teach the MBA basic marketing course and those who teach advanced or capstone undergraduate marketing management courses; each of these courses is appropriate for a marketing management book. Clearly many instructors are looking for a marketing management book that is:

- Written for today's students in an interesting and lively, yet professional, style.
- Up-to-date in all relevant aspects of how marketing is done today.
- A step up from the norm in terms of support materials for the instructor and students.

Marshall/Johnston's *Marketing Management 3e* continues its very successful tradition of taking great effort to represent marketing management the way it is actually practiced in successful organizations today. In our view, leading and managing the aspects of marketing in order to improve individual, unit, and organizational performance—**marketing management**—is a *core business activity*. Its relevance is not limited just to marketing departments or marketing majors. The ability to do great marketing management is relevant to, and an important knowledge and skill for, *everyone in a firm* and *all business majors*.

The table of contents for the third edition of the book reflects the major trends in the managerial practice of marketing, and the pedagogy is crafted around learning and teaching preferences in today's classroom. Above all, it is written in a style that is appealing for both students and instructors so that students will actually enjoy reading the material and instructors will be proud to teach from it and confident that they will feel good about presenting its up-to-date, professional approach to their classes.

The book contains 14 chapters, which we find is perfect for most course timetables. It has a fully developed array of application activities both in end-of-chapter materials and for student engagement on McGraw-Hill Connect. For instructors who craft their course around a marketing plan project, the book is ideal as these exercises clearly build on creating the elements of a marketing plan.

STRUCTURE OF THE THIRD EDITION

Marshall/Johnston's *Marketing Management 3e* has five major parts, reflective of the logical sequence of building blocks for the course.

- **Part One: Discover Marketing Management.** In this part, students gain an understanding of the dynamics of the field. Significant attention is paid to framing the importance of studying marketing to future success as a manager. In particular, doing marketing in a global, ethical, and sustainable way is highlighted. To kick off the marketing planning theme early in the course, Part One includes comprehensive coverage of strategy and planning along with an example marketing plan.

- **Part Two: Use Information to Drive Marketing Decisions.** It has often been said that information is the fuel that fires the engine of marketing management decision making. With this in mind, Part Two focuses on effective management of information to better understand customers, both in the consumer and business marketplaces. Market research elements, Customer Relationship Management (CRM), Big Data, marketing analytics, and marketing dashboards receive thorough coverage. Effective segmentation, target marketing, and positioning are at the core of successful marketing, and this part provides a modern managerial treatment of these critical topics along with other relevant competencies and capabilities of successful marketers.

- **Part Three: Develop the Value Offering—The Product Experience.** This part presents a clear and comprehensive drill-down into today's world of product strategy, branding, and new product development. Reflective of the rise of the concept of service-dominant logic in marketing and the notion that service is a key driver of product success, we devote a separate chapter to making important links between service and the overall value offering.

- **Part Four: Price and Deliver the Value Offering.** Part Four begins with a fresh, managerially relevant treatment of pricing decision making, followed by an integrative approach to the multitude of modes at a marketing manager's disposal today by which an offering can be made available to customers through channels and points of customer interface.

- **Part Five: Communicate the Value Offering.** With the rise of digital and social media marketing and the concurrent dramatic shifts in how marketing managers and their customers communicate, this part has been extensively revised for Marshall/Johnston's *Marketing Management 3e*. A key to successful marketing management today is the capability of marketing managers to create and execute the mix of digital, social media, and legacy promotional approaches most desired and preferred by customers.

KEY FEATURES

Management Decision Cases

At the end of each chapter is a case drawn from the business headlines. Students are engaged by the currency of the problem and asked to develop solutions using chapter material. The cases are just the right size for today's classroom use—not too short, but not too long!

Marketing Plan Exercises

Each chapter connects that chapter's key content to a semester-long marketing plan project activity. Marshall/Johnston's *Marketing Management 3e* is the only marketing management book to effectively thread a marketing planning focus throughout the textbook itself. Whether or not a semester marketing plan project is used by the instructor, the marketing plan exercise feature does a great job of tying together important planning concepts for students in a methodical, stepwise manner.

Glossary of Terms

A complete glossary of key terms and definitions is provided at the end of the book. The glossary serves as an important reference as well as a handy study aid for students preparing for exams.

Other Features in Each Chapter

- *Learning Objectives:* These set the stage at the beginning of the chapter for what students will achieve by reading and studying the chapter. Each objective reappears in the margin at the relevant point in the chapter so students can track their progress.

- *Summary:* At the end of each chapter, a summary reminds students of the highlighted topics.

- *Key Terms:* Terms are bolded throughout the chapter and connected with definitions in the Glossary.

- *Application Questions:* These engaging questions at the end of each chapter are designed to direct students' thinking about the topics to the next level of application. Throughout the book all of these questions have been specially designed to simulate managerial decision making.

NEW AND UPDATED CONTENT IN THE THIRD EDITION

Throughout this book, we've provided hundreds of new examples from a wide variety of practicing marketers and firms. Each chapter contains a brand-new Management Decision Case, and there are new and updated Application Questions at the end of each chapter. In addition, hundreds of new or replacement references have been added to the chapter end notes. Here are some highlights of specific changes, by chapter:

Chapter 1: Marketing in Today's Business Milieu
- Emphasis on the impact of the current "official" definition of marketing.
- New content around the major challenges facing marketing today.
- Coverage of the American Marketing Association's 7 Big Problems in Marketing.

Chapter 2: Marketing Foundations: Global, Ethical, Sustainable
- Updated discussion and examples of global marketing trends.
- Focus on the importance of ethical decision making in marketing and the marketing mix.
- In-depth coverage of sustainability and the "triple bottom line" in marketing.

Chapter 3: Elements of Marketing Strategy, Planning, and Competition
- Impact of marketing planning at the strategic business unit (SBU) level.
- Updated the JetBlue threaded marketing planning example.
- Updated the chapter appendix, which is an abbreviated example marketing plan.

Chapter 4: Market Research Essentials
- Updated coverage of new research methodologies with examples.
- Updated treatment of the marketing research industry.
- New content on data collection technologies.

Chapter 5: CRM, Big Data, and Marketing Analytics
- Updated discussion of the modern perils of potential customer information abuse and data security.

- Major new section on sources and types of Big Data.
- Major new section on marketing analytics as supported by Big Data.

Chapter 6: Understand Consumer and Business Markets

- Revised commentary on new trends in consumer and business markets.
- New and updated examples.
- Updated discussion of the consumer decision-making process.

Chapter 7: Segmentation, Target Marketing, and Positioning

- Updated census information for geographic segmentation.
- Extra emphasis on the millennial customer.
- Basics of CRM content moved from this chapter to earlier position in Chapter 5.

Chapter 8: Product Strategy and New Product Development

- New and updated content on product classifications.
- Revised and updated content to reflect changes in product strategy and new product development.
- Updated discussion on the product life cycle.

Chapter 9: Build the Brand

- Updated content about the most valuable brands today.
- Revised and updated content on brand definitions and concepts.
- Updated content around contemporary package designs.

Chapter 10: Service as the Core Offering

- New content on the service dominant logic.
- New content around the use of technologies to improve the customer service experience.
- Revised content to reflect changes in services strategy.

Chapter 11: Manage Pricing Decisions

- Revised table on price lining.
- Discussion of innovative pricing strategies.
- Discussion of pricing's role within the marketing strategy decision process.

Chapter 12: Manage Marketing Channels, Logistics, and Supply Chain

- Emphasis on the phenomenal growth of e-retailing.
- Attention to omnichannel retailing as firms deploy a number of channels in a customer's shopping experience.
- Enhanced treatment of customer communities.

Chapter 13: Promotion Essentials: Digital and Social Media Marketing

- New major section with full coverage of the role of digital marketing in communicating value.
- Clear delineation of types and approaches to digital marketing, including best practice tips and cautions for their use.
- New major section on managing social media marketing and engaging customers directly in the dialogue about a firm and its offerings.

Chapter 14: Promotion Essentials: Legacy Approaches

- Thoroughly revised discussion of legacy advertising tools to reflect changes in promotional strategy.
- Updated content on leading advertisers and the promotion industry.
- Updated and new content on crisis management.

ACKNOWLEDGMENTS

The task of writing a textbook requires the talents of many dedicated people. First and foremost, we want to thank the McGraw-Hill team for sharing the vision of this project with us from the very beginning. Particularly given the dynamic nature of marketing management both as a professional field and as a course of study, it was critically important that throughout the development process the entire team remain steadfast in believing in the vision of the project.

In particular, we want to recognize and thank the following individuals at McGraw-Hill who played a significant part in the successful development of *Marketing Management 3e*. Meredith Fossell, Executive Portfolio Manager, has been a visionary and strategic editorial leader throughout the project and we owe her a debt of gratitude for putting the project onto a great track. Lynn Huddon and Alyssa Lincoln, Product Developers, were instrumental in working with us daily to achieve this end result. Melissa Leick and Danielle Clement, Project Managers, were invaluable in keeping all elements of our product moving through production. And Nicole Young, Senior Marketing Manager, deserves high kudos for her excellence in communicating the value of our new edition to the marketplace. All of these great professionals made our job much more enjoyable. We have been McGraw-Hill authors for over 15 years and consider their team to be family.

Phillip Wiseman at the C. T. Bauer College of Business at the University of Houston provided able guidance and superior content in helping build the substantive revisions of Chapters 5 and 13. Phillip also led the process of developing new and updated interactive Connect exercises. His contributions to the third edition are exemplary. George Allen at the Howard Dayton School of Business at Asbury University and Andrew Thoeni at the Coggin College of Business at the University of North Florida did a masterful job in creating the new set of Management Decision Cases that add so much value to this new edition. Likewise, Jill Solomon at the University of South Florida developed the accompanying PowerPoints—she is truly an outstanding instructor of marketing management herself and that talent comes through in the materials she has created. In addition, we want to recognize the contributions of several members of the Rollins College Crummer Graduate School of Business team. Each of the following folks contributed to the plethora of great current business examples featured in this edition: Brandon Duncan, Richard Ross, Amy Crawford Weschler, and Courtney Wood. Courtney, along with Hannah Coyman from Crummer, also worked with Phillip Wiseman on the Connect interactives. We deeply appreciate the exceptional contributions of each of these individuals!

And finally, we want to offer a very special and heartfelt note of appreciation to our families, colleagues, and friends. Their encouragement and good humor throughout this process were integral to the end result.

Greg W. Marshall, ROLLINS COLLEGE

Mark W. Johnston, ROLLINS COLLEGE

REVIEWERS

Many colleagues have participated in the developmental process of Marshall/Johnston's *Marketing Management* from the first edition through this new third edition, via focus groups, chapter reviews, and other means. Our thanks go to each of the following people for their guidance and suggestions throughout this process:

Kalthom Abdullah, *INTERNATIONAL ISLAMIC UNIVERSITY OF MALAYSIA*

Denise Ammirato, *WESTFIELD STATE COLLEGE*

David Amponsah, *TROY UNIVERSITY MONTGOMERY*

Craig Andrews, *MARQUETTE UNIVERSITY*

David Andrus, *KANSAS STATE UNIVERSITY*

Maria Aria, *CAMDEN COUNTY COLLEGE*

Paul Arsenault, *WEST CHESTER UNIVERSITY OF PENNSYLVANIA*

Semih Arslanoglu, *BOSTON UNIVERSITY*

Chad Autry, *UNIVERSITY OF TENNESSEE–KNOXVILLE*

Parimal Baghat, *INDIANA UNIVERSITY OF PENNSYLVANIA*

William Baker, *SAN DIEGO STATE UNIVERSITY*

Roger Baran, *DEPAUL UNIVERSITY*

Danny Bellenger, *GEORGIA STATE UNIVERSITY*

John Bellenoit, *WESTFIELD STATE COLLEGE*

Parimal Bhagat, *INDIANA UNIVERSITY OF PENNSYLVANIA*

Subodh Bhat, *SAN FRANCISCO STATE UNIVERSITY*

Carol Bienstock, *RADFORD UNIVERSITY*

Diedre Bird, *PROVIDENCE COLLEGE*

George W. Boulware, *LIPSCOMB UNIVERSITY*

Douglas Boyd, *JAMES MADISON UNIVERSITY*

Samuel Bradley, *ALVERNIA UNIVERSITY*

Eileen Bridges, *KENT STATE UNIVERSITY*

Steve Brokaw, *UNIVERSITY OF WISCONSIN–LACROSSE*

Susan Brudvig, *INDIANA UNIVERSITY EAST*

Laura Buckner, *MIDDLE TENNESSEE STATE UNIVERSITY*

Tim Calkins, *NORTHWESTERN UNIVERSITY*

Barb Casey, *DOWLING COLLEGE*

Paul Clark, *COASTAL CAROLINA UNIVERSITY*

Bob Cline, *UNIVERSITY OF IOWA*

Cathy Cole, *UNIVERSITY OF IOWA*

Mark Collins, *UNIVERSITY OF TENNESSEE–KNOXVILLE*

David Conrad, *AUGSBURG COLLEGE*

Bob Cutler, *CLEVELAND STATE UNIVERSITY*

Geoffrey Da Silva, *TEMASEK POLYTECHNIC*

Lorie Darche, *SOUTHWEST FLORIDA COLLEGE*

Mahmoud Darrat, *AUBURN MONTGOMERY UNIVERSITY*

Patricia Daugherty, *MICHIGAN STATE UNIVERSITY*

Denver D'Rozario, *HOWARD UNIVERSITY*

F. Robert Dwyer, *UNIVERSITY OF CINCINNATI*

Jacqueline K. Eastman, *GEORGIA SOUTHERN UNIVERSITY*

Michael Edwards, *UNIVERSITY OF ST. THOMAS*

Adel El-Ansary, *UNIVERSITY OF NORTH FLORIDA*

Maurice Elliard, *ALBANY STATE UNIVERSITY*

Alexander Ellinger, *UNIVERSITY OF ALABAMA–TUSCALOOSA*

Ken Fairweather, *LETOURNEAU UNIVERSITY*

Bagher Fardanesh, *JOHNS HOPKINS UNIVERSITY*

Richard L. Flight, *EASTERN ILLINOIS UNIVERSITY*

Andrew Forman, *HOFSTRA UNIVERSITY*

Fred Fusting, *LOYOLA COLLEGE OF MARYLAND*

Jule B. Gassenheimer, *ROLLINS COLLEGE*

Mahesh Gopinath, *OLD DOMINION UNIVERSITY*

Shiv Gupta, *UNIVERSITY OF FINDLAY*

Liz Hafer, *UNIVERSITY OF COLORADO–BOULDER*

Angela Hausman, *UNIVERSITY OF NORTH CAROLINA AT PEMBROKE*

Jeffrey Heilbrunn, *COLUMBIA COLLEGE OF MISSOURI*

Chuck Hermans, *MISSOURI STATE UNIVERSITY*

Asep Hermawan, *UNIVERSITAS TRISAKTI*

Marjorie Carlson Hurst, *MALONE UNIVERSITY*

Mahmood Hussain, *SAN FRANCISCO STATE UNIVERSITY*

Donna Rue Jenkins, *WARREN NATIONAL UNIVERSITY*

Johny Johansson, *GEORGETOWN UNIVERSITY*

Amit Joshi, *UNIVERSITY OF CENTRAL FLORIDA*

Fred Katz, *JOHNS HOPKINS UNIVERSITY*

Craig Kelley, *CALIFORNIA STATE UNIVERSITY–SACRAMENTO*

Anthony J. Khuri, *BALDWIN WALLACE UNIVERSITY*

Vishnu Kirpalani, *CONCORDIA UNIVERSITY, MONTREAL, CANADA*

Elias Konwufine, *KEISER UNIVERSITY*

Robert Kopp, *BABSON COLLEGE*

Kate Lawrence, *CAMPBELL UNIVERSITY*

Sangwon Lee, *BALL STATE UNIVERSITY*

Michael Levens, *WALSH COLLEGE*

Jason Little, *FRANKLIN PIERCE UNIVERSITY*

Cesar Maloles, *CALIFORNIA STATE UNIVERSITY–EAST BAY*

Avinash Malshe, *UNIVERSITY OF ST. THOMAS*

Susan Mantel, *INDIANA UNIVERSITY–PURDUE UNIVERSITY–INDIANAPOLIS*

Norton Marks, *CALIFORNIA STATE UNIVERSITY–SAN BERNARDINO*

Thomas Maronick, *TOWSON UNIVERSITY*

H. Lee Mathews, *OHIO STATE UNIVERSITY*

Melvin Mattson, *RADFORD UNIVERSITY*

Denny McCorkle, *UNIVERSITY OF NORTHERN COLORADO*

Timothy McMahon, *CREIGHTON UNIVERSITY*

Michael Menasco, *CALIFORNIA STATE UNIVERSITY–SAN BERNADINO*

Morgan Miles, *UNIVERSITY OF TASMANIA*

Chad Milewicz, *UNIVERSITY OF CENTRAL FLORIDA*

Chip E. Miller, *DRAKE UNIVERSITY*

Herb Miller, *UNIVERSITY OF TEXAS*

Mark Mitchell, *COASTAL CAROLINA UNIVERSITY*

Thomas Noordewier, *UNIVERSITY OF VERMONT*

Nicholas Nugent, *SOUTHERN NEW HAMPSHIRE UNIVERSITY*

Carl Obermiller, *SEATTLE UNIVERSITY*

Azizah Omar, *UNIVERSITI SAINS MALAYSIA*

Barnett Parker, *PFEIFFER UNIVERSITY*

Vanessa Patrick, *UNIVERSITY OF GEORGIA*

Dennis Pitta, *UNIVERSITY OF BALTIMORE*

Jeffrey S. Podoshen, *FRANKLIN AND MARSHALL COLLEGE*

Abe Qastin, *LAKELAND UNIVERSITY*

Salim Qureshi, *BLOOMSBURG UNIVERSITY*

Lori Radulovich, *BALDWIN WALLACE UNIVERSITY*

Pushkala Raman, *TEXAS WOMAN'S UNIVERSITY*

K. Ramakrishna Rao, *MULTIMEDIA UNIVERSITY*

Molly Rapert, *UNIVERSITY OF ARKANSAS–FAYETTEVILLE*

Richard Rexeisen, *UNIVERSITY OF ST. THOMAS*

Subom Rhee, *SANTA CLARA UNIVERSITY*

Robert Richey, *UNIVERSITY OF ALABAMA–TUSCALOOSA*

Torsten Ringberg, *UNIVERSITY OF WISCONSIN–MILWAUKEE*

Ann Root, *FLORIDA ATLANTIC UNIVERSITY–BOCA RATON*

Al Rosenbloom, *DOMINICAN UNIVERSITY*

Jason Ryan, *CALIFORNIA STATE UNIVERSITY, SAN BERNARDINO*

David Rylander, *TEXAS WOMAN'S UNIVERSITY*

Mahmod Sabri Haron, *UNIVERSITI SAINS MALAYSIA*

Dennis Sandler, *PACE UNIVERSITY*

Matt Sarkees, *PENNSYLVANIA STATE UNIVERSITY*

Linda Saytes, *UNIVERSITY OF SAN FRANCISCO*

Victoria Seitz, *CALIFORNIA STATE UNIVERSITY, SAN BERNARDINO*

Shahid Sheikh, *AMERICAN INTERCONTINENTAL UNIVERSITY*

Kathy A. Skledar, *LAKE ERIE COLLEGE*

Susan Sieloff, *NORTHEASTERN UNIVERSITY*

Karen Smith, *COLUMBIA SOUTHERN UNIVERSITY*

Sharon Smith, *DEPAUL UNIVERSITY*

Jill Solomon, *UNIVERSITY OF SOUTH FLORIDA*

Ashish Sood, *EMORY UNIVERSITY*

Robert Spekman, *UNIVERSITY OF VIRGINIA, DARDEN SCHOOL*

James Spiers, *ARIZONA STATE UNIVERSITY*

Thomas Steenburgh, *UNIVERSITY OF VIRGINIA, DARDEN SCHOOL*

Geoffrey Stewart, *UNIVERSITY OF LOUISIANA–LAFAYETTE*

Derik Steyn, *CAMERON UNIVERSITY*

John Stovall, *GEORGIA SOUTHWESTERN STATE UNIVERSITY*

Ziad Swaidan, *UNIVERSITY OF HOUSTON AT VICTORIA*

Michael Swenson, *BRIGHAM YOUNG UNIVERSITY*

Victoria Szerko, *DOMINICAN COLLEGE*

Leona Tam, *OLD DOMINION UNIVERSITY*

John L. Teopaco, *EMERSON COLLEGE*

Niwet Thamma, *RAMKHAMHEANG UNIVERSITY*

Meg Thams, *REGIS UNIVERSITY*

Rungting Tu, *PEKING UNIVERSITY*

Bronislaw Verhage, *GEORGIA STATE UNIVERSITY*

Jolivette Wallace, *BELHAVEN UNIVERSITY*

Guangping Wang, *PENNSYLVANIA STATE UNIVERSITY*

Cathy Waters, *BOSTON COLLEGE*

Art Weinstein, *NOVA SOUTHEASTERN UNIVERSITY*

Darin White, *UNION UNIVERSITY–JACKSON*

Ken Williamson, *JAMES MADISON UNIVERSITY*

Dale Wilson, *MICHIGAN STATE UNIVERSITY*

Walter Wochos, *CARDINAL STRITCH UNIVERSITY*

John Wesley Yoest, Jr, *THE CATHOLIC UNIVERSITY OF AMERICA*

Khanchitpol Yousapronpaiboon, *KHONKHEN UNIVERSITY*

Zach Zacharia, *LEHIGH UNIVERSITY*

Jason Qiyu Zhang, *LOYOLA UNIVERSITY MARYLAND*

Yong Zhang, *HOFSTRA UNIVERSITY*

Shaoming Zou, *UNIVERSITY OF MISSOURI–COLUMBIA*

 **connect**®

McGraw-Hill Connect® is a highly reliable, easy-to-use homework and learning management solution that utilizes learning science and award-winning adaptive tools to improve student results.

Homework and Adaptive Learning

- Connect's assignments help students contextualize what they've learned through application, so they can better understand the material and think critically.
- Connect will create a personalized study path customized to individual student needs through SmartBook®.
- SmartBook helps students study more efficiently by delivering an interactive reading experience through adaptive highlighting and review.

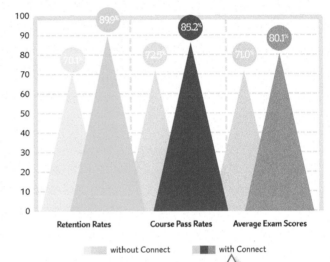

Connect's Impact on Retention Rates, Pass Rates, and Average Exam Scores

Retention Rates: 70.1% without Connect, 89.9% with Connect
Course Pass Rates: 72.5% without Connect, 85.2% with Connect
Average Exam Scores: 71.0% without Connect, 80.1% with Connect

without Connect | with Connect

Using **Connect** improves retention rates by **19.8%**, passing rates by **12.7%**, and exam scores by **9.1%**.

Over **7 billion questions** have been answered, making McGraw-Hill Education products more intelligent, reliable, and precise.

73% of instructors who use **Connect** require it; instructor satisfaction **increases** by 28% when **Connect** is required.

Quality Content and Learning Resources

- Connect content is authored by the world's best subject matter experts, and is available to your class through a simple and intuitive interface.
- The Connect eBook makes it easy for students to access their reading material on smartphones and tablets. They can study on the go and don't need Internet access to use the eBook as a reference, with full functionality.
- Multimedia content such as videos, simulations, and games drive student engagement and critical thinking skills.

Robust Analytics and Reporting

- Connect Insight® generates easy-to-read reports on individual students, the class as a whole, and on specific assignments.

- The Connect Insight dashboard delivers data on performance, study behavior, and effort. Instructors can quickly identify students who struggle and focus on material that the class has yet to master.

- Connect automatically grades assignments and quizzes, providing easy-to-read reports on individual and class performance.

©Hero Images/Getty Images

Impact on Final Course Grade Distribution

without Connect		with Connect
22.9%	A	31.0%
27.4%	B	34.3%
22.9%	C	18.7%
11.5%	D	6.1%
15.4%	F	9.9%

More students earn **As** and **Bs** when they use **Connect**.

Trusted Service and Support

- Connect integrates with your LMS to provide single sign-on and automatic syncing of grades. Integration with Blackboard®, D2L®, and Canvas also provides automatic syncing of the course calendar and assignment-level linking.

- Connect offers comprehensive service, support, and training throughout every phase of your implementation.

- If you're looking for some guidance on how to use Connect, or want to learn tips and tricks from super users, you can find tutorials as you work. Our Digital Faculty Consultants and Student Ambassadors offer insight into how to achieve the results you want with Connect.

BRIEF TABLE OF CONTENTS

DETAILED CONTENTS

PART ONE

Discover Marketing Management

CHAPTER 1

Marketing in Today's Business Milieu

LEARNING OBJECTIVES

LO 1-1 Identify typical misconceptions about marketing, why they persist, and the resulting challenges for marketing management.

LO 1-2 Define what marketing and marketing management really are and how they contribute to a firm's success.

LO 1-3 Appreciate how marketing has evolved from its early roots to be practiced as it is today.

LO 1-4 Recognize the impact of key change drivers on the future of marketing.

WELCOME TO MARKETING MANAGEMENT

Welcome to the world of marketing management! Now is a great time to be studying about marketing. In fact, marketing as a field of study has much to offer everyone, regardless of whether or not the word "marketing" appears in their job title. Whether your interest and training are in engineering, accounting, finance, information technology, or fields outside business, marketing is relevant to you. You can be confident that, when finished with this course about marketing management, you will emerge with a set of knowledge and skills that will not only enhance your personal effectiveness as a leader and manager regardless of your area of responsibility or job title, but will also positively impact the performance of your work group and firm. Mastering great marketing is useful for anyone!

Despite the strong case for the value of learning about marketing, marketing is often misunderstood for a variety of reasons. So before we go any further, let's start by clearing the air. Before you learn about great marketing and how to successfully manage it, it is important to address some misconceptions and stereotypes about marketing. Getting these out in the open will give you the opportunity to challenge your own perceptions of the field. After this section, attention will quickly turn from marketing misconceptions to *marketing realities* in today's business milieu.

MARKETING MISCONCEPTIONS

When you think of *marketing,* what sorts of ideas and images initially come to mind? Close your eyes and think about the essence of the word. What images flow in? The images will vary depending on your age, your professional background, and whether you have worked in some aspect of the marketing field. Here is a short list of perceptions commonly conjured up about marketing:

LO 1-1

Identify typical misconceptions about marketing, why they persist, and the resulting challenges for marketing management.

- Catchy and entertaining advertisements—or perhaps the opposite, incessant and boring advertisements.
- Pushy salespeople trying to persuade someone to *buy it right now.*
- Incessant spam in your e-mail inbox and unwelcome solicitations on your smartphone.
- Obtrusive tracking and recording of your every click and browsing activity online.
- Famous brands and their celebrity spokespeople, such as Nike's athlete endorsers.
- Product claims that turn out to be overstated or just plain false, causing doubt about the trustworthiness of a company.
- Marketing departments "own" an organization's marketing initiative.

Exhibit 1.1 expands on the common stereotypes and misconceptions about marketing.

Behind the Misconceptions

Several important factors have contributed to the development of these misconceptions, including marketing's inherent visibility and its tendency toward buzzwords and "spin."

Marketing Is Highly Visible by Nature Unlike most other key areas of business, marketing as a field is highly public and readily visible outside the confines of the internal business operation. Think of it this way: Most aspects of financial management, accounting, information technology, production, operations management, and human resource management take place behind the curtain of an organization, out of the general public's sight. But marketing is very different. A good portion of marketing is very public. Marketing is seen through the web page that stimulates interest in seeking more product information, the (hopefully) good service received from the salesperson representing a firm's products, the enjoyment and interest generated from a clever advertisement on Super Bowl Sunday, or the well-stocked shelves at the neighborhood Target store.

Of all the business fields, marketing is almost certainly the most visible to people outside the organization. While other fields also have negative stereotypical images (think accountants with green eyeshades or IT computer geeks), you'd be hard pressed to identify another business

EXHIBIT 1.1 | Marketing Misconceptions: What Marketing Is *Not*

MISCONCEPTION NO. 1: Marketing is all about advertising.

THE REALITY: Advertising is just one way that marketing is communicated to potential customers. Advertising is highly visible to the general public, so many people naturally think of advertising when they think of marketing. A famous axiom: *Good advertising makes a bad product fail faster.*

MISCONCEPTION NO. 2: Marketing is all about selling.

THE REALITY: The general public also experiences a lot of selling. Much of this day-to-day selling is in retail store environments. Selling, or more correctly "personal selling," is simply another method of marketing communication. Marketers have to decide on a mix of marketing communication approaches that (in addition to advertising and personal selling) might also include public relations/publicity, sales promotion, and direct marketing. Later chapters discuss how and when each might be most effective in communicating the message.

MISCONCEPTION NO. 3: Marketing is all fluff and no substance.

THE REALITY: Yes, some aspects of marketing are inherently fun and glitzy. Hiring Kevin Durant as a celebrity spokesperson had to be a real thrill for everybody at Nike, not to mention the pleasure and fun it gave Nike fans. But marketing also has aspects that involve sophisticated research, detailed analysis, careful decision making, and thoughtful development of strategies and plans. For many organizations, marketing represents a major investment and firms are naturally reluctant to invest major resources without a reasonable level of assurance of a satisfactory payback.

MISCONCEPTION NO. 4: Marketing is inherently unethical and harmful to society.

THE REALITY: Marketing is no more inherently unethical than other business areas. The extreme corporate financial misdeeds that led to the Great Recession of the late 2000s show that to be true. However, when some element of marketing proves to be unethical (or even illegal), it tends to be visible to the general public. Untrue advertising claims, arm-twisting sales tactics, and nonenvironmentally friendly product packaging are a few very visible examples of marketing not behaving at its best.

MISCONCEPTION NO. 5: Only marketers market.

THE REALITY: Everybody does marketing. Everybody has a stake in the success of marketing. Regardless of your position in a firm or job title, learning how to do great marketing is a key professional asset. People with strong marketing skills achieve greater success—both on the job and off. If you've never thought of yourself in the context of being a "personal brand" that needs to be effectively communicated, just consider how useful such an approach could be in job seeking or positioning yourself for a promotion.

MISCONCEPTION NO. 6: Marketing is just another cost center in a firm.

THE REALITY: The mind-set that marketing is a cost, rather than an investment, is deadly in a firm because costs are inherently to be reduced or avoided. When management doesn't view marketing as earning its keep—that is, marketing being able to pay back its investment over the long term—it becomes very easy for firms to suboptimize their success in the long run by avoiding investment in brand and product development in favor of cutting costs. This is the classic argument that successful firms must simultaneously monitor costs to ensure short-term financial performance while also investing in marketing to ensure long-term competitive strength.

field about which nearly everyone has formed a deeply held set of images and opinions or about which nearly everybody thinks they know enough to confidently offer advice! Think about how many times casual conversation in a social setting turns to something marketing related. Have you ever had similar social exchanges about the ins and outs of financial management or the complexities of computerized production systems? Of course not, but it seems almost anybody is comfortable talking (and tweeting!) about elements of marketing—from the week's advertised specials at the supermarket to this year's fashion for kids heading back to school to the service received at a favorite vacation hotel—marketing is a topic everyone can discuss!

In fact, companies are increasingly utilizing corporate social media presence to generate conversation itself as a marketing tool. For example, fast-food restaurant chain Wendy's gained over 1.5 million followers on Twitter as a result of its saucy social media strategy.[1] The company's Twitter account gained fame by surprising customers with its bold, humorous responses to customer tweets about the company and its competitors. Wendy's Twitter profile describes its strategy this way: "We like our tweets the same way we like to make hamburgers: better than anyone expects from a fast food joint."[2] With some Twitter users even requesting for Wendy's to "roast" them on Twitter, the online conversations often strayed from explicit product advertising. Yet the social media buzz itself brought attention to the company and served as an invaluable advertising tool.

Why is the notion that marketing is visible and accessible to nearly everyone so important to students of marketing management? The truth is, despite the fact that much of marketing is easily observable to just about anyone, marketing as a professional field worthy of serious study doesn't always get the respect it deserves, maybe in part because of its overexposure. The business functions of financial management, operations, IT, and the rest seem to be viewed by many MBA and undergraduate students (and also, unfortunately, by managers in many firms) as the more "serious" parts of an enterprise–topics that are perceived as more concrete, more scientific, and more analytical than marketing, thus implying they are topics worthy of more substantial investment in time, money, and other resources.[3] In the past, marketing has had few useful metrics or measures to gauge the performance impact of a firm's marketing investment, while other areas of the firm have historically been much more driven by measurement of results. The old adage "if it can't be measured, it can't be managed" has plagued marketing for years. This is changing, and today measurement of marketing's performance and contribution is a focal point in many firms.[4] In fact, as you progress through this book you will notice a very strong emphasis on marketing analytics, marketing metrics, and the preeminence of digital and social media marketing as both a source and a beneficiary of customer data.

Marketing Is More Than Buzzwords Given the inherently transparent nature of marketing and the prior lack of ways to effectively measure its impact on a firm's success, it should be no surprise that some managers consider marketing to be little more than a necessary evil–a *cost* they reluctantly have to incur.[5] They're not sure *how* marketing works, or even *if* marketing really does work, but for competitive reasons–or maybe just because it's always been done–they continue to invest large sums of money in its many facets including market research, brand development, advertising, salespeople, public relations, and so forth. With so much ambiguity historically surrounding the management and control of marketing, too often the field has been plagued by a coterie of consultants and authors looking to make a quick buck by selling their latest and greatest ideas complete with their own catchy buzzwords for the program.

Anyone who doubts the pervasiveness of quick-fix approaches to marketing should visit a bookstore or online bookseller. Go to the business section and look at the marketing titles. Among the buzzwords right in the book titles are such gems as *guerrilla marketing, permission marketing, holistic marketing, marketing warfare, marketing rainmaking, buzz marketing, integrated marketing* . . . the list goes on and on. Although these approaches may prove useful under certain circumstances, these quick-fix strategies contribute to the circus-like perception of marketing, which ultimately undermines the field's reputation as a respectable business function.

Beyond the Misconceptions and Toward the *Reality* of Modern Marketing

Of course, buzzwords are just window dressing, and most popular press prescription approaches to marketing don't do much to improve the *long-term* performance of an organization. Effective marketing management isn't about buzzwords or quick fixes. Nor is the essence of marketing really about the kinds of stereotypical viewpoints identified earlier in this section. In today's business milieu, marketing is a central function and set of processes essential to any enterprise.[6] Moreover, leading and managing the facets of marketing to improve individual, unit, and organizational performance–**marketing management**–is a *core business activity,* worthy of any student's study and mastery.

The chapters that follow lay the groundwork for developing the knowledge and skills around marketing that will allow you to build a more successful career as a leader and manager, regardless of your department, area of specialization, level in the organization, or job title. Is marketing relevant to *you?* You bet it is, because *everyone* in an organization does marketing in some way and must share ownership of its success or failure.

Learning about marketing management is not just about reading a book or taking a course, although dedication to these activities is a great starting point. Instead, great marketing is a lifelong journey that requires dedication to continuous learning and improvement of your knowledge and skills as a leader and manager. It is in this spirit that we enthusiastically invite you to begin your journey into the field of marketing management!

DEFINING MARKETING

Over 60 years ago, the late management guru Peter Drucker, often referred to as the father of modern management, set the stage for defining contemporary marketing and conceiving of its potential power. Consider this quote from Drucker, circa 1954 (emphasis added):

> If we want to know what a business is we have to start with its *purpose*. There is only one valid definition of business purpose: *to create a customer*. It is the customer who determines what a business is. For it is the customer, and he alone, who through being willing to pay for a good or service, converts economic resources into wealth, things into goods. What the business thinks it produces is not of first importance—especially not to the future of the business and its success. What the customer thinks he is buying, what he considers "value" is decisive. . . . Because it is the [purpose of a business] to create a customer, [the] business enterprise has two—and only two—business functions: *marketing* and *innovation*.[7]

Consider the power of these ideas: a business built around the customer with resources and processes aligned to maximize customer value. Within this context, Drucker is not talking just about "marketing departments," but rather marketing in much broader terms. More on that distinction later. For now, consider this subsequent quote from Drucker circa 1973:

> Marketing is so basic that it cannot be considered a separate function (i.e., a separate skill or work) within the business . . . it is, first, a central dimension of the entire business. It is the *whole business* . . . seen from the *customer's* point of view. Concern and responsibility for marketing must, therefore, permeate all areas of the enterprise.[8]

Clearly, Peter Drucker was a man whose business philosophy was way ahead of his time. Now fast forward to this decade. The American Marketing Association periodically reviews and updates its official definition of marketing. As of this book's publication, their definition is as follows:

> Marketing is the activity, set of institutions, and processes for creating, communicating, delivering, and exchanging offerings that have value for customers, clients, partners, and society at large.

This definition is quite good because it

- Focuses on the more *strategic* aspects of marketing, which positions marketing as a core contributor to overall firm success.

- Recognizes marketing as an activity, set of institutions, and processes—that is, marketing is not just a "department" in an organization.
- Shifts the areas of central focus of marketing to *value*—creating, communicating, delivering, and exchanging offerings of value to various stakeholders.

Just who are the relevant stakeholders of marketing? **Marketing's stakeholders** include any person or entity inside or outside a firm with whom marketing interacts, impacts, and is impacted by. For example, internal stakeholders—those inside a firm—include other organizational units that marketing interacts with in the course of business. Strong, productive relationships between marketing and finance, accounting, production, quality control, engineering, human resources,

Toyota's popular Scion line exemplifies the growing focus on stakeholders interested in green-friendly products.

Source: Toyota Motor Sales, U.S.A., Inc.

and many other areas in a firm are necessary in order for a firm to do business successfully.[9] The range of external stakeholders—those outside a firm—is even broader and includes customers, vendors, governmental bodies, labor unions, and many others. One important challenge in marketing management is deciding how to prioritize these internal and external stakeholders in terms of their relevance and importance to the firm.[10] Most firms place the customer first, but a key question is: how do you decide which of the others deserve the most attention?

At the broadest conceptual level, members of society at large can be viewed as stakeholders for marketing, a concept called **societal marketing.** As one example, the concept of environmentally friendly marketing, or *green marketing,* has been a growing trend in socially responsible companies. Today the movement has evolved into a part of the philosophical and strategic core of many firms under the label **sustainability,** which refers to business practices that meet humanity's needs without harming future generations.[11] Sustainability practices have helped socially responsible organizations incorporate *doing well by doing good* into their overarching business models so that both the success of the firm and the success of society at large are sustained over the long term. For example, Unilever brands implemented the "Unilever Sustainable Living Plan" as an integral part of the company's business model. This plan seeks to: (1) "Help more than a billion people to improve their health and wellbeing," (2) "Halve the environmental footprint of . . . products," and (3) "Source 100% of [the company's] agricultural raw materials sustainably and enhance the livelihoods of people across [the company's] value chain."[12] The company launched its "Brighter Future" marketing campaign to highlight how Unilever brands are creating a positive social impact and ensuring a brighter future through its commitment to sustainable living.[13]

"Purpose marketing," or "prosocial marketing," is growing as a marketing strategy. This growing popularity can be attributed to the increasing number of consumers who say that what a company stands for influences their purchasing decisions. Toms shoe company is renowned for its social entrepreneurism and socially conscious purpose marketing. Toms' "One for One" mission assures customers that with every purchase, "Toms will help a person in need."[14] An estimated 3.5 million people participated in Toms' annual One Day Without Shoes initiative in 2016 alone.[15] Purpose marketing with sincerity has the potential to appeal to consumers on an emotional level and further drive customer loyalty. This trend moves marketing beyond push brand messaging and instead engages consumers in a much more meaningful way.[16]

Value and Exchange Are Core Marketing Concepts

Throughout the various topics encompassed within this book, the idea of value as a core concept in marketing will be a central theme. From a customer's perspective, we define **value** as a ratio of the bundle of benefits a customer receives from an offering compared to the costs incurred by the customer in acquiring that bundle of benefits.[17] Another central tenet of marketing is the concept of **exchange,** in which a person gives up something of value to them for something else they desire to have.[18] Usually an exchange is facilitated by money, but not always. Sometimes people trade or barter nonmonetary resources such as time, skill, expertise, intellectual capital, and other things of value for something else they want. For any exchange to take place, the following five conditions must be present:

1. There must be at least two parties.
2. Each party has something that might be of value to the other party.
3. Each party is capable of communication and delivery.
4. Each party is free to accept or reject the exchange offer.
5. Each party believes it is appropriate or desirable to deal with the other party.

Just because these conditions exist does not guarantee that an exchange will take place. The parties must come to an agreement that results in both being better off, hence the phrase in the AMA definition of marketing ". . . exchanging offerings that *have value* . . . (emphasis added)." Value implies that both parties win from the exchange.

EXHIBIT 1.2 | **Marketing Yesterday and Today**

Pre-Industrial
Revolution

↓

Focus on Production
and Products

↓

Focus on Selling

↓

Advent of the
Marketing Concept

↓

Post-Marketing
Concept Approaches
- Differentiation Orientation
- Market Orientation
- Relationship Orientation
- One-to-One Marketing

A New Agenda for Marketing

We firmly believe that today is the best time ever to be engaged as a leader and manager in marketing. Recently, the American Marketing Association (AMA) announced their Intellectual Agenda 1.0, which seeks to serve as a "big tent" source of guidance and inspiration that includes both theoretical and applied knowledge, which will ultimately provide actionable insights, frameworks, tools, and resources for marketers around the world. Part and parcel to this Intellectual Agenda is the identification of AMA's 7 Big Problems in Marketing in order to provide context for the critical challenges all marketing managers face. These 7 Big Problems provide common ground for ongoing conversation and ideation about the marketing field. In summary form, they are:

1. Effectively targeting high-value sources of growth.
2. The role of marketing in the firm and the C-suite.
3. The digital transformation of the modern corporation.
4. Generating and using insight to shape marketing practice.
5. Dealing with an omni-channel world.
6. Competing in dynamic, global markets.
7. Balancing incremental and radical innovation.[19]

Importantly, the AMA is deeply committed to the idea that the role of marketing in enhancing the greater good of society and the planet through economic, environmental, and social sustainability transcends these 7 Big Problems. That is, for each of the problems, the only viable and acceptable solutions must take into account the big picture of the greater good. You will read more about the societal impact of marketing in Chapter 2.

The AMA definition of marketing highlights marketing's central role in creating (or developing), communicating, delivering, and exchanging offerings that have value. But marketing's central focus hasn't always been on value and customer relationships, and the truth is that even today some firms lag in these areas. The next section offers perspectives on marketing's roots and evolution, and explains why some firms today are frozen in past approaches to marketing.

MARKETING'S ROOTS AND EVOLUTION

LO 1-3

Appreciate how marketing has evolved from its early roots to be practiced as it is today.

In the spirit of the old adage that he who ignores history is doomed to repeat its mistakes, here's a short marketing history lesson. Exhibit 1.2 illustrates the flow of marketing's evolution as a field. It is important to note that there are still firms that are "stuck in the past" in the way they approach marketing. That is, not all organizations have "fully evolved"! But hopefully the majority of firms seek to approach marketing from a 21st-century perspective as we present throughout this book.

Pre-Industrial Revolution

Before Henry Ford and his contemporaries created assembly lines and mass production, marketing was done very much on a one-to-one basis between firms and customers, although the word *marketing* wasn't really used. Consider what happened when a person needed a new pair of shoes, pre-Industrial Revolution. One would likely go visit the village cobbler, who would take precise measurements and then send the customer away with instructions to return in a week or so to pick up the new shoes. Materials, styles, and colors would be limited, but customers likely would get a great fit since the cobbler created a customized pair of shoes for each person. And if they didn't fit just right, the cobbler would adjust the shoes to a customer's liking—right on the spot.

Focus on Production and Products

The Industrial Revolution changed nearly everything in business by shifting the focus from meeting demand one item at a time to mass production via assembly line. Maximizing production capacity utilization became a predominant concern. For the early part of the 20th century, the focus was on this **production orientation** of improving products and production efficiency without much regard for what was going on in the marketplace. In fact, consumers snapped up this new pipeline of reasonably priced goods, even if the products didn't give much choice in style or function. Having a Ford Model T was great, but as Henry Ford himself said, "People can have the Model T in any color—so long that it's black."[20]

A production orientation assumes that customers will beat a path to your door just because you have a great product that functions nicely; build a better mousetrap and they will come. You will learn throughout your study of marketing management that great products alone do not ensure success. Unfortunately, firms that are stuck in a production orientation mentality likely will have great difficulty competing successfully for customers.

Focus on Selling

Around the end of World War I, production capacity utilization began to decline for several reasons. First, capacity had been increased greatly for the war. Second, a number of firms that had dominated their respective industries before the war now found themselves with stiff competition for sales because many new competitors had flooded into the marketplace. And third, financial markets were becoming more sophisticated and were placing more pressure on firms to continually increase sales volume and profits.

These factors resulted in the rise of many of the great sales organizations of today. A **sales orientation** suggests that, to increase sales and consequently production capacity utilization, professional salespeople need to "push" product into the hands of customers, both businesses and end users. For years, the most vivid image of a salesperson in the public eye was that of the peddler, the classic outside salesperson pushing product on customers with a smile, a promise, and a handshake. Gradually, customers of all kinds grew wary of high-pressure selling, sparking laws at all levels to protect consumers from unscrupulous salespeople. For many customers, the image of marketing became permanently frozen as that of the pushy salesperson. And just as with the production orientation, to this day some firms still practice mainly a sales-oriented approach to their business.

Advent of the Marketing Concept

After World War II, business began to change in many long-lasting ways. Business historians point to a number of reasons for this shift, including:

- Pent-up demand for consumer goods and services after the war.

- Euphoric focus on family and a desperate need to regain a normalcy of day-to-day life after years of war (which produced the baby boomer generation).

- Opening up of production capacity dominated for years by war production.

- Advent of readily available mainframe computing capability, and especially the associated statistical analytic techniques that allowed for more sophisticated market research.

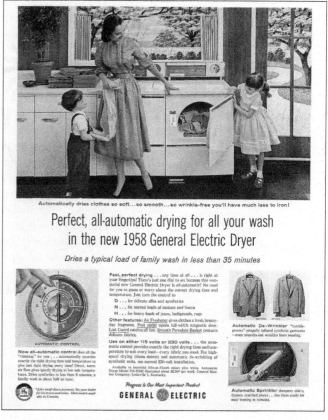

Perfect, all-automatic drying for all your wash in the new 1958 General Electric Dryer

This vintage GE ad from the late 1950s is a great example of how ads in that era were more "informative" and less "sexy" than much of today's advertising.

©The Advertising Archives/Alamy Stock Photo

In the 1950s, these forces, combined with growing frustration with high-pressure selling, sparked a shift in the focus of American business. The resulting business philosophy has been labeled the **marketing concept,** which is an organization-wide customer orientation with the objective of achieving long-run profits.[21] General Electric's *1952 Annual Report* is often cited as the first time the marketing concept was articulated in writing by a major corporation. Clearly delighted to herald its new-age management philosophy, GE wrote the following to stockholders in that report (in this historical period, the assumption was that business professionals would be male):

> [The marketing concept] . . . introduces the marketing man at the beginning rather than at the end of the production cycle and integrates marketing into each phase of the business. Thus, marketing, through its studies and research, will establish for the engineer, the design and manufacturing man, what the customer wants in a given product, what price he is willing to pay, and where and when it will be wanted. Marketing will have authority in product planning, production scheduling, and inventory control, as well as in sales distribution and servicing of the product.[22]

The articulation of the marketing concept was a major breakthrough in business, and in the 1960s and '70s it spread like wildfire throughout companies of all kinds. Soon firms everywhere were adopting the practice of letting the market decide what products to offer. Such an approach required substantial investment in ongoing market and consumer research and also necessitated an organization-wide commitment to marketing planning. As a result, the idea of the marketing plan became codified in most organizations' business processes. We'll come back to the idea of marketing planning in Chapter 3.

The Marketing Mix The articulation of the marketing concept and its quick adoption across a gamut of industries quickly led to a major focus on teaching marketing courses in colleges and universities. In the mid-1960s, a convenient way of teaching the key components was developed with the advent of the **marketing mix,** or **4Ps of marketing,** originally for *product, price, place,* and *promotion.*[23] The idea was that these fundamental elements comprise the marketer's "tool kit" to be applied in carrying out the job. It is referred to as a "mix" because, by developing unique combinations of these elements, marketers set their product or brand apart from the competition. Also, an important rubric in marketing is the following: making a change in any one of the marketing mix elements tends to result in a domino effect on the others.

Today, the basic concept of the marketing mix still persists, but with considerably greater sophistication than in the 1960s. The product is now regarded broadly in the context of an overall *offering,* which could include a bundle of goods, services, ideas (for example, intellectual property), and other components, often represented by strong overarching branding. Many marketers today are more focused on *solutions* than products—the characterization of an offering as a solution is nice because of the implication that a solution has been developed in conjunction with specific, well-understood customer wants and needs.[24] *Price* today is largely regarded in relationship to the concept of value. *Place* has undergone tremendous change. Rather than just connoting the process of getting goods from Point A to Point B, firms now understand that sophisticated, integrated supply chain approaches are a crucial component of business success.[25] And finally, to grasp the magnitude of changes in *promotion* since the 1960s one need only consider the proliferation of high-tech media options available to marketers today, from the Internet to cell phones and beyond.

Over the years some authors have proposed various additions to the original marketing mix—that is, adding "more Ps." Especially outside the setting of marketing physical goods, as in the context of marketing services or ideas, the case is frequently made for the need to add more elements to the marketer's tool kit.[26] This issue has been hotly debated for years. Pete Markey, brand communications and marketing director at Aviva, argues that the 4Ps are still relevant today because they remind businesses that marketing is not the responsibility of just one department; it is the responsibility of the entire business to understand customers' wants and needs, and to extract value from them. The 4Ps capture the essence of marketing in a simplified, repeatable process that needs to be communicated to the new generation of marketers.[27]

You will find as you progress in your reading of this book that later on we follow the basic topical flow of developing, pricing, delivering, and communicating offerings that have value. Put in terms of the 4Ps of the marketing mix, Part Three of the book focuses on *developing* the value offering through product strategy and new product development, building the brand, and attention to service (the product "P"). Part Four focuses on pricing and delivering the value offering (the "price and place Ps"). Finally, Part Five provides a comprehensive look at how firms communicate the value offering to customers (the "promotion P"). Thus, the core elements of the original 4Ps of marketing are there but presented within the context of the terminology and work processes used by *today's* marketing managers.

Post-Marketing Concept Approaches

Close perusal of the definition of the marketing concept reveals several issues that still resonate widely in today's business milieu. The decisions to place the customer at the core of the enterprise (often referred to as a **customer-centric** approach to business), focus on investment in customers over the *long term,* and focus on marketing as an *organization-wide* issue (that is, not just relegated to a "marketing department") are all relevant and important topics in business classes and boardrooms today, and each will be discussed further in later chapters.[28] Amazon is one of the leading companies pursuing a customer-centric approach to business, and its CEO, Jeff Bezos, has integrated this technique into Amazon culture, often leaving a seat open at his conference tables to remind everyone in the room that the most important person in any conversation is "the Customer."[29]

Referring again to Exhibit 1.2, the four evolutionary steps beyond the original marketing concept warrant further discussion now: differentiation orientation, market orientation, relationship orientation, and one-to-one marketing.

Differentiation Orientation More sophisticated research and analytical approaches have made it possible to do increasingly precise refinement of market segmentation, target marketing, and positioning of products to serve very specific customer groups, processes you will learn more about in Chapter 7. The idea is to create and communicate **differentiation**, or what clearly distinguishes your products from those of competitors in the minds of customers.[30] The ability for marketers to tailor and deliver different product messages to different groups also has been greatly enhanced by the proliferation of multiple types of media that can be used with great precision to communicate to very specifically defined customer groups. For example, during its "Share a Coke" campaign, Coca-Cola put 250 of the most popular names among teens and millennials on 20-ounce bottles, and created a website geared toward share-worthy content. Coca-Cola targeted the millennial generation by delivering personalization, trend, and social interaction in a Coke bottle, and increased sales by 2 percent after the campaign launched.[31]

Market Orientation A great deal of research has been devoted to learning how a firm can successfully put the marketing concept into practice. Think of **market orientation** as the implementation of the marketing concept. The notion of market orientation, one component of which is **customer orientation**—placing the customer at the core of all aspects of the enterprise—takes the guiding business philosophy of the marketing concept and works to more usefully define just how to implement it within a firm.[32] The focal point of Southwest Airlines is its customer experience, which manifests itself through the personality of its brand, the heart on the underbelly of its planes, its ticker symbol (LUV), and the employees who are hired for their attitude and trained for skill. The Southwest heart is a promise to customers and a reminder to employees that Southwest cares.[33]

Relationship Orientation Marketing managers today recognize the power of securing, building, and maintaining long-term relationships with profitable customers.[34]

The original marketing concept clearly recognized the need for an orientation toward the longer term in marketing—that is, not just making the next quarter's financial projections but rather cultivating customers for the long haul. The move toward a **relationship orientation** by firms has been driven by the realization that it is far more efficient and effective to invest in keeping and cultivating profitable current customers instead of constantly having to invest in gaining new customers that come with unknown return on investment.[35] Certainly most firms simultaneously focus on both current and new customers, but no company wants to be in a position of losing great customers and having to scramble to replace the associated lost revenue.

A relationship orientation draws its power from the firm's capability to effectively collect and use ongoing, real-time information on customers in marketing management decision making. Implementation of a relationship orientation is discussed in Chapter 5 in the context of customer relationship management (CRM). Much of CRM is designed to facilitate higher levels of customer satisfaction and loyalty, as well as to provide a means for identifying the most profitable customers—those worthy of the most marketing investment.[36] Dollar Shave Club has mounted a serious competitive threat to Gillette and other traditional razor and blade providers by using its in-house CRM system, customer support platform, and data analytics to gain deep customer insights. As a result, it delivers an outstanding customer experience to its over 1.5 million subscribers and aims to engage in a true relationship with each of them.[37]

One-to-One Marketing Remember the earlier example of the pre-Industrial Revolution cobbler who would customize a pair of shoes for each customer? In many ways marketing's evolution has come full circle back to a focus on creating capabilities for such customization. In a series of classic books and articles, Don Peppers and Martha Rogers popularized the term **one-to-one marketing,** which advocates that firms should direct energy and resources into establishing a learning relationship with each customer and then connect that knowledge with the firm's production and service capabilities to fulfill that customer's needs in as custom a manner as possible.[38]

Some firms come close to one-to-one marketing by employing **mass customization,** in which they combine flexible manufacturing with flexible marketing to greatly enhance customer choices.[39] Retailers have even entered into mass customization. The luxury brand Burberry allows customers to build their own trench coats. They are able to select from silhouettes of varying length, leather or fabric type, and several colors. Options also include sleeve length, lining, collar, buttons, and belts. Buyers are able to customize their perfect coat with the click of a few buttons.[40]

So far in this chapter we have explored common misconceptions about marketing and then moved well past the stereotypes to begin to gain a solid foundation for understanding what marketing management really is about today. Given the increasingly rapid pace of changes in today's business environment, it's highly likely that marketing's role will evolve even more rapidly than in the past. Now let's turn our attention to the future to identify important change drivers that are sure to impact marketing over the next decade and beyond.

CHANGE DRIVERS IMPACTING THE FUTURE OF MARKETING

<table>
<tr><td>

LO 1-4

Recognize the impact of key change drivers on the future of marketing.

</td><td>

A great way to systematically explore the future of marketing is by considering several well-documented broad trends that are clearly impacting the future of the field. These trends are well under way, but their ultimate impact on marketing and on business in general is not yet fully known. Five key areas of shift, or change drivers, are

</td></tr>
</table>

- Shift to product glut and customer shortage.
- Shift in information power from marketer to customer.
- Shift in generational values and preferences.

- Shift to distinguishing Marketing ("Big M") from marketing ("little m").
- Shift to demanding return on marketing investment.

Shift to Product Glut and Customer Shortage

Fred Wiersema, in his book *The New Market Leaders,* builds a powerful case that the balance of power is shifting between marketers and their customers in both business-to-consumer (B2C/end user) markets and business-to-business (B2B) markets. He identifies "six new market realities" in support of this trend: Competitors proliferate, all secrets are open secrets, innovation is universal, information overwhelms and depreciates, easy growth makes hard times, and customers have less time than ever.[41]

Blockbuster's demise did not happen because of technology or Netflix, but rather because it failed to focus on its customers. Blockbuster might have been salvaged if it had understood that it was in the business of retail customer service, restructured its strategy to consultative selling, and branded itself as "*the* movie expert" utilizing any platform necessary. Instead, Blockbuster continued to think of itself as a convenience chain for a product that (unfortunately) in reality was no longer convenient in the digital age, and eventually it shut down operations.[42]

Wiersema's central point is that not only is a customer orientation desirable, but also in today's market it is a *necessity for survival.* Coming to grips with the impact of Wiersema's six market realities greatly heightens the role of marketing in the firm as the nexus of an organization's customer-focused strategies.

The highly customizable brand Burberry has extended its product line to children.

Source: Burberry

Shift in Information Power from Marketer to Customer

Nowadays, customers of all kinds have nearly limitless access to information about companies, products, competitors, other customers, and even detailed elements of marketing plans and strategies. This is analogous to Wiersema's "All Secrets Are Open Secrets," but here we're talking about the customer's perspective. For decades, marketers held a degree of information power over their customers because firms had access to detailed and sophisticated information about their products and services that customers couldn't get without the help of somebody in the firm (usually a salesperson). Now, customers are empowered to access boundless information about all kinds of products and services on the Internet.[43]

For competitive reasons, firms have no choice but to be more open about their businesses and products. Even if they wanted to, firms can't stop chat rooms, independent websites, web logs or blogs, and other customer-generated modes of communication from filling web page after web page with information, disinformation, and opinions about a company's products, services, and even company dirty laundry. Consider Walmart, one of the world's most successful companies. In recent years Walmart from time to time has been caught off guard by the number and range of uncontrollable information sources about it and its activities (such as employee wage and benefit practices). Another example of this shift in information power is the physician/patient relationship. Between open direct-to-consumer advertising by pharmaceutical companies and innumerable websites devoted to every medical malady, more and more patients arrive at the doctor's office self-diagnosed and ready to self-prescribe![44]

GEICO
Sponsored · 🌐

You'll have a happy face too when you see how much you could save with GEICO.

Savings that will make you smile.

GEICO

Save big with GEICO.
Get your free quote today!
GEICO.com

Get Quote

GEICO has made major inroads with the younger generation of insurance purchasers by introducing clever themes and efficient rate quotes via the web.

Source: GEICO

The trend toward more information in the hands of the customer is not going to diminish. Marketing approaches must be altered to reflect and respond to this important change.

Shift in Generational Values and Preferences

Aspects of generational marketing will be discussed in more detail in Chapter 7. For now, the inexorable shift in values and preferences from generation to generation deserves mention as one of the key trends affecting the future of marketing. One clear impact is on the firm's message and the method by which that message is communicated. For example, GenY consumers tend to be much more receptive to electronic commerce as a primary mode of receiving marketing communication and ultimately purchasing than are prior generations.[45] Did you know that through the iTunes Store or Google Play you can secure the Girl Scout Cookie Finder app, which provides users with GPS coordinates for the nearest cookie sales location? For many, gone are the days of strictly relying on face-to-face selling.[46] This preference has clear implications for how marketing carries out its management of customer relationships across generations and also calls into question how much *value* younger customers derive from the different approaches to relationships. That is, do members of the younger generation appreciate, or even need, the kinds of close personal relationships companies like State Farm provide through their agents, or are they perfectly happy to interact with firms like GEICO, primarily through electronic sales and distribution channels?

Generational shifts also impact marketing in terms of human resources. Consider how generational differences in attitudes toward work life versus family life, expectations about job satisfaction and rewards, and preferred modes of learning and working (e.g., electronic versus face-to-face) affect the ability of firms to hire people into various marketing-related positions. For example, firms often wish to differentiate themselves by offering great service to their customers. Yet nearly all organizations are severely challenged today in hiring and keeping high-quality customer service personnel because of a severe shortage of capable, qualified customer care personnel.[47]

Generational changes are nothing new. In the context of both customers and organization members, understanding the generational differences and how to work to appeal to different generations' values and preferences is a critical part of marketing management. Today, the importance of this issue is accentuated and accelerated in marketing due to propensities among generational groups to differentially use technology and the impact of generational differences on workplace design and management practice.

We'd be remiss not to highlight the generation that is the apple of many a marketer's eye today—millennials. The millennial generation represents roughly 25 percent of the population and $200 billion in annual buying power. Millennials favor authenticity over content, are brand loyal (especially if those brands are active on social media), are highly connected through technology, and wish to be part of a company's product development process.[48] Chipotle's "build-your-own" business model provided a customer experience that was interactive, and its web series "Farmed and Dangerous" provided social media interaction, resulting in a young customer base that largely remained loyal during Chipotle's food-safety crisis in 2015.[49]

By 2025, millennials are expected to represent 75 percent of workers. They want their share of responsibility while at work, but they also value work-life balance and time away from work, and seek to join companies that are tuned in to ethical business practices and social responsibility. Millennials represent the best-educated generation in history.[50] The software firm Workday caters to the millennial mind through its "Generation Workday" program, inviting junior staffers to senior leader meetings, offering mentoring opportunities, and rotating employees through different divisions to gain new skills, experiences, and networks.[51] You'll learn more about generational marketing in Chapter 7.

EXHIBIT 1.3 | Strategic and Tactical Marketing

Shift to Distinguishing Marketing (Big M) from marketing (little m)

Earlier it was established that the marketing concept is intended to be an overarching business philosophy in which firms place the customer at the core of the enterprise. Also, you have learned through reading some of the stereotypical impressions of what marketing is (and is not) and that marketing—at least the *image* of marketing—can be fairly fragmented and often quite tactical in nature. How can marketing as a discipline that is both strategic and tactical be reconciled?

Begin by thinking of marketing as occurring on two dimensions within an organization. These dimensions exist in tandem, and even intersect on occasion, but harbor fundamental differences in goals and properties. For convenience, we can distinguish these dimensions by capitalizing the word for one ("Marketing"—"Big M") and leaving the word in lowercase for the other ("marketing"—"little m"). Exhibit 1.3 portrays this relationship. Let's investigate these concepts further.

Marketing (Big M) Marketing (Big M) serves as a core driver of business strategy. That is, an understanding of markets, competitors, and other external forces, coupled with attention to internal capabilities, allows a firm to successfully develop strategies for the future. This approach is often referred to as **strategic marketing,** which means a long-term, firm-level commitment to investing in marketing—supported at the highest organizational level—for the purpose of enhancing organizational performance.

Going back to the AMA definition, marketing's focus as ". . . the activity, set of institutions, and processes for creating, communicating, delivering, and exchanging offerings that have value for customers, clients, partners, and society at large" contains substantial elements of Marketing (Big M): The core concepts of customer value, exchange, customer relationships, and benefit to the organization and its stakeholders are all very strategic in nature and help form the core business philosophy of a firm. Earlier we saw that the marketing concept includes a strong Marketing (Big M) thrust: ". . . an organization-wide customer orientation with the objective of achieving long-run profits." Certainly the core marketing concept characteristics of an organization-wide customer orientation and long-run profits are very strategic. Both the AMA definition of marketing and the long-standing marketing concept provide evidence of the centrality of Marketing (Big M) to the firm as a core business philosophy.

The concept of Marketing (Big M) necessitates several important actions on the part of the organization to maximize marketing's impact. Consider these action elements required for successful Marketing (Big M):

- Make sure *everyone* in an organization, regardless of their position or title, understands the concept of customer orientation, which places the customer at the core of all aspects of the enterprise. It doesn't matter whether or not the organization member directly interfaces with customers outside the firm. The point is that everybody has customers within the organization, and through the process of effectively serving those internal customers, the firm can better serve its external customers. In this way, everyone in the firm has a stake in the success of Marketing (Big M).

- Align all internal organizational processes and systems around the customer. Don't let the IT system, telecommunications system, billing system, or any other internal process or system become an impediment to a customer orientation. If the people inside a firm understand the power of a customer-centric business approach, but the internal systems don't support it, Marketing (Big M) won't be successful.

- Find somebody at the top of the firm to consistently champion this Marketing (Big M) business philosophy. The CEO is the most appropriate person for this role, perhaps manifest through the CMO (chief marketing officer). Like anything else of importance in a business organization, Marketing (Big M) takes resources, patience, and time to acculturate and implement, and it won't happen unless someone at the top is consistently supportive, with both resources and leadership.

- Forget the concept that the marketing department is where Marketing (Big M) takes place. Marketing (Big M) is not about what one department does or does not do. Marketing (Big M) is the basis on which an organization approaches its whole enterprise—remember Peter Drucker's words: "[Marketing] is the *whole business* . . . seen from the *customer's* point of view. Concern and responsibility for marketing must, therefore, permeate all areas of the enterprise." Drucker was right!

- Create *market-driving,* not just *market-driven,* strategies. It is imperative to study the market and competition as part of the marketing planning process. Firms today must break out of linear thinking when developing new products and markets. Certainly research on markets and customers can uncover unmet needs and offer guidance on designing products to fulfill those needs. But the process contributes little toward **market creation**—approaches that drive the market toward fulfilling a whole new set of needs that customers did not realize was possible or feasible before. Classic examples of market creation include Microsoft's revolution of the information field, Disney's creation of the modern theme park industry, and Apple's innovations in integrated communications with the iPhone and iPad. These were all market-driving strategies that created really new markets.

marketing (little m) In contrast, **marketing (little m)** serves the firm and its stakeholders at a functional or operational level; hence, marketing (little m) is often thought of as **tactical marketing**. In fact, marketing (little m) almost always takes place at the functional or operational level of a firm. Specific programs and tactics aimed at customers and other stakeholder groups tend to emanate from marketing (little m).[52] But marketing (little m) always needs to be couched within the philosophy, culture, and strategies of the firm's Marketing (Big M). In this way, Marketing (Big M) and marketing (little m) should be quite naturally connected within a firm, as the latter tends to represent the day-to-day operationalization and implementation of the former. Everything from brand image, to the message salespeople and advertisements deliver, to customer service, to packaging and product features, to the chosen distribution channel—in fact, all elements of the marketing mix and beyond—exemplify marketing (little m).

Understanding these two dimensions of marketing helps clarify much of the confusion surrounding the field today. It certainly helps explain much of the confusion surrounding what marketing management is supposed to be, and how and why the field tends to have a bit of an identity crisis both inside firms and with the public at large. Occasionally throughout this book, the Marketing (Big M), marketing (little m) notion will be brought up to add explanatory power to important points. But for the most part, we'll just use one version of the word, assuming we all understand it contains both levels.

Shift to Justifying the Relevance and Payback of the Marketing Investment

The final change driver affecting the future of marketing is a topic on the minds of many CEOs and CMOs today. The issue is how management can effectively measure and assess the level of success a firm's investment in various aspects of marketing has had. Appropriate and effective **marketing metrics** must be designed to identify, track, evaluate, and provide key benchmarks for improvement just as various financial metrics guide the financial management of the firm.[53] Why the intense focus on metrics? Here are several important reasons:

- *Marketing is a fuzzy field.* Marketing has often historically viewed itself as working within gray area comfort zones of a business. That is, if what marketing contributed was mostly creative in nature, how can the impact of such activities be measured effectively? For the marketer, this can be a somewhat attractive position to be in, and historically many marketers probably took advantage of the idea that their activities were above measurement. Those days are over.

- *If it can't be measured, it can't be managed.* As with all aspects of business, effective management of the various aspects of marketing requires quantification of objectives and results. The marketing plan is one of the most important elements of a business plan. Effective planning requires metrics.

- *Is marketing an expense or an investment?* Practicing marketers tend to pitch marketing internally as an investment in the future success of the organization.

This AT&T-sponsored display in a local YMCA calls out the dark side of smartphone communication—texting while driving. Technology has increased the channels of marketing communications, but at the same time created important new responsibilities for marketers to promote proper use.

©Imeh Akpanudosen/Getty Images

As an investment, it is not unreasonable that expected returns be identified and measured.[54] Leading consulting firm McKinsey & Company uses its Marketing Navigator to translate complex marketing return on investment (MROI) data into simplified visualizations to help its clients make better marketing investment decisions. McKinsey believes that better MROI begins with better objectives, and communicating marketing as an investment, not a cost.[55] We'll take a close look at marketing analytics and metrics in Chapter 5.

- *CEOs and stockholders expect marketing accountability.* Marketers need to create tools for ongoing, meaningful measurement of marketing productivity. More and more, CMOs are being held accountable for marketing performance in the same manner as are CFOs and leaders of other functional aspects of the business.[56]

This section has identified and examined several key change drivers that are sure to impact the future of marketing. Clearly, many other trends in the macro-level environment of business also affect marketing, including the obvious examples of globalization, ethnic diversification, and the growth and proliferation of technology, such as a precipitous shift to digital and social media approaches to marketing communication. All of these issues, and more, will be thematic throughout your reading of the chapters ahead.

YOUR MARKETING MANAGEMENT JOURNEY BEGINS

Some students take the marketing management course because they "have to" take it in order to fulfill a degree requirement, not necessarily because they see inherent value in marketing for their career as a leader and manager. It is our hope that if you initially fell into this category, you can now see that gaining the knowledge and skills required for marketing management will increase your worth as an asset to any firm, regardless of your position or job title.

As you progress through this course, keep in mind that marketing management is not so much a position or a job title as it is a process and a way of approaching decision making about important business opportunities and challenges. Our presumption throughout this book is that you are seeking knowledge and skills that will enable you to use marketing to its fullest potential to positively impact organizational performance. Be assured from the outset that a high level of personal and career value can be derived by investing time and energy now in mastering the leadership and management of marketing.

SUMMARY

Marketing as an activity, set of institutions, and processes adds value to a firm and its internal and external stakeholders in many ways. For a marketing manager to be successful, he or she must approach the job with a strong understanding of what it takes to do great marketing *today,* which, because of a variety of change drivers, is very different from doing marketing in the past. Leading and managing the facets of marketing in order to improve individual, unit, and organizational performance—marketing management—is a core business activity in today's business milieu, worthy of study and mastery by any student of business regardless of job title or professional or educational background.

KEY TERMS

marketing management   5
marketing's stakeholders   6
societal marketing   7
sustainability   7
value   7
exchange   7
production orientation   9
sales orientation   9
marketing concept   10

marketing mix
  (4Ps of marketing)   10
customer-centric   11
differentiation   11
market orientation   11
customer orientation   11
relationship orientation   12
one-to-one marketing   12
mass customization   12

Marketing (Big M)   15
strategic marketing   15
market creation   16
marketing (little m)   16
tactical marketing   16
marketing metrics   16

APPLICATION QUESTIONS

More application questions are available online.

1. Consider the various marketing misconceptions introduced in this chapter.
   a. Pick any two of the misconceptions and develop a specific example of each from your own experience with firms and brands.
   b. How will it be beneficial for a new marketing manager to understand the misconceptions that exist about marketing?
   c. Can you come up with some other marketing misconceptions of your own—ones that are not addressed in the chapter?

2. In the chapter we make a strong case for the relevance of Peter Drucker's key themes today, even though much of his writing was done decades ago. Do you agree that his message was ahead of its time and is still relevant? Why or why not? Assume you are the CEO of a firm that wants to practice a market orientation. How will Drucker's advice help you to accomplish this goal?

3. Put yourself in the role of a marketing manager. From this perspective, do you agree with the concepts of societal marketing and sustainability? Why or why not? How does a focus on sustainability affect the marketing manager's role and activities? Identify two organizations that you believe do a great job of paying attention to sustainability and present the evidence that leads you to this conclusion.

4. Review the section on change drivers and select any two within the set that you want to focus on. Pick an organization of your choice and answer the following questions:
   a. In what ways does each of the change drivers impact the firm's ability to successfully do marketing?
   b. How is the firm responding to the change drivers in the way it approaches its business? What should it be doing that it is not doing at present?

c. What role do you believe the marketing manager has in proactively preparing for these and future change drivers?

5. In the chapter you learned that harmonious performance of Marketing (big M) and marketing (little m) within a firm can lead to greater levels of success. Why is this true? What does it mean that these two need to be "harmonious"? What would be some likely negative consequences if they were out of sync?

MANAGEMENT DECISION CASE
From Clydesdales to Talking Frogs: Budweiser's Strategic Adaptability Keeps It a Winner

In the rapidly changing world of today's marketing manager, for a brand to survive and thrive over the long run, its marketing strategy must stay ahead of the curve. It must continually evolve—responding to the changing needs and preferences of customers and taking advantage of the many new tools for connecting with its target markets. Over the course of its 150 years,[57] the Budweiser brand has not only survived but thrived, thanks to strong marketing management focused on providing value and effectively communicating that value to its customers.

In 1864, Adolphus Busch partnered with his father-in-law, Eberhard Anheuser, to begin brewing beer in St. Louis. Anheuser was a marketing pioneer in those early years, using a strong mix of the most cutting-edge promotional tools of the day: print and outdoor advertising, point-of-sale material in saloons, an inventory of giveaway items, and a large cadre of traveling salesmen (yes, they were all men back then).[58] Fast forward to 1908: anticipating Prohibition, Busch used newspaper ads to remind readers (and regulators) that the beer industry employed 750,000 people who touch 4 million women and children family members, and that 400,000 more people were employed on farms that produced crops needed to make beer. In a patriotic theme to be revisited in future years, Busch and Anheuser proclaimed to everyone that beer industry employees "love their homes," and "are good, honest citizens, temperate, patriotic, and true."[59]

Despite their best efforts to thwart it, Prohibition arrived in 1920, and the minds behind Budweiser responded with a major modification to the product component of the marketing mix: the introduction of nonalcoholic beer and soft drinks.[60] When Prohibition ended in 1933, the knee-jerk marketing approach of most beer brands was to simply announce they were back in business with ads in the key newspapers of the day (*The New York Times,* for example).

Budweiser took a bit bolder marketing approach. In an early example of event marketing, Budweiser celebrated the return of legal booze with six Clydesdale horses pulling a red, white, and gold beer wagon up New York's Fifth Avenue to the Empire State Building.[61] These majestic horses were a very early "brand character," and of course they would go on to appear many times in Budweiser promotions in the coming years.

After the Great Depression, Budweiser made a major product packaging innovation—beer in cans—that dramatically boosted product sales. The 1940s brought the now-famous slogan, or tagline, the "King of Beers," which is still in use today. In the 1980s, faced with more health-conscious consumers, Budweiser responded with one of its biggest product innovations: Bud Light. Although Budweiser grew to be the number 1 American beer brand in 1988, by 2001 the Bud Light brand line extension overtook its big brother for first place in U.S. beer sales. Also in the 1980s, Budweiser took the bold marketing strategy step of focusing almost exclusively on sports-watching males. So it was only natural that Budweiser would decide to dominate the premier sporting event—the Super Bowl, of course. While requiring a huge promotional expenditure, the annual event gave them instant access to a massive audience of these targeted sports-watching males, and it was also a great platform for some very memorable and creative advertising (search for "Budweiser Frogs commercial" or "Budweiser Whassup commercial" to see a couple of famous classics).[62] Budweiser was indeed the King of Beers—and the King of Marketers!

But alas, market preferences shifted in the 1990s toward wine and cocktails, causing a marked decline in beer sales and heightening the role of marketing management even more for Budweiser. Ultimately, the emerging microbrewery craze set in; in 2008, Anheuser-Busch was sold to the Belgian company InBev (the new corporate name is AB InBev).[63] Although no longer an "American-owned" beer, Budweiser continues to push its strong association with Americana through cutting-edge Super Bowl commercials and the return of the beloved Clydesdales. Budweiser's 2017 Super Bowl ad reached even further back into its American history, telling the story of Adolphus Busch's immigration to the United States.[64]

Budweiser continues to innovate with products focused on females and millennials. In 2012, it launched a blend of beer and cocktail called Lime-A-Rita, with additional flavors recently released.[65] In 2014, 200,000 millennials were invited to vie for 1,000 spots at Whatever, USA, a Budweiser-led event in Crested Butte, Colorado, where guests partied with celebrities, made many new friends, and, of course, drank Bud Light. The strategy was executed largely through digital and social media.[66]

Over all these years, Budweiser's longevity and continued success is a testament to the power of strong, adaptive marketing management—always staying fresh in the market, relevant to new groups of customers, and effective in using the day's most effective promotional tools to communicate the brand's value and differentiation.

Questions for Consideration

1. Over the course of its history, Budweiser's marketing responded to major regulatory and cultural changes, such as Prohibition and the changing role of women in society. What other changes are either happening now or are on the horizon to which today's marketing managers at Budweiser should respond? What should that response be?

2. In this account of Budweiser's history there is evidence of both "Big M" marketing and "little m" marketing. Which of these two types of marketing do you think is Budweiser's greater strength? Support your answer with examples to demonstrate your understanding of these concepts.

3. The most recent threat to Budweiser's dominance is the microbrewery craze, which has created (or resulted from) a set of more discriminating beer drinkers, not so different from wine aficionados. One approach Budweiser has taken in their commercials is to make fun of these enthusiasts. Do you believe this is an effective strategy? Why or why not? What alternative communication or product innovation strategies (if any) should be considered to reach this segment?

NOTES

1. @Wendy's. *Twitter,* 2017, https://twitter.com/Wendys?ref_src=twsrc%5Egoogle%7Ctwcamp%5Eserp%7Ctwgr%5Eauthor.

2. Source: Jayson DeMers. "What Your Business Should Know before Imitating Wendy's Twitter Feed." *Forbes,* January 17, 2017, https://www.forbes.com/sites/jaysondemers/2017/01/17/is-wendys-winning-or-losing-with-its-twitter-roasting-streak/#2129cb6a1944.

3. Pola B. Gupta, Paula M. Saunders, and Jeremy Smith, "Traditional Master of Business Administration (MBA) versus the MBA with Specialization: A Disconnection between What Business Schools Offer and What Employers Seek," *Journal of Education for Business* 82, no. 8 (2007), pp. 307–12.

4. David W. Stewart, "How Marketing Contributes to the Bottom Line," *Journal of Advertising Research* 48, no. 1 (2008), p. 94.

5. Malcolm A. McNiven, "Plan for More Productive Advertising," *Harvard Business Review* 58, no. 2 (1980), p. 130.

6. Mitchell J. Lovett and Jason B. MacDonald, "How Does Financial Performance Affect Marketing? Studying the Marketing-Finance Relationship from a Dynamic Perspective," *Journal of the Academy of Marketing Science* 33, no. 4 (2005), pp. 476–85; and Ramesh K. S. Rao and Neeraj Bharadwaj, "Marketing Initiatives, Expected Cash Flows, and Shareholders' Wealth," *Journal of Marketing* 72, no. 1 (2008), pp. 16–26.

7. Source: Peter F. Drucker, *The Practice of Management.* New York, NY: HarperCollins Publishers, pp. 37–38, 1954.

8. Source: Peter F. Drucker, *Management: Tasks, Responsibilities, Practices* (New York: Harper and Row, 1973), p. 63.

9. Shaun Powell, "The Management and Consumption of Organisational Creativity," *Journal of Consumer Marketing* 25, no. 3 (2008), pp. 158–66.

10. Rosa Chun and Gary Davies, "The Influence of Corporate Character on Customers and Employees: Exploring Similarities and Differences," *Journal of the Academy of Marketing Science* 34, no. 2 (2006), pp. 138–47.

11. John Grant, "Green Marketing," *Strategic Direction* 24, no. 6 (2008), pp. 25–27.

12. Source: "About Unilever," *Unilever,* n.d., https://www.unilever.com/about/who-we-are/about-Unilever/.

13. Leonie Roderick, "Unilever Puts Brands Front and Centre in Renewed Sustainability Push," *Marketing Week,* September 1, 2016, https://www.marketingweek.com/2016/09/01/unilever-puts-brands-front-and-centre-in-renewed-sustainability-push/.

14. *Toms,* n.d., http://www.toms.com/.

15. Charlotte Rogers, "How Toms Engaged 3.5 Million People in One Day," *Marketing Week,* June 29, 2016, https://www.marketingweek.com/2016/06/29/how-footwear-brand-toms-engaged-3-5-million-people-in-one-day-using-tribe-power/.

16. Stuart Elliot, "Selling Products by Selling Shared Values," *New York Times,* www.nytimes.com/2013/02/14/business/media/panera-to-advertise-its-socialconsciousness-advertising.html?pagewanted=all&_r=0.

17. Michael J. Barone, Kenneth C. Manning, and Paul W. Miniard, "Consumer Response to Retailers' Use of Partially Comparative Pricing," *Journal of Marketing* 68, no. 3 (2004), pp. 37–47; and Dhruv Grewal and Joan Lindsey-Mullikin, "The Moderating Role of the Price Frame on the Effects of Price Range and the Number of Competitors on Consumers' Search Intentions," *Journal of the Academy of Marketing Science* 34, no. 1 (2006), pp. 55–63.

18. Jyh-shen Chiou and Cornelia Droge, "Service Quality, Trust, Specific Asset Investment, and Expertise: Direct and Indirect Effects in a Satisfaction-Loyalty Framework," *Journal of the Academy of Marketing Science* 34, no. 4 (2006), pp. 613–28.

19. Source: Jaworski, Bernie , Rob Malcolm, and Neil Morgan. "7 Big Problems in the Marketing Industry," *Marketing News,* 2016.

20. Source: "Henry Ford Quotes," UBR Inc., www.people.ubr.com /historical-figures/by-first-name/h/henry-ford/henry-ford -quotes.aspx.

21. Louis E. Boone and David L. Kurtz, *Contemporary Marketing* (Hinsdale, IL: Dryden Press, 1974), p. 14.

22. Source: General Electric Company, *1952 Annual Report* (New York: General Electric Company, 1952), p. 21.

23. Neil H. Borden, "The Concept of the Marketing Mix," *Journal of Advertising Research* 4 (June 1964), pp. 2–7; and E. Jerome McCarthy, *Basic Marketing: A Managerial Approach* (Homewood, IL: Irwin, 1960).

24. Bernard Cova and Robert Salle, "Marketing Solutions in Accordance with the S-D Logic: Co-creating Value with Customer Network Actors," *Industrial Marketing Management* 37, no. 3 (2008), pp. 270–77.

25. Evangelia D. Fassoula, "Transforming the Supply Chain," *Journal of Manufacturing Technology Management* 17, no. 6 (2006), pp. 848–60.

26. Jonathan Bacon, "The Big Debate: Are the '4Ps of Marketing' Still Relevant?" *Marketing Week,* February 9, 2017, https://www.marketingweek.com/2017/02/09/big-debate -4ps-marketing-still-relevant/.

27. Mary Jo Bitner and Bernard H. Booms, "Marketing Strategies and Organizational Structures for Service Firms," in *Marketing of Services,* J. Donnelly and W. George, eds. (Chicago: American Marketing Association, 1981), pp. 47–51.

28. V. Kumar and J. Andrew Petersen, "Using a Customer-Level Marketing Strategy to Enhance Firm Performance: A Review of Theoretical and Empirical Evidence," *Journal of the Academy of Marketing Science* 33, no. 4 (2005), pp. 504–20; and Stephen L. Vargo and Robert F. Lusch, "Evolving to a New Dominant Logic for Marketing," *Journal of Marketing* 68, no. 1 (2004), pp. 1–17.

29. Liad Stein, "4 Examples of Successful Businesses Following a Customer-Centric Model," *Nanorep,* June 28, 2016, https:// www.nanorep.com/4-examples-of-customer-centric-models.

30. Sundar Bharadwaj, Terry Clark, and Songpol Kulviwat, "Marketing, Market Growth, and Endogenous Growth Theory: An Inquiry into the Causes of Market Growth," *Journal of the Academy of Marketing Science* 33, no. 3 (2005), pp. 347–60.

31. Mindy Weinstein, "A Trillion-Dollar Demographic: 10 Brands That Got Millennial Marketing Right," *Search Engine Journal,* July 23, 2015, https://www.searchenginejournal.com /trillion-dollar-demographic-10-brands-got-millennial -marketing-right/135969/.

32. Vargo and Lusch, "Evolving to a New Dominant Logic for Marketing."

33. Stan Phelps, "Southwest Airlines Understands the Heart of Marketing Is Experience," *Forbes,* September 14, 2014, https:// www.forbes.com/sites/stanphelps/2014/09/14/southwest -airlines-understands-the-heart-of-marketing-is-experience /#1677aefa2bda.

34. Mark W. Johnston and Greg W. Marshall, *Relationship Selling,* 2nd ed. (New York: McGraw-Hill/Irwin, 2008), p. 5.

35. George S. Day, "Managing Market Relationships," *Journal of the Academy of Marketing Science* 28, no. 1 (2000), pp. 24–31.

36. Simon J. Bell, Seigyoung Auh, and Karen Smalley, "Customer Relationship Dynamics: Service Quality and Customer Loyalty in the Context of Varying Levels of Customer Expertise and Switching Costs," *Journal of the Academy of Marketing Science* 33, no. 2 (2005), pp. 169–84; and Girish Ramani and V. Kumar, "Interaction Orientation and Firm Performance," *Journal of Marketing* 72, no. 1 (2008), pp. 27–45.

37. Joseph Pigato, "How 9 Successful Companies Keep Their Customers," *Entrepreneur,* April 3, 2015, https://www.entrepreneur.com/article/243764.

38. Don Peppers and Martha Rogers, *The One-to-One Manager: Real World Lessons in Customer Relationship Management* (New York: Doubleday Business, 2002).

39. Jagdish N. Sheth, Rajendra S. Sisodia, and Arun Sharma, "The Antecedents and Consequences of Customer-Centric Marketing," *Journal of the Academy of Marketing Science* 28, no. 1 (2000), pp. 55–67.

40. Cotton Timberlake, "Retailers Cater to Customization Craze," *San Francisco Chronicle,* January 18, 2013, www.sfgate .com/business/article/Retailers-cater-to-customization -craze-4207186.php.

41. Fred Wiersema, *The New Market Leaders: Who's Winning and How in the Battle for Customers* (New York: Free Press, 2001), pp. 48–58.

42. Jonathan Salem Baskin, "The Internet Didn't Kill Blockbuster, the Company Did It to Itself," *Forbes,* November 8, 2013, https:// www.forbes.com/sites/jonathansalembaskin/2013/11/08 /the-internet-didnt-kill-blockbuster-the-company-did-it-to -itself/#7a5c2cf6488d.

43. Efhymios Constantinides and Stefan J. Fountain, "Web 2.0: Conceptual Foundations and Marketing Issues," *Journal of Direct, Data and Digital Marketing Practice* 9, no. 3 (2008), pp. 231–45.

44. Anonymous, "Search and Seizure," *Marketing Health Services* 28, no. 1 (2008), p. 6.

45. Barton Goldenberg, "Conquering Your 2 Biggest CRM Challenges," *Sales & Marketing Management* 159, no. 3 (2007), p. 35.

46. Natalia Angulo, "Girl Scout Cookie Finder App Helps You Find Your Thin Mints," *Fox News,* February 7, 2013, www .foxnews.com/tech/2013/02/07/girl-scout-cookie-finder-app -helps-buyers-find-their-thin-mints/.

47. Ruth Maria Stock and Wayne D. Hoyer, "An Attitude-Behavior Model of Salespeople's Customer Orientation," *Journal of the Academy of Marketing Science* 33, no. 4 (2005), pp. 536–53.

48. Dan Schawbel, "10 New Findings about the Millennial Consumer," *Forbes,* January 20, 2015, https://www.forbes .com/sites/danschawbel/2015/01/20/10-new-findings-about -the-millennial-consumer/2/#6f5b812c1474.

49. Mindy Weinstein, "A Trillion-Dollar Demographic: 10 Brands That Got Millennial Marketing Right," *Search Engine Journal,* July 23, 2015, https://www.searchenginejournal.com/trillion-dollar -demographic-10-brands-got-millennial-marketing-right /135969/; "NPD Group: Millennials Not abandoning Chipotle," *Fast Casual,* February 18, 2016, https://www.fastcasual.com /news/npd-group-millennials-not-abandoning-chipotle/.

50. Micah Solomon, "You've Got Millennial Employees All Wrong; Here Are the Four Things You Need to Know Now," *Forbes,* January 26, 2016, https://www.forbes.com/sites

/micahsolomon/2016/01/26/everything-youve-heard-about -millennial-employees-is-baloney-heres-the-truth-and-how -to-use-it/#7b693dfe4904.

51. Katherine Reynolds Lewis, "Everything You Need to Know about Your Millennial Co-Workers," *Fortune,* June 23, 2015, http:// fortune.com/2015/06/23/know-your-millennial-co-workers/.

52. Marco Vriens, "Strategic Research Design," *Marketing Research* 15, no. 4 (2003), p. 20.

53. Lovett and MacDonald, "How Does Financial Performance Affect Marketing?"; and Steven H. Seggie, "Assessing Marketing Strategy Performance," *Journal of the Academy of Marketing Science* 34, no. 2 (2006), pp. 267–69.

54. Thomas S. Gruca and Lopo L. Rego, "Customer Satisfaction, Cash Flow, and Shareholder Value," *Journal of Marketing* 69, no. 3 (2005), pp. 115–30.

55. "Marketing Return on Investment," McKinsey & Company, 2017, http://www.mckinsey.com/business-functions/marketing-and -sales/how-we-help-clients/marketing-return-on-investment.

56. Frederick E. Webster, Jr., Alan J. Malter, and Shankar Ganesan, "Can Marketing Regain Its Seat at the Table?" *Marketing Science Institute Working Paper Series,* Report No. 03-113 (2004).

57. Fastco Studios, "Whassup?! 150 Years of Budweiser History, from Clydesdales to Talking Frogs, in 2 Minutes," *Fast Company,* web video, October 2, 2014, www.fastcompany .com/3036422/whassup-150-years-of-budweiser-history-from -clydsdales-to-talking-frogs-in-2-minutes.

58. "Anheuser-Busch," *Advertising Age,* September 15, 2003, http:// adage.com/article/adage-encyclopedia/anheuser-busch/98319/.

59. Jay R. Brooks, "Beer in Ads #623: Budweiser's 6000 Men," *Brookston Beer Bulletin,* June 4, 2012, http://brookstonbeerbulletin .com/beer-in-ads-623-budweisers-6000-men/.

60. Fastco Studios, "Whassup?!"

61. Anheuser-Busch, "Horse-Story in the Making: The Budweiser Clydesdales," *Anheuser-Busch,* November 21, 2016, http://www.anheuser-busch.com/about/clydesdale.html.

62. Fastco Studios, "Whassup?!"

63. Fastco Studios, "Whassup?!"

64. Will Burns, "Budweiser Tells Its Own Immigration Story in Super Bowl Ad," *Forbes,* January 31, 2017, https://www .forbes.com/sites/willburns/2017/01/31/budweiser-tells-its -own-immigration-story-in-super-bowl-ad/#446cab0e2907.

65. John Kell, "AB InBev Is Marketing Bud Light Lime-A-Rita Exclusively to Women," *Fortune,* March 13, 2017, http:// fortune.com/2017/03/13/ab-inbev-lime-a-rita-women/.

66. Kristina Monllos, "Inside Whatever, USA: Bud Light's Party Town as 'Content Factory,'" *Adweek,* June 2, 2015, www .adweek.com/brand-marketing/inside-whatever-usa-bud -lights-party-town-content-factory-165114/; Jeff Fromm, "The Secret to Bud Light's Millennial Marketing Success," *Forbes,* October 7, 2014, www.forbes.com/sites/jefffromm/2014/10/07 /the-secret-to-bud-lights-millennial-marketing-success /#5f0854ee7054.

CHAPTER 2

Marketing Foundations: Global, Ethical, Sustainable

LEARNING OBJECTIVES

LO 2-1 Identify the various levels in the Global Marketing Experience Curve.

LO 2-2 Learn the essential information components for assessing a global market opportunity.

LO 2-3 Define the key regional market zones and their marketing challenges.

LO 2-4 Describe the strategies for entering new global markets.

LO 2-5 Recognize key factors in creating a global product strategy.

LO 2-6 Learn the importance of ethics in marketing strategy, the value proposition, and the elements of the marketing mix.

LO 2-7 Recognize the significance of sustainability as part of marketing strategy and the use of the triple bottom line as a metric for evaluating corporate performance.

How do the three topics of this chapter—global, ethical, sustainable—fit together? You may have asked that question when you read the title. However, these topics represent the foundation of marketing and build on the ideas and concepts discussed in Chapter 1. Though they may seem unrelated, they are linked together because companies realize that success in the marketing place today is defined, in part, by a company's ability to consider global opportunities, clearly define its values, and develop a value proposition and marketing strategy that considers factors beyond profit (sustainability). In this chapter, we explore each of these topics, linking them back to the concepts in Chapter 1 and introducing information that you will use throughout the rest of the book.

MARKETING IS NOT LIMITED BY BORDERS

From large multinationals to small start-up companies, business is no longer confined to a company's local market. Worldwide distribution networks, sophisticated communication tools, greater product standardization, and the Internet have opened world markets. Large companies such as Nestlé, P&G, Amazon, and General Electric leverage their considerable assets to build global companies that do business anywhere in the world (see Exhibit 2.1). At the same time, with relatively minimal investment, small companies access international markets with only a website and an international shipping company.[1]

While the opportunities have never been greater, the risks have also never been higher. Global marketing mistakes are expensive. The international competitive landscape includes sophisticated global companies as well as successful local organizations. The operating environment varies dramatically around the world, creating real challenges for companies moving into new markets. Global customers demand different products, which means that successful products in a company's local market frequently have to be adapted to new markets.[2] All these factors establish global marketing as one of the most demanding but rewarding areas in marketing.

THE GLOBAL EXPERIENCE LEARNING CURVE

An understanding of marketing beyond home markets develops over time as a company gets more international business experience. This process is referred to as *the global experience learning curve.* In some cases this happens quickly. General Motors moved into Canada in 1918, only two years after being incorporated, and eBay opened in the United Kingdom during its first year of operation. However, other companies take much longer to push into global markets. Walmart opened its first international store in Mexico City in 1991, nearly 30 years after Sam Walton opened the first store in Bentonville, Arkansas. Exhibit 2.2 lists the global expansion histories of a number of companies.

> **LO 2-1**
>
> Identify the various levels in the Global Marketing Experience Curve.

EXHIBIT 2.1 | **World's Largest International Companies in 2016**

Company	Revenue ($ Millions)
Walmart	$484,130
State Grid	329,601
China National Petroleum	299,271
Sinopec Group	294,344
Royal Dutch Shell	272,156
ExxonMobil	246,204
Volkswagen	236,600
Toyota Motor	236,592
Apple	233,715
BP	225,982

Source: "Fortune Global 500," *Time Inc.,* July 3, 2016.

As a global airline, Emirates wants to promote international togetherness with the hope of more people traveling and, not surprisingly, choosing Emirates.

Source: The Emirates Group

The global experience learning curve moves a company through four distinct stages: no foreign marketing, foreign marketing, international marketing, and global marketing. The process is not always linear; companies may, for example, move directly from no foreign marketing to international marketing without necessarily engaging in foreign marketing. In addition, the amount of time spent in any stage can vary; some companies remain in a stage for many years.

Companies with No Foreign Marketing

Many companies with *no direct foreign marketing* still do business with international customers through intermediaries or limited direct contact. In these cases, however, there is no formal international channel relationship or global marketing strategy targeted at international customers. Of course, any company with a website is now a global company as someone can visit the site from anywhere in the world, but companies with no foreign marketing consider any sales to an international customer as incidental.

The typical company with no foreign marketing is usually small, with a limited range of products. Increasingly though, small companies move into international markets much faster than even a decade ago. This is due, in part, to domestic distributor relationships, local customers with global operations, and effective websites, which have all created international opportunities for many small companies with limited resources.

Companies with Foreign Marketing

Companies often develop a more formal international strategy by following their existing customers into foreign markets. Domestic customers with global operations may demand more service or place additional orders that require the company to work with their foreign

EXHIBIT 2.2 | Examples of Global Companies and Their Expansion into Global Markets

Years to Expansion	U.S. Company	First Expansion
29	Walmart (est. 1962)	1991: Walmart opens two units in Mexico City.
20	Hewlett-Packard (est. 1939)	1959: HP sets up a European marketing organization in Geneva, Switzerland, and a manufacturing plant in Germany.
26	Tyson Foods (est. 1963)	1989: Tyson establishes a partnership with a Mexican poultry company to create an international partnership.
25	Caterpillar (est. 1925)	1950: Caterpillar Tractor Co. Ltd. in Great Britain is founded.
19	Home Depot (est. 1979)	1998: Home Depot enters the Puerto Rican market, followed by entry into Argentina.
18	Gap (est. 1969)	1987: The first Gap store outside the United States opens in London on George Street.
12	Goodyear (est. 1898)	1910: Goodyear's Canadian plant opens.
10	FedEx (est. 1971)	1981: International delivery begins with service to Canada.
1	PepsiCo (est. 1965)	1966: Pepsi enters Japan and Eastern Europe.

subsidiaries. This stage of the global experience learning curve is called *foreign marketing* and involves developing local distribution and service representation in a foreign market in one of two ways. One method is to identify local intermediaries in appropriate international markets and create a formal relationship. The second approach is for the company to establish its own direct sales force in major markets, thereby expanding the company's direct market reach.

In either scenario, key activities (product planning and development, manufacturing) are still done in the company's home market, but products are modified to fit international requirements. Global markets are important enough for management to build international sales forecasts, and manufacturing allocates time specifically to international production. At this point, international markets are no longer an afterthought, but rather an integral, albeit small, part of the company's growth model.[3]

EXHIBIT 2.3 | Large U.S. Companies with over 50% of Revenue from International Markets

Company	Percent of Sales from International Markets
Qualcomm	98%
Intel	82
McDonald's	68
Dow Chemical	66
General Motors	63
Apple	62
Nike	55
Johnson & Johnson	53
General Electric	53

International Marketing

When a firm makes the commitment to manufacture products outside its domestic market, it is engaged in *international marketing*. While companies can be heavily involved in international markets with extensive selling organizations and distribution networks, the decision to manufacture outside its home market marks a significant shift toward an integrated international market strategy. Global markets become an essential component of the company's growth strategy, and resources are allocated to expand the business into those markets. The company incorporates an international division or business unit that has responsibility for growing the business in targeted foreign markets.

International marketing aligns the company's assets and resources with global markets, but, in the vast majority of companies, management still takes a "domestic first" approach to the business. As a result, the corporate structure still divides international and domestic markets.

Global Marketing

A *global marketing* company realizes that all world markets (including the company's own domestic market) are, in reality, a single market with many different segments. This frequently happens when a company generates more than half its revenue in international markets. Exhibit 2.3 highlights companies considered traditional American companies but that generate more than half their revenue outside the United States.

The most significant difference between international and global marketing organizations is management philosophy and corporate planning. Global marketers treat the world as a single, unified market with many different segments that may or may not fall along countries' political boundaries. International marketers, on the other hand, define markets along traditional political boundaries and, most often, assign unique status to their domestic market.

The first step in moving into global markets is to evaluate the market opportunities. Since a company's management team is usually less familiar with foreign markets, research helps fill in the blanks, providing critical information for decision makers.

Essential Information

Global market research focuses on five basic types of information.

Economic An accurate understanding of the current economic environment, such as gross domestic product (GDP) growth, inflation, strength of the currency, and business

LO 2-2

Learn the essential information components for assessing a global marketing opportunity.

EXHIBIT 2.4 | Top 5 Economies Based on GDP

Top 5 Economies	GDP (purchasing power parity) (US$ trillion)
China	$21.27
European Union	$19.18
United States	$18.56
India	$ 8.72
Japan	$ 4.93

Source: 2016 CIA World Fact Book

cycle trends, is essential. Also, depending on the company's target markets (consumer or business), additional economic data on consumer spending per capita (consumer products) or industrial purchasing trends (business products) are also needed to facilitate decision making. Exhibit 2.4 identifies the five largest economies in the world based on GDP, which is the total market value of all final goods and services produced in a country in a given year and one of the most widely used measures of economic growth.

Culture, Societal Trends Understanding a global market's culture and social trends is fundamental for consumer products and helpful for business-to-business marketers. Cultural values, symbols and rituals, and cultural differences affect people's perception of products while B2B companies must learn local cultural practices to recruit employees and establish good business relationships.[4]

Business Environment Knowledge of the business environment is essential for companies moving into foreign markets where they will invest significant resources. Ethical standards, management styles, degree of formality, and gender or other biases are all critical factors that management needs to know before entering a new market. Failure to understand the business environment can lead to misunderstanding and lost relationships as the company enters a new market. (See Exhibit 2.5 for examples.)

Political and Legal Local political changes can create significant uncertainties for a business. As witnessed in Bolivia and other countries, new governments sometimes alter the relationship of government to industry by exerting greater control and even nationalizing some industries.

Learning the legal landscape is fundamental before committing resources in a foreign market. Developing countries frequently limit the flow of money out of the country, making it harder for a foreign company to transfer money back home. Labor laws also vary widely around the world. Germany and France, for example, make it difficult to terminate someone once that person has

EXHIBIT 2.5 | Business Customs in Five Selected Countries

When you are doing business in...	Remember...
The Czech Republic	Relationship building is important. Start with small talk and get to know the individual you are working with.
France	You should address the French as Monsieur or Madame followed by his or her last name. Use first names only after you are encouraged to do so.
Japan	Exchanging business cards is a brief ceremony. Use both hands to accept the card and look over each side before you slip it into your jacket pocket or briefcase.
Germany	Punctuality is extremely important. Be on time or you may seem disrespectful.
Colombia	Colombians stand closer to each other than do Americans. Do not step back if you feel they are too close; you may seem rude.

Source: Kwintessential.co.uk

been hired, while Great Britain's termination policies are more consistent with those of the United States.

Specific Market Conditions Before entering a foreign market, a company has some understanding of the specific market conditions for its own products as a result of its existing business knowledge. However, it is unlikely a company has in-depth knowledge about market trends, competitors, and unique market characteristics. Unfortunately, many companies that follow customers into a particular market believe it is unnecessary to know a lot about local market conditions. This lack of understanding can limit growth opportunities. The more a company knows about the local market environment, the better it will be able to leverage its investment in that market.

EXHIBIT 2.6	Fastest-Growing World Economies

Country	2017 GDP Real Growth Rate (%)
Libya	13.73
Yemen	12.62
Côte d'Ivoire	7.98
Myanmar	7.70
India	7.61

Source: IMF, *World Economic Outlook*, October 2016.

Emerging Markets

World economic growth for much of the 20th century was fueled by the **developed economies** of Western Europe, the United States, and Japan. Over the past 25 years, however, while developed economies continue to grow, the most significant economic growth is found in **emerging markets**. Indeed, 75 percent of world economic growth over the next 20 years is projected to come from a new group of powerful economies, most notably China and India. These economic growth engines create market opportunities for companies, which, in turn, means marketers need to understand the unique challenges and opportunities of emerging markets.[5] Exhibit 2.6 highlights the fastest-growing economies in the world. Notice that, with the exception of India, the fastest-growing economies are small and their significant percentage growth is due in large part to the fact that the country's economy is starting from a much smaller economic base. Libya, for example, grew nearly 14 percent in 2017, but that does not mean it represents a good market opportunity.

The nature of emerging markets means traditional marketing methods will not be effective. For example, if the majority of a country lacks a television or radio and cannot read, traditional advertising campaigns will not work, or if a country lacks a distribution network, it will not be possible to deliver products to customers.

The challenge for marketers, particularly consumer products companies, is that demand for their products may be strong, but there is insufficient income to purchase the product and inadequate infrastructure to support sophisticated market programs. Soon after the Velvet Revolution in the Czech Republic, Estee Lauder opened a store in Prague targeted at Czech women living in the capital.[6] At first the company experienced problems because products that sold well in Western Europe and the United States simply were not being purchased. The company came to realize the products were sized and priced according to Western European standards and too expensive for the local Czech businesswoman. The solution was to sell sample sizes (which are often offered as premiums in promotional packages sold in the United States) for a fraction of the large product sizes. Czech women wanted to purchase Estee Lauder cosmetics, but at a size and price consistent with the local market.

Multinational Regional Market Zones

The single most significant global economic trend over the past 15 years is the emergence of regional market zones around the world. **Regional market zones** consist of a group of countries that create formal relationships for mutual economic benefit through lower tariffs and reduced trade barriers. In some cases, such as the European Union, their influence extends beyond economic concerns to political and social issues. Many countries believe membership in an economic alliance will be essential for access to markets in the future. As the world divides itself into a handful of powerful economic alliances, countries feel

LO 2-3

Define the key regional market zones and their marketing challenges.

EXHIBIT 2.7 | Top Four Regional Market Zones

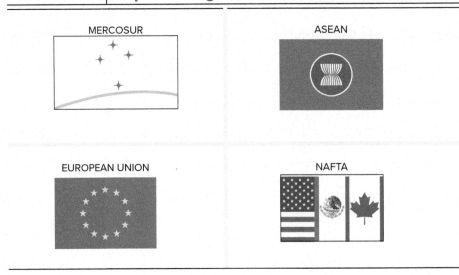

Source: ©Alliance Images/Alamy Stock Photo

pressure to align with a regional market zone. Exhibit 2.7 identifies four of the largest regional market zones.

Regional market zones generally form as a result of four forces. The first and most fundamental factor is *economic.* Many small and medium-sized countries believe growth in their own country will be enhanced by forming alliances with other countries. By enlarging the trading area and creating a market zone, each country benefits economically and the market zone has more power in the global marketplace. Second, research suggests *geographic proximity* to other alliance partners is advantageous in the development of a market zone. Transportation and communication networks are more likely to connect countries close to one another, making it easier to facilitate market zone activities. Other issues such as immigration also tend to be handled more effectively when the distance between partners is minimized. The third factor is *political.* Closely related to increased economic power is increased political clout, particularly as smaller countries form broad political alliances. A prerequisite for effective political alliances among countries is general agreement on government policies. Countries with widely disparate political structures find it difficult to accommodate those differences in a political alliance. *Cultural similarities,* such as having a shared language, among alliance partners also facilitate market zones as shared cultural experiences encourage greater cooperation and minimize possible conflicts from cultural disparities.

Europe The **European Union** is the most successful regional market zone and it is also one of the oldest. Founded more than 50 years ago by six countries (Belgium, France, Italy, Luxembourg, the Netherlands, and West Germany) with the Treaty of Rome, the EU now includes 28 countries spanning all of Europe. In addition, five countries are seeking membership in the European Union: Iceland, Macedonia, Montenegro, Serbia, and Turkey. The process of becoming a member of the EU takes many years, and applicants must meet a wide range of economic, social, and legal criteria. One of the most difficult challenges for many member states is meeting targeted government spending and total debt limits. France and Germany (the two largest members of the EU) have both failed to meet government spending limits in recent years, and the debt limits of countries like Italy and Greece exceed the EU guidelines. With few consequences for missing EU targets, many governments focus more on local country priorities than EU directives. This has been a factor in the ongoing challenges for the euro as countries like Greece experience significant budget problems. Other countries (Italy, Spain, Portugal) are also having significant problems meeting their financial obgliations.[7]

The EU is one of the most dominant economic entities in the world, with economic output approximately equal to that of the United States, but it is not without challenges. Its currency, the euro, has been considered one of the strongest in the world. However, recent challenges to the economic stability of several EU members (such as Greece) have caused significant fluctuations in its value. At the same time, some countries (notably Great Britain) have voted to leave the EU, creating a great deal of uncertainty about its future. Despite the challenges it faces, the EU maintains a great deal of power over member states, with the ability to enact laws, impose taxes, and exert tremendous social influence in the lives of citizens. For example, the EU has adopted strong socially responsible policies for companies doing business in member countries.

The WTO is the leading global organization to settle trade disputes between countries.
©Martin Good/Shutterstock

Americas The most significant market zone in the Americas is the alliance of the United States, Canada, and Mexico, which is commonly referred to by the treaty that created the alliance, **NAFTA (North American Free Trade Agreement)**. NAFTA created the single largest economic alliance and has eliminated tariffs between the member countries for more than 19 years. Exhibit 2.8 lists NAFTA's main provisions. Many industries, such as automaking, have manufacturing plants in Mexico to supply the U.S. market. Retailers have also benefited; Gigante, a large Mexican supermarket chain, operates in the United States while Walmart, a U.S. company, has over 800 stores in Mexico.[8]

NAFTA is not the only market zone in the Americas. **MERCOSUR**, the most powerful market zone in South America, was inaugurated in 1995 and includes Argentina, Bolivia, Brazil, Chile, Paraguay, and Uruguay. With over 200 million people and a combined GDP of more than $1 trillion, it is currently the third-largest free trade area in the world.[9] One of the drawbacks has been a limited transnational transportation network, which restricts the movement of goods between member countries. However, MERCOSUR has overcome this

---

EXHIBIT 2.8 | Key Provisions of NAFTA

NAFTA aims to:

- Eliminate barriers to trade in, and facilitate the cross-border movement of, goods and services between the territories of the Parties.

- Promote conditions of fair competition in the free trade area.

- Increase substantially investment opportunities in the territories of the Parties.

- Provide adequate and effective protection and enforcement of intellectual property rights in each Party's territory.

- Create effective procedures for the implementation and application of this Agreement, for its joint administration and for the resolution of disputes; and

- Establish a framework for further trilateral, regional, and multilateral cooperation to expand and enhance the benefits of this Agreement.

Source: Article 101: Establishment of the Free Trade Area, NAFTA.

problem by successfully leveraging the combined economic power of the individual member countries and creating additional economic benefits for its members.

Asia The most important Asian market zone is **ASEAN**, which was founded in 1967 and comprises 10 countries in the Pacific Rim (Brunei Darussalam, Indonesia, Malaysia, Philippines, Cambodia, Laos, Myanmar, Singapore, Thailand, and Vietnam). After the 1997–1998 Asian financial crisis, the group added China, Japan, and South Korea. While the relationships with these "plus 3" countries are less developed than among the full member countries, the combined economic activity of all participants makes ASEAN a powerful global economic force.[10] The GDP of the 10 full members is over $600 billion, and if the "plus 3" countries are included, the combined total is over $20 trillion. ASEAN is currently leading talks to create an Asian free-trade area that would encompass "30 percent of the world's total export volume." The Regional Comprehensive Economic Partnership would be second only to the WTO in size.

SELECT THE GLOBAL MARKET

Conducting a thorough assessment of potential global market opportunities is an essential first step in entering the global market. Once the analysis is completed, it is time to select specific countries for future investment. Deciding which countries to enter is difficult because the risk of failure is very high. Targeting the wrong country can lead to very high costs and unprofitable long-term investments. Walmart pulled out of the German market at an estimated cost of $400 million. On the other hand, moving too slowly into a market can hamper growth and limit profit potential in the future. eBay's decision to move slowly into China cost the company a dominant position in the market.

Identify Selection Criteria

Market selection criteria incorporate the nature of the competitive environment, including both local and global competitors, as well as target market size and future growth rates. Marketing managers need to know which markets will be the easiest and which will be the most difficult to enter. In addition, the size and future growth potential of international markets are critical in making the long-term commitment to manufacture in an international market. On the other hand, financial criteria focus on the cost of market entry and profitability estimates over given time periods. Decision makers are particularly interested in knowing the size of the investment and the length of time it will take before the company can expect to be profitable in a new market.[11]

Company Review

As a marketing manager you will need to evaluate global market opportunities against key company characteristics to look for markets that maximize the company's strengths while minimizing weaknesses. Moving into new foreign markets brings greater risk to the company. As a result, decision makers must consider whether their company philosophy, personnel skill sets (principally in critical areas such as marketing and logistics), organizational structure, management expertise, and financial resources support the move into new countries (see Exhibit 2.9). Comparing the

EXHIBIT 2.9 | **Key Company Characteristics in Global Market Expansion**

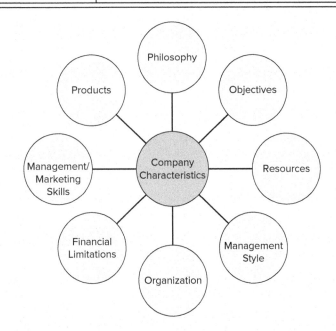

analysis of market opportunities with company characteristics drives the final selection as management looks for the best fit between each country's mix of opportunities/threats and the company's strengths/weaknesses.

DEVELOP GLOBAL MARKET STRATEGIES

After selecting a country, you must develop a comprehensive marketing strategy. International expansion requires a reassessment of existing marketing strategies. Companies often mistakenly believe they can adapt existing market strategies to new international markets. Unfortunately, successful market tactics in the company's home market often fail to translate well into foreign markets. As a result, it is necessary to construct a marketing plan specifically designed for entering global markets.

Market Entry Strategies

The first decision is how to enter the market. An entry strategy is the framework for entering a new global market, so choosing the right strategy is critical. This decision affects all other marketing decisions. In addition, deciding on a market entry strategy has long-term implications because once the strategy is selected it is difficult and expensive to change.

LO 2-4

Describe the strategies for entering new global markets.

Entry into new global markets follows one of four basic strategies: exporting, contractual agreements, strategic alliances, and ownership. Within these basic strategies are various options. Generally, companies enter new markets by exporting because it offers minimal investment and lower risk. At the same time, potential return on investment and profitability are lower and the company has very little control over the process. As a company strengthens its international involvement there is the potential for greater financial returns and control over the process; however, risk and company investments increase.

Exporting Exporting is the most common method for entering foreign markets and accounts for 10 percent of all global economic activity. Primary advantages include the ability to penetrate foreign markets with minimal investment and very little risk. Frequently, companies lack a coherent exporting strategy and take an opportunistic approach that simply fills orders without regard to any specific analysis or targeting.

Most people consider exporting an initial entry strategy and not a long-term approach to global marketing. However, some very large companies find exporting a viable strategy despite a global market presence. Boeing and Airbus, the two manufacturers of large jet airliners, both follow an exporting strategy, manufacturing the jets in their home markets (Boeing in the United States, Airbus in Europe) and then using a direct sales force to market their planes around the world.[12]

Internet. Without question, the Internet has expanded the global reach of every company with a website. Critical to the success of the Internet market entry strategy is easy payment and credit terms offered by global credit companies such as MasterCard, Visa, and American Express. Credit cards and other financial payment systems have greatly simplified transactions, making it easier for the customer to purchase and more secure for the company to sell products anywhere in the world. Another key is the ability to deliver products anywhere in the world on time and in good working order using global delivery companies such as UPS, FedEx, and DHL. This greatly enhances customer and company confidence in a successful transaction.

Internet retailers such as Amazon.com have moved aggressively into global markets. Amazon has opened sites for Germany, the United Kingdom, Canada, Japan, France, China, Italy, Spain, and Austria. In the United Kingdom and Germany, Amazon's sites are among the most visited commercial sites. The Internet has also expanded the international market reach of all retailers. For example, H&M uses an aggressive online strategy to drive business around the world.[13]

Exporter and Distributor. The next of level of exporting involves having country representation, which can take several forms. **Exporters** are international market specialists that help companies by acting as the export marketing department. They generally do not have much contact with the company, but exporters provide a valuable service with their knowledge of policies and procedures for shipping to foreign markets. For small companies with little or no international experience, exporters expedite the process of getting the product to a foreign customer.

Distributors represent the company and often many others in foreign markets. These organizations become the face of the company in that country, servicing customers, selling products, and receiving payments. In many cases, they take title to the goods and then resell them. The primary advantages are that distributors know their own local markets and offer a company physical representation in a global market, saving the company from committing major resources to hire and staff its own operations. The disadvantages are lack of control since distributors do not work directly for the company and lower profitability resulting from the distributor's markup.

Direct Sales Force. Staffing a direct sales force in foreign markets is a significant step for a company moving into global markets. It is expensive to staff and maintain a local sales team in a foreign market; however, companies will often make the commitment because of the level of control and expertise offered by company-trained salespeople. For some industries, creating a direct sales force is required because customers will demand that company salespeople be in the country. This is often the case in the technology and high-end industrial product industries.

Contractual Agreements

Contractual agreements allow a company to expand participation in a market by creating enduring, nonequity relationships with another company, often a local company in that market. Most often these agreements transmit something of value such as technology, a trademark, a patent, or a unique manufacturing process in return for financial compensation in the form of a licensing fee or percentage of sales.

Licensing. Companies choose **licensing** when local partnerships are required by law, legal restrictions prohibit direct importing of the product, or the company's limited financial resources limit more active foreign participation. Companies seeking to establish greater presence in a market without committing significant resources can choose to license their key asset (patent, trademark) to another company, effectively giving that company the right to use that asset in that market. Small and medium-sized companies with a specific product competence that lack the willingness or expertise to invest heavily in foreign operations can identify a license partner in a particular foreign market to manufacture products or provide critical services such as local distribution. In addition, larger companies use this approach to help in exporting and even manufacturing products where more extensive investments are not justified. Pharmaceutical companies are global manufacturers but also license their products in a number of foreign markets. For example, Hammock Pharmaceuticals and MilanPharm/TriLogic Pharma signed an agreement giving Hammock the global rights to an innovative new women's health technology that transforms a liquid into a gel at body temperature, opening new treatment opportunities for women around the world.[14] In these situations, there is limited direct risk to the company, though selecting the wrong licensing partner can be a major problem. On the other hand, licensing does not offer high profit potential and can limit long-term opportunities if a company awards an extended licensing contract.

Franchising. This market entry method has been growing over the last decade; it enables companies to gain access to a foreign market with local ownership. The franchisor, usually a company seeking to enter a foreign market, agrees to supply a bundle of products, systems, services, and management expertise to the franchisee in return for local market knowledge, financial consideration (franchisee fee, percentage of sales, required purchasing of certain products from franchisor), and local management experience. Franchisors exert a great deal of control with extensive franchise agreements that dictate how the franchisee will operate the business.[15] In this way, the franchisor is able to maintain some level of quality control at the point of customer contact.

Franchising, as a global market entry strategy, really took off in the 1990s and has been the first point of entry for many retailers looking to expand international operations. McDonald's, Burger King, KFC, and others have created large franchising networks around the world. Nearly two-thirds of McDonald's restaurants are outside the United States. Combining low capital investments, rapid expansion opportunities, and local market expertise, franchising offers many advantages as a market entry strategy. However, there are also challenges. Worldwide, consumer tastes vary significantly and franchisors need sufficient resources to create products that will meet demands of global customers while maintaining quality control.

Strategic Alliances As a market entry strategy, **strategic alliances** have grown in importance over the past 20 years in an effort to spread risk to other partners. In some industries, strategic alliances now dominate the competitive landscape. Nowhere is this more noticeable than the airline industry. **one**world Alliance (American Airlines, British Airways, Qantas, Cathay Pacific), Sky Team (Air France, KLM, Delta, Korean Air, AeroMexico), and Star (United, Lufthansa) have created a worldwide network of airline partnerships that include code-sharing, frequent flyer mileage partnerships, and some logistical support. All these alliances are designed to make each airline stronger at its weakest point. Building a global airline is extremely expensive and it is much more cost-effective for Delta to partner with Air France to reach cities inside Europe than it is to build its own network. In reality, it would not even be possible with local legal restrictions favoring local airlines.[16] As a result, creating strategic alliances is a necessity, and airlines create broad global partnerships to extend their reach (see Exhibit 2.10).

International Joint Venture. A specific type of strategic alliance called joint venture enables many companies to enter a market that would otherwise be closed because of

EXHIBIT 2.10 | **Airline Strategic Alliances**

ADRIA Airways, Aegean Airlines, Air Canada, Air China, Air India, Air New Zealand, ANA, Asiana Airlines, Austrian, Avianca, Brussels Airlines, Copa Airlines, Croatia Airlines, EgyptAir, Ethiopian Airlines, EVA Air, LOT Polish Airlines, Lufthansa, SAS, Shenzhe Airlines, Singapore Airlines, South African Airlines, SWISS, TAP Portugal, Thai, Turkish Airlines, United Airlines

Aeroflot, Aerolineas Argentinas, AeroMexico, AirEuropa, Air France, Alitalia, China Airlines, China Eastern, China Southern, Czech Airlines, Delta, Garuda Indonesia, Kenya Airways, KLM Royal Dutch Airlines, Korean Air, Middle East Airlines, Saudia, TAROM Romanian Air Transport, Vietnam Airlines, Xiamen Airlines

Airberlin, American Airlines, British Airways, Cathay Pacific, Finnair, Iberia, Japan Airlines, LATAM Airlines, Qatar Airways, Malaysia Airlines, Qantas, SriLankan Airlines, Royal Jordanian, S7 Airlines

legal restrictions or cultural barriers.[17] Additionally, like all strategic alliances, it reduces risk by spreading risk to other partners. **Joint ventures** are a partnership of two or more participating companies and differ from other strategic alliances in that (1) management duties are shared and a management structure is defined; (2) other corporations or legal entities, not individuals, formed the venture; and (3) every partner holds an equity position. Since both partners have equity in the joint venture and share in management duties, it is essential to choose the right partner. To avoid problems, each partner must define what it brings to the joint venture in terms of reputation, resources, and management expertise. Additional critical topics include management structure, cost sharing, and control.

Direct Foreign Investment The market entry strategy with the greatest long-term implications is **direct foreign investment**. Risks go up substantially when a company moves manufacturing into a foreign market. Although this is the riskiest market entry strategy, future market potential can position it for long-term growth. A company must consider a number of factors including:

- *Timing*–unknown political or social events, competitor activity.
- *Legal issues*–growing complexity of international contracts, asset protection.
- *Transaction costs*–production and other costs stated in various currencies.
- *Technology transfer*–key technologies are more easily copied in foreign markets.
- *Product differentiation*–differentiating a product without increasing cost.
- *Marketing communication barriers*–local market practices vary a great deal.

The size of the investment and the risk to the company mean a company should consider a wide range of costs and potential problems as well as the market opportunity. Issues like loss of product technologies can be overlooked as the company considers the opportunity to expand into new markets.[18] All too often companies have committed significant resources before they realize that a critical issue has substantially raised the investment and risk.

Organizational Structure

Once marketing managers decide on a specific market entry strategy, they must create an efficient and effective global market organizational structure. This challenge requires constant monitoring and adaptation. No one ideal structure exists. A recent study of 43 multinational U.S. companies reported they planned to make a total of 137 organizational changes to their international operations over the next five years. This suggests that the best organizational structure is, at best, a moving target that evolves over time.

Before a company decides on its organizational structure, it must make two critical decisions. The first involves **decision-making authority**. As companies grow, lines of authority become longer and more complicated, so clearly defined protocols regarding which decisions are made at each level of the organization are important. A decision normally made by senior management becomes more difficult when executives are eight time zones away.[19]

The **degree of centralization** is a second critical decision since it affects resource allocation and personnel. Three primary organizational patterns employed by organizations around the world are centralized, decentralized, and regionalized. The primary advantages of a more centralized structure include greater control and, as a result, more consistency across the organization. It is also more efficient in creating centers of expertise that bring together knowledgeable people to address key organizational issues (for example, R&D, legal, and IT). Decentralized organizations, on the other hand, offer a hands-on management approach that facilitates rapid response to changing market conditions. The regional organization seeks to combine advantages of both approaches by centralizing key functions while pushing decision making closer to the global market.[30]

Once decision-making authority has been established and degree of centralization defined, companies usually adopt one of three organizational structures in building their international operations. First, **global product lines** work well for companies with a broad, diverse range of products. This model is based on the global functionality and appeal of the products and enables companies to target similar products to customers around the world. A product line structure can also be divided by customer, providing an even closer link between product usage and customer need. The disadvantage is that some organizational functions such as the direct sales force may be duplicated in markets where the company believes there is significant market opportunity. Siemens, the large German conglomerate, maintains specialized direct sales forces by product and customer. This approach works for Siemens because its diversified product portfolio includes everything from large power generators to sophisticated medical equipment. A second structure, **geographic regions**, divides international markets by geography, building autonomous regional organizations that perform business functions in their geographic area. This model works particularly well when local government relationships are critical to the success of international operations as it affords company management a closer connection to local customers. Large construction and engineering companies such as Halliburton maintain operations geographically with specific operations in each area that are suited to the environments in which they operate. The **matrix structure** is the third form and is a hybrid of the first two. Not surprisingly, most companies today use some form of matrix structure that encourages regional autonomy while building product competence in key areas around the world.

Product

Global market expansion is based on the belief that people or other businesses outside the company's home market will purchase its products. Acceptance of that belief depends largely on what products the company will sell in those new markets. Does it, for example, simply take its existing product with no modifications? Does it create a new product developed specifically for foreign markets, or something in between? The answers to these questions are fundamental to global market expansion.

LO 2-5

Recognize key factors in creating a global product strategy.

Some products are more easily accepted than others in new markets around the world. Several consumer electronics products such as digital music players and digital cameras are essentially the same product around the world. But many products, like food, do not travel well across borders. Those products usually need to be adapted to fit local tastes. A company may select from three basic product options:[21]

- **Direct product extension:** Introduce a product produced in the company's home market into an international market with no product changes. Advantages include no additional R&D or manufacturing costs. Disadvantages are that the product may not fit local needs or tastes.

- **Product adaptation:** Alter an existing product to fit local needs and legal requirements. Adaptation can range from regional levels all the way down to city-level differences.

- **Product invention:** Create a new product specifically for an international market. Sometimes old products discontinued in one market can be reintroduced in a new market, a process known as backward invention. Cell phone manufacturers have adopted this strategy, taking phones that have been replaced in European or Asian markets and introducing them in Latin America. Another strategy is forward invention, or creating new products to meet demand in a specific country or region.

Consumers

Moving into global consumer markets creates significant challenges because companies with little international experience find it difficult to assess, develop, and market products targeted at consumers with widely different needs, preferences, and product usage demands. Even experienced global marketers sometimes fail to identify specific consumer trends in foreign markets. Four specific product issues face international consumer marketers—quality, fitting the product to the culture, brand strategy, and country of origin.

Coke, despite displaying a different name, displays the same fun feeling in this ad as it does in their U.S. advertising.

Source: The Coca-Cola Company

Quality The perception of quality varies drastically around the world, which makes it hard for a company developing or adapting a product for a global market. What works in one market may fail in another, as cell phone manufacturers have learned. In Europe, Japan, and the United Sates, cell phones must have a roaming capability to be successful, but Chinese consumers do not consider it an important feature.

Global consumers are knowledgeable about product quality and have a clear understanding of what they are willing to pay for at a given quality level. Research suggests the relationship of price and quality, or the value proposition that we focus on in this book, remains a key factor in consumer decision making. The test for many organizations is providing quality when they lack control over the delivery of key quality dimensions such as service. As we discussed earlier, in many situations companies do not provide key elements of the product experience, which is one reason good international partners are so important.

Fitting the Product to the Culture Cultural differences exert tremendous influence on consumer product choices and are critical in international markets. Brand names as well as product colors and features are heavily influenced by the culture in local foreign markets.

Language differences have created unique and occasionally humorous examples of marketing mistakes. When Coca-Cola introduced Diet Coke in Japan, initial sales were disappointing until the company realized that Japanese women do not like the concept of dieting and the Japanese culture relates dieting to sickness (not a desired connection with a product). The company changed the name to Coke Light, which has been much more effective around the world. Companies also have to adapt their products to fit local markets. Manufacturers of kitchen products have found the Japanese market difficult to penetrate. Mr. Coffee and Philips Electronics NV found their coffeemakers did not sell well in Japan because Asian kitchens in general are much smaller than Western kitchens. The larger coffeemakers sold in the United States did not fit on Japanese kitchen counters.

Brand Strategy As we will explore in Chapter 9, companies often seek to create a unified branding strategy around the world. In some cases this is effective. Coca-Cola, Caterpillar, Apple, Kellogg, BMW, and others have created powerful global brands. As companies acquire local brands, one of the first decisions is whether to fold a local brand into a global brand. Companies have to consider local conditions, but, when possible, companies are harmonizing brands to build brand awareness and extend marketing communication dollars.

Local brands, on the other hand, offer companies distinct awareness and built-in market loyalty. Nestlé, for example, follows a local branding strategy for individual products (the company carries more than 7,000 brands) but also promotes the Nestlé corporate brand globally. It believes that local branding helps differentiate its products.

Country of Origin Increasingly, customers apply what is known as the country-of-origin effect in their purchase decisions. The **country-of-origin effect** is the influence of the country of manufacture, assembly, or design on a customer's positive or negative perception of a product.[22] "Made in Japan," "Made in Italy," "Made in the United States"—each has meaning to customers and infers that a product has certain qualities based on its country of origin. Such perceptions can change over time. Immediately after World War II, products made in Japan were considered of poor quality and inexpensive, which may seem hard to believe in light of the preeminent view of Japanese quality in the 21st century. Budweiser is a product with a very strong country-of-origin effect. Consumers around the world identify the product as American. After the purchase of Anheuser-Busch by InBev, based in Belgium, InBev announced that maintaining the strong American identity of Budweiser was a focus of the company.

Companies use ethnocentric messages to differentiate their products from foreign brands. Ford and Chrysler have both used their American heritage in advertising to foster a "buy American" feeling among consumers. Interestingly, Japanese automobiles manufactured in the United States frequently carry a higher percentage of U.S. parts than cars assembled in Mexico for American automobile manufacturers.[23] Research reports the following regarding country of origin:

- People in developed countries prefer products manufactured in their own country.
- Manufacturers from countries viewed favorably in the world tend to highlight their country of origin more than those from less developed countries.
- Countries have developed certain areas of influence in which the country of origin makes a difference, such as Japan and Germany for cars, the United States for technology, and France for wine and luxury goods.

Market Channels

One of the thorniest issues facing global marketers is getting their product to the customer.[24] American and European companies, in particular, are used to sophisticated channels of distribution that seamlessly move products from manufacturing sites to the customer at relatively low cost. Well-coordinated transportation and logistics systems lower distribution costs and increase customer choices at the point of sale.

Many companies have to rethink their distribution strategy when they enter global markets and find inadequate transportation networks, poorly organized or not easily accessible distribution systems, as well as an almost unlimited number of fundamentally different channel structures. Companies are frequently unprepared for the complexity of penetrating a foreign distribution system. The stakes are high because channel decisions are, at least in the short run, difficult and expensive to adjust. Companies able to develop successful channel strategies gain a competitive advantage in that market and effectively limit the options of other competitors.

Channel Structures Unless the product is manufactured in the country where it is sold, all products pass through a global channel of distribution (see Exhibit 2.11). The product must

EXHIBIT 2.11 | International Channel Structure

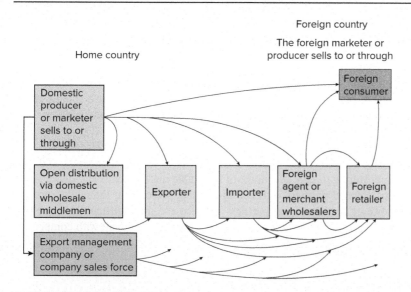

Source: Cateora, Philip R. , John Graham, and Mary C. Gilly, *International Marketing* New York, NY: McGraw-Hill Education, 2016.

move from the country of manufacture through an international channel between countries to the local international market distribution channel. Obviously the manufacturer is most familiar with the distribution network in its home country. However, goods going to international markets use different intermediaries such as trading companies or international agents that require modifications to existing channels. Coordinating the movement of products between countries usually means hiring specialists familiar with legal issues as well as the most effective and efficient means of transportation. Companies have a number of transportation choices and, in addition to cost, should consider risk and length of time in transit. The producer faces the greatest challenge in the last stage, getting the product into the local channel and ultimately to the customer. International shipping specialists can help identify local distribution partners, but the company is more likely to look for channel alliances that fit overall business objectives and not simply distribution channels.

Channel Factors In selecting a channel partner, companies should consider six strategic objectives known as the Six Cs of channel strategy: Cost, capital, control, coverage, character, and continuity offer a checklist for evaluating channel options.

Cost Estimating channel costs includes (1) the initial investment in creating the channel and (2) the cost of maintaining the channel. As companies expand into new markets, many search for ways to increase the efficiency of local distribution systems by eliminating unnecessary middlemen, thereby shortening the channel to the customer.[25]

Capital An inadequate global market distribution system is expensive in terms of both adding cost to the product and creating long-term damage to the brand and the company's reputation. If a channel network is already in place, the investment is low; however, if the company needs to develop or greatly improve an existing system, the cost can be very high.

Control The more control the company wants in the channel, the more expensive it is to maintain. As a result, companies generally look for a balance between channel control and cost. The complexity of global supply chains coupled with lack of local market knowledge make the task of creating a distribution system so expensive that all but the most accomplished global marketers rely on local distribution networks in foreign markets.

Coverage Local distribution networks around the world may lack full exposure to a given market. Even in the United States, for example, complete coverage of a consumer market necessitates multiple distribution channels. As a result, it is necessary to evaluate which distribution network best reaches the target customers, which may not necessarily be the network with the widest distribution. Targeting upper- and middle-class consumers in China requires extensive distribution in cities along the coast (Beijing, Shanghai, and Guangzhou) but minimal distribution in the rest of the country.

Character The long-term nature of channel decisions makes character an issue in selecting the best channel partner.[26] The capabilities, reputation, and skills of the local channel partner should match the company's characteristics. A service-oriented company should look for local channel partners with a reputation for excellent service and high customer satisfaction.

Continuity Changing a distribution system creates anxiety among customers and gives competitors an opportunity to take advantage of inevitable inefficiencies and disruption of service. Identifying channel partners with a long-standing presence in the market provides some security; however, the best local partners are also the most difficult to establish a relationship with as they frequently already have established involvement with competitors.

Marketing Communications

Another factor to consider is global marketing communications, which place additional demands on an organization's communication strategy. The core elements of communicating to a customer in a home market (language, images, color, cultural contextual cues) can be vastly different in foreign markets.[27] In addition, media are different and companies that rely on one form of media in their home market will have to adapt to other media.

Advertising Global market advertising follows one of four basic approaches that vary by degree of adaptation. The first strategy creates **global marketing themes,** adjusting only the color and language to local market conditions. The basic ad template remains unchanged throughout the world. A second strategy, **global marketing with local content**, keeps the same global marketing theme as the home market but adapts it with local content. Local content is incorporated in a standardized template to encourage a local look and feel to the ad. This includes images as well as written copy, but the ad still relates to the same global marketing message. A third approach is a **basket of global advertising themes**. Here related but distinct ads built around several marketing messages are generated, often by the company's lead advertising agency, and local marketers select the ads that best fit their specific market situation. Finally, some companies allow **local market ad generation**. Marketers have the authorization to create local ads that do not necessarily coordinate with global marketing messages. However, this strategy still requires coordination at higher levels in the company to ensure consistent quality. It takes considerable resources to market products globally, and the leading global advertisers all spend well in excess of $2 billion advertising globally every year.

Personal Selling The salesperson–customer relationship is dramatically different around the world. In the United States, the relationship is very business-focused and less personal. In Latin America and Asia, the relationship is much more personal. Actual business negotiations often do not begin until a personal relationship has been established. Companies need sensitivity in selecting, hiring, and training their global sales force to accommodate local business cultures.

Sales Promotion A relatively small part of U.S. marketing communication budgets is allocated to sales promotion; however, this can be a significant component of marketing communication strategy in global markets. The need to stimulate consumer trial and purchase can be greater. Both PepsiCo and Coca-Cola sponsor traveling carnivals to outlying villages in Latin America with the purpose of encouraging product trial.[28]

Public Relations The expansion of global communications has greatly increased the importance of international public relations. Companies realize that dealing with crises must be done quickly and effectively as global news organizations move instantly on stories around the world. Getting the company's perspective on a story requires coordination by the company and public relations consultants before release to the public. Public relations can also enhance other elements of a marketing communications strategy.[29] When companies introduce new products, they frequently schedule them to coincide with press conferences and news cycles in other countries.

Pricing

There are three main pricing strategies. No single pricing strategy accommodates every local foreign market, so most companies follow a combination of cost-based and market-conditions-based pricing in setting a final price to market.[30]

One World Price The company assigns one price for its products in every global market. In theory, this approach enables a company to standardize other elements in the marketing mix and simplifies financial forecasting. In reality, this strategy is not followed very often. While price is constant, the cost to produce, distribute, and market the product varies dramatically, creating wide fluctuations in profit margins. Furthermore, local conditions such as competitive pressures, economic circumstances, and other local market factors can have a significant effect on the final product price.

Local Market Conditions Price The company assigns a price based on local market conditions with minimal consideration for the actual cost of putting the product into the market. Responding to the market is certainly vital in assigning the final price, but local conditions may not reflect the reality of bringing the product to market for an international company. Local competitors do not incur the transportation costs, potential tariffs, and other related expenses of bringing a product to a foreign market. As a result, companies must be particularly sensitive to local market pricing when setting their price. Strong local or even global competitors that dictate local market prices should be considered in assessing the attractiveness of a global market opportunity. One solution is to identify valued-added product features that allow a higher final price to the customer.

Cost-Based Price This strategy considers cost plus markup to arrive at a final price. While the focus on costs precludes charging an unprofitable price, it does not consider actual market conditions. If costs are high as a result of tariffs or transportation, the final price may be too high for the market.

Price Escalation A considerable quandary for companies in global marketing is that the costs of doing business globally are often higher than in their home market. Many people are surprised that products sold in their home country frequently cost twice as much in foreign markets. Four primary forces drive higher costs and create price escalation.

- **Product export costs:** Differences in the product configuration, packaging, and documentation raise the cost of many products for international markets. A key internal cost issue is **transfer pricing**, or the cost companies charge internally to move products between subsidiaries or divisions. If companies charge too high a price internally, it can make the final product price uncompetitive because the local subsidiary must add a markup to arrive at a final price.
- **Tariffs, import fees, taxes:** Governments all around the world impose tariffs, fees, and taxes on imported products to protect industries in their home market and increase their revenue.
- **Exchange rate fluctuations:** For many years, the U.S. dollar was the standard for all international contracts, which tended to minimize currency fluctuations as everything was priced in dollars. Now, currencies float and products are priced using a market basket of currencies. Since currencies can easily float 15 to 20 percent against each other, the assigning of currency values in international contracts is critical. Increasingly, companies want contracts written in their home currency to protect their risk of loss due to currency fluctuations.[31]
- **Middlemen and transportation costs:** Creating a channel for global markets extends the number of channel members and increases costs. Each channel partner requires compensation, which raises the final price to the customer. Moreover, transportation costs increase as the distance to a local market increases.

Global Pricing Issues In addition to price escalation, there are two other global pricing issues. The first, **dumping**, refers to the practice of charging less than actual costs or less than the product price in the company's home markets.[32] The World Trade Organization and most national governments have outlawed this practice and, if dumping is proven, a government can impose a tax on those products. Dumping is generally not a problem when global markets are strong; however, the willingness to price export goods based on marginal costs rather than full costs increases when markets weaken. The second major issue is the **gray market**, which involves the unauthorized diversion of branded products into global markets. Gray market distributors (who are often authorized distributors) divert products from low-price to high-price markets. Companies should carefully watch unusual order patterns among their distributors because that can signal a gray market problem.[33]

ETHICS: AT THE CORE OF SUCCESSFUL MARKETING MANAGEMENT

Ethics is an essential element of a successful marketing strategy and, more broadly, a company's overall business strategy. Indeed, many companies know—and research supports—the substantial benefits of ethical leadership, culture, and policies. Unfortunately, it is difficult to go a week without the news reporting some ethical lapse in business. Often the issue may seem like a poorly conceived strategy or implementation, but a more careful review frequently reveals a failure of ethical decision making. For example, take the ongoing challenges Volkswagen faces as it deals with the crisis created by deceptive practices in the reporting of emissions by their diesel-powered cars around the world. To date, the company has incurred costs in the billions of dollars and experienced significant loss of trust in its brand and cars. While the investigation into the installation of deceptive software that masked true diesel engine emissions revealed a number of poor decisions, it is clear the culture of the company supported, or least did not discourage, individuals from making decisions that ultimately had serious negative effects on the company.

LO 2-6

Learn the importance of ethics in marketing strategy, the value proposition, and the elements of the marketing mix.

Ethics in marketing plays a fundamental role in developing and maintaining strong customer relationships in both business and consumer markets.[34] The marketplace rewards companies that exhibit ethical behavior with greater loyalty, resulting in increased financial performance.[35] In addition, ethical companies accrue benefits such as greater employee loyalty, resulting in lower turnover and recruiting costs. Ethics plays a role in every aspect of marketing, from the value proposition through all the critical elements in the marketing mix, and even in marketing strategy and implementation. Realizing the importance of ethics in marketing and business, companies create policies and "codes of ethics" to help direct ethical decisions in the organization. We will look at all of these topics in the next sections.

Some argue that companies only need to meet legal obligations in their marketing activities. However, successful marketers today understand that the law is only the "baseline" of expected behavior and generally lags behind societal norms and opinion. In some respects, this is good, as opinions can change quickly and companies need stability in strategic planning and implementation. However, following the law does not mean the company is doing all it can do or even should do in its marketing efforts. On the other hand, **marketing ethics** encompasses a societal and professional standard of right and fair practices that are expected of marketing managers in their oversight of strategy formulation, implementation, and control.[36]

Ethics and the Value Proposition

Value is a core concept in marketing, as we discussed in Chapter 1. You will recall that value is the net benefits (or costs) associated with a product or service. The buyer considers all the benefits, then subtracts all the costs, and arrives at a value for the product. One of the key considerations is the buyer's trust or belief that the company will keep its promises with regard to the product experience, warranty, service, and a host of other interactions. When the customer does trust the company, that is a major benefit, but when trust does not exist, it is a significant cost. In either case, the buyer's evaluation of the company's ethics plays an essential role in the defining value to the customer, and the research is clear—buyers (businesses or consumers) consider a company's ethics in evaluating the value proposition and ultimately the decision to purchase.[37]

Wells Fargo has been one of most successful banks in the United States over the last decade, but a scandal involving the creation of fake accounts to drive sales at the bank altered the company's value proposition to its customers (large and small), and caused major harm to the company's long-term relationship with many customers. The immediate impact of the scandal was to drive away existing customers and potential new business.[38] The challenge for Wells Fargo, or any company, is that once trust with a customer is broken it is very difficult to get it back. In an industry like banking, trust and ethics are a fundamental part of the value proposition.

As a company's ethics play an increasingly important role in defining the value proposition, it is important to remember that trust is developed slowly but lost quickly. Johnson & Johnson's line of baby products has built a strong connection with customers over a long period of time. However, when its baby powder containing talc was linked with ovarian cancer, there were a number of lawsuits. Johnson & Johnson maintains that its baby powder is safe, but has settled a number of the suits and increased its marketing communications budget to offset the negative publicity. In addition, internal company documents suggest the company knew there may be some risk. This highlights the pressure companies face when ethical decisions and business decisions are not aligned.[39] Johnson & Johnson baby powder remains on the market and commands a market-leading position, but the long-term effects to the product's brand image have not been determined.

Ethics and the Elements of the Marketing Mix

Ethics impacts all the elements of the marketing mix. In addition, ethical decisions in marketing can also have legal and financial consequences, such as Volkswagen's decision to use deceptive software in its diesel cars. It is not surprising then that companies spend time and resources considering the ethical and legal implications of their marketing decisions. Let's consider some of the ethical implications for each marketing mix element, as seen in Exhibit 2.12.

Product There are a number of ethical issues related to product strategy. It begins with what markets should be targeted. For example, certain markets—such as children and the elderly—are considered vulnerable, and special consideration is given to products targeted at those markets. Food manufacturers need to be concerned about the quality and amounts of ingredients, as well as other decisions that directly impact the quality of the product. At the same time, there is a concern that some products may target some groups while excluding others. For many years, some clothing companies did not manufacture their clothes in plus sizes despite the fact that plus-size clothing represents 20 percent of the market.

There are also a number of ethical issues surrounding the collection and use of market research data critical in developing product strategy. Companies today are collecting a great deal of data on their customers, and there is a question as to how the data will be used as well as concerns about the security and privacy of the data.

EXHIBIT 2.12 | Examples of Ethical Decisions in the Marketing Mix

Product
- Use marketing research data that ensures privacy and confidentiality.
- Define market segments that do not discriminate against any particular segment.
- Develop products that are safe and select materials that are not harmful to users.
- Manufacture products using materials that are safe for users, in conditions that are safe for employees.
- Clearly define and honor warranties and service agreements.

Price
- Disclose the full price to customers before purchase.
- Do not engage in unethical pricing practices such as price discrimination, price fixing, or predatory pricing.
- Fully disclose any other bundled pricing before customer's purchase.

Distribution
- Unfair pressure should not be put on channel members.
- Channel members should not use manipulative sales techniques on other channel members.
- Data privacy confidentiality should occur throughout the channel.
- No channel members should exert undue pressure on customers to purchase products that are unnecessary or not needed.

Marketing Communications
- No deception or misrepresentation should occur in any marketing communications to any stakeholders (customers, investors, employees).
- High-pressure or manipulative sales techniques should not be used by salespeople or messaged in advertising.

One of the primary ethical product issues is the quality and safety of materials used in the product. Companies seek to keep costs down, which puts pressure on decision makers to use product components that are unsafe or fail to meet quality standards. Even before making decisions about the materials in the manufacturing process, companies must consider the safety of the product in the product development phase. For example, because children are considered a vulnerable market, special care is given to the design of toys to minimize sharp objects or parts that can be easily broken and swallowed.

Price Ethical questions are an integral part of pricing strategy and implementation. For example, it is unethical (and illegal) for companies to use certain pricing strategies, such as predatory pricing (selling below cost to push a competitor out of the market) or price fixing (collusion between companies to set prices at a mutually beneficial high level) to gain competitive advantage in the marketplace. (Both of these terms are explained in more detail in Chapter 11.)

Another issue is the "actual" price of a product. For example, sometimes companies charge a low price but then add on fees and other charges to substantially raise the actual price to the customer. Consider the purchase of airline tickets; while the fare may be low, many airlines charge you to check your luggage or book a certain type of seat. Some airlines, such as Spirit Airlines, even charge the customer to print a boarding pass or take carry-on luggage on board the plane.

Distribution Among the ethical challenges in distribution is the ability of key channel members to exert undue influence on the channel. This can manifest itself in the demand for special terms or deals with other channel members. In some cases, powerful channel members will ask for "gifts," usually money, to help secure contracts or to carry a certain product.

At the same time, the sourcing of products can lead to ethical dilemmas. For example, companies that manufacture products globally are often faced with the decision of whether to use suppliers that employ child labor. By Western society standards, child labor is not ethical, but in other parts of the world child labor is accepted as part of the culture.

Promotion No area in marketing presents more ethical challenges than promotion. A persuasive, effective marketing message is an important element in any successful marketing strategy. However, marketing managers must be careful to avoid deceptive or false claims. This is true for all marketing communications, including advertising, personal selling, and digital messaging (such as e-mail).

In sales, there is the additional ethical issue of manipulating or coercing customers to purchase products or accept unfavorable terms. There is always the question of bribery when salespeople offer incentives for the customer to purchase a product. While this is considered unethical in much of the world, it is also illegal in many countries to use bribery in order to gain additional customer sales.

Code of Marketing (Business) Ethics

Everyone lives by their own "code of ethics" that guides their choices and behavior. Most individuals never formally write it down, but simply make decisions using their internal code. Companies face a unique challenge because employees must work together within the culture to ethically accomplish organizational goals and objectives. As a result, the vast majority of companies today create a code of ethics that defines the company's values. Often, a second document called a code of conduct seeks to operationalize the company's value by defining appropriate behaviors and decisions. The American Marketing Association, the premier organization of marketing professionals in the world, has a code of ethics which defines the norms and values for marketers.[40] The code speaks to six primary ethical values: honesty, responsibility, fairness, respect, transparency, and citizenship.

Many companies embrace similar ethical values in their corporate codes of ethics. At the same time, companies increasingly see a need to supplement their corporate codes of ethics with a discussion of specific ethical marketing practices. The goal is to provide clarity for marketing managers as they make critical marketing decisions that frequently involve an ethical component. The focus on ethics in marketing speaks to the essential role of marketing in the organization and the impact of ethical (and unethical) decisions on organizational performance.

SUSTAINABILITY: NOT JUST THE RIGHT THING TO DO BUT A GOOD MARKETING STRATEGY

Is "doing the right thing" a good marketing strategy? Yes; as presented in Chapter 1, the concept of sustainability includes all business practices that seek to balance business success and societal success over the long term. Unfortunately, while there is agreement on general principles, there is also a lot of ambiguity about the scope of sustainability. It is often summed up as "doing well by doing good," but other terms such as "green" or "corporate responsibility" are considered part of being sustainable.

The concept of sustainability goes back many years. For example, a number of U.S. environmental laws grew out of the need to better manage resources such as water, air, and even farmland as a result of the Great Depression in the 1930s. This awareness was built on the realization that utilizing resources efficiently and effectively was good for society but also beneficial to business. The "green" movement was founded on the environmental concerns and resource utilization issues that have come to be known as sustainability.

Today, however, the definition of sustainability has been expanded to include issues like an educated workforce, greater connection to and support of local communities, as well as clear linkage between policies and good marketing (business) strategy. The result has been a redefining of the term *sustainability* to include this broader scope. Put simply, sustainability can be summarized as "people, planet, profit," or what has come to be known as the "triple bottom line."

Triple Bottom Line: The Link between Doing Well and Doing Good

In Chapter 1 we identified the various groups, called marketing stakeholders, that interact with or are impacted by marketing, and they are key to understanding the triple bottom line. These stakeholders are shown again in Exhibit 2.13. Originally presented by John Elkington in his book *Cannibals with Forks: The Triple Bottom Line of 21st Century Business,* the triple bottom line brings accountability to the various interests of marketing (business) stakeholders. The traditional approach, financial accounting, was useful for shareholders, but what about customers, suppliers, government agencies, and many others? The **triple bottom line (TBL)** is a metric for evaluating not only the financial results of the company but the broader social equity, economic, and environmental considerations as well.[41] Consider the impact of the TBL in marketing management using the people, planet, and profit approach outlined graphically in Exhibit 2.14.

Many, if not most, organizations still focus exclusively on profit as the sole metric of success. However, companies are increasingly realizing that success needs to include other metrics, like people. This type of change begins with management acknowledging that there are success objectives beyond profit, then creating metrics, strategies, and tactical plans to implement that change. From there, training and education is needed to raise employee awareness that, over time, leads to a change in culture. As marketing employees

EXHIBIT 2.13 | Stakeholders in Marketing

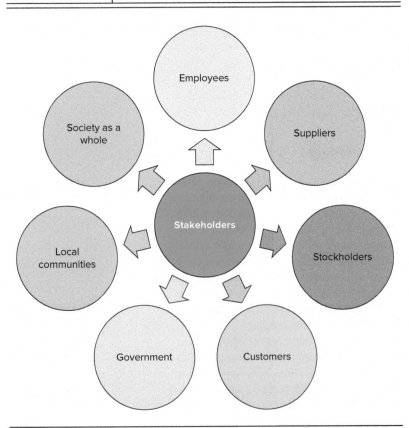

EXHIBIT 2.14 | Triple Bottom Line

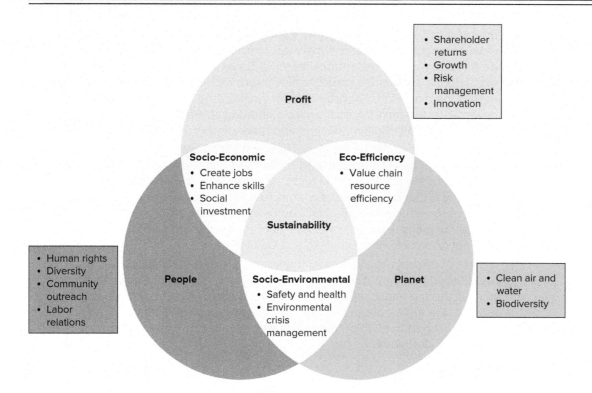

Profit
- Shareholder returns
- Growth
- Risk management
- Innovation

Socio-Economic
- Create jobs
- Enhance skills
- Social investment

Eco-Efficiency
- Value chain resource efficiency

Sustainability

People

Socio-Environmental
- Safety and health
- Environmental crisis management

Planet

- Human rights
- Diversity
- Community outreach
- Labor relations

- Clean air and water
- Biodiversity

(sales, customer service, and others) are often the customer's point of contact with the company, this becomes an important first step. Ultimately, companies today now actively look for ways to "give back" to the community. Disney, for example, allows employees time off to work with community organizations of their choice. In addition, the company will match donations from employees to community organizations.

A second TBL metric is the planet, and marketers are very involved in decisions that impact the planet. From sustainable sourcing of materials to efficient, environmentally sensitive supply chains, marketers are evaluating critical processes to maximize the environmental impact while meeting corporate objectives related to cost and product quality. Over time, companies like Starbucks have been successful in developing "ethically sourced" coffee that is socially responsible and environmentally safe. The company was instrumental in creating the C.A.F.E. (Coffee and Farmer Equity) practices, which set forth guidelines around four key areas: quality, economic accountability and transparency, social responsibility, and economic leadership. Companies are accepting greater responsibility not only for their own manufacturing but for their suppliers' business practices as well. In some cases, such as Nike, this was the result of public pressure to reduce unhealthy employee work conditions at their suppliers. Nike and others are now proactively evaluating their suppliers to maintain the same environmental standards and working conditions as they themselves do.

Finally, profit remains an important metric in a sustainable company. While considering the impact of marketing decisions on people and the planet, marketing managers must still meet financial objectives for the company to be successful. For example, consider the impact of a company's sustainability decisions on customer product choice decisions. Some target markets, such as millennials, consider sustainability an important factor in their decision making. This means companies have to adapt their products, distribution, marketing communications, and pricing to incorporate sustainability into their overall marketing strategy. The challenge is not limited to B2C markets, but is increasingly prevalent in B2B markets as well. IBM, for example, invests heavily in a variety of sustainable activities and has won awards for its focus on the environment and sustainable development. Customers, employees, and other stakeholders—not to mention shareholders—expect companies to be able to balance profit goals and objectives with people and planet objectives.

SUMMARY

Global marketing is now synonymous with marketing. Technology and sophisticated distribution systems make it easy for a company anywhere in the world to become an international marketer. However, companies generally go through a global experience learning curve as their international business expands. As companies consider new international markets they must first assess the marketing opportunity and consider the impact moving into the new market will have on their entire marketing strategy, from product development through distribution, pricing, and marketing communications.

Ethics is one of the foundational elements in marketing; it impacts the development and implementation of the marketing strategy as well as all elements of the marketing mix and even the value proposition. Companies understand that being an ethical company means developing a culture that encourages ethical decisions and behavior. A primary tool in developing an ethical company is a code of ethics that defines the company's values and sets out codes of conduct.

One of the keys to successful marketing is sustainability, which is often understood to mean "doing well by doing good." However, it can be difficult to evaluate the impact of doing good on a company's overall performance. As a result, the triple bottom line metric—focused on people, planet, and profit—was developed to enable companies to evaluate financial performance and other considerations.

KEY TERMS

developed economies   29
emerging markets   29
regional market zones   29
European Union   30
NAFTA (North American
  Free Trade Agreement)   31
MERCOSUR   31
ASEAN   32
exporting   33
exporters   34
distributors   34

contractual agreements   34
licensing   34
franchising   35
strategic alliances   35
joint ventures   36
direct foreign investment   36
decision-making authority   36
degree of centralization   36
global product lines   37
geographic regions   37
matrix structure   37

country-of-origin effect   38
global marketing themes   41
global marketing with
  local content   41
basket of global advertising
  themes   41
local market ad generation   41
transfer pricing   42
dumping   42
gray market   42
marketing ethics   43
triple bottom line (TBL)   46

APPLICATION QUESTIONS

connect

More application questions are available online.

1. You are the marketing manager for a small company located in the United States that manufactures specialized parts for high-end ink-jet printers. The company's largest customer (Hewlett-Packard) has asked your company to supply parts to 10 of its distribution and repair sites around the world. The company has never sold products outside the United States, so this represents a significant step for the company. What stage in the global experience learning curve is the company likely entering and why? Identify the activities the company should undertake at this stage.

2. You are the market research director for a consumer product company. You have been asked to evaluate China as a potential market for your company's products and begin a search of secondary data. What types of information

would you consider in assessing China? How would you find information on these issues?

3. You are the marketing manager for Oxymoron detergent and have been instructed to introduce this product into Argentina. What six factors would you need to consider in determining the proper channel of distribution for the introduction of Oxymoron detergent?

4. The marketing manager for McDonald's has been asked to develop a code of marketing ethics for the company. Develop a marketing code of ethics for McDonald's, keeping in mind that the the company has stores all over the world.

5. The CEO of Timberland has called and asked you to develop a triple bottom line report for the company. What might be included in a TBL report for Timberland?

MANAGEMENT DECISION CASE
Selling to the Bottom of the Pyramid: Marketing Unilever Products in Rural Villages around the World

When assessing the viability of a country or region for global expansion, one of the first factors marketers examine is the ability of consumers to afford the product being offered. With that criterion in mind, would you consider marketing your product to people making only $1,500 a year? What if there were *4 billion* of those potential customers?[42]

This is the challenge and opportunity that marketers face when expanding into *bottom of the pyramid* markets (BOPM). Successfully (and profitably) marketing to this group requires a focus on two key priorities: changing consumers' behavior and changing the way products are made and delivered. The first can require innovative forms of education. The second may mean a change in features, quality, or portion size to bring costs and prices to an affordable level. These often remote areas create special challenges in the distribution and promotional parts of the marketing mix as well.[43]

Unilever, known in the United States for its Dove soap and shampoos, took on this challenge when it decided to sell its Wheel brand of detergent in India. The company had a head start in that it already had well-established distribution and retail channels serving the middle and poorer classes. Also, detergent was already a known product class, so they did not have to educate the population on the purpose of the product. However, to get the word out about Wheel, they used an unusual sales force: an army of approximately 70,000 *shakti* women (and later, their husbands) to sell their product in 165,000 rural villages. Shakti—which means "strength" or "power" in Hindi—gave Unilever the power of a large, informal sales staff that reached into rural areas across India.[44] With intimate knowledge of the geography and communication styles, as well as having existing relationships with people in the villages, the women in this group could quickly become effective brand ambassadors for Unilever's new product.

The product also had to be packaged in a small and affordable size. Unilever pioneered the use of "sachets"—single-use packages that met the price target and conformed to the shopping habits of Indian consumers, who often shop daily for necessities. Sales of these packets reached a quantity of 27 billion per year.[45]

Since that success in India, Unilever has expanded these concepts into rural areas in other countries. In Pakistan, women are trained as beauticians, learning how to apply makeup and shampoo hair, as well as how to sell Unilever products. In Thailand, Unilever's Platinum store initiative supports rural retailers by helping with layout and promotions. A 10-cent deodorant packet innovation in the Philippines led to a market penetration rate of 60 percent for their Rexona product.[46]

Unilever's BOPM innovations have also included novel approaches in communicating with customers. Many rural customers in India have cell phone service, but they limit their costs by using the "missed call" strategy. Mobile users dial a number, then hang up—avoiding a charge, but letting someone know you want to reach them. Unilever exploited this practice in a promotion for its Active Wheel detergent. Consumers were asked to call a special number programmed to cut off after two rings, costing the caller nothing. They then automatically received a call back from Unilever with a comic message from a Bollywood star—and an ad for Wheel. The result? Sixteen million calls and triple the sales for Wheel detergent in the region.[47]

While these ventures led to Unilever becoming the world's fifth-largest consumer goods manufacturer, it also allowed them to "do well by doing good." Their education programs have helped reduce child mortality by teaching more than 300 million consumers to use soap. The agricultural practices of 600,000 farmers in the Unilever supply chains have been strengthened through the company's "Sustainable Living Plan," a program that helped put Unilever in the number one spot in GlobalScan's survey of companies most respected for their sustainability efforts.[48]

Unilever's success has not gone unnoticed, particularly by rival Procter & Gamble.[49] As global companies like these and others continue to stretch the boundaries of customer viability, they will also have to continue to innovate in the production of affordable products, in their distribution methods, and in finding creative ways to reach consumers in remote parts of the world with their promotional messages.

Questions for Consideration

1. Is Unilever providing *value* to their Indian customers? In what ways? Consider the four types of utility when forming your answer.

2. Considering the competition Unilever is receiving from Procter & Gamble and other companies, in what creative ways could Unilever change their Wheel detergent product offering to differentiate it from competitors' offerings?

3. What principles should be used to determine if a product is a good fit for a BOPM market? Are there products that should not be offered to BOPM consumers? Should this issue be decided by marketers, governments, or consumers?

4. Is it ethical for marketers to try to make money off people who are living at a subsistence level? Should companies only market their products to people in certain income classes? What factors should a marketer take into consideration when trying to answer these questions?

NOTES

1. Peter Gabrielsson, Mika Gabrielsson, John Darling, and Reijo Luostarinen, "Globalizing Internationals: Product Strategies of ICT Manufacturers," *International Marketing Review* 23, no. 6 (2006), pp. 650–67.

2. M. Theodosiou, and L. C. Leonidou, "International Marketing Policy: An Integrative Assessment of the Empirical Research," *International Business Review* 12, no. 2 (2003), pp. 141–71.

3. Katrijn Gielens and Marnik G. Dekimpe, "The Entry Strategy of Retail Firms into Transition Economies," *Journal of Marketing* 71, no. 2 (2007), pp. 196–210; and Jasmine E. M. Williams, "Export Marketing Information-Gathering and Processing in Small and Medium-Sized Companies," *Marketing Intelligence and Planning* 24, no. 5 (2006), pp. 477–92.

4. Kristian Moller and Senja Svahn, "Crossing East-West Boundaries: Knowledge Sharing in Intercultural Business Networks," *Industrial Marketing Management* 33, no. 3 (2004), pp. 219–28.

5. "Growth Still Quite Strong: Inflation Remains the Key Concerns for Emergers, with Many Countries Still Tightening Policies," *Emerging Marketing Weekly*, April 14, 2008, pp. 1–13; and Luiz F. Mesquita and Sergio G. Lazzarini, "Horizontal and Vertical Relationships in Developing Economies: Implications for SME's Access to Global Markets," *Academy of Management Journal* 51, no. 2 (2008), pp. 359–71.

6. Jennifer Hoyt, "Innovations in Beauty," *The Prague Post*, April 7, 2005, www.praguepost.cz/archivescontent/40872 -innovations-in-br-br-beauty.html.

7. Cristina del Campo, Carlos M. F. Monteiro, and Joao Oliveira Soares, "The European Regional Policy and the Socioeconomic Diversity of European Regions: A Multivariate Analysis," *European Journal of Operational Research* 187, no. 2 (2008),

pp. 600–12; and David Floyd, "Have 'European Politics' and EU Policymaking Replaced the Politics of Member State Countries?" *International Journal of Social Economics* 35, no. 5 (2008), pp. 338–43.

8. "Wal-Mart Banks on the 'Unbanked,'" *BusinessWeek*, December 13, 2007, and www.giganteusa.com.

9. Kerry Campbell, "McDonald's Offers Ethics with Those Fries," *BusinessWeek*, January 7, 2007, www.businessweek .com/globalbiz/content/jan2007/gb20070109_958716 .htm?chan=search.

10. *BBC News*, "Profile Association of SouthEast Asian Nations," May 20, 2008, http://news.bbc.co.uk/2/hi/asia-pacific/country _profiles/4114415.stm.

11. Richard A. Owusu, Maqsood Sandhu, and Soren Kock, "Project Business: A Distinct Mode of Internationalization," *International Marketing Review* 24, no. 6 (2007), pp. 695–714; and Terence Fan and Phillip Phan, "International New Ventures: Revisiting the Influences behind the 'Born-Global' Firm," *Journal of International Business Studies* 38, no. 7 (2007), pp. 1113–32.

12. Judith Crown and Carol Matlack, "Boeing Delays Dreamliner Again," *BusinessWeek*, April 9, 2008, www.businessweek.com /print/bwdaily/dnflash/content/apr2008/db2008049 _424569.htm; and Carol Matlack, "Airbus Cost-Cuts Don't Fly," *BusinessWeek*, May 7, 2008, www.businessweek.com/global -biz/content/may2008/gb2008057_379072.htm?chan=search.

13. Deloitte Global Powers of Retailing 2017, Top 250 Stats, http:// www.nxtbook.com/nxtbooks/nrfe/STORES_globalretail 2017/index.php#/1.

14. "Hammock Pharmaceuticals Announces Licensing of Women's Health and Urological Technology Platform from

MilanaPharm," *Yahoo Finance,* January 2017, http://finance.yahoo.com/news/hammock-pharmaceuticals-announces-licensing-womens-130000627.html.

15. B. Elango, "Are Franchisors with International Operations Different from Those Who Are Domestic Market Oriented?" *Journal of Small Business Management* 45, no. 2 (2007), pp. 179–85.

16. Sergio G. Lazzarini, "The Impact of Membership in Competing Alliance Constellations: Evidence on the Operational Performance of Global Airlines," *Strategic Management Journal* 28, no. 4 (2007), pp. 345–60; and Kerry Capell, "Skirmishing in the Open Skies," *BusinessWeek,* January 14, 2008, www.businessweek.com/print/globalbiz/content/jan2008/gb20080114_431564.htm.

17. Jane W. Lu and Xufei Ma, "The Contingent Value of Local Partners' Business Group Affiliations," *Academy of Management Journal* 51, no. 2 (2008), pp. 295–305; and Eric Rodriguez, "Cooperative Ventures in Emerging Economies," *Journal of Business Research* 61, no. 6 (2008), pp. 640–55.

18. Lance Eliot Brouthers, Yan Gao, and Jason Patrick McNicol, "Corruption and Market Attractiveness Influences on Different Types of FDI," *Strategic Management Journal* 29, no. 6 (2008), pp. 673–81; and Jan Hendrik Fisch, "Investment in New Foreign Subsidiaries under Receding Perception of Uncertainty," *Journal of International Business Studies* 39, no. 3 (2008), pp. 370–87.

19. Riki Takeuichi, Jeffrey P. Shay, and Jiatao Li, "When Does Decision Autonomy Increase Expatriate Managers' Adjustment? An Empirical Test," *Academy of Management Journal* 51, no. 1 (2008), pp. 45–60.

20. Andrea Dossi and Lorenzo Patelli, "The Decision-Influencing Use of Performance Measurement Systems in Relationships between Headquarters and Subsidiaries," *Management Accounting Research* 19, no. 2 (2008), pp. 126–39.

21. Michael G. Harvey and David A. Griffith, "The Role of Globalization, Time Acceleration, and Virtual Global Teams in Fostering Successful Global Product Launches," *Journal of Product Innovation Management* 24, no. 5 (2007), pp. 486–501; and Thomas L. Powers and Jeffrey J. Loyka, "Market, Industry, and Company Influences on Global Product Standardization," *International Marketing Review* 24, no. 6 (2007), pp. 678–94.

22. Sadrudin A. Ahmed and Alain d'Astous, "Antecedents, Moderators, and Dimensions of Country-of-Origin Evaluations," *International Marketing Review* 25, no. 1 (2008), pp. 75–84; and Saikat Banerjee, "Strategic Brand-Culture Fit: A Conceptual Framework for Brand Management," *Journal of Brand Management* 15, no. 5 (2008), pp. 312–22.

23. "Made in the USA? The Truth behind the Labels," *Consumer Reports* 73, no. 3 (2008), p. 12.

24. Eric Gang, Robert W. Paellmatier, Lisa K. Scheer, and Ning Li, "Trust at Different Organizational Levels," *Journal of Marketing* 72, no. 2 (2008), pp. 80–98; Janice M. Payan and Richard G. McGarland, "Decomposing Influence Strategies: Argument Structure and Dependence as Determinants of the Effectiveness of Influence Strategies in Gaining Channel Member Compliance," *Journal of Marketing* 69, no. 3 (2005), pp. 66–79; Eric M. Olson, Stanley F. Slater, and G. Tomas M. Hult, "The Performance Implications of Fit among Business Strategy, Marketing Organization Structure, and Strategic Behavior," *Journal of Marketing* 69, no. 3 (2005), pp. 49–65; and Carlos Niezen and Julio Rodriguez, "Distribution Lessons from Mom and Pop," *Harvard Business Review* 86, no. 4 (2008), pp. 23–46.

25. Abel P. Jeuland and Steven M. Shugan, "Managing Channel Profits," *Marketing Science* 27, no. 1 (January/February 2008), pp. 49–54.

26. Neil Herndon, "Effective Ethical Response: A New Approach to Meeting Channel Stakeholder Needs for Ethical Behavior and Socially Responsible Conduct," *Journal of Marketing Channels* 13, no. 1 (2005), pp. 63–67; and Emma Kambewa, Paul Ingenbleek, and Aad Van Tilbury, "Improving Income Positions of Primary Producers in International Marketing Channels: The Lake Victoria–DU Nile Perch Case," *Journal of Macromarketing* 28, no. 1 (2008), pp. 53–64.

27. Michelle R. Nelson and Hye-Jin Paek, "A Content Analysis of Advertising in a Global Magazine across Seven Countries: Implications for Global Advertising Strategies," *International Marketing Review* 24, no. 1 (2007), pp. 64–78.

28. Wagner A. Kamakura and Wooseong Kang, "Chain Wide and Store Level Analysis for Cross Category Management," *Journal of Retailing* 83, no. 2 (2007), pp. 159–70.

29. Piet Verhoeven, "Who's In and Who's Out? Studying the Effects of Communication Management on Social Cohesion," *Journal of Communication Management* 12, no. 2 (2008), pp. 124–30; and Tom Watson, "Public Relations Research Priorities: A Delphi Study," *Journal of Communication Management* 12, no. 2 (2008), pp. 104–11.

30. George S. Yip and Audrey J. M. Bink, "Managing Global Accounts," *Harvard Business Review* 85, no. 9 (2007), pp. 102–19; and Kenneth D. Ko, "Optimal Pricing Model," *Journal of Global Business Issues* 2, no. 1 (2008), pp. 143–48.

31. Magda Kandil, "The Asymmetric Effects of Exchange Rate Fluctuations on Output and Prices: Evidence from Developing Countries," *Journal of International Trade and Economic Development* 17, no. 2 (2008), pp. 257–70.

32. Benjamin Eden, "Inefficient Trade Patterns: Excessive Trade, Cross-Hauling and Dumping," *Journal of International Economics* 73, no. 1 (2007), pp. 175–87.

33. William Vetter and C. Jeanne Hill, "The Hunt for Online Trademark Infringers: The Internet, Gray Markets, and the Law Collide," *Journal of the Academy of Marketing Science* 34, no. 1 (2006), pp. 85–88; Jen-Hung Huang, Bruce C. Y. Lee, and Shu Hsun Ho, "Consumer Attitudes toward Gray Market Goods," *International Marketing Review* 21, no. 6 (2004), pp. 598–611; and Barry Berman, "Strategies to Combat the Sale of Gray Market Goods," *Business Horizons* 47, no. 4 (2004), pp. 51–70.

34. P. M. Madhani, "Marketing Ethics: Enhancing Firm Valuation and Building Competitive Advantages,:" *SCMS Journal of Indian Management* 13, no. 3 (2016), pp. 80–99.

35. P. M. Madhani, "Compensation, Ethical Sales Behavior and Customer Lifetime Value," *Compensation & Benefits Review* 46, no. 4 (2014), pp. 204–18.

36. Patrick E. Murphy, Gene R. Laczniak, and Andrea Prothero, *Ethics in Marketing* (New York: Routledge, 2012), p. 9.

37. V. Gruber, "Exploring the Positioning of Sustainable Products and Its Impact on Consumer Behavior," *Proceedings of the Marketing Management Association* (Spring 2015), p. 25.

38. Jen Wieczner, "Here's How Much Wells Fargo's Fake Accounts Scandal Is Hurting the Bank," *Fortune,* January 13, 2017, http://fortune.com/2017/01/13/wells-fargo-fake-accounts-scandal-closing-branches-earnings/.

39. Susan Berfield, Jef Feeley, and Margaret Cronin Fisk, "Johnson & Johnson Has a Baby Powder Problem," *Bloomberg Businessweek,* March 31, 2016, https://www.bloomberg.com/features/2016-baby-powder-cancer-lawsuits/.

40. American Marketing Association, "Statement of Ethics," 2017, https://www.ama.org/AboutAMA/Pages/Statement-of-Ethics.aspx.

41. John Elkington, *Cannibals with Forks: The Triple Bottom Line of 21st Century Business* (Oxford: Capstone, 1999).

42. E. Simanis and D. Duke, "Profits at the Bottom of the Pyramid," *Harvard Business Review* 92, no. 10 (2014), pp. 86–93.

43. Simanis and Duke, "Profits at the Bottom of the Pyramid"; and V. Mahajan, "How Unilever Reaches Rural Consumers in Emerging Markets," *Harvard Business Review Digital Articles* (2016), pp. 2–6.

44. Simanis and Duke, "Profits at the Bottom of the Pyramid"; Mahajan, "How Unilever Reaches Rural Consumers in Emerging Markets"; and Kim Bhasin, "Unilever Now Has an Army Of 50,000 'Shakti Women' Selling Its Products in India," *Business Insider,* July 3, 2012, http://www.businessinsider.com/unilevers-shakti-women-fight-pg-in-india-2012-7.

45. Mahajan, "How Unilever Reaches Rural Consumers in Emerging Markets."

46. Mahajan, "How Unilever Reaches Rural Consumers in Emerging Markets."

47. Mahajan, "How Unilever Reaches Rural Consumers in Emerging Markets."

48. Jack Nelson, "Unilever's Responsible Capitalism Should Be Lauded," *Financial Times* 10 (March 6, 2017); and Globescan, "The 2016 Sustainability Leaders," June 7, 2016, http://www.globescan.com/component/edocman/?view=document&id=250&Itemid=591.

49. Bhasin, "Unilever Now Has an Army of 50,000 'Shakti Women' Selling Its Products in India."

CHAPTER 3

Elements of Marketing Strategy, Planning, and Competition

LEARNING OBJECTIVES

LO 3-1 Examine the concept of value and the elements and role of the value chain.

LO 3-2 Understand the conditions required for successful marketing planning, that marketing planning is focused on the value proposition, and that marketing planning is a dynamic process.

LO 3-3 Identify various types of organizational strategies.

LO 3-4 Conduct a situation analysis.

LO 3-5 Use the framework provided for marketing planning, along with the content in future chapters, to build a marketing plan.

VALUE IS AT THE CORE OF MARKETING

In Chapter 1, the concept of value was introduced as a core element of marketing. Value was defined from a customer's perspective as a ratio of the bundle of benefits a customer receives from an offering compared to the costs incurred by the customer in acquiring that bundle of benefits. From the late management guru Peter Drucker's early writings in the 1950s through to today's American Marketing Association official definition of marketing, it is clear that marketing plays a central role in creating, communicating, delivering, and exchanging offerings that have value.

Let's examine the idea of value a bit more carefully now. One can think of value as a ratio of benefits to costs, as viewed from the eyes of the beholder (the customer). That is, customers incur a variety of costs in doing business with any firm, be those costs financial, time, opportunity costs, or otherwise. For the investment of these costs, the customer has a right to expect a certain bundle of benefits in return. A **benefit** is some type of utility that a company and its products (and services) provide its customers. **Utility** is the want-satisfying power of a good or service.[1] Four major kinds of utility exist: form, time, place, and ownership. *Form utility* is created when the firm converts raw materials into finished products that are desired by the market. The other three utilities—*time, place,* and *ownership*—are created by marketing. They are created when products are available to customers at a convenient location when they want to purchase them, and facilities of *exchange* are available that allow for transfer of the product ownership from seller to buyer. Chapter 1 mentioned that facilitating exchange between buyers and sellers is another core element of marketing.

Since value is a ratio of benefits to costs, a firm can impact the customer's perceptions of value by altering the benefits, the costs, or both. Assume that a person is faced with the decision of buying one of two automobiles. One should expect that a purchase decision will be greatly influenced by the ratio of costs (not just monetary) versus benefits for each model. That is, it is not just pure price that drives the decision. It is price compared with all the various benefits (or utilities) that Car 1 brings versus Car 2.[2] These benefits could relate to availability, style, prestige, features—all sorts of factors beyond mere price. In the *U.S. News Best Car for the Money 2017 Awards,* Toyota and its luxury brand, Lexus, won the most awards, including "Best Hybrid Car" (Toyota Prius) and "Best Luxury Compact SUV" (Lexus NX). This, despite charging higher prices than the competition! It seems their vehicles deliver consistently high quality and thus represent an excellent value. In particular, the Toyota Prius has outstanding fuel economy estimates and excellent cargo room, and the Lexus NX has an upscale, modern interior and plenty of passenger space.[3]

Recall that marketing is charged not just with *creating* offerings that have value, but also with *communicating, delivering,* and *exchanging* those offerings. When a firm communicates the **value proposition** of its products to customers, the value message may include the whole bundle of benefits the company promises to deliver, not just the benefits of the product itself.[4] For example, when South Korean–based Samsung first brought its brand to the United States, it communicated a message centered primarily on functionality at a moderate price—a strategy designed to provide an advantage over pricier Japanese brands. But over time, Samsung's value proposition has expanded to include innovativeness, style, and dependability—the latter of which was helped significantly by high ratings of many of the company's products by sources such as *Consumer Reports.*[5] Software firm Intuit states its unique value proposition as "simplifying the business of life." Widely known for TurboTax, Mint, and QuickBooks, Intuit creates business and financial management solutions aimed at small businesses, consumers, and accounting professionals. The firm recently realized growth of 41 percent for QuickBooks online subscribers and 17 percent for payroll customer growth in Intuit's small business segment alone, providing clear evidence that their value proposition resonates.[6]

For years, firms have been preoccupied with measuring **customer satisfaction**, which at its most fundamental level means how much the customer likes the product. However, for firms interested in building long-term customer relationships, having satisfied customers is not enough to ensure the relationship is going to last. A firm's value proposition must be strong enough to move customers past mere satisfaction and into a commitment to a

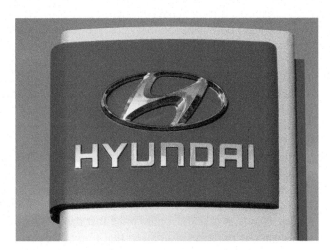

Korean firms such as these have gained global market share by associating their brands with a strong value proposition for consumers.
(LG) ©Grisha Bruev/Shutterstock; (Samsung) ©360b/Shutterstock; (Kia) ©Toni Genes/Shutterstock, (Hyundai) ©josefkubes/Shutterstock

company and its products and brands for the long run. Such a commitment reflects a high level of **customer loyalty**, which increases **customer retention** and reduces **customer switching**.[7] In Hewlett-Packard's hypercompetitive space, keeping high customer satisfaction and loyalty along with low levels of customer switching is critical. To improve these factors along with customer retention, HP has increased its number of U.S.-based call center agents, invested in IVR software, and leveraged remote diagnostic tools to provide superior and expedited customer support. It also has customer support available on its website, Twitter, Facebook, and an app that is preinstalled on every HP laptop.[8]

Customer loyalty almost always is directly related to the various sources of value the customer is presently deriving from the relationship with the company and its brands. Except in situations of monopoly (which creates forced loyalty), loyal customers by definition tend to also experience a high level of satisfaction.[9] However, not all satisfied customers are loyal. If a competitor comes along with a better value proposition, or if a value proposition begins to slip or is not effectively communicated, customers who are currently satisfied become good candidates for switching to another company's products.[10]

The Value Chain

A highly useful approach to bringing together and understanding the concepts of customer value, satisfaction, and loyalty is the **value chain**. Created by Michael Porter in his classic book *Competitive Advantage,* the value chain serves as a means for firms to identify ways to create, communicate, and deliver more customer value within a firm.[11] Exhibit 3.1 portrays Porter's value chain concept.

EXHIBIT 3.1 | Porter's Value Chain

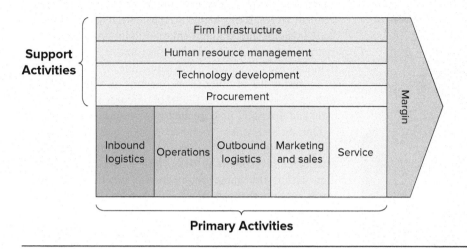

Source: Porter, Michael E., *Competitive Advantage: Creating and Sustaining Superior Performance*, New York, NY: Free Press, 1985.

Basically, the value chain concept holds that every organization represents a synthesis of activities involved in designing, producing, marketing, delivering, and supporting its products. The value chain identifies nine relevant strategic activities the organization can engage in that create/impact both sides of the value equation: benefits and costs. Porter's nine **value-creating activities** include five primary activities and four support activities.[12]

The five *primary activities* in the value chain are:

1. *Inbound logistics*—how the firm goes about sourcing raw materials for production.
2. *Operations*—how the firm converts the raw materials into final products.
3. *Outbound logistics*—how the firm transports and distributes the final products to the marketplace.
4. *Marketing and sales*—how the firm communicates the value proposition to the marketplace.
5. *Service*—how the firm supports customers during and after the sale.

The four *support activities* in the value chain are:

1. *Firm infrastructure*—how the firm is set up for doing business; are the internal processes aligned and efficient?
2. *Human resource management*—how the firm ensures it has the right people in place, trains them, and keeps them.
3. *Technology development*—how the firm embraces technology usage for the benefit of customers.
4. *Procurement*—how the firm deals with vendors and quality issues.

The value chain concept is highly useful in understanding the major activities through which a firm creates, communicates, and delivers value for its customers. CEOs in recent years have been concentrating on *aligning* the various elements of the value chain, meaning that all facets of the company are working together to ensure that no snags will negatively impact the firm's value proposition.[13] From a customer's perspective, when the supplier's value chain is working well, all the customer tends to see are the *results* of a well-aligned value chain: quality products, good salespeople, on-time delivery, prompt service after the sale, and so on. However, it takes only one weak link in the value chain and the whole process of cultivating satisfied and loyal customers can be circumvented.

The U.S. Army does sophisticated marketing that leads to its ability to effectively appeal to recruits.
Source: US Army

Consider, for example, what happens if a glitch in the value chain of one of Walmart's vendors delays delivery of products at the peak selling season, resulting in stock-outs in Walmart stores. If this happens repeatedly, it can damage the overall relationship Walmart enjoys with its customers as well as the relationship between Walmart and that supplier. To minimize the potential for this happening, Walmart, as well as a growing list of other firms, requires all vendors to link with its IT system so that the whole process of order fulfillment and inventory management is as seamless as possible.[14]

One final element depicted at the end of the value chain is margin, which refers to profit made by the firm. Intelligent investment in the primary and support activities within the value chain should positively enhance profit margin through more efficient and effective firm performance.[15]

Planning for the Value Offering

The remainder of this chapter presents the approach that marketing managers use to plan for creating, communicating, and delivering the value offering. This is often referred to as **marketing planning**—the ongoing process of developing and implementing market-driven strategies for an organization—and the resulting document that records the marketing planning process in a useful framework is the **marketing plan**.[16]

MARKETING PLANNING IS BOTH STRATEGIC AND TACTICAL

Recall that one key trend identified in Chapter 1 was the practice of marketing on two dimensions or levels within an organization. Although these dimensions exist in tandem and even intersect on occasion, each holds fundamental differences in goals and properties. At the strategic level, Marketing (Big M) serves as a core driver of business strategy. That is, an understanding of markets, competitors, and other external forces, coupled with attention to internal capabilities, allows a firm to successfully develop strategies for the future. At the functional or operational level, marketing (little m) represents the specific programs and tactics aimed at customers and other stakeholder groups and includes everything from brand image, to the message salespeople and advertisements deliver, to customer service, to packaging and product features—in fact, all elements of operationalizing the marketing mix and beyond.[17] As an example of a marketing program and tactics (marketing, little m) as an outcome of a marketing strategy (Marketing, Big M), Nike launched its now legendary "Just Do It" campaign in the late 1980s at a pivotal moment in company history. Realizing it needed to widen its access point to include all sorts of potential athletes beyond just the elite few, Nike needed one clean and clear phrase that captured the attention of the masses and could be easily reproduced through most any communication channels. The "Just Do It" campaign instantly resonated with people's feelings toward exercise and the drive needed to push beyond one's limits, and the phrase is ubiquitous worldwide today well beyond just Nike.[18]

Although these two levels of marketing are distinctly different in scope and activities, the common link is in the process of marketing planning. Marketing managers must be able to grasp both the big picture of strategy formulation and the details of tactical implementation. In fact, many a marketing plan has failed because either the formulation of the strategies was flawed or their implementation was poorly executed.

A well-written marketing plan must fully address both Marketing (Big M) and marketing (little m) elements. Ultimately, the following must be in place for effective marketing planning to occur:

- *Everyone* in an organization, regardless of his or her position or title, must understand and support the concept of customer orientation, which, as you learned in Chapter 1, places the customer at the core of all aspects of the enterprise. Firms that promote and practice a high level of customer focus are often referred to as *customer-centric* organizations.[19] Rite Aid is a customer-centric company. The company is the third-largest pharmacy in the United States and is expanding its "NowClinic Online Care" services in stores. This program allows customers to go online and chat or have a video consultation with a doctor or nurse about an illness or injury and then retain a record of the consultation so they are able to share it with their primary care physician. The price for a 10-minute consultation with a doctor varies depending on factors such as employer discounts or insurance co-pays, but even at full price is very reasonable. And after the consult, doctors can order prescriptions or refer patients to a specialist for more extensive care. Understanding and analyzing consumer trends and motivations led Rite Aid to pursue this strategy. Gone are the days when the customer has to wait to see a doctor. With the trend for technology also increasing, this concept addresses the desire for convenience as well.[20]

- To operationalize a customer-centric approach, all internal organizational processes and systems must be aligned around the customer. A firm's internal structure and systems cannot be allowed to become an impediment to a customer orientation.[21] Anyone who has ever placed a phone call for service and been driven through a maze of phone transfers with a string of people (or machines) unable to help knows how poor structure and systems can impact customer satisfaction and loyalty!

- The CEO and others at the top of the organization must consistently set the tone for market-driven strategic planning through the customer-centric business philosophy. As with a firm's internal structure and systems, its culture must be supportive of such an approach in order for a marketing plan to be successful. Upper management must also support the process through consistent investment of resources necessary to make it work. Marketing planning is not a "sometimes" process; rather, it should be a driving force in the firm day in and day out.[22] Tableau's CEO, Adam Selipsky, is optimistic about Tableau's continued growth—that is, so long as going forward the company always makes decisions with the customer at top of mind. Selipsky plans to focus Tableau more on developing capabilities for larger companies, while also maintaining good service for its current customer base in data analytics. For Tableau, improving their stake in enterprise customers is a key to future success.[23]

At this point in the learning process about marketing management, you may begin to feel concerned that you are getting a lot of structure for marketing planning but not enough specific content to fill in the elements of the marketing plan template. That reaction is quite natural, as by design the depth of content for most of the various sections of a marketing plan is covered later in the book. Your next task is to familiarize yourself with the overall process and framework for marketing planning so that as the content pieces unfold chapter by chapter, it will be very clear how those pieces fit together into a complete marketing plan. Beginning with this one, each chapter ends with a "Marketing Plan Exercise." These are designed to help you make the connections between the content in each chapter and the requirements of your marketing plan template.

ELEMENTS OF MARKETING PLANNING

To get you started, we'll first walk through the process and content involved in marketing planning. A condensed framework for this process is presented in Exhibit 3.2. Then at the end of this chapter you'll find an abbreviated marketing plan example for the fictitious company CloudCab Small Jet Taxi Service. You'll want to look at that appendix for an example of what the key elements of a marketing plan look like in practice.

EXHIBIT 3.2 | Condensed Framework for Marketing Planning

- Ensure the marketing plan is connected to the firm's business plan including organizational-level mission, vision, goals, objectives, and strategies.
- Conduct a situation analysis.
  - Macro-level external environment
  - Competitive environment
  - Internal environment
- Perform any needed market research.
- Establish marketing goals and objectives.
- Develop marketing strategies.
  - Product-market combinations
  - Market segmentation, target marketing, positioning

- Marketing mix strategies:
  - Product/branding strategies
  - Service strategies
  - Pricing strategies
  - Supply chain strategies
  - Promotional strategies
- Develop implementation plans.
  - Programs/action plans for each strategy including timetable, assignment of responsibilities, and resources required
  - Forecasts and budgets
  - Metrics for marketing control
- Provide for contingency planning.

Connecting the Marketing Plan to the Firm's Business Plan

How does a marketing plan fit into a firm's overall business planning process? As we have learned, marketing is somewhat unique among the functional areas of business in that it has the properties of being both a core business philosophy (Marketing, Big M) and a functional/operational part of the business (marketing, little m). As such, all business-level strategy must be market-driven in order to be successful. Hence, the term **market-driven strategic planning** is often used to describe the process at the corporate or strategic business unit (SBU) level of marshaling the various resource and functional areas of the firm toward a central purpose around the customer.[24] A **strategic business unit (SBU)** is a relatively autonomous division or organizational unit of a large company that operates independently but within the corporate umbrella, exercising control over most of the factors affecting its long-term performance.

A great example of how these levels of planning fit together is General Electric. GE contains numerous SBUs that compete in very different markets, from lighting to jet engines to financial services. GE's CEO oversees a **corporate-level strategic plan** to serve as an umbrella plan for the overall direction of the corporation, but the real action in marketing planning at GE is at the individual SBU level. Each GE business has its own **SBU-level strategic plan**, and part of GE's historical leadership culture has been to turn SBU management loose to run their own businesses under their own plans, so long as they meet their performance requirements and contribute satisfactorily to the overall corporate plan.

Before going deeper into our study of planning, it's important to emphasize at the outset that great planning and strategy often are game-changing for organizations. For a number of years McDonald's was the unchallenged leader in

For McDonald's and many other firms, marketing planning and strategy, while analytical in nature, often yield very funny marketing communications.

Source: McDonald's

quick-serve restaurants. But over the years its strength in the market waned as new and innovative competitors captured the business from a new generation of consumers. But when Steve Easterbrook took over as president and CEO in 2015, things immediately began to change, thanks largely to an aggressive turnaround plan that included many innovative new strategies for growth. Fast-forward to today: business is booming, as is investor confidence that McDonald's is back on course strategically for the future.[25]

Portfolio Analysis **Portfolio analysis**, which views SBUs and sometimes even product lines as a series of investments from which it expects maximization of returns, is one tool that can contribute to strategic planning in a multi-business corporation. Two of the most popular approaches are the **Boston Consulting Group (BCG) Growth-Share Matrix** and the **GE Business Screen**. These are portrayed in Exhibits 3.3 and 3.4.

EXHIBIT 3.3 | **Boston Consulting Group Growth-Share Matrix**

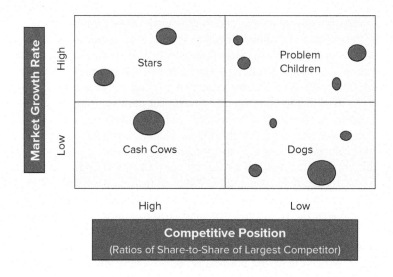

Source: Henderson, Bruce, *Henderson on Corporate Strategy,* New York, NY: Wiley, 1979.

EXHIBIT 3.4 | **GE Business Screen**

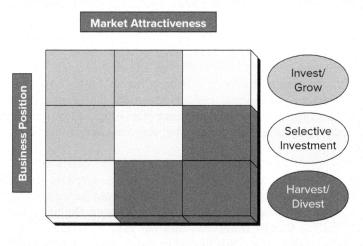

Business Position (high, medium, and low): Assess the firm's ability to compete. Factors include organization, growth, market share by segment, customer loyalty, margins, distribution, technology skills, patents, marketing, and flexibility, among others.

Market Attractiveness (high, medium, and low): For the market, assess size, growth, customer satisfaction levels, competition (quantity, types, effectiveness, commitment), price levels, profitability, technology, governmental regulations, sensitivity to economic trends, among others.[26]

Source: "GE Business Screen," *Business Resource Software Online,* www.brs-inc.com/pwxcharts.asp?32, accessed April 22, 2017.

The concept of the BCG approach to portfolio analysis is to position each SBU within a firm on the two-dimensional matrix shown in Exhibit 3.3. The competitive market-share dimension is the ratio of share to that of the largest competitor. The growth dimension is intended as a strong indicator of overall market attractiveness. Within the BCG matrix you find four cells, each representing strategy recommendations:

- *Stars* (high share, high growth): important to building the future of the business and deserving any needed investment.
- *Cash Cows* (high share, low growth): key sources of internal cash generation for the firm.
- *Dogs* (low share, low growth): potential high cash users and prime candidates for liquidation.
- *Problem Children,* or *Question Marks* (low share, high growth): high cash needs that, if properly nurtured, can convert into stars.[27]

For purposes of strategy development, the BCG matrix approach is seductively simple and has contributed to decision making about internal cash generation and usage across SBUs. It has also morphed in application downward to often be applied to product lines and product groups, which is nominally possible so long as costs and returns can be properly isolated for investment decisions. But because of its simplicity, BCG ignores other important factors that should go into this decision making and also ignores the viability of generating cash externally.

The GE Business Screen, shown in Exhibit 3.4, is a more realistic and complex portfolio model. It also evaluates the business on two dimensions—market attractiveness and business position, which refers to its ability to compete. The investment decision is again suggested by the position on a matrix. A business that is favorable on both dimensions should usually be a candidate to grow. When both market attractiveness and business position evaluations are unfavorable, the harvest (maximizing the remaining profits with minimal or no further investment in the SBU) or divest (selling off or closing down the SBU) options should be raised. Cisco's Flip was introduced in 2006 and discontinued in 2011. A pocket-sized camera that could record up to an hour of video could no longer compete with phone-based video cameras that eliminated the need for a separate video-recording device. Thus, the product had clearly played out and had been harvested to the degree possible. Cisco's statement explained that reallocating resources was going to allow the firm to focus on other key company priorities.[28] When the matrix position is neither unambiguously positive nor negative, the investment decision will require more analysis.

For now, it is important to note that portfolio analysis does not offer a panacea for corporate strategy formulation. Wise firms are thoughtful in its application and recognize that it is but one approach to strategy decision making.[29]

Functional Level Plans A firm's SBU plans all incorporate **functional-level plans** from operations, marketing, finance, and the other operational areas. Just as the individual SBU CEOs are held accountable to GE's corporate CEO for their unit's performance within the context of GE's plan, the chief marketing officer, chief financial officer, and other operational-level executive of each SBU are held accountable to their own business unit CEO for the performance of their portion of the SBU plan.[30] While GE's system certainly may be larger in scope and complexity than many business planning situations, the logic is the same regardless of the type or size of an organization. Hence, the marketing plan is nested within the context of an overall corporate and/or business-level strategic plan.

Before each of the sections of the marketing plan is identified and described, you are referred to JetBlue Airways as an example of a firm that has become noted for successful marketing planning. Why JetBlue as an example? Clearly, JetBlue's not perfect, and in the turbulent airline industry it's really tough to do great marketing planning. During his tenure as chairman and CEO, JetBlue founder David Neeleman was quite transparent about his strategies and plans for the company, not only discussing them openly with the business press but also placing a substantial amount of organizational information on the company website. This approach has continued in the post-Neeleman era of the firm. And when JetBlue has made missteps, the company has been forthright in recognizing and addressing the errors. As each of the elements of the marketing planning process is described below, JetBlue will be used as a thematic example of each piece in practice.

Organizational Mission, Vision, Goals, and Objectives

Marketing planning does not occur in a vacuum; it must connect with the firm's overall mission and vision. A **mission statement** articulates an organization's purpose, or reason for existence. A well-conceived mission statement defines the fundamental, unique purpose that sets a company apart from other firms of its type and identifies the scope of a company's operations, products, and markets.[31] IKEA, a furniture company, defines its mission as making everyday life better for its customers. IKEA buys in bulk and has a very efficient supply chain so that it can offer very attractive prices. Strategically, though, instead of defining its mission as providing affordable furniture, IKEA, chooses instead to define a unique purpose beyond low price that is experiential and relatable to its loyal fans.[32]

Most mission statements also include a discussion of what the company would like to become in the future—its **strategic vision**. According to iconic GE former chairman and CEO Jack Welch, "Good business leaders create a vision, articulate the vision, passionately own the vision, and relentlessly drive it to completion."[33] The vision of what the firm is capable of in the future and where it *wants* to go, as championed by its top leadership, sets the tone for everything that follows in the planning process. **Goals**, general statements of what the firm wishes to accomplish in support of the mission and vision, eventually become refined into specific, measurable, and (hopefully) attainable **objectives** for the firm.[34] Objectives at the corporate and SBU level provide the benchmarks by which organizational performance is assessed. Unfortunately, despite a formal mission, vision, goals, and objectives, it is all too easy for senior management and even the board of directors to become distracted and stray off course. Such action can create major problems both inside and outside the company.

JetBlue Airways took to the air February 11, 2000, flying from John F. Kennedy International Airport in New York to Fort Lauderdale in Florida. Today, the upstart airline is rapidly becoming a major player, serving more than 50 cities (including several Caribbean locations) with nearly 100 aircraft, and it has ambitious plans for continued growth. The company's vision is to offer great service with low fares—and make a profit—even when other air carriers are struggling to survive. Several important goals back up this vision:

- Start and remain well-capitalized.
- Fly new planes.
- Hire the best people.
- Focus on service.
- Practice responsible financial management.

To date, JetBlue has mostly stayed true to this course. While most of the major carriers continuously bleed red ink, JetBlue, though not perfect in bringing in every quarter's sales and profit goals, appears to be much more stable financially than the majority of other airlines. Much of the airline's success can be attributed to great market-driven strategic planning.

In terms of specific and measurable objectives, Neeleman established high performance expectations for financial results, operational processes, and customer satisfaction and loyalty. As mentioned earlier, JetBlue's website is very transparent in laying out company leaders' plans for the firm—Neeleman was always quite confident that the company had created a unique value offering that few (if any) competitors could readily duplicate. During one winter some years ago, JetBlue suffered a highly publicized operational meltdown at its JFK airport home base due to a massive snow and ice storm, and Neeleman was right there on the website and in the public media. In addition to offering an apology, he also provided full refunds, free replacement tickets, and travel vouchers to stranded passengers and established the first passengers' bill of rights in the industry.

In developing a marketing plan, the marketing manager must proceed with a strong understanding of and commitment to the firm's mission, vision, goals, and objectives. JetBlue's well-conceived and executed marketing plan is an integral element in its success.

Organizational Strategies

LO 3-3

Identify various types of organizational strategies.

At the firm level, a **strategy** is a comprehensive plan stating how the organization will achieve its mission and objectives. Put another way, strategy is like a road map to get the organization where it wants to go, based on good information gathered in advance. The choice of which direction a firm should go ultimately boils down to a *decision* by a firm and its managers. Strategy has two key phases: formulation (or development) and execution. And it occurs at multiple levels in the firm: corporate level, SBU (or business) level, and functional level (marketing, finance, operations, etc.). As we have discussed, the strategies developed and executed at each of these levels must be aligned and directed toward the overall organizational mission and goals.

A firm's **generic strategy** is its overall directional strategy at the business level.[35] Fundamentally, all firms must decide whether they wish to (or are able to) *grow,* and if not, how they can survive through *stability* or *retrenchment.* Exhibit 3.5 provides options for generic strategies for each of these three directions. Kroger is the largest supermarket chain and third-largest retailer overall in the nation. This distinction was reached by executing an aggressive growth strategy through multiple acquisitions during a time frame in which many of its competitors primarily pursued a different growth strategy—opening their own new stores. A defining acquisition for Kroger was its takeover of Fred Meyer, at the time the fifth-largest supermarket chain. That deal paved the way for Kroger's recent successes by allowing it to achieve huge economies of scale. At peak after that acquisition, revenues have nearly doubled and the stock price tripled.[36]

The choice of generic strategy is usually driven by resource capabilities of the firm, as well as the competitive landscape. In the growth-oriented business culture in the United States, stockholders and financial analysts are constantly interested in knowing a firm's next growth strategy and can become quickly disenchanted, even with firms that are growing but at a slower than predicted rate. Yet, sometimes for reasons related to the competitive landscape or resource constraints, the best generic strategy for a firm may not actually be growth but stability or retrenchment instead. Interestingly, the pressure to constantly achieve accelerated growth is much less intense in many business cultures outside the United States.

Michael Porter identifies three primary categories of **competitive strategy**: low cost, differentiation, and focus (or niche). Exhibit 3.6 describes each of these, and

---

EXHIBIT 3.5 | Generic Business Strategies

Growth

- Organizations that do business in dynamic competitive environments generally experience pressure to grow in order to survive. Growth may be in the form of sales, market share, assets, profits, or some combination of these and other factors. Categories of growth strategies include: *Concentration*—via vertical or horizontal integration. *Diversification*—via concentric or conglomerate means.

Stability

- The strategy to continue current activities with little significant change in direction may be appropriate for a successful organization

operating in a reasonably predictable environment. It can be useful in the short term but potentially dangerous in the long term, especially if the competitive landscape changes.

Retrenchment

- An organization in a weak competitive position in some or all of its product lines, resulting in poor performance and pressure on management to quickly improve, may pursue retrenchment.
- Essentially, retrenchment involves pulling assets out of underperforming parts of the business and reinvesting in aspects of the business with greater future performance potential.

Source: J. David Hunger and Thomas H. Wheelen, *Essentials of Strategic Management,* 5th ed. (Upper Saddle River, NJ: Prentice Hall, 2011).

EXHIBIT 3.6 | Competitive Strategy Options

Cost Leadership

- The organization strives to have the lowest costs in its industry and produces goods or services for a broad customer base. Note the emphasis on *costs*, not *prices*.

Differentiation

- The organization competes on the basis of providing unique goods or services with features that customers value, that they perceive as different, and for which they are willing to pay a premium.

Focus (or Niche)

- The organization pursues either a cost or differentiation advantage, but in a limited (narrow) customer group. A focus strategy concentrates on serving a specific market niche.

Source: Porter, Michael E., *Competitive Advantage: Creating and Sustaining Superior Performance*, New York, NY: Free Press, 1985.

EXHIBIT 3.7 | Competitive Strategy Matrix

Competitive Advantage

	Lower Cost	Differentiation
Broad Target	Cost Leadership	Differentiation
Narrow Target	Cost Focus	Focused Differentiation

Competitive Scope (vertical axis label spanning Broad Target / Narrow Target)

Source: Porter, Michael E., *Competitive Advantage: Creating and Sustaining Superior Performance*, New York, NY: Free Press, 1985.

Exhibit 3.7 illustrates them further within a matrix format. Porter's overarching premise is that firms must first identify their **core competencies**, or the activities the firm can do exceedingly well. When these core competencies are superior to those of competitors, they are called **distinctive competencies**. Firms should invest in distinctive competencies, as they offer opportunity for **sustainable competitive advantage** in the marketplace, especially if the competencies cannot be easily duplicated or usurped by competitors. Sources of differential advantage will be developed further in Chapter 7.

As illustrated in Exhibit 3.8, Miles and Snow propose several categories of firms within any given industry based on **strategic type**. Firms of a particular strategic type have a common strategic orientation and a similar combination of structure, culture, and processes consistent with that strategy. Four strategic types are prospectors, analyzers, defenders, and reactors—depending on a firm's approach to the competitive marketplace.

JetBlue has historically followed an internal growth strategy. As some of its rivals continue to falter, it will be interesting to see how aggressive JetBlue might become in terms of growth through concentration via acquisitions. Like its much larger competitor Southwest Airlines, JetBlue executes a low-cost strategy in the competitive marketplace. Because it has no unions, hedges on fuel prices, and standardizes the types of planes flown, JetBlue enjoys numerous cost advantages over the competition. However, JetBlue differs from Southwest in that its strategy (in the context of Exhibit 3.8) is more of a cost focus, while Southwest's is

EXHIBIT 3.8 | Miles and Snow's Strategy Types

- **Prospector:** Firm exhibits continual innovation by finding and exploiting new product and market opportunities.
- **Analyzer:** Firm relies heavily on analysis and imitation of the successes of other organizations, especially prospectors.

- **Defender:** Firm searches for market stability and production of only a limited product line directed at a narrow market segment, focusing on protecting established turf.
- **Reactor:** Firm lacks any coherent strategic plan or apparent means of effectively competing; reactors do well to merely survive in the competitive marketplace.

Source: Miles, Raymond E. and Charles C. Snow, *Organizational Strategy, Structure, and Process,* New York, NY: McGraw-Hill Education, 1978.

SOMEONE HAS TO STAND UP FOR TALL PEOPLE.

The most legroom in coach.
Fly now at jetblue.com

jetBlue
YOU ABOVE ALL

One way JetBlue differentiates itself is by providing more legroom in the main cabin.
Source: JetBlue Airways

LO 3-4

Conduct a situation analysis.

cost leadership. The difference is that Southwest—especially with its acquisition of AirTran Airways—has defined the scope of its competitive marketplace much more broadly than has JetBlue, although JetBlue is getting bigger all the time. Southwest carries more passengers domestically than any other U.S.-based carrier! But don't think that these two lower-cost strategy airlines don't also offer differentiation. For example, JetBlue very successfully relies on in-flight entertainment and comfortable seats, while Southwest hangs its hat on its fun atmosphere. The point is, it's very possible for cost leadership firms to also execute differentiation as a competitive strategy.

In terms of strategic type, JetBlue can be labeled a prospector. When a firm introduces a new offering to a market that the market hasn't experienced before, this defines (or redefines) the scope of the competitive marketplace and is called **first-mover advantage.** JetBlue gained first-mover advantage by providing television, movies, and games in every seat along with comfy leather accoutrements and plenty of legroom—all at bargain prices! Exhibit 3.8 provides typical characteristics of firms that fall into each of the strategy types.

To summarize, for purposes of marketing planning, it is necessary to be mindful of the organizational strategies in play when developing marketing strategies. One could reasonably argue that a fine line exists between organization-level strategies and marketing strategies, and, in many firms, the market-driven strategies developed within the context of the marketing plan ultimately rise to the organizational level.[37] Fortunately, the distinction is moot so long as the strategies developed and implemented are fully supportive of the organization's mission, vision, and goals.

Situation Analysis

The marketing manager must perform a complete **situation analysis** of the environment within which the marketing plan is being developed. The situation includes elements of the macro-level external environment within which the firm operates, its industry or competitive environment, and its internal environment.[38] Think of external environmental factors as those a firm must be mindful of and plan for, yet has little or no direct ability to impact or change. On the other hand, internal environmental factors include the firm's structure and systems, culture, leadership, and various resources, all of which are under the firm's control. Ironically, when undertaking a situation analysis, managers often have more difficulty assessing the internal environmental components than the external, perhaps because it is much more difficult to self-assess and potentially criticize that for which the managers are responsible.[39]

Macro-Level External Environmental Factors

Major categories for analysis within the external environment include:

- *Political, legal, and ethical.* All firms operate within certain rules, laws, and norms of operating behavior. For example, JetBlue has myriad regulations administered by the Federal Aviation Administration, the National Transportation Safety Board, and the Transportation Security Administration. In the airline industry, the regulatory environment is a particularly strong external influence on firms' marketing planning.

- *Sociocultural/demographic.* Trends among consumers and in society as a whole impact marketing planning greatly. Many such trends are demographic in nature, including changing generational preferences and the rising buying power of minority groups domestically and consumers in developing nations in the global marketplace.[40] Speaking of generational preferences, JetBlue jumped on the video game trend among children and teens by providing in-seat games, much to the delight of parents who no longer have to entertain the kids for the duration of the flight.

  Demographic factors influence a company's marketing strategy. Sonic Drive-In uses social media to advertise, sell, and even inspire the designs of its food in order to attract younger customers. Toward this end, Sonic launched its Square Shakes Instagram marketing campaign at the popular Coachella Valley Music and Arts Festival in California. Shakes were hawked as "The world's first shakes designed for Instagram."[41] Merging food art and social technology trends, the campaign portrayed Sonic's new milkshakes with square cups, straws, and cherries against quirky backgrounds as eye-catching Instagram posts. In an interview, former Sonic President and CMO Todd Smith explained that the company wanted to be "the first brand, and especially the first food brand, to have a product that was designed for Instagram, offer it exclusively for sale on Instagram, and then deliver that product within minutes of your order on Instagram."[42] This initiative was part of a broader strategy by Sonic to ramp up digital and social media marketing, in support of the brand and its more than 3,500 drive-ins nationwide, and attract and appeal to the next generation of Sonic customers.

- *Technological.* Constantly emerging and evolving technologies impact business in many ways. The goal is to try to understand the future impact of technological change so a firm's products will continue to be fresh and viable. As JetBlue has grown, it has put into service more and more of the new downsized "regional jets," planes that carry about 100 passengers and allow for entry into smaller, underserved markets. The airline is banking on these attractive, comfortable new aircraft to provide a market edge over the competition.

- *Economic.* The economy plays a role in all marketing planning. Part of a marketing plan is a forecast and accompanying budget, and forecasts are impacted by the degree to which predicted economic conditions actually materialize.[43] Fuel prices are a major economic cost element for any airline. JetBlue was a pioneer in hedging against rising fuel prices—that is, making speculative long-term purchase commitments betting on fuel prices going up.

- *Natural.* The natural environment also frequently affects marketing planning.[44] JetBlue's highly publicized winter weather fiasco at JFK airport some years ago prompted immediate changes in the way the company communicates with its customers. And on a broader scope, the concept of environmentally friendly marketing, or *green marketing,*

Panera BREAD®
Perfect Pick for Fall
Rethink homemade.

Fuji Apple Chicken Salad
Chicken raised without antibiotics, mixed field greens, romaine lettuce, vine-ripened tomatoes, red onions, pecans, Gorgonzola cheese and apple chips tossed in our white balsamic apple vinaigrette. Available in whole and half. (Nutritional values below are based on whole serving

For locations or online orders visit www.panerabread.com

Panera Bread and other competitors in the fast casual restaurant category have benefited from macro-level and competitive environmental factors including consumer preferences changing toward healthier items and the reluctance of many millennials to frequent traditional "fast food" places such as McDonald's and KFC.
Source: Panera Bread

has been a growing trend in socially responsible companies. *Sustainability,* which refers to business practices that meet humanity's needs without harming future generations, has evolved into a part of the philosophical and strategic core of many firms.

Competitive Environmental Factors The competitive environment is a particularly complex aspect of the external environment. Let's identify several factors, or forces, that comprise a basis for assessing the level and strength of competition within an industry. The forces are portrayed in Exhibit 3.9 and summarized below:

- *Threat of new entrants.* How strong are entry barriers based on capital requirements or other factors? A cornerstone of JetBlue's initial market entry success was the fact that it was exceptionally well-capitalized. Not many new airlines are.

- *Rivalry among existing firms.* How much direct competition is there? How much indirect competition? How strong are the firms in both categories? JetBlue's industry contains a number of firms that are much larger, but based on JetBlue's unique value proposition, few of them can deliver the same customer experience at reasonable prices that JetBlue can.

- *Threat of substitute products.* Substitutes appear to be different but actually can satisfy much or all of the same customer need as another product. Will teleconferencing PC-to-PC reach a point in the near future such that business travel is seriously threatened, thus impacting JetBlue and other airlines?

- *Bargaining power of buyers.* To what degree can customers affect prices or product offerings? So far, JetBlue has not been in much head-to-head competition with Southwest, Spirit, Allegiant, Frontier, or other low-fare carriers in its primary markets. Should this change, passengers will have more power to demand even lower fares and/ or additional services from JetBlue.

EXHIBIT 3.9 | Forces Driving Industry Competition

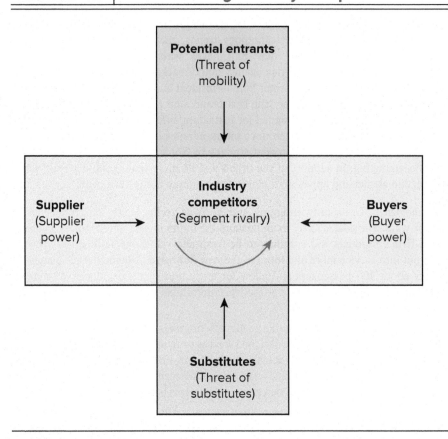

Source: Porter, Michael E., *Competitive Advantage: Creating and Sustaining Superior Performance,* New York, NY: Free Press, 1985.

- *Bargaining power of suppliers.* Suppliers impact the competitive nature of an industry through their ability to raise prices or affect the quality of inbound goods and services. Jet fuel literally fires the airline industry's economic engine. Also, few manufacturers of commercial aircraft still exist. Both of these factors point to a competitive environment with strong supplier power.

One other competitive force not directly addressed by Porter is the *relative power of other stakeholders.* This force is becoming more and more relevant in assessing industry competitiveness. The level of activity by unions, trade associations, local communities, citizens' groups, and all sorts of other special-interest groups can strongly impact industry attractiveness.[45] Founder David Neeleman established JetBlue as a non-union shop with the goal of keeping it that way by hiring the very best people and treating those people right. The union environment in the airline industry adds multiple complexities to the ability to stay competitive.[46]

Internal Environmental Factors Major categories for analysis in the internal environment include:

- *Firm structure and systems.* To what degree does the present organizational structure facilitate or impede successful market-driven strategic planning? Are the firm's internal systems set up and properly aligned to effectively serve customers? David Neeleman had his organizational chart right on the company website and talked openly about being a lean and mean operation. It's hard to find much evidence that JetBlue's structure and systems offer impediments to its marketing planning.

- *Firm culture.* As discussed previously, successful marketing planning requires a culture that includes customer orientation as a core value. If a firm's culture does not value and support a customer orientation and customer-centric approach to the overall business, marketing planning will likely disappoint.[47] Although every airline has its detractors, overall, JetBlue scores high points for its communication with customers as well as the generally positive tone of social media chatter. This provides evidence that customer orientation is a core value at the company.

- *Firm leadership.* Of course, the CEO must believe in and continuously support (financially and otherwise) the structure, systems, and culture necessary for market-driven strategic planning.[48] JetBlue's employee-friendly—and customer-friendly—approach epitomizes such leadership and commitment.

- *Firm resources.* Finally, internal analysis involves taking an honest look at all aspects of a firm's functional/operational-level resources and capabilities and how they play into the ability to develop and execute market-driven strategies.[49] Key resources for study are:
  - Marketing capabilities.
  - Financial capabilities.
  - R&D and technological capabilities.
  - Operations and production capabilities.
  - Human capabilities.
  - Information system capabilities.

JetBlue historically has performed better than almost all the competition on all these resource dimensions.

Summarize the Situation Analysis into a SWOT Upon completion of the situation analysis, a convenient way to summarize key findings is into a matrix of strengths, weaknesses, opportunities, and threats—a **SWOT analysis**. Exhibit 3.10 provides a template for a SWOT analysis. Internal analysis reveals strengths and weaknesses, while external analysis points to potential opportunities and threats. Based on the situation analysis and SWOT, it is now possible to begin making decisions about the remainder of the marketing plan.

Besides helping a marketing manager organize the results of a situation analysis, the SWOT analysis template is also useful in beginning to brainstorm marketing strategies that might be appropriate depending on which of four possible combination scenarios predominate

EXHIBIT 3.10 | SWOT Analysis Template

INTERNAL FACTORS ⟍ EXTERNAL FACTORS	Strengths (S) List 5–10 *internal* strengths here	Weaknesses (W) List 5–10 *internal* weaknesses here
Opportunities (O) List 5–10 *external* opportunities here	**S/O Based Strategies** Generate strategies here that use **strengths** to take **advantage** of **opportunities**	**W/O Based Strategies** Generate strategies here that take **advantage** of **opportunities** by **overcoming weaknesses**
Threats (T) List 5–10 *external* threats here	**S/T Based Strategies** Generate strategies here that use **strengths** to **avoid threats**	**W/T Based Strategies** Generate strategies here that **minimize weaknesses** and **avoid threats**

Source: Weihrich, H. "The TOWS Matrix --A Tool For Situational Analysis," *Long Range Planning* 15, no. 2, 1982, p. 60.

in a firm's situation: internal strengths/external opportunities, internal strengths/external threats, internal weaknesses/external opportunities, or internal weaknesses/external threats. During the situation analysis it is essential to begin to critically and realistically examine the degree to which a firm's external and internal environments will impact its ability to develop a marketing strategy. The more honest and accurate the portrayal provided by the SWOT analysis, the more useful the remainder of the marketing planning process will be.

Additional Aspects of Marketing Planning

Additional elements of marketing planning are identified below. As they derive their content primarily from future chapter topics, reference is made where relevant to the chapters from which the content can be derived.

Perform Any Needed Market Research Part Two of the book focuses on using information to drive marketing decisions. In those chapters, you will learn about collecting and analyzing market information; gain insights on CRM, Big Data, and marketing analytics and dashboards; and discover how to best understand consumer and business markets—all focused on making better decisions as a marketing manager. JetBlue has an effective CRM system that is supported through its TrueBlue loyalty program and other means. The firm also engages in ongoing market and consumer research to pinpoint trends and opportunities to better enhance the customer experience.

The Mall of America in Minneapolis, Minnesota, is the largest mall in the United States. Managing and measuring customer satisfaction can be a challenging process, given that the mall welcomes 40 million shoppers annually. Despite the widespread news of failing shopping malls, this one continues to pack 'em in. A good part of its continued success is attributable to customer data collection and analysis. Mall administration sensed that some additional analytical power was needed and found a revolutionary product called Kipsu. This sophisticated CRM system allows the users to text a specified phone number and anonymously report about their experiences. The Mall of America began using the product in the early 2010s. To give an example of the impact, custodians at the mall now have an informal competition to determine which bathrooms receive the fewest complaints! Mall management staff members receive real-time metrics and updates from both the customers and the employees. Joseph Reuter, cofounder of Kipsu, said, "We are revolutionizing the service cultures of our clients. By scientifically dissecting the nuances of communication in service environments, we provide discipline over data and accountability." The success of the Mall of America is proving his statement is correct.[50]

Establish Marketing Goals and Objectives What is expected to be accomplished by the marketing plan? Based on what is learned from the situation analysis, competitor analysis, and market research, goals and objectives can now be developed related to what the marketing manager intends to accomplish with the marketing plan. JetBlue's marketing goals focus on enhancing the safety, comfort, and fun of customers' travel experience, building high satisfaction and loyalty among JetBlue users, and attracting new users to the brand.

Develop Marketing Strategies As we mentioned earlier, marketing strategies provide the road map for creating, communicating, and delivering value to customers. An overarching decision that must be made is which combinations of products and markets to invest in. A product-market combination may fall into one of four primary categories, as illustrated by Exhibit 3.11, Igor Ansoff's Product-Market Matrix.

- **Market penetration strategies** involve investing in existing customers to gain additional usage of existing products.
- **Product development strategies** recognize the opportunity to invest in new products that will increase usage from the current customer base.
- **Market development strategies** allow for expansion of the firm's product line into heretofore untapped markets, often internationally.
- **Diversification strategies** seize on opportunities to serve new markets with new products.

JetBlue began business with a primary focus on product development. The clean new planes, comfy leather seats, full spectrum entertainment console, and friendly staff were all welcomed by fliers as a long overdue change from other airlines' cattle-call mentality. However, more recently the company has focused on taking its winning formula into a number of new geographic markets. This market development strategy dramatically increased the number of cities on JetBlue's

EXHIBIT 3.11 | Product-Market Combinations

	Product Emphasis	
	Existing Products	New Products
Existing Markets	Strategy = Market penetration Seek to increase sales of existing products to existing markets	Strategy = Product development Create growth by selling new products in existing markets
New Markets	Strategy = Market development Introduce existing products to new markets	Strategy = Diversification Emphasize both new products and new markets to achieve growth

(Row labels under **Market Emphasis**)

Source: H. Igor Ansoff, *The New Corporate Strategy*, New York, NY: John Wiley & Sons, 1988.

route system and especially increased opportunities for customers from underserved smaller cities using smaller regional jets. JetBlue has also added numerous international destinations into the travel mix such as Bermuda and Havana, Cuba (JetBlue's 100th destination).

Create an Implementation Plan Including Forecast, Budget, and Appropriate Marketing Metrics As pointed out earlier, strategy *development* is only part of marketing planning. The other part is strategy *implementation,* including measuring results. The process of measuring marketing results and adjusting the marketing plan as needed is called **marketing control**.

In a marketing plan, every strategy must include an implementation element. Sometimes these are called action plans or programs. Each must discuss timing, assign persons responsible for various aspects of implementation, and assign resources necessary to make the strategy happen.[51] Forecasts and their accompanying budgets must be provided. Then, appropriate metrics must be identified to assess along the way to what degree the plan is on track and the strategies are contributing to achievement of the stated marketing objectives. Chapter 5 provides more information on marketing dashboards and metrics for marketing control.

On the JetBlue website, the Investor Relations and Press Room sections provide compelling evidence that the company is highly oriented toward measurement of marketing results. And although the airline industry as a whole has suffered in recent years due to increased costs, JetBlue has generally received better reviews than most other airlines from Wall Street analysts in part because of the clarity of JetBlue's goals, metrics, and controls.

Develop Contingency Plans A final step marketing managers should take is to develop contingency plans that can be implemented should something happen that negates the viability of the marketing plan.[52] As you've learned, in marketing planning, flexibility and adaptability by managers are critical because unexpected events and drastic changes in various aspects of the external environment are the norm rather than the exception. To address this eventuality, a firm should incorporate contingency plans into the process.

Contingency plans are often described in terms of a separate plan for a worst-case, best-case, and expected-case performance against the forecast. That is, the implementation of the marketing strategies would be different depending on how performance against the forecast actually materializes. If better, the firm could quickly shift to a best-case implementation scenario. If worse, then the shift would be to a worst-case scenario. Having these contingency plans in place avoids scrambling to decide how to adjust marketing strategies when performance against a forecast is higher or lower than expected.

When developing contingency plans, the firm should be realistic about the possibilities and creative in developing options for minimizing any disruption to the firm's operations should it become necessary to implement them. Some firms use contingency planning to reduce the chances they would make a public relations blunder when confronted with an unexpected challenge that generates negative publicity in the media such as product tampering or failure, ethical or legal misconduct of an officer, or some other aspect of their operation that garners bad press.[53]

For JetBlue, as with all airlines, the ultimate external resource contingency is jet fuel. Over the past decade fuel prices have swung from very high to very low, and other than hedging (investing to reduce the risk of adverse price movements of an asset), there's not much JetBlue can do to combat these swings short of buying a refinery (which Delta, in fact, actually did!). As such, JetBlue no doubt has in place contingency plans for different future jet fuel price levels. Having those plans codified helps ensure that a dramatic swing in the price is met with an actionable strategy change immediately.

Lego has executed a highly successful strategy by expanding into Legoland theme parks with locations in California, Florida, Denmark, Germany, Malaysia, and the UK.
©Jason Knott/Alamy Stock Photo

TIPS FOR SUCCESSFUL MARKETING PLANNING

Developing a marketing plan is an essential process for firm success. In addition to its direct impact on a firm's ability to compete, ongoing marketing planning also has the strong internal organizational benefit of providing a rallying point for developing creative ideas and for gaining input from important stakeholders throughout the various areas within an organization.[54] Who should be involved in marketing planning? The answer is: anyone from any unit at any level whose contribution and participation in the process will enhance the likelihood of a successful outcome. Marketing planning provides a unique opportunity for organization members to contribute to the success of a firm in a very concrete and visible way.

Here are a few final tips for having a successful marketing planning experience.

LO 3-5

Use the framework provided for marketing planning, along with the content in future chapters, to build a marketing plan.

1. *Stay flexible.* Don't forget that marketing plans are not set in stone. Markets and customers change, competitors do unexpected things, and the external environment has a nasty habit of creating unexpected surprises. Great marketing managers understand when to adjust a plan. Nimble organizations tend to be much more successful in their marketing strategies.

    In his provocative book, *The Rise and Fall of Strategic Planning,* strategy expert Henry Mintzberg builds the case that organizations sometimes spend so much time focused on planning for the long term that they miss the opportunities presented by the next customer who walks through the door.[55] Mintzberg's concern is valid and points to the need to view planning as an ongoing, organic process in which managers exhibit flexibility and adaptability to changing market conditions. Marketing plans are not written in stone—that is, after a plan is prepared, myriad changes in the firm's external and internal environments may create a need for marketing managers to quickly alter their strategies in the marketplace.[56] The more nimble a company is in changing course to address new conditions as they arise, the more successful its marketing strategies will be.

2. *Utilize input, but don't become paralyzed by information and analysis.* Great marketing managers value research and analytics, but also know when to move forward with action.

3. *Don't underestimate the implementation part of the plan.* This is such a common mistake it is nearly synonymous with poor marketing planning. The quality of the action plans and metrics often make or break the success of the plan. Put another way, a good plan on paper is useless without effective implementation.

4. *Stay strategic, but also stay on top of the tactical.* Remember that marketing has these two levels of interrelated issues, and both the strategic and tactical elements have to be right for the plan to be successful.

5. *Give yourself and your people room to fail and try again.* Marketing planning is by no means a predictable science. It is more realistic to think of it as both science and art, and creativity and risk-taking are to be rewarded. All great marketing managers have experienced both success and failures in marketing planning. As in baseball, it's not one or two times at bat but rather the long-term batting average that separates the great from the average performer.

VISIT THE APPENDIX FOR A MARKETING PLAN EXAMPLE

Often the best way to learn is through example, so in the appendix to this chapter we have provided an abbreviated example marketing plan for the fictitious company CloudCab Small Jet Taxi Service. Take this opportunity early in the course to familiarize yourself with the flow and content, albeit abbreviated, of a typical marketing plan.

In addition, at the end of each chapter starting with this one you will find a Marketing Plan Exercise that is designed to highlight aspects of the chapter as they pertain to a manager's ability to build an effective marketing plan. Use these activities to build your own knowledge and skill in the marketing planning process.

SUMMARY

Marketing planning is an ongoing process of developing and implementing market-driven strategies for an organization. Great marketing planning is essential for success in the marketplace. Once established, marketing plans are not set in stone. Instead, marketing managers must be flexible enough to constantly assess changes in the external and internal environments and adjust strategies and tactics accordingly. The chapter introduces a framework for marketing planning. The essential elements of that framework are covered in the chapters throughout the remaining three parts of the book.

KEY TERMS

benefit   55
utility   55
value proposition   55
customer satisfaction   55
customer loyalty   56
customer retention   56
customer switching   56
value chain   56
value-creating activities   57
marketing planning   58
marketing plan   58
market-driven strategic
  planning   60
strategic business unit (SBU)   60

corporate-level strategic plan   60
SBU-level strategic plan   60
portfolio analysis   61
Boston Consulting Group (BCG)
  Growth-Share Matrix   61
GE Business Screen   61
functional-level plans   62
mission statement   63
strategic vision   63
goals   63
objectives   63
strategy   64
generic strategy   64
competitive strategy   64

core competencies   65
distinctive competencies   65
sustainable competitive
  advantage   65
strategic type   65
first-mover advantage   65
situation analysis   66
SWOT analysis   69
market penetration strategies   71
product development
  strategies   71
market development strategies   71
diversification strategies   71
marketing control   72

APPLICATION QUESTIONS

More application questions are available online.

1. What is a value proposition? For each of these brands, articulate your perception of their key value proposition:
   a. Disney theme parks
   b. Target
   c. Instagram
   d. Chick-fil-A
   e. Netflix

2. Consider the concept of the value chain. Identify a firm that you believe does an especially good job of investing in elements in the value chain to gain higher profit margins versus its competition. Which two or three elements in the value chain does that firm handle especially well? For each of those elements, what does it do that is better than its competition?

3. Why is it so important for marketing managers, when engaged in marketing planning, to successfully deal with both Marketing (Big M) and marketing (little m) elements? What would be the likely negative outcome if a marketing

plan paid a lot of attention to strategies and little attention to tactics? What would be the likely negative outcome of the reverse?

4. Select any industry of interest to you and identify several competing firms. Using Miles and Snow's strategy types, identify the following: (1) a firm that you believe is a prospector; (2) a firm that you believe is an analyzer; (3) a firm that you believe is a defender; and (4) a firm that you believe is a reactor. What characteristics of each led you to conclude they belong in their respective strategy type?

5. Historically, the theme park industry in Orlando is heavily affected by a large number of macro-level external environmental factors. From each of the five major categories of macro-level external factors, identify a specific example of how some element within that category might impact a theme park's marketing planning for the next couple of years. Be sure to explain *why* you believe each of your examples will be important for marketing managers to consider as they develop their marketing plans.

MANAGEMENT DECISION CASE
Marketing Planning Helps Dunkin' Donuts Score Big in Coffee Customer Loyalty

A key goal for a marketing manager is to make sure that the company's brand stays relevant. Successfully realizing this goal requires a marketing planning process that is both thorough and grounded in best practices, and also flexible enough to allow the firm to react to (and hopefully stay ahead of) changing customer preferences and shifts in values. Over its 67 years in business, Dunkin' Donuts has shown that it can stick to its core mission while also regularly updating its marketing strategy, and thus remain relevant within the highly competitive "out-of-home coffee" category.[57]

In 1950, Dunkin' Donuts was a single restaurant in Quincy, Massachusetts, with a simple mission: serve high-quality donuts and coffee at affordable prices with fast and friendly service. Today, with over 12,000 restaurants in 45 countries, the chain's mission is still basically the same, but many aspects of its marketing strategy have changed to keep the brand fresh and relevant against fierce competition.[58]

In the first five decades of its history, Dunkin' was mostly about the donuts. In the early 2000s, it decided to shift the focus more to the drink into which the donut was about to be dunked—the coffee. It squarely took on market leader Starbucks by offering a less expensive (yet really tasty) alternative, one that was faster and more user-friendly—the "average Joe's average joe." In 2006, Dunkin' got even more serious about coffee with its famous and highly successful "America Runs on Dunkin'" campaign. Today, although it certainly still sells plenty of donuts, Dunkin' sells an incredible 1.9 billion cups of coffee per year—that's 60 cups *per second!*[59]

In recent years, a major focus of Dunkin' Donuts' marketing planning has been its digital strategy, especially by enabling engagement with customers through social media. Examples include the "create Dunkin's next donut" contest a few years back, and the more recent integrated #mydunkin campaign on Twitter. In the latter, fans were encouraged to share their experiences via Facebook and Twitter with how Dunkin' keeps them running, with the most enthusiastic fans appearing in Dunkin' TV ads. Using these tools has helped the company hear the stories of its customers, retell the stories, and interact with these loyal fans on a regular basis.[60]

Although Dunkin' scores lower than Starbucks in the number of social media interactions, experts importantly give Dunkin higher marks in terms of the *quality* of those interactions. According to Dunkin's ad agency executives, "More than ever, Dunkin' is a brand that listens to its guests, through multiple channels, at all levels of the organization. Dunkin' puts its fans at the center of its social media strategy—they're an active and passionate tribe that's fueled by interactions with the brand." And Dunkin' also manages to take a jab at the competition now and then. Recently, its top Facebook post was a photo of a Dunkin' T-shirt emblazoned with the message "Friends don't let friends drink Starbucks."[61]

Marketing (Big M) and marketing (little m) combine strategic and programmatic/tactical approaches to provide a comprehensive focus on a company's most important stakeholder: the customer and his or her experience with the brand. Witness Dunkin's highly successful loyalty program, DD Perks Rewards, which is a key competitive differentiator for the company. With over 5 million members, this program is one of the fastest-growing loyalty programs in the quick service restaurant (QSR) industry. As a member of DD perks, customers earn points for every dollar spent and receive a free drink when they accrue 200 points. On becoming a DD Perks Rewards member, the customer receives a personalized welcoming e-mail message explaining the benefits of the program. Additional e-mails are also sent, and customers receive special offers on their device through Dunkin's mobile app (which has been downloaded over 16 million times since its launch). The app is also the platform for Dunkin's On-the-Go-Ordering, with which customers can place their order in advance and pick it up on arrival.[62]

The superior customer experience that Dunkin' Donuts provides has earned them industry accolades. No doubt to the ultimate chagrin of Starbucks, in the Brand Keys Customer Loyalty Engagement Index®, Dunkin' Donuts has been number 1 in coffee customer loyalty *for the past 11 years* in the out-of-home coffee category and the number 1 brand for packaged coffee category for the last five years. This index recognizes brands that surpass competitors in delighting customers and meeting their expectations for taste, quality, and service, as well as brand value.[63]

Because of superior marketing planning and marketing strategy execution, Dunkin' Donuts has successfully made the shift in focus from donuts to coffee, but it does operate in the shadow of Starbucks, which has 36 percent of the U.S. market to Dunkin's 24 percent. And make no mistake about it, Starbucks is also very committed to digital and social media marketing and also has a loyalty program and a mobile app.[64] As each company engages with its customers, Dunkin's marketing managers will have to stay at the top of their game and continue to deploy a strong market planning process, monitor and adapt to customer trends, and respond with strategies designed to keep the Dunkin' Donuts brand relevant and strategically differentiated against the competition.

Questions for Consideration:

1. Dunkin' Donuts made a strategic decision to make its business about the coffee, not just the donuts. What are the risks when a company that is so closely identified with one product (it's in their name!) decides to change its focus to a different product? What marketing strategies can help reduce the risks and increase the probability of success?

2. What are the key differences between the marketing strategy of Dunkin' Donuts and its chief competitor, Starbucks? What else could the company do from a marketing manager's standpoint to successfully compete with and clearly differentiate Dunkin' from Starbucks?

3. Loyalty programs like DD Perks can get customers engaged with the brand and incentivize them to stay loyal. But loyalty programs alone are relatively easy for competitors to match and top, and thus they often aren't sufficient to retain customers and thwart switching. In addition to reward programs, what other factors drive loyalty to a brand, and which of these do you presently see in play at Dunkin' Donuts? Is there more that Dunkin' could do to increase customer loyalty?

MARKETING PLAN EXERCISES

ACTIVITY 1: Elements of a Marketing Plan

In the chapter, you learned that marketing planning drives the activities of the marketing manager and you were provided a framework for marketing planning. Before you move further through this course, it is important to be sure that you understand the flow and content of a typical marketing plan.

1. Read the annotated marketing plan example presented in the appendix to this chapter.

2. Make notes about any questions you may have about the example plan, and be prepared to bring those questions to class for clarification.

ACTIVITY 2: Situation Analysis

In the chapter you also learned about the key situation analysis areas of external macro-level environmental factors, competitive forces, and internal environmental factors that marketing managers must consider in marketing planning. You also saw how this information can be conveniently summarized and portrayed in a SWOT analysis.

1. Using the chapter discussion on situation analysis along with Exhibit 3.10 as a guide, develop a short list of internal strengths and weaknesses and external opportunities and threats. Focus on issues that you believe will be most important to your marketing planning over the next year or so.

2. Exhibit 3.10 suggests that you consider the four different scenario combinations of the SWOT to begin to brainstorm possible strategies. Based on what you know at present, develop one idea for a marketing strategy that might be appropriate for each of the four situational scenario combinations represented in the exhibit—that is, one strategy that uses internal strengths to take advantage of external opportunities you have identified; one strategy that uses internal strengths to avoid external threats you have identified; one strategy that takes advantage of opportunities by overcoming internal weaknesses you have identified; and one strategy that minimizes internal weaknesses and avoids external threats.

NOTES

1. Peter C. Verhoef, "Understanding the Effect of Customer Relationship Management Efforts on Customer Retention and Customer Share Development," *Journal of Marketing* 67, no. 4 (October 2003), pp. 30–45.

2. Stephanie Coyles and Timothy C. Gokey, "Customer Retention Is Not Enough," *Journal of Consumer Marketing* 22, no. 2/3 (2005), pp. 101–06.

3. Jamie Page Deaton, "2017 Best Cars for the Money," *U.S. News & World Report,* February 7, 2017, https://cars.usnews.com /cars-trucks/Best-Cars-for-the-Money/; Mel Anton, "2017 Toyota Prius Review," *U.S. News & World Report,* March 23, 2017, https://cars.usnews.com/cars-trucks/toyota/prius; and Cody Trotter, "2017 Lexus NX Review," *U.S. News & World Report,* March 3, 2017, https://cars.usnews.com/cars-trucks/lexus/nx.

4. Anders Gustafsson, Michael D. Johnson, and Inger Roos, "The Effects of Customer Satisfaction, Relationship Commitment Dimensions, and Triggers on Customer Retention," *Journal of Marketing* 69, no. 4 (October 2005), pp. 210–18.

5. Seongjae Yu, "The Growth Pattern of Samsung Electronics: A Strategy Perspective," *International Studies of Management & Organization* 28, no. 4 (Winter 1998/1999), pp. 57–73.

6. "QuickBooks Online Passes 1.5 Million Paid Subscribers." *Intuit,* August 8, 2016, http://investors.intuit.com/press-releases/press -release-details/2016/QuickBooks-Online-Passes-15-Million -Paid-Subscribers/default.aspx; Intuit Inc., "Form 10-K." *Securities and Exchange Commission,* September 1, 2016, https://www .sec.gov/Archives/edgar/data/896878/000089687816000286 /fy16q410-kdocument.htm.

7. Michael D. Johnson, Andreas Herrman, and Frank Huber, "The Evolution of Loyalty Intentions," *Journal of Marketing* 70, no. 2 (April 2006), pp. 122–32.

8. "Top 10 Customer-Centric Companies of 2014." *Talk Desk,* January 13, 2015, https://www.talkdesk.com/blog/top-10

-customer-centric-companies-of-2014; and Michael A. Prospero, "Is HP Customer Service Good? 2017 Rating," *LAPTOP,* March 9, 2017, http://www.laptopmag.com/articles/hp-tech-support.

9. Kusum L. Ailawadi and Bari Harlam, "An Empirical Analysis of the Determinants of Retail Margins: The Role of Store-Brand Share," *Journal of Marketing* 68, no. 1 (January 2004), pp. 147–65.

10. Frederick F. Reichheld, *Loyalty Rules! How Leaders Build Lasting Relationships in the Digital Age* (Cambridge, MA: Harvard Business School Press, 2001).

11. Michael E. Porter, *Competitive Advantage* (New York: Simon & Schuster, 1985).

12. J. David Hunger and Thomas H. Wheelen, *Essentials of Strategic Management,* 4th ed. (Upper Saddle River, NJ: Prentice Hall, 2007).

13. Eric M. Olson, Stanley F. Slater, and G. Tomas M. Hult, "The Performance Implications of Fit among Business Strategy, Marketing Organization Structure, and Strategic Behavior," *Journal of Marketing* 69, no. 3 (July 2005), pp. 49–65.

14. Thomas L. Friedman, *The World Is Flat: A Brief History of the Twenty-First Century* (New York: Farrar, Straus and Giroux, 2005).

15. Wayne McPhee and David Wheeler, "Making the Case for the Added-Value Chain," *Strategy and Leadership* 34, no. 4 (2006), pp. 39–48.

16. Roland T. Rust, Katherine N. Lemon, and Valarie A. Zeithaml, "Return on Marketing: Using Customer Equity to Focus Marketing Strategy," *Journal of Marketing* 68, no. 1 (January 2004), pp. 109–27.

17. Richard W. Mosley, "Customer Experience, Organisational Culture, and the Employer Brand," *Journal of Brand Management* 15, no. 2 (November 2007), pp. 123–35.

18. Riley Jones, "How Nike's 'Just Do It' Slogan Turned the Brand into a Household Name," *Complex,* August 17, 2015,

http://www.complex.com/sneakers/2015/08/nike-just-do-it-history; and Lindsay Kolowich, "12 of the Best Marketing and Advertising Campaigns of All Time," *Hub Spot,* June 26, 2015, https://blog.hubspot.com/blog/tabid/6307/bid/32763/The-10-Greatest-Marketing-Campaigns-of-All-Time.aspx#sm.0000peftmpa6qd6rphv169ukue3b8.

19. P. Rajan Varadarajan, Satish Jayachandran, and J. Chris White, "Strategic Interdependence in Organizations: Deconglomeration and Marketing Strategy," *Journal of Marketing* 65, no. 1 (January 2001), pp. 15–29.

20. Ron Southwick, "$45 for 10 Minutes: Rite Aid Ex-pands Online Doctor's Appointments to Four More Cities," *MedCity News,* March 3, 2013, http://medcitynews.com/2013/03/45-for-10-minutes-rite-aid-expands-online-doctors-appointments-to-four-more-cities/.

21. Karen Norman Kennedy, Jerry R. Goolsby, and Eric J. Arnold, "Implementing a Customer Orientation: Extension of Theory and Application," *Journal of Marketing* 67, no. 4 (October 2003), pp. 67–81.

22. Rust, Lemon, and Zeithaml, "Return on Marketing."

23. Rachel Lerman, "Tableau's New CEO Vows to Put Customer First on His Agenda," *Seattle Times,* November 9, 2016, http://www.seattletimes.com/business/technology/tableaus-new-ceo-vows-to-put-customer-first-on-his-agenda/.

24. Karen Dubinsky, "Brand Is Dead," *Journal of Business Strategy* 24, no. 2 (March/April 2003), pp. 42–43.

25. Haley Peterson, "McDonald's CEO Reveals His Massive Plan to Save the Business," *Business Insider,* May 4, 2015, http://www.businessinsider.com/mcdonalds-ceo-reveals-turnaround-plan-2015-5.

26. "GE Business Screen," *Business Resource Software,* www.brs-inc.com/pwxcharts.asp?32.

27. "The Experience Curve—Reviewed: IV. The Growth Share Matrix or The Product Portfolio," *Boston Consulting Group,* www.bcg.com/documents/file13904.pdf.

28. Dylan Love and Karyne Levy, "12 Discontinued Tech Products That We Miss So Much," *Business Insider,* March 29, 2014, http://www.businessinsider.com/discontinued-tech-we-miss-2014-3#.

29. Andrew E. Polcha, "A Complex Global Business' Dilemma: Long Range Planning vs. Flexibility," *Planning Review* 18, no. 2 (March/April 1990), pp. 34–40.

30. Robert Slater, *Jack Welch and the GE Way: Management Insights and Leadership Secrets of the Legendary CEO* (Boston: McGraw-Hill, 1998).

31. Hunger and Wheelen, *Essentials of Strategic Management.*

32. Lindsay Kolowich, "12 Truly Inspiring Company Vision and Mission Statement Examples," *Hub Spot,* August 4, 2015, https://blog.hubspot.com/marketing/inspiring-company-mission-statements#sm.0000peftmpa6qd6rphv169ukue3b8.

33. Noel Tichy and Ram Charan, "Speed, Simplicity, Self-Confidence: An Interview with Jack Welch," *Harvard Business Review,* September–October 1989, p. 113.

34. Mohanbir Sawhney and Jeff Zabin, "Managing and Measuring Relational Equity in the Network Economy," *Journal of the Academy of Marketing Science* 30, no. 4 (Fall 2002), pp. 313–33.

35. Bishnu Sharma, "Marketing Strategy, Contextual Factors, and Performance: An Investigation of Their Relationship," *Marketing Intelligence & Planning* 22, no. 2/3 (2004), pp. 128–44.

36. Jeremy Bowman, "Why Kroger Co's Growth Strategy Beats Its Rivals," *The Motley Fool,* August 23, 2015, https://www.fool.com/investing/general/2015/08/23/why-kroger-cos-growth-strategy-beats-its-rivals.aspx.

37. Mark B. Houston, Beth A. Walker, Michael D. Hutt, and Peter H. Reingen, "Cross-Unit Competition for Market Charter: The Enduring Influence of Structure," *Journal of Marketing* 65, no. 2 (April 2001), pp. 19–35.

38. David Mercer, *Marketing Strategy: The Challenge of the External Environment* (Thousand Oaks, CA: Sage, 1998).

39. Robert L. Cardy, "Employees as Customers?" *Marketing Management* 10, no. 3 (September/October 2001), pp. 12–14.

40. Regina D. Woodall, Charles L. Colby, and A. Parasuraman, "Evolution to Revolution," *Marketing Management* 16, no. 2 (March/April 2007), p. 29.

41. Sonic Drive-In, "#squareshakes," *Instagram,* n.d., https://www.instagram.com/explore/tags/squareshakes/.

42. Tim Nudd, "Sonic Is Making Awesome Square Shakes Designed for Instagram, Sold through Instagram," *Adweek,* April 4, 2017, http://www.adweek.com/creativity/sonic-making-awesome-square-shakes-designed-instagram-sold-through-instagram-170602/.

43. Chaman L. Jain, "Benchmarking the Forecasting Process," *Journal of Business Forecasting Methods & Systems* 21, no. 3 (Fall 2002), pp. 12–16.

44. Rajdeep Grewal and Patriya Tansuhaj, "Building Organizational Capabilities for Managing Economic Crisis: The Role of Market Orientation and Strategic Flexibility," *Journal of Marketing* 65, no. 2 (April 2001), pp. 67–81.

45. Hunger and Wheelen, *Essentials of Strategic Management.*

46. Gary Chaison, "Airline Negotiations and the New Concessionary Bargaining," *Journal of Labor Research* 28, no. 4 (September 2007), pp. 642–57.

47. Kennedy et al., "Implementing a Customer Orientation."

48. Ross Goodwin and Brad Ball, "What Marketing Wants the CEO to Know," *Marketing Management* 12, no. 5 (September/October 2003), pp. 18–23.

49. Robert Inglis and Robert Clift, "Market-Oriented Accounting: Information for Product-Level Decisions," *Managerial Auditing Journal* 23, no. 3 (2008), pp. 225–39.

50. Patrick Hanlon, "Google Pushes Marketing Talk-Back Button," *Forbes,* February 8, 2013, www.forbes.com/sites/patrickhanlon/2013/02/08/google-pushes-marketing-talk-back-button/.

51. Robert L. Cardy, "Employees as Customers?" *Marketing Management* 10, no. 3 (September/October 2001), pp. 12–14.

52. Denis Smith, "Business (Not) as Usual: Crisis Management, Service Recovery, and the Vulnerability of Organisations," *Journal of Services Marketing* 19, no. 5 (2005), pp. 309–21.

53. Tobin Hensgen, Kevin C. Desouza, and Maryann Durland, "Initial Crisis Agent-Response Impact Syndrome (ICARIS)," *Journal of Contingencies and Crisis Management* 14, no. 4 (December 2006), pp. 190–98.

54. William B. Locander, "Staying within the Flock," *Marketing Management* 14, no. 2 (March/April 2005), pp. 52–55.

55. Henry Mintzberg, *The Rise and Fall of Strategic Planning* (New York: Financial Times Prentice Hall, 2000).

56. Polcha, "A Complex Global Business' Dilemma."

57. Steve Olenski, "Time to Make the Donuts: How the Dunkin' Donuts Brand Stays Relevant," *Forbes.com,* March 6, 2017, https://www.forbes.com/sites/steveolenski/2017/03/06/time-to-make-the-donuts-how-the-dunkin-donuts-brand-stays-relevant/#14b3b3575556; Dunkin' Donuts, "Brand Keys Names Dunkin' Donuts #1 in Coffee Customer Loyalty for 11th Consecutive Year," *Dunkin' Donuts corporate website,* January 26, 2017, https://news.dunkindonuts.com/news/brand-keys-names-dunkin-donuts; and Linda Tucci, "Dunkin'

Sees Growth from Digital Tech," *TechTarget.com,* February 9, 2017, http://searchcio.techtarget.com/news/450412715/Dunkin-pins-growth-on-digital-tech.

58. Olenski, "Time to Make the Donuts."

59. Christine Champagne and Teresa Iezzio, "Dunkin' Donuts and Starbucks: A Tale of Two Coffee Marketing Giants," *FastCompany.com,* August 21, 2014, www.fastcompany.com/3034572/dunkin-donuts-and-starbucks-a-tale-of-two-coffee-marketing-giants; Linda Tischler, "It's Not about the Doughnuts," *Fast Company.com,* December 1, 2004, https://www.fastcompany.com/51444/its-not-about-doughnuts; Dunkin' Donuts, "Brand Keys Names Dunkin' Donuts #1 in Coffee Customer Loyalty"; and Dunkin' Donuts, "Facts ABOUT Dunkin' Donuts," *Newsday.com,* April 17, 2017, http://www.newsday.com/business/facts-about-dunkin-donuts-including-munchkins-coffees-iced-coffee-quincy-and-first-store-1.10435725.

60. Ali Aceto, "Behind the Scenes of #mydunkin with Dunkin' Donuts Fan Meg A," *Dunkin' Donuts corporate website,* October 17, 2013, https://news.dunkindonuts.com/blog/behind-the-scenes-of-mydunkin-with-dunkin-donuts-fan-meg-a; and Champagne and Iezzio, "Dunkin' Donuts and Starbucks."

61. Champagne and Iezzio, "Dunkin' Donuts and Starbucks."

62. Dunkin' Donuts, "Brand Keys Names Dunkin' Donuts #1 in Coffee Customer Loyalty"; Olenski, "Time to Make the Donuts"; Jim Tierney, "Dunkin' Donuts Look to Strengthen Customer Loyalty," *Customer 360,* October 7, 2016, https://www.loyalty360.org/content-gallery/daily-news/dunkin-donuts-look-to-strengthen-customer-loyalty; and James Geddes, "Dunkin' Donuts Introduces New App with On the Go Ordering and Free Beverage Signup Promo," *Tech Times,* April 19, 2016, http://www.techtimes.com/articles/150873/20160419/dunkin-donuts-introduces-new-app-with-on-the-go-ordering-and-free-beverage-signup-promo.htm.

63. Dunkin' Donuts, "Brand Keys Names Dunkin' Donuts #1 in Coffee Customer."

64. Champagne and Iezzio, "Dunkin' Donuts and Starbucks."

Cloudcab Small Jet Taxi Service

Abbreviated Example Marketing Plan

NOTE TO READER

This is an *abbreviated version* of a marketing plan for a fictitious firm, CloudCab Small Jet Taxi Service. This appendix is designed to walk you through the main steps of marketing planning. The idea is to provide you with an example early in the course so you will have a better understanding throughout the chapters of how the pieces of a marketing plan come together. Chapter 3 is devoted to the topic of marketing planning, providing a marketing plan framework and explaining the parts. That framework is used to develop this abbreviated example. Note that in practice most marketing plans contain more depth of detail than is provided here. Also, remember that each chapter ends with a Marketing Plan Exercise designed to guide you in applying the concepts from that chapter to a marketing plan.

SITUATION ANALYSIS

CloudCab seeks to provide solutions for the time-conscious traveler using quick, luxurious jet transportation. The small company was founded by former pilot Travis Camp and is now poised to be a first-mover into the California/Nevada/ Arizona market. CloudCab will provide an alternative to frustrating waits at the airport and long car rides at a fair price for its customers.

CloudCab will use small, underutilized airports and a new class of Very Light Jet (VLJ) to quickly and comfortably transport customers from one city to another. Its customers will come primarily from businesses needing quick, on-demand transportation. Initially, CloudCab will not face much direct competition, so its biggest challenge will be to convince customers of its benefits over more traditional products.

Macro-Level External Environment

Political and Legal

Like all companies using the skies, CloudCab is subject to the rules set forth by the Federal Aviation Administration and other regulatory bodies. Fortunately, smaller jets have many of the same air privileges as their larger counterparts. This ensures access to needed airspace and air traffic control services.

The political and legal environment has the potential to become an even more positive factor for CloudCab as business expands. CloudCab uses smaller, underutilized airports, thereby drawing traffic away from congested major hubs and increasing the efficiency of the entire system. If CloudCab is successful, this may actually induce lawmakers to provide incentives for companies like CloudCab.

Furthermore, larger airports are already facing capacity strain. If CloudCab ties up the governmental resources needed by larger planes carrying more passengers, there may be pressure to limit the use of small jets at large airports.

Sociocultural

The macro-trend of consumers leading time-poor lives continues as both individuals and companies strive to be more efficient in their day-to-day operations. Coupled with an increase in waiting times at major airports due to heightened security procedures, this has led today's consumers to be even more conscious of the time spent in transit. Many are willing to spend extra money on faster, more convenient travel options.

Technological

Until recently, small jet service on a large scale was prohibitively expensive. The limited number of people willing to pay for such service could not compensate for the high cost of the jet itself. Due to changes in technology and the advent of the VLJ, this has begun to change. Several companies have been able to produce VLJs for the relatively low price range of $1 million to $3 million each. Using these efficient three-to-six-passenger jets, a taxi-like air service is now economically feasible.

Economic

The overall state of the economy will have a large impact on CloudCab's success, since business travel declines precipitously during economic downturns. Since some industries inherently require more travel than others (e.g., consulting, sales) and thus have a larger impact on demand for CloudCab services, CloudCab should particularly watch the health of these industries as predictors of demand for its own services.

CloudCab is also heavily dependent on the availability and price of oil. Higher oil prices will erode CloudCab's margins, while shortages may effectively stall the business. The risk involved in relying on a potentially price-volatile resource must be effectively managed to ensure success.

Competitive Environment

Threat of New Entrants

If CloudCab is successful it may entice others to enter the market. CloudCab's business is very capital intensive, though not as much so as a traditional airline due to smaller, lower-cost jets and a limited operating area. Still, the capital needs are sufficient to deter entry by many.

The biggest hurdle facing new entrants is the lead time necessary to procure the VLJs. This requires planning years in advance of actual operation due to backlogs in manufacturing and high demand. Thus, if a company is not in the business now, it would likely be at least a few years until it was able to enter. In the meantime, CloudCab would have some warning that a new competitor was coming.

Rivalry among Existing Firms

Fortunately, CloudCab will be one of the first to market, so initially there will not be many direct competitors. For a while, companies currently pursuing similar strategies should have ample market share to coexist peacefully, especially since most are geographically concentrated. However, it is just a matter of time before a few establish themselves as the dominant brands and expand nationally, increasing the rivalry and pushing some weaker players out of business.

CloudCab will face some indirect competition from the start from other private jet options. These include partial ownership plans and pay-by-the-hour membership cards. Until now, these have been the solutions of choice for speedy, luxurious travel.

Threat of Substitute Products

CloudCab's greatest threat will likely come from substitute products. Consumers have a variety of options when it comes to transportation. For regional travel, they can choose to fly on a traditional airline, drive their car, or in some cases take a bus or train. These options do not provide nearly the same level of comfort and speed as air taxis, but they do accomplish the task of getting a person from Point A to Point B at a significantly lower cost. Also, for business travelers, technology solutions such as videoconferencing make physical travel to some types of meetings nonessential. If national security travel limitations develop or an economic downturn forces firms to cut business travel, these substitutes will predominate.

Bargaining Power of Buyers

CloudCab primarily competes in the business-to-business (B2B) market space, and it will be catering to only a few customers per flight on a limited number of flights. This means that any one customer's decision to use CloudCab has a large proportional impact, especially during CloudCab's early years. CloudCab will have to treat each customer well because it cannot afford to lose any. Still, a single traveler will not be able to demand, or bargain for, changes from CloudCab because the cost of making those changes will likely be larger than the revenue collected from that one buyer. On the other hand, a major corporate client—supplying many passengers over time—would wield considerable power.

Bargaining Power of Suppliers

CloudCab uses a single manufacturer for its jets; thus the level of dependency is high. If the jets are not ready in time or do not meet specifications, CloudCab could be put out of business. If CloudCab's manufacturer is not able to fulfill its contract, CloudCab might have to wait years to have an order filled with another supplier. Consequently, CloudCab's supplier is in a strong position to bargain for better terms.

At present, the supplier has relatively few buyers, one of them being CloudCab. So as a buyer, CloudCab also has some bargaining power. This makes the two interdependent and reduces the incentive for the supplier to treat CloudCab unfairly.

Internal Environment

Firm Structure

CloudCab, being relatively new, is far smaller than most businesses in the airline industry. Having few employees makes communication easy and response to change quick to occur. Realizing that the company's success depends heavily on customer adoption of the new offering, CloudCab executives' actions are driven primarily by the needs of the market.

CloudCab is led by founder and CEO Travis Camp. Robert Fray, chief operating officer and close friend of Camp, has been crucial in developing cost-saving measures to ensure CloudCab's prices are as competitive as can be. Other officers include Thomas Puck, chief financial officer; Elizabeth Vars, chief marketing officer; and Jeffery Brown, chief technology officer. All have airline industry experience, and Camp and Fray are former commercial pilots. The firm is in the entrepreneurial stage of its corporate development.

CloudCab is privately held and funded primarily through the investments of Travis Camp and Robert Fray, who combined have a controlling interest in the company. The rest of the funding has been obtained mostly from venture capital firms seeking returns based on a five-year time horizon.

Firm Culture

CloudCab is built on seizing opportunities to better serve the customer. It epitomizes a "lean and mean" culture. New ideas for improvements in efficiency and service quality are encouraged in this customer-centric culture. CloudCab has formalized reward systems for outstanding performance and attitude to promote high morale and productivity among its employees.

Firm Resources

Marketing capabilities: CloudCab has a strong, close-knit marketing team with a combination of experienced hands and recent college graduates. Several employees have ties with local media in major cities that can be used upon product launch.

Financial capabilities: CloudCab is well-financed through equity investments. It has purchased outright the 15 VLJs it plans to use in its operations. Current cash reserves should easily cover initial marketing and ongoing operating expenses, though investors have pledged further funds if needed.

R&D and technological capabilities: Lacking R&D capabilities in-house, CloudCab has chosen to purchase all aircraft and related systems from qualified vendors and outsource needed maintenance on those aircraft and systems. CloudCab values keeping its systems current and ensuring the firm is in a position to take advantage of any oncoming industry breakthroughs in jet technology.

Operations capabilities: CloudCab currently has the capacity to serve four city locations in California and Nevada (see the Market Research section of this document). Following success in these markets, CloudCab will be able to expand using its fully scalable communications and logistics tracking systems.

Human capabilities: CloudCab's employees are capable and committed. Many employees have received stock and stock options as part of their compensation, tying the interests of company and employee together. CloudCab is presently staffed with 45 people and has plans to employ a total of 80 people when fully operational. Many functions such as maintenance, security, and janitorial work will be outsourced.

Information systems capabilities: CEO Camp is a strong believer in customer relationship management (CRM). Every time a customer flies, he or she will be given the option to fill out a comment card, the contents of which will be entered into CloudCab's central database. Employees of CloudCab with customer contact will also be able to make notes on customer observations. Both of these data sources will be coded categorically and used to assist in customer development and planning. Popular flight times and routes will also be tracked to better assist in modification of product offerings.

SWOT SUMMARY/ANALYSIS

Internal / External	Key Strengths (S)	Key Weaknesses (W)
	Customer focus Speed to market Industry knowledge	Untested product Unknown brand Limited geographic reach
Key Opportunities (O) Time-conscious travelers VLJ availability Small airports underutilized	**S/O Based Strategies** Use VLJs to provide quick transportation between small airports	**W/O Based Strategies** Focus on and invest in building the brand and offering in a small market first
Key Threats (T) Traditional flights and cars Larger airports overcrowded Possibility of new, better jets	**S/T Based Strategies** Demonstrate benefits over alternatives, avoid large airports, and stay tech aware	**W/T Based Strategies** Don't try to compete against bigger airlines for mainstream customers

MARKET RESEARCH

To determine which locations to serve, CloudCab first gathered secondary data on air traffic patterns, popular destinations among private jet owners, and travel frequency for business and leisure. This allowed CloudCab to see where similar services were already being used for comparison.

CloudCab then gathered primary data on travelers' aspirations for where they would like to see CloudCab operate and what features they would want the service to have. This was done through a combination of focus groups and surveys. Focus groups were comprised of travel purchasers within businesses, business travelers themselves, and upper-income leisure travelers. Surveys were distributed via e-mail with a goal of gaining responses from both business and leisure travelers.

All of the data were analyzed to form a complete picture of what travel patterns are like now, what they may be in the future, and what factors (translated into customer benefits) would create demand for CloudCab services. CloudCab used the data to select its first four cities for operation: San Francisco, Los Angeles, Reno, and Las Vegas.

Research also revealed the following findings:

- In general, there seems to be a greater demand for sky taxis from business than from leisure travelers.
- Leisure travelers plan further ahead and have less need of on-demand service.
- Both leisure and business travelers want luxurious accommodations.
- Business travelers have more need of one-way flights than do leisure travelers.
- Time is the biggest priority for business travelers, while comfort is the biggest for leisure travelers.
- Some businesses, such as consulting and sales, have a greater need for on-demand travel than others.
- There is a "sweet spot" in income level among leisure travelers where they are wealthy enough to afford CloudCab services but not wealthy enough to own their own jet.

MARKETING GOALS AND OBJECTIVES

Goal

The goal of CloudCab is to be the preferred provider of on-demand short flight service.

Objectives

Aiming for a May 1 launch, within its first partial year of operation CloudCab will:

1. Sell 5,500 flight itineraries.
2. Attain a rating of "highly satisfied" customer satisfaction scored by 90 percent of customers.
3. Achieve repeat purchase by 50 percent of customers.

MARKETING STRATEGIES

Product-Market Combinations

CloudCab will use a product development strategy to introduce its new on-demand jet service into the California/Nevada/Arizona market. Based on CloudCab's market research, the product will first be made available in San Francisco, Los Angeles, Reno, and Las Vegas. If the product is successful there, then CloudCab will gradually add more service locations. Once a firm foothold in the region is established, CloudCab will expand into new markets in other regions.

Initially, CloudCab will depart only from the four selected cities. However, customers will be able to use the service to fly round-trip to *any airport* they choose within the region of operation. For one-way flights, CloudCab will provide service only between selected cities, making the plane instantly available at that location for the next flight.

Market Segmentation, Target Marketing, Positioning

Segmentation

The market for on-demand small jet service can be easily divided between business travelers and leisure travelers. Leisure travelers can be further divided based on income levels, and business travelers can be further divided based on industry and other variables such as firm size. Of all possible segments, CloudCab has identified three that have especially high potential to be CloudCab customers:

- Leisure travelers with annual incomes between $300,000 and $1 million.
- Business travelers making B2B sales calls.
- Business travelers on assignment for mid- to large-size consulting firms.

Target Marketing

CloudCab evaluated each of these segments to determine its focus for initial investment. The first segment, leisure travelers, has the means to afford CloudCab's service and could be a highly profitable market if effectively reached. However, its preference for round trips over one-way and its tendency to book travel arrangements in advance does not fit well with CloudCab's on-demand service. Leisure travelers are also far less concentrated and thus harder to reach with marketing communications.

The second segment, business travelers in sales, would be easier to reach and would need CloudCab's one-way flights between select cities. Sales calls are a combination of previously scheduled appointments and client requests, making the demand for on-demand service in this group mixed. Sales professionals are often under pressure to keep traveling costs down, though, making the profitability of serving this segment questionable.

The third segment, business travelers in consulting, shares sales professionals' need for one-way flights and on-demand service. Yet compared to sales professionals, there is less pressure to keep travel costs down since time and level of service to the client take precedence, and travel and other expenses are often billable to the client. Additionally, these travelers are largely concentrated in fewer firms, making it easier for marketing communications to reach this segment. Also, there is a substantial submarket of independent consultants from which to draw. For these reasons, CloudCab has decided to concentrate on the business consulting traveler segment as its primary target market. CloudCab will make its services available to other segments if they desire to use CloudCab, but CloudCab will not make any concentrated efforts to invest marketing dollars toward them in the beginning. Thus, high-income leisure travelers and sales professionals may be viewed as secondary target markets at present. No tertiary target markets have been identified as of yet.

Positioning

On one end of the travel spectrum, there exists the low-price, low-benefits group. This includes such offerings as traditional airfare and car transportation. Both involve a great deal of hassle, wasted time, and discomfort. The one advantage of this group is that it is affordable to the masses.

On the opposite end of the spectrum, there exists the high-price, high-benefits group. This group consists of private sole jet ownership, partial jet ownership similar to a time-share, and, on the lower side, pay-by-the-hour jet service. These options afford their customers a high degree of luxury and many time-saving features, but at a price well outside the range of most travelers, business or leisure.

In the middle of these two groups of travel options is a wide chasm. Until now, no company has been able to strike a happy medium between the two. Utilizing new technology and a unique business model, CloudCab seeks to position itself in this void with a focus on the B2B consulting market. Using its on-demand small-jet service, customers flying from select cities will be able to access many of the same benefits private jet owners enjoy, but without the exorbitant cost associated with it. CloudCab's service will be faster and more enjoyable than traditional airline flights or ground transportation, yet cost far less than private jet ownership. This appears to be a strong positioning with high upside potential for messaging to the primary target market.

Marketing Mix Strategies

Product/Branding Strategies

CloudCab's product benefits center on convenience, dependable service, and a quality image. CloudCab will primarily focus on service to small "executive airports" near the four start-up cities, with the exception of Las Vegas, for which travelers will have direct access to McCharren (the main Las Vegas airport) due to its proximity to the "strip."

To use CloudCab, customers will have two options. They will be able to either call a qualified customer service representative to book their flight or go online and enter their flight and payment information themselves.

Branding of CloudCab will evoke in customers the imagery of being quickly and comfortably transported "by a cloud" from one location to another. This will be communicated through the product name CloudCab as well as its logo, an airplane seat lightly resting in a fast-moving cloud.

Service Strategies

Customer service representatives and airport attendants will be noticeably a cut above the ordinary—polite and professional at all times, both on the phone and in person. Because of the firm's CRM capabilities to provide personalized service to its most valued customers, CloudCab employees will be able to easily enter information into an internal database under individual customer profiles. This will allow CloudCab to consistently meet the expectations of its customers without the customer having to express preferences every time CloudCab is used.

Pricing Strategies

The pricing decision for CloudCab is made more difficult due to the newness of its product offering and lack (so far) of strong competitors in its markets. In the early stages, penetration pricing can be effective to gain customer trial, expose customers to the excellent service quality, and build customer loyalty for the brand. Such an approach can also serve to keep planes in full service, making the most of a small fleet.

However, the penetration pricing strategy has to be tempered by attention to CloudCab's financial objectives for revenue, margins, and ROI. Chances are that, once a loyal customer base is developed, some incremental price increases can be taken without major disruption in the customer base.

CloudCab can communicate its positioning through price. Being first to market, CloudCab has the opportunity to set the value of its product in the mind of the customer. In setting a price, CloudCab must be careful to realistically assess the actual time savings and comfort customers can expect to receive, and what those benefits are worth to them. In this way, the price will work together with CloudCab's promotional strategies to effectively position the product and communicate value.

Supply Chain Strategies

CloudCab has purchased the needed operational systems to properly track its planes and ensure they are always where they need to be. Customer service representatives will use these systems to give customers information on flight availability and schedule new flights. CloudCab's outsource firms and supply chain partners will also have access to the system to ensure needed materials arrive where and when they are needed for everything from pillows to jet fuel.

Promotional Strategies

CloudCab will first use promotion to *create awareness* of CloudCab and *build interest* in the benefits of its service. All efforts will be focused on conveying a clear and consistent message. CloudCab's unique selling proposition will be that it is akin to a taxi service in the air, much quicker and more comfortable than other travel modes.

To convey this message, CloudCab will use targeted advertising, direct marketing, personal selling, and buzz marketing. Advertising will be limited to publications with high readership among the target market. Various forms of digital and social media marketing—will be used to provide sales promotion incentives to customers to try CloudCab's service. Personal selling efforts will be made at consulting firms to attempt to gain contracts to make CloudCab one of the firm's transportation methods of choice. Finally, to generate buzz through public relations (PR), CloudCab will pitch stories to the media about its official launch date and first flight as a revolutionary way to travel.

Although these strategies should get CloudCab off the ground, over the long run the company will rely heavily on buzz generated by positive customer experiences to grow the business. The more people CloudCab effectively serves, the more potential brand ambassadors there will be. This should translate into an exponential sales growth for CloudCab.

IMPLEMENTATION

CloudCab possesses the needed resources for a successful launch early next year. The action plan below details the promotional initiatives CloudCab will undertake to increase market share and reach its goal of 5,500 flights in its first partial year of operation.

Marketing Action Plan for Initial Launch

Action	Date	Duration	Cost	Responsibility
Targeted print ads	December 1	4 months	$265,000	CMO Vars
CloudCab direct marketing to identified targets	February 1	3 months	$170,000	CMO Vars
Personal sales calls on key target firms	March 1	2 months	$210,000	CEO Camp and others
First CloudCab flight	May 1			COO Fray
Media coverage of first CloudCab flight	May 1	1 week	$ 3,000	CMO Vars

Monthly Sales Forecast to End of First Year

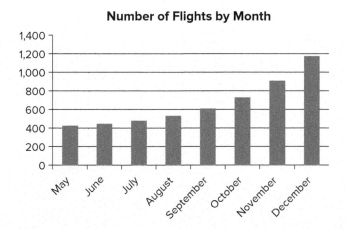

Number of Flights by Month

First-Year Budget

Using its forecasted sales volume, CloudCab can begin to establish a budget for its first partial year of operation. For now, CloudCab will use an estimated price of $1,200 per flight.

Revenue	5,287 × $1,200	$ 6,600,000
Fuel Costs		2,600,000
Promotional Activities		648,000
Salaries		1,200,000
Outsourced Systems		700,000
Operating Income		1,452,000
VLJ purchases		9,500,000
Net Income		$(8,048,000)

Marketing Control and Metrics

CloudCab must continually evaluate its marketing efforts to ensure its performance is on track against stated objectives for its first partial year of operation. The following metrics are associated with each objective.

Objective 1: Sell 5,500 Flight Itineraries

CloudCab will track sales to monitor if monthly targets are being met. If they are not, the market will have to be surveyed to determine awareness levels, and direct-mail response rates and personal selling closing ratios will be examined. In doing this, problem areas should be identified and resolved. If the problem cannot be addressed via CloudCab's current promotional mix, other elements may be added to the mix to find better ways of reaching the target audience.

Objective 2: Attain a Rating of "Highly Satisfied" Customer Satisfaction Scored by 90 Percent of Customers

Progress will be monitored by ongoing customer satisfaction measurement.

Objective 3: Achieve Repeat Purchase by 50 Percent of Customers

The CRM system will be utilized to track frequency of usage by customers.

CONTINGENCY PLANNING

CloudCab's product requires significant capital investment to bring to market and cannot be easily modified. Consequently, if CloudCab's target market does not respond to the product as planned, it would likely be easier to change the market to fit the product than to change the product to fit the market. If consultants do not find sufficient value in CloudCab and purchase at the anticipated level, then investment will be made against the secondary target market of salespeople.

In addition, CloudCab needs to closely track usage by leisure travelers. If it happens that, despite CloudCab's intentions, a larger than anticipated number of customers are leisure travelers or represent some business segment besides consulting, then CloudCab would consider refocusing its marketing efforts on both of these targets. It will have a contingency promotional plan in place that anticipates this eventuality.

PART TWO

Use Information to Drive Marketing Decisions

CHAPTER 4

Market Research Essentials

LEARNING OBJECTIVES

LO 4-1 Describe the difference between market information systems and market research systems.

LO 4-2 Identify how critical internal (inside the firm) information is collected and used in making marketing decisions.

LO 4-3 Explain essential external (outside the firm) information collection methods.

LO 4-4 Recognize the value of market research and its role in marketing.

LO 4-5 Define the market research process.

LO 4-6 Illustrate current research technologies and how they are used in market research.

MAKING GOOD MARKETING DECISIONS—THE NEED TO KNOW

Information is power speaks to the importance of good information in decision making. Companies realize the right information at the right time and in the right format (a critical but often neglected part of the process) is essential for decision makers. Marketers are usually the ones entrusted with scanning the environment for changes that might affect the organization. They are able to analyze a great deal of data quickly to better understand consumer trends and behavior. Companies are creating a new position, chief data officer, to manage the information and make more informed decisions linking corporate strategy with customer-driven information. As a result, creating procedures that collect, analyze, and access relevant information is a critical part of marketing management.[1]

A significant problem for most managers today is not having too little information but having too much. They frequently see interesting information that has no relevance to the immediate problem. As a result, companies need information systems that can collect and analyze huge amounts of information and then keep it for the right time and circumstance. Pulte Homes is one of the largest home builders in the United States. The company conducts research to learn how people move around in a home (the design flow), what features consumers want (for example, large master bedrooms and bathrooms), and what extras they want (upgraded countertops and wood trim). Also, Pulte studies demographic changes. For example, a large segment of the population, baby boomers (ages 53–71), is moving toward retirement; this has led the company to design and build smaller homes with more special features. Also, volatility in the real estate market has led the federal government to adopt changes in real estate financing, and many states have followed suit with additional legislation. Finally, Pulte also needs to study changes in federal and state laws that affect home construction. These changes affect the homes people buy and, as a result, Pulte needs to be knowledgeable in all these areas.[2]

In addition to storing large amounts of data, marketing managers need a system to design and execute research that generates precise information. Consider the Apple iPhone. Before introducing a new model, Apple conducts tests with actual users to be sure the product fits their needs and performs as promised. The company also studies a wide range of other issues including competitors such as Samsung and long-term technology trends to identify key technologies for the iPhone now and in the future. Marketing managers need this information to make critical decisions as the iPhone is improved and the marketing plan put together. The success of the iPhone led competitors to incorporate similar features in their phones.

These examples highlight the two fundamental types of market information decision makers need today. The first is data related to broad areas of interest such as demographic and economic trends, or the customer order fulfillment process inside the company. These data are used in strategic planning to help forecast potential new opportunities for company investment or to deal with possible problems before they become major issues for the company.[3] The second type of information needed addresses a specific question, for example, what is the best kitchen design for a retired baby boomer couple? Or what features would a young urban professional want in an iPhone? Questions like these require unique research designed to answer specific questions.[4] This chapter will examine both types of information needs. We'll start by discussing the market information system, which is designed to bring together many different kinds information useful to the marketing decision maker. Then we'll look at market research, which is the process marketers use to conduct research on specific market questions.

Apple seeks to improve each iteration of the iPhone based on user experiences.

©Leszek Kobusinski/Shutterstock

MARKET INFORMATION SYSTEM

The Nature of a Market Information System

As noted earlier, marketing decision makers need limited amounts of the right data at any given time. Put simply, managers need what they need when they need it. When there is too much information, managers tend to either spend an excessive amount of time analyzing or get overwhelmed and ignore all the data. If they have too little information, managers

LO 4-1

Describe the difference between market information systems and market research systems.

are more likely to make poor decisions because they don't have all the facts. In either case, incorrect decisions are often the result. Exhibit 4.1 summarizes the various ways market research is used in making marketing decisions. As you can tell from Exhibit 4.1, market research takes many forms both inside and outside an organization.

EXHIBIT 4.1 | Market Research Is Critical to Marketing Decisions

STAGES OR PROCESSES WITHIN MARKETING PLANNING	APPROPRIATE MARKET RESEARCH
Situation Analysis • Identification of competitive strengths and weaknesses • Identification of trends (opportunities and threats)	• Competitive barrier analysis • Analysis of sources of competitive advantage • Trend analysis • Positioning analysis • Identification of public and key issues concerns • Measure of market share
Selection of a Target Market • Analysis of the market • Selection of a target market	• Identification of segmentation bases • Market segmentation study • Needs assessment • Determination of purchase criteria • Buyer behavior analysis • Market demand estimation
Plan of the Marketing Mix • Product	• Product design assessment • Competitive product analysis • Competitive packaging assessment • Packaging trends assessment • Definition of brand image descriptors • Identification of brand name/symbol • New product ideation (concept development) • Package development or redesign
• Price	• Measure of price elasticity • Industry pricing patterns • Price-value perception analysis • Analysis of the effects of various price incentives
• Distribution	• Merchandising display assessment • Inventory management assessment • Location analysis (site analysis) • Market exposure assessment
• Promotion	• Message assessment • Content analysis • Copy testing • Media assessment • Media buy assessment
Marketing Control • Marketing audit	• Promotion effectiveness study • Assessment of effectiveness of marketing mix

Source: Cooper, Donald R. and Pamela S. Schindler, *Business Research Methods,* 12th ed. New York, NY: McGraw-Hill Education, 2014.

A **market information system (MIS)** is not a software package but a continuing process of identifying, collecting, analyzing, accumulating, and dispensing critical information to marketing decision makers. The MIS is really an "information bank" where data relevant to the company's marketing efforts are collected and stored until such time as management needs to "withdraw" them. Generally, this information is not specific to a particular problem or question; rather, it is important information that the marketing decision maker will need at the appropriate time.[5] A company needs to consider three factors in creating an MIS.

First, what information should the system collect? In evaluating internal and external information sources, companies need to consider not only what information is important but also the source of the data. Think about all the ways a company gets competitor data—salespeople and customers in the field, competitor materials and websites, business-related websites such as Hoover's, and many others. Because there are so many sources of information, decisions must be made about what information will be collected and where it will come from.

Second, what are the information needs of each decision maker? Not all managers need the same information. The CEO probably doesn't want or need daily sales figures across individual product lines, but the local sales manager does. A good MIS is flexible enough for managers to customize the information they receive and, in some cases, the format they receive it in.

Third, how does the system maintain the privacy and confidentiality of sensitive information? Company databases hold a great deal of confidential data on customers, suppliers, and employees. By limiting access to the data to those with a need to know, companies protect relationships and build trust. As more data is collected and the ability to analyze it becomes more accurate, the need for a market information system becomes more critical. Although we will discuss Big Data in Chapter 5, it is important to note that companies like Google and Amazon are analyzing vast amounts of data collected through a variety of sources to prescribe (looking at what you have done and offering alternatives) and predict (making predictions of future behavior based on past behavior) customer behavior. It is no surprise, then, that companies are investing in building and enhancing their market information systems.

Internal Sources—Collecting Information Inside the Company

At the heart of marketing is the relationship among the company, its products, and its customers. Critical to that relationship is a clear understanding of what is, and is not, working in the customer interface. Think about the senior manager at Microsoft who is concerned about rising dissatisfaction with customer support among its Office suite users. While there could be a number of reasons for this increase, the manager will first want to look at internal customer service metrics that include call wait times, ability of customer service representatives to handle the problems efficiently and effectively, number of customers who call back to address a problem, and a host of other metrics. In addition, web traffic monitoring by companies like Google Web Analytics can show customer service managers what areas of the website are creating problems for customers (for example, lack of clarity or direction, inconsistency with other customer messaging, not helpful to the customer), which can improve customer service. These are all internal sources of data. By looking at such critical internal metrics collected as part of the market information system, management is able to do two things. First, in our example, management might see that an increase in call wait times has led to higher customer dissatisfaction. Here information is used to identify the problem. A second and more effective use of market information systems is to proactively address issues before they become problems.[6] For example, management can set a benchmark stating that call wait times will not exceed two minutes. In this way, management can deal with a problem before it becomes a significant concern for the company. Of course, the investment in time and money needed to create and monitor such a system is significant.

A market information system can be as complicated as the company wants or can afford. It is expensive to collect and analyze data, and most companies don't maximize their existing information. Often, simply checking secondary sources such as legitimate websites will

EXHIBIT 4.2 | Internal Information Sources

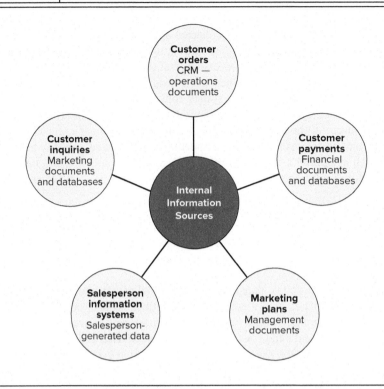

provide sufficient information for the marketing manager to make a decision in a particular situation. More formal information systems, however, provide a great deal more information that can help guide strategic decisions (changes in demographics can lead to new market opportunities) or address critical tactical issues (shorten call wait times for customer service).[7] Exhibit 4.2 identifies five common internal sources of data collected as a regular part of doing business. Unfortunately, managers are often not aware of all the information in their own company.

From the Customer's Order to Order Fulfillment Tracking a customer's initial inquiry through to order placement, delivery, payment, and follow-up after the purchase offers insight about the customer as well as insight about how well the company is working. CRM systems use customer data collected through market information systems to help drive customer-centric strategies, as discussed in Chapter 5. More specifically, the data collected and analyzed in a CRM system enable companies to:

- **Identify the frequency and size of customer orders.** By charting the frequency, size, and specific items included in an order, it's possible to assess customer satisfaction.
- **Determine the actual cost of a customer order.** Tools such as activity-based cost accounting can allocate time and overhead costs to specific customers. By combining that with information from each customer order, it is possible to get accurate cost and profitability measures of individual customers.
- **Rank customers based on established criteria like profitability.** Not all customers are equal, and the customer mix changes over time. Companies need to understand how each customer rates on a defined set of criteria to better allocate current resources and develop strategies for future growth. Starbucks' reward system actually adjusts based on profitability and usage. Frequent users, for example, have to earn more stars (buy more products) for rewards than newer, less frequent customers.
- **Calculate the efficiency of the company's production and distribution system.** Tracking customer orders makes it possible to assess many of the company's critical functions.

Heard on the Street—Sales Information System One of the best internal information sources is the sales force. Salespeople are on the front lines of the company-customer interface and have unique access to the customer. As a result, they are an excellent information source not only about the customer but also about market trends and even the competition.[8] This is particularly true in a business-to-business environment where salespeople are often the primary method for communicating with customers. Salespeople are usually the first to hear about changes with the customer, such as new personnel or the need for new products. What's more, as they interact with customers, salespeople frequently learn a great deal about competitors' tactics and plans.

Regrettably, companies time and again fail to maximize this information source. While salespeople may share what they learn with local management or other salespeople, companies have traditionally not had formal systems of collecting and analyzing data from the sales force.[9] This is changing, however, as management creates formal sales information systems to collect, analyze, store, and distribute information from the field to appropriate decision makers in the company.[10] A sales information system includes:

Salesforce.com has been successfully providing online CRM applications that allow salespeople to access customer data easily. Moreover, its customizable applications encourage salespeople to input customer data into the company sales information system.

Source: Salesforce.com, inc.

- **Formal systems for collecting data (getting the data).** Many salespeople write call reports summarizing each sales call. Much of the information on a call report is relevant in a sales information system. This includes products discussed with the customer, customer concerns, and changes in personnel.

- **Interpretation of data (analysis).** This may be done at the local level by sales managers who add additional insight to the "raw" data from the salesperson. In more sophisticated sales information systems, people at regional or national offices will analyze data from many salespeople looking for broad trends.

- **Distribution of data (getting the analysis to decision makers and back into the field).** A sales information system needs to distribute the information to management as part of a larger market information system. At the same time, it is important to get the information back out to the sales force. When trends, problems or solutions to problems, and opportunities are identified, salespeople benefit from learning quickly so they can respond in the field. Much of this information has a time value. If salespeople do not get the analysis in a timely manner, much of the benefit will be lost. For example, suppose a company learns from several salespeople that a major competitor is contacting customers about a new product. Getting this information to the entire sales force quickly will enable them to develop responses for their own customers.

External Sources—Collecting Information Outside the Company

Staying connected to the business environment is no longer optional. Success is based, in part, on both the quality and quantity of information available to management. As a result, most companies engage in collecting, analyzing, and storing data from the macro environment on a continuous basis; this is known as **marketing intelligence**. The ability to do this well is a competitive advantage; successful companies accurately analyze and interpret environmental information, then develop strategies to take advantage of opportunities and deal with threats before they become problems (see Exhibit 4.3).

> **LO 4-3**
>
> Explain essential external (outside the firm) information collection methods.

EXHIBIT 4.3 | External Forces Affect Marketing Decisions

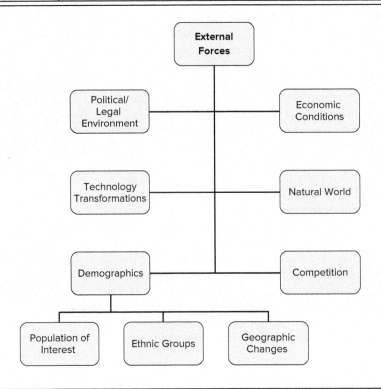

Demographics Populations change over time, and companies must be aware of those changes. Not tracking and responding to demographic changes is a management failure because the data are easy to obtain and major changes occur slowly. Surprisingly, many companies do not do a good job of either learning about demographic trends or responding to them.

Demographics can be defined as the statistical characteristics of human populations, such as age or income, used to identify markets. They provide a statistical description of a group of people and are extremely useful in marketing, for two reasons. First, *demographics help define a market.* How old is a typical customer? How educated? What is the typical customer's income? These are all demographic characteristics that help describe a market. For example, a typical Mercedes-Benz automobile owner in the United States is a male, successful, and over 50 years old. By analyzing demographics, a company can define not only the "typical" customer but also its market at large. Second, *studying demographics helps identify new opportunities.* As baby boomers age, they will need, among other things, retirement communities. This represents an opportunity for companies to build unique retirement properties specifically for baby boomers.

Companies that deal directly with consumers develop customer profiles based on demographic information and compare their profiles against those of competitors. For example, the typical Mercedes-Benz owner tends to be older than a BMW owner. Companies even create pictures of their "average" customer, highlighting key demographic data (age, gender, and ethnicity).

Populations of Interest Marketers are not interested in all groups, only populations of interest. The difficult part for many marketers is separating relevant demographic data from irrelevant. For example, does cell phone maker Samsung need to know that world population growth is faster in less developed countries (among less developed countries the population is growing at 2 percent per year while developed countries are growing at less than 1 percent)? Your first response might be no as Samsung is likely interested in more developed countries with established cellular networks and people who can afford the technology.

However, while less developed countries do not need the more expensive Samsung Galaxy phones, they could use older, less expensive technology to encourage economic development and build a communication network. Targeting less developed countries may offer Samsung an opportunity to establish a market presence in these countries even as they develop economically.

Ethnic Groups Many countries are becoming more ethnically diverse as individuals increase their mobility. While some countries, such as the United Arab Emirates in the Middle East, have populations composed of a single ethnic group, others like the United States are much more ethnically diverse. Nearly three-quarters of the U.S. population is white, but trends project that whites will be less than 50 percent of the population in less than 30 years. Hispanics have shown the greatest increase among ethnic groups in the United States over the past 10 years. They are currently the second-largest minority group and are expected to continue growing as a percentage of the U.S. population.

The European Union has made it possible for individuals to move freely around member countries. While many of the member countries are still dominated by local ethnic groups, the European continent is becoming more ethnically diverse. For the most part, this leads to greater opportunities; however, some countries such as France find it difficult to assimilate certain groups into their culture. The market challenge then becomes developing effective marketing strategies across different ethnicities living in the same area.

As the Hispanic population grows, advertisers continue to seek endorsements from Hispanic celebrities like Sofia Vergara.

Source: Procter & Gamble

Geographic Changes People are moving not only in the United States but around the world. As we just noted, the opening of borders in the European Union has increased the mobility of those living in the EU. A decades-old trend—people moving from the countryside to the city—continues around the globe and some cities, such as Mexico City, São Paulo, and others, find it difficult to cope with the influx of people that stretches their ability to provide social services (see Exhibit 4.4).

The changes present opportunities but also challenges. The growth of Asian cultures means many companies must adjust their marketing strategies to fit the unique needs of Asian consumers. Appliance companies such as Whirlpool have redesigned their products to fit in smaller Asian kitchens. Coincidentally, downsizing products is a strategy consistent with the migration of people to urban centers. Mr. Coffee, Braun, and others have created coffeemakers designed for single households in the smaller living environments often found in large cities.

Economic Conditions

Companies are keenly interested in the ability of their customers to purchase products and services. It is not surprising then that a good understanding of current and future economic trends is important in an effective market information system. There are two principal types of economic knowledge. The study of individual economic activity (firm, household, or prices) is known as **microeconomics**. At the other end of the spectrum, **macroeconomics** refers to the study of economic activity in terms of broad measures of output (gross national product or GNP) and input as well as the interaction among various sectors of an entire economy. Both are important for marketing managers. Microeconomics helps marketing managers understand how individuals set priorities and make buying decisions. Macroeconomics, on the other hand, gives a "big picture" perspective for an economy and can be helpful at looking for broad economic trends.

Indicators such as the GNP measure the health of an economy and are helpful in spotting trends. For example, if the GNP goes up, it is generally viewed as a sign the economy is doing well. As an economy slows, the GNP will slow.

EXHIBIT 4.4 | Selected Cities' Population with Projected Growth Rates

Urban Area	Population (millions)			Rank		
	1990	2025	2050	1990	2025	2050
Tokyo, Japan	32.5	6.40	32.62	1	1	7
Delhi, India	8.3	22.2	35.19		4	4
Mexico City, Mexico	15.3	21.01	24.33	3	6	10
New York–Newark	16.1	20.63	24.77	2	7	9
Shanghai, China	13.3	19.41	22.32		9	15
São Paulo, Brazil	14.8	21.43	22.83	4	5	14
Mumbai (Bombay), India	12.4	26.39	42.40	5	2	1
Beijing, China	10.8	14.55	15.97		16	23
Dhaka, Bangladesh	6.7	22.50	36.16		3	2
Kolkata (Calcutta), India	10.9	20.56	33.04	7	8	5

Source: Daniel Hoornweg and Kevin Pope, "Population Projections of the 101 Largest Cities in the 21st Century," Global Cities Institute Working Paper No. 4, January 2014.

Technology Transformations Few areas in business have been more affected by technology than marketing. Technology has been one of the major catalysts for change in the marketplace. Faster, smaller, and easier-to-use computers and powerful software facilitate sophisticated analyses right on the desks of front-line managers from anywhere in the world. Complex supply chain and manufacturing processes coupled with Internet connectivity allow customers real-time access to the entire manufacturing process. Consider the online order process for HP. A consumer places the order online, gets a final price and expected delivery date, then follows it from the assembly plant literally to their front door with a tracking number from the shipping company.

Marketing managers need to know the role of technology in their business today and also, perhaps even more importantly, its role in the future. Successfully assimilating technology into a business takes time and money. Almost every organization has had at least one negative experience with technology. Hershey Foods, for example, tried to bring a new CRM system online at the busiest selling season of the year for candy, Halloween, only to find problems implementing the system. The company estimated it was unable to fill $100 million worth of candy orders as a result of issues related to integrating the new software. At the same time, companies know they must remain open to new technologies that can significantly impact their business. For example, YouTube, Netflix, and others have changed the way people watch videos, creating opportunities for companies to reach new markets with creative messaging.[11]

Natural World Everyone lives on planet Earth, and business operates within the constraints of available natural resources. Two key issues drive marketers' need to know about the natural world. First, individuals, governments, and business all recognize the need to manage the available resources well. It took the world roughly 150 years to use 1 trillion barrels of oil; however, it is predicted the world will use the next trillion barrels by 2030 and, while there may be a lot of oil left, it will be harder to get and more expensive. Governments and businesses are concerned about the effect of increasing energy costs on economic growth. Other resources such as water are also becoming increasingly scarce in parts of the world. In the western United States, for example, growth in communities such as Phoenix is considered in the context of water access, which limits future development as water becomes scarcer.

A second concern regarding the natural world is pollution. In some parts of the world, pollution takes a significant toll on the quality of life and economic growth in a community. In Mexico City, driving is limited for everyone to certain days during the week as congestion and smog create huge clouds of pollution that hang over the city. In China, government statistics show that of the lakes and rivers monitored for pollution levels, nearly 20 percent contained water considered unusable even for agricultural irrigation, causing losses in the billions of dollars.[12] These concerns influence marketers as they make decisions about how and where products are manufactured. For example, energy companies such as Chevron are investing billions to identify and develop more environmentally safe energy.

Political/Legal Environment Political judgments and, more broadly, the legal environment significantly affect company decisions and sometimes an entire industry. In 2003, the National Do Not Call Registry was created to minimize intrusive telemarketing calls. By registering, individuals protect themselves from telemarketing calls. Telemarketing companies are subject to significant fines if they call someone listed on the register. Millions of people signed up, and many companies were forced to reconfigure their marketing communications strategy.[13]

Local, state, and federal legislatures pass more business-related legislation than ever before. In addition, government agencies are more active in monitoring business activity. During the 1990s the Securities and Exchange Commission actively pursued several antitrust actions, the largest against Microsoft for illegal monopoly activity. As a result, Microsoft made changes to Windows 8 that opened it up to outside software vendors. More recently, the Dodd–Frank Wall Street Reform and Consumer Protection Act, passed in 2010, required banks and other financial institutions to dramatically change many aspects of their businesses including lending practices.

Competition One of the most important external environmental factors to consider is the competition. Companies want to know as much as possible about competitors' products and strategies. In highly competitive markets, companies are constantly adjusting their strategies to the competition. Airlines, for example, track competitors' pricing and adjust their pricing almost immediately to changes in the marketplace. When one airline offers a sale in a specific market, competitors will soon follow with sales in the same market. Identifying, analyzing, and effectively dealing with competitors is the focus in Chapter 2.

MARKET RESEARCH SYSTEMS

Marketing managers are confronted with an unlimited number of problems, opportunities, and issues that require specific answers. Sometimes the information needed is not available from other sources or even from the company's own market information system. To get specific answers to important management questions, market research is necessary.

The Importance of Market Research to Managers

Consider the following:

LO 4-4

Recognize the value of market research and its role in marketing.

- You are a marketing manager for Harley-Davidson Motorcycles, and 90 percent of your bikes are sold to men. You believe women are a great potential target market but have had little success selling Harleys to them. What do you do?
- You are the director of advertising for McDonald's, and the company is getting ready to roll out a new advertising campaign designed to increase sales of a new sandwich. However, senior management wants to know if it will work. What do you do?

The answers to situations like these lie in market research. **Market research** is the methodical identification, collection, analysis, and distribution of data related to discovering and then

EXHIBIT 4.5 | Top Five Market Research Companies in the World

Organization	Headquarters	Total Revenue
The Nielsen Company	New York	$6.288 Billion
Kantar	London/Fairfield, CT	$3.785 Billion
IMS Health	Danbury, CT	$2.641 billion
Ipson SA	Paris, France	$2.219 billion
GfK SE	Nuremberg, Germany	$1.932 billion

Source: American Marketing Association, *2016 AMA Gold Global Report*, p. 36.

solving marketing problems or opportunities and enhancing good decision making. Several things come out of this definition. Good market research:

- **Follows a well-defined set of activities and does not happen by accident.** Rather, it comes as a result of the methodical identification, collection, analysis, and distribution of data.
- **Enhances the validity of the information.** Anyone can "Google" a topic and come up with a lot of information. However, following the market research process enhances the confidence that the research will discover and then solve marketing problems and opportunities.
- **Is impartial and objective.** It does not prejudge the information or develop answers to fit an already decided outcome; rather, it enhances good decision making.

Market research is also big business. In 2017 nearly $40 billion was spent on market research worldwide, with the United States ($18 billion) conducting the most research.[14] Some of these departments, such as McDonald's internal research group, are larger than many research companies and spend hundreds of millions of dollars a year conducting market research for their own organizations. Exhibit 4.5 lists the top market research companies in the world.

The Market Research Process

LO 4-5

Define the market research process.

At the heart of the market research process is a search for understanding. Sometimes management seeks answers to a particular problem. In other situations, an opportunity needs to be evaluated before committing resources. By following the market research process, marketing managers can have greater confidence in the information they are receiving and, hopefully, make better informed decisions. As shown in Exhibit 4.6, the process consists of six steps.

Define the Research Problem One of the biggest challenges facing a market researcher is accurately defining the problem. What exactly is the issue/opportunity/problem? Often managers are not clear about the problem and need help defining it. It is not uncommon for a market research professional to get a call that starts something like this: "I have a problem. Sales have been falling for six months and I am losing business to my competitors." The researcher knows that the real problem is not the company's declining sales; falling sales are the result, a symptom, of the real issue. Market research can be a useful tool helping senior managers identify and deal with the real issue.[15]

Given that management often does not have a clear understanding of the problem, defining the research problem involves two distinct steps. First, management, working with researchers and marketing decision makers, defines the **management research deliverable**. Exactly what does management want to do with this research? Keep in mind that decision makers are looking for information to help them make better, more informed decisions. For example, if you are the director of advertising for McDonald's, you want to increase sales of a new sandwich, and a new advertising campaign can help accomplish that goal. However, before you decide to spend a lot of money on the campaign, you want to know if it is going to be successful.

Once the management research deliverable has been identified, the next step is to define the **research problem**. Exactly what information is needed to help management in this situation? In our example, that means assessing the target market's response to the new advertising campaign.

In the McDonald's example, the research problem is fairly straightforward. However, there are often multiple research problems, and researchers will have to prioritize which problems to study first. Consider the example of Harley-Davidson motorcycles and targeting more female riders. Management may want to know: (1) How many women would be in the market for a motorcycle and, more specifically, how many women would be in the market for a large bike like a Harley? (2) What kind of motorcycle would they want to buy? (3) If Harley-Davidson were to create a new bike, how would loyal, dedicated Harley-Davidson owners react to it? You can begin to see why it is necessary for management and researchers to prioritize the problems and identify which research issues to address first.[16]

Establish the Research Design Following problem definition, companies must establish a research design, or a plan of action for attacking the research problem. Research designs consist of five activities, each of which is designed to address a specific question about the research process, as shown in Exhibit 4.7. It is critical that researchers develop and execute a research design so that decision makers can have confidence in the research findings. Effective market research is dependent on creating a research design and then executing it.[17] Conversely, and this is a problem for decision makers, bad market research cannot yield good information. When this happens, it severely limits management's confidence in the results.

While multiple designs often could work in any research situation, it is important to specify one design and follow it throughout the research. Decisions made at the research design stage affect the rest of the project, and it is not appropriate to start over once a project has begun. Let's examine each of these activities.

Type of Research: What Kind of Research Needs to Be Done? Not all market research involves complex, costly studies. People do market research all the time and don't think of it that way. For example, a salesperson who visits a website to learn more about a customer before a sales call is engaged in market research. The key is to fit the research to the unique requirements of the situation.

There are three basic types of research: exploratory, descriptive, and causal. While the complexity and methodology change for each type of research, it is not necessarily true that causal research is better than exploratory. Let's look at each research type more closely.

EXHIBIT 4.6 | **The Market Research Process**

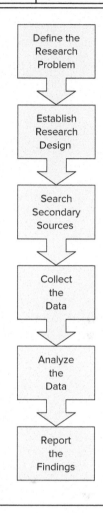

Define the Research Problem

Establish Research Design

Search Secondary Sources

Collect the Data

Analyze the Data

Report the Findings

EXHIBIT 4.7 | **Research Design Activities**

Activity	Question to Be Answered
Type of research	What kind of research needs to be done?
Nature of data	What kind of data do we need?
Nature of data collection	How should we collect the data?
Information content	What do we need to know?
Sampling plan	Who should be included in the research?

As the name implies, **exploratory research** is really about discovery. Reasons for conducting exploratory research include:

- Clarifying the research problem.
- Developing hypotheses for testing in descriptive or causal research.
- Gaining additional insight to help in survey development or to identify other research variables for study.
- Answering the research question.

Many times conducting exploratory research will provide sufficient information to answer the research question. Even if more sophisticated research is needed, exploratory research is usually the first step.

Descriptive research seeks to describe or explain some phenomenon. Often this involves something going on in the marketplace and can include issues such as:

- Identifying the characteristics of our target market.
- Assessing competitors' actions in the marketplace.
- Determining how customers use our product.
- Discovering differences across demographic characteristics (age, education, income) with respect to the use of our product or that of our competitors.

Descriptive research uses many different methods including secondary data, surveys, and observation. Some of these methods are also used in exploratory research. The difference is how you use the information. Descriptive research uses a different, more restrictive and rigorous methodology than exploratory research.

Descriptive research identifies associations between variables; for example, the customers for Harley-Davidson motorcycles tend to be middle-aged, successful men. **Causal research** tries to discover the cause and effect between variables.

In our Harley-Davidson example, does an increase in Harley-Davidson advertising directed toward men lead to increased sales of Harley-Davidson motorcycles? This can be particularly useful in making important marketing decisions. Consider a critical decision faced by all marketing managers: What effect will a price increase have on sales? Causal research can determine the change in the number of sales for different price levels. The types of research vary a great deal, so the question becomes: What kind of research is appropriate in a given circumstance? The following factors help make that determination.

Benefit versus cost: Before making any other decisions about the type of marketing research to use, it is essential to assess the benefits versus the costs. Put simply, if the benefits of doing the research do not exceed the cost, don't do the research.

Time until decision: Decision makers sometimes have very little time between realizing a need for additional information and making the decision. When time is very short (a matter of days), it is simply not possible to conduct in-depth market research. The Internet can cut the time needed for a study from months to weeks, but when time is short researchers may have to rely on more exploratory research and the use of secondary data.

Nature of the decision: The more strategic the decision, the more important the information and the greater the need for primary data. Conversely, if the decision is primarily tactical (for example, decisions about where to place advertising), secondary data, like reviewing a medium's demographics and rate card, will likely be sufficient to make the decision.

Availability of data: Companies already have a lot of data as a result of CRM and other internal information systems. Consequently, it may not always be necessary to collect primary data when existing or secondary data will provide the necessary answers to the research problems.

Nature of Data: What Kind of Data Do We Need? Once the type of research has been determined, the next step is to evaluate what kind of data is needed for the research. The nature of the data will determine how the data are collected and is driven by the kind of research the company is undertaking.[18] The basic question is, does the research require **primary data**—data collected specifically for this research question—or will **secondary data**—data collected for some other purpose than the problem currently being considered—be sufficient? Even if primary data are collected, almost all research involves some secondary data collection, which we will talk about in the next section.

Primary data are collected using one of two approaches: qualitative and quantitative. **Qualitative research** is less structured and can employ methods such as surveys and interviews to collect the data; qualitative research employs small samples and is not meant to be used for statistical analyses. **Quantitative research** is used to develop a more measured understanding using statistical analysis to assess and quantify the results.[19] Now let's look at the nature of data collection.

Nature of Data Collection: How Should the Data Be Collected? No one technique is better than another, but it is important to use the right technique based on an assessment of the research problem and research type. Let's evaluate the various approaches to collecting primary data. Exploratory research techniques include focus groups and in-depth interviews.

Without question, the most widely used qualitative research technique is focus groups. Perhaps for this reason, it is also one of the most misused.[20] A **focus group** is a meeting (either in person or increasingly online) of 6 to 10 people that is moderated by a professional who carefully moves the conversation through a defined agenda in an unstructured, open format. Generally, the participants are selected on the basis of some criteria. Companies like Walmart and Unilever make use of web panels that allow companies to collect relevant information quickly and cost-effectively.[21] For example, they may be current customers or possess certain demographic characteristics (age, income, education), but they will all have at least one shared attribute.

The value of focus groups lies in the richness of the discussion. A good moderator can draw out a lot of information from the participants. For example, the marketing manager for Harley-Davidson might use focus groups to learn how women relate to motorcycles. The trade-off is a deeper understanding of each participant versus a more superficial knowledge of additional people. Herein lies the mistake many people make with focus groups. They assume that the results of a focus group are generalizable to a population of interest. This is not the case. Focus groups are not a representative sample, and care should be taken to interpret the results properly. However, focus groups do provide insights on an issue that are useful to researchers as they develop quantitative research techniques. Focus group data provide a good starting point from which researchers can develop specific questions used in survey instruments.[22]

Another common qualitative technique is the in-depth interview. An **in-depth interview** is an unstructured (or loosely structured) interview with an individual who has been chosen based on some characteristic of interest, often a demographic attribute. This technique differs from focus groups in that the interview is done one on one rather than in a small group. The same advantages and disadvantages are present here as with focus groups, so researchers most often use this technique to help formulate other types of research (surveys, observational research).

Descriptive research techniques include surveys, behavioral data, and observational data. Of the quantitative research techniques used to collect primary data, surveys, in their various forms, are the most prevalent. While they can be used informally in exploratory research, their most common purpose is in descriptive research. **Surveys** are structured questionnaires given to a sample group of individuals representing the population of interest and are intended to solicit specific responses to explicit questions.[23]

There are a number of survey methods. Historically, mail and telephone surveys were the most common. Today, electronic surveys have become widely adopted for their speed, ease of use, and relatively low cost. E-surveys can easily be done over the Internet using services such as SurveyMonkey.[24]

Behavioral data include information about when, what, and how often customers purchase products and services as well as other customer "touches" (for example, when they contact the organization with a complaint or question). When companies match this kind of information with demographic and psychographic information, they can see differences in purchase patterns. Behavior is usually more reliable than surveys because it is based on what the respondents actually do rather than what they say they are going to do.

Harley-Davidson does market research to learn more about developing products that appeal to women.

©Ramzi Haidar/AFP/Getty Images

It is possible to get a lot of insight about people by simply watching what they do in various situations. **Observational data** are the behavioral patterns among the population of interest. One of the most common uses of this type of research is in retailing. Retailers watch how people move through a store, noting what aisles they go down and where they spend their time. In recent years a more intrusive approach to observational data has been used to actually examine people in a personal setting (for example, their homes). In this approach, the observer enters into the world of the individual rather than standing back and simply watching activities. Researchers see people in a very personal environment to better understand how people use and interact with products.

A variation of observational data is mechanical observation. **Mechanical observation** uses a device to chronicle activity. Some forms of mechanical observation are benign and not intrusive on the individual. Turnstiles, for example, record people coming into or going out of an area. Traffic counters record the number of cars on a given street for a set time period.

There are, however, mechanical devices that are more invasive. *Mechanical devices* can be very useful for researchers but are often used sparingly because of the cost and also the bias associated with the respondent's awareness of the device. Eye cameras can track the movement of an eye as the individual watches an ad. From this researchers can determine what the person sees first, what he is focusing on in the ad, and how his eyes move around the ad. Another device, the galvanometer, is attached to the skin and measures subtle changes in skin temperature. Researchers can then determine if the respondent found the ad interesting. With the advent of sophisticated home assistants, it is possible to track people right in their homes. Alexa, from Amazon, is a home assistant that helps users carry out various functions around the home. At the same time, it collects all the information generated around each interaction and sends it to Amazon.

Information Content: What Do We Need to Know? A critical part of research design involves determining exactly what information is needed and how to frame the questions to get that information. From the questions used in focus groups to long questionnaires, it is important to consider the structure and wording as well as the response choices. Most often this issue comes up in designing questionnaires. As the most commonly used primary research technique, the survey questionnaire allows a lot of variability in its design and structure. Some surveys, such as comment cards, are short and ask only a few questions. Others, such as new car satisfaction surveys, can be much longer and ask dozens of questions. No matter what the situation, careful attention must be paid to the design, structure, and format of each question. For years marketers have been interested in building and measuring customer loyalty.

Today, researchers must also consider the method of survey delivery. For example, mail surveys differ significantly from telephone surveys because respondents interact with the questions differently. Electronic surveys present a different challenge, although their structure is more easily adapted from a mail questionnaire.

Researchers must consider which of the many types of question formats is most appropriate for the situation. One of the most basic decisions is whether to use open-ended or closed-ended questions. **Open-ended questions** encourage respondents to be expressive and offer the opportunity to provide more detailed, qualitative responses. As a result, these kinds of questions are often used in exploratory research. **Closed-ended questions**, on the other hand, are more precise and provide specific responses. As a result, they allow for more quantitative analysis and are most often used in descriptive research. Frequently, questionnaires will contain a mix of open-ended and closed-ended questions to get both qualitative and quantitative information in a single survey.

Sampling Plan: Who Should Be Included in the Research? Once the other elements of the research design have been developed, it is time to consider who will be selected for the research. The most basic decision is whether to conduct a census or to sample a group of individuals from the population. A **census** is a comprehensive record of each individual in the population of interest, while a **sample** is a subgroup of the population selected for participation in the research. A census may seem like the better approach because everyone in the population is included in the study. Unfortunately, most of the time the number and diversity of the population are so large that it is simply not physically or financially possible to communicate with everyone. As a result, sampling is by far the preferred method of selecting people for market research.[25]

There are two basic approaches to sampling: probability and nonprobability sampling. It is important to keep in mind that one is not necessarily better than the other; rather, the key to making the right choice is to match the sampling approach with the research. Budgetary constraints will also likely influence the decision. **Probability sampling** uses a specific set of procedures to identify individuals from the population to be included in the research. From here, a specific protocol is identified to select a number of individuals for the research. As an example, suppose Bank of America is interested in finding out more about a group of its customers holding a certain kind of credit card. Let's assume there are 10 million customers holding this particular card. The bank wants to randomly choose 5,000 individuals for the survey. That means that everyone has a $5,000/10,000,000 = .0005$ chance of being selected. Next, Bank of America will create an algorithm to randomly identify 5,000 individuals from the list of 10 million. The algorithm ensures that, while everyone has a .0005 chance of being selected, only 5,000 will be sampled from the entire group.

A second approach is called **nonprobability sampling** and, as the name implies, the probability of everyone in the population being included in the sample is not identified. The chance of selection may be zero or not known. This type of sampling is often done when time and/or financial constraints limit the opportunity to conduct probability sampling. The most significant problem with nonprobability sampling is that it significantly limits the ability to perform statistical analyses and generalize conclusions beyond the sample itself.

Search Secondary Sources Secondary data are almost always part of market research. Searching a wide variety of sources and compiling additional information provide greater insight to the research problem and supplement the primary data collected for a specific study. We have already discussed the availability of information inside the company, so let's turn our attention to external sources of secondary data.

Government Sources Federal, state, and local governments are an important resource in collecting information on a variety of topics. For example, the U.S. Census Bureau publishes a library full of reports on business and consumer demographic trends. In 2012, the Census Bureau released the most recent Economic Census providing an in-depth analysis of business activity in the United States. Often, data are available by zip code, which can be useful for marketers in targeting specific groups of people. Updated Census Bureau data is set for release in 2019. States also publish additional data on economic activity. Finally, local governments publish records such as business licenses as well as general economic activity in that area. Governments provide a great deal of information on a variety of activities. From here marketers can identify areas, even down to specific streets, and get detailed demographic information, which is very useful in a number of ways including targeted marketing communications campaigns.

Market Research Organizations A number of market research organizations publish data helpful to marketers. One resource many people are familiar with is Nielsen Media Research's TV ratings. The ratings are the basis for establishing national, cable, and local advertising rates. Another service well known to automobile enthusiasts is the J.D. Power automobile quality and customer satisfaction rankings. While automobile manufacturers pay a fee for more detailed information, the public has access to the overall rankings.

Other organizations publish data that can be useful to marketers in particular industries. For example, MMGY Global publishes several reports on both the leisure and business travel markets every year. These reports profile travel patterns and market segments in the travel industry. They are very useful for any business connected to the travel industry such as airlines, hotels, and cruise lines.

There are also information data services such as Information Resources, InfoScan, and Nielsen's ScanTrack that track scanner data from thousands of retailers. These organizations match sales data with demographic records to give a detailed picture of how well a product is doing in a particular area or within a certain target market. This information is useful for consumer products companies that want to assess the success of specific marketing activities (for example, how well an advertising campaign is working with a target market).

The Internet It is now possible to access a huge amount of information using search engines to identify hundreds, even thousands, of information sources. Care should be taken, however, to evaluate the validity of the data and the reliability of the source. Generally two kinds of data sources can be found on the Internet. The first is market research organizations (such as the ones we just discussed) willing to share or sell market data. A second source is "general knowledge" sites such as business publications, academic research sites, or other independent sources that have data applicable to the research problem.[26]

Advantages and Disadvantages of Secondary Data Sources As we discussed earlier, secondary data are almost always the first place to go in conducting a market research project. Even if primary data are collected, it is a good idea to see what has been done already that may be applicable now. Secondary data come with two primary advantages. First, it's a fast way to get information. Just a few minutes on a search engine can yield a lot of information. Of course, it takes much longer than that to look through it all. A second and related advantage is cost. Secondary data are relatively less expensive. Even if a company chooses to subscribe to organizations such as J.D. Power and Associates, thereby getting access to more detailed data, it is still more cost-effective than conducting a primary research study.

Of course, there are very distinct disadvantages. First and most important, secondary data will, almost by definition, not fit the research problem exactly. As a result, a specific answer to the research problem will not be possible using secondary data alone. Second, secondary data are not current. Sometimes the information may be only a few weeks or months old, or it may be dated to the point where it is no longer useful for the current project. Third, without a clear understanding of the methodology used to collect and interpret the secondary data, one should be a little skeptical about its validity.[27]

Collect the Data Now it is time to find and engage the respondent to collect the data. **Data collection** involves access and distribution of the survey to the respondent, then recording the respondent's responses and making the data available for analysis. A company can choose to collect the data using its own resources or hire a market research firm to administer the data collection. The choice often depends on the company's internal expertise in market research as well as the resources required to complete the job.

This stage in the market research process presents several unique challenges. First, data collection is often the most costly element in the market research process. Second, the greatest potential for error exists as data are collected.[28] For example, respondents may not respond to certain questions or may fill out the survey incorrectly. Finally, the people collecting the survey may be biased or make mistakes.

Technology, in the form of online surveys, can help to mitigate some of the issues with data collection. For example, electronic survey methods are often more cost-effective than other survey methodologies. In addition, there is less chance of transcription error as no one has to input the data into a computer. Unfortunately, not everyone has access to a computer. As a result, certain target markets may be underrepresented if a survey requires completion of an online survey. Additionally, people may still input inaccurate responses.[29] We will talk about online research tools in the next section.

Photodex ProShow Gold is one of many software packages designed to enhance presentations. The presentation of a research report often includes sophisticated software designed to clearly present research findings and recommendations.

Source: Photodex Corporation

Analyze the Data Once the data are collected, coded, and verified, the next step is to analyze the information. The appropriate analysis is performed based on the research questions developed at the beginning of the research. A common mistake is using unsuitable analyses that are not supported by the data.

Analysis of the data will lead to findings that address the research questions. These findings are, in a sense, the "product" of the research. In most cases, researchers will also interpret the findings for decision makers.

Report the Findings The best research projects are only as good as the final report and presentation. If the research is done well but the report is poorly written and presented, managers will not benefit from the research. Exhibit 4.8 provides a basic framework for a research report. Note that, for managers, the key section of the report is the Executive Summary as it presents a summation of the analysis and essential findings. Keep in mind that managers are not really interested in the number of secondary data sources, the questionnaire design, or the sampling plan; rather, they want to see the findings.

EXHIBIT 4.8 | Outline of a Research Report

Report Modules	Short Report — Memo or Letter	Short Report — Short Technical	Long Report — Management	Long Report — Technical
Prefatory Information		1	1	1
Letter of transmittal		√	√	√
Title page		√	√	√
Authorization statement		√	√	√
Executive summary		√	√	√
Table of contents			√	√
Introduction	1	2	2	2
Problem statement	√	√	√	√
Research objectives	√	√	√	√
Background	√	√	√	√
Methodology		√ (briefly)	√ (briefly)	3
Sampling design				√
Research design				√
Data collection				√
Data analysis				√
Limitations		√	√	√
Findings		3	4	4
Conclusions	2	4	3	5
Summary and conclusions	√	√	√	√
Recommendations	√	√	√	√
Appendices		5	5	6
Bibliography				7

Source: Cooper, Donald R. and Pamela S. Schindler, *Business Research Methods,* 12th ed. New York, NY: McGraw-Hill Education, 2014.

Market Research Technology

LO 4-6

Illustrate current research technologies and how they are used in market research.

Market research has benefited from better, more cost-effective technology. The use of powerful software tools and online technologies brings research to any level in the organization. Sales managers can survey customers, analyze the results, and make decisions without costly, time-consuming external studies. Sophisticated software incorporating CRM and marketing decision support systems can do in-depth analyses that offer unique insights about customers or market trends not possible just a few years ago. In most respects, making market research tools available throughout the company has been a big success. Unfortunately, as the access to market research technology has increased, so has the misapplication of the technology. Without implementing the market research process presented earlier, no amount of technology can create worthwhile results.

Online Research Tools Online research tools fall into three categories: databases, focus groups, and sampling. Each of these three categories offers unique opportunities to expand the reach and usefulness of market research. Let's examine each more closely.

Online (Cloud) Databases An **online database** is data stored on a server that is accessed remotely over the Internet or some other telecommunications network. Many, if not most, companies now have databases available to employees, suppliers, even customers. Information on orders, shipments, pricing, and other relevant information is available to salespeople and customer service personnel who need to access it.[30]

Independent online databases available from government and other sources are extremely useful tools in market research. Organizations such as the National Archives and Records Administration offer a wide range of databases with topic-specific data, all of which can be accessed for free. Fee-based services, while expensive, offer access to a wide range of information. Lexis/Nexis, for example, enables market researchers to access thousands of business and trade publications and market studies. Another company, IBISWorld, allows members to access hundreds of industry overviews and analyses that have been conducted through research. These services make it possible to review market research reports, industry and company analyses, even market share information.[31]

Online Focus Groups The virtual focus group is becoming a viable alternative to the traditional focus group format (6 to 10 people in a room). Offering distinct advantages in terms of convenience and cost-efficiency, online focus groups provide data quickly and in a format that is usually easier to read and analyze. Traditional focus groups require someone to transcribe the spoken words into a transcript. With online focus groups, everything is already recorded by computer. With the increased use of mobile devices, it is even easier to conduct online focus groups and collect data even as the customer is experiencing the product or service.[32]

The primary disadvantage of online focus groups is that participants are limited to those with access to a computer or workstation. In addition, as people often participate remotely, it is not possible to verify who is actually responding to the questions. Measures can be employed to verify participation (for example, passwords), but the reality is that, in most cases, you must rely on the individual to be honest. One final problem is the lack of control over the environment. Traditional focus groups create an environment where participants are required to focus on the questions. Online focus groups enable participants to be at home, work, or even a remote location with wireless access. As a result, participants can become distracted and environmental factors can affect their concentration and responses.

SAS offers powerful analysis tools to help managers more clearly understand market data.

Source: SAS Institute Inc.

Online Sampling If someone has access to a computer with an Internet connection, that person can complete a questionnaire. Online sampling has become increasingly popular as a data collection methodology. As with online focus groups, the primary advantages are convenience and cost-efficiency. Respondents are free to complete the survey when it is best for them, and sending a survey online is essentially free. Online survey companies such as QuestionPro offer a complete service from survey design and a variety of delivery methods (traditional e-mail, popup surveys, company newsletter integration, and others) to data analysis and presentation of findings.

Statistical Software One of the real benefits of market research technology today is the ability to put powerful statistical software in the hands of front-line managers. With the proper training and data, it is now possible for managers to conduct analyses that were not possible even five years ago. Two software packages dominate desktop statistical analysis—IBM SPSS and SAS. IBM SPSS offers a range of marketing analytical tools. Its statistical software combines an easy-to-use interface with powerful statistical tools in a format that managers at all levels can use. The other widely used package is called SAS, and it offers many of the same features. One of the real advantages of these packages is their ability to take the findings of the data analysis and create tables and reports.[33]

Interestingly, while dedicated statistical packages offer powerful analytical tools and outstanding reporting capabilities, probably the most widely used tool for analyzing business data is one almost everyone already has on his or her computer—Excel spreadsheets. Part of the Microsoft Office suite of products, Excel offers the ability to analyze data using formulas created by the user or statistical functions already embedded in the software. While not a dedicated statistical package, it is certainly a useful tool in basic data analysis.

Market Research Challenges in Global Markets

The primary difference between domestic and international research is that international market data are more difficult to get and understand than domestic data. In most Western European countries and the United States, it is much easier to access quality data than in the rest of the world. Let's examine some of the challenges market researchers face in finding, collecting, and then analyzing market data in foreign markets.

Secondary Data Exhibit 4.9 identifies the ten most expensive countries for marketing research. Note that while the United States and, to a lesser extent, Japan and the European Union are data-rich market environments, they are also among the most expensive countries in which to conduct marketing research. Unfortunately, that level of information is not found anywhere else in world. In certain areas, such as Central Europe, this is because they have only recently moved to open market economies. In other parts of the world, such as China and India, the culture does not encourage the free flow of information. This makes it difficult for any organization, even governments, to collect good information. Let's consider three major challenges researchers face as they collect data around the world.

EXHIBIT 4.9 | The Ten Most Expensive Countries for Research

Country	Global Index Scale
United States of America	241
Switzerland	239
Canada	229
Japan	222
United Kingdom	187
Sweden	168
Germany	165
Denmark	162
France	161
The Netherlands	156

Source: "US the Most Expensive Country for Market Research," *Marketing Charts*, October 17, 2014.

Data Accessibility In the United States, businesspeople are accustomed to easily accessing information that simply does not exist in much of the world. The U.S. Census Bureau provides detailed information across a wide range of business sectors, including retailing and distribution, as well as specific data on many different economic and personal criteria such as income per capita, population by county, and zip code (broken down by gender, age, ethnic mix, and many other characteristics). From government sources (U.S. Census Bureau, Department of Commerce, EU Business Development Center), nongovernment business organizations (U.S. Chamber of Commerce, OECD), and private research organizations, a great deal of information is available to managers. The quantity and quality of data found in the United States are not available in most of the world.

Data Dependability A second major issue is the reliability of the data. Can the information be considered accurate? Regrettably, in many cases it cannot. Govrnment agencies, particularly in developing countries, will distort data to present a more favorable analysis. The data are often reported incorrectly because people do not want the government to know the true figures, usually because of higher tax concerns. In other cases, governments want to present optimistic results that support government policies, so they alter the data to reflect government accomplishments.

Data Comparability Comparing secondary data from foreign markets risks three other problems. First, developing countries often lack historical data, making it much harder to assess long-term economic or business trends. Second, the available data are outdated so they are ineffective for making decisions in the current economic environment. Finally, terms used in reporting information are not consistent. Standardized business terminology used in industrialized countries has not been adopted by many developing regions, making it difficult for researchers to interpret data.

Primary Data
Essential information about economic and general business trends can be gathered from secondary sources, but to get specific market data such as customer preferences, primary data are necessary. Collecting primary data presents many challenges for marketers that are almost always compounded in global markets. Some of the specific problems of international primary data collection include the following issues.

Unwillingness to Respond Cultural, gender, and individual differences create wide disparities in the willingness to provide personal information. The United States has an open information culture and people are much more willing to respond, but this openness is not shared around the world. In addition, government agencies such as the Securities and Exchange Commission require publicly traded companies to provide accurate business information including valid financial results. Nongovernment agencies such as trade associations report studies widely used in business. The National Realtors Association, for example, publishes quarterly data on the housing industry that is considered an accurate assessment of the real estate market in the United States.

As we discussed earlier, many people don't respond because they are concerned about government interference or additional taxes. However, concerns about privacy and how personal data are used generate a broad distrust of surveys among consumers and businesses. It is not difficult to understand these concerns. In countries formerly under the control of the Soviet Union (Czech Republic, Poland, Hungary, and others), for example, people were concerned that personal information provided to authorities could be used against them. After the fall of the Soviet Union, the historical problems created by decades of living in a closed society made it very difficult for companies such as A.C. Nielsen to collect valid consumer opinions and business data.

Unreliable Sampling Procedures Related to the quality of data noted earlier is the problem of unreliable or inadequate demographic information to conduct primary research. In many countries, there is no way to locate or identify who lives where or even how many people live in a given location, something businesspeople in the United States take for granted. In the United States, sophisticated global positioning system (GPS) devices can direct people to specific locations based on maps and other data stored on a hard drive. Consider the problem, then, if you are in a medium or small South American or Asian city where maps do not exist and street names are not even posted. The lack of reliable census information coupled with an inadequate infrastructure leaves market researchers in many countries with no accurate sampling frame from which to draw respondents.

Inaccurate Language Translation and Insufficient Comprehension Getting people in global markets to actually complete a survey presents three challenges. First, simply translating surveys can be a challenge. For example, Chinese is written with characters known as hànzi, with each character representing a syllable of spoken Chinese with its own meaning. To read fluently in Chinese requires knowledge of more than 3,000 symbols. Second, word usage changes dramatically around the world. In the United States and Western Europe, "family" generally refers to the immediate family unit, including a father, mother, and their children, while in many Latin and Asian cultures "family" almost always includes the extended family, including all aunts, uncles, cousins, and grandparents. When a survey asks about family members, then, the responses could vary dramatically.

A final problem is insufficient language comprehension. In many parts of the world illiteracy rates are high, which rules out most survey methodologies. In addition, some countries use multiple languages, making translation costly and increasing the likelihood of mistranslation. India, for example, recognizes 14 official languages, with many additional nonofficial languages. Imagine writing a survey that would translate well into over a dozen languages.

SUMMARY

Marketers know that accurate, relevant, and timely information is an essential element in marketing management. There are two sources of information: that which comes from outside the company and that which can be found internally. Being aware of environmental forces such as demographic profiles and changes, economic conditions, emerging technologies, changes in the natural world, and the political and legal environment enables marketers to create more effective short- and long-term marketing strategies.

Critical to assessing marketing information is a thorough understanding of the market research process. The process involves six specific steps: define the problem, establish the research design, search secondary sources, collect the data, analyze the data, and present the research findings. Researchers must follow the market research process to ensure the data are valid and useful for decision makers.

KEY TERMS

market information system (MIS)   91
marketing intelligence   93
demographics   94
microeconomics   95
macroeconomics   95
market research   97
management research deliverable   98
research problem   99
exploratory research   100

descriptive research   100
causal research   100
primary data   100
secondary data   101
qualitative research   101
quantitative research   101
focus group   101
in-depth interview   101
surveys   101
behavioral data   101

observational data   102
mechanical observation   102
open-ended questions   102
closed-ended questions   102
census   102
sample   102
probability sampling   103
nonprobability sampling   103
data collection   104
online database   106

APPLICATION QUESTIONS

More application questions are available online.

1. Imagine you are the vice president of sales for a large security company and you have been asked to put together a sales information system that collects, analyzes, interprets, and distributes information from the sales force. How would you do it? What information would you ask salespeople to collect?

2. As a market manager at Lenovo, what key information from outside the company would be important to help in the design of a new laptop for small and medium-sized businesses?

3. The marketing manager for Disney Cruise Line wants to know what demographic trends will affect the cruise line business over the next five years. What kind of research is needed to address this question? Conduct some secondary research and try to identify two or three important demographic trends that might affect the cruise line business.

4. The market research director for John Deere has just received a call from the marketing manager in the company's lawn tractor division. The manager wants to know how the new advertising campaign is being received by current customers. Design a research study for this research. Be sure to include a problem definition and research design.

5. The alumni director at your institution wants to know how to serve the alumni better. Design a survey of no more than 10 questions that the alumni director can use to ask alumni about their interest in getting more involved with their school.

MANAGEMENT DECISION CASE
BMW's Road to Higher Customer Satisfaction: Just Tell Me What You Think!

Customer satisfaction and loyalty are critical elements in any successful marketing strategy, but they are essential when the product is purchased only once every few years. It was, therefore, of great concern to luxury automakers like Acura, Audi, and BMW when in 2014 their customer satisfaction scores all dropped below the average for the entire automobile industry.[34] For years these companies had been gathering and using external primary data from their own surveys, and also relying on secondary data from sources like the American Consumer Satisfaction Index, yet satisfaction was falling. Assuming the luxury automakers were listening and responding to the data they received from existing research, it appeared the old modes of research were missing key insights. Management had a new research deliverable—learn how we can improve customer satisfaction—and a new research question—what specific product attributes or service components are not satisfying our customers?

In situations like this, you don't know what you don't know. Were less-expensive competitors adding features that satisfied customers at a lower price? Were service amenities like free loaner cars not valued by the customers? What were the features or service components that were failing, missing, or just not valued? Finding a method to ask questions that exposed areas of dissatisfaction (or missed opportunities to satisfy), and ask these questions in a way that was representative of the target customers, became the market research problem. One of these companies—BMW—learned how to listen and greatly improved its customer satisfaction scores. It now ranks above the industry average for customer satisfaction and higher in satisfaction than its luxury automobile competitors.[35] BMW's focus on understanding its customers has helped it reach the top of its market, but its path was only possible with an understanding of important trade-offs different types of marketing research require.

Through a worldwide dealer network, BMW makes 10 promises to its customers and then measures how well the company (and dealers) keep those promises. Walk into (or visit on the web) nearly any BWM dealership, from Idaho Falls, Idaho, to Hastings, New Zealand, and you will see a display of the 10 promises of service quality.[36] What you don't see is how difficult it is to measure and make sense of hundreds, thousands, or, at a country level, hundreds of thousands of opinions about customers' satisfaction with activities such as response timeliness, explaining the bill, or offering a test drive.

In an effort to gather better satisfaction information, BMW UK set about to solve two problems at once. Like most companies, it had a difficult time getting customers to respond to its surveys.[37] And, with 10 promises to measure, the surveys were fairly long and time-consuming to complete. This led to a falloff in customer response rates. The second problem was making sense of the incoming survey data. To make surveys easier for respondents and for later analysis, market researchers use closed-ended quantitative questions, typically with a one-to-five- or one-to-seven-point scale of very unsatisfied to very satisfied. Customers who responded answered by bubbling in the appropriate number on their survey. But, without context as to why they were very satisfied (or not), it was difficult for BMW to know exactly what to keep doing and what to fix. More context meant more questions, and more questions meant fewer responses.

To address this problem and get deeper context, market researchers often seek to gather deeper, qualitative information through in-depth interviews, which are often one on one and quite expensive to administer, or by inviting a small number of customers (usually around a dozen) to a focus group, where a professional moderator asks open-ended qualitative questions, digging out nuances of why customers are expressing a given level of satisfaction. One downside of both in-depth interviews and focus groups is that they are not a statistically valid representation of the population of interest (for example, a target segment such as Lexus buyers). BMW recognized that focus groups enable the company to gain deeper context and actionable insights through qualitative data but do not allow for generalizing the findings to a large group, so they only provide guidance on what should be focused on in a broader, statistically valid study.

BMW faced what is, for all market researchers, a series of trade-offs between different research methods. Qualitative methods, such as focus groups, brought deeper insights, but at the cost of being able to apply the findings to a more general customer target. Other methods, such as quantitative surveys, brought speed, generalizability, and a higher level of numerical precision and statistical validity, but lacked an ability to delve deeper and understand the heart of what customers value. And, in both cases, the more information BMW sought, the fewer customers responded. Realizing a need for richer and more representative information, BMW set out to find a way to analyze representative samples of large amounts of open-ended qualitative customer responses.

Questions for Consideration

1. Assuming BMW wants to learn more about what customers value in a luxury driving experience, and then make decisions based on that research, what kind(s) of market research would you recommend that might improve BMW's understanding?

2. BMW is facing the classic quality–quantity–cost trade-off; when it seeks higher-quality information (represented by more questions), fewer responses are received or research costs are higher. Since BMW's executives all have 25 to 30 years of experience in the automotive market, what would be the advantages and disadvantages of trusting their own experience versus spending more on market research?

3. When problems develop, like what BMW is experiencing in its research data gathering, a new, often technological solution is developed to address the issue. What might be some innovative ways to approach gaining both statistical significance (through higher response rate) and deeper context (through open-ended qualitative data)?

MARKETING PLAN EXERCISE

ACTIVITY 3: Identify Critical Information

This exercise asks you to identify the critical information needed to create the marketing plan. In that regard it is important to evaluate existing information (internal and secondary data) as well as new information gathered through primary research. This assignment includes:

1. Catalog internal sources of information available to you inside the organization and what information you will receive from each source.

2. Identify secondary data sources and the specific information you need from each source.

   a. List sources.

   b. Date.

   c. Assess the relevance of the data to the project.

3. List primary data needs to create the marketing plan. Then develop the specific instruments (focus group questions, surveys) that you will use later in the marketing plan.

NOTES

1. David Barton, "Data Analytics Top Trends in 2017," *Innovation Enterprise*, March 2017, https://channels.theinnovationenterprise.com/articles/data-analytics-top-trends-in-2017.

2. Dana Varinsky, "An American Cultural Revolution Is Killing Cookie-Cutter Homes," *Business Insider*, March 9, 2017, http://www.businessinsider.com/the-dream-of-owning-a-cookie-cutter-home-is-dying-heres-where-people-are-moving-instead-2017-2.

3. Roger Bennett, "Sources and Use of Marketing Information by Marketing Managers," *Journal of Documentation* 63, no. 5 (2007), p. 702; and Hean Tat Keh, Thi Mai Nguyen, and Hwei Ping Ng, "The Effects of Entrepreneurial Orientation and Marketing Information on the Performance of SME's," *Journal of Business Venturing* 22, no. 4 (2007), pp. 592–611.

4. Paul Ingenbleek, "Value-Informed Pricing in Its Organizational Context: Literature Review, Conceptual Framework, and Directions for Future Research," *Journal of Product and Brand Management* 16, no. 7 (2007), pp. 441–58.

5. Gerrit H. Van Bruggen, Ale Smidts, and Berend Wierenga, "The Powerful Triangle of Marketing Data, Managerial Judgment, and Marketing Management Support Systems," *European Journal of Marketing* 35, no. 7 (2001), pp. 796–816.

6. Shreyas Tanna, "Research Delivers Insight into the Global Predictive Analytics market to 2021," *WhaTech*, March 17, 2017, https://www.whatech.com/market-research/it/275294-research-delivers-insight-into-the-global-predictive-analytics-market-forecast-to-2021.

7. João F. Proença, Teresa M. Fernandez, and P. K. Kannan, "The Relationship in Marketing: Contribution of a Historical Perspective," *Journal of Macromarketing* 28, no. 1 (2008), pp. 90–106.

8. Sandra S. Liu and Lucette B. Comer, "Salespeople as Information Gatherers: Associated Success Factors," *Industrial Marketing Management* 36, no. 5 (2007), pp. 565–79.

9. Joel Le Bon and Dwight Merunka, "The Impact of Individual and Managerial Factors on Salespeople's Contribution to Marketing Intelligence Activities," *International Journal of Research in Marketing* 23, no. 4 (2006), pp. 395–412.

10. Jean Michel Moutot and Ganael Bascoul, "Effects of Sales Force Automation Use on Sales Force Activities and Customer Relationship Management Process," *Journal of Personal Selling and Sales Management* 28, no. 2 (2008), pp. 167–82.

11. K. Michel, "OTT: The Future of Content Delivery." *Broadcasting & Cable* 146, no. 40 (2016), p. 49.

12. Brad Plumer, "Will China Ever Get Its Pollution Problem under Control?" *Washington Post,* March 11, 2013, www.washingtonpost.com/blogs/wonkblog/wp/2013/03/11/will-china-ever-get-its-pollution-problem-under-control/; "Plan to Reduce Air Pollution Chokes Mexico City," *Phys Org,* February 2, 2017, https://phys.org/news/2017-02-air-pollution-mexico-city.html.

13. Connie R. Bateman and JoAnn Schmidt, "Do Not Call Lists: A Cause for Telemarketing Extinction or Evolution," *Academy of Marketing Studies Journal* 11, no. 1 (2007), pp. 83–107; and Herbert Jack Rotfeld, "Misplace Marketing: Do-Not-Call as the U.S. Govern-ment's Improvement to Telemarketing Efficiency," *Journal of Consumer Marketing* 21, no. 4/5 (2004), pp. 242–59.

14. "2017 U.S. Industry and Market Outlook (Marketing Research and Public Opinion Polling)," *Barnes Reports,* October 2016.

15. Alan Tapp, "A Call to Arms for Applied Marketing Academics," *Marketing Intelligence and Planning* 22, no. 5 (2004), pp. 579–96.

16. Dianne Altman Weaver, "The Right Questions," *Marketing Research* 18, no. 1 (2006), pp. 17–18.

17. Janice Denegri-Knott, Detiev Zwick, and Jonathan E. Schroeder, "Mapping Consumer Power: An Integrative Framework for Marketing and Consumer Research," *European Journal of Marketing* 40, no. 9/10 (2006), pp. 950–71.

18. Gordon A. Wyner, "Redefining Data," *Marketing Research* 16, no. 4 (2004), pp. 6–7.

19. Naomi R. Henderson, "Twelve Steps to Better Research," *Marketing Research* 17, no. 2 (2005), pp. 36–37.

20. David Stokes and Richard Bergin, "Methodology or 'Methodolatry'? An Evaluation of Focus Groups and Depth Interviews?" *Qualitative Market Research* 9, no. 1 (2006), pp. 26–38.

21. B. J. Allen, U. M. Dholakia, and S. Basuroy, "The Economic Benefits to Retailers from Customer Participation in Proprietary Web Panels," *Journal of Retailing* 92, no. 2 (2016), pp. 147–61. http://dx.doi.org.ezproxy.rollins.edu:2048/10.1016/j.jretai.2015.12.003.

22. Jennifer Comiteau, "Why the Traditional Focus Group Is Dying," *Adweek,* October 31, 2005, pp. 24–27.

23. Gordon Wyner, "Survey Errors," *Marketing Research* 19, no. 1 (2007), pp. 6–7.

24. Catherine A. Roter, Robert A. Rogers, George C. Hozier Jr., Kenneth G. Baker, and Gerald Albaum, "Management of Marketing Research Projects: Does Delivery Method Matter Anymore in Survey Research," *Journal of Marketing Theory and Practice* 15, no. 2 (2007), pp. 127–45; and Sharon Loane, Jim Bell, and Rob McNaughton, "Employing Information Communication Technologies to Enhance Qualitative International Marketing Enquiry," *International Marketing Review* 23, no. 4 (2006), pp. 438–53.

25. Edward Blair and George M. Zinkhan, "Nonresponse and Generalizability in Academic Research," *Academy of Marketing Science Journal* 34, no. 1 (2006), pp. 4–8.

26. Peter Keliner, "Can Online Polls Produce Accurate Findings?" *International Journal of Market Research* 46 (2004), pp. 3–15; and Olivier Furrer and D. Sudharshan, "Internet Marketing Research: Opportunities and Problems," *Qualitative Market Research* 4, no. 3 (2001), pp. 123–30.

27. N. L. Reynolds, A. C. Simintiras, and A. Diamantopoulos, "Theoretical Justification of Sampling Choices in International Marketing Research: Key Issues and Guidelines for Researchers," *Journal of International Business Studies* 34, no. 1 (2003), pp. 80–90.

28. Bill Blyth, "Mixed Mode: The Only 'Fitness' Regime?" *International Journal of Marketing Research* 50, no. 2 (2008), pp. 241–56.

29. Nick Sparrow, "Quality Issues in Online Research," *Journal of Advertising Research* 47, no. 2 (2007), pp. 179–91; and Elisabeth Deutskens, Ad de Jong, Ko de Ruyter, and Martin Wetzels, "Comparing the Generalizability of Online and Mail Surveys in Cross National Service Quality Research," *Marketing Letters* 17, no. 2 (2006), pp. 119–32.

30. Kai Wehmeyer, "Aligning IT and Marketing—The Impact of Database Marketing and CRM," *Journal of Database Marketing & Customer Strategy Management* 12, no. 3 (2005), pp. 243–57; Joshua Weinberger, "Database Marketers Mine for Perfect Customer Segmentation," *Customer Relationship Management* 8, no. 10 (2004), p. 19; and Hoda McClymont and Graham Jocumsen, "How to Implement Marketing Strategies Using Database Approaches, "*Journal of Database Marketing & Customer Strategy Management* 11, no. 2 (2003), pp. 135–49.

31. R. Dale Wilson, "Developing New Business Strategies in B2B Markets by Combining CRM Concepts and Online Databases," *Competitiveness Review* 16, no. 1 (2006), pp. 38–44.

32. K. Brosnan, B. Griin, and S. Dolnicar, "PC, Phone or Tablet?" *International Journal of Market Research* 59, no. 1 (2017), 35–55. doi:10.2501/IJMR-2016-049.

33. Steve Ranger, "How Firms Use Business Intelligence," *BusinessWeek,* May 24, 2007, www.businessweek.com/globalbiz/content/may2007/gb20070524_006085.htm?chan=search; and Colin Beasty, "Minimizing Customer Guesswork," *Customer Relationship Management* 10, no. 6 (2006), p. 45.

34. Aimee Picchi, "Some Surprises in Customers' Car Rankings," *CBS News,* August 26, 2014, http://www.cbsnews.com/news/some-surprises-in-customers-car-rankings/.

35. "Benchmarks by Company: BMW," *American Customer Satisfaction Index,* 2016, http://www.theacsi.org/customer-satisfaction-benchmarks/benchmarks-by-company.

36. "Customer Promise | BMW of Idaho Falls," 2017, http://www.bmwofidahofalls.com/customer-promise.htm; and "BMW Customer Promise - Hawkes Bay BMW," 2017, http://www.hawkesbaybmw.co.nz/com/en/insights/aboutus/customer_promise.html.

37. "Shorter BMW Customer Surveys Increase Response Rates by 10%," *Feedback Ferret,* 2016, http://www.feedbackferret.com/wp-content/uploads/sites/2/2016/02/Feedback-Ferret-Automotive-Case-Studies-USA.pdf.

CHAPTER 5

CRM, Big Data, and Marketing Analytics

LEARNING OBJECTIVES

LO 5-1 Define CRM and articulate its objectives and capabilities.

LO 5-2 Describe the CRM process cycle.

LO 5-3 Understand the concept of customer touchpoints and why touchpoints are critical in CRM.

LO 5-4 Identify and appreciate the types of data used in marketing management decision making.

LO 5-5 Recognize key approaches to marketing analytics.

LO 5-6 Understand the concept of a marketing dashboard and how it improves marketing planning for a firm.

LO 5-7 Explain return on marketing investment (ROMI), including cautions about its use.

OBJECTIVES AND CAPABILITIES OF CRM

We've mentioned CRM briefly in earlier chapters of this book. But what exactly is CRM? **Customer relationship management (CRM)** is a comprehensive business model for increasing revenues and profits by focusing on customers. Significantly, this definition does not speak to who should "own CRM" within the organization. In the mid-1990s, the introductory days of CRM systems, CEOs tended to relegate the operation of a firm's CRM system to the information technology group. After all, CRM is technology-based, isn't it? But legendary horror stories abound about CEOs who purchased multimillion-dollar CRM installations purely on the recommendation of the IT department, without any significant consultation with those in the firm who would be the system's primary *users*, such as salespeople, marketing managers, and customer service representatives. In the end, through the school of hard knocks, firms learned that no one group should have "ownership" of the CRM system. Positioning CRM as a comprehensive business model provides the impetus for top management to properly support it over the long run and for various internal stakeholder groups to have the opportunity to both use it and impact how it is used.[1]

Fortunately, with many of the initial CRM adoption misfires relegated to the past, most companies are now adopting CRM as a mission-critical business strategy. It is considered mission-critical largely because of competitive pressures in the marketplace; nobody can afford to be the lone wolf that does not have a handle on the customer side of an enterprise in a competitive space.

To optimize CRM's potential for contribution to the bottom line, companies are redesigning internal structures, as well as internal and external business processes and systems, to make it easier for customers to do business with them. Although marketing does not "own" CRM, because of CRM's focus on aligning the organization's internal and external processes and systems to be more customer-centric, marketing managers are a core contributor to the success of CRM by virtue of their expertise on customers and relationships.[2] And in particular, as Chapter 14 will discuss in detail, the sales force in CRM-driven organizations has taken center stage in executing a firm's customer management strategies, complete with new titles befitting the new sales roles such as "client manager," "relationship manager," and "business solution consultant."

Ultimately, CRM has three major objectives:

1. *Customer acquisition*–acquisition of the *right* customers based on known or learned characteristics that will drive growth and increase margins.

2. *Customer retention*–retention of satisfied and loyal profitable customers and channels, and thus growing the business profitably over the long run.

3. *Customer profitability*–increased individual customer margins, while offering the right products at the right time.[3]

Accomplishing these objectives requires a clear focus on the product and service attributes that represent value to the customer and that create customer satisfaction and loyalty. **Customer satisfaction** means the level of liking an individual harbors for an offering–that is, to what level is the offering meeting or exceeding the customer's expectations? **Customer loyalty** means the degree to which an individual will resist switching, or defecting, from one offering to another. Loyalty is usually based on high satisfaction coupled with a high level of perceived value derived from the offering and a strong relationship with the provider and its brand(s). Customer satisfaction and loyalty are two extremely popular metrics used by marketing managers to gauge the health of their business and brands.[4]

All of this implies strong integration of CRM into the overall marketing planning process of a firm. Perusal of the elements of marketing planning presented in Chapter 3 reveals numerous

Salesforce offers state-of-the-art CRM capabilities that are cloud-based and operate well on multiple devices.

Source: Salesforce.com Inc.

points at which information derived from a CRM system can assist in the strategy development and execution process. Key parts of a marketing plan that rely on CRM-generated information include the situation analysis, market research, strategy development, implementation, and measurement phases of marketing planning. In fact, many of the metrics that marketing managers use to assess their success are derived directly from the firm's CRM system.[5]

One of the most important metrics in CRM is that of the **customer lifetime value (CLV).** Fredrick Reichheld in his books on customer loyalty has demonstrated time and again that investment in CRM yields more successful long-term relationships with customers, and that these relationships pay handsomely in terms of cost savings, revenue growth, profits, referrals, and other important business success factors. It is possible to actually calculate an estimate of the projected financial returns from a customer, or **return on customer investment (ROCI)**, over the long run. This analysis provides a very useful strategic tool for deciding which customers deserve what levels of investment of various resources (money, people, time, information, etc.). Many of the most useful marketing metrics derive their power and functionality from CRM.

Proliferation of ROCI analysis has raised the prospects of **firing a customer** who exhibits a low predicted lifetime value, and instead investing resources in other more profitable customers. Of course, such action assumes other more attractive customers exist.[6]

THE CRM PROCESS CYCLE

LO 5-2

Describe the CRM process cycle.

The process cycle for CRM may be divided into the following four elements: (1) knowledge discovery, (2) marketing planning, (3) customer interaction, and (4) analysis and refinement. Elements of the process cycle are portrayed in Exhibit 5.1 and discussed below.

Knowledge Discovery

Knowledge discovery is the process of analyzing the customer information acquired through various customer touchpoints. At their essence, **customer touchpoints** are where the selling firm touches the customer in some way, thus allowing for information about him or her to be collected. These might include point-of-sale systems, call-center files, Internet accesses, records from direct selling or customer service encounters, or any other customer contact experiences. Touchpoints occur at the intersection of a business event that takes place via a channel using some media, such as online inquiry from a prospect, telephone follow-up with a purchaser on a service issue, face-to-face encounter with a salesperson, and so on.[7]

A **data warehouse** environment is the optimal approach to handling all the customer data generated through the touchpoints and transforming those data into useful information for marketing management decision making and marketing planning. A data warehouse affords the opportunity to combine large amounts of information and then use data mining techniques to learn more about current and potential customers.[8]

Data mining is a sophisticated analytical approach to using the massive amounts of data accumulated through the CRM system to develop segments and micro-segments of customers for purposes of either market research or development of market segmentation and target marketing strategies. The knowledge discovery phase of the CRM process cycle becomes the focal point for many direct marketers. Direct marketing involves utilizing the data generated through this phase to develop "hit lists" of customer prospects, who are then contacted

EXHIBIT 5.1 | Process Cycle for CRM

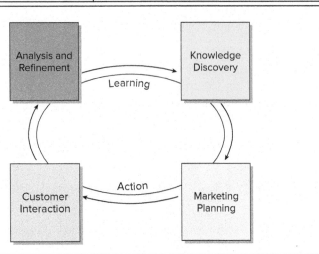

Source: Swift, Ronald S. *Accelerating Customer Relationships: Using CRM and Relationship Technologies.* Upper Saddle River, NJ: Prentice Hall, 2001.

individually by various means of marketing communication. This activity is often referred to as **database marketing**.[9] Clearly, this knowledge discovery phase has much to do with the market research and the management of market information that you learned about in Chapter 3.

Marketing Planning

The next phase in the CRM process cycle is marketing planning, which represents a key use of the *output* from the knowledge discovery phase. That is, the information enables the capability to develop marketing and customer strategies and programs. CRM input into the marketing planning process is particularly useful in developing elements of the marketing mix strategies, including employing the marketing communication mix in integrated ways to customize approaches to different customer groups (issues of marketing communication will be discussed in Part Five of the book).[10]

Customer Interaction

The customer interaction phase represents the actual implementation of the customer strategies and programs. This includes the personal selling effort, as well as all other customer-directed interactions. These must be aimed at all the customer touchpoints, or channels of customer contact, both in person and electronically.[11]

Analysis and Refinement

Finally, the analysis and refinement phase of the CRM process is where **organizational learning** occurs based on customer response to the implemented strategies and programs. Think of it as market research in the form of a continuous dialogue with customers, facilitated by effective use of CRM tools. With such an ongoing commitment and capability related to customer research, continuous adjustments made to the firm's overall customer initiatives should result in more efficient investment of resources and increasing ROCI.[12]

MORE ON CUSTOMER TOUCHPOINTS

You have read that CRM initiatives depend heavily on interactions with customers, suppliers, or prospects via one or more touchpoints—such as a call center, salesperson, distributor, store, branch office, website, or e-mail. CRM entails both acquiring knowledge about customers and (where feasible) deploying information to customers at the touchpoint. Some touchpoints are *interactive* and allow for such two-way information exchange. That is, they involve *direct interface* between a customer and a firm's customer contact person in the form of a salesperson, telemarketer, customer service representative, interactive website, and so on. Other touchpoints are *noninteractive;* that is, the customer may simply provide information on a static website's data entry form or by mail, without the capability of simultaneous direct interface with a company representative. To maximize a firm's ability to successfully use touchpoints, an ongoing concerted effort must be undertaken to (1) identify *all* potential touchpoints, (2) develop specific objectives for what kind of information can be collected at each touchpoint, (3) determine how that information will be collected and ultimately integrated into the firm's overall customer database, and (4) develop policies on how the information will be accessed and used.

LO 5-3

Understand the concept of customer touchpoints and why touchpoints are critical in CRM.

CRM, Touchpoints, and Customer Trust

The aspect of CRM involving customer information collected through touchpoints raises substantial ethical and legal issues for the firm regarding privacy, particularly in the consumer marketplace. Clearly, a key component of a strong customer relationship with a firm is a high level of *trust*.[13] Customers must be absolutely certain that the information a firm collects and stores about them will not be used for unintended purposes. Often referred to as the "dark side of CRM," this issue has become so prominent in some industries that firms are beginning to publicly promote guarantees of nonabuse of stored customer information as a means of attracting customers.[14] It is a feature that resonates well with customers and likely provides a strong point of differentiation over competitors.

In many industries, firms having access to sensitive customer information, such as social security numbers, necessitates more heavy regulation of information usage (financial services is a good example). In such cases, firms may be required to communicate the different ways that customers' personal information may be used and which of those potential uses a customer can opt out of. In addition, marketing managers must consider regulatory requirements, which may impose constraints such as what information can be conveyed to the firm within a given marketing campaign or at any touchpoint.

Potential abuse of information provided by customers is one source of concern, but not the only one that a customer may have when relinquishing his or her personal information at a given touchpoint. The increasing prevalence of malicious activity online intended to gain access to private information for personal benefit, generally for financial gain, is something that all organizations must be sensitive to. As mentioned before, *trust* is an important component of an organization's relationship with its customers. For any firm that collects large amounts of data through CRM, customers' perceptions of the organization's ability to securely handle and protect information can substantially influence that trust. For an online retailer, trust, and the resulting customer commitment to the firm, requires establishing a perception of security in the ability of the retailer's website to guarantee absolute security of the sensitive personal information. This is accomplished through such components as the use of advanced transaction processing technology, and a track record free of data breaches.[15]

Although the administration of information security is not generally viewed as a part of the marketing manager's job per se, one can play a pivotal role in enabling the firm's information security capabilities to deliver additional customer value. Marketing managers who understand how their organizations protect customer information can help develop more effective strategies for proactively communicating the most relevant elements of the organization's information security strategy to customers in a manner that engenders trust and greater commitment to the firm and its brand. Marketing also gets involved reactively in the aftermath of an information security breach by helping determine ways to mitigate the negative impact of the incident on consumer perceptions of the organization and to lead the way toward regaining customer trust.

Retailing giant Target's marketing managers had to determine how best to rebuild trust after a massive data breach that resulted in the loss of the personal information of about 40 million customers. This also meant quickly altering already planned marketing communication, including postponing a major campaign focused on Target's corporate citizenship.[16]

CRM Facilitates a Customer-Centric Culture

As you know, a firm that is customer-centric places the customer at the core of the enterprise including everything that happens, both inside and outside the firm. Customers are the lifeblood of any business—without them a firm has no sales, no profits, and ultimately no business. As such, marketing managers must approach their role with the attitude that customers are worth investing considerable resources in so long as an acceptable return on that investment can be anticipated.

At the strategic marketing level, a customer-centric culture includes, but is not limited to, the following major components:

1. Adopting a relationship or partnership business model overall, with mutually shared rewards and risk management.

2. Redefining the selling role within the firm to focus on customer business consultation and solutions.

3. Increasing formalization of customer analysis processes.

4. Taking a proactive leadership role in educating customers about value chain opportunities available by developing a business relationship.

5. Focusing on continuous improvement principles stressing customer satisfaction and loyalty.[17]

The effort a firm makes toward cultivating a customer-centric culture requires a high degree of formalization within the firm. **Formalization** means that structure, processes and tools, and managerial knowledge and commitment are formally established in support of the culture. With these elements in place, strategies and programs can be successfully developed and executed toward the goals related to customers, accompanied by a high degree of confidence they will yield the desired results. Today, the most prevalent formalization mechanism of a customer-centric culture is CRM.

As mentioned in Chapter 1, firms that are customer-centric have a high level of customer orientation. Organizations practicing a customer orientation place the customer at the core of all aspects of the enterprise and:

1. Instill an organization-wide focus on understanding the requirements of customers.

2. Generate an understanding of the customer marketplace and disseminate that knowledge to everyone in the firm.

3. Align system capabilities internally so that the organization responds effectively to customers with innovative, competitively differentiated, satisfaction-generating products and services.[18]

How do the concepts of customer-centricity and customer orientation connect to the actions required by individual members of a firm? One way to think about how an organization member might exhibit a customer orientation is through a **customer mind-set**, which is a person's belief that understanding and satisfying customers, whether internal or external to the organization, is central to the proper execution of his or her job.[19] It is through organization members' customer mind-set that a customer orientation "comes alive" within a firm. Exhibit 5.2 provides example descriptors of customer mind-set in the context of both customers outside the firm as well as people inside the firm with whom one must interact to get the job done (internal customers). Concepts of internal customers and internal marketing are developed further in Chapter 10 on service as the core offering.

In the end, the software part of CRM will work, and can probably do far more for any firm than expected. CRM's real strengths, as well as its fragilities, rest with how the organization chooses to use CRM as a means of enabling a customer-centric culture and operationalizing a customer orientation as an ongoing driver of the enterprise. CRM across all

EXHIBIT 5.2 | Do You Have a Customer Mind-Set?

External Customer Mind-Set

I believe that . . .

- I must understand the needs of my company's customers.

- It is critical to provide value to my company's customers.

- I am primarily interested in satisfying my company's customers.

- I must understand who buys my company's products/services.

- I can perform my job better if I understand the needs of my company's customers.

- Understanding my company's customers will help me do my job better.

Internal Customer Mind-Set

I believe that . . .

- Employees who receive my work are my customers.

- Meeting the needs of employees who receive my work is critical to doing a good job.

- It is important to receive feedback from employees who receive my work.

- I focus on the requirements of the person who receives my work.

Score yourself from 1 to 6 on each item such that 1 = strongly disagree and 6 = strongly agree. Total up your score; a higher total score equates to more of a customer mind-set.

Source: Kennedy, Karen Norman, Felicia G. Lassk, and Jerry R. Goolsby, "Customer Mind-Set of Employees Throughout the Organization," *Journal of the Academy of Marketing Science,* vol. 30, 2002, pp. 159–171.

dimensions—as a business strategy, set of processes, and analytic tools—has amazing potential to facilitate great marketing planning and management.

BIG DATA AND MARKETING DECISION MAKING

LO 5-4

Identify and appreciate the types of data used in marketing management decision making.

Advances in information technology have changed the ways that customers and organizations function. Laptops, smartphones, and other smart devices have changed how individuals perform work, access and organize information, and communicate with each other. In addition, these tools have enabled the collection of vast amounts of data, with significant implications for comprehending how various phenomena can be better understood and acted on. Before we consider the topics of data and analytics from a marketing management perspective, here's a general example. In New York's bustling midtown, close to 300 sensors, cameras, and EZ-Pass readers have been deployed to enable the city's Traffic Management Center both to adjust traffic light patterns in real time and to enhance traffic signal plans within a 270-block region, to better account for traffic flow. The initial results of this program indicate a greater than 10 percent decrease in travel times.[20] In short, the union of large quantities of data and advanced capabilities to analyze patterns in those data resulted in solutions that benefit large segments of the population.

Big Data refers to the ever-increasing quantity and complexity of data that is continuously being produced by various technological sources. Four characteristics generally characterize Big Data; taken together, these characteristics are commonly referred to as the four "Vs" of Big Data: volume, velocity, variety, and veracity.[21] *Volume* relates to the amount of data produced, which is generally measured in bytes, given the digital media in which data is most commonly stored. *Velocity* relates to the frequency at which data is generated over time and the speed at which it can and should be analyzed and used. *Variety* relates to the different types of data, including text, video, images, and audio, to name a few types. And *veracity* relates to the reliability and validity of the data.[22]

For marketing managers, the rise of Big Data has provided significant opportunities to better understand several important elements of customer behavior. These include the varying experiences that make up the process through which customers choose to purchase a product or service, the different touchpoints that customers have with an organization through their use of a product or service, and the ways in which customers interact with and experience different products and services. In fact, some managers often include a fifth "V" when considering the different characteristics of the Big Data their firms possess—*value*. Without a clear idea of the value that can be obtained from Big Data, there is a limited justification for the expense of its collection and storage.

Categories of Big Data: Structured and Unstructured

Exhibit 5.3 provides a summary of key issues in structured versus unstructured data. **Structured data** refers to data that is generated in such a way that a logical organization is imposed on it during its generation, thus enabling it to be more readily analyzable for knowledge creation. Structured data can easily be placed into specific categories and stored within information systems for future analysis. Structured data is typically either numeric or text that is substantially limited to a certain set of input values (female/male, for example). This is the type of data that is generally found in relational databases or spreadsheets such as Microsoft Excel or Google Sheets; it is generally organized into tables with columns that make it clear what types of information will be included in each of the entries within a given column.

To help make the idea of structured data seem less abstract, consider the process of creating an account on a retailer's website so you can conveniently purchase items online. You often must fill out a webform that requests information such as your name, gender, date of birth, e-mail, mailing address, and other standard inputs. Because of the method by which this data is collected—separate boxes in a webform—it qualifies as structured data that can

EXHIBIT 5.3 | Structured versus Unstructured Data

	Structured Data	Unstructured Data
Storage	Generally stored in relational databases or other information system structures that contain a well-defined row and column structure.	Generally stored in files with a limited degree of organization imposed within the files (e.g., data entries may be logged and organized chronologically).
Characteristics	Generally easier and less costly to store and analyze because of its readily available structural characteristics (e.g., each record may be restricted to a single data type such as numeric, date, time, alphabetic).	Generally harder and more costly to analyze because of its lack of readily available structural characteristics.
Examples	• Data input into specific fields within a webform (e.g., Age, Gender, Birthday) • Data created through specific transactions (e.g., purchasing a clothing item online).	• Text and images within e-mail messages. • Text, images, audio, and video within social media posts. • Text, images, audio, and video within blog posts.

populate a relational database or spreadsheet. Each row within the table would contain a different person who signed up for an account. This structure enables many different analyses and other types of actions to be more easily conducted (for example, determining the average age of the company's male customers who shop online). While structured data is generally easier for marketing managers to work with, it has limitations in terms of the types of insights it can provide, and in reality only represents a small percentage of the data that is available for use. By some past estimates, it is believed that structured data only accounts for 10 to 20 percent of all data available to organizations.[23]

Unstructured data refers to data that is generated in such a way that it does not possess a specific organizational structure that renders it readily analyzable for knowledge creation. Unstructured data may not be immediately actionable in the way that structured data is, but it has become the most common form of data available to organizations, and is a potentially rich source of deep insights on customer behavior and customer/provider relationships. Unstructured data can include posts that people make on social media, e-mails sent to customer service representatives (CSRs), call logs from salespeople and CSRs, information that salespeople and CSRs input into CRM systems to describe interactions with current and potential customers, videos that people make discussing their experiences with products, images (including memes) that people use to express their feelings about brands or experiences as customers, as well as many other types of input.

For the marketing manager, a key challenge with unstructured data in the past has been determining how to extract meaning from the data so that it can be used in subsequent analyses. From an application standpoint, the question basically becomes determining how to create structured data from unstructured data that is not lesser in value than the information contained within its initial unstructured form.[24] To help provide a more general understanding of the objective of this process, it is worth considering some examples of the information contained in an electronic message from a customer that has potential value to a marketing manager. For example, if a product is mentioned in the customer's message, then capturing the specific product's name in a structured form should provide some valuable context for future analytically oriented applications. In addition, if there appears to be a specific way that the customer feels about the product, then it would most likely be useful to capture that feeling in a structured form for future study.

In the context of Big Data, the extraction of structured data from unstructured data is primarily accomplished using automated technologies. Given the amount of data available to organizations, it would not be economically feasible for people to manually sift through the data being generated to perform this function. Fortunately, advances in technology have provided for increasingly efficient and sophisticated means of extracting structure from unstructured data in order to provide useful fodder for running a variety of marketing analytics.

At this point it is worth noting that although we have used the convention of structured and unstructured data to classify data, in reality not all data fits neatly into these two classifications. **Semi-structured data** fits between structured and unstructured data in the sense that it contains some elements of structure that make it easier for machines to understand its organization, but still contains parts that do not possess an appropriate level of structure to make them readily analyzable by automated means for knowledge creation. Semi-structured data does not readily adhere to a strict set of standards.[25] A typical example from the web would be Extensible Markup Language (XML) files. XML files contain tags (markings within an XML file that provide a degree of organization to the data and offer some semantic meaning), but additional effort is required to create structured data from these files so that the output can be stored in a manner that enables a wider range of analyses to be applied.

Big Data Sources and Implications

Big Data comes from a wide range of sources. The most valuable sources for marketers are those that capture data on both potential and current customers to yield actionable insights. Six key sources that serve this purpose are business systems, social media platforms, Internet-connected devices, mobile apps, commercial entities, and government entities. Each is described and discussed below.

Data from Business Systems The information systems that companies use for different internally and externally facing business functions provide valuable information for better understanding how to maximize the value of customers. CRM systems often act as central hubs of customer-related data and many contain capabilities that enable them to easily integrate with other applications utilized by an organization. The advantage of centralizing information in one place through integration of multiple applications is that it facilitates a more holistic view of the firm's current and potential customers and allows for analyses of differing levels of sophistication to be conducted using the related data.

The collection of transaction data from customers through point-of-sales (POS) systems in retail locations, as well as online transaction processing systems, can be tied to other rich information about a customer and used to determine that customer's relative value. It can also provide insight into what kinds of products, services, and promotional offerings would most appeal to that customer. Kroger uses the massive amount of transaction and personal data it has collected through its POS system and loyalty card program to develop direct mail campaigns customized for each individual customer, yielding coupon return rates more than 18 times higher than the industry average, significantly impacting financial performance.[26]

Web-related activity is a major source of data generation that will continue to grow in importance as more people rely on the Internet and various technologies that enable Internet access to search for information, communicate with others, and transact business. Every action that a customer takes on a website creates data that through analysis has the potential to provide valuable insights for marketing managers. This data can be collected in a web log, which records specific actions that a user takes on a website in reverse chronological order (that is, displayed from newest to oldest). One particular element of interest captured within a web log is clickstream data, which includes the specific sequence of mouse clicks that the user made while visiting one or more websites. Data originating from web logs is of value for multiple reasons, including gaining insights on improving the way a website functions, as well as the effect that different marketing actions have on firm outcomes.

The use of clickstream data at an early stage in a customer's exploration of an e-commerce website can provide insight into the state of his or her intentions (which may in fact change during a single browsing session on the site). One implication of this type of knowledge is that it is possible to increase the likelihood that a customer will make a purchase during a browsing session by dynamically altering aspects of the site based on that customer's predicted intentions at a given stage during the browse.[27] For instance, for a customer who appears to be in a state where he or she is interested in making a purchase decision, a website can be modified to provide greater attention to pricing information and remove promotional elements around the periphery of the page that might distract from that customer's focus on making the purchase decision at hand.

Since customers now use several different technologies to access the Internet, it is important to be able to delineate between web log data, such as what's generated by individuals who are using a smartphone versus a laptop. Differences in web-related behavior that may be observed between these two devices may offer valuable insight to marketing managers intent on delivering better online experiences across multiple devices.

Data from Social Media Platforms An increasingly valuable source of data comes from the vast number of social media sites that customers use to communicate with each other and various organizations. Data generated through social media platforms is very diverse in nature, related to the different means of communication that are emphasized or enabled by different social networking sites. As an example, consider that Facebook lets users post messages in text form, react to posts with different emotional responses (visually captured as emojis), share images, and post a video (or record it live). In addition to the data generated by communicating using a platform such as Facebook, large amounts of data are generated as users set up and further augment their profiles on the site. All this data, which is a mix of structured and unstructured data, offers marketing managers unique opportunities to provide targeted marketing communications to different customers as well as gain greater insight into the thoughts, feelings, opinions, and interests of those customers.

The way that users communicate with each other on social media platforms, and who they communicate with, offers chances to better understand relationships between specific individuals and groups and differences in influence that certain individuals and groups wield on others. For a marketing manager developing a campaign for a specific product, identifying individuals on social media with high levels of influence who have an interest in a product and involving them in the marketing campaign can yield substantial benefits through the positive word of mouth those influencers are able to create.[28]

Data from Internet-Connected Devices As more smart devices enter the market and more products gain the capability to become network-connected, an increasing source of structured and unstructured data is being generated and transmitted to organizations via these devices. Many include sensors that enable the collection of large amounts of unstructured data. Data generated from the use of these products has the potential to provide greater understanding of how customers use products and services, such as informing the design of future features and helping identify opportunities to communicate information about features that a customer is not utilizing to their fullest potential benefit.

The value of communicating information on underutilized features may be most apparent in the case of products or services with a wide range of features, such as an automobile or a financial services provider. Because of the complexity of certain products, a customer may over time focus on using a certain set of features within a product and forget about the existence of other features. Being able to identify these patterns could provide an opportunity for the development of marketing communications to let customers know later in their consumption experiences of a product about one or more of the features that they may not be using, but that may be of value to them based on the analyzed data. For more complex features, the marketing communications provided could include an educational component to help

USAA, a pioneer in the use of CRM, collects a great deal of data on its members and utilizes that data to enhance the customer experience. USAA is consistently rated the top insurance company in the U.S. on member satisfaction.

Source: USAA

the customer understand how to utilize the promoted feature (for example, different investment options). This type of just-in-time training may be particularly effective for customers who prefer to learn incrementally.

Data from Mobile Apps Data generated from a customer's use of different mobile applications (apps) can provide insight into how different customers use mobile apps, and what elements within a mobile app are the most effective from a general standpoint. Mobile apps used to assist customers in finding in-store deals, such as Cartwheel from Target, provide opportunities for retailers to maximize the value of in-store shopping experiences; understand a customer's response to different price levels for different products, categories, and brands; and gain better insights on how shopping behavior that blends online and offline experiences might differ from traditional offline shopping behavior. In the case of mobile games, it can generally be determined which elements of the game appeal specifically to different segments of customers. One implication of this knowledge is identifying cross-promotional opportunities. For instance, if it is determined that one customer seems to enjoy that a game awards badges for accomplishments (as evidenced by a choice to share accomplishments with friends online), then that customer may be provided in-game advertisements for other games that have a badge-awarding feature at the point where it is expected the customer will soon stop playing the first game.

Data from Commercial Entities Several organizations collect Big Data on customers in order to sell it to other organizations as their primary business model. Some organizations, such as retailers and credit card processors, engage in this practice to generate additional revenue. Since these organizations already have the data available as a by-product of their primary business functions, it makes good business sense for them to find additional ways to extract value from it. Retailers that collect transaction data on customers and record data on pricing and store environmental factors can provide this data in aggregate to organizations interested in purchasing it.[29] The data does not enable purchasers to discern one customer's purchases from another, but it can provide significant insight into factors influencing customer behavior within different product categories and related to specific brands.

Data from Government Agencies Finally, data collected by governments can also be a valuable source of information for organizations interested in understanding demographic characteristics within different parts of a population and identifying specific patterns or trends on a large scale. In the U.S. government, at the state and federal level, there has been an increase in efforts to make the data that government agencies collect available and easily accessible to the public. A great example is the U.S. Bureau of Labor Statistics, a unit within the Department of Labor, which has greatly enhanced its website to provide more of a commercial flair and easier access. In many cases the transfer of government data to the public realm has been formalized through the development of open data policies.[30] Consider how access to census data related to the demographics within a region can help organizations identify attractive geographic areas where there is a higher concentration of individuals who fit an organization's demographic profile of an ideal customer, based on factors such as age, gender, and income. Census data can also provide insight into the attractiveness of a region related to the level of competition in that industry, based on the inclusion of data on the number of businesses within an industry that operate within a region as well as data on how that number has changed over time.[31]

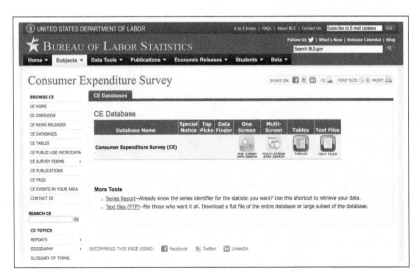

The U.S. Bureau of Labor Statistics is a governmental agency, but it clearly views itself as a valued provider of data to a wide range of stakeholders and customers.

Source: U.S. Department of Labor

MARKETING ANALYTICS

For marketing managers, a crucial component of extracting value from Big Data is the effective use of marketing analytics. **Marketing analytics** include a set of methods facilitated by technology that utilize individual-level and market-level data to identify and communicate meaningful patterns within the data for the purpose of improving marketing-related decisions.[32] Marketing analytics is not technically a new concept, but with the explosion of data available to marketing managers, organizations have become increasingly interested in finding new ways to extract maximum value from the data that they continue to accumulate. To help gain a greater appreciation of just how "big" Big Data can be, consider these factoids about Google and Facebook—massive generators of such data. Users of Google input more than 4 million search queries per minute, and the organization processes more than 20 million petabytes (1 petabyte is equivalent to 1 million gigabytes) of data per day. Users of Facebook produce about 2.5 million pieces of content each minute.[33] Truly incredible scales of data!

So given the escalating volume, availability, and accessibility of Big Data, the central question for marketing managers is how to use the data to gain customer insights and for marketing planning. Answering this question requires knowledge about marketing analytic approaches, and marketing analytics are significantly changing the whole field of marketing management based on the increased capability and speed of gaining valuable customer insights.

Marketing Analytic Approaches

Marketing analytic approaches can be thought of by considering the level of analytic complexity and the value that is created from employing each within the specific research project. Generally, greater levels of complexity come with a higher cost in the form of the level of expertise and effort required on the part of the **marketing analyst,** an individual familiar with different forms of market and customer data and who is trained to conduct different market analyses, as well as the computational costs associated with those analyses. But more complex analytical approaches also tend to yield higher-value customer insights. In the sections that follow, we introduce you to four key types of marketing analytics: descriptive analytics, diagnostic analytics, predictive analytics, and prescriptive analytics. Each has its place in taking Big Data and providing valuable insights for marketing management decision making. These are illustrated in Exhibit 5.4 according to increasing complexity.

Descriptive Analytics An approach using **descriptive analytics** utilizes data to provide summary insights. Data in raw form is transformed into measures that provide insight into the past and hopefully a basis for further explorations of the data.[34] Customers who are members of a company's loyalty program, such as that of the online shoe and clothing shop Zappos, constitute a rich data source for use in descriptive analytics. Measurements produced from descriptive analysis can include sums (such as total number of new customers acquired per month by an online insurance company), averages (such as the average dollar amount of purchases made by a customer who is a member of a clothing company's loyalty program), or measures of changes in variables of interest (such as percent increase or decrease in number of e-mail subscribers to a company's blog for a given month compared to the same month in the prior year). Information produced from descriptive analyses is often presented in a visual format to assist in its interpretation by a broader audience. For instance, histograms, scatter plots, or pie charts may make it easier to see patterns in the information produced via descriptive analysis.

Customer loyalty programs such as "Zappos Rewards" provide data that enables descriptive analytics.

Source: Zappos.com Inc.

EXHIBIT 5.4 | Marketing Analytics Approaches

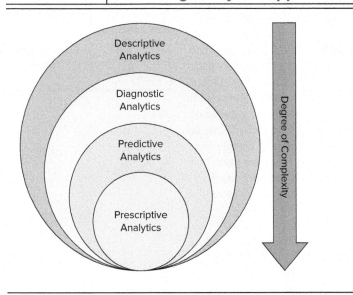

Descriptive Analytics

Diagnostic Analytics

Predictive Analytics

Prescriptive Analytics

Degree of Complexity

The use of descriptive analytics is generally an appropriate first step to consider before employing more complex (and costly) analyses. The resulting information can provide some initial evidence that an event has occurred that has implications for marketing management decision making. For instance, a significant increase in sales observed for a product for a month that historically sees much lower sales, as captured through a descriptive analysis, might prompt a marketing manager to request more complex analyses to understand what caused the observed spike in sales if the cause is not readily known. If the identified cause is one that can be reproduced or enabled by the organization, then the marketing manager can exploit this knowledge in the future to the benefit of the firm.

Diagnostic Analytics An approach using **diagnostic analytics** utilizes data to explore the relationships between different marketing-relevant factors that influence the organization's performance either directly or indirectly. There is significant value in understanding how marketing-relevant factors (for example, advertising frequency, advertisement placement, or product pricing) that can be influenced or controlled by the marketing managers can influence important firm outcomes such as product sales or customer satisfaction scores. Diagnostic analytics provide insights into the relationships of different factors with the implication being that an understanding of their relationships can have value for future marketing decisions. Statistical methods such as linear regression, which in this context provide a quantifiable relationship between a marketing outcome and specific marketing-relevant factors believed to influence that outcome, can provide evidence of any relationships that exist, as well as evidence of the relative magnitudes of those identified relationships.

As an example, consider a marketing manager for a television network who is interested in exploring the impact that conversations in online forums have on the television ratings of new shows. The marketing manager believes that the number of conversations and the spread of the conversations across different online forums are important determinants of the success of a new show. He or she collects data on the number of conversations within a set of online forums (representing different communities of television viewers), the spread of conversations across those online forums that occur during each week, and the weekly ratings of new shows during the period of analysis. Using diagnostic analytics, the marketing manager then looks at the relationship between the number of conversations and the spread of the conversations for a new show in a given week and the ratings of the show in the following week, and discovers that the spread of conversations is far more impactful on future ratings of the show than the sheer number of conversations. This finding might motivate the marketing manager to invest greater resources into encouraging a smaller but more diverse set of viewers to engage in discussions online to increase the spread of conversations across online forums, as opposed to engaging with a group of similar customers who might engage in conversations within a more limited set of online forums that subsequently limits the diffusion of engagement.

Predictive Analytics An approach using **predictive analytics** utilizes data to make predictions about future marketing outcomes of interest. Predictive analytics can be divided into those that use historical measurements of the outcome of interest to determine a pattern that can be extrapolated in the future, and those that make predictions based on the examination of relationships between a set of factors and an outcome of interest that the factors are believed to influence. For the latter, there is a close relationship between predictive analytics and diagnostic analytics. Specifically, the relationships identified using diagnostic analytics can be used to predict how, as different marketing-relevant factors are expected to change over time, their influence on a marketing outcome leads to changes in that outcome over time.[35]

Consider as an example a car dealership that has identified through diagnostic analytics that a customer's exposure to different elements of the dealership's marketing mix (the marketing-relevant factors in this case) is associated with different probabilities of the customer actually coming into the dealership for a test drive (which most of us know really amps up the likelihood that a car is going to be purchased). Elements of the marketing mix in this example could include exposure to advertising (for the model of interest), viewing specific pages on the dealership's website (especially the product page for the model of interest), and an online chat with a customer service representative through that website. As the customer is exposed to each of these elements, his or her probability of making a purchase would be expected to increase incrementally, and this can be captured through predictive analytics. Now consider that another element that has a significant impact on the probability of a customer coming into the dealership is the offering of free floor mats with any purchased model, but this offer only has a significant impact if a customer's probability of coming into the dealership is above 50 percent at the point that the offer is made; otherwise the offer has a negligible effect. Using predictive analytics, the point at which the floor mat offer should be made can be determined by calculating the customer's current probability of coming into the dealership and providing the offer only after the threshold of 50 percent is met. Pretty sophisticated, isn't it?

The value of predictive analytics stems from its ability to help provide greater clarity into the impact that changes that are expected to occur in different marketing-relevant factors may have on related marketing outcomes. Importantly, a predictive approach can be applied on a wide continuum anywhere between the macro level for the prediction of market level outcomes, such as the effect on market share that will be observed based on expected spending allocations for the marketing mix, and the micro level for predicting customer-level responses, such as the probability that a customer will make a purchase and the effect that an expected level of exposure to one or more specific elements of the marketing mix will have on that probability (as illustrated in the example above). American Express looks at specific indicators within its data that have been identified as key to predicting loyalty, and through predictive analytics zeros in on accounts that are likely to churn within a short time period. This enables the marketing team to reach out to these at-risk customers proactively and mitigate churn, resulting in a noticeable impact on the organization's bottom line.[36]

Prescriptive Analytics An approach using **prescriptive analytics** involves determining the optimal level of marketing-relevant factors for a specific context by considering how adjusting their levels in varying ways will impact different marketing outcomes.[37] For instance, prescriptive analytics can be used to look at how adjusting the level of spending on different marketing communication channels (such as print ads, television commercials, online video ads, online banner ads, and social media ads) will impact one or more marketing outcomes related to marketing communications spending (key outcomes might be total sales of products or services, or changes in market share). Prescriptive analytics is the most advanced of the marketing analytics approaches (and the most costly), because it draws on the results and insights derived from the other three approaches to provide a framework for making specific (and in many cases quantifiable) marketing management decisions. In another sense, prescriptive analytics allows marketing managers to engage in questions of "what if we do this, or what if we do that" to assess the relative value of those decisions. The "what if" questions generally would be derived from the observation of results stemming from the use of the other analytic approaches. The ability to look at multiple possible scenarios using this approach enables marketing managers to more carefully consider how to most effectively allocate resources and prepare for potential risks that may arise in the future related to actions by competitors and other external factors that could have an impact on different critical marketing outcomes.

EXHIBIT 5.5 | Examples of Types of Marketing Analytics and Related Applications

Types of Marketing Analytics	Description	Examples of Relevant Data	Examples of Specific Applications
Web Analytics	Analysis of data produced through the different actions taken by consumers while using the Internet.	• Referral source (such as search engine, website, email) • Website page views	Data on the referral source that lead a customer to a website can be analyzed to see which sources bring in the most traffic and which sources bring in the highest value traffic (in the case of an online retailer, those sources that yield the visitors who spend the most on average).
Social Media Analytics	Analysis of data produced through the usage of social media platforms by consumers.	• Likes for posts • Shares of posts	Data on the pattern of shares that an organization's posts have received can be analyzed to understand what factors and characteristics related to a post (such as topic, tone, timing, audience targeted) have the greatest impact on a given post's propensity to be shared.
CRM Analytics	Analysis of data collected within CRM systems.	• Customer demographics • Dates of interactions with sales and service employees	Customer demographic data and data on customer interactions with sales and customer service employees can be used to identify those demographic characteristics of a given customer that suggest a higher level of service and thus more expense investment is required to maintain the customer relationship.
Retail Analytics (In-store)	Analysis of data collected via the in-store retail environment as well as data produced as a result of in-store consumer purchases.	• Products sold • In-store marketing mix	Data collected on the products sold by a retailer in-store combined with data from the retailer's customer loyalty program (which among other things enables individual transactions to be associated with a specific customer) can be used to develop customized promotions that can increase the share of a customer's wallet an organization is able to capture.

Capabilities of Marketing Analytics Supported by Big Data

Marketing analytics that leverage Big Data provide significant capabilities for organizations in the form of deep customer insights that can be achieved. Advances in technology have made it easier than ever to deliver dynamic and personalized experiences to customers at lower costs, and to adjust investments in the marketing mix as deemed appropriate. Many believe that today is the best time ever to be a marketing manager due to the capabilities available for better decision making and strategy execution. Exhibit 5.5 provides a variety of examples of types of marketing analytics and related marketing management applications. Below, we consider two specific capabilities that result from Big Data and applied marketing analytics in more detail: marketing mix enhancement and increased personalization of products, services, and customer experiences.

Marketing Mix Enhancement Optimizing the marketing mix (the 4Ps) is largely dependent on the ability to understand the different effects that the mix elements (and different levels of those elements) have on different marketing outcomes. Big Data has enhanced this capability by providing customer-level data in quantities that were not available in the past from sources that provide insights into specific aspects of a customer's experience with a product or service that heretofore were not easily measured. For example, the experience of a customer attending a theme park is easier to gather data on today than it has been in the past, thanks to the widespread use of social media. Messages that customers post on one or more social media platforms while at a theme park serve as a valuable source of information about their experiences, as well as what may be working well and not so well within the park. The practical challenge associated with this example is that such insights might be contained within unstructured data. Advances in marketing analytics have made it more feasible to maximize the value of unstructured data using methods such as **sentiment analysis,** a type of analytic method that identifies the general attitude (for example, positive, negative, or

Major theme parks such as Universal Orlando use data from patrons to gain rich insight into which aspects of the customer experience add or detract from customer satisfaction and repeat purchase.

©Kamira/Shutterstock

neutral) contained within a message through an analysis of its content. Thus, the identified attitude is the structured data extracted from the unstructured data that can be used in subsequent analyses. Capturing the attitude within a given message as well as any references to a specific part of the theme park or ride within the park that are contained within the related message (as structured data) can provide richer insight into how particular aspects of a customer's experience within the park are adding to or detracting from overall customer satisfaction and likelihood to be a repeat customer. The more data that can be collected related to a customer's exposure to the various elements of the marketing mix, the more possible it is to determine the different effects of those elements (individually and in combinations) on specific important organizational outcomes.

A key consideration that arises when assessing the impact of the marketing mix is **attribution,** which can be thought of as determining how to give appropriate credit to different elements of the marketing mix through the measurement of their effects. In the digital context, it is generally straightforward to tie exposure to marketing mix elements online to a desired outcome (for example, clicking the purchase button). With this data alone it might be possible to estimate, in a quantifiable sense, the impact that different online elements of the marketing mix have on the desired outcome, but with some caveats. Consider the case where a marketing manager believes that there are elements of the marketing mix that the customer is exposed to offline that have a substantial effect on the decision to make a purchase online. For example, note that it has been demonstrated for some products that exposure to television advertisements influences the number of brand-specific keyword searches conducted online by customers.[38] Presumably, some proportion of these keyword searches would lead to online purchases. Without accounting for this influence of the television advertisements, a marketing manager's efforts at improving the value of their search engine results and search engine advertising could be given too much credit for the resulting outcome (clicking the purchase button). An important takeaway is that as long as the organization has access to the required data on marketing mix elements, marketing analytics should be able to help disentangle the various effects that both *individual elements* of the marketing mix and *specific combinations* of those elements have on marketing outcomes.

Increased Personalization The ability to effectively provide more personalized products, services, and customer experiences (for convenience we'll refer to this trio as "offerings") to customers is dependent on understanding the characteristics of different customers and what types of offerings customers value the most. One of the most prominent applications of personalization using marketing analytics is the recommendation systems that many electronic retailers and digital content providers employ. Recommendation systems can be divided into content filtering, collaborative filtering, and hybrid methods.[39] **Content filtering** is an analytic method that identifies which products or services to recommend based on a determination of how similar a product or service seems to be to those that the customer has demonstrated a preference for in the past, or is currently considering. Such an approach is dependent on products or services being assigned different characteristics stored as data that can be used to quantitatively determine the degree of similarity between any two products or services in a way that enables relative comparisons between different pairs. **Collaborative filtering** predicts a customer's preferences for products or services based on the observed preferences of customers who are perceived to be similar. Determining which customers are similar is generally based on the analysis of data related to each customer's behaviors and preferences on the related website. Netflix uses its data and marketing analytics capabilities to develop personalized home page video recommendations for its users. Through advanced analytics, including machine learning techniques, the organization can determine which videos to recommend and how to group them to enable users to understand what they have in common and potentially why they are being recommended. This approach allows Netflix to determine how to best maximize the limited space on the home page (and the attention span of users). Providing users with relevant content recommendations in an efficient manner is key to keeping users happy and engaged.[40]

Personalization can be achieved at three possible levels of granularity, as illustrated in Exhibit 5.6: mass personalization, where everyone receives the same offering; segment-level

EXHIBIT 5.6	Levels of Granularity of Personalization Achievable with Marketing Analytics

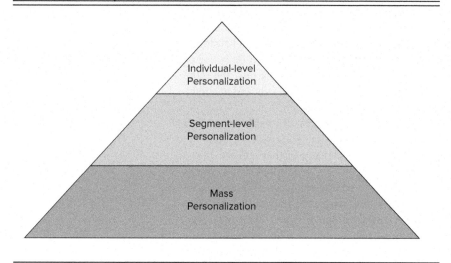

personalization, in which groups of customers with similar preferences are identified and an offering is developed for each segment; and individual-level personalization, in which each customer receives an offering customized to his or her specific tastes. It is often sensible to set the level of granularity of personalization for an element of the offering based on a consideration of the costs and benefits.[41] Consider, as an example, how an automobile company might manufacture specific cars for different segments of a market, but customize its sales efforts and product pricing for individual customers via an empowered salesforce. Data at the customer level makes personalization at each level of granularity feasible.

THE MARKETING DASHBOARD

LO 5-6

Understand the concept of a marketing dashboard and how it improves marketing planning for a firm.

Consider how the dashboard of a car, airplane, or even a video game provides you with a lot of crucial information in real time and in a convenient format. So it should be with a **marketing dashboard**, which is a comprehensive system providing managers with up-to-the-minute information necessary to run their operation including data on actual sales versus forecast, progress on marketing plan objectives, distribution channel effectiveness, sales force productivity, brand equity evolution, and whatever metrics and information are uniquely relevant to the role of the marketing manager in a particular organization.[42] Clearly, a dashboard metaphor for this process of capturing, shaping, and improving marketing effectiveness and efficiency is a good one.[43]

How does a marketing dashboard manifest itself? It could appear in your inbox weekly or monthly in the form of a color printout, be beamed through cyberspace as an e-mail update, or be accessible on a password-protected website on your company intranet. Its physical form and layout should be developed within your organization *by* managers *for* managers. Search the Internet for "Marketing Dashboards" and you will be amazed at how many consulting firms come up, each working hard to convince you that its proprietary approach to a marketing dashboard is the right one for you. To successfully compete in today's market, firms must focus on marketing planning so that managers and executives have the core information about progress toward relevant goals and metrics at their fingertips *at all times.* This is what a dashboard approach delivers.

A marketing dashboard approach to enhance marketing planning delivers several key benefits summarized below.

- Aligns marketing objectives, financial objectives, and firm strategy based on the selected dashboard metrics.
- Enhances alignment within the marketing function and also clarifies marketing's relationships with other organizational functions. Cross-functional alignment contributes greatly to a shared spirit for organizational success.
- Portrays data in a user-friendly manner. Creates a direct, understandable link between marketing initiatives and financial results.
- Fosters a learning organization that values fact-based, logical decision making about allocation of marketing resources to achieve desired organizational results.
- Creates organizational transparency about marketing's goals, operations, and performance, increasing marketing's credibility and trust by organizational leadership and other areas of the firm.[44]

Goals and Elements of a Marketing Dashboard

An effective dashboard is organic, not static. The dashboard must adapt and change with the organization as objectives are clarified and redefined, as causal relationships are established between metrics and results, and as confidence in predictive measures grows. About the only thing you know for certain about your first version of a marketing dashboard is that it will likely look very different in a year or two.

Two primary goals of any dashboard are diagnostic insight and predictive foresight—with a special emphasis on the latter. Some dashboard metrics are diagnostic, looking at what has happened and trying to discern why. Probably the most important metrics you'll come to rely on, however, are predictive, using the diagnostic experience to better forecast results under various assumptions about circumstances and resource allocations.[45]

A great marketing dashboard is comprised of the following key elements:

- Company goals translated into a set of marketing objectives.
- Measurement of financial impact of marketing programs.
- Tracking of how marketing assets such as the brand and customer relationships are progressing.
- Execution of skills and competencies of the marketing team.
- Execution of other business processes necessary to deliver customer value.
- Continuous refinement of tools to increase access to and usability of customer insights.
- Insight on not only what is happening in the market but also why it is happening.
- A diagnostic for prediction, forecasting, and of course remediation.
- Ultimately, enhanced return on marketing investment (ROMI).[46]

Potential Pitfalls in Marketing Dashboards

Although taking a dashboard approach to marketing metrics goes a long way toward enabling successful marketing planning, several potential pitfalls exist in its execution, including the following:

- *Overreliance on "inside-out" measurement.* Having too many internal measures puts the focus on what you already know instead of on the unpredictably dynamic external marketplace. A focus on monitoring external factors likely to cause significant changes to the marketing plan is what makes a dashboard especially valuable.

- *Too many tactical metrics; not enough strategic insight.* Because of the focus over the past decade on holding marketing accountable for financial results, tactical, or "intermediary," metrics have proliferated. Numerous books and articles provide list after list of calculations and ratios to assess all sorts of marketing programmatic results (brand awareness, customer trial, lead conversion, etc.). Although these are valuable and having the right set of intermediary metrics on the dashboard is important, it is critical that they do not overshadow measures of strategic importance to the firm.

- *Forgetting to market the dashboard internally.* One measure of the success of a marketing dashboard is the level at which it is embraced and *used* by managers and executives throughout the firm. As we've emphasized consistently, marketing is not just a department, but rather a part of the strategic and cultural fabric of the enterprise. As such, it is important to market the dashboard internally to key stakeholders, not just to marketers. You want the percentage of senior executives who both believe in and understand what the dashboard is presenting to be very high. Obviously, the CEO should be a target for internal marketing, but just as important is your CFO. The greater the affinity a CFO has for marketing, and especially for marketing as a contributor to the firm's long-term success, the better.[47]

RETURN ON MARKETING INVESTMENT (ROMI)

LO 5-7

Explain return on marketing investment (ROMI), including cautions about its use.

CEOs today expect to know exactly what impact an investment in marketing has on a firm's success, especially financially. Hence, it has become critical to consider **return on marketing investment (ROMI).**[*] Throughout this book we have focused on marketing as an *investment,* not as an expense, because a goal-driven investment approach to marketing maximizes the opportunity for a firm's offerings to reach their full potential in the marketplace. The alternative viewpoint—approaching marketing as an expense tied to a percentage of historical or forecasted sales—both limits market opportunities and thwarts the ability to meaningfully plan for and measure marketing results.[48]

Similar to other investment decisions, investment decisions in marketing must consider four basic elements:

- Level of investment.
- Returns.
- Risks.
- Hurdle rates.

As with any investment, the projected results (returns minus costs) must exceed a certain investment hurdle rate for a given level of risk (both defined by the firm). Hence, ROMI represents either the revenue or the margin generated by a marketing program divided by the cost of that program at a given risk level. The ROMI hurdle rate is defined as the minimum acceptable, expected return on a program at a given level of risk. Consider an example of a relatively low-risk marketing program with costs of $1 million and new revenue generated of $5 million. This program has a ROMI of 5.0. If the company has a marketing budget of $5 million and needs to generate $20 million in revenue, then the ROMI hurdle rate for any low-risk marketing program is 4.0. This means that any marketing program must generate at a minimum $4.00 in revenue for every $1.00 in marketing expenditure. The example ROMI of 5.0 above surpasses the ROMI hurdle rate and is therefore an acceptable marketing program.[49]

Companies have to set their own hurdle rates based on differing levels of potential risk across marketing programs. Risk also tends to vary quite a bit by industry and by whether the marketing plan involves a start-up or an established product line. At its core, ROMI is a tool to help yield more out of marketing. This tool and the way of thinking promoted by the use of the tool within an organization will help marketing managers better conceptualize and execute marketing plans and programs. It puts them in a much better position to connect their planning, measurement, and results to the firm's goals and expectations and, when successful, provides gravitas for the CMO to go back to the CEO for more investment money for marketing.

Cautions about Overreliance on ROMI

Given the above, it's no wonder that ROMI is the *metric du jour* for many firms' marketing bottom line. Several offshoots of ROMI have been developed that apply the same principles to customers (ROCI), brands (ROBI), and promotion (ROPI).[50] Overall, the trend in boardrooms and executive suites of expecting more quantification of marketing's contributions has been a positive one. But remember that within the marketing dashboard concept, what organizations should be reviewing is an *array of relevant metrics,* selected for inclusion on the dashboard because together they paint a picture of firm performance. Managers should always temper the interpretation of ROMI results with review of other appropriate metrics.

In addition, it is important to remember that ROMI was originally designed for comparing capital projects, where investments are made once and the returns flow in during the periods that follow. In marketing, capital projects are analogous to discrete marketing

---

[*]One of the single best sources for understanding ROMI is the following book, which is highly recommended for marketing managers: Guy R. Powell, *Return on Marketing Investment: Demand More from Your Marketing and Sales Investments,* Albuquerque, NM: RBI Press, 2002. The ideas in this section are drawn from that source.

programs or campaigns that have well-defined goals and clear points of beginning and end. However, in practice, ROMI is often applied in situations that have no clear beginning or end. Here are six other commonly expressed objections about an overreliance on ROMI:

1. While a firm may "talk the talk" of marketing as an investment, not an expense, typically marketing expenditures are not treated as an investment in a company's accounting system.

2. ROMI requires the profit to be divided by expenditure, yet all other bottom-line performance measures consider profit or cash flow *after* deducting expenditures.

3. The truth is, ROMI is maximized during the period when profits are still growing. Pursuit of ROMI during flat periods can be viewed as "causing" underperformance and suboptimal levels of activity; thus firms tend to reduce marketing reinvestment at that time in an attempt to maximize profits and cash flow. The result is a self-fulfilling prophecy of downward performance.

4. Calculating ROMI requires knowing what would have happened if the incremental expenditure hadn't occurred. Few marketers have those figures or can conjure up something meaningful to replace them.

5. ROMI has become a fashionable surrogate for "marketing productivity" in executive suites and boardrooms, yet there is mounting evidence that firms interpret the appropriate calculation of ROMI quite differently. When executives discuss ROMI with different metrics in mind, confusion results and the value of the metric degrades.

6. ROMI by nature ignores the effect of the marketing assets of the firm (for example, its brands) and tends to lead managers toward a more short-term decision perspective. That is, it typically considers only short-term incremental profits and expenditures without looking at longer-term effects or any change in brand equity.[51]

Proceed with Caution

The expectation is that ROMI and other metrics of marketing performance will continue to proliferate, as firms home in on attempting to better quantify marketing's contribution to various dimensions of organizational success. Marketing managers should embrace the opportunity to quantify their contributions, and by taking a more holistic dashboard approach to goal-driven measurement, the potential downsides to focusing on one or a few metrics are largely mitigated.

In the end, marketing management is both a science and an art. The scientific side craves quantification and relishes the ability to provide numeric evidence of success to superiors in a firm and to stockholders. But the artistic side understands that sometimes the difference between an average new-product introduction and a world-class one rests largely on creativity, insight, and the good fortune to have a great idea that is hitting the market at just the right time.

An interesting question, given the current focus in business toward sustainability and socially responsible business practices, is how would metrics related to such aspects (say, for example, ROSI, or return on social investment) operate in tandem with other more traditional performance measures? Firms such as the venerable H. J. Heinz Company have drawn a line in the sand that establishes a balance between traditional performance metrics such as ROMI and broadly beneficial metrics such as ROSI.

H. J. Heinz Company takes ROSI (return on social investment) seriously with their "plant bottle" that is fully recyclable and up to 30 percent made from plants—at no additional cost to ketchup lovers!

Source: The Kraft Heinz Company

SUMMARY

Customer relationship management (CRM) is a comprehensive business model for increasing revenues and profits by focusing on customers. CRM works effectively by focusing on acquisition and retention of profitable customers, thus enhancing customer satisfaction and loyalty. Successful CRM runs on information acquired through various customer touchpoints such as a salesperson, customer care representative, or website. Importantly, CRM facilitates a customer-centric culture, and it is critical that all organization members exhibit a customer mind-set as they approach their jobs.

Big Data can be characterized by the four "Vs": volume, variety, velocity, and veracity (and for many managers, a fifth "V," value). Valuable customer-related data is generated through a wide range of sources, both internal and external to the organization, with a wide range of potential uses for marketing managers. Big Data can be generated from a variety of sources in the more readily analyzed form of structured data as well as the less readily analyzed form of unstructured data (and in some cases in a semi-structured form falling in between).

Marketing analytics play a critical role in extracting value from Big Data. Four key types of marketing analytics in order of increasing complexity are descriptive analytics, diagnostic analytics, predictive analytics, and prescriptive analytics. Generally, more complex approaches come with a higher cost. For marketing managers, effective use of marketing analytics yields important customer insights as well as marketing performance indicators. Marketing dashboards offer a comprehensive approach to providing marketing managers relevant, timely, and accurate information in a convenient format for use in decision making. Metrics play an important role for marketers in assessing the relative performance of various marketing investments. One particular metric, return on marketing investment (ROMI), frames marketing's contribution in financial terms, thus conveying both the potential and realized value of a given marketing effort to a broader organizational audience and promoting greater accountability.

KEY TERMS

APPLICATION QUESTIONS

More application questions are available online.

1. Consider each of the brands below. Assuming that a strong CRM system is in place in each brand's parent firm, what specific actions can marketing managers take in each case to ensure high satisfaction and loyalty among the most profitable customers?

   a. Aeropostale

   b. Wynn Las Vegas

   c. Your own college or university

   d. Subaru automobiles

   e. GE home appliances

2. Consider the CRM process cycle of knowledge discovery, market planning, customer interaction, and analysis and refinement. Pick a company of interest to you and identify one of its important brands or product lines (it can be a good or a service). Chart what you believe the CRM process cycle should be for that firm, paying particular attention to identifying the relevant customer touchpoints. Be as specific as you can in describing each of the cycle elements.

3. In the chapter you read about several Big Data sources. For each Big Data source listed below, identify an organization that you believe uses (or could use) that data source and then briefly describe how you believe the organization currently uses (or could use) data from each source to answer a specific marketing question or make a marketing-related decision (questions and decisions you identify can be different for each data source).

   a. Business systems

   b. Social media platforms

   c. Customers' Internet-connected devices

   d. Mobile applications

   e. Commercial entities

   f. Government agencies

4. Select an organization that employs a highly personalized approach to selling products or services to its customers online. Ideally, this is one that you have used in the past so that you are more familiar with it.

   a. What are some different ways that the selected organization employs personalization in its marketing efforts?

   b. What are some specific actions/behaviors that customers engage in on the organization's website that enable personalized marketing efforts you identified above?

   c. What are some specific actions/behaviors that an organization could collect data on that might provide evidence that the personalization efforts identified above have had a positive effect? Which type of marketing analytics approach(es) discussed in this chapter would be best suited for establishing the value of personalization for the organization?

5. Pick a firm that interests you and for which you have some knowledge of its offerings.

   a. How would this firm benefit from a marketing dashboard approach?

   b. What elements would you recommend it put onto its dashboard? Why do you recommend the ones you do?

   c. How could the firm avoid some of the pitfalls potentially associated with marketing dashboards?

MANAGEMENT DECISION CASE
Outline India: Enabling the Jump from Data to Decisions

In more developed countries, having access to market data that is both high in quality and high in quantity is a given. High ownership rates of smartphones, tablets, and laptops, along with high rates of Internet connectivity, make it easy to gather data from people anywhere in the country. But most of the world is not so developed! Hence, a key question is how can you apply modern marketing analytic methods to make informed choices in countries where it's a lot harder to gather data? A firm called Outline India is working hard to successfully answer that question. But before we can understand why Outline India's work is so important, let's delve into how more developed countries collect data.

In the United States, commercial data vendors of many types provide demographic, behavioral, and attitudinal data on consumers. In addition, the governments of the United States and many European countries fund research that involves data gathering, intended to aid government agencies and officials in making better-informed decisions, and with results made available publicly at little or no cost. A prime example of this type of data gathering is the U.S. census, which is updated annually through sample-based surveys and statistical extrapolation of trends, and once every decade door-to-door data gathering from every person in the United States is completed. The data gathered on U.S. citizens as part of the census helps establish a factual basis on which estimates are made and by which policy decisions are informed. (As an aside, it has been demonstrated empirically that taking a statistical sample would be more accurate than attempting a full census, but that's another story.)

This works well for a country like the United States, which has many resources at its disposal. But let's go back to the question we asked in the first paragraph: How can we apply marketing analytic methods when a country struggles to collect valuable data? Consider India. More than 1.3 billion people populate the country, but only 35 percent have Internet access, and in some rural areas only 25 to 35 percent have electricity.[52] This makes data gathering difficult, and the data that does come in tends to be biased toward urban areas. This is where Outline India comes in.

Started in 2012 and based outside New Delhi, Outline India trains locals to gather and record key data elements sought by Outline India's clients. So far, its grassroots effort has been successful. Data have been gathered from more than 2,300 villages to help commercial and governmental clients answer pressing questions about the needs of Indian consumers and constituents. For example, if your company's marketing objective is to identify locales in India that have a need for solar water pumps, you'd call Outline India. Outline India works in rural areas to improve data gathering, so firms that support corporate social responsibility (like H&M, through its Conscious Foundation), start-ups and commercial businesses, and government agencies can get the analytical results they need to make informed decisions.[53]

Outline India's founder, Prerna Mukharya, learned how to extract value from raw data at Boston University, where she earned her postgraduate degree, and through research done at the Centre for Policy Research in Delhi. Mukharya says data have always been a useful and valuable tool for combating poverty, gender gaps, child labor, and other social issues in India, and one of Outline India's goals is to help clients apply data through the use of more advanced analyses.[54] In addition to gathering data, Outline India performs descriptive and predictive analyses on the data it gathers, and then communicates the analyzed results directly to its clients. The data are also often made available to nonprofit organizations.

Thus far, Outline India has built a team of 250 surveyors, with an ability to reach 1 million individuals. But while the reach is impressive for a company that is essentially a start-up, and the data it has collected so far has proven to be useful, Outline India still faces challenges. Outline India certainly helps provide a greater *quantity* of data, but due to the size of India's population it still covers only one-tenth of 1 percent of the country's population. Data *quality*—how accurate and complete the data it gathers are—is another important issue. To address this, Outline India not only trains locals on how to gather data but also qualifies them through testing—individuals must undergo different levels of professional examination depending on the complexity of the data they will be handling, and thus are proven to be proficient.[55]

Outline India faces further barriers to gathering more and different types of data, barriers that are pertinent to any marketer entering a developing country. One of the main communication channels in rural India is cellular, and although *basic* cell-phone use is very high in India (upwards of 77 percent), smartphone usage—which would allow more sophisticated data gathering apps—is relatively low, at about 12 percent.[56] While basic cell phone usage creates an effective "last mile" connection to consumers (and potential data touchpoints), it limits data gatherers to very simple tools and makes it difficult to communicate large amounts of data, due to a lack of reliable high-bandwidth connections. Furthermore, large, unstructured data—such as aerial images showing village infrastructure—requires the most sophisticated smartphones or laptops to capture and deliver data.

Fortunately, though, these communication challenges may soon ease up. Boston Consulting Group projects that rural smartphone ownership in India will grow 2.6 times by 2020, resulting in 315 million rural Indians gaining the ability to communicate their needs to marketers and companies like Outline India.[57] In the end, no matter what obstacles it faces, Outline India strives to provide a large quantity of high-quality field data to help inform the decisions of policymakers and companies, which will ultimately continue to positively impact the population of India. Outline India's end goal is to use data gathering and data analysis to improve the lives of many rural Indians.

Questions for Consideration

1. What general and specific types of market data would you need to perform an analysis of the Indian market? Which of these data might be less available in a developing country?

2. If you were faced with the problem Outline India faces—trying to gather not only a large amount of data, but making sure that data is of high quality—how might you go about helping to ensure that the data are accurate and complete?

3. What are some non-technological barriers Outline India may face when trying to gather data in the field?

MARKETING PLAN EXERCISES

ACTIVITY 4: Plan for a CRM System

In this chapter, you learned about the value of CRM in fostering a customer-centric culture and establishing a relationship-based enterprise. At this point in the development of your marketing plan, the following steps are needed:

1. Establish the objectives of your CRM system with regard to customer acquisition, customer retention, and customer profitability. Pay particular attention to driving high customer satisfaction and loyalty among profitable customers.

2. Map out the CRM process cycle you will employ in your business. Identify all the relevant touchpoints you plan to utilize—both interactive and noninteractive.

3. Prepare a set of guidelines on the ethical handling of customer data, with a focus on avoiding misuse and theft.

4. Consider the reasons for CRM failure identified in the chapter. Develop an approach to ensure that each can be avoided in your firm.

NOTES

1. Ronald S. Swift, *Accelerating Customer Relationships: Using CRM and Relationship Technologies* (Upper Saddle River, NJ: Prentice Hall PTR, 2001).

2. Stephen F. King and Thomas F. Burgess, "Understanding Success and Failure in Customer Relationship Management," *Industrial Marketing Management* 37, no. 4 (June 2008), pp. 421–31.

3. Stanley A. Brown, ed., *Customer Relationship Management: A Strategic Imperative in the World of E-Business* (Toronto: Wiley Canada, 2000), pp. 8–9.

4. Anders Gustafsson, Michael D. Johnson, and Inger Roos, "The Effects of Customer Satisfaction, Relationship Commitment Dimensions, and Triggers on Customer Retention," *Journal of Marketing* 69, no. 4 (October 2005), pp. 210–18.

5. Mohanbir Sawhney and Jeff Zabin, "Managing and Measuring Relational Equity in the Network Economy," *Journal of the Academy of Marketing Science* 30, no. 4 (Fall 2002), pp. 313–33.

6. Frederick F. Reichheld, *Loyalty Rules! How Leaders Build Lasting Relationships in the Digital Age* (Cambridge, MA: Harvard Business School Press, 2001).

7. Timothy W. Aurand, Linda Gorchels, and Terrence R. Bishop, "Human Resource Management's Role in Internal Branding: An Opportunity for Cross-Functional Brand Messaging Synergy," *Journal of Product and Brand Management* 14, no. 2/3 (2005), pp. 163–70; and Scott Davis, "Marketers Challenged to Respond to Changing Nature of Brand Building," *Journal of Advertising Research* 45, no. 2 (June 2005), pp. 198–200.

8. Sawhney and Zabin, "Managing and Measuring Relational Equity."

9. Werner Reinartz, Jacquelyn S. Thomas, and V. Kumar, "Balancing Acquisition and Retention Resources to Maximize Customer Profitability," *Journal of Marketing* 69, no. 1 (January 2005), pp. 63–79.

10. Nicole E. Coviello, Roderick J. Brodie, Peter J. Danaher, and Wesley J. Johnston, "How Firms Relate to Their Markets: An Empirical Examination of Contemporary Marketing Practices," *Journal of Marketing* 66, no. 3 (July 2002), pp. 33–47.

11. Peter C. Verhoef, "Understanding the Effect of Customer Relationship Management Efforts on Customer Retention and Customer Share Development," *Journal of Marketing* 67, no. 4 (October 2003), pp. 30–45.

12. Neil A. Morgan, Eugene W. Anderson, and Vikas Mittal, "Understanding Firm's Customer Satisfaction Information Usage," *Journal of Marketing* 69, no. 3 (July 2005), pp. 131–51.

13. James E. Richard, Peter C. Thirkell, and Sid L. Huff, "An Examination of Customer Relationship Management (CRM) Technology Adoption and Its Impact on Business-to-Business Customer Relationships," *Total Quality Management & Business Excellence* 18, no. 8 (October 2007), pp. 927–45.

14. Bob Lewis, "The Customer Is Wrong," *InfoWorld* 24, no. 2 (January 14, 2002), pp. 40–41.

15. Avinandan Mukherjee and Prithwiraj Nath, "Role of Electronic Trust in Online Retailing: A Re-Examination of the Commitment-Trust Theory," *European Journal of Marketing* 41, no. 9/10, pp. 1173–1202.

16. Natalie Zmuda, "Target's CMO Navigates Marketing Post-Security Breach," *Advertising Age*, March 10, 2014, http://adage.com/article/news/target-s-cmo-navigates -marketing-post-security-breach/292032/.

17. George Day, "Capabilities for Forging Customer Relationships," *MSI Report* #00–118 (Cambridge, MA: Marketing Science Institute, 2000).

18. Patricia Kilgore, "Personalization Provides a Winning Hand for Borgata," *Printing News,* December 11, 2006, pp. 7–8.

19. Karen Norman Kennedy, Felicia G. Lassk, and Jerry R. Goolsby, "Customer Mind-Set of Employees throughout the Organization," *Journal of the Academy of Marketing Science* 30 (Spring 2002), pp. 159–71.

20. New York City Mayor's Office of Tech and Innovation, "INYC DOT Announces Expansion of Midtown Congestion Management System, Receives National Transportation Award," June 5, 2012, http://www.nyc.gov/html/dot/html/pr2012 /pr12_25.shtml.

21. Michel Wedel and P. K. Kannan, "Marketing Analytics for Data-Rich Environments," *Journal of Marketing* 80, no. 6, pp. 97–121.

22. Amir Gandomi and Murtaza Haider, "Beyond the Hype: Big Data Concepts, Methods, and Analytics," *International Journal of Information Management* 35, no. 2, pp. 137–44.

23. Jaikumar Vijayan, "Solving the Unstructured Data Challenge," June 25, 2015, http://www.cio.com/article/2941015/big-data/ solving-the-unstructured-data-challenge.html;andDarinStewart, "Big Content: The Unstructured Side of Big Data," May 1, 2013, http://blogs.gartner.com/darin-stewart/2013/05/01/big -content-the-unstructured-side-of-big-data/.

24. Alexandros Labrinidis and H. V. Jagadish, "Challenges and Opportunities with Big Data," *Proceedings of the VLDB Endowment* 51, no. 12, pp. 2032–33.

25. Gandomi and Haider, "Beyond the Hype."

26. Lisa Morgan, "Big Data: 6 Real-Life Business Cases," May 27, 2015, *Information Week,* http://www.informationweek. com/software/enterprise-applications/big-data-6-real-life -business-cases/d/d-id/1320590?image_number=5.

27. Alan L. Montgomery, Shibo Li, Kannan Srinivasan, and John C. Liechty, "Modeling Online Browsing and Path Analysis Using Clickstream Data," *Marketing Science* 23, no. 4, pp. 579–95.

28. V. Kumar and Rohan Mirchandani, "Increasing the ROI of Social Media Marketing," *MIT Sloan Management Review* 54, no. 1, pp. 55–61.

29. "Nielsen Datasets," https://research.chicagobooth.edu/nielsen /datasets#simple1.

30. Jason Shueh, "Open Data: What Is It and Why Should You Care?" March 17, 2014, *Government Technology,* http:// www.govtech.com/data/Got-Data-Make-it-Open-Data-with -These-Tips.html.

31. "Jenny," "3 Ways You Can Use Census Data," *MacKenzie Corporation,* October 23, 2013, http://www.mackenziecorp .com/3-ways-you-can-use-census-data-2/.

32. Gary Lilien, "Bridging the Academic-Practitioner Divide in Marketing Decision Models," *Journal of Marketing* 75, no. 4, pp. 211–24.

33. Wedel and Kannan, "Marketing Analytics for Data-Rich Environments."

34. Wedel and Kannan, "Marketing Analytics for Data-Rich Environments."

35. Joe F. Hair Jr., "Knowledge Creation in Marketing: The Role of Predictive Analytics," *European Business Review* 19, no. 4, pp. 303–15.

36. Nadia Cameron, "How Predictive Analytics Is Tackling Customer Attrition at American Express," April 11, 2013, http://www.cmo.com.au/article/458724/how_predictive _analytics_tackling_customer_attrition_american_express/.

37. Wedel and Kannan, "Marketing Analytics for Data-Rich Environments."

38. Mingyu Joo, Kenneth C. Wilbur, Bo Cowgill, and Yi Zhu, "Television Advertising and Online Search," *Management Science* 60, no. 1, pp. 56–73.

39. Wedel and Kannan, "Marketing Analytics for Data-Rich Environments."

40. Chris Alvino and Justin Basilico, "Learning a Personalized Homepage," April 9, 2015, http://techblog.netflix .com/2015/04/learning-personalized-homepage.html.

41. Wedel and Kannan, "Marketing Analytics for Data-Rich Environments."

42. A number of concepts in this section are derived from the following outstanding book, which is the best single source for understanding marketing dashboards. It is highly recommended as a guidebook on the topic for marketing managers: Patrick LaPointe, *Marketing by the Dashboard Light: How to Get More Insight, Foresight, and Accountability from Your Marketing Investments* (New York: ANA, 2005).

43. Gail J. McGovern, David Court, John A. Quelch, and Blair Crawford, "Bringing Customers into the Boardroom," *Harvard Business Review* 82, no. 11 (November 2004), pp. 70–80.

44. Patrick LaPointe, *Marketing by the Dashboard Light: How to Get More Insight, Foresight, and Accountability from Your Marketing Investments* (New York: ANA, 2005).

45. Thorsten Wiesel, Bernd Skiera, and Julián Villanueva, "Customer Equity: An Integral Part of Financial Reporting," *Journal of Marketing* 72, no. 2 (March 2008), pp. 1–14.

46. LaPointe, *Marketing by the Dashboard Light.*

47. Leigh McAlister, Raji Srinivasan, and MinChung Kim, "Advertising, Research, and Development, and Systematic Risk of the Firm," *Journal of Marketing* 71, no. 1 (January 2007), pp. 35–49.

48. Claes Fornell, Sunil Mithas, Forrest V. Morgeson III, and M. S. Krishnan, "Customer Satisfaction and Stock Prices: High Returns, Low Risk," *Journal of Marketing* 70, no. 1 (January 2006), pp. 3–14; and Roland T. Rust, Katherine Lemon, and Valarie A. Zeithaml, "Return on Marketing: Using Customer Equity to Focus Marketing Strategy," *Journal of Marketing* 68, no. 1 (January 2004), pp. 109–27.

49. Behram Hansotia and Brad Rukstales, "Incremental Value Modeling," *Journal of Interactive Marketing* 16, no. 3 (Summer 2002), pp. 35–46.

50. Dominique M. Hanssens, Daniel Thorpe, and Carl Finkbeiner, "Marketing When Customer Equity Matters," *Harvard Business Review* 86, no. 5 (May 2008), p. 117; and Rick Ferguson, "Word of Mouth and Viral Marketing: Taking the Temperature of the Hottest Trends in Marketing," *Journal of Consumer Marketing* 25, no. 3 (2008), pp. 179–82.

51. Don E. Schultz, "The New Branding Lingo," *Marketing Management* 12, no. 6 (November/December 2003), pp. 8–9.

52. "Internet Users by Country," 2016, http://www.internetlivestats.com/internet-users-by-country/; and Deepak Patel, "All Villages Electrified, but Darkness Pervades," *Indian Express*, September 14, 2016, http://indianexpress.com/article/india/india-news-india/electricity-in-india-villages-problems-still-no-light-poverty-3030107/.

53. "We Are Currently Collaborating with H&M's for a WASH Project across Four Indian States," *Outline India*, February 1, 2017, http://www.outlineindia.com/.

54. Suparna Dutt D'Cunha, "This Startup Is Using Data Analytics and Technology to Solve Social Challenges in India," *Forbes*, April 6, 2017, https://www.forbes.com/sites/suparnadutt/2017/04/06/this-startup-is-using-data-analytics-and-technology-to-solve-social-challenges-in-india/#162503f06c22.

55. D'Cunha, "This Startup Is Using Data Analytics and Technology."

56. Saritha Rai, "India Just Crossed 1 Billion Mobile Subscribers Milestone and the Excitement's Just Beginning," *Forbes*, January 6, 2016, https://www.forbes.com/sites/saritharai/2016/01/06/india-just-crossed-1-billion-mobile-subscribers-milestone-and-the-excitements-just-beginning/#726816627db0.

57. Vidhi Choudhary, Sounak Mitra, Harveen Ahluwalia, "Internet Usage Picks Up in Rural India," *Mint*, August 12, 2016, http://www.livemint.com/Consumer/QgM23BLpCo4ovHxA0jpOGM/Rural-India-getting-online-faster-BCG-report.html.

CHAPTER 6

Understand Consumer and Business Markets

LEARNING OBJECTIVES

LO 6-1 Understand the value of knowing the consumer.

LO 6-2 Consider the role of personal and psychological factors in consumer decision making.

LO 6-3 Appreciate the critical and complex role of cultural, situational, and social factors in a consumer purchase decision.

LO 6-4 Understand the consumer decision-making process.

LO 6-5 Understand the differences between B2C and B2B markets.

LO 6-6 Understand the critical role of the buying center and each participant in the B2B process.

LO 6-7 Learn the B2B purchase decision process and different buying situations.

LO 6-8 Comprehend the role of technology in business markets.

Understanding the behavior of a target market is essential in developing an effective marketing strategy. This is true whether the target market is a group of consumers or another business. In this chapter we will examine both B2C and B2B behavior, as there are distinct differences between the two. First, we will consider consumer behavior, which has been an area of significant interest to marketers for decades. Knowing how consumers make decisions—and the tools marketers use to influence that process—is important to companies that sell directly to consumers and to companies that sell to other businesses. Later, we will discuss how business-to-business behavior differs from consumer behavior, and review the tools marketers use to reach other businesses.

Teenage couple watching 3D movie.
©Image Source

THE POWER OF THE CONSUMER

It's a Friday night and a group of people are considering how to spend the evening. A consensus forms around watching a movie. The discussion focuses on two choices: visit the local multiplex theater to see a first-run showing of the latest hit movie or go to a friend's house and watch a classic on the 55-inch LED TV with surround sound. Ultimately, they decide to watch *Justice League* at the friend's house. This interaction is repeated thousands of times each weekend and represents just one example of consumer decision making.

> **LO 6-1**
>
> Understand the value of knowing the consumer.

Marketers are fundamentally interested in learning about the process people use to make purchase decisions. In our example, the implications of the seemingly innocuous decision to watch a movie at home are very significant. Movie theaters are concerned because attendance has been falling for a decade while sales of video on demand have been growing at double-digit rates. Theater owners are investing millions of dollars to get people to choose a night out at the movies instead of going home. At the same time, movie studios such as Paramount, Sony, Time Warner, and Disney are paying attention. Because they want to maximize revenue, they have shortened the time between theatrical release and DVD sales, in addition to making first-run movies available via video on demand.[1] Finally, theme parks such as Universal Orlando Resort are interested because they invest millions to combine successful movies with live-action shows and rides to extend the movie's experience.

Delivering value to the customer is the core of marketing, and a company can only do that with a thorough, accurate, and timely understanding of the customer. Complex forces influence consumer choices, and these forces change over time, which adds to the challenges marketers face. Exhibit 6.1 displays a model of the consumer decision process, which is a complex interaction of internal (personal and psychological characteristics) and external (cultural, situational, and social stimuli) forces that, joined with a company's marketing activities and environmental forces, affect the purchase decision process. This chapter will identify the internal and external forces affecting the process, then focus on the consumer decision process itself.

INTERNAL FORCES AFFECT CONSUMER CHOICES

Among the most difficult factors to understand are those internal to the consumer. Often, consumers themselves are not fully aware of the role these important traits play in their decision making. Compounding the challenge is the fact that these characteristics vary by individual, change over time, and affect decisions in complex ways that are difficult to know. Exhibit 6.2 identifies examples of internal forces.

> **LO 6-2**
>
> Consider the role of personal and psychological factors in consumer decision making.

Personal Characteristics

Personal attributes are frequently used to define an individual. Age, education, occupation, income, lifestyle, and gender are all ways to identify and classify someone. The *American Heritage Online Dictionary* defines **demographics** as "[t]he characteristics of human populations and population segments, especially when used to identify consumer markets." It is helpful

EXHIBIT 6.1 | Model of the Consumer Decision Process

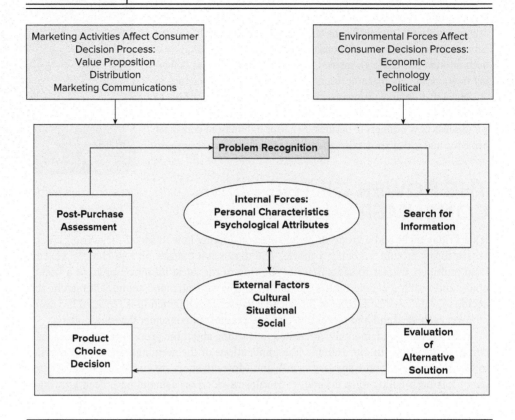

to understand the demographics of a target market for two reasons. First, knowing the personal characteristics of a target market enables marketers to evaluate relevant statistics against competitors and the overall population using broad demographic studies like the U.S. Census Bureau reports. Comparing demographic data such as age and income to competitor data enables you to assess how your target markets match up with those of competitors. Second, personal characteristics like age, income, and education play a critical role in consumer decision making, affecting information search, possible product choices, and the product decision itself.[2] Demographics are also an important tool in market segmentation, and Chapter 7 will explore how demographics are used to make decisions about targeting customer groups.

Life Cycle Stage (Age) As individuals age, their lives change dramatically, and as a result, so do their purchase patterns. From childhood to retirement, purchase behavior is shaped by a person's stage of life, and while specific aspects of the marketing mix change from one generation to the next, children still want to play, families still need homes and

EXHIBIT 6.2 | Internal Forces Affecting Consumer Choices

Personal Characteristics	Psychological Attributes
Age	Motivation
Education	Attitude
Occupation	Perception
Income	Learning
Lifestyle	Personality
Gender	

everything that goes in them, and seniors still focus on retirement. Marketers realize that changes in life stage (for example, graduating from college, getting married, or having a child) transform an individual's buying habits and are referred to as the **family life cycle**. These life changes mirror the individual's family environment and include the number, age, and gender of the people in the immediate family.

Historically, age has been a primary construct for identifying a person's life cycle. A new trend is emerging, however, as people move beyond traditional roles. Young adults are marrying and having kids later in life, altering the traditional view of 30-somethings as family builders. Concurrently, American couples are having children far into their 40s, significantly changing the buying behavior of individuals who might normally be planning retirement. Let's consider U.S. population trends by age. For example, one important marketing insight from examining population trends is that while the population is growing, it is also getting older. As we have discussed, the aging population leads to market opportunities for products, such as Dove's Real Beauty, that have surged in the past 10 years.

Occupation People are influenced by their work environment. From the executive suite to the plant floor, people who work together tend to buy and wear similar clothes, shop at the same stores, and vacation at the same places.[3] As a result, marketers identify target groups based on an individual's position in an organization.

In addition to broad occupational categories (union worker, management) marketers also target specific occupations. Physicians, for example, have a host of products, from smartphone apps to vacations, designed specifically for them. Given the amount of time spent working, it is not surprising that individuals develop similar interests and purchase behaviors.

Lifestyle Even though people share the same life cycle stage or occupation, their lifestyles may be dramatically different. **Lifestyle** references an individual's perspective on life and manifests itself in that person's activities, interests, and opinions (AIO). By learning about what the person likes to do, his or her hobbies, and views about the world, marketing managers develop a holistic view of the individual. As the name implies, lifestyle is how people choose to live, and how a person lives dictates what she or he buys. By choosing particular activities, developing unique interests, and holding on to specific opinions, an individual identifies what is really important. Marketers seek to match their products and services with the consumer's lifestyle.[4] New technologies enable marketers not only to know a great deal about their customers but also to direct targeted marketing messages. However, privacy issues and the intrusive nature of these technologies can increase ethical concerns.

Just as women's roles in the workforce have changed over the past several decades, so has their purchasing behavior. Increased purchasing power and wealth for women have led to new purchasing roles. Auto purchases, for example, were historically dominated by men; however, women now influence 80 percent of vehicle purchases and 40 percent of SUV sales. The cosmetics industry, while offering some products to men, focuses primarily on women.

Gender roles are behaviors regarded as proper for men and women in a particular society. These roles change over time and across cultures. In general, women have been adding new roles as they move into the workforce and positions of political power. In the United States, this means that men and women are more likely to share responsibilities than to live in a traditional household where the men work and women stay at home to raise the children.

Differences in women's roles have created vastly different market segments. At one end

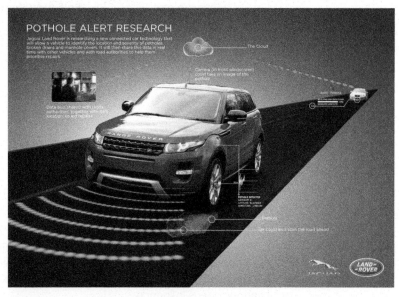

Land Rover connects its models to specific target markets with enhanced features like technology to make drivers aware of road hazards such as potholes.

Source: Jaguar Land Rover North America, LLC

are traditional homemakers who derive satisfaction primarily from maintaining the household and nurturing the family. At the other extreme is the career woman who is either single or married and who makes a conscious choice to work and derives personal satisfaction from her employment. Other segments include trapped housewives (and husbands) who are married but prefer to work and trapped working women who would prefer to be at home but must work because of financial necessity or family pressure.

Marketing managers understand that men and women vary not only in the products they require but also in the marketing communications they are receptive to. For example, the websites that men and women visit most often vary a great deal. Consequently, the messages they see are different.[5] Men prefer automotive and sports websites while women choose health and epicurean websites. In addition, the message itself varies by gender, with men preferring a "self-help" message and women responding to a "help others" communication. All this suggests that gender roles are a critical personal characteristic affecting consumer choices.[6]

Psychological Attributes

The consumer decision process involves a number of psychological forces that profoundly affect the consumer choice process. These forces drive the need, shape the content and format of information stored in memory, and have an effect on point of view about products and brands.

Motivation At any given time people experience many different needs. Most are not acted upon; however, when need reaches a particular strength or intensity, it becomes a motive that drives behavior. People prioritize needs, making sure that stronger, more urgent needs get met first. **Motivation** is the stimulating power that induces and then directs behavior. It is the force by which powerful unmet needs, or motives, prompt someone to action. Many theories have been developed over the years to explain human motivation. Exhibit 6.3 provides a summary of four popular theories of motivation and how they are used in marketing.

EXHIBIT 6.3 | Contemporary Theories of Motivation

	Theory	Key Elements	Marketing Implications
Maslow's Hierarchy of Needs Theory	Humans have wants and needs that influence their behavior. People advance to the next level only if the lower needs are met.	1. **Physiological** 2. **Safety** 3. **Love/Social** 4. **Self-Esteem** 5. **Self-Actualization**	Individuals are not interested in luxuries until they have had basic needs (food, shelter) met.
Herzberg's Two-Factor Theory	Certain factors in the workplace result in job satisfaction.	1. **Motivators:** challenging work, recognition, and responsibility 2. **Hygiene factors:** status, job security, salary, and benefits	Satisfying hygiene factors does not create a loyal employee or customer. For a company to really create satisfied employees it is important to focus on motivators.
Aldelfer's ERG Theory	Expansion on Maslow's hierarchy, placing needs in three categories.	1. **Existence** 2. **Relatedness** 3. **Growth**	People need a sense of belonging and social interaction. Creating a relationship with the customers extends the customers' satisfaction with the product.
McClelland's Achievement Motivation Theory	There are three categories of needs and people differ in the degree to which the various needs influence their behavior.	1. **Need for Achievement** 2. **Need for Power** 3. **Need for Affiliation**	Companies can be successful targeting one of three basic needs.

Attitude From religion to politics, sports to tomorrow's weather, people have an attitude about everything. An **attitude** is defined as a "learned predisposition to respond to an object or class of objects in a consistently favorable or unfavorable way."[7] Several key points come from this definition. First, attitudes are learned or at least influenced by new information. This is important for marketers because they seek to affect a person's attitude about a product. Second, attitudes are favorable or unfavorable, positive or negative. In other words, attitudes are seldom, if ever, neutral. As a result, marketers pay close attention to people's attitudes about their products because they play an important role in shaping a person's purchase decision.

Initially, a person's attitudes are formed by their values and beliefs. There are two categories of values. The first refers to cultural values based on national conscience. Americans, for example, value hard work and freedom, among other things. In Japan, national values include reciprocity, loyalty, and obedience. The second category is personal values held by the individual. Products possessing characteristics consistent with a person's value system are viewed more favorably.

While values may be based, in part, on fact, beliefs are a subjective opinion about something. Since they are subjective (emotional and not necessarily based on fact) marketers become concerned that a negative product belief will create a negative attitude about that product, making the attitude more difficult to overcome.[8] It is also important to note that beliefs, once formed, are resistant to change. Personal experiences, marketing communication, and information from trusted sources, such as family members or friends, all shape a person's belief system.

Values and beliefs come together to shape attitudes about an object whether it is Coke, the environment, or your favorite sports team. This overall predisposition is the result, generally, of an individual's assessment of that object on several attributes. For example, an attitude about Coke could be based on attributes such as health, which could be a positive belief—Coke's caffeine gives you energy—or a negative belief—Coke has a lot of sugar and calories. Coke is presented as a fun, youthful drink and youth is an American value.[9]

Because people's beliefs/values impact their purchase decisions, marketing managers try to learn about those beliefs/values. They do that by having customers check off rating scales that evaluate a product's performance on a list of attributes. This is important information because most attitudes result from an individual's assessment of an object using a **multiattribute model** that evaluates the object on several important attributes. Learning which attributes are used and how individuals rank those attributes is particularly helpful to marketers in creating specific marketing messages as well as the overall value proposition.[10] For instance, individuals who value the environment and ecology will place a higher priority on fuel economy and other environmentally friendly characteristics in the purchase of a car.

Perception People are inundated with information. Indeed, there is so much information that it is not possible to make sense of everything, so people use a process called perception to help manage the flow of environmental stimuli. **Perception** is a system to select, organize, and interpret information to create a useful, informed picture of the world.

In marketing, perception of a product is even more important than the reality of that product because, in a very real sense, an individual's perception is his or her reality. Perception drives attitudes, beliefs, motivation, and, eventually, behavior. Since each individual's perception is unique, everyone's perceptual response to a given reality will vary. Two people will see an ad for a new Samsung OLED flat-panel television, but

Coke promotes its fun brand image with thoughtful, amusing, and interesting graphics designs.
Source: The Coca-Cola Company

their perception of the ad will be very different. One may see a high-quality television worth the money, while the other sees an overpriced television that does not warrant a premium price. Their attitudes toward the ad and the product are affected by their perceptions.

Perception is shaped by three psychological tools: selective awareness, selective distortion, and selective retention.

Selective Awareness An individual is exposed, on average, to between 2,000 and 3,000 messages daily. People cannot process, let alone retain, all those messages, so they employ a psychological tool known as **selective awareness** to help them focus on what is relevant and eliminate what is not. The challenge for marketers is breaking through people's decision rules, which are designed to reject the vast majority of stimuli they see every day.

Research provides several insights about these decision rules. First, not surprisingly, people are more likely to be aware of information that relates to a current unmet need. Someone looking to change cellular providers will pay more attention to ads from cellular companies than someone who is happy with her current service. Second, people are more receptive to marketing stimuli when they expect them. Customers entering an AT&T or Verizon Wireless store anticipate seeing mobile telephones and tablet computers and, as a result, pay more attention to them. Finally, people are also more likely to become aware of marketing stimuli when they deviate widely from what are expected. For several years, Allstate Insurance has run a series of ads called "Mayhem" in which a man in a business suit points out the problems someone might have without Allstate. In addition to the creativity behind this approach, one of the reasons the campaign has done well is because it deviated from normal insurance ads. People didn't expect to see "Mayhem" talking about insurance.[11]

Selective Distortion Breaking through the customer's selective awareness is an important first step. However, even if a stimulus is noticed, there is no guarantee it will be interpreted accurately. Information can be misunderstood or made to fit existing beliefs, a process known as **selective distortion**.

The issue for marketers is that selective distortion can work for or against a product. If an individual has a positive belief about a powerful brand or product, information that is ambiguous or neutral will likely be interpreted positively. Even negative data can be adjusted to align with an individual's existing beliefs. For example, despite the negative implications of the information, a recall of Toyota Prius cars did not slow sales, in part, because people's perception of Toyota's overall quality offset the negatives associated with a product recall. On the other hand, a negative belief can lead to negative interpretation. In the 1990s, General Motors worked hard to improve the quality of its cars. This came after several decades of being rated below Toyota and Honda in terms of quality. Despite significant quality improvements validated by independent researchers like J.D. Power and Associates, people continue to believe GM car quality is inferior to that of Toyota and Honda. Sometimes a positive belief can work against a marketer, particularly when the belief leads to an incorrect interpretation.[12] When P&G ran a campaign called "Irresistible Superiority," experts and consumers were confused. No one knew how it connected to P&G products. So while P&G wanted consumers to think its products were superior, consumers were simply left wondering what it meant.

Selective Retention Even if a stimulus is noticed and interpreted correctly, there is no guarantee it will be remembered. While selective awareness significantly controls the amount of information available to the individual's consciousness, selective retention acts as an additional filter. **Selective retention** is the process of placing in one's memory only those stimuli that support existing beliefs and attitudes about a product or brand. This is significant because **memory** is where people store all past learning events; in essence it is the "bank" where people keep their knowledge, attitudes, feelings, and beliefs.[13] There are two types of memory—short and long term. **Short-term memory** is what is being recalled at the present time and is sometimes referred to as working memory, while **long-term memory** is enduring storage, which can remain with the individual for years and years. Marketing managers are particularly interested in understanding an individual's long-term memory recall about their brand. Selective retention tends to reinforce existing attitudes and creates a real challenge for marketers trying to overcome negative beliefs and attitudes since people are less likely to be aware of or retain information to the contrary.

One last point about perception concerns a controversial issue—the effect of subliminal stimuli on perception. While people are aware of most stimuli around them, a number of other stimuli go unnoticed. In most cases, either the stimuli are presented so fast they are not recognized or they overload the individual and are "lost" in the person's consciousness. These stimuli are termed *subliminal,* and many critics of advertising suggest the stimuli can affect consumer behavior. Despite many claims to the contrary, however, research has uncovered no evidence that a subliminal message, whether sent deliberately or accidentally, has any effect on product attitudes or choice behavior.

Given the psychological processes people use to limit their awareness of marketing stimuli and control retention of any remaining information, it is easy to see why marketers must deliver a message over and over. Without repetition, the message is not likely to break through selective awareness and even less likely to be retained by the individual.[14]

Learning How does an individual become a consumer of a particular product? Most consumer behavior is learned through a person's life experiences, personal characteristics, and relationships.

Learning is any change in the content or organization of long-term memory or behavior. Learning occurs when information is processed and added to long-term memory. Marketers can therefore affect learning by providing information using a message, format, and delivery that will encourage customers to retain the information in memory.

There are two fundamental approaches to learning. The first, **conditioning**, involves creating an association between two stimuli. There are two types of conditioning: classical and operant. Classical conditioning seeks to have people learn by associating a stimulus (marketing information, brand experience) and response (attitude, feeling, behavior).[15] Many companies today use a variety of music genres in their ads, designed to connect with specific target audiences. Ads for products targeted at young people use current artists, while older target markets like baby boomers respond to music from the 1960s and 1970s. This is conditioned learning, connecting the stimulus—music—with a response—a positive association with a particular brand.

The other type of conditioning, operant conditioning, entails rewarding a desirable behavior, for example, a product trial or purchase, with a positive outcome that reinforces that behavior.[16] For example, many different types of food retailers offer product samples in their stores. Frito-Lay, for instance, offers free in-store samples of Doritos for the express purpose of getting people to try the product, enjoy the product, and finally purchase a bag of Doritos. Enjoying the Doritos reinforces the positive attributes of the product and increases the probability of a purchase. Since the consumer must choose to try the product for operant conditioning to occur, Frito-Lay wants to make the trial as easy as possible.

While conditioning requires very little effort on the part of the learner, **cognitive learning** is more active and involves mental processes that acquire information to work through problems and manage life situations.[17] Someone suffering from the flu and seeking information from their friends, doctors, or medical websites about the best over-the-counter remedy for their specific symptoms is engaged in cognitive learning. They are looking for information to help solve a problem. Marketers must understand that consumers sometimes engage in this type of activity and be proactive in providing the information sought by the consumer. Consider a box of Theraflu caplets; Theraflu Daytime lists six symptoms right on the front of the box that the product will help relieve. This kind of information is critical at the point of purchase as an individual considers which product will help him feel better faster.

GoPro initially targeted extreme athletes and other people who identified with excitement and ruggedness.

©Purestock/SuperStock

Personality When people are asked to describe someone, most of us do not talk about the person's age or education. Rather, our response generally reflects the individual's personality and is based on our interactions with that person in different situations. Our descriptions usually include various personality dimensions such as kind, outgoing, or gentle. **Personality** is a set of unique personal qualities that produce distinctive responses across similar situations.

Many theories of personality have been developed, but marketers tend to focus on personality trait theories because they offer the greatest insights on consumers. Personality trait theories all have two basic assumptions: (1) each person has a set of consistent, enduring personal characteristics, and (2) those characteristics can be measured to identify differences between individuals. Most believe personality characteristics are formed at a relatively early age and can be defined in terms of traits such as extroversion, instability, agreeableness, openness to new experiences, and conscientiousness. These core traits then lead to outward characteristics, which are what people notice. For example, an extrovert would favor the company of others and be comfortable meeting new people. A conscientious person would exhibit behaviors that are considered careful, precise, and organized. Knowing the personality tendencies of a target audience can help marketers develop specific product features, such as chat options in many applications that allow people to engage with others who have similar interests.

EXTERNAL FACTORS SHAPE CONSUMER CHOICES

LO 6-3

Appreciate the critical and complex role of cultural, situational, and social factors in a consumer purchase decision.

While internal factors are fundamental in consumer decision making, forces external to the consumer also have a direct and profound effect on the consumer decision process. These factors shape individual wants and behavior, define the products under consideration, target the selection of information sources, and shape the purchase decision. Three wide-ranging external factors that have the most significant impact on consumer choices are cultural, situational, and social.

Cultural Factors

Culture is a primary driver of consumer behavior because it teaches values and product preferences and, in turn, affects perceptions and attitudes. Beginning in childhood and continuing on throughout life, people respond to the culture in which they live. In recent years, despite the globalization of communications and the universal nature of the Internet, people have developed a heightened awareness of their own culture and subculture.

Marketers need to be aware of culture for two reasons. First, learning a target market's culture is essential to an effective marketing strategy. Creating a value proposition that incorporates cultural cues is a prerequisite to success. Second, failing to understand cultural norms has a significant negative effect on product acceptance.

Culture **Culture** assimilates shared artifacts such as values, morals, beliefs, art, law, and customs into an organized system that enables people to function as members of society. In school, children learn basic cultural values through interaction with classmates and formal classroom learning. At a very early age, young people learn values and concepts about their culture. Among the values shared by Americans, for example, are achievement, hard work, and freedom, while Japanese value social harmony, hierarchy, and devotion.

EXHIBIT 6.4 | Nonverbal Communication

Nonverbal Communication: the means of communicating through facial expressions, eye behavior, gestures, posture, and any other body language	
Positive nonverbal communication during a presentation	• Eye contact • Smiling • Steady breathing • Tone of voice • Moving closer to the person
Negative nonverbal communication during a presentation	• Swaying • Stuttering • Hands in pockets • Fidgeting • Looking at watch or clock
Caution: Nonverbal communication can contradict what is spoken if not used correctly.	

While culture affects people in many ways, three factors are particularly relevant in consumer behavior: language, values, and nonverbal communications. **Language** is an essential cultural building block and the primary communication tool in society. At the most basic level it is important to understand the language, making sure that words are understood correctly.[18] However, language conveys much more about a society and its values. Scandinavian cultures, for example, place a high value on spending time together. They have more words to express "being together" than English does, and their meaning implies a more intimate sharing of thoughts and ideas. These concepts do not translate into the Anglo-American language and are not easily understood.

Cultural values are principles shared by a society that assert positive ideals. These principles are often viewed on a continuum. Consider the value of limited versus extended family. In the United States, the obligation and commitment to family are often limited to an individual's immediate family, including his or her parents, children, and siblings. Most Latin American cultures, on the other hand, have a more wide-ranging definition of family that includes extended family members such as cousins and grandparents and is also more inclusive, with extended family members living together.

The last cultural factor is **nonverbal communication**. While a number of factors fall into this category (refer to Exhibit 6.4 for a more complete discussion), let's focus on two: time and personal space. The perception of time varies across cultures. Americans and Western Europeans place a high value on time and view it in discrete blocks of hours, days, and weeks. As a result, they focus on scheduling and getting as much done in a given period as possible. Latin Americans and Asians, on the other hand, view time as much more flexible and less discrete. They are not as concerned with the amount of work that gets done in a given time block. How does this affect marketing? Salespeople who have been trained in an American sales environment are often frustrated to find their Asian and Latin American customers less concerned about specific meeting times and more concerned about spending time building a personal relationship.

Personal space is another example of nonverbal communication that varies across cultures. In the United States, for example, most business conversations occur between three and five feet, which is a greater distance than in Latin American cultures. Salespeople used to a three- to five-foot distance can find it a little disconcerting when the space shrinks to 18 inches to three feet. Not understanding these differences can lead to confusion and embarrassment and even create a problem in the business relationship.[19]

Subculture As consumer behavior research has discovered more about the role of culture in consumer choices, it has become evident that beyond culture, people are influenced even more significantly by membership in various subcultures. A **subculture** is a group within the culture that shares similar cultural artifacts created by differences in ethnicity, religion, race, or geography. While part of the larger culture, subcultures are also different from each other. The United States is perhaps the best example of a country with a strong national culture that also has a number of distinct subcultures.

Several subcultures in the United States have become such powerful forces that companies now develop specific marketing strategies targeted at those groups. Large companies such as L'Oréal and General Motors have begun targeting the Hispanic and African-American markets with specific products, distribution channels, and marketing communications. For example, L'Oreal, the cosmetics company, has a research center in New Jersey that focuses exclusively on the African-American market and has resulted in a number of products in its Soft-Sheen Carson and Mizani brands.[20]

Situational Factors

At various points in the consumer decision process, situational factors play a significant part. Situational factors are time-sensitive and interact with both internal and external factors to affect change in the consumer. Because they are situational, they are difficult, if not impossible, for the marketer to control. However, it is possible to mitigate their effects with a good marketing strategy.

Physical Surroundings People are profoundly affected by their physical surroundings. An individual viewing an ad during an NFL football game will react differently when watching the game alone or at a party with friends. Same game, same ad, but a different reaction as a result of the physical surroundings at the time the marketing message is being delivered. As we will see in Chapter 12, retailers devote a lot of time and resources to creating the right physical surrounding to maximize the customer's shopping experience. They know people respond differently to changes in color, lighting, or location of the product within the store; indeed, almost every element of the customer's experience is considered important in the consumer choice process.

Personal Circumstances An individual's behavior is always filtered through his or her immediate personal circumstances. Parents with crying children shop differently than parents with small kids enjoying the experience, and parents without the kids along shop differently than parents with their children present. At the point of consumer choice, many things can influence the final purchase. If the line at the checkout is too long, people may eliminate certain discretionary items or forgo the entire purchase.

While it is not possible for marketers to control personal circumstances, it is important to understand how personal situations influence the choice process. Consider cold medicines such as Tylenol Cold Relief. Johnson & Johnson, maker of Tylenol Cold medicine, knows that people frequently purchase the product when they are not feeling well. As a result, the company makes the product readily available using a wide distribution channel.

Time Time is a critical situational factor that affects individuals throughout the consumer choice process. An emerging consumer trend in many industrialized countries is the willingness to trade time for money. This is evidenced in a study that reported a majority of Americans would like to have more time for family and are seeking ways to simplify their lives.[21] For many people, time is a resource to be used, spent, or wasted and, for these people, the issue is not always the best price but, rather, the best service. Increasingly, customers are asking if the purchase of this product will give them more time or be less of a hassle than another product. Automobile manufacturers and dealers have responded by creating more "hassle-free" shopping experiences. Instead of going through a difficult negotiation process to get the lowest price, dealers are offering low, fixed prices that reduce some of the hassle.

Social Factors

Humans are social beings. Everyone seeks social interaction and acceptance on some level. As people move through life, they affect and, in turn, are affected by various social factors. These factors include groups like their family, social class, and reference groups, as well as individual opinion leaders.

Family The first group any individual belongs to is the family. Families are the single most important buying group, and they influence the consumer choice process in two ways. First, the family unit is the most influential teacher of cultural values. Children are socialized into a community and its values primarily through the family unit as they interact with parents, siblings, and extended family members. Second, children learn consumer behavior from their parents. As adults and later parents, they model the behavior first learned as a child.

The most basic definition of a **family** is a group of two or more people living together and related by birth, marriage, or adoption. Historically, in the United States and much of the world, the traditional family included a married couple with children of their own or adopted children. However, the last 40 years have witnessed changes in the family structure. In the 1970s the traditional family comprised 70 percent of all households. Today that number has dropped to a little under half of all households (48 percent).

New family structures are now much more prevalent. These emerging family structures create a number of challenges for marketers.[22] Single-parent households, for example, often report discretionary time is in short supply. Grocery stores have seized on this opportunity by creating deli bars that cater to working fathers and mothers who pick up dinner on their way home from work.

The **household life cycle (HLC)** is fundamental to understanding the role of family in the consumer choice process. The traditional family life cycle consists of a fairly structured set of activities that begins when single people get married (20s), start a family (30s), raise kids (40s to 50s), watch as the kids grow up and leave home (50s to 60s), and finally enter into retirement (60s and beyond). However, while the basic tenets of the traditional household life cycle are valid, people are marrying later and putting off the start of a family. Women are having children later in life for a variety of reasons (marry later, focus on career). Couples raise kids then divorce and remarry, creating blended families, or they start new families of their own.

Each group offers opportunities and challenges for marketing managers. From basic needs that motivate individuals to engage in the process through information search and then on to final purchase decision, each group thinks and behaves differently. Each group makes completely different choices based on its stage in the life cycle.[23] For example, two couples (35 years old, married, professionals)—one with two children, the other without—have very different lifestyles, values, and purchase priorities. As a result, marketers are interested in age trends as an indicator of future life cycle stages. (Exhibit 6.5 shows age trends in the United States over the next 40 years.)

Individual responsibility in family decision making references the way individuals inside the family make decisions. There has been a great deal of research on the roles of various family members in the decision-making process. Across all the purchases in a household, research suggests, not surprisingly, that husbands and wives each dominate decision making in certain categories and jointly participate in others. For example, husbands tend to dominate insurance purchase decisions while wives are primary decision makers in grocery shopping.[24] Children, even at an early age, exert influence and dominate decisions for products such as cereal and indirectly influence decisions on things like vacations. However, traditional family responsibilities are changing as family units change. Single-parent households have shifted traditional purchase decisions. For example, single fathers must take on the responsibility for selecting their child's school.

Social Class In every society, people are aware of their social status; however, explaining the social class system to someone from outside the culture is often a challenge. People learn about social class and their social status at a very early age from their

EXHIBIT 6.5 | Projections of the Population Selected Age Groups for the United States

Sex and Age	2020	2030	2040	2050	2060
BOTH SEXES	334,503	359,402	380,219	398,328	416,795
Under 18 years	74,128	76,273	78,185	79,888	82,309
Under 5 years	20,568	21,178	21,471	22,147	22,778
5 to 13 years	36,824	38,322	39,087	39,887	41,193
14 to 17 years	16,737	16,773	17,627	17,854	18,338
18 to 64 years	203,934	209,022	219,690	230,444	236,322
18 to 24 years	30,555	30,794	31,815	32,717	33,300
25 to 44 years	89,518	95,795	96,854	99,653	103,010
45 to 64 years	83,861	82,434	91,021	98,074	100,013
65 years and over	56,441	74,107	82,344	87,996	98,164
85 years and over	6,727	9,132	14,634	18,972	19,724
100 years and over	89	138	193	387	604

Source: "Projections of the Population by Sex and Selected Age Groups for the United States: 2015 to 2060," Table 3. Washington, DC: U.S. Census Bureau, Population Division, December 2014.

parents, school, friends, and the media. **Social class** is a ranking of individuals into harmonized groups based on demographic characteristics such as age, education, income, and occupation.

Most Western cultures have no formal social class system; however, there is an informal social ranking. These informal systems exert influence over an individual's attitudes and behavior. Two factors drive social status. Success-driven factors have the greatest effect on social status and include education, income, and occupation. Innate factors, the second category, do not result from anything the individual has done but, rather, are characteristics the individual has inherited from birth. Gender, race, and parents are the primary innate factors determining social status.

Social class is not the result of a single factor, such as income, but rather a complex interaction among many characteristics. While some social class drivers are not in the individual's control, people do make choices about their education and occupation. Therefore, it is possible for people, particularly in societies providing educational opportunities, to move into new social classes based on their achievements. In addition, the availability of easy credit, creative pricing, and new financing arrangements enable and even encourage people to engage in aspirational purchases. **Aspirational purchases** are products bought outside the individual's social standing. Over 50 percent of the luxury cars sold in the United States are leased. By offering special financing terms, individuals with lower income levels now drive a BMW, Mercedes-Benz, or Audi. This enables people to drive a car they normally could not afford, an aspirational purchase.

From a marketing perspective, the impact of social status on consumption behavior is profound, affecting everything from the media people choose to view (lower classes watch more TV while upper classes tend to read more) to the products they buy (lower classes tend to buy more generics while the upper classes select more branded products).

Opinion Leaders The previous discussion on external factors focused primarily on group influences such as social and cultural factors; however, external factors also include personal influences. Consider, for example, Elon Musk, CEO of Tesla, who has dramatically changed the automobile industry with his Tesla electric vehicles and is considered a technology visionary. He speaks out on a number of issues, including new technologies like Augmented Reality. Musk's interviews are widely disseminated and discussed not just because he is CEO of Tesla, but because he is considered an opinion leader. His insights are considered harbingers of the future.

Opinion leaders fulfill an important role by classifying, explaining, and then bestowing information, most often to family and friends but occasionally to a broader audience, as is the case with Elon Musk. People seek out opinion leaders for a variety of reasons, including unfamiliarity with a product, reassurance about a product selection before purchasing, and anxiety resulting from high involvement with the purchase of a particular product. Anyone whose opinions are valued by the individual can be an opinion leader. For instance, the friend who enjoys cars could be an opinion leader about automobiles; the relative with a background in information technology might be the expert on technology.

While opinion leaders are often defined by product class, such as Musk's expertise in technology, another influential group has emerged. This new group, whose members are called **market mavens**, has information about many kinds of products, places to shop, and other facets of markets, and the members initiate discussions with consumers and respond to requests from consumers for market information.[25] The key difference between opinion leaders and market mavens is the focus on their market knowledge. Market mavens have a broader understanding and expertise that goes beyond product to include other elements of the purchase decision such as shopping experience and price.

In their role as information gatekeepers, opinion leaders and market mavens exert influence over an individual's product and brand choice. As a result, marketers seek to understand the roles of these two groups so they can identify the members and, in turn, encourage them to try a particular product. Marketers encourage these individuals using these activities:

- Market research. As a primary source of information for interested individuals, it is critical that opinion leaders and market mavens be familiar with a product and understand its advertising so they can convey the information accurately. Many market researchers focus on the way these individuals interpret messages to ensure the marketing mix is working correctly.

- Product sampling. Testing a product is an essential part of any gatekeeper's acceptance. As a result, the leaders are prime targets for product sampling.

- Advertising. Companies use opinion leaders and market mavens to influence decision makers, whether it is a business leader or an individual consumer. Tag Heuer (a watch manufacturer) hired Cristiano Ronaldo, one of the world's best soccer players, as one of its ambassadors because he is an opinion leader. The company hopes that Ronaldo's qualities—successful, focused, and a winner—influence individuals looking to buy a watch.

Reference Groups Everyone identifies with and is influenced by groups. In most cases, the individual may belong to the group or seek membership, while in other situations the group is perceived negatively and the individual works to disassociate himself. A **reference group** is a group of individuals whose beliefs, attitudes, and behavior influence (positively or negatively) the beliefs, attitudes, and behavior of an individual.[26] Three characteristics are used to categorize reference groups: association, desirability, and degree of affiliation.

The association with reference groups can be formal or informal. Students, for example, have a formal relationship with their college or university and, as a result, respond to and connect with other students at the school. At the same time, a student has a number of informal relationships with other groups. Circles of friends and classmates, while not a formal group, can exert a lot of influence over an individual.

Tag Heuer hopes that Ronaldo's success as one of the world's best and most visible athletes will carry over to people's perceptions of the company's watches.
Source: Tag Heuer

A key characteristic impacting the degree a group affects the individual is the extent to which an individual desires to be associated with the group. **Desirability** is the extent and direction of the emotional connection an individual wishes to have with a particular group. Individuals can really want to belong to a group or not, and the linkage can be either positive or negative. Sports teams encourage participation at many levels. Like many cities, Boston has a number of established sports teams, including the Red Sox, Patriots, Celtics, and Bruins, each with thousands of supporters, though the level of support varies widely. Dedicated fans with the available resources become season-ticket holders, spending thousands of dollars a year to attend every game of the season. Many Boston residents are not actively involved with any team or are ardent fans of one team but show less interest in the others. Some Boston residents may even support teams from other cities, perhaps the New York Yankees, and hold negative perceptions of the local team. As a result, the desirability of belonging to the reference group known as a "Boston sports fan" is person- and even team-specific.

The **degree of affiliation** indicates the amount of interpersonal contact an individual has with the reference group. **Primary groups** are marked by frequent contact, while less frequent or limited dealings are known as **secondary groups**. Individuals come in frequent contact with co-workers, close friends, and other groups such as religious, special-interest, or hobby groups that may be primary or secondary depending on the level of contact. Over time, the degree of affiliation will likely change; for example, when someone changes jobs, the primary group of co-workers will also change.

THE LEVEL OF INVOLVEMENT INFLUENCES THE PROCESS

One significant outcome of motivation, discussed earlier, is **involvement** with the product because it mediates the product choice decision. Involvement is activated by three elements: the individual's background and psychological profile, the aspirational focus, and the environment at the time of the purchase decision. As we noted, motivation is unique to each individual and drives purchase decisions. Aspirational focus is anything of interest to the buyer and is not limited to the product itself. It is possible to be involved with a brand, advertising, or activities that occur with product use.

Many people ride motorcycles, but far fewer ride Harley-Davidson motorcycles and, among Harley riders, some get tattoos of the Harley-Davidson logo. Clearly these people are highly involved beyond the product and associate strongly with the Harley lifestyle. Finally, the environment changes the level of involvement. Time, for example, can limit involvement if there is pressure to make a decision quickly but can enhance involvement if there is sufficient time to fully engage in the decision process. Involvement influences every step in the choice decision process, and, as a result, marketers create strategies based on high and low levels of involvement. For example, high-involvement purchases drive buyers to more cognitive learning such as the new car buyer who visits car dealers, checks out automotive websites, and seeks out the advice of automotive experts for information on cars in an effort to make an informed purchase decision. On the other hand, conditioning works well with low-involvement purchases such as the purchase of gasoline where people frequently purchase from the same station because of various factors such as price and location.[27]

Decision Making with High Involvement

Greater motivation that leads to greater involvement results in a more active and committed choice decision process. When someone is concerned with the outcome of the process, they will spend more time learning about product options and become more emotionally connected to the process and the decision. Someone stimulated to acquire new information is engaged in **high-involvement learning**. For example, someone interested in purchasing a new high-end digital camera will seek out product reviews on CNET.com or other online sources to discover information that will assist in the choice decision. Some, despite a brand preference, may be willing to experiment with other brands and seek out additional information looking for a new alternative. A high level of involvement usually means the entire process takes longer. High-involvement consumers report high levels of satisfaction in their purchase decision. This is not surprising since these consumers spend more time engaged in the decision process and, therefore, are more comfortable in their decision.

Decision Making with Limited Involvement

While high-involvement purchases are more significant to the consumer, the vast majority of purchases involve limited or low involvement. From the purchase of gasoline to the choice of restaurants, decisions are often made almost automatically, often out of habit, with little involvement in the purchase decision. The reality is that consumers tend to focus their time and energy on high-involvement purchases while making many purchases with little or no thought at all.

Low-involvement learning happens when people are not prompted to value new information. This is more prevalent than high-involvement learning because the vast majority of marketing stimuli occur when there is little or no interest in the information. People do not watch TV for the commercials; they watch for the programming, and advertising is just part of the viewing experience. Likewise, print advertising exists alongside articles and is often ignored. While people are not actively seeking the information, they are exposed to advertising and this, in turn, affects their attitudes about a brand. Research suggests that people shown ads in a low-involvement setting are more likely to include those brands in the choice decision process. Low-involvement consumers spend little time comparing product attributes and frequently identify very few differences across brands. Because the decision is relatively unimportant, they will often purchase the product with the best shelf position or lowest price with no evaluation of salient product characteristics.[28]

Marketers consider several strategies in targeting low-involvement consumers. The objective of these strategies is to raise consumer involvement with the product. Generally, time is the defining characteristic for these strategies. Short-term strategies involve using sales promotions such as coupons, rebates, or discounts to encourage trying the product and then hoping the consumers will raise their product involvement. Long-term strategies are more difficult to implement. Marketers seek to focus on the product's value proposition, creating products with additional product features, better reliability, or more responsive service to increase customer satisfaction. Additionally, strong marketing communications campaigns that speak to consumer issues or concerns can raise involvement with the product. A classic example of this tactic is Michelin's highly effective and long-running advertising campaign that links a relatively low-involvement product, tires, with a significant consumer concern, family safety. Tires are not typically a high-involvement product; however, when the voiceover on the commercial says, "Because so much is riding on your tires," or more recently "What matters most," while showing children in the car, consumer involvement in the product—and more specifically the brand—increases.

While a low-involvement consumer demonstrates little or no brand loyalty, he or she is also, by definition, open to brand switching. As a result, brands can experience significant gains in consumer acceptance with an effective, comprehensive marketing strategy.

THE CONSUMER DECISION-MAKING PROCESS

Every day, people make a number of consumer decisions. From breakfast through the last television show watched before going to bed, people are choosing products as a result of a decision-making process. Learning about that process is a vital step for marketers trying to create an effective marketing strategy.

Years of consumer research have resulted in a five-stage model of consumer decision making. While not everyone passes through all five stages for every purchase, all consumers apply the same fundamental sequence beginning with problem recognition, followed by search for information, evaluation of alternatives, product choice decision, and finally post-purchase evaluation. Each time a purchase decision is made, the individual begins to evaluate the product in preparation for the next decision (see Exhibit 6.6).

> **LO 6-4**
>
> Understand the consumer decision-making process.

EXHIBIT 6.6 | Consumer Decision-Making Process

Problem Recognition → Search for Information → Evaluation of Alternatives → Product Choice Decision → Post-Purchase Decision

However, as noted earlier, someone driving home from work does not go through an extensive search for information or evaluate a number of alternatives in purchasing gasoline for the car. In all likelihood, the consumer buys from a station he or she knows well and shops at regularly. Nevertheless, this model is helpful because it illustrates what can be called the "complete decision-making process," which occurs when people are fully involved in the purchase.

Problem Recognition

Every purchase decision made by an individual is initiated by a problem or need that drives the consumer decision-making process. Problems or needs are the result of differences between a person's real and preferred states.

People live in the perceived reality of present time or **real state**. At the same time, people also have desires that reflect how they would like to feel or live in the present time, and this is known as a **preferred state**. When the two states are in balance, the individual does not require anything and no purchase occurs. However, where there is a discrepancy in the two states, a problem is created and the consumer decision-making process begins.

The discrepancy, or gap, can be created by internal or external drivers. Internal drivers are basic human needs such as hunger and security. Someone is hungry (real state) and wants to eat (preferred state). This will lead to a number of choices: eat at home, dine out, or go to the grocery store. It may even trigger other options such as calling a friend, which addresses a need for social interaction. External drivers happen as people interact with the world. Some of these triggers result from a company's marketing efforts, but most arise when an individual experiences something that creates a desire, like seeing a friend driving a new car or hearing about a good new restaurant.

Despite internal or external stimuli, people do not respond to every gap between a real and preferred state. Sometimes the disparity is not sufficient to drive the person to action. A person may want a new car but does not act on that feeling because he or she lacks the financial resources or simply cannot justify the purchase. When the conflict between real and preferred states reaches a certain level, the decision-making process begins.

Marketers need to understand problem recognition for several reasons. First, it is essential to learn about the problems and needs of the target market to create value-added products. Second, key elements of an effective marketing strategy, particularly communication, are predicated on a good knowledge of problem recognition triggers.

Search for Information

Once a problem is recognized and action is required, people seek information to facilitate the best decision. The search for information is not categorical; rather, it operates on a continuum from limited to extensive. Consider the following examples. A couple notices the low-fuel light comes on as they are driving home from a party. The driver recalls their "local" station is on the way home and, without any additional information, stops at the station and fills up the car. This is an example of **minimal information search**. The same couple now finds out they are going to have a baby and realizes their Mercedes-Benz C-class coupe has to be replaced with a more practical vehicle. They engage in a thorough information search reviewing car magazines, soliciting opinions from friends and family, conducting online research on sites like Edmunds or KBB, and test-driving a number of new cars and SUVs before making a final purchase decision. This is an example of **extensive**

information search. Between these two extremes is **limited information search**, which, as the name implies, involves some, albeit restricted, search for information. Suppose the wife from the couple in our previous examples has a cold. The husband stops at the drugstore to get her some medicine. At the cold medicine aisle he scans the boxes looking for the one that will provide "maximum relief" for his wife's symptoms. He may even ask the pharmacist for help in selecting the best choice. At this point he is engaged in a limited search for information. Generally, people do only the amount of information search they believe is necessary to make the best decision.

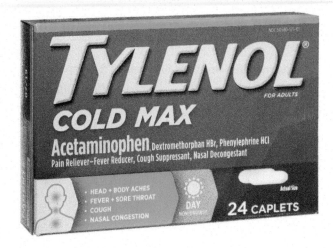

Tylenol Cold provides a great deal of information on the package to help consumers make a decision in the store at the point of purchase.
©Editorial Image, LLC

Information Sources There are two basic sources of information: internal and external. **Internal information sources**, as the name implies, are all information stored in memory and accessed by the individual. This is always the first place people consider for information. Past experiences, conversations, research, preexisting beliefs, and attitudes create an extensive internal database that is tapped by the individual once the problem is recognized. In our example of the car low on gas, the driver searched internal information and found past experiences provided sufficient information to make a decision.

Even when additional information is needed, internal information is used to frame the external search. Price limits and key performance metrics, criteria often used in the evaluation of alternatives, are frequently derived from information stored in memory. People gather and process information even if they are not actively involved in the purchase decision process. Consequently, an individual's internal information is changing all the time. As people gain more experience with a product or brand, and gather more information, they often rely more on internal information and conduct a less external information search.

The second fundamental source of information is external. Once people have determined internal information is not sufficient to make the purchase decision, they seek information from outside sources. **External information sources** include independent groups (sources), personal associations (friends and family), marketer-created information (automobile manufacturer website, advertising), and experiences (product trial and demonstrations).

An organization's marketing communications represent only one source, albeit an important one, among several external information source options. However, company marketing communications can play an important role in influencing other sources of information such as personal contacts. For example, when Johnson & Johnson introduces new baby care products, it spends a lot of money providing product samples and information to pediatricians and nurses in an effort to support the company's direct marketing communications to young mothers. So even though consumers indicate company-sponsored marketing information is of limited value in making purchase decisions, the company's marketing efforts can play a more significant role when considered in light of their effect on other external information sources. Exhibit 6.7 is a summary of external information sources and highlights the diversity of available information resources.

Defining the Set of Alternatives At some point in the search for information, often during the internal information search, people begin to limit the number of alternatives under consideration. From a practical perspective, it is simply not possible to gather and process information on many different options. This is known as bounded rationality and defines people's limited capacity to process information.

People begin with a very large set of possible alternatives known as the **complete set**. This set includes a variety of options across different brands and perhaps even products. Consider a person looking for mobile, wireless Internet access. The complete set could include different product options (cell phone, laptop, or tablet computer) and brands (Apple, Dell, Sony, Samsung, Hewlett-Packard, and Lenovo). Based on the individual's

EXHIBIT 6.7 | Sources of External Information

External Information Sources	Example	Marketing Implications
Independent groups	*Consumer Reports* Consumer's Union	Favorable reviews from independent sources are an important source of external information. Marketers need a strategy to reach independent sources with relevant information.
Personal associations	Family/friends	These associations can be an important external source of information in certain decisions. Marketers seek to influence reference groups and opinion leaders through favorable product reviews and effective marketing communications.
Marketer information	Advertising, manufacturer website	Effective marketing communications reinforce messages to other external information sources such as independent groups.
Experiential	Product trials	Product samples for certain categories such as food are easy to provide. Encourage people to seek out product trials and demonstrations when a sample is not appropriate (electronics, automobiles).

choice criteria, however, this large set of possible options will be reduced. Keep in mind that the complete set is not *all* options available to the buyer; rather, the set is the options that the buyer is aware of when the search process begins. The extent of the buyer's knowledge about the problem and available options determines the set of possible alternatives in the complete set.

As consumers move through the search for information, certain products (laptop computer) may be eliminated in favor of others (tablet computer) and brands will be evaluated and discarded. The **awareness set** reduces the number of options. At a minimum, the number of different product categories, if considered, will be reduced and some brands discarded. Interestingly, the awareness set can include choices across product categories. In our example, it is still possible for a particular brand of cell phone to remain in the awareness set despite the fact they are different product categories. From the awareness set, individuals conduct an additional information search. Based on additional information and evaluation, a **consideration (evoked) set** is created, which encompasses the strongest options. It is from the consideration set that the product decision is made.

Marketers are vitally interested in learning about the information search process for two reasons. First, marketers must identify important external information sources so they can direct their resources to the most effective external sources. Second, they must learn how consumers choose products for inclusion in their awareness and consideration sets to create marketing strategies that increase the probability of being in the consideration set.

Evaluation of Alternatives

Concurrent with the search for information are the analysis and evaluation of possible product choices. As we discussed previously, consumers move, sometimes quickly, from many options to a more restricted awareness set and from there to a final consideration set from which a decision is made. During this process, the individual is constantly evaluating the alternatives based on internal and external information.

The consumer choice process is complex and ever changing. Environmental and personal factors at the moment of decision dramatically affect the purchase decision. As a result, it is impossible to develop a consumer choice model for every purchase. However, years of research suggest consumers make product choices primarily from three perspectives: emotional, attitude based, and attribute based.

Emotional Choice Not all purchases are made strictly for rational reasons. Indeed, product choices can be **emotional choices**, based on attitudes about a product, or based on attributes of the product depending on the situation. Frequently, the product choice encompasses a mix of all three. An individual enjoys yogurt and taking a break to enjoy a snack (emotional based). That same person considers Chobani Greek Yogurt the best choice for a healthy yogurt (attitude based). Finally, the individual considers Chobani Greek Yogurt to be better tasting than other competitors (attribute based).

While emotions have been considered an important factor in decision making for many years, it was only recently that marketers began to develop specific marketing strategies targeting emotion-based decisions. Product design and execution even focus on creating an emotional response to the product. From there, marketing communications connect the product to the target audience using images and words that convey an emotional connection. Exhibit 6.8 shows an ad that communicates emotion to the reader.

Attitude-Based Choice Early in the evaluation of alternatives, people regularly use beliefs and values to direct their assessment. As consumers create the awareness set, they discard or include products and brands using existing attitudes. **Attitude-based choices** tend to be more holistic, using summary impressions rather than specific attributes to evaluate the options, and affect even important purchases such as a car or house. It is not uncommon for beliefs to affect the actual product decision. For example, "it is important to buy cars made in America" or the opposite, "foreign cars are better than American products." When two brands are judged to be relatively the same, people frequently look to existing attitudes to guide their decision. When someone responds to a question about why he bought a particular product with, "I always buy . . ." or "this is the only brand I use . . . ," they are likely making an attitude-based choice decision.

Attribute-Based Choice By far the most prevalent approach to product decisions is **attribute-based choice** based on the premise that product choices are made by comparing brands across a defined set of attributes. These evaluative attributes are the product features or benefits considered relevant to the specific problem addressed in the purchase decision. Antilock brakes are a product feature that translates into a consumer benefit—better control in a hazardous situation. Most consumers could not describe how antilock brakes actually work but are quite aware of the benefits and would eliminate a car from the choice process if it failed to have that product feature. Not all evaluative attributes are tangible. Brand image, prestige, and attitudes about a brand or product can also be used as evaluative criteria.

Product Choice Decision

The end result of evaluating product alternatives is an intended purchase option. Until the actual purchase, it is still only an "intended" option because any number of events or

EXHIBIT 6.8 | Ketel One Offers an Emotional Choice

GENTLEMEN, THIS IS VODKA.

Ketel One is connecting to their customers on an emotional level, reinforcing the appeal of a beautiful woman saying that "This is Vodka."
Source: Ketel One

interactions can happen to dissuade or alter the final purchase decision. Four purchase event characteristics affect the actual choice decision:

Physical surroundings–the environment for the purchase. From store colors to the employees, consumers respond to their physical environment. For example, while the color red creates awareness and interest, it also creates feelings of anxiety and negativity. Blue is calmer and considered the most conducive in creating positive feeling with the customer. Crowding can have a negative effect on purchase decisions because, if the store becomes too crowded, people will forgo the purchase, perhaps going somewhere else.

Social circumstances–the social interaction at the time of purchase. Shopping is a social activity and people are influenced by the social interaction at the time of purchase. Trying on an outfit alone may lead to the purchase; however, when putting on the outfit while shopping with a friend, it is unlikely the clothing will be purchased if the friend does not like it.

Time–the amount of time an individual has to make the purchase. The product choice decision can be affected by time pressure. The consumer will be less willing to wait for the best solution and more likely to purchase an acceptable alternative.

State of mind–individual's state of mind at time of purchase. An individual's mood influences the purchase decision. People in a positive state of mind are more likely to browse. Negative mood states are less tolerant and lead to increased impulse and compulsive purchases.

As a result of these purchase event characteristics, the intended purchase can be altered despite the information search and evaluation process. Some of these characteristics are at least nominally in the marketer's control. Other characteristics, such as an individual's state of mind, are uncontrollable and must be dealt with at the moment of purchase by employees who, it is hoped, have the skills and training needed to handle difficult situations.[29]

The final purchase decision is not a single decision; rather, the consumer confronts five important decisions:

What: select the product and, more specifically, the brand. Included as part of the product choice are decisions about product features, service options, and other characteristics of the product experience.

Where: select the point of purchase. Select the retailer and, increasingly, the channel–retail store (bricks) or online (clicks)–through which the product is to be purchased.

How much: choose the specific quantity to be purchased. For example, warehouse clubs, such as Sam's Club and Costco, offer consumer options on purchase quantity. If you have the ability to store products, it is possible to save money by purchasing in larger quantities.

When: select the timing of the purchase. The timing of the purchase can make a difference in the final purchase price. Car dealers traditionally offer better deals at the end of the month as they try to meet monthly sales quotas. Through sales and other marketing communications, marketers encourage consumers to purchase sooner rather than later.

Payment: choose the method of payment. The selection of a payment method makes a big difference to the consumer and marketer. Marketers want to make it easy for the consumer to purchase; however, not all payment methods are equal. Credit cards charge the retailer a fee that, in turn, is passed back to the consumer. One payment method, the debit card, is becoming popular, combining the convenience of a credit card with the fiscal responsibility of using cash. Finally, electronic payment methods using smartphones eliminate the need to carry credit cards or cash.

Consumers make a number of decisions at the point of purchase. Often, the selection of where the product will be purchased is done in conjunction with the product evaluation.

Post-Purchase Assessment

Once the purchase is complete, consumers begin to evaluate their decision. Attitudes change as they experience and interact with the product. These attitudinal changes include the way the consumer looks at competitors as well as the product itself. At the same time, marketers want to foster and encourage the relationship and, as we will discuss in Chapter 7, increasingly focus resources to build the customer relationship. Most of a CRM program is built around the customer's experience after the purchase. The four critical characteristics of post-purchase assessment are dissonance, use/nonuse, disposition, and satisfaction/dissatisfaction.

Dissonance High-involvement, large purchases often lead to a level of doubt or anxiety known as **post-purchase dissonance**. Most purchases occur with little or no dissonance.[30] The likelihood of dissonance increases if one or more of the following purchase decision attributes are present: (1) a high degree of commitment that is not easily revoked; (2) a high degree of importance for the customer; (3) alternatives that are rated equally and a purchase decision that is not clear. Also, the individual's own predisposition for anxiety can create additional dissonance. Big-ticket purchases frequently include several of those characteristics. For example, buying a house, the single biggest purchase most people will ever make, is a big commitment that can be complicated when two or three homes are evaluated as more or less equal by the consumer.

How do consumers reduce dissonance? The single most effective method is a thorough information search and evaluation of alternatives. When consumers are confident that due diligence has been done, they have less anxiety after the purchase. If dissonance remains a problem, additional information can be sought to reduce anxiety and reinforce the decision. Marketers can direct marketing communications to reduce dissonance, particularly with large purchases such as automobiles. As part of a CRM program, many companies follow up with customers after the purchase to assess their satisfaction.

Use/Nonuse Consumers buy a product to use. Marketers are acutely interested in learning how customers use the product for several reasons. First, it is important the customer knows how to use the product correctly. Buying a new television can quickly become a negative experience if it is not set up properly. As a result, marketers want to be sure the customer understands how the product is to be used and any setup procedures that may be needed to ensure proper function. Second, a satisfied customer means a greater likelihood of additional purchases. Buying and riding a bicycle means the consumer is more likely to buy a helmet, light, bike rack, and other accessories.

Building customer relationships and making sure the customer understands the product and how it is to be used reduce the probability of consumers returning the product. Another potential post-purchase problem can be that the product is purchased and not used. In these situations, marketers seek to stimulate product usage. Campbell Soup Co. found customers frequently had several cans of soup on their shelf for long periods of time. The company developed a marketing communications program to encourage faster consumption of the product. Many packaged foods include expiration dates encouraging consumers to use the product quickly and repurchase.

Disposal Increasingly, marketers are concerned about how products are disposed of once they are no longer in use. Environmental concerns consistently rank as a major issue for consumers in many parts of the world. People living in the United States, for example, produce nearly 2,000 pounds (1 ton) of garbage per person every year. Once a product is consumed, in most cases, a physical object remains and needs to be disposed of. New technologies such as laptops and mobile devices are particularly difficult to discard because they contain dangerous chemicals.

Environmentally friendly products encourage proper use and disposal. Companies including Coca-Cola use recycled materials in their manufacturing and packaging. At the same time, companies are encouraging consumers to recycle on their own. Dell and other computer companies have a program that encourages consumers to recycle their old computers.

Satisfaction/Dissatisfaction Consumers evaluate every aspect of the product. As previously noted, this includes any dissonance present at the time of purchase, use or nonuse of the product, the product disposition, the purchase experience, and

Seventh Generation is one of many companies that use recycled materials in their packaging.
©Editorial Image, LLC

even the value equation. This results in the consumer's satisfaction or dissatisfaction with the product and purchase decision. In addition, various dimensions of the overall experience will be satisfactory or unsatisfactory. A customer may love the product but dislike the dealer or retailer.

Most products are evaluated on two dimensions—instrumental performance and symbolic performance. **Instrumental performance** relates to the actual performance features of the product and answers the question: Did the product do what it is supposed to do? **Symbolic performance** refers to the image-building aspects of the product and answers the question: Did the product make me feel better about myself? A product that performs poorly on instrumental dimensions will ultimately lead to dissatisfaction. However, for a consumer to be fully satisfied with the product, it must perform well both instrumentally and symbolically. A new Kia automobile may score high on instrumental performance but low on symbolic performance. Is the customer dissatisfied? No, but it is not certain that person will purchase another Kia.

There are two primary outcomes of consumer dissatisfaction with a product: a customer will either change his or her behavior or do nothing. When a customer has an unfavorable experience at the bank, she may not leave, but her opinion of the bank diminishes. Over time, this will erode the consumer's evaluation of the bank. The second result of consumer dissatisfaction is a change in behavior. The consumer may simply choose to stop shopping at that store or purchasing a particular product. Another option is to complain to management. Marketers are aware that for every complaint, there are eight "quiet" but dissatisfied consumers who chose to walk away. An even greater concern is consumers telling friends about a bad experience or complaining to government agencies. Finally, dissatisfied consumers who believe their legal rights have been violated may take legal action for damages related to the purchase experience.

ORGANIZATIONAL BUYING: MARKETING TO A BUSINESS

Many people believe marketing is focused primarily on consumers—the ultimate users of the product. This is due at least in part to the fact that most people experience marketing as a consumer. The reality, however, is that large consumer products companies purchase hundreds of billions of dollars of products and services every year. General Motors, for example, spends over $60 billion a year on products and services. Everyone knows Hewlett-Packard (HP) and General Electric (GE) because of the products they sell to consumers, but these companies derive most of their revenue from selling to other businesses.

In many cases, companies are selling products that end up as components in a finished product. GE is a world manufacturing leader in commercial jet engines that power half of the jets flying today. Also, companies must purchase products to help them maintain their business. Lenovo is a global company providing IT solutions to companies worldwide. Its products are not a component of another product but, rather, help a business run better. While many companies serve business-to-consumer markets, all companies operate in a business-to-business market, as we will see in this chapter. From GE to Walmart, companies must understand and work with other companies as part of their business operations.

In this section, we explore **B2B markets**. The first part of the chapter defines business-to-business markets and delineates the differences between B2B markets and consumer markets. Next, we discuss the business market purchase decision process, which is different from the process consumers use in making a purchase decision. Finally, the significant role of technology in business-to-business market relationships will be presented.

Lenovo markets its products to both consumers and businesses.
Source: Lenovo

DIFFERENCES BETWEEN BUSINESS AND CONSUMER MARKETS

Business markets and consumer markets are not the same. Six distinct differences dramatically affect marketing strategy and tactics (see Exhibit 6.9). These differences create unique opportunities and challenges for marketing managers because success in consumer marketing does not translate directly to business markets and vice versa.

LO 6-5

Understand the differences between B2C and B2B markets.

Relationship with Customers

As we will discuss in Chapter 7, many consumer product companies now focus on building strong relationships with their customers. However, even when a relationship is cultivated with the customer, it is impersonal and exists primarily through electronic communication or direct mail.

The opposite is true in business markets. The nature of business markets requires a more personal relationship between buyer and seller. Every relationship takes on additional significance as the sales potential of each customer increases. A strong personal relationship is critical because business customers demand fast answers and good service and, in general, want a close relationship with suppliers.[31] As a result, companies selling in a B2B market invest more resources to foster and maintain personal contact with their customers than in a consumer market. Consider a company like HP, which certainly sells their products to consumers but has a separate, dedicated sales staff focused solely on selling into B2B markets. In some cases, companies even invest in their suppliers to strengthen the relationship.

A more personal relationship most often connotes a greater emphasis on personal selling and, increasingly, technology. Customers want direct communication with company representatives and prefer someone they know and trust. The individual most responsible for maintaining a relationship is the salesperson. Personal selling also offers companies the most effective method for direct communication with the customer. Technology has greatly improved the quality and quantity of communications between buyer and seller.

EXHIBIT 6.9 | Differences between Business and Consumer Markets

	B2B Market (Business)	B2C Market (Consumer)
Relationship with customers	Invest more in maintaining personal relationships	Impersonal; exist through electronic communication
Number and size of customers	Fewer but larger customers	More customers but buy in smaller, less frequent quantities
Geographic concentration	Suppliers located strategically by the buyers	Could be anywhere in the world
Complexity of buying process	Complex process that can take a long time (years in some cases) and involve more people	Fewer people, often just one, directly involved in the purchase decision and the purchase decision is often based on personal and psychological benefits
Complexity of supply chain	Direct from supplier to manufacturer	Complex with products moving through the channel to reach the consumer
Demand for products	Derived from consumer demand, fluctuates with changes to consumer demand, and more inelastic (less price sensitive)	Consumer perceptions about their own needs mitigated by environmental factors and marketing stimuli

However, one-on-one personal communication is still the most important tool in developing and maintaining a strong customer relationship in business markets.

At the same time, technology plays a critical role in connecting buyer and seller. Integrating IT systems that enhance sales response times, provide better customer service, and increase information flow is now an accepted element in a successful B2B customer relationship. Customers demand not only a personal relationship with their vendors but also an efficient one. Most companies now require vendor Internet connectivity to increase efficiency.

Number and Size of Customers

Business markets are characterized by fewer but larger customers. Goodyear, for example, may sell one set of tires to a consumer over the course of three years, but every year the company sells millions of tires to Ford Motor Company. Add up all the major automobile companies, and there are fewer than 25 business customers for Goodyear. Not surprisingly, the company maintains a dedicated sales force just for the automobile manufacturers.

The large size and small number of customers place a higher value on each customer. Although consumer products companies value customer relationships, it is not possible to satisfy every customer every time, nor is it economically feasible. However, in a business market setting, losing even one large customer has striking implications for a company.[32] Walmart is Procter & Gamble's single biggest customer, accounting for 14 percent of company sales (roughly equivalent to $10 billion). At its Arkansas office, P&G has a 300-member staff dedicated to one customer—Walmart.

Geographic Concentration

Business markets tend to concentrate in certain locations.[33] Historically, the automobile industry concentrated in the Midwest, particularly Detroit, and technology firms dominated Silicon Valley in California. As a result, their suppliers congregated nearby. A software developer, for example, that wants to be close to its primary customers should set up an office in San Jose, California. While the Internet allows people to live anywhere, the nature of business relationships means companies want to have a strong presence near their best customers.

Complexity of the Buying Process

The B2B customer buying process, discussed later in the chapter, is more complex than the consumer purchase decision process. It takes longer and involves more people, making the seller's job more challenging. In addition, as companies connect with customers, the number of relationships increases and it is difficult for one individual, the salesperson, to keep up with the complexity of the relationships.[34]

Complexity of the Supply Chain

The movement of goods through a channel to the ultimate consumer requires a high level of coordination among the participants. A **supply chain** is the synchronized movement of goods through the channel. It is far more integrated than ever before as companies seek to keep production costs low, provide maximum customer input and flexibility in the design of products, and create competitive advantage. At the same time, the supply chain in B2B markets is generally more direct, with suppliers and manufacturers working closely together to ensure efficient movement of products and services.

Demand for Products and Services Is Different in a Business Market

Product demand in business markets is different from consumer demand on three critical dimensions: derived demand, fluctuating demand, and inelastic demand. All three offer unique challenges and opportunities for marketers. For example, two of the three differences (derived and fluctuating demand) deal with the relationship between B2B and B2C demand and suggest B2B marketing managers must first understand their customer's markets before they can sell to the customer. The final dimension (inelastic demand) is an opportunity for a seller but must be managed carefully to maintain a successful relationship.

Derived Demand Demand for B2B products originates from the demand for consumer products, or, put another way, demand for B2B products is **derived demand**. If consumers are not buying Ford cars and trucks, then there is no need for Ford to purchase Goodyear tires. Therefore, it is important for Goodyear to understand the consumer market for automobiles for two reasons. First, knowing what consumers are looking for in a car is critical to designing tires for those cars. Second, knowing the consumer automobile market is essential to create a value proposition that speaks to Ford's need to sell more cars and trucks to consumers.

In addition to the demand for specific Ford products, such as the Flex or Mustang, Goodyear scans the environment for anything that might affect consumer demand. Environmental factors have long-term and short-term effects on consumer product choices. For example, long-term economic factors such as dramatic changes in the price of gasoline can have significant positive or negative effects on the sale of SUVs, and short-term factors like a hurricane in Florida or the Southeast can limit distribution and sale of products in those areas for a while. B2B sellers understand that business customer success frequently means finding ways to assist them in their consumer markets. This is a challenge for business marketers because, despite having a great product and providing great service at a competitive price, they may still not get the business because consumer demand for their business customer's product is weak.

Goodyear appeals to consumers by pointing out that they make tires for snow rescue vehicles, which demand high-quality snow tires.

Source: The Goodyear Tire & Rubber Company

Fluctuating Demand The relationship between consumer demand and demand for business products presents a real challenge for business-to-business marketers. Small changes in consumer demand can lead to considerable shifts in business product demand and is referred to as the **acceleration effect**. This makes forecasting the sale of consumer products important because making even a small mistake in estimating consumer demand can lead to significant errors in product production.

Inelastic Demand Business products experience fairly **inelastic demand**, meaning changes in demand are not significantly affected by changes in price. Apple, for example, will not buy more processors from Intel if Intel lowers the price, nor will it buy fewer chips if Intel raises the price until the price increase becomes so high that Apple considers alternative vendors. Apple designs some of its computers around Intel processors and changing vendors creates disruption and costs in other areas of the manufacturing process. Price increases, particularly incremental changes, are often accepted because manufacturers are hesitant to disrupt manufacturing processes, which, in turn, creates inelastic demand in the short run. Exhibit 6.10 has two demand curves, D_1 and D_2. As price rises from P_1 to P_2, the demand changes. The more elastic demand curve is the one with the largest shaded area—B. Demand in business-to-business markets is generally more inelastic than in consumer markets, which means changes in price have less effect on demand—the smaller shaded area A. This makes D_2 an example of inelastic demand.

EXHIBIT 6.10 | **Examples of Elastic and Inelastic Demand**

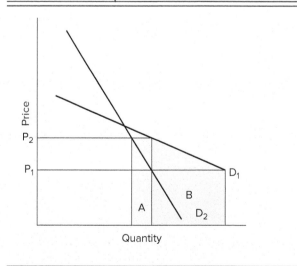

Source: Slavin, Stephen. *Economics,* 10th ed. New York: NY: McGraw-Hill Education, 2011.

BUYING SITUATIONS

People involved in making business **buying decisions** face many choices as they move through the purchase decision process. Business buying decisions vary widely based on the

- Nature of the purchase (large capital outlay like that needed for a new manufacturing plant versus simply ordering office supplies).
- Number of people involved in the decision (one or many).
- Understanding of the product being purchased (new to the firm or a familiar product purchased many times before).
- Time frame for the decision (short time requiring an immediate purchase decision or a longer lead time).

Some decisions require little or no analysis before the purchase decision. Others require updating information or changing existing purchase orders before the purchase decision can be made. Finally, some decisions require an in-depth analysis of the product. These three scenarios are referred to as straight rebuys, modified rebuys, and new purchases.

Straight Rebuy

Many products are purchased so often that it is not necessary to evaluate every purchase decision. Companies use a wide range of products on a consistent basis (office supplies, raw materials) and simply reorder when needed. This type of purchase is called a **straight rebuy**. Increasingly, this is done automatically via secure Internet connections with approved or preferred suppliers. Far fewer people are involved with the purchase decision; often it is handled by one person in the purchasing department.

The goal of business sellers in straight rebuy situations is to become the preferred supplier. A company given approved status must be diligent and mindful of competitors seeking to displace it. Companies not on the approved list are called **out suppliers**. Their primary task is to obtain a small order, an opening, then leverage that opportunity to gain additional business. This is a challenge, however, if the approved supplier is doing a good job of meeting the customer's needs. From time to time, many companies order small quantities from nonapproved suppliers just to keep the approved supplier from becoming too complacent or to evaluate a potential new vendor.[35]

Modified Rebuy

A **modified rebuy** occurs when the customer is familiar with the product and supplier but is looking for additional information. Most often this need for change has resulted from one or more of three circumstances. First, the approved supplier has performed poorly or has not lived up to the customer's expectations. Second, new products have come into the market, triggering a reappraisal of the current purchase protocols. Third, the customer believes it is time for a change and wants to consider other suppliers.

All three situations create opportunities for out suppliers to gain new business. When a purchase contract is opened up for a modified rebuy, it represents the best opportunity for a new supplier. At the same time, however, the current approved supplier seeks to maintain the relationship. The approved supplier almost always has the advantage, particularly if it has a close relationship with the customer, because it knows the people involved and usually gets access to critical information first.

New Purchase

The most complex and difficult buying situation is the new purchase. A **new purchase** is the purchase of a product or service by a customer for the first time. The more expensive, higher the risk, and greater the resource commitment, the more likely the company will engage in a full purchase decision process (outlined later in the chapter).

This process almost certainly involves a group throughout the entire decision process, even though the final decision may rest with a single individual. Because the company's purchasing personnel have had very little experience with the product, they seek information from a variety of sources. First and foremost, vendor salespeople are a key source of information about the product's capabilities. If they do their job well, they help the customer define its needs and how best to address them. Another avenue of information for companies is to hire consultants who, as unbiased experts, can assess and educate customers on their needs and possible solutions. Finally, the company must scan its own resources, including past purchase records, for relevant information.

BUYING CENTERS

As we discussed, business purchases are seldom made by just one person, particularly in modified rebuy and new purchase situations. A number of individuals with a stake in the purchase decision come together to form a **buying center** that manages the purchase decision process and ultimately makes the decision. The individuals included in the buying center may have direct responsibility over the decision (purchasing department) or financial control of the company (senior management). In other cases, the individuals might have a specific expertise helpful to the decision (engineer, consultant).[36]

LO 6-6

Understand the critical role of the buying center and each participant in the B2B process.

Buying centers usually are not permanent groups but are convened to make the decision and then disband. Also, individuals may participate in more than one buying center at any given time. Purchasing agents are apt to be members of several buying centers. In addition, while the vast majority of buying center participants work for the customer, others, such as outside consultants, are invited into the group because of their expertise. This happens, for example, in new purchases when a company believes it lacks sufficient internal knowledge and experience to make an informed decision. Most buying centers include a minimum of five people; however, they can be much larger. In larger multinational corporations, buying centers for companywide purchase decisions, such as a new corporate CRM system, can include dozens of people from all over the world.

Members of the Buying Center

Every participant in a buying center plays a certain role and some may play multiple roles (see Exhibit 6.11). In addition, an individual's role may change. As people move up in an organization, they can move from user to influencer and finally to a decider. These functions can be defined formally by the company or informally as a result of an individual's expertise or influence. Let's examine each of the five major roles.

User Users are the actual consumer of the product and play a critical role. While typically not the decision makers, they do have a lot of input at various stages of the process. They are the first to recognize the problem based on a need, and they help define the product specifications. Finally, they provide critical feedback after the product purchase. As a result, their responsibility is enhanced in new purchase and modified rebuy situations when product specifications are being set for the purchase decision.

Initiators The **initiator** starts the buying decision process, usually in one of two ways. In one scenario the initiator is also the user of the product, as in the secretary who reorders when office supplies run low. A second scenario occurs when senior executives make decisions that require new resources (manufacturing sites, product development, and information technology). In these

EXHIBIT 6.11 | Buying Center Participants

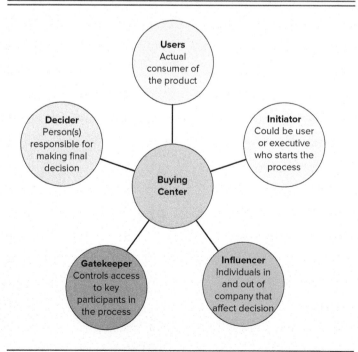

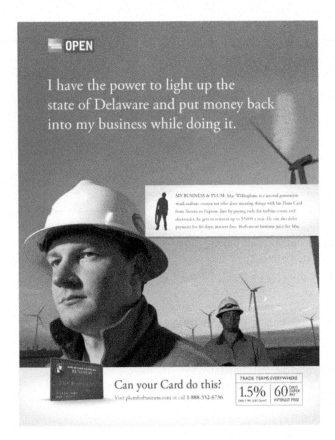

OPEN

I have the power to light up the state of Delaware and put money back into my business while doing it.

Can your Card do this?

Visit plumforbusiness.com or call 1-888-352-6736

TRADE TERMS EVERYWHERE
1.5% | 60 DAYS

American Express communicates to small and medium-sized business owners by reinforcing the financial benefits of using their card for business expenses.

Source: American Express Company

situations the executives act as initiators to the purchase decision process.

Influencers Individuals, both inside and outside the organization, with relevant expertise in a particular area act as **influencers**, providing information that is used by the buying center in making the final decision. Engineers are frequently called on to detail product requirements and specifications. Purchasing agents, based on their experience, are helpful in evaluating sales proposals. Marketing personnel can provide customer feedback. In all of these cases, the influencer's knowledge on a given topic relevant to the purchase decision can affect the purchase decision.

Gatekeepers Access to information and relevant individuals in the buying center is controlled by **gatekeepers**. Purchasing departments act as gatekeepers by limiting possible vendors to those approved by the company. Similarly, engineering, quality control, and service department personnel create product specifications that, in essence, limit the number of vendors. At the same time, basic access to key people is controlled by secretaries and administrative assistants. One of the toughest challenges facing salespeople in a new purchase or modified rebuy situation is getting access to the right people.

Deciders Ultimately, the purchase decision rests with one or more individuals, **deciders**, in the buying center. Often it will be the most senior member of the team; however, it can also include other individuals (users, influencers), in which case the decision is reached by consensus. The more expensive and strategic the purchase, the higher in the organization the decision must go for final authority.[37] It is not uncommon for the CEO to sign off on major strategic decisions about technology, new manufacturing plants, and other key decisions that affect fundamental business processes. Costly capital equipment purchases often include the chief financial officer (CFO), who will most likely be a key decider. CFOs will employ a wide range of financial tools, including discounted cash flow analysis of the proposed investment, as they determine the most appropriate purchase decision.

Pursuing the Buying Center

Buying centers present marketers with three distinct challenges, as presented in Exhibit 6.12. First, who is part of the buying center? Simply identifying the members of a buying center can be difficult and is made more challenging by gatekeepers whose role, in part, is to act as a buffer between buying center members and outside vendor representatives. The job of identifying membership in the buying center is made even more complex

EXHIBIT 6.12 | Marketing Challenges in Buying Centers

| Who is part of the buying center? | Who are the most significant influencers? | What are the decision criteria for evaluating the various product options? | **Buying Center Target Market** |

as participants come and go over time. Second, who are the most significant influencers in the buying center? This is critical in both preparing a sales presentation and following up. Targeting influencers is important in persuading the buying center to purchase the salesperson's product. Finally, what are the decision criteria for evaluating the various product options? A very real concern for salespeople is making sure their products perform well on critical evaluation criteria; however, without a good understanding of evaluation criteria, it is not possible to assess the probability of the product's success.

THE PLAYERS IN BUSINESS-TO-BUSINESS MARKETS

B2B markets are not homogenous. The complexity of business markets rivals that of consumer markets, with more than 20 million small businesses in the United States alone. The number grows dramatically when you include large corporations, nonprofit institutions, and government entities. The diversity of businesses coupled with the unique characteristics of business-to-business markets means companies selling in B2B markets need to know their markets very well. Let's explore each of the major categories of business markets to better understand their similarities and differences.

The North American Industrial Classification System (NAICS)

Historically, the basic tool for defining and segmenting business markets was a classification system known as the Standard Industrial Classification (SIC) codes developed by the U.S. government in the 1930s. The SIC system organized businesses into 10 groups that further broke down business categories based on their output (what they produced or their primary business activity). For many years, it was the foundation for business segmentation in the United States.

The SIC codes were updated in the 1990s and are now called the **North American Industrial Classification System (NAICS)**. The system has been expanded to include businesses in Mexico and Canada. NAICS defines 20 major business sectors based on a six-digit hierarchical code. The first five digits are standardized across Mexico, Canada, and the United States, while the sixth digit enables countries to adjust the code to fit the country's own unique economic structure.[38]

The NAICS is not perfect; companies are classified on the basis of their primary output, which means that large companies with multiple businesses across different sectors are not accurately represented as they receive only one NAICS code. However, the system does offer a great starting point for researching a particular business market. It is possible to purchase detailed information on each of the codes in the system. This information includes data on companies listed in each code, number of employees, sales revenue, their location, and contact information. Exhibit 6.13 provides an example.

Manufacturers

One of the largest groups of business customers is manufacturers, which consume two types of products. First, components used in the manufacturing process are called **original equipment manufacturer (OEM)** purchases. Companies selling OEM products work to convince the OEM customer their products offer the best value (price and quality) to the OEM's customers. Intel's reputation for overall value among consumers has enabled the company to build a strong business with OEM computer manufacturers such as Lenovo to the point that Lenovo and others promote "Intel Inside."

OEM customers purchase in large quantities to support their own product demand. Two important outcomes result from this purchase power. First, OEM customers seek the very "best" prices from sellers. *Best* does not always mean lowest; other factors play an important role.[39] The assurance of product quality, ability to meet demand, just-in-time product delivery schedules, and other factors frequently figure into the final selection of product

EXHIBIT 6.13 | NAICS Example

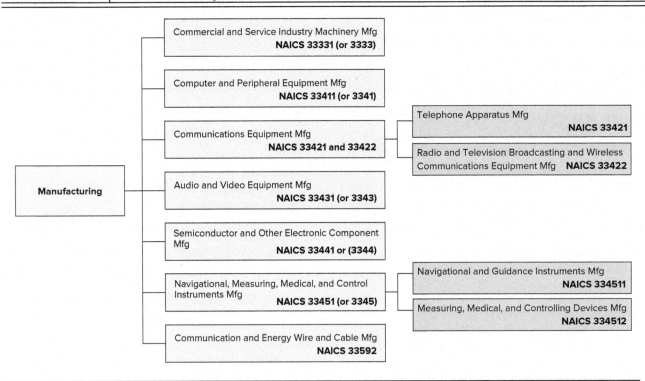

Source: North American Industry Classification System (NAICS).

and vendor. The second result of large purchase quantities is the ability to dictate specific product specifications. OEM customers often compel suppliers to modify existing products and even develop new products. Sellers work closely with the OEM engineers and technicians to develop products that will fit the need of the OEM customer. The benefit is a high volume of product sales and the opportunity to develop a long-term strategic relationship.[40]

A second category of products purchased by manufacturers is called **end user purchases** and represent the equipment, supplies, and services needed to keep the business operational. There are two major types of end user purchases: **capital equipment** and **materials, repairs,** and **operational (MRO)** supplies and services. Capital equipment purchases involve significant investments and include major technology decisions (mainframe computers, ERP and CRM software packages) or critical equipment needed in the manufacturing process (large drill presses, robotic assembly systems). Since these purchases are considered a long-term investment, customers evaluate not only the purchase price but also other factors such as cost of ownership, reliability, and ease of upgrading. The cost and long-term commitment of these purchases mean senior management is often involved in the final decision. Frequently a buying center will evaluate options and make a recommendation to senior management.

MRO supplies, on the other hand, are products used in everyday business operations and are typically not considered a significant expense. Purchasing agents or individuals close to the purchase decision, such as an office manager, are responsible for MRO purchases. Many of these purchases are straight rebuys; the individuals involved do not want to spend a lot of time making the purchase. Vendors in these industries are well aware that once they have a customer, the business is assured until the company does not perform up to customer expectations. Put another way, the business is theirs to lose.

Resellers

Companies that buy products and then resell them to other businesses or consumers are called **resellers**. Home Depot, for example, buys home products and then resells them to consumers, building contractors, and other professionals in the construction industry. Chapter 12 provides an in-depth discussion of consumer resellers, but it is important to note that resellers have unique needs when it comes to purchase decisions. Just as manufacturers need end user products, resellers also need equipment and supplies to run their businesses. Retailers need technology such as computers and checkout counters to keep track of sales and inventory. Distributors need stocking and inventory management systems to maintain their distribution centers and also have the same MRO needs.

Government

The single largest buyer of goods and services in the world is the U.S. government. Combined with state and local governments, the value of purchases is over $2 trillion. Local, state, and particularly federal **government** entities have unique and frequently challenging purchase practices. Detailed product specifications must be followed precisely, and the purchase process is often long. The purchase decision by the Department of Defense on the USS *Gerald R. Ford* aircraft carrier took many years and involved hundreds of thousands of product specifications.[41] While the government is theoretically open to all vendors, the reality is that experience with the government purchase process is usually a prerequisite to success.

Federal and state governments make a number of resources available to potential vendors; it is possible to obtain guidelines from the federal government. Furthermore, some private companies exist to offer assistance in learning about the process. The National Association of State Purchasing Officials publishes information on selling products and services to each of the 50 states. In addition, small-business organizations, such as the Small Business Administration, provide information on federal government contracts and contact personnel at government agencies.

Institutions

Institutions, such as nonprofits, hospitals, and other nongovernmental organizations (NGOs), represent a large and important market that has some unique characteristics. First, profitability does not play as significant a role in many of these organizations; rather, the delivery of service to the targeted constituency is the primary objective. Profit, or surplus as it is often called in the nonprofit community, is important but is not the fundamental driver in decision making. For example, Adventist Health System, which owns and operates health care facilities in more than a dozen states, is a large nonprofit health care provider that considers a range of priorities in making important strategic decisions.[42] A second unique characteristic is a limited number of resources. Even the largest NGOs, including the Red Cross, do not have access to the capital and resources of most large for-profit organizations.

THE BUSINESS MARKET PURCHASE DECISION PROCESS

In some respects business market purchase decisions follow the same basic process as consumer decisions. As presented in Exhibit 6.14, a problem is recognized, information is collected and evaluated, a decision is made, and the product experience is then evaluated for future decisions. However, there are also significant differences between business market purchase decisions and consumer purchase decisions. These differences make the process more complex and require the involvement of more people. One key difference is that, while consumer decisions often include an emotional component, business goals and performance specifications drive organizations toward a more rational decision process.

As we discussed, the process is not used for every purchase decision. In straight rebuy situations, the problem is recognized and the order is made. Defining product

> **LO 6-7**
>
> Learn the B2B purchase decision process and different buying situations.

EXHIBIT 6.14 | Model of Business Market Purchase Decision Process

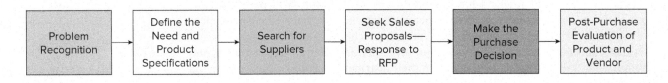

specifications, searching for suppliers, and other steps in the process were probably done at one time, but, once a supplier is selected, the purchase decision process becomes more or less automatic. A selected or approved list of suppliers shortens the decision process dramatically. Buyers go to the targeted vendor or choose from a list of suppliers and make the purchase. This process is consistent across organizations. Modified rebuys, on the other hand, are much more organization and situation specific. In some situations, the process may be more like a straight rebuy with some changes to product specifications or contract terms. In other situations, it may resemble a new purchase with an evaluation of new suppliers and proposals. New purchases will include all the steps in the process. As a rule, a new purchase takes longer because going through each of the steps takes time. In some cases, the process may take years, as in the building of a new oil refinery or automobile assembly plant.

Problem Recognition

The business market purchase decision process is triggered when someone inside or outside the company identifies a need. In many cases, the need is a problem that requires a solution. The paper supply is running low and the office manager reorders more. A company's manufacturing facilities are at full capacity and it must consider options to increase production. In other situations, the need may be an opportunity that requires a new purchase. New technology can increase order efficiency or a new design of a critical component can improve the effectiveness of a company's own products, giving it an edge with consumers. As companies struggle to deal with higher energy prices, new alternative solutions, sometimes using older technologies, are being adopted for use in interesting ways.

Employees frequently activate the purchase process as part of their job. The office manager is responsible for keeping the office stocked with enough supplies. The vice president of strategic planning is tasked with planning for future manufacturing needs. However, salespeople from either the buying or selling company's sales force or channel partners also initiate the purchase process by helping identify a need or presenting an opportunity to increase efficiency or effectiveness. This is most likely to happen when the salesperson has established a trusted relationship with the company. Trade shows are also a source of new ideas; attendees often go to see what is new in the marketplace. Traditional marketing communications such as advertising and direct mail are less effective in business markets but are important in supporting the more personal communication efforts of salespeople.

Define the Need and Product Specifications

Once a problem has been identified, the next step is to clearly define the need. Individuals from across the organization clarify the problem and develop solutions. Not all problems lead to a new purchase. A vice president of information technology may notice an increase in call waiting times, but the issue could be a lack of training or a shortage of employees. The solution might include a new, expanded phone and call management system, but it will be up to management, working with other employees, to determine what is needed.

As part of describing the need, product specifications should be defined so that everyone inside and outside of the company knows exactly what is needed to solve the problem. This serves two important purposes. First, individuals inside the organization can plan for the future. Purchasing agents identify possible vendors while managers estimate costs and build budgets based on the specifications. Users plan how to assimilate the new purchase into existing work processes. The buying center will use the product specifications to help evaluate vendor proposals. Putting product specifications into a document for distribution is known as a **request for proposal (RFP)**. The second purpose of outlining product specifications is to guide potential suppliers. Product specifications as contained in the RFP become the starting point from which vendors put together their product solution. In the best-case scenario, there is a good fit between what the customer is asking for and the supplier's existing products.[43] Much more often, however, there are some specifications in which the potential products compare favorably and others where competitors excel. Exhibit 6.15 identifies the key sections of a request for proposal. RFPs generally require a great deal of information, and it takes a significant amount of time for a company to prepare a successful sales proposal.

The challenge for salespeople is to get involved in the purchase decision process as early as possible. If the salesperson, for example, has a strategic relationship with the customer, it may be possible to help define the product specifications. This is a real advantage because the vendor's salespeople can work to create specifications that present their products in the most favorable way. Product specifications are often written in such a way as to limit the number of vendors. Companies realize that not knowing the product specifications puts them at a disadvantage over other vendors. It is still possible to win the order, but the job becomes more difficult.

EXHIBIT 6.15 | Sections of a Request for Proposal

1. *Statement of Purpose:* Describe the extent of products and services your organization is looking for, as well as the overall objectives of the contract.

2. *Background Information:* Present a brief overview of your organization and its operations, using statistics, customer demographics, and psychographics. State your strengths and weaknesses honestly. Don't forget to include comprehensive information on the people who will handle future correspondence.

3. *Scope of Work:* Enumerate the specific duties to be performed by the provider and the expected outcomes. Include a detailed listing of responsibilities, particularly when subcontractors are involved.

4. *Outcome and Performance Standards:* Specify the outcome targets, minimal performance standards expected from the contractor, and methods for monitoring performance and process for implementing corrective actions.

5. *Deliverables:* Provide a list of all products, reports, and plans that will be delivered to your organization and propose a delivery schedule.

6. *Term of Contract:* Specify length, start and end dates of the contract, and the options for renewal.

7. *Payments, Incentives, and Penalties:* List all the terms of payment for adequate performance. Highlight the basis for incentives for superior performance and penalties for inadequate performance or lack of compliance.

8. *Contractual Terms and Conditions:* Attach standard contracting forms, certifications, and assurances. You may include requirements specific to this particular contract.

9. *Requirements for Proposal Preparation:* A consistent structure in terms of content, information, and document types simplifies things for the people evaluating the proposals. Therefore, you should request a particular structure for the proposal and provide an exhaustive list of documents you want to receive.

10. *Evaluation and Award Process:* Lay down the procedures and criteria used for evaluating proposals and for making the final contract award.

11. *Process Schedule:* Clearly and concisely present the time line for the steps leading to the final decision, such as the dates for submitting the letter of intent, sending questions, attending the preproposal conference, submitting the proposal.

12. *Contacts:* Include a complete list of people to contact for information on the RFP, or with any other questions. Incorporate their name, title, responsibilities, and the various ways of contacting them into this list.

Source: Technology Evaluation Centers, "Writing an RFP," 2017.

Search for Suppliers

Once the company's needs have been identified and product specifications have been outlined, business customers can identify potential suppliers. Two methods are commonly used to determine the list of vendors. First, companies create a list of preferred or approved suppliers and go to that list whenever a new purchase is being considered. The list can result from the company's cumulative experience. In this situation it is important to keep the list current with respect to existing vendors and also any new vendors.

A second, more complex, method is to search for and identify potential suppliers. The Internet has become a valuable tool for companies in identifying potential suppliers. General search engines and even dedicated supplier search websites, such as Thomas Global Register, are easy to use and enable customers to identify specific potential vendors. Of course, companies still need to perform due diligence by checking vendor customer references, and in critical purchases it is advisable to research the vendor's financial stability and management capabilities.

Seek Sales Proposals in Response to RFP

Companies frequently solicit proposals from a number of vendors for two reasons. First, even if there is a preferred vendor, getting more information about available options from other suppliers is a good idea. If it is an open vendor search, then the proposal becomes a valuable source of information as well as the primary evaluation tool. Second, getting additional proposals helps in negotiating with the preferred vendor. When a vendor is aware that other proposals are under consideration, that vendor works harder to meet the expectations of the customer.

This step is usually characterized by limited vendor contact. Again, many companies are asked to submit proposals from which a smaller set of potential vendors will be selected. As a result, the sales proposal plays a critical role in marketing to businesses. Most of the time it is the first and best chance to impress the customer. In general, proposals accomplish two objectives. First, the proposal clearly specifies how the company's products will meet the product specifications detailed in the RFP. Second, the proposal makes the case for selecting the company by presenting any additional information such as unique product features, service programs, or competitive pricing to help persuade the customer.

EXHIBIT 6.16	Critical Choice in the Purchase Decision

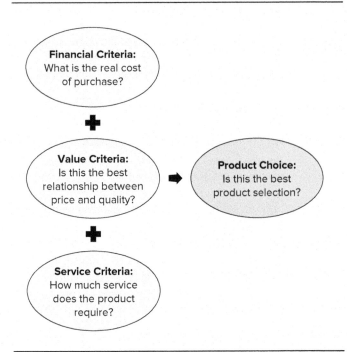

Make the Purchase Decision

Once the proposals are submitted, the next step is the purchase decision. Given the time and analysis companies put into the decision process, one might think the decision is straightforward. The reality, however, is more complex, as detailed in Exhibit 6.16. Often the final decision involves trade-offs between equally important evaluation criteria and equally qualified vendors.

Product Selection The first purchase decision is the **product choice**. In many cases the product decision is based on a single criterion, for example, product cost (the office manager purchasing printer paper at the lowest price). Single-criterion decisions usually fall into a straight rebuy or very limited modified rebuy situation and do not require a buying center to assist in the new purchase decision. Much of the time, however, no one product fits all the product specifications exactly. As a result, the final decision assesses the product against the product evaluation criteria and determines the optimal solution.[44] Consider a company purchasing a new office copier. The first response might be, "pick the best copier," but what is the definition of "best"? One person might define best as most copies per minute, another as lowest cost per copy, and a third may consider the lowest maintenance costs to be the best. As a result, it is important to define the evaluation criteria and then follow a consistent and fair methodology in evaluating the sales proposals. Three primary criteria are used to evaluate the product choice.

Financial Criteria Financial criteria are a set of analyses and metrics grouped together to assess the cost of ownership. The actual purchase price is just one consideration in determining the real cost of a purchase. Maintenance and operating costs, repair charges, and supplies are all costs associated with ownership that can vary across product choices. These costs are then evaluated against the stated life of the product. This is important as some products with a higher initial price actually cost less over time because of the product's longer life. Financial analysis also evaluates the time it takes to break even on the investment. A company considering new equipment designed to lower manufacturing costs will want to know how long it will take to recoup the investment given the projected savings.

Business-to-business marketers understand that presenting a strong financial case for their products is an essential part of selling the product. As a result, many of these financial analyses are performed by the supplier and included in the sales proposal. Buyers then compare, and verify, the analyses across vendors.

Value Criteria Value is the relationship between price and quality and it is a significant facet of the purchase decision. B2B buyers are aware that the lowest-cost product may not be the right product, especially in critical OEM equipment where failure can mean customer dissatisfaction or in strategic purchases such as a new IT system where failure can cause serious business disruption. On the other hand, it is costly to overengineer a product and purchase more than is needed for the situation. A computer network that must work 100 percent of the time is much more costly when considering the backup systems and redundant hardware and software needed to maintain it than a system with 95 percent run time. It is up to the buying center to determine the specifications needed to do the job.[45]

Buyers do not always need the highest-quality product, which is why most businesses carry multiple lines with different quality and price levels. Offering customers a choice increases the likelihood of success and minimizes the opportunity for competitors to target gaps in a company's overall product line.[46]

Service Criteria Buyers are concerned with the service requirements of a product because servicing equipment costs a company in two ways. First, there is the direct cost of service, including labor and supplies. Second, there is the indirect cost of downtime when a system is out of service, which means the equipment is not being used for its intended purpose.[47] Southwest flies only Boeing 737s in part because maintenance crews need to know only one plane, which makes it easier to maintain and service the 737.

Products are designed, in part, to minimize service costs. There are trade-offs, however, as companies seek the best compromise between product performance and lower service costs. Knowing the buyer's specific priorities with regard to performance, service, and other critical criteria is essential to designing and building the product that best fits the product specifications.

Supplier Choice Businesses buy not just a product; they also make a **supplier choice**. Often, multiple sellers will be offering the same product or very similar product configurations. As a result, supplier qualifications become part of the purchase decision. Decision makers know a purchase decision can turn out badly if the wrong vendor is selected, even if the product choice is correct.[48]

The most fundamental criterion in vendor selection is **reliability**, which is the vendor's ability to meet contractual obligations including delivery times and service schedules. Strategic business-to-business relationships are based, in part, on a high level of trust between organizations. In those situations, the supplier's reliability becomes an

IT'S REALLY A HYBRID OF MAN AND MACHINE.

JOHN DEERE

John Deere is a long-standing supplier in the construction industry.

Source: Deere & Company

essential factor in the final selection. Furthermore, a judgment is often made about the seller's willingness to go above and beyond what is specified in the contract. All things being equal, the seller with the best reliability and intangibles, like a willingness to do a little more than required, usually gets the order.[49]

Personal and Organizational Factors Several additional factors affect product and supplier choices. Suppliers often find it difficult to understand the role these factors play in the final decision, but their influence can be profound. The first, **personal factors**, refers to the needs, desires, and objectives of those involved in the purchase decision. Everyone in the buying center comes with his or her own needs and goals. Someone might see this as an opportunity for promotion, another believes he will receive a raise if he can be successful, and a third may want to impress management. It is not possible to separate the individual agendas people bring to the buying center from the purchase decision. In addition, individuals in the buying center come to the group with their own perspective of the decision. Engineers, for example, tend to focus on product performance and specifications. Accountants often concentrate on the cost and other financial considerations. Purchasing agents give attention to vendor quality and ease of ordering. One reason buying centers are effective is their ability to bring individuals with different perspectives together to evaluate possible product options.

Another influence on the product and supplier choice is organizational factors. The primary **organizational factor** is risk tolerance. Individuals and companies all have a certain tolerance for risk. Their product decisions will be influenced by their aversion to or acceptance of risk.[50] Consider the IT manager looking to purchase a new network for his company. Two suppliers have submitted proposals that meet the product specification. One is a local vendor with an excellent reputation. This vendor has quoted a lower price and guaranteed better service. The other is Cisco Systems, the world leader in network equipment and software. The manager for the company with a low risk tolerance will probably choose Cisco Systems. It represents the "safe" choice. His superiors would never question purchasing from the market leader. If the same individual works for a risk-tolerant organization, the decision might be to go with the vendor offering better price and service. The cost of a mistake is high. If the network goes down and the company suffers a business disruption because the supplier has performed poorly, questions about the supplier selection arise. Risk tolerance does play a role as the buying center moves closer to a final decision.

Post-Purchase Evaluation of Product and Supplier

Once the purchase decision is made, buyers begin the process of evaluation (see Exhibit 6.17). Initially, they assess product performance and the seller's response to any problems or issues. A key

EXHIBIT 6.17 | **Post-Purchase Evaluation Criteria**

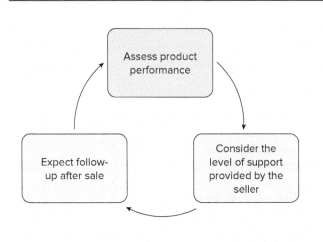

Assess product performance

Consider the level of support provided by the seller

Expect follow-up after sale

for business marketers is to make sure the customer understands the proper operation and maintenance of the product. At the same time, buyers consider the level of support provided by the seller and expect follow-up after the sale to be sure there are no problems. Dealing with complaints, resolving customer problems, and making sure the company is meeting customer expectations are critical to ensuring customer satisfaction.

The evaluation process is designed, in part, to help customers make better purchase decisions in the future. Being the current seller is a distinct advantage because, if the customer evaluates the purchase decision positively, there is no need to change the decision next time. In essence, the evaluation process, if handled properly, can be the best sales tool for the seller when it comes time for the next purchase decision.

Naturally, the opposite is also true. If the product performs poorly or the seller does not meet customer expectations, competitors can use those mistakes to trigger a modified rebuy or even a new purchase decision process that increases their probability of success. Losing a customer is disappointing; however, it also represents an opportunity. By using well-developed service recovery strategies, companies can reacquire customers (Chapter 10 discusses service recovery strategies).

THE ROLE OF TECHNOLOGY IN BUSINESS MARKETS

Technology has transformed the business purchase decision process. From the Internet to portable handheld optical scanning devices, technology has made the purchase decision process more efficient and effective. Technology has also pushed the purchase decision process closer to the product user because front-line managers can now make purchases directly.[51]

LO 6-8

Comprehend the role of technology in business markets.

Sophisticated programs manage inventories and automatically replenish supplies. By linking directly with **electronic data interchange (EDI)**, customer computers communicate directly with supplier computers to reorder as needed. Late deliveries, defective products, and other issues related to supplier performance can be identified and dealt with before they become a major problem. Collaboration between business buyers and sellers has increased significantly as a result of technology linkages.[52]

E-Procurement

B2B transactions have been growing at a phenomenal rate with online B2B commerce worldwide in excess of $1 trillion, a much larger amount than that generated by B2C online sales. The process of business purchasing online is referred to as **e-procurement**.[53] Let's examine the various e-procurement methods:

Industry purchasing sites: Industries have formed websites to streamline and standardize the e-procurement process. Steel, chemicals, paper, and automobile manufacturers have created integrated websites to assist their own purchasing departments in online purchasing and supplier selection.

Business function sites: Certain business functions have websites to standardize purchasing. For example, individual utilities used to negotiate by phone to buy and sell electricity with each other; however, today the purchase of electricity by utility companies is done over a website dedicated to energy management.

Extranet to major suppliers: Many companies have set up direct links to approved suppliers to make the purchase easier and move it closer to front-line decision makers.[54] Office Depot, for example, has a number of direct relationships using EDI with thousands of companies.

Company buying sites: Many large companies have created their own websites to assist vendors. RFPs and other relevant supplier information as well as some contact information are accessible for review.

SUMMARY

A thorough knowledge and understanding of customers is an essential element in developing an effective value proposition. For business-to-consumer companies this means learning about how and why consumers buy products and services. This chapter talks about the consumer buying decision process. We discuss the two complex, critical forces (internal and external) that shape the consumer decision-making process. We offer an in-depth analysis of the process a consumer uses in making a purchase decision. The distinction is made between high- and low-involvement decisions, which dramatically affects the degree to which the consumer engages in the entire buying decision process.

Several significant characteristics differentiate business and consumer markets, including the concentration and number of customers found in business markets. Different types of selling situations lead to very different types of customer decision processes. Business customers interact with their suppliers in very different situations, from a straight rebuy to new purchases. The buying center is a team of individuals, from inside and outside the organization, which engages in the purchase decision process and either makes or recommends to the decision maker the final product selection. The purchase decision process includes six steps, from problem identification through purchase decision and post-purchase evaluation of the product and supplier. Technology plays a major role in business-to-business marketing. The growth of online purchasing, also known as e-procurement, has transformed B2B alliances and made the process faster and more accurate.

KEY TERMS

APPLICATION QUESTIONS

connect

More application questions are available online.

1. As we have discussed, understanding the consumers in a target market is critical to creating an effective value proposition. Assume you are the vice president of marketing for Regal Cinemas. What do you think is the demographic profile (including the age, income, and life cycle stage) of your largest target market? As part of a mini-market research project, visit a movie theater on a weekend and track the people entering. How old are they? Are they families or people meeting friends?

2. You are the marketing manager for the Bowflex Revolution Home Gym. You believe the product appeals to both men and women. As you develop the marketing strategy, what differences might you consider in the product based on whether a man or woman is buying? What about the marketing communications (message, choice of media)?

3. You are the marketing manager for Lenovo laptop computers. Identify and briefly discuss the differences between the consumer market for laptops and the business market. Then give an example of each difference using college students as the consumer market and defense-related companies as the business market.

4. You work for Siemens Power Generation Systems and are responsible for the sale of large, expensive ($2 million to $5 million) turbine generators to power utility companies. You have been contacted by the Ever-Sure Utility Corporation in Any Town, USA. Identify the buying center you are likely to find inside the company and how you would market the generators to the buying center group.

MANAGEMENT DECISION CASE
Taking the Nike Experience Direct to Consumers

Let's say you're upping your game and want to exercise more. Maybe that means walking in the mornings, playing a pickup game after work, or running a marathon. Whatever your goal is, you need some new shoes, and Nike is your favored brand. If you're like the majority of consumers, you head to a retail store to purchase a pair. Until recently, this was your only choice. Just a short while ago, if you tried to connect to Nike directly you'd find yourself squarely in a system focused on B2B (business-to-business) marketing channels. While Nike is no stranger to B2C (business-to-consumer) marketing—it opened its first NikeTown retail store in 1990—these stores were as much museums as retail outlets, and more about brand promotion than retail sales.

In 2014, with more than 700 Nike-contracted factories moving shoes and apparel through 57 distribution centers to 140,000 retail stores, Nike garnered 82 percent of its revenue through B2B channels and just 18 percent from B2C.[55] But this is changing fast. Competitors such as Under Armour already get 30 percent of their sales direct from consumers.[56] Acknowledging trends in both B2C and B2B behaviors and needs, Nike announced that by 2020 it will grow its B2C e-commerce business seven-fold, from $1 billion to $7 billion. Total B2C business, including company-owned retail, will rise to $16 billion, or 32 percent of its total global revenue, almost doubling in just six years.[57]

As discussed in this chapter, demographic trends plus changes in consumers' motivations and behaviors are guiding Nike to expand its target markets and channels. For example, broad consumer trends suggest e-commerce B2C sales will continue to grow, from $1.9 trillion in 2016 (8.7 percent of total worldwide retail sales) to $4 trillion by 2020.[58] More specifically, consumers' desire to have healthier lifestyles suggests an increase in Nike's overall business. But the continued rise in the number of working women, who have less time to shop, suggests more spending power in the women's sector and a greater need for access to online purchasing. In addition, demographic trends show younger cohorts, who are very comfortable with online shopping, are now the largest consumer segment. Nike, intent on serving customers in ways that meet their needs, has addressed these trends by increasing its attention to its women's line of training footwear and apparel, and expanding its e-commerce presence.

But trends in B2B also suggest that Nike should target more of its business with direct-to-consumer models. Threatening the traditional B2B distribution model in the eyeglass, razor, and shoe industries, companies like Warby Parker, the Dollar Shave Club, and TOMS Shoes are selling products directly to the consumer instead of through wholesale distribution channels.[59] This has placed traditional manufacturers, those who make the product but rely on a distribution channel to reach consumers, on the defensive.

Prior to the Internet, it was difficult to purchase directly from a manufacturer. B2B firms didn't have the operational systems to take and fill small orders from individual consumers. But the Internet makes one-to-one communication easier, and readily available e-commerce tools make fulfilling orders much simpler. With these tools, small manufacturers can compete with the large. Today, even the smallest of manufacturers can pitch their product directly to consumers. Before a product is made, companies can pitch their value though sites like Kickstarter—an online crowd-sourced funding site—sourcing their "investor-customers" directly and then continuing to sell B2C instead of starting with distribution channels.

Consumers often like the direct model too. Disappointments encountered in retail shopping, where limited inventory may mean the right size, color, or quantity is out of stock, are almost never a problem when shopping directly with the manufacturer, where inventory is largest and the ability to make more quickly is right at hand. Likewise, consumers are often pleased when they get to interact directly with a brand by providing input into product design or sharing feedback on their experience with the product. Manufacturers are also perceived as being the truest experts on the product, and a better place to get advice or help.[60] Such interactions can lead to improved brand loyalty.

Manufacturers are recognizing this disruption in the marketplace, so much so that Unilever, one of the world's largest consumer goods conglomerates, recently paid $1 billion for the Dollar Shave Club. And the reason? Not the excellent e-commerce site operated by Dollar Shave Club, but the firm's ability to build a relationship directly with consumers.[61] For manufacturers, the opportunity to own the relationship with the customer, and to be able to define their own brand without intermediaries, is an attractive reason to go direct. And for Nike, one of the world's top 20 most valuable brands, owning the relationship as trends move toward B2C will be important.[62]

Questions for Consideration

1. This chapter highlights how marketing efforts are different for B2B and B2C firms. As Nike and other manufacturers continue to expand into B2C channels, what are some differences in B2C and B2B behavior that might affect Nike's approach to these channels?

2. What are some hurdles Nike may face as it expands its B2C business? Consider this question both internally, with new skills Nike needs to amass, and externally, with challenges it may face from its B2B channel partners.

3. What would be some negative consequences to consumers if all manufacturers sold only B2C and eliminated wholesaler distributors who supply retail stores?

MARKETING PLAN EXERCISE

ACTIVITY 5: Define Consumer Markets

For those marketing products to consumers (or through a channel that sells directly to consumers), understanding the purchase decision process of the target market is an essential element of the marketing plan. This exercise includes the following activities:

1. Develop a demographic profile of the customer to include
   a. Age
   b. Income
   c. Occupation

d. Education

e. Lifestyle (activities, interests, opinions)

2. Describe the motivation of the target consumer. Why is the consumer buying the product?

3. What external forces will influence the target consumer as he or she considers the purchase? For example, will the consumer's culture or subculture affect the purchase decision? How?

4. Describe the consumer's typical consumer purchase decision process. What is the likely process a consumer will go through in making the decision to purchase the product?

ACTIVITY 6: Determine Business Market Relationships

This exercise has four primary activities:

1. Conduct an analysis of your key market opportunities to assess the fundamental nature of these markets. This analysis should include a description of:

a. What are the key companies in this market? How much business do you do with the industry leaders? What share of their total business do you have?

b. Where are these companies located?

2. Identify the probable company structure and business center participants you would encounter in selling to your key B2B customer.

3. Put together a probable buying decision process for key B2B customers and discuss your internal process in selling to these customers.

4. Develop a list of second-tier customers in key B2B markets that represent future potential customers.

NOTES

1. S. Mark Young, James J. Gong, and Wim A. Van der Stede, "The Business of Selling Movies," *Strategic Finance* 89, no. 9 (2009), pp. 35–42; and Jon Silver and David Lieberman, "Movie Theater Stocks Hit after Analyst Warns of Slowing Growth," *Deadline,* February 1 2017, http://deadline.com/2017/02/movie-theater-stocks-hit-analyst-warns-slowing-growth-1201899794/.

2. P. Sullivan and J. Heitmeyer, "Looking at Gen Y Shopping Preferences and Intentions: Exploring the Role of Experience and Apparel Involvement," *International Journal of Consumer Studies* 32, no. 3 (2008), pp. 285–99.

3. Paul G. Patterson, "Demographic Correlates of Loyalty in a Service Context," *Journal of Services Marketing* 21, no. 2 (2007), pp. 112–21.

4. Lisa E. Bolton, Americus Reed II, Kevin G. Volpp, and Katrina Armstrong, "How Does Drug and Supplement Marketing Affect a Healthy Lifestyle?" *Journal of Consumer Research* 34, no. 5 (2008), pp. 713–26.

5. Maureen E. Hupfer and Brian Detior, "Beyond Gender Differences: Self-Concept Orientation and Relationship-Building Orientation on the Internet," *Journal of Business Research* 60, no. 6 (2007), pp. 613–28; and J. Michael Pearson, Ann Pearson, and David Green, "Determining the Importance of Key Criteria in Web Usability," *Management Research News* 30, no. 11 (2007), pp. 816–29.

6. Parimal S. Bhagat and Jerome D. Williams, "Understanding Gender Differences in Professional Service Relationships," *Journal of Consumer Marketing* 25, no. 1 (2008), pp. 16–29.

7. M. Fishbein and I. Ajzen, *Belief, Attitude, Intention, and Behavior: An Introduction to Theory and Research* (Reading, MA: Addison-Wesley, 1975).

8. Maxwell Winchester and Jenni Romaniuk, "Positive and Negative Brand Beliefs and Brand Defection/Update," *European Journal of Marketing* 42, no. 5/6 (2008), pp. 553–68.

9. John Davis, "Did Seth Go to the Dark Side," *Inc.,* May 2008, pp. 21–24.

10. Pamela Miles Horner, "Perceived Quality and Image: When All Is Not 'Rosy,'" *Journal of Business Research* 61, no. 7 (2008), pp. 715–31.

11. E. J. Schultz, "Inside Allstate's Strategy to Start Mayhem on Twitter," *Ad Age,* October 15, 2013, http://adage.com/article/digital/inside-allstate-s-strategy-start-mayhem-twitter/244690/.

12. Joseph B. White, "Eyes on the Road: Good News, Bad News at Buick; Models Get Safer, Says J. D. Power, Then Get Dumped," *Wall Street Journal,* August 14, 2007, p. D5.

13. Elizabeth Cowley, "How Enjoyable Was It? Remembering an Affective Reaction to a Previous Consumption Experience," *Journal of Consumer Research* 34, no. 4 (2007), pp. 494–510; and Moonhee Yang and David R. Roskos-Ewoldsen, "The Effectiveness of Brand Placements in the Movies: Levels of Placements, Explicit and Implicit Memory, and Brand Choice Behavior," *Journal of Communication* 57, no. 3 (2007), pp. 469–82.

14. Ming-tiem Tsai, Wen-ko Liang, and Mei-Ling Liu, "The Effects of Subliminal Advertising on Consumer Attitudes and Buying Intentions," *International Journal of Management* 24, no. 1 (2007), pp. 3–15; and Sheri J. Broyles, "Subliminal Advertising and the Perpetual Popularity of Playing to People's Paranoia," *Journal of Consumer Affairs* 40, no. 2 (2006), pp. 392–407.

15. Brian D. Till and Sarah M. Stanley, "Classical Conditioning and Celebrity Endorsers: An Examination of Belongingness

15. and Resistance to Extinction," *Psychology and Marketing* 25, no. 2 (2008), pp. 179–94.

16. Gordon R. Foxall, M. Mirella, and Yani de Soriano, "Situational Influences on Consumers' Attitudes and Behaviors," *Journal of Business Research* 58, no. 4 (2005), pp. 518–33.

17. Marcus Cunha Jr., Chris Janiszewski, and Juliano Laran, "Protection of Prior Learning in Complex Consumer Learning Environments," *Journal of Consumer Research* 34, no. 6 (2008), pp. 850–68.

18. Katja Magion-Muller and Malcolm Evans, "Culture, Communications, and Business: The Power of Advanced Semiotics," *International Journal of Marketing Research* 50, no. 2 (2008), pp. 169–82.

19. Mark W. Johnston and Greg W. Marshall, *Contemporary Selling,* 4th ed. (New York: Routledge, 2013), p. 180.

20. "Softsheen.Carson," *L'Oréal,* 2017, http://www.lorealusa.com/brand/consumer-products-division/softsheencarson.

21. Alexandra Montgomery, "U.S. Families 2025: In Search of Future Families," *Futures* 40, no. 4 (2008), pp. 377–89.

22. Julie Tinson, Clive Nancarrow, and Ian Brace, "Purchase Decision Making and the Increasing Significance of Family Types," *Journal of Consumer Marketing* 25, no. 1 (2008), pp. 45–56.

23. Rex Y. Du and Wagner A. Kamakura, "Household Life Cycles and Lifestyles in the United States," *Journal of Marketing Research* 43, no. 1 (2006), pp. 121–32.

24. Palaniappan Thiagarajan, Jason E. Lueg, Nicole Ponder, Sheri Lokken Worthy, and Ronald D. Taylor, "The Effect of Role Strain on the Consumer Decision Process of Single Parent Households," *American Marketing Association, Conference Proceedings 17* (Summer 2006), p. 124.

25. Caroline Goode and Robert East, "Testing the Marketing Maven Concept," *Journal of Marketing Management* 24, no. 3/4 (2008), pp. 265–81; and Lawrence F. Feick and Linda L. Price, "The Market Maven: A Diffuser of Marketplace Information," *Journal of Marketing* 51, no. 1 (1987), pp. 83–98.

26. Katherine White and Darren W. Dahl, "Are All Out-Groups Created Equal? Consumer Identity and Dissociative Influence," *Journal of Consumer Research* 34, no. 4 (2007), pp. 525–40; Jennifer Edson Escalas and James R. Bettman, "Self-Construal, Reference Groups, and Brand Meaning," *Journal of Consumer Research* 32, no. 3 (2005), pp. 378–90; and Terry L. Childers and Akshay R. Rao, "The Influence of Familiar and Peer-Based Reference Groups on Consumer Decisions," *Journal of Consumer Research* 19, no. 2 (1992), pp. 198–212.

27. Hans H. Baurer, Nicola E. Sauer, and Christine Becker, "Investigating the Relationship between Product Involvement and Consumer Decision Making Styles," *Journal of Consumer Behavior* 5, no. 4 (2006), pp. 342–55; Salvador Miquel, Eva M. Capillure, and Joaquin Aldas-Maznazo, "The Effect of Personal Involvement on the Decision to Buy Store Brands," *Journal of Product and Brand Management* 11, no. 1 (2002), pp. 6–19; and Laurent Gilles and Jean-Noel Kapferer, "Measuring Consumer Involvement Profiles," *Journal of Marketing Research* 22, no. 1 (1985), pp. 41–54.

28. Zafar U. Ahmed, James P. Johnson, Xiz Yang, and Chen Kehng Fatt, "Does Country of Origin Matter for Low Involvement Products?" *International Marketing Review* 21, no. 1 (2004), pp. 102–15; and Wayne D. Hoyer, "An Examination of Consumer Decision Making for Common Repeat Purchase Product," *Journal of Consumer Research* 11, no. 3 (1984), pp. 822–30.

29. On Amir and Jonathan Levav, "Choice Construction versus Preference Construction: The Instability of Preferences Learned in Context," *Journal of Marketing Research* 45, no. 2 (2008), pp. 145–61.

30. Mohammed M. Nadeem, "Post-Purchase Dissonance: The Wisdom of 'Repeat' Purchase," *Journal of Global Business Issues* 1, no. 2 (2007), pp. 183–94.

31. Brian N. Rutherford, James S. Boles, Hiram C. Barksdale Jr., and Julie T. Johnson, "Buyer's Relational Desire and Numbers of Suppliers Used: The Relationship between Perceived Commitment and Continuance," *Journal of Marketing Theory and Practice* 16, no. 3 (2008), pp. 247–58.

32. Ruben Chumpitaz Caceres and Nicholas G. Paparoidamis, "Service Quality, Relationship Satisfaction, Trust, Commitment and Business-to-Business Loyalty," *European Journal of Marketing* 41, no. 7/8 (2007), pp. 836–48; and Papassapa Rauyruen and Kenneth E. Miller, "Relationship Quality as Predictor of B2B Customer Loyalty," *Journal of Business Research* 60, no. 1 (2007), pp. 21–35.

33. Avik Chakrabarti, Yi-Ting Hsieh and Yuanchen Chang, "Cross Border Mergers and Market Concentration in a Vertically Related Industry: Theory and Evidence," *Journal of International Trade and Economic Development* 26, no. 1 (2017), pp. 111–30.

34. Tao Gao, M. Joseph Sirgy, and Monroe M. Bird, "Reducing Buyer Decision Making Uncertainty in Organizational Purchasing: Can Supplier Trust, Commitment, and Dependency Help?" *Journal of Business Research* 58, no. 4 (2005), pp. 397–409.

35. Leonidas C. Leonidou, "Industrial Manufacturer-Customer Relationships: The Discriminating Role of the Buying Situation," *Industrial Marketing Management* 33, no. 8 (2004), pp. 731–45.

36. G. Tomas M. Hult, David J. Ketchen Jr., and Brian R. Chabowski, "Leadership, the Buying Center, and Supply Chain Performance: A Study of Linked Users, Buyers, and Suppliers," *Industrial Marketing Management* 36, no. 3 (2007), pp. 393–408.

37. Marcel Paulssen and Matthias M. Birk, "Satisfaction and Repurchase Behavior in a Business to Business Setting: Investigating the Moderating Effect of Manufacturer, Company and Demographic Characteristics," *Industrial Marketing Management* 36, no. 7 (2007), pp. 983–95.

38. Marydee Ojala, "SIC Those NAICS on Me: Industry Classification Codes for Business Research," *Online* 29, no. 1 (2005), pp. 42–45; and Robert P. Parker, "More U.S. Economic Data Series Incorporate the North American Industry Classification System," *Business Economics* 38, no. 2 (2003), pp. 57–60.

39. Kun Liao and Paul Hong, "Building Global Supplier Networks: A Supplier Portfolio Entry Model," *Journal of Enterprise Information Management* 20, no. 5 (2007), pp. 511–23; and Chiaho Chang, "Procurement Policy and Supplier Behavior—OEM vs. ODM," *Journal of Business and Management* 8, no. 2 (2002), pp. 181–98.

40. Masaaki Kotabe, Michael J. Mol, and Janet Y. Murray, "Outsourcing, Performance, and the Role of e-Commerce: A Dynamic Perspective," *Industrial Marketing Management* 37, no. 1 (2008), pp. 37–48; and Bruno Schilli and Fan Dai, "Collaborative Life Cycle Management between Suppliers and OEM," *Computers in Industry* 57, no. 8/9 (2006), pp. 725–29.

41. Kyle Mizokami, "First of Its Class, America's Newest Aircraft Carrier Is Underway at Sea," *Popular Mechanics,* April 10, 2017, http://www.popularmechanics.com/military/navy-ships/news/a26014/gerald-ford-carrier-is-underway-at-sea/.

42. Adventist Health System Website, April 2017, http://adventisthealthsystem.com/page.php?section=locations.

43. Jesus Cerquides, Maite Lopex-Sanchez, Antonio Reyes-Moro, and Juan A. Rodruguez-Aguilar, "Enabling Assisted Strategy Negotiations in Actual World Procurement Scenarios," *Electronic Commerce Research* 7, no. 3/4 (2007), pp. 189–221; and Mike Brewster, "Perfecting the RFP," *Inc.,* March 1, 2005, p. 38.

44. S. Y. Chou, C. Y. Shen, and Y. H. Chang, "Vendor Selection in a Modified Re-Buy Situation Using a Strategy Aligned Fuzzy Approach," *International Journal of Production Research* 45, no. 14 (2007), pp. 3113–24.

45. Alptekin Ulutas, Nagesh Shukla, Senevi Kiridena, and Peter Gibson, "A Utility-Driven Approach to Supplier Evaluation and Selection: Empirical Validation of an Integrated Solution Framework," *International Journal of Production Research* 54, no. 5 (2016), http://www.tandfonline.com/doi/abs/10.1080/00207543.20.15.1098787.

46. Nicolas G. Paparoidamis, Constantine S. Katsikeas, and Ruben Chumpitaz, "The Role of Supplier Performance in Building Customer Trust and Loyalty: A Cross Country Examination," *Industrial Marketing Management,* February 2017, http://www.sciencedirect.com/science/article/pii/S0019850117301372.

47. Ruth N. Bolton, Katherine N. Lemon, and Peter C. Verhoef, "Expanding Business to Business Customer Relationships: Modeling the Customer's Upgrade Decision," *Journal of Marketing* 72, no. 1 (2008), pp. 46–60; and Paul Jeremy Williams, M. Sajid Khan, Rania Semaan, Earl R. Naumann, and Nicholas Jeremy Ashill, "Drivers of Contract Renewal in International B2B Services: A Firm-Level Analysis," *Marketing Intelligence & Planning* 35, no. 3 (2017), pp. 358–76, doi: 10.1108/MIP-05-2016-0079.

48. Maria Holmlund, "A Definition, Model and Empirical Analysis of Business to Business Relationship Quality," *International Journal of Service Industry Management* 19, no. 1 (2008), pp. 32–46.

49. Havard Hansen, Bendik M. Samuelsen, and Pal R. Siseth, "Customer Perceived Value in B-to-B Service Relationships: Investigating the Importance of Corporate Reputation," *Industrial Marketing Management* 37, no. 2 (2008), pp. 206–20; and Jeffrey E. Lewin and Wesley J. Johnston, "The Impact of Supplier Downsizing on Performance, Satisfaction over Time, and Repurchase Decisions," *Journal of Business and Industrial Marketing* 23, no. 4 (2008), pp. 249–63.

50. Wayne A. Neu and Stephen W. Brown, "Manufacturers Forming Successful Complex Business Services: Designing an Organization to Fit the Market," *International Journal of Service Industry Management* 19, no. 2 (2008), pp. 232–39.

51. Blanca Hernandez Ortega, Julio Jimenez Martinez, and Ja Jose Martin De Hoyos, "The Role of Information Technology Knowledge in B2B Development," *International Journal of E-Business Research* 4, no. 1 (2008), pp. 40–55.

52. Christian Tanner, Ralf Wolffle, Petra Schubert, and Michael Quade, "Current Trends and Challenges in Electronic Procurement: An Empirical Study," *Electronic Markets* 18, no. 1 (2008), pp. 8–19.

53. Juha Mikka Nurmilaakso, "Adoption of e-Business Functions Migration from EDI Based on XML Based e-Business Frameworks in Supply Chain Integration," *International Journal of Production Economics* 113, no. 2 (2008), pp. 721–41.

54. T. Ravichandran, S. Pant, and D. Chatterjee, "Impact of Industry Structure and Product Characteristics on the Structure of Be2 Vertical Hubs," *IEEE Transactions on Engineering Management* 54, no. 3 (2007), p. 506.

55. Phalguni Soni, "An Overview of Nike's Supply Chain and Manufacturing Strategies," *Market Realist,* December 2, 2014, http://marketrealist.com/2014/12/overview-nikes-supply-chain-manufacturing-strategies/; and Phalguni Soni, "Why Is Nike Focusing on the Direct-to-Consumer Channel?" *Market Realist,* March 15, 2016, http://marketrealist.com/2016/03/nikes-focusing-higher-dtc-channel-growth/.

56. Soni, "An Overview of Nike's Supply Chain and Manufacturing Strategies"; and Soni, "Why Is Nike Focusing on the Direct-to-Consumer Channel?"

57. "Nike, Inc. Announces Target of $50 Billion in Revenues by End of FY20," October 14, 2015, http://s1.q4cdn.com/806093406/files/doc_events/NIKE-Inc-FY16-Investor-Day-Summary-Press-Release-FINAL.pdf.

58. "Worldwide Retail Ecommerce Sales Will Reach $1.915 Trillion This Year," *eMarketer,* August 22, 2016, https://www.emarketer.com/Article/Worldwide-Retail-Ecommerce-Sales-Will-Reach-1915-Trillion-This-Year/1014369.

59. Zachary Hanlon, "Why Direct-to-Consumer Is a Powerful Business Model for B2B Companies," *Oracle,* December 8, 2016, https://blogs.oracle.com/cx/commerce/why-direct-to-consumer-is-a-powerful-business-model-for-b2b-companies.

60. Jon MacDonald, "16 Powerful Benefits of Selling Direct-to-Consumer Online," *The Good,* November 22, 2016, https://thegood.com/insights/benefits-direct-to-consumer/.

61. Jing Cao, Melissa Mittelman, "Why Unilever Really Bought Dollar Shave Club," July 20, 2016, *Bloomberg Technology,* https://www.bloomberg.com/news/articles/2016-07-20/why-unilever-really-bought-dollar-shave-club.

62. "Best Global Brands," *Interbrand,* 2016, http://interbrand.com/best-brands/best-global-brands/2016/ranking/.

CHAPTER 7

Segmentation, Target Marketing, and Positioning

LEARNING OBJECTIVES

LO 7-1 Explain the criteria for effective segmentation.

LO 7-2 Identify the various approaches to market segmentation.

LO 7-3 Describe the steps in target marketing.

LO 7-4 Define positioning and link it to the use of the marketing mix.

LO 7-5 Use and interpret perceptual maps.

LO 7-6 Identify sources of differentiation.

LO 7-7 Avoid potential positioning errors.

FULFILLING CONSUMER NEEDS AND WANTS

The triad of activities illustrated in Exhibit 7.1—market segmentation, target marketing, and positioning—get at the heart of marketing's ability to successfully create, communicate, and deliver value to customers and thus successfully fulfill their needs and wants. This capability is enabled by CRM, which was introduced as a concept in Chapter 1 and developed extensively in Chapter 5. What distinguishes much of marketing today from that of the past is that today's marketing managers can more precisely home in on specific customers and customer groups and offer products or services that have a clear and compelling value proposition for those specific customers.[1]

Accomplishing this first requires the use of **market segmentation** to divide a market into meaningful smaller markets or submarkets based on common characteristics. Once a segmentation approach is developed, marketing managers engage in **target marketing**, which involves evaluating the segments and deciding which shows the most promise for development. In most ways, selecting target markets (also called market targets) is truly an *investment* decision. That is, a company must decide where to best invest its limited resources in developing markets for future growth. Everything else being equal, it should invest in the target markets that promise the best overall return on that investment over the long run.[2]

Finally, the way the firm ultimately connects its value proposition to a target market is through its positioning. **Positioning** relies on the communication of one or more sources of value to customers in such a way that the customer can easily make the connection between his or her needs and wants and what the product has to offer. Execution of this approach is referred to as a firm's **positioning strategy.** Positioning strategies are executed through the development of unique combinations of the marketing mix variables, introduced in Chapter 1 as the 4Ps: product (or more broadly—the offering), price, place (distribution/supply chain), and promotion.[3]

The process of effective market segmentation, target marketing, and positioning is one of the most complex and strategically important aspects of marketing management. It bridges the overall process of creating, communicating, and delivering value to customers in that if the segmentation is flawed, target selection is incorrect, or positioning is unclear, there is no *value* because the customer doesn't connect with the product. Having a product whose value proposition is a well-kept secret is not a good thing in marketing—marketing managers want the right customers to clearly recognize their products' value-adding capabilities.[4]

Let's first take a closer look at segmentation. Then we will go on to gain an understanding of target marketing. Finally, we will introduce positioning as a lead-in to the chapters that follow, which focus on developing, pricing, and delivering the value offering. These three concepts are equally relevant in both the consumer and business marketplaces. The criteria used for developing segments are somewhat different between the two markets, but the general concepts and importance of the process are similar.

EXHIBIT 7.1 | Market Segmentation, Target Marketing, and Positioning

Market Segmentation
Dividing a market into meaningful smaller markets or submarkets based on common characteristics.

↓

Target Marketing
Evaluating the market segments, then making decisions about which among them is most worthy of investment for development.

↓

Positioning
Communicating one or more sources of value to customers in ways that connect needs and wants to what the product has to offer. Positioning strategies are executed through the development of unique combinations of the marketing mix variables.

WHAT IS SEGMENTATION?

From a marketing manager's perspective, one way to think about markets is on a continuum that ranges from *undifferentiated,* where everybody essentially needs and wants the same thing, to *singular,* where each person has unique needs and wants. The territory between these two extremes is where segmentation approaches come into play.

LO 7-1

Explain the criteria for effective segmentation.

Segmentation seeks to find one or more factors about members of a heterogeneous market that allow for dividing the market into smaller, more homogeneous subgroups for the purposes of developing different marketing strategies to best meet the segments' distinct needs and wants.[5] The operative word is *different,* as in **differentiation**, which means communicating and delivering value in different ways to different customer groups.[6] It is important to note that the basic logic and principles behind segmentation are sound, regardless of the basis on which a market is segmented:

- Not all customers are alike.
- Subgroups of customers can be identified on some basis of similarity.
- The subgroups will be smaller and more homogeneous than the overall market.
- Needs and wants of a subgroup are more efficiently and effectively addressed than would be possible within the heterogeneous full market.

Effective Segmentation

Before developing and executing a segmentation approach, the marketing manager must be assured that several criteria for successful segmentation are met, as listed in Exhibit 7.2. The manager must satisfactorily answer these questions:

1. *Is the segment of sufficient size to warrant investing in a unique value-creating strategy for that segment as a target market?* Ultimately, there is no point doing market segmentation unless a positive return on investment is expected. Size of a segment doesn't necessarily mean number of customers—when Bombardier markets its small Learjets, it knows the number of potential buyers is limited. Yet segmentation is still a valid approach because of differences in needs and wants among customers and the financial size of the transaction.

2. *Is the segment readily identifiable and can it be measured?* Effective segmentation relies on the marketing manager's ability to isolate members of a submarket to create a unique appeal. Segmentation most often requires data, and if secondary data on the markets of interest aren't available or if primary data can't be easily collected, it may not be possible to do segmentation.

3. *Is the segment clearly differentiated on one or more important dimensions when communicating the value of the product?* For segmentation to work properly, it must allow for the creation and execution of different marketing strategies to the different submarkets identified. Segments should be expected to respond differently to different marketing strategies and programs. Otherwise, there is no reason to differentiate.

4. *Can the segment be reached (in terms of both communication and physical product) in order to deliver the value of the product, and subsequently can it be effectively and efficiently managed?* Barriers to reaching a segment might include language, physical distance, or, as in the case of some developing markets, transportation, technology, and infrastructure challenges. Firms have to be able to sustain their management of a target segment over time—if this activity becomes problematic, it can be a drain on resources and result in poor ROI.

When considering segmentation, it is important to remember that an essential part of Marketing (Big M)—strategic marketing—is not just *identifying* existing segments but also *creating* new ones through product development strategies. The sensational initial introduction of Apple's iPhone stimulated needs

Old Spice is a venerable brand in the men's toiletries market. In fact, it's so strong with the male segment that it's doubtful a product could be branded Old Spice and be successful with women.

Source: Procter & Gamble

EXHIBIT 7.2 | Criteria for Effective Segmentation

1. Segment is of sufficient size to warrant investing in a unique value-creating strategy for that segment as a target market.
2. Segment is readily identifiable and can be measured.
3. Segment is clearly differentiated on one or more important dimensions when communicating the value of the product.
4. Segment can be reached (in terms of both communication and physical product) to deliver the value of the product, and subsequently can be effectively and efficiently managed.

and wants on the part of consumers in uncharted areas in terms of a single product's capabilities to fulfill, thus creating a new market by opening up new avenues of value-enhancing apps.[7]

SEGMENTING CONSUMER MARKETS

In the consumer marketplace, the categories of variables used by marketing managers to develop segments can be conveniently grouped into four broad categories as illustrated by Exhibit 7.3: geographic, demographic, psychographic, and behavioral. Let's consider each of these segmentation approaches in turn.

Geographic Segmentation

One of the most straightforward approaches to segmentation is when evidence exists that consumers respond differently to marketing strategies and programs based on where they live. Thus, **geographic segmentation** divides consumer groups based on physical location. The key question is, do consumption patterns vary among the geographic submarkets identified? If so, firms can make tailored adjustments in their products to satisfy those regional differences in needs and wants.[8]

Within the United States, some of the more popular approaches to geographic segmentation include:

- *By region*—Northeast, Southeast, Midwest, and West, for example.
- *By density of population*—urban, suburban, exurban, and rural, for example.
- *By size and growth of population*—Exhibit 7.4 shows the top 20 standard metropolitan statistical areas (SMSAs) in the United States.
- *By climate*—colder Northern states versus warmer Southern states.

EXHIBIT 7.3 | **Consumer Market Segmentation Approaches**

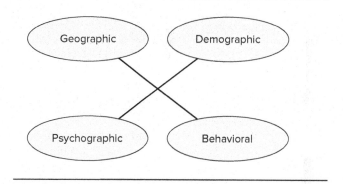

EXHIBIT 7.4 | **Top 20 U.S. SMSAs**

Rank	SMSA	Pop. Millions	Rank	SMSA	Pop. Millions
1	New York	20.2	11	San Francisco	4.7
2	Los Angeles	13.3	12	Phoenix	4.7
3	Chicago	9.5	13	Riverside, CA	4.5
4	Dallas	7.2	14	Detroit	4.3
5	Houston	6.8	15	Seattle	3.8
6	Washington, D.C.	6.1	16	Minneapolis	3.6
7	Philadelphia	6.1	17	San Diego	3.3
8	Miami	6.1	18	Tampa	3.0
9	Atlanta	5.8	19	Denver	2.8
10	Boston	4.8	20	St. Louis	2.8

Source: U.S. Census Bureau, population estimates. Largest city in each SMSA is listed.

Again, the key questions are whether segmenting by one or more of these geographic qualities means satisfying the criteria for effective segmentation and whether it will ultimately facilitate better communication and delivery of value to the submarkets than could be accomplished within the aggregate market. Target, for example, segments its target market by geographic climate. Starting in early September, Target begins marketing winter coats in its Minneapolis-area stores, an activity that won't begin until much later in Houston, where customers are still expecting several more months of 80 to 90 degrees. The chain's South Florida stores might never even stock traditional cold-weather apparel except in small quantities for travelers. Target wisely recognizes different customer needs across different climates and builds its marketing plans accordingly.

Geographic segmentation is useful but, in most instances, is an insufficient segmentation criterion in and of itself. Because people in the United States are extremely mobile and because the demand for many products is not determined by where a person lives, additional types of segmentation are needed to successfully target customers.

Demographic Segmentation

Another straightforward approach to segmentation is via demographic variables. In Chapter 6, you learned that demographics are the statistical characteristics of human populations such as age or income that are used to identify markets. **Demographic segmentation** divides consumer groups based on a variety of readily measurable descriptive factors about the group. Many different demographic variables are available for measurement including age, generational group, gender, family, race and ethnicity, income, occupation, education, social class, and geodemographic group. Demographic segmentation is one of the most popular segmentation approaches because customer needs and wants tend to vary with some degree of regularity based on demographic differences and because of the relative ease of measurement of the variables.[9] Let's look at the major demographic variables more closely (see Exhibit 7.5).

Age *Age segmentation* presumes some regularity of consumer needs and wants by chronological age.[10] It is important to make the distinction between chronological age, actual age in years, and psychological or attitudinal age, which reflects how people see themselves.

McDonald's employs age segmentation to execute different marketing strategies to attract young children for a Happy Meal and older consumers for an early morning Egg McMuffin and coffee with friends. But marketers must take care to understand that age alone often is not sufficient for successful segmentation. Older consumers exhibit great differences from person to person on such things as income, mobility, and work status. In fact, marketing managers in companies ranging from travel to insurance to health care have come to realize that lumping older consumers into one group is not an effective segmentation approach because of the vast differences in other important variables.

EXHIBIT 7.5 | **Demographic Segmentation Variables**

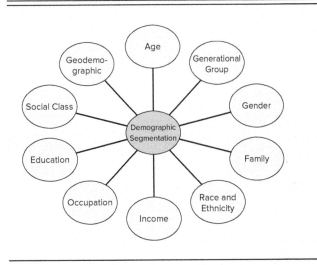

Generational Group One approach to age segmentation that helps get at the heart of differences in needs and wants is *generational segmentation*. Much research has been done on understanding differences in groups of people by generation. What defines a generational group and how does one know when a new generational group is emerging? Sociologists look for defining events such as wars, major economic upheaval, or sociocultural revolution as triggers for generational change. As with other segmentation approaches, the notion that different positioning strategies can be developed and executed for different generational groups assumes some degree of homogeneity among the generational cohort.[11] The most recent generational groups, from oldest to youngest, along with their birth years

EXHIBIT 7.6 | Generational Groups and Representative Values

GI (16 million born 1901–1924)

- Financial security and conservative spending (shaped by hard times and the economic depression of the 1930s)
- No such thing as problems—only challenges and opportunities
- Civic minded
- Duty to family, community, and country
- Unified and team oriented

Silent (35 million born 1925–1945)

- Strength in human relation skills
- Respectful of others' opinions
- Trusting conformists
- Health, stability, and wisdom
- Civic life and extended families

Baby boomer (78 million born 1946–1964)

- Forever young
- Individualistic
- Conspicuous consumption—great acquirers of goods and services
- Idealistic: value- and cause-driven despite indulgences and hedonism
- The end justifies the means

Generation X (57 million born 1965–1977)

- Lack of trust in society
- Cynical and media-savvy
- Entrepreneurial
- Accept diversity
- Environmentally conscious
- Work to live, not live to work

Generation Y or millennial (60 million born 1978–1994)

- Pragmatic
- Optimistic
- Team players
- Savvy consumers
- Edgy
- Focused on urban style
- More idealistic than Gen X
- Technology comes naturally

Generation Z (42 + million born after 1994)

- Multicultural
- Highly tech-savvy
- Educated
- Grown up in affluence
- Big spending power

are the GI Generation (1901–1924), Silent Generation (1925–1945), baby boomers (1946–1964), Generation X (1965–1977), Generation Y or millennials (1978–1994), and Generation Z (after 1994). It is important to recognize that Generation Z is a "work in progress" and as such it is way too soon to know what that next group after the millennials might ultimately be like, although there is much speculation. Also, a caveat is necessary at this point because there is no universal agreement on birth year ranges, especially for the more recent generations. We've presented a commonly used version here, but others may vary by a few years. Exhibit 7.6 describes each of these generational cohorts through Generation Z, including some of the core representative values of each.

The generational group that for years has been the apple of the marketing manager's eye is the baby boomers. This is because there are so many of them and because they personify conspicuous consumption—acquiring products for the pure enjoyment of the purchase. An interesting aspect of boomers is that, unlike prior generations, many of them don't seem to have any plans to retire. The reason may be financial, personal preference, or both. Much of the research on baby boomers indicates that—at least in their minds—they don't age.[12] Recall that a marketer must be cognizant of the difference between chronological age and attitudinal age. It is anticipated that this forever-young generation will enter the segment we would traditionally label as "older consumer" without an old outlook on life and the future. This has profound implications for marketers in that it turns on end the stereotypical approaches to what products are marketed to them and how they are marketed.[13] Many boomers will become more active, spend more money, and want to experience more new things after retirement than they ever did while they were employed—that is, if you can get them to retire. Many smart marketers who happen to be of Generation X or Y would do well to rethink the potential impact of successful strategies aimed at these ageless boomers.

Generation X is often thought of as a transitional generation. Its members are comfortable with much of the new-age technology but, unlike Gen Y, they didn't grow up with it, they had to learn it. Gen X is pegged as being a very entrepreneurial group, partly

Unilever's Axe product line appeals heavily to millennial guys.

Source: Unilever

because many advancement opportunities in traditional firms have been thwarted by the overabundance of boomers who occupy those positions. It has been estimated that Gen X entrepreneurs are responsible for more than 70 percent of the new business start-ups in the United States. Gen X is not as consumption-crazed as the boomers, preferring more of a work-family life balance. For the marketing manager, this knowledge about the Gen X segment offers the opportunity to develop appeals to their independent spirit and practical nature.

Gen X is often referred to as the "baby bust" because it represents a natural cyclical downturn in birthrate. Because Gen X is such a small segment of the consumer market, many marketers have their eye squarely on Gen Y—the millennials—as the next great consumer frontier. Millennials are now the largest single generational segment in the population, and they don't balk at using any and every sort of communication media available to enhance their lives, including making purchases. Millennials are made-to-order consumers for marketers who are equipped to engage them on their own turf—especially through digital marketing and social media. Chapter 13 provides many ideas about how best to engage millennials (and others) through these types of media.[14]

Millennials are a digitally adept generation, but Generation Z—the post-millennials—are the first generation to be born into the world of smartphones, social media, and cloud computing technology. Consider the effects of Twitter character limits, the vertical scroll/automatic refresh formats of social media apps, and other digital designs on younger generations' attention spans. Millennial Branding, an advertising consultancy firm in New York City, advises companies to communicate to millennials and Gen Z in "five words and a big picture." The success of this brief, visually captivating strategy is evidenced in the popularity of Facebook ads. Facebook allows businesses to design the ad format, select ad placement, and specify a target audience. Facebook ads limit words and employ videos and photos to engage younger audiences, focusing on storytelling rather than overt advertising.[15]

Gender Target Corporation claims that about 80 percent of the dollar sales in its stores are made to women. Many firms note that men account for the majority of online purchases. Such knowledge provides evidence of the power of *gender segmentation,* which recognizes differences in needs and wants of men versus women. Certainly, a wide variety of products are clearly marketed for the primary consumption of either men or women, but not both—think Rogaine, cigars, and athletic supporters versus pregnancy tests, lipstick, and bras, for example. In such cases, marketers can concentrate on linking the product's value-adding properties to its corresponding gender segment. What about cases in which a product appeals to both men and women, but on the basis of satisfying different—maybe subtly different—needs and wants?[16]

Take, for example, razors. Gillette learned some years ago that, generally, women don't like to use a man's razor, which they had to do for decades because no thought was given to differences in gender usage preference. Research revealed that most women viewed men's razors as too bulky, with too many bells and whistles, and not feminine in color or design. Suddenly, Gillette found an underserved new submarket for segmenting its razor line: the female shaver! The result was a completely new brand and product line called Gillette Venus, and today the brand comes in numerous product forms including Venus Original, Venus Bikini, Simply Venus, Venus Swirl, Venus Comfortglide, and Venus Embrace. And if you want carefree reordering of replacement blades, you can sign up for automatic delivery through P&G, Amazon, or elsewhere![17]

Recent research has shown that millennials generally still align with traditional gender differences in buyer behavior—for example, women are more attracted to health and beauty supplies while men tend to prefer technology and electronics.[18] Lush Ltd. is a UK-based body/beauty cosmetics brand that has capitalized on female consumer preferences to artfully market its fresh handmade cosmetics. The company focuses on natural elements, touting its vegetarian, non-animal-tested products and highlighting its "charity pot" product offerings, in which 100 percent of pot proceeds are donated to grassroots organizations.[19] Lush initiatives are communicated to shoppers as personal stories that unfold through masterful photography and poetic, blog-style articles. The result is high appeal to the millennial woman's interest in health, appreciation of beauty and art, and desire to join social causes.

Family and Household In years past, the concepts of family and household were fairly easy for marketers to define—a married man and woman, likely with children, and sometimes with other relatives such as a grandparent who had moved back in. Now, *family and household segmentation* can be more complex. Marketing managers are cognizant of all kinds of different family arrangements including singles, unmarried cohabitating couples, gay and lesbian couples, parents with 30-something offspring who boomeranged back home, very large extended families living in one household, and so forth. Many of these changes in the concept of family have evolved based on changing economic realities, social norms, and cultural/subcultural mores. These changes have created many new opportunities for marketers. Following the U.S. Supreme Court ruling that legalized same-sex marriage in 2015, Campbell's soup launched its "Real, Real Life" marketing campaign. It highlighted real American families, with one commercial featuring a same-sex couple feeding their son Star Wars Campbell's soup. The commercial signaled a shift in mainstream marketing's portrayal of U.S. families, stirring controversy and eliciting both praise and outcry.[20]

Marketers who want to use family and household in segmentation need to understand the overall picture. One way to portray this variable is through the **family life cycle**, which represents a series of life stages defined by age, marital status, number of children, and other factors.[21] When Amana introduced the microwave oven in the 1960s, it started out as a product that was marketed to the busy homemaker as a way to supplement her (yes, it was marketed exclusively to women) food preparation and make her day at home more efficient. Now, most new microwaves are sold to singles, both men and women, who, in many instances, don't use or even own a traditional oven.

Race and Ethnicity *Race and ethnicity segmentation* has become of prime importance in the United States as the number of natural-born citizens of ethnic minorities grows and the number of immigrants has increased.[22] In recent years, most firms have jumped on the bandwagon of segmenting by race and ethnicity, partly because many of these submarkets are growing quite rapidly in terms of both size and buying power and partly because they have historically been ignored by mainstream marketers.[23] African Americans account for slightly more than 12 percent of the U.S. population, a figure that has not been growing. In years past, very few products were marketed specifically to the African-American segment other than by firms specializing only in that segment. Hair and beauty product pioneer Johnson Products, founded in 1954, was an early believer in the power of developing products such as Ultra Sheen, Afro Sheen, Classy Curl, and others that brought the company consistent double-digit sales increases throughout the 1970s and 1980s. Ultimately, the product line became so attractive that it was acquired by mainstream beauty care manufacturer L'Oréal and eventually by Wella Corporation, another broad-line marketer of beauty care products. Today, almost all major cosmetic and beauty aid firms, from Avon to P&G, market products specifically designed to appeal to this vital market segment.

Several diverse ethnic groups comprise a major growth market segment for Cover Girl and other makeup manufacturers as they work hard to satisfy the beauty care needs of these consumers.
Source: Procter & Gamble

In contrast to the stable numbers in the African-American segment, the Hispanic/Latino and Asian-American segments are both growing at a rapid rate, with the Hispanic and Latino segment overtaking African Americans as a percentage of the U.S. population (almost 17 percent). An obvious challenge with the Hispanic/Latino segment, at least from the perspective of recent immigrants, has been the language barrier.[24] In the past, marketers' use of the Spanish language and symbolism in communicating with customers has mostly been through tacky attempts at humor. Go to YouTube and take a look at the 1990s ads featuring Taco Bell's "Yo quiero Taco Bell"–uttering Chihuahua dog or the 1970s Frito-Lay ads featuring the Frito Bandito, for example. But today, marketers are taking Spanish-speaking Americans very seriously.[25] Compared to other groups, these segments are younger, are more oriented toward developing long-term relationships with people and brands, have more people per family and household, and have experienced a tantalizingly strong increase in disposable income.

Income *Income segmentation* is based on a very quantifiable demographic variable, and it is usually analyzed in incremental ranges. Until the Great Recession that began in the late 2000s, the average income of U.S. families had been rising steadily, but at a declining rate of increase compared to prior decades. However, during the Great Recession, average household income dropped significantly and it is difficult to predict when and at what magnitude it may begin to rise.[26]

Marketers use income as a segmenting approach very frequently. Examples on the lower-income side include deep-discount retailers and dollar menus at fast-food restaurants. Examples at the higher end include luxury automobiles, gourmet restaurants, and exotic travel experiences. Interestingly though, there is not necessarily a direct correlation between income and price preferences. Southwest Airlines, for example, is a low-priced carrier yet maintains a certain cachet with many high-income customers largely because of its fun style and spirit.[27]

Using income alone as a segmentation approach has some problems. First, many people either purposely misstate or refuse to reveal their income on questionnaires and in interviews used in collecting data for identifying segments. Second, with the readily available credit that is pervasive in the U.S. consumer marketplace, actual income may not necessarily drive one's ability to purchase products that in prior days were reserved for those with more income.[28] Cars costing tens of thousands of dollars can be had by nearly anyone nowadays by extending payments out six or more years. Even the old standby of income segmentation, home ownership, has fallen victim to wild mortgage schemes during many years of low initial interest, no-interest, and 40- and 50-year terms to entice buyers to go ahead and sign their financial lives away (which we now know had the unintended consequence of facilitating a meltdown of the mortgage banking industry).

The health of a country's economy influences its citizens' spending habits and overall buyer behavior. Looking internationally, Japanese millennials' spending reflects a sense of frugality that stems from being raised in a long-stagnant economy. One consumer research report found that over 60 percent of Japanese high school students, college students, and adults in their early 20s would prefer to be perceived as frugal rather than generous. Such cautious spending behaviors have impacted the popularity of high-end luxury brands among Japanese millennials, but luxury brands such as LVMH have continued to flourish in Japan due to tourism and sales largely generated by Chinese visitors.[29]

Occupation *Occupational segmentation* recognizes that there may be a number of consistent needs and wants demonstrated by consumers based on what type of job they have. The U.S. Census Bureau lists numerous standardized categories of occupations including Professional/Managerial, Technical, Government, Trades, Agricultural, Educator, Student, and Unemployed.[30] In the United States, the workplace and our peer group of fellow workers is one of the strongest reference groups, and reference groups can be very powerful influencers on consumer behavior. All sorts of product lines are directly affected by occupation, including the clothing, equipment, and other personal support materials needed to fit in with the occupational peer group. Sometimes the employer influences purchase choice by offering tuition reimbursement, health care preferred provider networks, or discounts on products and services for employees. As a segmentation variable, occupation is very closely related to income, although the two are not perfectly correlated.[31] That is, many traditionally blue-collar jobs may pay higher wages than white-collar positions depending in part on the strength of the union within the firm and industry. Obviously, occupation is also related to education in that the latter usually enables the former.

Education In U.S. society, research consistently shows that education is one of the strongest predictors of success in terms of type of occupation, upward mobility, and long-term income potential. Everything else being equal, *educational segmentation* might lead a firm to offer its products based on some anticipated future payoff from the consumer. Take credit cards, for example. Why are credit card providers so eager to market themselves to college-bound high school seniors? Because they know that, even with low beginning credit limits, gaining usage early increases the chances of loyalty to the card over the long run—after the student finishes college, gains professional employment, and starts making a bigger salary. Unfortunately, educational segmentation works the other direction as well, which is a potential dark side of segmentation in general. Unscrupulous marketers have been accused of using educational segmentation (often combined with a language barrier) to intentionally take advantage of uneducated consumers in a host of ways including pushing unhealthy or untested products, encouraging bad financial investments, and promoting various illegal sales approaches such as taking the money for household or automobile repairs up front and employing illegal pyramid schemes.[32]

Social Class *Social class segmentation* involves grouping consumers by a standardized set of social strata around the familiar lower class, middle class, and upper class, and each of these contains several substrata. Exhibit 7.7 shows a traditional approach to segmentation by social class in the United States.

The composition of social classes takes into account several important demographic variables, including income, occupation, and education.[33] However, nowadays many mitigating factors might affect one's inclusion in one or the other of the class strata. Readily available credit has flattened the classes and made many luxury products affordable to a broad spectrum of consumers who in the past would not have been able to purchase them. And who doesn't know someone who is quite wealthy that also shops at Target for staple goods?

Although the very upper and very lower strata are still potentially useful for segmentation, it has become increasingly difficult to segment among the groups within the big middle stratum. Because of this, most marketing managers today prefer either to defer to other demographic variables for segmentation or, more likely, to look at psychographics and behavioral segmentation approaches that capture much of what used to be evidenced by social class.[34]

Geodemographics A hybrid form of segmentation that considers both geographic and demographic factors is called *geodemographic segmentation*. Typically, marketers turn to firms that specialize in collecting such data on an ongoing basis to purchase data relevant to their geographic area of focus.[35] Let's say, for example, that you are interested in coming into the Orlando metropolitan area with a new upscale type of convenience store and gas station to compete for customers, especially females, who don't like the ambience at a typical convenience store. In fact, recently cutting-edge convenience and gas retailer WaWa did just that. Your research shows that it will be important to place your stores in neighborhoods trafficked by consumers who are more likely to be attracted to your upscale merchandise and more pleasant surroundings. Where do you turn for data on segments that might be a good match for your product?

One source is Claritas, which continually updates a large database called PRIZM that is zip-code driven. PRIZM profiles every zip code in the United States by both demographic and lifestyle (psychographic) variables. Over time, PRIZM has discovered 68 "neighborhood

EXHIBIT 7.7 | **Traditional Social Class Strata in the United States**

UPPER CLASS
- Upper-upper
- Middle-upper
- Lower-upper

↓

MIDDLE CLASS
- Upper-middle
- Middle-middle
- Lower-middle

↓

LOWER CLASS
- Upper-lower
- Middle-lower
- Lower-lower

EXHIBIT 7.8 | Sample PRIZM Clusters

Winner's Circle (Wealthy Middle Age, Mostly with Kids)

Among the wealthy suburban lifestyles, Winner's Circle is the youngest, a collection of mostly 35- to 54-year-old couples with large families in new-money subdivisions. Surrounding their homes are the signs of upscale living: recreational parks, golf courses, and upscale malls. With a median income over $100,000, Winner's Circle residents are big spenders who like to travel, ski, go out to eat, shop at clothing boutiques, and take in a show.

Money and Brains (Upscale Older, Mostly without Kids)

The residents of Money and Brains seem to have it all: high incomes, advanced degrees, and

sophisticated tastes to match their credentials. Many of these city dwellers are married couples with few children who live in fashionable homes on small, manicured lots with expensive cars in the driveway.

Executive Suites (Upscale Middle Age, Mostly with Kids)

The residents of Executive Suites tend to be prosperous and active professionals who own multiple computers, large-screen TV sets, and are above average in their use of technology. Executive Suites also enjoy cultural activities, from reading books to attending theater and watching independent movies.

Source: www.claritas.com.

---

types" into which all zip codes fall. You can go to Claritas and look under "MyBestSegments" to plug in your own zip code if you like. "Segment Details" provides the geodemographic descriptions for each segment. Exhibit 7.8 describes several PRIZM clusters that might be potential customers for your new upscale convenience and gas store.

Judging from the description of the product, these PRIZM clusters seem to be likely segments of interest: Winner's Circle, Money and Brains, and Executive Suites. Certainly, other clusters not shown in Exhibit 7.8 might also fit your profile of assumed consumer needs and wants. The next step would be to seek zip codes whose location involves traffic patterns that will feed these consumer clusters into your convenience stores. These locations might involve being either close to housing additions or on key routes that members of these clusters take between home and work.

Psychographic Segmentation

Another approach to segmenting consumer markets is through **psychographic segmentation**, which relies on consumer variables such as personality and *AIOs* (activities, interests, and opinions) to segment a market. Psychographic segmentation is sometimes also referred to as segmentation by lifestyle or values. Psychographic segmentation builds on a purely demographic approach in that it helps flesh out the profile of the consumer as a human being and not just a location or demographic descriptor.[36] Psychographic segmentation brings individual differences into the profile along with the more readily measurable descriptive variables we have discussed so far.

Lifestyle brands are especially popular among younger consumers who are often attracted to belonging and community. GoPro is an adventurous, outdoors lifestyle brand whose mission is to help "people capture and share their lives' most meaningful experiences with others." To encourage video/photo

PROVE YOU DID WHAT THEY SAID YOU COULDN'T. GO PRO, OR GO HOME.

Individuals who engage in paraskiing and other extreme sports are a lucrative psychographic market segment for many products targeted to their sport.

Source: GoPro, Inc.

sharing, the company launched "GoPro Awards" in 2015, awarding up to $5 million in prizes to customers who produced and shared the best GoPro videos and photos.[37]

An important challenge of using psychographic segmentation involves the reliability and validity of its measurement. Unlike geographic and demographic measures, which are relatively objective in nature, psychographic measures attempt to "get into the head" of the consumer. One way to better assure that such measures are reliable and valid is through the use of standardized questionnaires that reflect the experiences of a large number of users over an extended period. One popular psychographic instrument is **VALS**™ owned and operated by Strategic Business Insights (SBI). Want to know your own VALS™ type? Just go to the Strategic Business Insights website, click on "VALS™ Survey," and complete a questionnaire.

VALS™ segments U.S. adults age 18 and older into eight consumer groups on the basis of a standardized questionnaire and proprietary algorithm. Exhibit 7.9 portrays the basic VALS™ framework. According to SBI, "Each of us is an individual. Yet each of us also has personality traits, attitudes, or needs that are similar to those of other people. VALS™ measures the underlying psychological motivations and resources that groups of consumers share that explain and predict each group's most likely choices as consumers." VALS™ has shown consistently strong evidence of reliability and validity.[38]

Assume that you take the survey and discover you are an Achiever. Lots of hard-driving MBA students and undergraduate business majors are Achievers. According to the VALS™ website, members of this group typically may be expected to:

- Have a "me first, my family first" attitude.
- Believe money is the source of authority.
- Be committed to family and job.
- Be fully scheduled.
- Be goal oriented.
- Be hardworking.
- Be moderate.
- Act as anchors of the status quo.
- Be peer conscious.
- Be private.
- Be professional.
- Value technology that provides a productivity boost.

A marketing manager might appeal to Achiever consumers through products that reflect success. It is important to note that although Achievers want to appear successful, they do not want to stand out from the crowd. Brands that connect well with this type currently incllude Nike, Honda, iPhone, Samsung, and Old Navy.

EXHIBIT 7.9 | VALS™ Framework

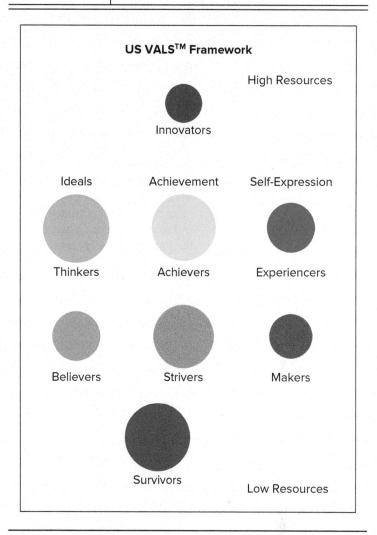

Behavioral Segmentation

Behavioral segmentation divides customers into groups according to similarities in benefits sought or product usage patterns.

Benefits Sought Why do people buy? That is, what are the crucial value-adding properties of an offering? For many people, a Walmart Supercenter offers the ultimate in one-stop shopping. The idea of going to one store and getting everything from groceries to CDs to kitty litter has a lot of appeal, if the critical benefit sought is broad selection, low prices, and infrequent, extended trips to the store. On the other hand, in recent years Walgreens drugstores have been cropping up on corner after corner on high-traffic streets. Walgreens has been extremely successful in appealing to a shopper seeking a different set of benefits, namely less time in the store and a lower level of hassle. The chain caters to consumers for whom the convenience of having a store that is close to home or en route to work trumps other potential benefits such as selection and price.[39]

For many marketing managers, segmentation by benefits sought is the best place to start the process of market segmentation. You might begin by identifying groups interested in the specific bundle of benefits afforded by your offering and then move toward utilizing the other segmentation variables to further hone the profile of the core group that is attracted to your product's benefits.

Usage Patterns Segmentation by usage patterns includes usage occasions, usage rate, and user status. An occasion means specifically when the product is used. Why do you buy greeting cards? What causes you to take your significant other out for that special dinner? What makes you break down and rent that tux or buy that formal? Each of these purchases is driven by an occasion, and marketers are very savvy at playing to consumers' desires to use occasions as a reason to buy.[40]

Listerine in an example of usage-based segmentation. Back when Listerine was marketed as just a mouthwash, it tended to be used sporadically or in the morning as part of the day's hygiene routine. But now that the product also addresses such oral concerns as gingivitis and gum disease, the usage rate is way up, with many people developing a regular, twice-a-day regimen. This greatly enhanced the usage rate for the product.[41] Marketers often segment based on whether a consumer is a light, medium, or heavy user. Many firms subscribe to the concept of the *80/20 rule*–that 80 percent of the business is done by 20 percent of the users.

Degree of customer loyalty is another important focus for segmentation. As you've learned, CRM is a powerful tool for marketing managers in identifying, tracking, and communicating with especially loyal patrons so they can implement strategies to keep those patrons loyal and reduce temptation to switch. In practice, loyalty programs for airlines and hotels, as well as frequent shopper cards for supermarkets and other retailers, all play on the notion of keeping the segment of heaviest users satisfied and using the product and of building a relationship between the customer and the brand and company.[42]

Finally, segmenting users into groups such as former users, current users, potential users, first-time users, and regular users can be very advantageous. Often, firms will come up with extra incentives for former users to retry a product or for potential users to make that initial purchase. It is critical to influence the segment of first-time users to take the plunge and purchase. CRM programs enable marketing managers to customize the value offering, thus maximizing the appeal to each of these user status segments.

Firms Use Multiple Segmentation Approaches Simultaneously

We have seen that geographic, demographic, psychographic, and behavioral approaches to segmenting consumer markets all have strong potential. In practice, these approaches are not applied one at a time. Firms develop a profile of a segment that might include aspects of any or all of the segmentation approaches we have discussed. Exhibit 7.10 provides visual examples of a range of segmentation approaches, including combinations of several types of segmentation.

EXHIBIT 7.10 | Examples of Segmentation Approaches

No market segmentation

Complete market segmentation

Market segmentation by
age groups A, B

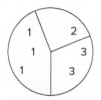

Market segmentation by
psychographic categories 1, 2, 3

Market segmentation by
psychographics and age

Developing the right segmentation strategy is one of the most important aspects of the marketing manager's role. Expertise in market segmentation is highly valued by companies across many industries because of the complexity of the process and the potential for effective segmentation to have a major impact on a firm's success in the marketplace.[43]

Segmenting Business Markets

Chapter 6 provided an extensive treatment of the many important characteristics of business markets. The variables relevant to segmentation of business markets share some overlap with those in consumer markets, but it is worth highlighting several unique segmentation approaches here as well. Exhibit 7.11 summarizes several key approaches to business market segmentation.

EXHIBIT 7.11 | Key Business Market Segmentation Variables

- Demographic
  - Industry
  - Company size
  - Location
- Operating Variables
  - Technology
  - User status
  - Customer capabilities
- Purchasing Approaches
  - Purchasing function organization
  - Power structure

- Nature of existing relationship
- General purchasing policies
- Purchasing criteria
- Situational Factors
  - Urgency
  - Specific application
  - Size of the order
- Personal Characteristics
  - Buyer-seller similarity
  - Attitudes toward risk
  - Loyalty

Source: This listing is derived from an influential early book on business markets—Source: Bonoma, Thomas V., and Shapiro, B. P. *Segmenting the Industrial Market* Lexington, MA: Lexington Books, 1983. The concepts are still fully valid today.

Raymond James provides financial services to a variety of market segments including individuals, corporations, and municipalities. The services are tailored to accomplish the different financial goals of each segment. For example, in the business segment corporations facing financial distress can hire the Restructuring Investment Banking team at Raymond James to receive a full range of restructuring solutions, including exchange offers, prepackaged bankruptcies, and out-of-court restructurings.[44]

In some ways, business market segmentation is more straightforward than that of consumer markets. This is partly because there is often a more defined universe of potential customers.[45] For example, using one variable from each set in Exhibit 7.11, a firm might create a profile segment for focus that includes one industry, current nonusers, price-focused, large quantity, and strong loyalty. In any given industry in the business-to-business market, this segmentation profile would probably narrow the segment to include just a few firms. This would allow for a focused approach to communicating and delivering value to this profile of firms. Of course, as with consumer markets, segments must meet the criteria for effective segmentation, and if the profile above appears too narrow, one or more of the variables can be removed.

TARGET MARKETING

LO 7-3

Describe the steps in target marketing.

Target marketing is the process of evaluating market segments and deciding which among them shows the most promise for development. The decision to invest in developing a segment into a target market represents an important turning point in the marketing planning process because, from this point forward, the direction of a firm's marketing strategies and related programs are set.[46] The three steps in target marketing are:

1. Analyze market segments.
2. Develop profiles of each potential target market.
3. Select a target marketing approach.

Analyze Market Segments

A number of strategic factors come into play when analyzing whether a segment is a good candidate for investment as a target market. Many different factors should be considered in the analysis. The goal is to determine the relative attractiveness of the various segments using an ROI (return on investment) approach. Everything else being equal, it is prudent to assign a high level of attractiveness to segments that provide the quickest, highest-level, and longest-sustaining anticipated ROI.[47]

Several factors should be considered when analyzing segment attractiveness. The following are among the most important: segment size and growth potential, competitive forces related to the segment, and overall *strategic fit* of the segment to the company's goals and value-adding capabilities.

Segment Size and Growth Potential Reckitt Benckiser is a British consumer goods company known for brands such as Dettol (the best-selling antiseptic in the world), Veet (the best-selling depilatory brand globally), and smaller brands such as Clearasil, Lysol, and Vanish. Its biggest brands, however, are less well known in the United States, so to move into U.S. markets, where it was not well represented, the company acquired Mucinex, Delsym, and eventually Cepacol, which positioned it squarely in the cough-and-cold market. With rising numbers of cases of the flu and a growing market for quick remedies, particularly with people more interested in dosing themselves (thanks in part to WebMD and other sites that allow sufferers to self-diagnose), the market was an attractive one, with a lot of growth potential and strong tie-ins to many of Reckitt Benckiser's other brands, particularly cleaners and disinfectants.[48]

Competitive Forces Related to the Segment In Chapter 3 we identified Michael Porter's competitive forces that firms must be cognizant of when considering investment in new target markets. For Reckitt Benckiser's cough-and-cold business, several of these forces predominate. First, rivalry among existing firms is fierce. Reckitt Benckiser entered a market dominated by Johnson & Johnson, but with fierce competition from brands like P&G as well. Second, a strong threat of substitute products is present in the form of a variety of cough-and-cold remedies, from homeopathic treatments to prescription medication to less conventional treatments like nasal irrigation (through neti pots and other sinus washes). New entrants are less of a threat, as patents and R&D make the barriers to entry high, and suppliers are not highly concentrated.

Strategic Fit of the Segment Strategic fit means there is a good match of a target market to the firm's internal structure, culture, goals, and resource capabilities. In the case of the Reckitt Benckiser acquisition of Mucinex and Delsym, the advantages and strategic fit were clear. The company already possessed similar international brands, and so it had experience with sourcing, production, and marketing. The brands also fit in well with the existing cleaning and disinfectant lines owned by Reckitt Benckiser, such as Lysol, since purchases of disinfectants often go hand-in-hand with purchases of cough or cold medication. The nature of the acquired brands was a great strategic fit for much of what Reckitt Benckiser already does in the market.

Develop Profiles of Each Potential Target Market

Once the market segments have been analyzed, marketing managers need to develop profiles of each segment under consideration for investment as a target market. Especially within the context of marketing planning, specifying the attributes of each segment and describing the characteristics of a "typical" consumer within that segment—from a geographic, demographic, psychographic, and behavioral perspective—are invaluable to gaining a better understanding of the degree to which each segment meets the criteria set out by a firm for segment attractiveness and target market ROI. Subsequently, a decision can now be made on prioritizing the segments for investment to develop them as target markets.[49]

Usually, this analysis results in segments that fall within four basic levels of priority for development:

1. **Primary target markets**—those segments that clearly have the best chance of meeting ROI goals and the other attractiveness factors.

2. **Secondary target markets**—those segments that have reasonable potential but for one reason or another are not best suited for development immediately.

3. **Tertiary target markets**—those segments that may develop emerging attractiveness for investment in the future but that do not appear attractive at present.

4. **Target markets to abandon for future development**.

Select a Target Marketing Approach

The final step in target marketing is to select the approach. Exhibit 7.12 portrays a continuum of approaches to target marketing from very broad to very narrow. Four basic options in target marketing strategy are undifferentiated, differentiated, concentrated (also called focus or niche), and customized (or one-to-one).

EXHIBIT 7.12 | Continuum of Target Marketing Approaches

Very Broad			Very Narrow
Undifferentiated target marketing	Differentiated target marketing	Concentrated target marketing	Customized target marketing

I make the crust by hand.
I make the filling by hand.
But to build my business,
I need a hand.

SMALL BUSINESS: YOU'RE NOT ALONE OUT THERE. Sandy, owner of The Right Slice, makes pies. Amazing pies. And when tourists asked to ship pies from her Hawaiian island shop in Kauai to the mainland, she went to The UPS Store® in her neighborhood. Because while Sandy knows all about flaky crust and fruit filling, The UPS Store experts know all about packing and shipping. And they can even put together professionally printed flyers, business cards and menus, easy as Mango Passion Fruit Pie. Locally owned and ready to help. At The UPS Store, we love small businesses. We love logistics.

Bring this ad to life. Download Aurasma Lite from your app store. Then hover your device over the ad to see how The UPS Store helped Sandy. Make sure "Location Services" is enabled on your phone. Or simply visit theupsstore.com/smallbiz

The UPS Store

WE ♥ LOGISTICS

POSTERS · FLYERS · MENUS · BUSINESS CARDS · CERTIFIED PACKING EXPERTS

In recent years, UPS has done a great job of target marketing small businesses to offer a wide range of logistics and supply chain expertise.

Source: United Parcel Service of America, Inc.

ChristianMingle, a Christian online dating site, has been extremely successful by targeting a very specific—and growing—market. Meeting online is second only to introductions by mutual friends as the way couples connect, with over 25 percent of U.S. couples first connecting through online dating sites. ChristianMingle is owned by Spark Networks, a small player against mainstream competitors like Match.com, eHarmony, and OkCupid, but has avoided direct competition by focusing on more niche markets. With well over 8 million users, Christian-Mingle is the largest of Spark Networks' 28 sites, but the company also owns JDate (a Jewish dating site) and much smaller networks such as Silver Singles, Deaf Singles Connection, and LDS (Latter-Day Saints) Singles. Although still relatively small, Spark Networks has experienced remarkable success so far and expects continued growth.[50]

Undifferentiated Target Marketing The broadest possible approach is **undifferentiated target marketing**—which is essentially a one-market strategy, sometimes referred to as an unsegmented *mass market.* Firms whose market approach is grounded in Porter's competitive strategy of low cost may use a relatively undifferentiated target marketing strategy based primarily on the resulting price advantage.[51] Southwest Airlines and Walmart are two firms that have built their businesses on their inherent internal cost advantages, passing along a price advantage to the mass market. But most firms don't have the kind of cost efficiencies it takes to operate such a target marketing approach and instead have to rely on developing sources of differentiation other than price.

Differentiated Target Marketing A differentiated target marketing approach, often referred to as simply *differentiation,* as you read earlier in this chapter, means developing different value offerings for different targeted segments. Possible sources of differentiation are many and include innovation/R&D, product quality, service leadership, employees, convenience, brand image, technology, corporate social responsibility, and many others. A significant challenge with differentiation as a core market strategy is that competitors are constantly coming to market with new differentiators that trump the efficacy of the current ones. Overnight a new technological innovation or other strategic shift by a competitor can doom a firm's current source of differentiation to the junk heap.[52]

FedEx famously differentiates based on speed of delivery and dependability of overall service to appeal to a target market willing to pay a price premium for these attributes. When UPS moved full force into the overnight package segment, its differentiating message was about full integration of services for the user through a smorgasbord of services including ground, overnight, and integrated supply chain solutions even for small to medium-size businesses. About the same time, FedEx entered UPS's lucrative over-the-road transport space with FedEx Ground. Initially, because of UPS's domination, FedEx had a difficult time differentiating itself in a meaningful way and only recently has FedEx Ground begun to gain widespread usage at a level that would even come close to affecting UPS's domination of that market.

Concentrated Target Marketing A **concentrated target marketing** approach, which Michael Porter refers to as a *focus strategy* and is also popularly called a *niche strategy,* involves targeting a large portion of a small market. Many start-up firms enter a marketplace as focus players. Because they are not saddled with keeping up with competitive demands in the broader market, firms using concentrated target marketing can realize cost and operational efficiencies and better margins than many first positioned as differentiators.[53] The danger of being a focus player is that sometimes these firms get too successful and are no longer able to fly under the radar of the differentiators, especially if the niche they occupy is a growing niche within the larger market.

Blackbaud competes in the software market against such powerhouses as MYOB and Quickbooks, but despite this it has managed to sustain annual revenue growth greater than 15 percent for the last 10 years. The secret to its success is its laser-focused concentrated target marketing to nonprofit organizations. Blackbaud tailors all its products and services to meet multiple needs specific to running a nonprofit organization and powering social good.[54]

Customized (One-to-One) Marketing With the proliferation of CRM, firms are able to develop more customized approaches to target marketing. In Chapter 1 we said that **customized (one-to-one) marketing** advocates that firms should direct energy and resources into establishing a learning relationship with each customer and then connect that knowledge with the firm's production and service capabilities to fulfill that customer's needs in as custom a manner as possible.[55] The related approach of mass customization allows flexible manufacturing, augmented by highly efficient ordering and supply chain systems, to drive the capability for a consumer to essentially build a product from the ground up. Today, many online clothing retailers offer a high degree of customization in ordering. Consumers enjoy "building their own outfit" by completing a form that includes all the necessary body dimensions along with style and color choices, and within a few days a custom garment arrives via FedEx or UPS!

Netflix takes pride in its algorithm's ability to predict and recommend content based on the individual tastes of Netflix users, the epitome of customized marketing. However, for some time, if multiple users shared a Netflix account, the algorithm struggled to find a pattern in the content interests of the account users. Netflix rectified this problem by creating a profile feature that allows users to create multiple profiles under one Netflix account. This enables Netflix to continue to recommend content for individual users.[56]

POSITIONING

Once market segments have been defined and analyzed and target markets have been selected for development, the firm must turn its attention to creating, communicating, delivering, and exchanging offerings that have value to the target markets—that is, positioning the product so that customers understand its ability to fulfill their needs and wants. The marketing mix of product, supply chain, price, and promotion is at the heart of positioning, and positioning strategies for a target market are executed through the development of unique combinations of these marketing mix variables.[57] Effective positioning is so important that the remaining chapters in this book are devoted to the various marketing mix elements.

Positioning doesn't occur in a vacuum; firms must position their offerings against competitors' offerings. Although McDonald's might like to think that their customers come because they're "lovin' it," the truth is that consumers of fast food can be fickle and they are constantly bombarded with the output of positioning strategies not just by direct hamburger competitors to McDonald's (such as Burger King and Wendy's) but also by many other types of quick-service restaurant cuisines.

In practice, much of the market research and marketing analytics described in Chapters 4 and 5 is designed to facilitate successful positioning. Many positioning studies start with focus groups that allow participants to talk about aspects of their experiences with a product. From the focus groups, a set of attributes is developed for further analysis. Attributes of a product represent salient issues that consumers consider when evaluating the product. For quick-service restaurants like McDonald's, the set of relevant attributes includes items such as cleanliness of the restaurant, speed of service, breadth of menu offerings, healthy food options, prices, employee courtesy, and numerous others.

LO 7-4

Define positioning and link it to the use of the marketing mix.

Founded in 1922, State Farm for years was known as a reliable, albeit rather quiet, brand. While not necessarily a bad reputation, it didn't help the company connect with its target market. Furthermore, until recently the insurance giant still relied nearly totally on an agent model, while other companies like GEICO and Progressive aggressively pushed self-service options. State Farm knew it had to act, and act fast, to create a more modern positioning. To that end, the company retired the "Auto-Fire-Life" ovals from its logo since it now offers a much broader range of services, and began an ad campaign centered around Aaron Rodgers' "Discount Double Check" along with other clever ads like the now-famous "Jake from State Farm" and "Internet and the French Model" commercials. Interactive media campaigns have also helped boost customer interaction, with the result that State Farm, at over 90 years old, is more agile and more connected to its core customer base than ever.[58]

Typically, after a series of focus groups to develop or confirm the relevant attributes, the positioning research moves to a survey methodology in which respondents rate the importance of each attribute, as well as the degree to which each of several competitors' products exhibit the attributes of interest.[59] For example, McDonald's might survey consumers about how important cleanliness of the restaurant, speed of service, breadth of menu offerings, healthy food options, prices, and employee courtesy are, and then ask them to provide their perceptions of how well McDonald's, Burger King, and Wendy's stack up in actually delivering these desired attributes.

The results of such a survey can be analyzed through a gap analysis that shows not only gaps by attribute in importance versus delivery, but also gaps among the competitors in delivery. Perhaps the analysis would reveal that McDonald's excels at healthy food options and cleanliness of the restaurant, but Burger King excels at breadth of menu offerings and prices. If that's the case, each firm has to decide if it is comfortable continuing to invest in these elements of positioning or if investment in other elements is warranted. Recently, edgier Burger King has deliberately invested in positioning itself as the "non-healthy menu" choice, blatantly featuring in ads its bigger and much more decadent food items in terms of fat and calorie content than either McDonald's or Wendy's advertises (although each certainly offers a fair share of unhealthy items).[60]

Perceptual Maps

LO 7-5

Use and interpret perceptual maps.

The data generated from the above analysis can be used to develop a useful visual tool for positioning called a **perceptual map**, which displays paired attributes in order to compare consumer perceptions of each competitor's delivery against those attributes.[61] Today, this is usually accomplished by computer statistical software applications that plot each competitor's relative positioning on the attributes.

Exhibit 7.13 provides three different examples of paired attributes on a perceptual map. The first map shows a generic pairing of price and quality and identifies several quadrants of feasible positions based on price-quality pairings that result in positive perceived value by the customer. The logic is compelling as to why the other two quadrants are not feasible positioning. In the upper-left quadrant, marketing an inferior offering at a high price is the antithesis of good marketing management. It may seem that in the short run an opportunity exists to make a quick buck, but the approach runs counter to everything we've learned so far about value and building customer relationships as the core of successful marketing over the long run. The bottom-right quadrant's positioning of high quality at a low price seems attractive, but only firms that can legitimately sustain Porter's notion of low-cost strategy can reasonably consider such positioning. And even for those players, the idea of nurturing cost and efficiency savings in operations is not that you will take the entire savings to price; rather, Porter advocates that a low-cost strategy should afford the opportunity to take much of the savings to improved margins and increased reinvestment in product development, only reflecting perhaps a small price differential. Chapter 11 reveals the inherent dangers in positioning primarily based on low price.

Audi, Volkswagen's luxury brand, delivers high-quality automobiles that rank at the top in nearly every vehicle category. Audis are stylish, powerful, and reliable, outshining the competition and allowing the company to successfully execute a premium pricing approach. For example, in recent years the Audi R8 featured an MSRP about $7,000 above the comparable Acura NSX.[62]

The other two perceptual maps in Exhibit 7.13 show where existing competitors are in the market based on the attributes reported. Such perceptual maps can be very useful in helping visualize where to make strategic changes to either move your product closer to the main market (clusters of competition) or further differentiate your product away from the competitive cluster and into more unique market space. In this way, perceptual maps aid in **repositioning** a product, which involves understanding the marketing mix approach necessary to change present consumer perceptions of the product. McDonald's has recently been engaged in a repositioning strategy into more healthy food options to appeal to an important target market of health-conscious consumers.

In actual practice, pairing just two attributes for consideration in making positioning decisions is overly simplistic. Data such as we described above are actually analyzed through a technique called multidimensional scaling that allows for interpretation of multiple attribute perceptions at the same time.

Sources of Differentiation

Effective differentiation is absolutely central to successful positioning strategies. Michael Porter, in his classic book *Competitive Advantage*, explains differentiation as follows:

> When employing a differentiation strategy, the organization competes on the basis of providing unique goods or services with features that customers value, perceive as different, and for which they are willing to pay a premium.[63]

Marketing managers can seek to create differentiation for their offerings in a variety of ways. The following are some of the most often used sources of differentiation.

- *Innovative leadership:* constantly developing the "next new thing." Example: Apple.

- *Product leadership:* performance, features, durability, reliability, style, and so on. Example: BMW.

- *Image leadership:* symbols, atmosphere, and creative media. Example: Harley-Davidson.

- *Price leadership:* Efficiencies in cost of labor, materials, supply chain, or other operational elements enabling the price leader to charge less. Example: Walmart.

- *Convenience leadership:* making the product or service significantly easier to obtain. Example: Amazon.com.

EXHIBIT 7.13 | **Examples of Perceptual Maps Used in Positioning Decisions**

Generic Price-Quality Perceptual Map

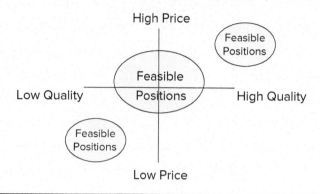

Perceptual Map for Hotel

Positioning involves trade-offs among other relevant attributes, not just price and quality.

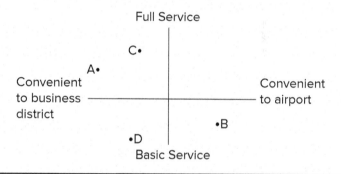

Perceptual Map for Automobile

Another example set of attributes.

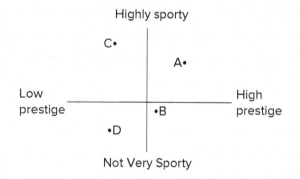

LO 7-6

Identify sources of differentiation.

A key differentiator for Chick-fil-A is personnel leadership. Their hiring and training practices are among the best in the quick-service restaurant industry, and the result is excellence in service leadership—another key differentiator for them.

©Rob Wilson/Shutterstock

- *Service leadership:* having an unusual and notable commitment to providing service to customers. Example: Ritz-Carlton.
- *Personnel leadership:* hiring employees who are competent, reliable, courteous, credible, responsive, and able to communicate clearly. Examples: Chick-fil-A, Southwest Airlines.

It is important to note that firms and brands often rely on multiple sources of differentiation simultaneously. For example, Chick-fil-A likely stakes a claim to differentiation by service, product leadership, and convenience in addition to the aspect of personnel leadership noted above.

Positioning Errors

Sometimes, positioning strategies don't work out as planned. The following positioning errors can undermine a firm's overall marketing strategy:[64]

- *Underpositioning:* when consumers have only a vague idea about the company and its products, and do not perceive any real differentiation. Until recently, both Audi and Volkswagen suffered from underpositioning as many consumers struggled to identify salient points of differentiation between those brands and their competitors. However, both brands have beefed up their marketing communication to better clarify exactly what each stands for in the marketplace.
- *Overpositioning:* when consumers have too narrow an understanding of the company, product, or brand. Dell became so entrenched as a brand of PCs that it has been a bit of a struggle to extend the brand into other lucrative product lines. In contrast, Apple and Samsung certainly are not overpositioned, having broadened the scope of their brands and products substantially during the same time frame.
- *Confused positioning:* when frequent changes and contradictory messages confuse consumers regarding the positioning of the brand. McDonald's has found itself the victim of confused positioning as it has worked to appeal to new segments of customers. It had tried (and failed) at so many diverse new product launches in the restaurants that many customers lost track of what the core of the brand was. Since then, under new top leadership, McDonald's has embraced its core differentiators of consistency of products and dependability of service, while growing new products at a much more conservative rate.
- *Doubtful positioning:* when the claims made for the product or brand are not regarded as credible by consumers. Sadly, firms that engage in unethical business practices often do not realize the magnitude of damage being done to their brand. Also, you will learn in the chapters on products and branding that trial is only the initial goal of marketing communication. After initial trial, firms need to ensure that the offering consistently meets or exceeds customer expectations so that repurchase—and loyalty—will occur, which is a process of customer expectations management. When FedEx promises 8 a.m. next-day delivery, it has to be sure its systems can actually produce such a level of performance all the time. In the aftermath of the 2008 financial crisis, insurance company American International Group (AIG) received a bailout from the U.S. Treasury because it was among the financial institutions deemed "too big to fail." Receiving this bailout seriously jeopardized AIG's credibility and positioning. AIG has long since paid off its $182 billion bailout, and in 2016 it received the "Double I" award from the Insurance Industry Charitable Foundation, recognizing AIG's corporate and philanthropic leadership.[65]

SUMMARY

Effective segmentation, target marketing, and positioning are central to marketing management because these decisions set the direction for the execution of the marketing plan. First, potential appropriate segmentation approaches must be identified. Second, the segments must be evaluated and decisions made about which to invest in for the most favorable ROI—these become your target markets. Finally, sources of differentiation must be identified that will result in customers perceiving fulfillment of needs and wants based on the value proposition of the offering.

KEY TERMS

market segmentation   185
target marketing   185
positioning   185
positioning strategy   185
differentiation   186
geographic segmentation   187
demographic segmentation   188
family life cycle   191

psychographic segmentation   194
VALS™   195
behavioral segmentation   196
primary target markets   199
secondary target markets   199
tertiary target markets   199
undifferentiated target marketing   200

concentrated target marketing   201
customized (one-to-one) marketing   201
perceptual map   202
repositioning   203

APPLICATION QUESTIONS

1. Go to the Claritas website, click on MyBestSegments, and find the Zip Code Look-Up. There you will find a demo that allows you to type in a zip code of your choice and find out what PRIZM clusters predominate in that geographic area.

   More application questions are available online.

   a. What do the findings tell you about the overall composition of potential customers within that zip code?

   b. Based on the array of clusters represented, what kinds of start-up businesses might flourish within the geographic area? Why do you believe those businesses in particular would be successful?

2. Go to the Strategic Business Insights (SBI) website and click through to the section on VALS™. Find the VALS™ survey and complete the questionnaire.

   a. Are the results surprising? Why or why not? Do you see yourself as part of the identified VALS™ segment?

   b. If you are comfortable doing so, share your results with a few other people in the class and ask if they mind sharing their results with you. What is the consensus among the group about whether the survey actually captured a relevant profile about yourself and your classmates?

   c. How might each of these brands benefit from the use of VALS™ as a psychographic segmentation tool?

      i. Chipotle

      ii. Walt Disney World Theme Park

      iii. Target Stores

      iv. Samsung

      v. Porsche

3. Assume for a moment that you are in marketing for Staples (the office supply company) and that the clients you are responsible for are business users (not end-user consumers). What five business market segmentation variables do you think will be most useful to consider as you move toward homing in on the Staples business target markets with the best ROI? Justify your choice of each.

4. Consider each of the brands below. Review the list of potential sources of differential competitive advantage (differentiation) highlighted in the chapter. For each: (*a*) indicate which one differentiation source you believe is most important to them currently and (*b*) indicate which other differentiation sources you believe might hold promise for development for them in the near future and *why*.

   a. Norwegian Cruise Line

   b. Sears Craftsman Tools

   c. Avon

   d. Lowe's Home Improvement Stores

   e. The Salvation Army

5. McDonald's is interested in your opinion of how it would stack up on a perceptual map against Burger King, Wendy's, Taco Bell, and Chick-fil-A on the attributes of convenience and product quality. Create the map by putting convenience as the vertical axis (high at the top and low at the bottom) and product quality as the horizontal axis (low on the left and high on the right). Then indicate your perceptions of the five brands on these attributes by placing a dot for each in the spot that indicates your view (see Exhibit 7.13 for examples).

   a. What does the result reveal about McDonald's current positioning on these attributes, based strictly from your perception?

   b. If possible, compare notes with others in your class. Do you find consistency?

   c. In general, what opportunities for repositioning do you see for any of the brands to take advantage of current perceptions revealed on the perceptual map? What would they have to do to accomplish this repositioning?

MANAGEMENT DECISION CASE
Crafty Credit Card Competitor "Chases" Amex for Share of Millennials' Wallets

American Express (Amex for short) is one of the most venerable brands in all of financial services. Unfortunately, Amex and its stockholders recently saw profits in the credit card business fall by nearly 20 percent, with an accompanying revenue plunge of $2 billion![66] How is it that a successful firm like Amex can hit such a rough patch? One key reason is changing customer demographic trends, Amex's aging and somewhat pompous brand image (which makes it appear out of touch with younger up-and-coming market segments), and a wily competitor in the form of Chase Bank (more on Chase later).

Amex, founded in 1850 as an express mail service, didn't offer its first charge card—which was technically not a credit card, since the balance had to be paid off each month—until 1958. Over its history, the firm created the once popular "Traveler's Cheques" business (1891–1990s), founded and spun off an investment bank to Lehman Brothers (1981–1994), and formed a joint venture with Warner Communications that led to the creation of television channels MTV and Nickelodeon (1979–1984). Today, Amex has over 100 million cardholders worldwide, some of whom see enough value in their cards to pay a $7,500 initial fee and a

$2,500 annual fee to obtain the rarefied Centurion card (a.k.a. their "black card").[67]

To call Amex a venerable brand would be a gross understatement, as it ranks as one of the top 25 brands in the world and has been valued by Interbrand at $18 billion.[68] Amex's branding power provides a lot of cachet with customers—especially those from Generation X and older—and it has significant pricing power with merchants worldwide. However, Amex recently has been steadily losing customers and key merchants, including dropped exclusive deals with Costco and JetBlue—losses that cost Amex massive amounts of revenue. Warren Buffett, whose holding company Berkshire Hathaway owns more than 10 percent of Amex, has said that the "brand is under attack." But why under attack now, in particular? The brand most responsible for the recent vulnerability at Amex is Chase. Chase has boldly taken advantage of an opportunity by segmenting, targeting, and positioning in Amex's market to craft and present a new image to the highly desirable and hard-to-reach millennials.

To explain Chase's approach, we must first understand that Amex has traditionally positioned itself as a premier offering, providing a posh credit card for the elite, successful, and (typically) older professional. But Chase decided to take a different approach. Following demographic trends, Chase saw that market growth potential was much greater for millennials (Generation Y) than any other generational segment. According to the U.S. Census Bureau, millennials now outnumber every other generational cohort and will hold this position for at least two decades.[69] Millennial consumers behave differently from those from previous generations. They are known to ignore much traditional advertising, and often postpone marriage and home purchases—but they may not hesitate to jump right into car and travel purchases. They check blogs and social media for product reviews, and also tend to be more brand loyal than other generational segments. The value that millennials place on brand authenticity and brand involvement with social causes, as well as their desire to participate in product creation processes and dialogues (usually virtually), provide strong clues to marketing managers about how to win them over.[70] It seems that Amex largely missed these cues, and Chase was only too happy to cash in on the oversight.

So Chase developed and marketed a card rich with rewards, designed to appeal to millennials' value-seeking behavior and attitudes. They positioned the Sapphire Reserve card as "not your father's credit card," directly opposite to Amex's positioning. Chase smartly set out to provide a different value proposition by offering up a brand image based on *experiences* rather than conspicuous consumption (meaning "showing off" one's ability to buy). Using basic demographic segmentation, but deepening the insights with psychographics of the millennial target segment, Chase discovered that younger consumers typically shunned the Amex card because, as one consumer stated, using the Amex card felt "braggy" (an antithetical value for millennials). But Chase's Sapphire card, tinted dark blue and made of metal, feels more authentic to the younger consumer. It says, "If I have this card I'm interesting."[71]

To be sure, the Sapphire Reserve card offers plenty of benefits, especially for travelers—a 100,000-mile reward sign-up bonus, credit toward TSA-Pre√ enrollment, an automatic extended warranty on purchases, trip insurance, and access to airport lounges. But Chase's main brand message is that these rewards are designed to get you to the snowboard slopes and the after-parties at the hottest local venues, rather than to an exclusive upscale wine tasting in the Loire Valley. To say that Chase's Sapphire Reserve card has been a slam dunk would be an understatement. In the first seven months after its release, Chase signed up more than 1 million new cardholders, half of whom were under age 35![72] But don't count Amex totally out of the millennial ballgame—they are working hard for a comeback, but how well they do is "all in the cards."

Questions for Consideration

1. Why is the millennial generation, in particular, so important to Amex?

2. This case focuses primarily on the battle between Chase and Amex over millennial consumers. But, as the content in this chapter points out, lumping all older consumers into a generalized segment overlooks some important variables. Looking at the generational groups and their representative values (see Exhibit 7.7), where would you suggest Amex focus its marketing efforts, and why?

3. As noted in the chapter, an external positioning statement is not just about being able to describe how your product benefits the customer—it also needs to explain how your product is *different* from the competition. Chase's "It's not your father's credit card" external positioning statement sums up in six words the idea that Chase is young while its competitors are old. The statement leads millennial consumers to consider what this card could do for them, beyond what their father's card could. Amex's positioning has always been that its card is for the successful professional—what would happen if Amex changed that positioning? (As a bonus, try to create a short external positioning phrase for Amex to use with millennials.)

MARKETING PLAN EXERCISES

ACTIVITY 7: Identify Target Markets

In this chapter you learned that effective segmentation, target marketing, and positioning favorably impact marketing management. For purposes of your marketing plan, we'll leave the specifics of developing your overall positioning strategies to the upcoming chapters on the marketing mix. At this point, the following steps are needed.

1. Consider the various approaches to segmenting your market(s). What segmentation approaches do you recommend? Why do you recommend those approaches over other available approaches?

2. Evaluate your proposed segments against the criteria for effective segmentation. What does this evaluation lead you to conclude about the best way to proceed?

3. Systematically analyze each potential segment on your list using the three steps you learned in the chapter: (1) assess each in terms of segment size and growth potential, segment competitive forces, and strategic fit of the segment; (2) for the short set that emerges, develop profiles of each potential target market, then identify each of your final set as primary, secondary, tertiary, or abandoned; (3) select the target marketing approach for each of your primary targets.

4. Identify the likely sources of differential advantage on which you will focus later in developing your positioning strategies.

NOTES

1. Nicole E. Coviello, Roderick J. Brodie, Peter J. Danaher, and Wesley J. Johnston, "How Firms Relate to Their Markets: An Empirical Examination of Contemporary Marketing Practices," *Journal of Marketing* 66, no. 3 (2002), pp. 33–57.

2. Jacquelyn S. Thomas and Ursula Y. Sullivan, "Managing Marketing Communications with Multichannel Customers," *Journal of Marketing* 69, no. 4 (October 2005), pp. 239–51; and Stephen L. Vargo and Robert F. Lusch, "Evolving to a New Dominant Logic for Marketing," *Journal of Marketing* 68, no. 1 (January 2004), pp. 1–17.

3. Javier Rodriguez-Pinto, Ana Isabel Rodriguez-Escudero, and Jesus Gutierrez-Cilian, "Order, Positioning, Scope, and Outcomes of Market Entry," *Industrial Marketing Management* 37, no. 2 (April 2008), pp. 154–66.

4. Anders Gustafsson, Michael D. Johnson, and Inger Roos, "The Effects of Customer Satisfaction, Relationship Commitment Dimensions, and Triggers on Customer Retention," *Journal of Marketing* 69, no. 4 (October 2005), pp. 210–18; and Ajay Kalra and Ronald C. Goodstein, "The Impact of Advertising Positioning Strategies on Consumer Price Sensitivity," *Journal of Marketing Research* 35, no. 2 (May 1998), pp. 210–25.

5. Cenk Koca and Jonathan D. Bohlmann, "Segmented Switchers and Retailer Pricing Strategies," *Journal of Marketing* 72, no. 3 (May 2008), pp. 124–42.

6. Allan D. Shocker, Barry L. Bayus, and Namwoon Kim, "Product Complements and Substitutes in the Real World: The Relevance of 'Other Products,'" *Journal of Marketing* 68, no. 1 (January 2004), pp. 28–40.

7. Arik Hesseldahl, "The iPhone Legacy: Pricier Smartphones?" *BusinessWeek,* November 1, 2007, www.businessweek.com/technology/content/oct2007/tc20071031_825744.htm?chan=search.

8. Leonard M. Lodish, "Another Reason Academics and Practitioners Should Communicate More," *Journal of Marketing Research* 44, no. 1 (February 2007), pp. 23–25.

9. Tat Y. Chan, V. Padmanabhan, and P. B. Seetharaman, "An Econometric Model of Location and Pricing in the Gasoline Market," *Journal of Marketing Research* 44, no. 4 (November 2007), pp. 622–35; and Jeff Wang and Melanie Wallendorf, "Materialism, Status Signaling, and Product Satisfaction," *Journal of the Academy of Marketing Science* 34, no. 4 (Fall 2006), pp. 494–506.

10. Subim Im, Barry L. Bayus, and Charlotte H. Mason, "An Empirical Study of Innate Consumer Innovativeness, Personal Characteristics, and New-Product Adoption Behavior," *Journal of the Academy of Marketing Science* 31, no. 1 (Winter 2003), pp. 61–74; and Sudhir N. Kale and Peter Klugsberger, "Reaping Rewards," *Marketing Management* 16, no. 4 (July/August 2007), p. 14.

11. Charles D. Schewe and Geoffrey Meredith, "Segmenting Global Markets by Generational Cohorts: Determining Motivations by Age," *Journal of Consumer Behaviour* 4, no. 1 (October 2004), pp. 51–64.

12. Anne L. Balazs, "Expenditures of Older Americans," *Journal of the Academy of Marketing Science* 28, no. 4 (Fall 2000), pp. 543–46; and Christopher D. Hopkins, Catherine A. Roster, and Charles M. Wood, "Making the Transition

to Retirement: Appraisals, Post-Transition Lifestyle, and Changes in Consumption Patterns," *Journal of Consumer Marketing* 23, no. 2 (2006), pp. 89–101.

13. Stuart Van Auken, Thomas E. Barry, and Richard P. Bagozzi, "A Cross-Country Construct Validation of Cognitive Age," *Journal of the Academy of Marketing Science* 34, no. 3 (Summer 2006), pp. 439–56.

14. Mark Andrew Mitchell, Piper McLean, and Gregory B. Turner, "Understanding Generation X . . . Boom or Bust Introduction," *Business Forum* 27, no. 1 (2005), pp. 26–31.

15. Alex Williams, "Move Over, Millennials, Here Comes Generation Z," *New York Times*, September 18, 2015, https://www.nytimes.com/2015/09/20/fashion/move-over-millennials-here-comes-generation-z.html?_r=0; "Get Started with Ads," *FacebookBusiness*,n.d.,https://www.facebook.com/business/learn/facebook-ads-basics; and "Ad Formats," *Facebook Business*, n.d., https://www.facebook.com/business/learn/facebook-create-ad-basics.

16. Qimei Chen, Shelly Rodgers, and William D. Wells, "Better Than Sex," *Marketing Research* 16, no. 4 (Winter 2004), pp. 16–22.

17. www.gillettevenus.com/en-us, accessed May 8, 2017.

18. Daniel Newman, "Research Shows Millennials Don't Respond to Ads," *Forbes*, April 28, 2015, https://www.forbes.com/sites/danielnewman/2015/04/28/research-shows-millennials-dont-respond-to-ads/#3568f89e5dcb.

19. "Charity Pot," *Lush Ltd.*, n.d. http://www.lushusa.com/on/demandware.store/Sites-Lush-Site/en_US/Stories-Show?tag=charity-pot.

20. "Campbell's New Portfolio Advertising Campaign Celebrates Real Life Moments," *Campbell's Newsroom*, October 5, 2015, https://www.campbellsoupcompany.com/newsroom/press-releases/?date=2015/10; Olivia Waxman, "Watch This Heartwarming Ad Showing Two Dads Impersonating Star Wars' Darth Vader," *Time*, October 9, 2015, http://time.com/4068363/campbells-soup-star-wars-gay-dads-father-ad/; and Michael Tanenbaum, "Campbell's Defends 'Star Wars' Commercial with Gay Fathers," *Philly Voice*, October 9, 2015, http://www.phillyvoice.com/campbells-star-wars-commercial-gay-fathers/.

21. Rex Y. Du and Wagner A Kamakura, "Household Life Cycles and Lifestyles in the United States," *Journal of Marketing Research* 43, no. 1 (February 2006), pp. 121–32.

22. Andrew Lindridge and Sally Dibb, "Is 'Culture' a Justifiable Variable for Market Segmentation? A Cross-Cultural Example," *Journal of Consumer Behaviour* 2, no. 3 (March 2003), pp. 269–87.

23. Frederick A. Palumbo and Ira Teich, "Market Segmentation Based on Level of Acculturation," *Marketing Intelligence & Planning* 22, no. 4 (2004), pp. 472–84.

24. Frederick A. Palumbo and Ira Teich, "Segmenting the U.S. Hispanic Market Based on Level of Acculturation," *Journal of Promotion Management* 12, no. 1 (2005), pp. 151–73.

25. Mark R. Forehand and Rohit Deshpande, "What We See Makes Us Who We Are: Priming Ethnic Self-Awareness and Advertising Response," *Journal of Marketing Research* 38, no. 3 (August 2001), pp. 336–48.

26. Carmen DeNavas-Walt, Bernadette D. Proctor, and Jessica Smith, "Income, Poverty, and Health Insurance Coverage in the United States: 2006," *U.S. Census Bureau*, August 2007, www.census.gov/prod/2007pubs/p60-233.pdf.

27. C. B. Bhattacharya and Sankar Sen, "Consumer-Company Identification: A Framework for Understanding Consumers' Relationships with Companies," *Journal of Marketing* 67, no. 2 (April 2003), pp. 76–88.

28. Ben Levisohn and Brian Burnsed, "The Credit Rating in Your Shoe Box," *BusinessWeek*, April 10, 2008, www.businessweek.com/magazine/content/08_16/b4080052299512.htm?chan=search.

29. Reuters, "Why Japan's Thrifty Millennials Are a Bad Omen for Its Economy," *Fortune*, December 8, 2016, http://fortune.com/2016/12/09/japan-economy-millennials/; and Kate Abnett, "In Japan, Luxury Flourishes While Economy Flounders," *Business of Fashion*, February 11, 2016, https://www.businessoffashion.com/articles/global-currents/in-japan-luxury-flourishes-while-economy-flounders.

30. www.census.gov.

31. Paul G. Patterson, "Demographic Correlates of Loyalty in a Service Context," *Journal of Services Marketing* 21, no. 2 (2007), pp. 112–21.

32. Madhubalan Viswanathan, Jose Antonio Rosa, and James Edwin Harris, "Decision Making and Coping of Functionally Illiterate Consumers and Some Implications for Marketing Management," *Journal of Marketing* 69, no. 1 (January 2005), pp. 15–31.

33. Charles M. Schaninger and Sanjay Putrevu, "Dual Spousal Work Involvement: An Alternative Method to Classify Households/Families," *Academy of Marketing Science Review* (2006), pp. 1–21.

34. Rob Lawson and Sarah Todd, "Consumer Lifestyles: A Social Stratification Perspective," *Marketing Theory* 2, no. 3 (September 2002), pp. 295–308.

35. David J. Faulds and Stephan F. Gohmann, "Adapting Geodemographic Information to Army Recruiting: The Case of Identifying and Enlisting Private Ryan," *Journal of Services Marketing* 15, no. 3 (2001), pp. 186–211.

36. Geraldine Fennell, Greg M. Allenby, Sha Yang, and Yancy Edwards, "The Effectiveness of Demographic and Psychographic Variables for Explaining Brand and Product Category Use," *Quantitative Marketing and Economics* 1, no. 2 (June 2003), pp. 223–44.

37. "About Us," *GoPro Inc.*, n.d., https://gopro.com/about-us; and Tim Peterson, "How GoPro Will Use an Awards Campaign to Grow Its Media Biz," *Advertising Age*, October 14, 2015, http://adage.com/article/media/gopro-invests-media-biz-5-million-award-program/300876/.

38. "VALS Survey," *Strategic Business Insights,* www.strategicbusinessinsights.com/VALS.

39. James Frederick, "Walgreens Leaders Reaffirm Strategy, Outlook," *Drug Store News,* February 16, 2004.

40. Florian V. Wangenheim and Tomas Bayon, "Behavioral Consequences of Overbooking Service Capacity," *Journal of Marketing* 71, no. 4 (October 2007), pp. 36–47; and Ruth N. Bolton, Katherine N. Lemon, and Peter C. Verhoef, "The Theoretical Underpinnings of Customer Asset Management: A Framework and Propositions for Future Research," *Journal of the Academy of Marketing Science* 32, no. 3 (Summer 2004), pp. 271–93.

41. Sarah Plaskitt, "Listerine Boosts Sales by 20%," *B&T Magazine,* May 22, 2003, www.bandt.com.au/news/49/0c016749.asp.

42. Yuping Liu, "The Long-Term Impact of Loyalty Programs on Consumer Purchase Behavior and Loyalty," *Journal of Marketing* 71, no. 4 (October 2007), pp. 19–35.

43. V. Kumar and J. Andrew Petersen, "Using Customer-Level Marketing Strategy to Enhance Firm Performance: A Review of Theoretical and Empirical Evidence," *Journal of the Academy of Marketing Science* 33, no. 4 (Fall 2005), pp. 504–20; and David Feldman, "Segmentation Building Blocks," *Marketing Research* 18, no. 2 (Summer 2006), p. 23.

44. "About Us," *Raymond James*, https://www.raymondjames.com/about-us; and "Restructuring Investment Banking," *Raymond James*, https://www.raymondjames.com/corporations-and-institutions/investment-banking/capabilities-and-coverage-areas/restructuring.

45. Thomas L. Powers and Jay U. Sterling, "Segmenting Business-to-Business Markets: A Micro-Macro Linking Methodology," *Journal of Business & Industrial Marketing* 23, no. 3 (2008), pp. 170–77.

46. Peter R. Dickson, Paul W. Farris, and Willem J. M. I. Verbeke, "Dynamic Strategic Thinking," *Journal of the Academy of Marketing Science* 29, no. 3 (Summer 2001), pp. 216–38.

47. Eric Almquist and Gordon Wyner, "Boost Your Marketing ROI with Experimental Design," *Harvard Business Review* 79, no. 9 (October 2001), pp. 135–47.

48. Jack Neff, "Flu Gives Reckitt, Johnson & Johnson a Shot in the Arm," *Advertising Age* 14 (January 2013), http://adage.com/article/news/flu-reckitt-johnson-johnson-a-shot-arm/239156/.

49. Gary L. Frazier, "Organizing and Managing Channels of Distribution," *Journal of the Academy of Marketing Science* 27, no. 2 (Spring 1999), pp. 226–51; and Darren W. Dahl and Page Moreau, "The Influence and Value of Analogical Thinking during New Product Ideation," *Journal of Marketing Research* 39, no. 1 (February 2002), pp. 47–61.

50. Logan Hill, "At ChristianMingle and JDate, God's Your Wingman," *Bloomberg Businessweek,* February 28, 2013, www.businessweek.com/articles/2013-02-28/at-christianmingle-and-jdate-gods-your-wingman.

51. J. David Hunger and Thomas H. Wheelen, *Essentials of Strategic Management,* 4th ed. (Upper Saddle River, NJ: Prentice Hall, 2007).

52. Subin Im and John P. Workman Jr., "Market Orientation, Creativity, and New Product Performance in High-Technology Firms," *Journal of Marketing* 68, no. 2 (April 2004), pp. 114–32.

53. Bruce Buskirk, Stacy M. P. Schmidt, and David L. Ralph, "Patterns in High-Tech Firms Growth Strategies by Seeking Mass Mainstream Customer Adaptations," *Business Review, Cambridge* 8, no. 1 (Summer 2007), pp. 34–40.

54. Charles Gaudet, "Five Go-To Market Leaders That Dominate Their Niche," *Forbes,* March 25, 2014, https://www.forbes.com/sites/theyec/2014/03/25/five-go-to-market-leaders-that-dominate-their-niche/#51c232733650; and "Company Overview," *Blackbaud,* https://www.blackbaud.com/company/.

55. Don Peppers and Martha Rogers, *The One-to-One Manager: Real World Lessons in Customer Relationship Management* (New York: Doubleday Business, 2002).

56. Scott Yates, "6 Kick-Ass Examples of Marketing Personalization," *Hub Spot,* December 17, 2013, https://blog.hubspot.com/insiders/marketing-personalization-examples.

57. David A. Schweidel, Eric T. Bradlow, and Patti Williams, "A Feature-Based Approach to Assessing Advertisement Similarity," *Journal of Marketing Research* 43, no. 2 (May 2006), pp. 237–43.

58. E. J. Schultz, "Agent of Change: How State Farm Used New Logo, Tagline to Stay Relevant at 90," *Advertising Age,* November 26, 2012, http://adage.com/article/special-report-marketer-alist-2012/state-farm-reinvents-90-logo-tagline-digital/238419/.

59. Andrew Curry, Gill Ringland, and Laurie Young, "Using Scenarios to Improve Marketing," *Strategy & Leadership* 34, no. 6 (2006), pp. 30–39.

60. "Burger King's Monster 923 Calorie Burger," *Metro News,* November 6, 2006, www.metro.co.uk/news/article.html?in_article_id=23982&in_page_id=34.

61. Detelina Marinova, "Actualizing Innovation Effort: The Impact of Market Knowledge Diffusion in a Dynamic System of Competition," *Journal of Marketing* 68, no. 3 (July 2004), pp. 1–20.

62. Cherise Threewitt, "14 Best Luxury Car Brands," *U.S. News & World Report,* November 22, 2016, https://cars.usnews.com/cars-trucks/best-luxury-car-brands; and "Compare 2017 Acura NSX vs 2017 Audi R8," *Car Connection,* http://www.thecarconnection.com/car-compare-results/acura_nsx_2017-vs-audi_r8_2017.

63. Michael E. Porter, *Competitive Advantage* (New York: Simon & Schuster, 1985).

64. David W. Cravens and Nigel F. Piercy, *Strategic Marketing,* 9th ed. (Boston: McGraw-Hill/Irwin, 2009).

65. Gregory Gethard, "Failing Giant: A Case Study of AIG," *Investopedia,* August 31, 2016, http://www.investopedia.com/articles/economics/09/american-investment-group-aig-bailout.asp; "AIG: America's Improved Giant," *Economist,* February 2, 2013, http://www.economist.com/news/finance-and-economics/21571139-insurer-has-done-good-job-rehabilitating-itself-can-it-stand-its-own; and "AIG Recognized for Corporate and Philanthropic Leadership." *AIG,* June 22, 2016, http://www.aig.com/about-us/awards-and-recognition/aig-recognized-for-corporate-and-philanthropic-leadership.

66. Charles Duhigg, "Amex, Challenged by Chase, Is Losing the Snob War," *New York Times,* April 14, 2017, https://www.nytimes.com/2017/04/14/business/american-express-chase-sapphire-reserve.html?_r=0.

67. Matthew Frankel, "5 Things You Didn't Know about American Express," *Motley Fool,* April 28, 2017, https://www.fool.com/investing/2017/04/28/5-things-you-didnt-know-about-american-express.aspx?yptr=yahoo.

68. "Best Global Brands," *Interbrand,* 2016, http://interbrand.com/best-brands/best-global-brands/2016/ranking/.

69. Richard Fry, "Millennials Overtake Baby Boomers as America's Largest Generation," *Pew Research,* April 25, 2016, http://www.pewresearch.org/fact-tank/2016/04/25/millennials-overtake-baby-boomers/.

70. Dan Schawbel, "10 New Findings about the Millennial Consumer," *Forbes,* January 20, 2015, https://www.forbes.com/sites/danschawbel/2015/01/20/10-new-findings-about-the-millennial-consumer/.

71. Duhigg, "Amex, Challenged by Chase, Is Losing the Snob War."

72. Duhigg, "Amex, Challenged by Chase, Is Losing the Snob War."

PART THREE

Develop the Value Offering– The Product Experience

CHAPTER 8

Product Strategy and New Product Development

LEARNING OBJECTIVES

LO 8-1 Understand the essential role of the product experience in marketing.

LO 8-2 Define the characteristics of a product.

LO 8-3 Recognize how product strategies evolve from one product to many products.

LO 8-4 Understand the life of a product and how product strategies change over time.

LO 8-5 Recognize the importance of new product development to long-term success.

LO 8-6 Understand the new product development process.

LO 8-7 Identify how new products become diffused in a market.

PRODUCT: THE HEART OF MARKETING

As we discussed in Chapter 1, the primary function of marketing and, more broadly speaking, the entire organization is to deliver value to the customer. The essential component in delivering value is the product experience, which is why it is considered the heart of marketing. Consider Nespresso, a single-serve, high-end espresso maker and one of the fastest-growing brands in the Nestlé company. The company's focus on delivering the "perfect coffee in the perfect portion" has led to global growth and demonstrated that customers are willing to pay for a product that delivers value. Indeed, many Nespresso customers argue that the Nespresso single-serve coffee experience rivals the best espressos in any restaurant.[1]

LO 8-1

Understand the essential role of the product experience in marketing.

Instead of focusing solely on its product, Starbucks has been successful selling "the Starbucks experience," which extends beyond drinking coffee to social interaction and lifestyle. The company defines the "product" (coffee) and the coffee-drinking experience in a way that delivers value to millions of customers around the world every day. Given the importance of the product experience in delivering customer value, it is not surprising that companies place a great deal of significance on getting the product experience right.

When the product is wrong, no amount of marketing communications and no degree of logistical expertise or pricing sophistication will make it successful. Apple is widely regarded as a product innovator with the iPhone, Apple Watch, iPad, iMac, and other products. However, the company has also experienced some product missteps. One of the most notable was Newton, the first PDA, introduced in the early 1990s but discontinued after Palm brought out its line of smaller, more user-friendly products. While technically superior to Palm, Apple did not understand the key value drivers in the product. People wanted PDAs with connectivity to other computers, a reasonable combination of features, and a realistic price (early Newtons cost over $1,000).[2] Newton's failure highlights an interesting fact: the best product technically is not always the most successful product. People look for the product that delivers the best overall product experience.

The Apple Newton, while technically better than similar PDAs, failed in the marketplace because it did not deliver a better product experience than competitors such as Palm.

©Chris Willson/Alamy Stock Photo

Product Characteristics

Define the Product What does the term *product* mean? Most people define a product as a tangible object; however, that is not accurate. The product experience encompasses a great deal more, as we will learn over the next several chapters. Consider the customer walking into Starbucks; is he or she just buying a cup of coffee? Did the owner of a new Toyota Prius buy just a new car? Is a pair of Madewell jeans just a pair of jeans? The answer is that, while customers are buying a cup of coffee, a new car, and a pair of jeans, they are also buying a product experience. It is important for the marketer to understand exactly what the customer includes in that experience. This is a particularly difficult challenge because different target markets will view the same product in completely different ways. Parents buying their daughter a pair of jeans would probably consider Madewell jeans to be just another pair of jeans; however, to the teenager, the same purchase makes an important statement about herself and her choice of clothes.[3]

LO 8-2

Define the characteristics of a product.

Product can be defined as anything that delivers value to satisfy a need or want and includes physical merchandise, services, events, people, places, organizations, information, even ideas. Most people have no problem considering a computer or car a product, but would these same individuals consider a get-away weekend at the Amelia Island Ritz-Carlton in Florida a product? The Ritz-Carlton does, and it develops a specific marketing strategy around the resort.

It is important to differentiate between a product and a product item. A product is a brand such as Post-it Notes or Tide detergent. Within each product a company may develop a number of product items, each of which represents a unique size, feature, or price. Tide powder detergent offers 12 "scents," including fragrance-free, in a variety of sizes designed to reach a variety of target markets.[4] Each combination of scent and size represents a unique product item in the Tide product line and is known by a **stock-keeping unit (SKU)**. An SKU is a unique identification number used to track a product through a distribution system, inventory management, and pricing.

Essential Benefit Why does someone purchase a plane ticket? The answer quite obviously is to get from one place to another. Simply stated, the essential benefit of purchasing a plane ticket is getting somewhere else; therefore, the essence of the airline product experience is transporting people. Successful airlines, indeed all companies, understand that before anything else, they must deliver on the essential benefit.

The **essential benefit** is the fundamental need met by the product. No matter what other value-added product experiences are provided to the customer, the essential benefit must be part of the encounter. For example, an airline can offer low fares, an easy-to-navigate website, or in-flight Wi-Fi, but unless the customer receives the essential benefit (getting from Point A to Point B), the other items have very little meaning to the customer. Without the essential benefit, other benefits may actually increase the customer's dissatisfaction with the experience. What good are low fares if the customer doesn't arrive at the destination?

Core Product Aircraft, pilots, flight attendants, baggage handlers, reservation agents, managers, and an IT system are a few of the elements needed to get people and their luggage from one place to another. An airline brings all those pieces together to create a product that efficiently and effectively delivers the essential benefit, transporting someone from Point A to Point B.

Companies translate the essential benefit into physical, tangible elements known as the **core product**. Some companies do it better than others, making this critical challenge an important differentiator separating successful companies from their competitors.[5] Southwest Airlines, for example, has done a very good job of translating the essential benefits of air travel. By using one kind of airplane, identifying efficiencies in everything from reservations to flight routes, and taking care of employees, the company is the industry leader in low-cost air travel and, in the process, has revolutionized the entire airline industry. Contrast Southwest with the long list of carriers over the past 15 years that defined the core product experience in ways many customers found unsatisfying. Many of the "legacy" carriers such as United, American, and Delta experienced financial problems, even bankruptcy, in part because they did not adequately deliver a positive core product experience to the customer.

As a company creates the core product experience, it is vital to clearly understand customer expectations. Every aspect of the product experience is evaluated by the customer and then considered against a set of expectations. When an airline creates a flight, there is an expectation that the flight will arrive at its stated time. If the flight does not arrive on time, the passenger assesses the reasons. Was it the airline's fault, the weather, or something else? Airlines are sensitive about their on-time arrival percentage and where they rank relative to the competition because they know customers believe this is an important characteristic of the core product experience. The customer's evaluation of a product experience against a set of defined expectations is a critical element contributing to overall satisfaction or dissatisfaction with the product.[6]

Enhanced Product The core product is the starting point for the product experience. All cell phones deliver on the essential benefit of mobile communication, but there is a vast difference between the low-end feature phone offered by many service providers and the latest iPhone or Android. Features, cutting-edge designs, and functionality differentiate one product from another. As consumers around the world become more sophisticated, companies are required to look beyond delivering great core products to creating products that enhance, extend, and encourage the customer.

The **enhanced product** extends the core product to include additional features, designs, and innovations that exceed customer expectations. In this way, companies build on the core product, creating opportunities to strengthen the brand. Consider Southwest Airlines once again, which has done a good job of delivering people on time and meeting customer expectations regarding low-cost air travel. Southwest added features such as frequent flyer

EXHIBIT 8.1 | Defining the Product at Southwest Airlines

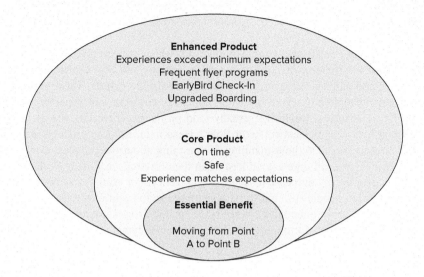

opportunities, EarlyBird Check-In, and Upgraded Boarding to further augment the customer's air travel experience. Exhibit 8.1 shows how the essential benefit, core product, and enhanced product are created for Southwest Airlines.

Product Classifications

Products can be classified in four ways. Two of the four classifications define the nature of the product: tangibility and durability. The other two classification criteria deal with who uses the product: consumers or businesses. It is important to understand the nature and use of a product because marketing strategies differ among the various product classifications.

Tangibility: Physical Aspects of the Product Experience Products, as opposed to services, have a physical aspect referred to as **tangibility**. Tangible products present opportunities (customers can see, touch, and experience the product) and also some challenges (customers may find the product does not match their personal tastes and preferences). Services, which we will explore in Chapter 10, are intangible. A significant challenge for marketers today is that many tangible products have intangible characteristics.[7] For example a significant element in an individual's satisfaction with a new car is the customer service before and after the purchase. Intangible products, on the other hand, such as services, have tangible characteristics. Airlines, for example, introduce new seats on their planes to create a competitive advantage.

Durability: Product Usage Durability references the length of product usage. **Nondurable products** are usually consumed in a few uses and, in general, cost less than durable products. Examples of consumer nondurables include personal grooming products such as toothpaste, soap, and shampoo, while business nondurables include office supplies such as printer ink, paper, and other less expensive, frequently purchased items. Because these products are purchased frequently and are not expensive, companies seek a wide distribution to make them as readily available as possible, create attractive price points to motivate purchase, and heavily advertise these products. **Durable products** have a longer product life and are often more expensive. Consumer durables include microwave ovens, washer/dryers, and certain electronics such as televisions. Business durables include products that may be used in the manufacturing process such as IT networks, as well as equipment such as office furniture and computers to facilitate the running of the business.[8]

Consumer Goods Consumers purchase thousands of products from an assortment of millions of choices. On the surface it may seem difficult to develop a classification system for the variety of products consumers purchase, but the reality is that consumer purchase habits fall into four broad categories: convenience, shopping, specialty, and unsought.

Frequently purchased, relatively low-cost products for which customers have little interest in seeking new information or considering other options and rely heavily on prior brand experience and purchase behavior are called **convenience goods**. These products include most items people buy regularly such as toiletries, gasoline, and paper products and fall into four categories. Staples are usually food products people buy weekly or at least once a month such as Folgers coffee or Boar's Head ham. Impulse products, as the name implies, are purchased without planning. If you think about the products available in vending machines, you will have a good idea of an impulse product. Finally, there are a host of products people only purchase in times of emergency. For example, as hurricanes approach communities, people rush out to purchase extra supplies of food, gas, batteries, and other products. It is not uncommon to see occasional shortages of some products as distribution systems are strained to meet unplanned spikes in demand for these everyday products.

Products that require consumers to do more research and compare across product dimensions such as color, size, features, and price are called **shopping goods**. Consumer products that fall into this category include clothes, furniture, and major appliances such as refrigerators and dishwashers. These products are purchased less frequently and are more costly than convenience goods. Price concerns, a variety of choices at various price levels, many different features, and a fear of making the wrong decision are among the factors that drive consumers to research these purchases. As a result, companies often develop product strategies that target product price points with particular features to appeal to the broadest range of consumers. For example, Whirlpool brand makes over 40 different electric dryers ranging in price from $599 to $1,899.

Specialty goods are a unique purchase made based on a defining characteristic for the consumer. The characteristic might be a real or perceived product feature such as Apple iPhone's easy user interface or brand identification like Porsche's reputation for building sports cars. Whatever the attribute(s), consumers apply decision rules that frequently minimize the number of different product choices and focus less on price. They are also more willing to seek out the product; however, expectations about product service, salesperson expertise, and customer service are higher. Bang & Olufsen's line of high-end electronic equipment is not available in regular retail outlets. Rather, the company has a limited number of retail stores in major cities. Consumers wanting to purchase Bang & Olufsen equipment must seek out those stores.

The final categories of goods, **unsought goods**, are products that consumers do not seek out and, indeed, often would rather not purchase at all. Insurance, particularly life insurance, is not a product people want to purchase. In general, customers do not want to purchase products or services related to sickness, death, or emergencies because, in part, the circumstances surrounding the purchase are not pleasant. As a result, companies have well-trained salespeople skilled in helping customers through the purchase process. These salespeople often must be supported by extensive marketing communications.

Business Goods Businesses buy a vast array of products that can be classified into three broad areas based on two dimensions: (1) whether or not they are used in the manufacturing process and (2) cost. Goods incorporated into the company's finished product as a result of the manufacturing process are either materials or parts. **Materials** are natural (lumber, minerals such as copper) or farm products (corn, soybeans) that become part of the final product. **Parts** consist of equipment either fully assembled or in smaller pieces that will be assembled into larger components and, again, used in the production process.

In addition to the products that are used directly in the production process, companies purchase a number of products and services to support business operations. These can generally be placed on a continuum from low-cost/frequent purchases to very high-cost/infrequent purchases. **MRO (maintenance, repair, operating) supplies** are the everyday items that a company needs to keep running. While per unit cost is low, their total cost over a year can be high.

At the other end of the cost/purchase-frequency continuum are **capital goods**, which are major purchases in support of a significant business function. Building a new plant or a new IT network can require large equipment purchases that cost millions of dollars and require significant customization. These purchases are negotiated over a period of months, sometimes years. Consider that it takes two to five years to build a new data center for companies like Apple or Amazon, and the cost is between $1.5 and $2.5 billion. Companies selling capital goods to businesses focus on personal selling and a high level of customer service with significant product customization.

Product Discrimination: Create a Point of Differentiation

A fundamental question in the product purchase decision-making process is what makes this product different? As a result, marketing managers must identify important characteristics that successfully differentiate their product from others in the customer's mind. Then they must produce those elements in the product itself, balancing a number of factors including customer preferences, costs, and company resources.

Form The most elemental method of differentiating a product is to change its **form**—size, shape, color, and other physical elements. Many products considered very similar in functionality can be differentiated by variations in packaging or product delivery. Among the reasons cited for the growth of Guinness in the U.S. over the past several years has been new product variations and packaging (Exhibit 8.2). Bombardier is a leader in business and regional jet production. Bombardier recently announced its C Series airliners, its first product to compete against Boeing and Airbus in the mainline market. The C Series has two planes: the CS300, a 130-seater, and the CS100, a 108-seater. The C Series' lightweight aluminum and composite body makes for attractive efficiency, and its turbofan engines are more fuel efficient than current airplanes, making the plane 15 percent cheaper to operate. Delta Airlines placed an order for 75 CS100 airliners with Bombardier—a deal that is worth about $5.6 billion.[9]

Bombardier builds a wide range of small to medium-size jets to meet transportation needs around the world.

©Graham Hughes/Alamy Stock Photo

Features When asked what makes a product different, many people will respond by talking about features. A **feature** is any product attribute or performance characteristic and is often added to or subtracted from a product to differentiate it from competitors. However, while delivering consumer value is the primary driver in making product decisions, a company must balance the features customers want with what they will pay at a given quality level.[10]

Interestingly, based on their research, competitors often create products with very different feature configurations. Cell phone manufacturers, for example, are constantly assessing the feature mix across their product line. When comparing similar Samsung versus Apple models, a number of feature differences will be easily identified. One of the great challenges for marketers is determining the feature mix that best

EXHIBIT 8.2 | Form and Product Variations for Guinness Products

©Editorial Image, LLC

satisfies the needs and wants of the target audience and at what price. No competitors ever arrive at the same feature mix, which means decisions about which features to include and exclude are critical to a product's success.

Performance Quality Should a company always build the highest-quality product? Some people would say the answer is yes. However, the answer is more complex than that. Essentially, companies should build products to the performance quality level that their target audience is willing to pay for. Often this means a company will build products at multiple performance levels to meet demand at various price points. Keep in mind that the key is to deliver value to the customer. Consider the airline industry. With the exception of a few airlines, such as Southwest, every airline offers different classes of service. On domestic flights, many offer economy class and first class. On international flights, airlines often offer three or four different classes of service—economy, premium economy, business, and first. These different experiences come with very different prices. For example, a round-trip flight from New York to London could be as low as $700, while a first-class ticket on the same flight could cost over $16,000. The key is to define the experience so that customers are willing to pay for the value received.[11]

The market's perception of the company's performance quality is critical in defining its market space. Companies generally try to match product performance quality with the market's perception of the brand. Timex will not develop a $25,000 watch because the market would not expect, and may not accept, a watch with production quality at that level from Timex, although they do expect it from Rolex.[12] At the same time, companies need to be careful not to lower performance quality too dramatically in an effort to cut costs or reach new markets. Losing control of a quality image can do significant harm to a brand's image. For example, product safety remains a critical concern for consumers. Products that fail to meet quality standards can lead to a loss of consumer confidence.

Conformance Quality An important issue for consumers is **conformance**, which is the product's ability to deliver on features and performance characteristics promised in marketing communications. The challenge for marketers and manufacturing is that every product must deliver on those promises. A product is said to have high conformance quality when a high percentage of the manufactured products fulfill the stated performance criteria.[13] If someone opened a Coke and there was no "fizz," it wouldn't be a Coke. The challenge for Coca-Cola and its bottlers is to ensure that every Coke has just the right carbonation when the consumer opens the can or bottle anywhere in the world.

Durability Consumer research and purchase patterns affirm that people find **durability,** the projected lifetime of the product under specific operating conditions, an important discriminating product characteristic and are willing to pay a premium for products that can demonstrate greater durability.[14] KitchenAid appliances have a reputation for durability that has translated into a price premium for their products.

Reliability A similar discriminator references the dependability of a product. **Reliability** is the percentage of time the product works without failure or stoppage. Businesses and consumers consistently report this is an important discriminator in their purchase decision; however, a product can be too reliable. While it is possible to build computers that will last for years and cost a premium, most computer manufacturers do not build them because computer technology changes so quickly and product improvements happen so fast that people will not pay the premium for a computer that will last for many years.[15] They know that better, cheaper technology will be available before the computer actually malfunctions.

Repairability Increasingly, consumers and businesses evaluate the **repairability**, ease of fixing a problem with the product, as part of the product evaluation process. As a result, companies have built better diagnostics into their products to help isolate, identify, and repair products without the need for the costly repairs of a professional service.[16] Many car companies, including most of the luxury car manufacturers, now offer run-flat tires that enable the driver to continue driving even after a tire has been damaged. At the same time and where appropriate, products are designed to "call in" to repair services online or on the phone. Cell phone manufacturers and service providers work together to build self-diagnostic phones that can be accessed in the field by service technicians. The technician can look at the phone's functionality and actually do minor software upgrades or repairs during a phone call. Of course, repairability has a cost, and companies must constantly evaluate the costs and benefits of this dimension. For example, General Motors reduced the free trial period for its OnStar Guidance Plan from six months to three months, but reminds consumers that new vehicles still come with the OnStar Basic Plan for five years, free of charge. OnStar's Protection Plan offers the most important safety-related features offered by OnStar for several hundred dollars annually. Similar services are offered by Ford and Kia without a subscription cost to customers. This change comes shortly after GM reduced its powertrain warranty to cover up to five years or 60,000 miles. These changes in service reduced the perceived value of GM vehicles, and hurt GM's operating margins.[17]

Style One of the most difficult discriminators to accurately assess and build into a product is the look and feel of the product, or **style**. It is easy for someone to say a particular product has style, but designing it into a product can be a challenge. More than any other discriminator, style offers the advantage of being difficult to copy. Many companies, from Samsung to Fitbit to Microsoft, have tried to develop a successful wearable device, but none of them have been able to develop a "must have" wearable that can compete with the Apple Watch. Despite issues with battery life and missing functions, Apple Watch is the leader in the wearables market. A key to the Apple Watch's success has been the product's style, which builds on Apple's strong reputation for creating products, such as the iPhone and iMac, that not only perform well but look great while doing their job.

The real challenge is that style can be difficult to create consistently. Consumer tastes change over time, and what is considered stylish can quickly lose its appeal. Companies invest in information systems that help them spot trends. Once a trend is identified, product development teams must be able to translate it into design elements that can be incorporated into the product.[18] In some industries this is critical; for example, clothing manufacturers anticipate future trends, then use efficient production processes to design, build, and distribute their clothes while a particular style is still popular.

Exhibit 8.3 identifies product discriminators and gives examples.

EXHIBIT 8.3 | Product Discriminators

Form

With a large number of spray heads, ambient rain shower panels provide luxurious water delivery.

(cont.)

EXHIBIT 8.3 | **Product Discriminators** *(cont.)*

Features		The new London Taxi TX 5 is a completely redesigned version of the classic London Taxi. It incorporates a number of new features, such as in-car entertainment, and is completely electric to meet the most demanding emissions standards.
Performance Quality		Oil companies produce several grades of gasoline to meet the demands of consumers.
Conformance Quality		Crest Whitestrips are a good low-priced teeth whitener. The system also comes with a standard 60-day money-back guarantee, should you not care for the results.
Durability		Timberland has a reputation for building high-quality, durable products like these boots that come with a commitment to customer satisfaction.
Reliability		Carrier promotes the fact that its air conditioners are reliable. In addition, it provides different quality levels with varying warranties.
Repairability		Many bicycle manufacturers highlight the easy repair of their bikes. A key point is that anyone can fix most of the problems that may occur.

(cont.)

Style  Apple Watch promotes style in the design of the watch as well as the ability to customize through color choice and a variety of watch bands.

Sources: (shower head): ©Nalinratana Phiyanalinmat/Alamy Stock Photo; (Taxi TX 5): ©Adrian Dennis/AFP/Getty Images; (gas pumps): ©David Muscroft/SuperStock/Alamy Stock Photo; (Crest Whitestrips): Procter & Gamble; (Timberland boot): ©xMarshall/Alamy Stock Photo; (Carrier air conditioner): ©Editorial Image, LLC; (woman repairing bike): ©Jetta Productions/Blend Images; and (Apple watch): ©Neil Godwin/MacFormat Magazine via Getty Images.

Product Plan: Moving from One Product to Many Products

Our discussion thus far has focused on a single product; however, companies generally create a range of products. These products can be variations or extensions of one basic product or completely different products. Most people would consider Post-it Notes, 3M's iconic brand of self-adhesive notes, a single product, but over 600 Post-it products are sold in more than 100 countries.[19] When you couple the extensive range of Post-it products with the thousands of products offered by 3M across more than 40 core product lines, it becomes apparent why management must understand how a product fits into the company's product strategy. Developing a plan sets strategy not only for a single product, but also for all the products in the company's catalog.

Product Line A **product line** is a group of products linked through usage, customer profile, price points, and distribution channels or needs satisfaction. Within a product line, strategies are developed for a single product, but also for all the products in the line. For example, 3M develops a strategy for each Post-it product, such as Post-it cards, that identifies possible product uses, different target markets, and marketing messages. At the same time, the company combines individual products for specific markets to create consumer-based solution catalogs. Students can find Post-it products targeted for them and teachers can find a separate listing of products.

Companies must balance the number of items in a product line. Too many items and customers find it difficult to differentiate between individual products. In addition, cost inefficiencies involved in producing multiple products lower margins for the entire product line. Too few products and the company runs the risk of missing important market opportunities. Consumers are gravitating toward small and boutique brands, and younger consumers have increased their fresh food consumption by 23 percent. For Campbell Soup, these trends require a new recipe for the future, as the former cold-weather staple is getting hammered. In response, the company has developed three new lines of soup: Well Yes!, Garden Fresh Gourmet, and Souplicity. Garden Fresh Gourmet and Souplicity are refrigerated products sold in plastic containers instead of the traditional metal can. Souplicity is completely organic and the highest-end line of the three. Garden Fresh Gourmet soups are family-sized, and although they are not completely organic it is still a health-focused brand. Well Yes! is more traditional, still appearing in can form, but it uses healthful ingredients and puts a twist on traditional recipes. At a low price point, Well Yes! is geared toward consumers who try to make positive changes to better their health, but do not follow strict rules, and already buy canned soups.[20]

Product Mix Combining all the products offered by a company is called the **product mix**. Small, start-up companies frequently have a relatively limited product mix, but, as companies grow, their list of products grows as well. Developing strategies for the entire product mix is

EXHIBIT 8.4 | **3M's Product Mix of 55,000 Products**

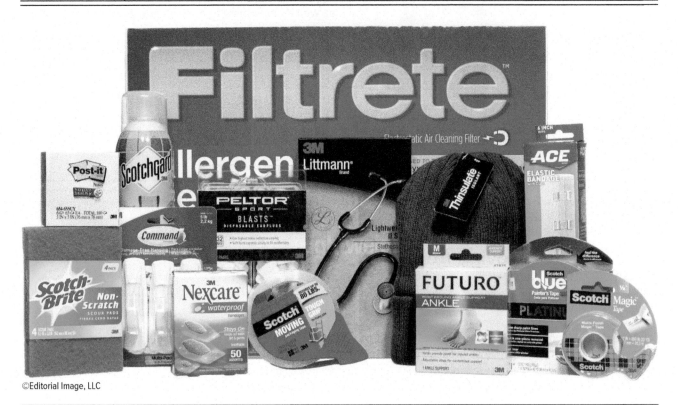

©Editorial Image, LLC

done at the highest levels of the organization.[21] Large companies, like 3M or GE, have widely disparate product lines that encompass hundreds of products and thousands of product items. Exhibit 8.4 lists some of the more than 55,000 products in 3M's product mix, which range from Post-it Notes to communication technology systems and a host of industrial applications.

Product Decisions Affect Other Marketing Mix Elements

Decisions about the product affect other elements of the marketing mix. Let's look at how two key marketing mix elements, pricing and marketing communications, are influenced by product decisions.

Pricing Pricing is one of the key marketing mix components and will be covered in detail in Chapter 11; however, several key issues related to product line pricing are appropriately covered here. Individual product pricing within the context of a broader product line requires a clear understanding of the price points for all the products in the line. Often multiple price points are targeted at specific markets with unique features following a "good, better, best" product line strategy. This strategy develops multiple product lines that include products with distinct features at each particular price point to attract multiple target markets. When new products are introduced, marketers carefully consider customer perceptions of the product's feature mix and price point to avoid customer confusion.

Technology companies, for many years, have faced the challenge of pricing new products that are less expensive but with more features than previous models. Dell and HP are sensitive to pricing new products because as new, more-powerful, less-expensive products come into the product mix, demand often drops for existing products. Dell prices new computer models to minimize disrupting demand for its existing products while, at the same time, lowering prices of existing products to create greater separation between the new product and current products (see Exhibit 8.5).

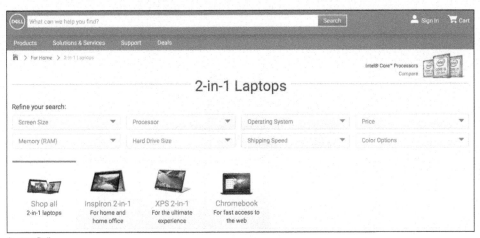

Source: Dell

Marketing Communications A key strategic decision for marketers is the degree to which marketing communications focuses on a single product item versus a product brand. Usually, companies do both, but the emphasis on one approach versus the other makes a big difference in the communications strategy. For example, 3M focuses much of its Post-it marketing communications on the Post-it product line, emphasizing the brand. Contrast that with Häagen-Dazs, which focuses on specific products (ice cream, sorbet, and yogurt) and specific product items within each product (chocolate, almond hazelnut swirl, pineapple coconut).

A second communications issue is the allocation of communications budget dollars across product items in a product line. Häagen-Dazs has more than 30 specific kinds of ice cream and dozens of other products across its entire product line. The company must make decisions about the allocation of budget dollars to each product, then each specific product item. This raises several challenges for marketing managers. Do they allocate dollars based on the most popular flavors like chocolate and vanilla? Or do they focus on new product items such as Mayan chocolate to build a competitive edge with products that are not offered by the competition? New products almost always have additional communication budgets to support the product's introduction. The assumption is that, once the product is established, it will be possible to cut back on the heavy expenditure of a new product communications campaign (see Exhibit 8.6).

THE LIFE OF THE PRODUCT: BUILDING THE PRODUCT EXPERIENCE

Companies create, launch, and transform products as market conditions change over time. This product evolution is referred to as the **product life cycle (PLC)** and defines the life of a product in four basic stages: introduction, growth, maturity, and decline (see Exhibit 8.7).[22]

The PLC generally refers to a product category (fitness bicycles) rather than a product item (Cannondale Quick bicycles), although companies often track their own product items against an industry PLC. The PLC is a useful tool because it (1) provides a strategic framework for market analysis, (2) tracks historical trends, and (3) identifies future market conditions. Cannondale Bicycles, for example, can evaluate the current fitness bike market and then consider growth opportunities for the Quick brand based on that product's position in the PLC.

LO 8-4

Understand the life of a product and how product strategies change over time.

EXHIBIT 8.6 | Häagen-Dazs Promotes One Product Item

Source: HDIP, INC

Häagen Dazs has been successful building a product line that features old favorites but also frequently introduces new product flavors.

EXHIBIT 8.7 | The Product Life Cycle

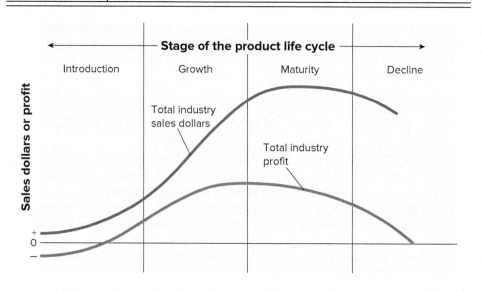

Product Life Cycle Sales Revenue and Profitability

Notice there are two lines on the PLC graph. The top line charts the industry sales revenue for the product over time. The sales revenue line increases dramatically in the introduction and growth stages as the product moves through the consumer adoption process. At some point, sales begin to decline. However, a sales decline does not necessarily mean the death of the product. Companies may create new products or market conditions may change, which can reinvigorate the product and start a new growth phase. Bottled water was long considered a product in decline until Evian, Dasani, Voss, and others developed new packaging, added new flavors, and emphasized the healthy aspects of water. Now the product category is experiencing a period of significant growth around the world.

The second line on the PLC graph is the total profits from the companies that compete in that industry. When the product is introduced, the category pioneer, the company introducing the product, has incurred product development costs. At the same time, new companies entering the market also sustain product development and initial marketing costs associated with the product launch. As a result, the industry starts the PLC "in the red" (no profits). As the product category grows, successful companies recoup their initial costs and begin to realize a return on their investments. A good example of the challenge around revenue and profitability in the product life cycle is Elon Musk's Tesla car company. The electric vehicle pioneer has a soaring stock price and a group of loyal followers right alongside a growing group of skeptics. Tesla has continued to report losses, and analysts suggest the losses will continue, at least in the short to medium term, which calls into question the company's long-term viability. Demand for the Tesla Model S and Model X is plateauing, as customers look for newer models like the Model 3. In addition, Tesla has experienced quality control issues after a recall of 53,000 cars with a parking brake problem. Growing sales is one thing, but increasing profitability can be more difficult, particularly for new products.[23]

Product Life Cycle Timeline

The speed at which products within a category move through the PLC is not consistent, and there is a great deal of variability across product categories. In some cases, a product moves through an entire cycle in a period of months and is replaced with the next product design. **Fads** come and go quickly, often reaching only a limited number of individuals but creating a lot of buzz in the marketplace.[24] Often, women's fashion is seasonal, with a product line being introduced in the spring, moving through its growth cycle in the summer and fall, then finally going into decline by winter. The cycle takes one selling season, in this case, one year. With other products such as men's suits, it may take decades from introduction to decline. Men's classic two-piece suits experience incremental changes every season, but the same basic design has been around for many years. The functionality of the product has made it an enduring style for men.

Product Life Cycle Caveats

It is important to note several caveats about the product life cycle. The PLC is a helpful conceptual tool that works best when viewed as a framework for studying a product category. It can be difficult to know with certainty what stage a product is in, particularly at transition points in the PLC. Rather, the PLC enables marketing managers to assess historical trends in the category and track how the product has behaved over time. Naturally, there may be different interpretations of the same data as marketing managers in one company look at the numbers and arrive at one conclusion while managers in another company arrive at a different conclusion.

The PLC is also useful when marketing managers focus on historical precedent—Where has the product been?—and future possibilities—How do we plan now to be successful in the next stage? By using the PLC as a planning tool for developing new products, it is possible to avoid getting caught in the immediacy of volatile market fluctuations. Exhibit 8.8 summarizes the phases of the product life cycle.

EXHIBIT 8.8 | Product Life Cycle

	Introduction Phase	Growth Phase	Maturity Phase	Decline Stage
Objective	Build market awareness for the product leading to trial purchase.	Differentiate product from those of new competitors, promoting rapid expansion.	Transition product from high growth to sales stability.	Determine the future of the product.
Profitability	Sales are low, typically high failure rate. High marketing and product costs.	Sales grow at increasing rate. Profits become healthier as operations are streamlined.	Sales continue to increase but at a decreasing rate. Cost minimization has reached full extent.	Long-run drop in sales. Profit margins dramatically reduced.
Market Conditions				
Market Segment	Nonexistent.	New market segment now established.	Market is approaching saturation.	Changing consumer tastes and substitute products eat away at market segment.
Targeted Consumers	Innovators and Early Adopters	Early Adopters to Majority Adopters	Majority Adopters	Laggards
Competitive Environment	Little competition.	Many competitors enter market.	Marginal competitors dropping out.	Falling demand forces many out of market.
Competitor Reaction	Market followers will release product similar to that of the pioneer.	Large companies may acquire small pioneering firms.	Typified by models of products with an emphasis on style over function.	Firms that remain focus on specialty products.
Strategies				
Product	High-quality, innovative design providing new benefit to consumers. Features well received and understood by target consumers.	More features and better design, learning from issues from first generation. Diversification of product and release of complementary products/ services.	Product lines are widened or extended. Work to further differentiate product from those of competitors.	Consider product expenses in terms of return on investment. Decide whether to invest further in product or allocate funding to new project(s).

(cont.)

	Introduction Phase	Growth Phase	Maturity Phase	Decline Stage
Price	**Market penetration:** Attractive price point to gain market share and discourage competitors.	New and improved models sold at high price points.	Target high-end market with differentiated product and higher price point.	Offer product at low price point to try to stimulate any remaining demand.
	Market skimming: High initial price point targeting less price-sensitive consumers to recoup R&D costs before competitors enter market.	Existing models or earlier generations move down in price.	Established competition makes price pressures more pronounced, forcing lower-price strategy if product not well-differentiated.	Significant price pressures from both competitors and more price-sensitive consumers.
Marketing Communications	Inform and educate target audience about the product's features and benefits.	Link the brand with key product features and highlight differentiation between competitors.	Challenge of deciding between short-term sales promotions or investing more in the brand.	Cost of continued investment in marketing communications not justified by market conditions.
	Promotion focused on product awareness and to stimulate primary demand.	Promotion emphasizes brand advertising and comparative ads.		
Distribution	Wide distribution network with limited product availability: Create anticipation by promoting excitement and sense of scarcity.	Broaden distribution networks to keep up with expanding market demand.	Product has reached its maximum distribution.	Reduced distribution channels.
	Limit distribution but increase product availability: Release to limited number of target markets with high availability. Intensive personal selling to retailers and wholesalers.	Maintain high levels of product quality and boost customer service efforts to keep up with product.	Channel members identify weak products and begin dropping out if necessary.	Channel members cease to support the product.

NEW PRODUCTS—CREATING LONG-TERM SUCCESS

No matter how good a company's current products are, long-term growth depends on new products. This can be done in one of two basic ways: acquisition or internal development. Both approaches have their advantages and disadvantages.

"New" Defined

LO 8-5

Recognize the importance of new product development to long-term success.

What does the term *new* mean? Every day, consumers see or hear marketing communications that talk about "new and improved." At the same time, people speak about buying a new car (which may in fact be a used car) as well as a new TV (which may be last year's model). Let's look at how the term is defined by the product's manufacturer and customers.

Company Perspective Most people would define *new* as a product that has not been available before or bears little resemblance to an existing product, and one type of new product is actually referred to as a **new-to-the-world product** because it has not been available before. Sometimes new-to-the-world products are so innovative they create a fundamental change in the marketplace and are known as *disruptive innovation*. They are called disruptive because they shift people's perspective and frequently alter their behavior by offering dramatically simpler, more convenient, and usually less-expensive products than currently exist. In the process they frequently make existing products less desirable. A Google search of "new-to-the-world products" reveals a list of self-proclaimed "new-to-the-world" items on Google Shopping, including a veggie bullet spiralizer, a nose irrigation device, and an air horn. Ironically, while such results demonstrate the importance of defining "new," Google itself is intent on developing innovative, groundbreaking products. Through Project Jacquard, Google has partnered with Levi to develop and embed technology into fabrics to create connected clothing and interactive surfaces. This technology aims to revolutionize the way that consumers interact with spaces around them.[25]

A second type of new-to-the-world product, *sustaining innovations,* are newer, better, faster versions of existing products that target, for the most part, existing customers. Sustaining innovations can be revolutionary by taking the market in a new direction. They can also be **upgrades or modifications to existing products** and represent incremental enhancements to current products.[26]

Once a product has been developed and is on the market, the company can extend the product by creating **additions to existing product lines**. For years, Coca-Cola has added new products to the Coke line, first with Diet Coke in the early 1980s and now with many different Coke-branded products including Coke Life. These products are also available in various sizes and packaging, giving Coke many different product items.

Another "new" product approach is to **reposition existing products** to target new markets. The cell phone market used this strategy successfully to introduce cell phones in the mid-1990s. Originally cell phone service providers positioned the phones as a tool for businesspeople or as a safety tool targeting individuals such as working women and moms. As the product became more widely adopted, the positioning of the product changed to become an important work tool. As the market for cell phones has expanded, the positioning has evolved to include younger users. Cell phones are the dominant communication device for teenagers, and phones have been created for kids as young as seven.

Cost reduction, as the name implies, is a specific method for introducing lower-cost products that frequently focus on value-oriented product price points in the product mix. Generally this approach involves eliminating or reducing features, using less-expensive materials, or altering the service or warranty to offer the product at a lower price point to the market.[27]

Customer's Perspective While the company follows a specific strategy in creating a new product, the customer is unaware and, in reality, often does not really care about how the product arrived in the marketplace. The customer's perspective is much more narrow and self-directed. The customer is most interested in an answer to the fundamental question—is this product new to me? From the company's perspective it is important to realize that every customer approaches a new product a little differently. For example, an individual going in to buy his or her first car can find the process intimidating. As a result,

EXHIBIT 8.9 | Why Do Products Fail?

Company
Inadequate value proposition

Poor marketing communications

Product does not meet customer expectations

Failure to fully develop product

Customers
Change in purchase priorities

Higher expectations

Competitors
Aggressively attack new competition

Environment
Changes in government regulation or legislation

Changes in societal demands

Economic changes

salespeople at the car dealer handle those customers carefully to reduce anxiety, concentrating on things like basic features, a low-stress selling environment, and friendly service. Experienced car buyers are interested in talking about the latest product updates, new leasing options, and extended service plans. One challenge companies face is dealing with historical customer perceptions. When Infiniti updated its line of luxury cars, it decided to change the names of many of its models to reflect significant updates to the models as well as a new, more modern image.

Reasons for New Product Success or Failure

Since new product development is such a critical factor in the long-term success of an organization, you might think companies are good at the development process. Unfortunately, this is not the case; 70 to 80 percent of all new products worldwide fail. While it is true that many of those products are developed by small entrepreneurs, no company is immune to product failure. Have you ever heard of Levi's business wear or Dunkin' Donuts cereal? Probably not, because these new products failed despite the fact they were introduced by companies with a track record of marketing success. Consider also the disastrous failure of Samsung's Galaxy Note 7, due to repeated instances of the phones exploding or catching fire. The phones were banned from all airline flights by the U.S. Department of Transportation as a fire hazard after over 100 instances of problems and injuries caused by the phone malfunctioning were reported. Similar bans were imposed by airlines in Europe, Asia, and Australia after persistent problems with the phone. Ultimately, the product was withdrawn from the market, which severely impacted Samsung's market leadership—at least in the short term.[28] The reasons vary, but it is possible to identify the role of the company, customers, and competitors in the success or failure of a new product.[29] Exhibit 8.9 summarizes the reasons for new product failure.

NEW PRODUCT DEVELOPMENT PROCESS

The new product development process consists of three main activities and eight specific tasks. Failure at any step significantly lowers the probability of long-term success. The three major activities in new product development are to (1) identify product opportunities, (2) define the product opportunity, and (3) develop the product opportunity.

There is a great deal of variability in the new product development timeline. Marketers must balance the product development process with the ever-changing demands of the marketplace. Take too long in product development and the market may have changed; rush the process and the product may be poorly designed or lack quality.[30]

Identify Product Opportunities

LO 8-6

Understand the new product development process.

The first step in the new product development process, identify potential product opportunities, has two specific tasks. First, companies must generate sufficient new product ideas. Very few product ideas make it through the entire process and, as we have seen already, far fewer products actually become successful. As a result, it is important to have a steady flow of new ideas into the development process. Second, ideas need to be evaluated before resources are committed to development.

Generate New Ideas Product ideas are generated in one of two ways: internal or external to the firm. While companies develop a preference for one approach over the other, the reality is that both internal and external sources produce good new product ideas. A number of factors, including the company's commitment to innovation, the reputation of competitors for new product development, and customer expectations, affect which approach a company prefers.[31]

Kimberly-Clark's Huggies brand of disposable diapers has developed dozens of different diaper products for newborns, older babies, and toddlers, as well as specialized products for extra comfort, overnight, and swimming diapers. K-C even manufactures six different kinds of baby wipes.

©McGraw-Hill Education/Jill Braaten, photographer

Internal Sources include employees from R&D, marketing, and manufacturing. Key employees know both the capabilities of the company and the needs of the market. Therefore, it is not surprising that internal sources are the single best source for new product ideas. Funding product research is expensive; companies spend billions of dollars every year to generate product ideas.

People who work directly with customers are another source of ideas. As salespeople, customer service representatives, and others interact directly with customers, it is possible to identify new product ideas. Often these ideas are incremental changes to existing products that solve a particular problem; however, occasionally the customer challenge requires a truly innovative solution.

Working with academia helps support the research activities of many organizations. Under Armour (UA) established a partnership with Johns Hopkins Medicine to conduct health and fitness research and develop UA's connected fitness platforms. UA currently has the largest connected fitness community in the world with over 190 million registered users. Through this agreement, UA is able to develop and market new products based on medical research as experts from Johns Hopkins provide research, insights, and recommendations on sleep, fitness, activity, and nutrition to improve UA's connected fitness community.[32]

External An excellent source of ideas comes from individuals and organizations not directly connected with the company. In some industries, such as Internet applications, small entrepreneurs drive innovation. Instagram is a popular Internet destination owned by Facebook. Started by entrepreneurs in 2010 who wanted to share files across social media platforms, the company has over 1200 million registered users. The company's acquisition by Facebook exemplifies how larger companies continue to grow by acquiring smaller companies with innovative products. Google, Microsoft, and Apple all maintain dedicated staff whose job it is to identify and acquire new start-up organizations with great product ideas.

Customers Customers are also an excellent source of product ideas. Solving their problems can lead to innovative solutions that have market potential beyond the immediate customer. Many companies encourage customer input directly online through e-mail and online discussion groups. Ford, BMW, Mercedes-Benz, and others sponsor user group bulletin boards that discuss improvements to existing products. While this will not likely lead to "new-to-the-world" products, it can lead to incremental or even substantial enhancements to existing products.

Distributors Distributors are a good source for new product ideas, particularly when they are the primary link between the customer and the company. Small organizations generally do not have the resources for a national sales force and use distributors in many markets. The distributor network is a key partner in the development of new products for the company. In actuality, almost anyone outside the organization can generate a new product idea.

Companies understand that even though the majority of ideas from external sources will not pass the screening process, they still want to encourage people to submit their product concepts. HP gets thousands of product ideas from a variety of individuals every year; however, very few are actually developed.

Screen and Evaluate Ideas Ideas need to be screened and evaluated as quickly as possible. The screening process has two primary objectives. The first objective is to eliminate product ideas judged unworthy of further consideration. New product development is expensive and resources are scarce, so ideas are evaluated early to assess their viability. An idea is rejected for several reasons. Perhaps the proposal is just not very good or it may be reasonable but inconsistent with the company's overall business strategy. Evaluating ideas can sometimes create difficult choices for managers as they wrestle with broader societal issues.[33] Consider the challenge of creating "kid friendly" television for young children. Netflix has created a number of shows that seek to provide an educational experience in an entertaining way to kids of various ages. Shows like *Ask the Storybots* answer questions on a variety of topics—with a group of friendly, funny bots.

Two types of mistakes are associated with rejecting or moving forward with a new product design, and both are potentially expensive for the company. The first is the **go-to-market mistake** made when a company fails to stop a bad product idea from moving into product development. This mistake runs on a continuum from very costly (the new product is not accepted and the company loses its initial investment) to not meeting targeted ROI projections (the product does not hit established benchmarks for profitability, or unit sales). Expensive mistakes often initiate a review of the screening process to figure out how the product made it through the development process. When the product fails to hit targeted benchmarks for success, the review may focus on errors in marketing strategy, target market adjustments, or competitive response to the product launch.

A **stop-to-market mistake** happens when a good idea is prematurely eliminated during the screening process. Almost every CEO can relate a story of the product success that got away. Most often companies are reluctant to talk about stop-to-market mistakes because it makes management uncomfortable and provides additional information about product development to competitors. For example, we have talked a lot about Apple, pointing out its wildly successful iPhone and iPad. But in addition to its failed Newton, which we discussed earlier, the company has also developed a number of other products that never made it to market. For example, the Macintosh PowerBook Duo Tablet was, arguably, the first tablet PC and was created in the early 1990s during the same period as Newton. Apple stopped development of the product, code-named PenLite, to avoid confusion with Newton. Among PenLite's many features was a wireless, full-function computer that connected with all PowerBook accessories.[34]

A second objective of the screening process is to help prioritize ideas that pass the initial screening and evaluation. All new product concepts are not equal, and it is important to focus resources on those that best match the success criteria. The criteria used to prioritize ideas vary by company but often include:

- Time to market (how long will it take to develop and get the product to market).
- ROI (what is the expected return for the dollars invested in the project).
- New product fit with overall company product portfolio.

This analysis includes an internal assessment by a team from specific areas across the company (finance, marketing, R&D, manufacturing, logistics).[35] Often these people are directly involved in new product development and have a thorough understanding of the success criteria and the company's overall product portfolio. Additionally, a relevant member of senior management provides continuity with

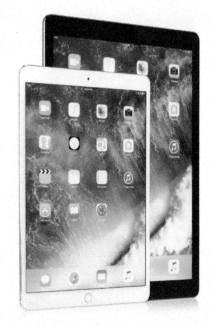

Apple's iPad was a smash success, unlike the Newton.

© Leszek Kobusinski/Alamy Stock Photo

long-term strategic goals and leadership in the screening process. Members of the team are rotated to ensure fresh ideas as there is often a significant time commitment required and members of the assessment team have other responsibilities in the company.[36]

Define the Product Opportunity

Ideas that pass through the screening process move into a development phase to define the product potential and market opportunity. Three specific tasks in this stage are to (1) define and test the product idea, (2) create a marketing strategy for the product, and (3) analyze the product's business case.

Define and Test Product Concept The product idea now needs to be clearly defined and tested. Ideas at this stage are frequently not fully developed or operational. At this point, depending on the concept, people and resources are allocated to move the product development forward and a budget is created to develop the product.

Product definition has three objectives. First, it defines the product's value proposition: what customer needs are being addressed and, in broad terms, at what price. Second, the definition briefly identifies the target market(s) and the purchase frequency. Third, the definition delineates the product's characteristics (look, feel, physical elements, and features of the product). As the product moves through development, the physical characteristics become more defined and particular features, often at different price points, are included in the prototypes.[37]

Target customers are useful in defining the product concept. Companies present models, limited prototypes, and verbal or written descriptions of the product concept to customers, individually or in focus groups. Computer graphics are also used to depict elements of the product and even functionality. For example, in the development of new jet airliners, Boeing and Airbus develop sophisticated simulations that allow passengers to *virtually* sit in the airplane. In this way, customers get a more realistic perspective at a fraction of the cost to develop a full-scale working prototype.

During this phase, companies start getting market input to refine and develop the concept. Customers are asked about their attitudes toward the product idea and if they perceive the idea as different from other products on the market. Product developers want to know, Would you buy this product and how much are you willing to pay? The company needs to know if the product is appealing to the target audience. A second question is also essential in this testing: What would you like to change about the product concept? If customers suggest changes that are not feasible (too costly to implement, not technically possible), it dramatically reduces the viability of the project. Whenever possible, however, customer feedback is incorporated into the product's development. By making adjustments during this phase rather than waiting until after the launch, companies can increase the probability of success. Since the information is so critical, researchers use large samples of target customers to ensure confidence in the findings.

In creating an effective new product marketing strategy, it is important to clearly identify the product benefits to the target audience. Here Mini is identifying a benefit: buy a mini and get better gas mileage as well as have more fun.

Source: MINI USA

Create Marketing Strategy The product development process leads to a distinct set of physical characteristics and a detailed feature mix. As the product becomes better defined, marketing specialists develop a tentative, but detailed, marketing strategy. Even though the product is still under development, there are several reasons for preparing a marketing strategy now. First, defining the target market is helpful to the product developers. In addition to the basic market information (size, geography, and demographics), product developers appreciate knowing how the product will be used (context, environment) and the psychographics of the market (the market's activities, interests, and opinions). Marketers also assess the market share potential at critical points in time (how much market share can the new product get after one year?). At this point, tentative pricing, distribution, and marketing communications strategies are created that will be adapted as the product gets closer to roll-out.[38] Often, as part of the initial marketing communications, appropriate publications will include articles about a new product. Finally, marketing managers begin to develop budgets for the product launch and estimates of the marketing communications budget, manufacturing capacity, and logistical needs.

Conduct Business Case Analysis As the product definition is developed and a tentative marketing strategy created, a critical "go–no go" decision is made before the next product development stage. At this point, the costs have been small relative to the cost of moving to full product development, market testing, and launch. There is a lot of pressure to get the decision right because a mistake is expensive. The **business case analysis** is an overall evaluation of a product and usually assesses the product's probability of success. It is often done when there are changes to an existing marketing plan, such as an increase in the marketing communications budget. The business case would assess the feasibility of increasing the communications budget.[39] In new product development, the business case focuses on two key issues. First, the total demand for the product over a specified period of time, usually five years, is determined. Second, a cash flow statement is developed that specifies cash flow, profitability, and investment requirements.

Total Demand   Sales are defined in two ways: revenue (unit sales × price) and unit sales. Each provides important information. Revenue is the top line number in a profitability analysis and is affected by price variations common to global products with substantial price differences around the world. Because currencies fluctuate, which can lead to wide variations in revenue, and price increases can also dramatically affect total revenue, unit sales is often considered a more realistic picture of product growth and represents the number of units sold, in various product configurations, around the world.

Estimating total demand is a function of three separate purchase situations.

- **New purchases**—first-time sales. With new products, these sales are called trial purchases. This is also calculated as the trial rate (how many individuals in a particular target market have tried the product).

- **Repeat purchases**—the number of products purchased by the same customer. This can be important with frequently purchased products such as convenience goods that rely on frequent repeat purchases for success.

- **Replacement purchases**—the number of products purchased to replace existing products that have become obsolete or have malfunctioned. Estimates are made on the number of product failures in any given year based on the expected product life. As more products are sold into a market through first-time and repeat purchases, the number of replacement sales will increase.

Profitability Analysis   To this point, costs have been primarily in R&D and market research. However, at the next step, the company will incur manufacturing, marketing, accounting, and the logistical costs of bringing the product to market. As a result, a thorough analysis is conducted of the short- and long-term product profitability.

Develop the Product Opportunity

If the result of the previous analysis is a "go" decision, then the number of people and the resources allocated to the product's development increase substantially. For much of the 20th century, companies would move a substantial number of new product concepts through to this stage and use product development and market testing to screen and eliminate ideas. That changed in the 1990s as the cost of taking products to market increased dramatically while failure rates remained high. Companies now screen product ideas much earlier in the development process. As a result, far fewer product ideas make it to this stage, and those products targeted for further development and market testing have a much higher probability of actually being launched in the marketplace.[40] In a classic article in the *Harvard Business Review* on the myths of product development, Thomke and Reinertsen define one main fallacy as the belief that more features create a better product. Increasing the number of features on a product can sometimes simply lead to confusion and frustrate customers. Often, customers desire simplicity and want a product that is easy to use. Amazon's Echo, for example, is a successful high-tech but easy-to-use product. Consumers of all ages can easily use the hands-free Bluetooth speaker and access the Alexa Voice Service by simply speaking.[41]

Develop the Product So far the product exists primarily as a concept, or, at most a working prototype, but if the product idea is to go forward, it must move from viable product concept to a working product that meets customer needs profitably. The challenge for the development team is to design and build a product the customer wants to buy while hitting the company's success metrics—sales price, revenue, profit margins, unit sales, and cost to build.[42]

Previous research during concept testing provides substantial information about what customers are looking for in the product. Coupled with input from engineers, designers, and marketing specialists, the product definition developed earlier is operationalized. This process moves from a strategic understanding of the customer's basic needs to a specific operational definition of the product's characteristics. Following this process, the product's physical characteristics are defined by targeting the essential benefits delivered to the customer.[43]

There are two product development models. The first incorporates more planning and follows a sequential timeline with key process metrics being met at each stage before moving on through the process. In this scenario, product development spends a lot of time creating a product that is considered close to the final product that will be rolled out to customers. Consequently, product testing is used primarily to affirm the extensive development done earlier in the process.

The next approach encourages more prototypes that incrementally move the product through the development process. Here the product does not need to be "perfect" before testing; rather, the idea is to continuously test the product and use the testing process to enhance the product and solicit customer feedback. Through this process, the market becomes aware of the product, and if properly managed, interest in the product is increased during development.

In this second method, the goal is to shorten the time spent in development, moving from development to testing as quickly as possible to minimize cost and get the product in the hands of potential users. The longer a company takes at this stage, the greater the likelihood that competitors learn of the product, customer preferences change, or external environment conditions dictate further product adjustments.

Product Testing Generally a product undergoes two types of testing. As the product's characteristics are being finalized, most of the testing is done internally by engineers, product specialists, and other employees. This type of testing, called alpha testing, helps clarify the basic operationalization of the product such as the physical characteristics and features.

At some point, the company will want potential customers to begin testing the product. Beta testing encourages customers to evaluate and provide feedback on the prototype. The product may be close to the final configuration, but beta tests allow for further product testing and refinement.[44]

Test the Market Once the product has reached the point where the product development team is satisfied with its performance, physical characteristics, and features, it is ready to be tested in the marketplace. To maintain security, minimize product information leaks, and disrupt competitor intelligence, products are often given code names. Once the product moves to the marketplace testing stage, a marketing strategy is created for the test using the product's market name. Some elements of the strategy such as brand name and packaging will have been tested with consumers during product development.[45] For example, engineers work with package design professionals to ensure that, first, the product is protected and, second, the packaging maximizes marketing communications opportunities.

The amount of market testing is a function of several critical factors that are in conflict with one another. First, a company must evaluate the cost of being wrong. While a great deal of money has been spent to this point, the cost of launching a product failure is much higher. The greater the risk of failure, the more market testing a company will want to do before a full product launch.

At the same time, market testing takes time, and competitors can take advantage to enhance their product mix or develop marketing strategies to counter a successful product launch. In addition, depending on the product, the selling season may dictate faster product rollout because waiting too long may cost the company significant sales. Ultimately, management must balance these factors and choose the optimum market testing strategy.[46]

Consumer Product Market Tests   In creating the market test, management must make four key decisions:

- *Where:* The location of the market test is based on how well it reflects the potential target markets. Most market tests involve somewhere between two and five cities to mitigate regional differences in purchase patterns (if there are any).

- *How long:* Most test markets run less than a year. The test should be long enough to include several purchase cycles. With many consumer products, purchase cycles are relatively short (days or weeks) so there is less need for a long market test.

- *Data:* Critical information needed to make necessary decisions must be identified. Management frequently wants to know how long it takes for the product to move through the distribution system, tracking the product from manufacturing plant through to the point of sale (matching inventory as it leaves the plant with store sales). In addition, buyers are interviewed on their product experience.

Trader Joe's conducts a great deal of analysis before it introduces a new product in its stores. The company considers hundreds of new products every year, but only a few make it onto store shelves.

©J. Emilio Flores/The New York Times/Redux

- *Decision criteria:* Metrics for further action must be identified. At this stage it is difficult to pull a product, but if the product fails in the market test, management is faced with a difficult decision—drop the product or send it back for major redesign. If the product is a success, then the product launch decision is much easier. Exhibit 8.10 is a summary of the decision criteria used in market tests.

EXHIBIT 8.10 | Summary of Decision Criteria in Market Tests

Category	Criteria
Financial	Gross margin
	Profit per unit shelf space
	Opportunity cost of capital needed to obtain the new item
Competition	Number of firms in the trading area
	Number of competing brands
Marketing strategy	Product uniqueness
	Vendor effort
	Marketing support
	Terms of trade: slotting allowances, off-invoice allowances, free cases, bill-back provisions
	Price
Other	Category growth
	Synergy with existing items

Source: www.emeraldinsight.com.

Consumer product market testing has two goals. The first is to provide specific numbers to the business case estimates including new (trial purchases), repeat, and, if appropriate, initial replacement purchases. Additionally, information about buyer demographics is evaluated against earlier target market scenarios and is compared against company business case models and historical data. The company takes data from the market test and projects the future.

The second objective of market testing is to get feedback on the tactics that can be used to adjust the marketing plan before product launch. While a company will often hold back implementing the entire marketing plan for security reasons, input from customers, distributors, and retailers is helpful in adjusting the final marketing plan.

Business Product Market Test   Products designed for business markets are tested differently than their consumer product counterparts. Essentially, the tests are smaller in scope and involve fewer individuals and companies; however, they are no less important in the new product development process. Because business markets are smaller, beta testing often includes only a few key customers with a long-standing company relationship. If, on the other hand, the company has independent distributors, it identifies a limited number for the market test and provides additional support to them as the product is being tested.[47]

Often in parallel with beta testing, companies will use trade shows to solicit customer feedback. Trade shows are a cost-effective way to get customer input because they are an efficient and convenient location to introduce new products or test new product ideas.

Product Launch   At this point in the new product process, it is time to implement the marketing plan. By now, considerable time, money, and human capital have been expended in the development of the product. Management has made the decision to launch the product. Now it is time to define the product's objectives (sales, target markets, success metrics), specify the value proposition, plan the marketing tactics, and implement the marketing plan. As we mentioned earlier, all of this will already have been done, but any necessary adjustments are made after the market test.

The product launch is critical to the long-term success of the product. Products that start poorly seldom recover from a poor launch. The pressure to create excitement, particularly for consumer products, leading to consumer trial purchase is a primary reason companies spend millions of dollars on a product launch. Netgear, a leading provider of networking devices, introduced the world's first tri-band mesh network to good reviews and broad customer acceptance. While other companies were earlier to market with mesh network systems, Netgear took a different approach with a unique tri-band system that outperforms the competition.[48]

Many marketing communication dollars are front-loaded at the product launch with the goal of creating sufficient product interest that will turn into repeat and replacement purchases later. If the product is not successful early, management is often unwilling to spend additional dollars as the product becomes widely distributed. The end result can be a downward spiral with low product interest generating fewer sales, which leads to more cutbacks in marketing support.[49]

CONSUMER ADOPTION AND DIFFUSION PROCESS

LO 8-7

Identify how new products become diffused in a market.

A target market consists of many people with different predispositions to purchase a product. Some will want to adopt a product early; others will wait until much later. The rate at which products become accepted is known as the adoption process. Marketers are interested in knowing the rate at which a product will be adopted into a market as well as the timeline (how long it will take for the product to move through the process). Of particular interest in a new product launch are the groups at the beginning of the process, innovators and early adopters.[50]

Consumer Product Adoption Process

As we have discussed, new products come in various forms, from new-to-the-world products to incremental changes to existing products, but the consumer adoption process is less concerned with the product definition and more concerned with the individual consumer's perception of the product. A product can be in the market for a long time and still be considered an innovation to an individual consumer. The **innovation diffusion process** is how long it takes a product to move from first purchase to last purchase (the last set of users to adopt the product). An individual moves through five stages before adopting a product:

1. **Awareness**—know of the product, but insufficient information to move forward through the adoption process.

2. **Interest**—receive additional information (advertising, word of mouth) and motivated to seek out added information for further evaluation.

3. **Evaluation**—combine all information (word of mouth, reviews, advertising) and evaluate the product for trial purchase.

4. **Trial**—purchase the product for the purpose of making a value decision.

5. **Adoption**—purchase the product with the intent of becoming a dependable user.

Marketers, particularly those involved in a new product launch, want to move consumers through the process as quickly as possible. One reason to spend heavily at the product launch phase is to move people through awareness, interest, and evaluation, getting them to try the product quickly. Sales promotion tools (coupons, product sampling), endorsements, third-party reviews, and other marketing communications methods are all part of a strategy to move people toward trial purchase. Trial purchase is the focus of a product launch marketing plan because if you can get consumers to try the product, you can win them over with superior product design, features, and value.[51]

The Diffusion of Innovations

Everyone in a target market falls into one of five groups based on his or her willingness to try the innovation (see Exhibit 8.11). A person can be an innovator or early adopter in one product category and a laggard in another. However, marketers want

EXHIBIT 8.11 | Consumer Product Adoption Chart

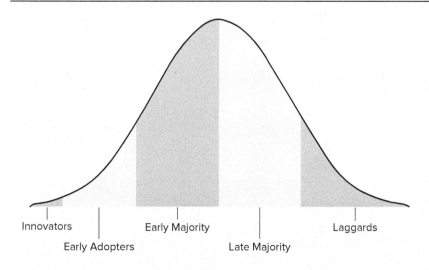

Innovators   Early Adopters   Early Majority   Late Majority   Laggards

Rubicon Consulting, www.rubiconconsulting.com.

to identify where individuals fall on the innovation curve for a particular product or product class. Interestingly, the process by which products become diffused in a market remains remarkably constant. Research into the adoption of the Internet in the United States found it very similar to the adoption of color television in the United States in the 1960s.

The process begins with a very small group who adopt the product, perhaps through targeted marketing (they are given the product to try, for example) or high involvement with the product. From there, larger numbers in the different groups move through the adoption process. Two-thirds of all adopters for a given product fall in the early and late majority. The final group, laggards, may not move into the adoption process until late in the product's life cycle.[52]

- **Innovators** (2.5 percent)—Product enthusiasts enjoy being the first to try and master a new product. Individuals in this group are prime candidates for beta testing and represent a good source of feedback late in the product development process or early in the product launch phase.

- **Early Adopters** (13 percent)—Product opinion leaders seek out new products consistent with their personal self-image. This group is not price-sensitive and is willing to pay the price premium for a product. At the same time, early adopters demand a high level of personalized service and product features.

- **Early Majority** (34.5 percent)—Product watchers want to be convinced of the product's claims and value proposition before making a commitment. This group is considered critical to long-term success as they take the product into the mainstream.

- **Late Majority** (34 percent)—Product followers are price-sensitive and risk-averse. They purchase older-generation or discontinued models with lower prices and fewer product features.

- **Laggards** (16 percent)—Product avoiders want to evade adoption as long as possible. Resistant to change, they will put off the purchase until there is no other option.

SUMMARY

The product experience is the essential element in delivering value to the customer. Organizations understand that, no matter what else happens in the customer experience, the product must deliver on its value proposition to the customer. Products have a detailed set of characteristics that include defined customer benefits as well as core and enhanced product attributes. Companies develop individual product strategies consistent with broader product line and category strategies that, in turn, achieve corporate goals and objectives. Products follow a product life cycle that includes introduction, growth, maturity, and decline. As a product moves through the cycle, marketing strategies change to meet new market conditions.

A key to the long-term success of any company is the development of new products. New product development can take many forms from "new to the world" to variations of existing products. The new product development process has three elements: identify the product opportunity, define the product opportunity, and develop the product opportunity. A new product moves through a diffusion process with a market as different people purchase the product at different times.

KEY TERMS

product   213
stock-keeping unit (SKU)   214
essential benefit   214
core product   214
enhanced product   214
tangibility   215
durability   215
nondurable product   215
durable product   215
convenience goods   216
shopping goods   216
specialty goods   216
unsought goods   216
materials   216

parts   216
MRO supplies (maintenance, repair, operating)   217
capital goods   217
form   217
feature   217
conformance   220
durability   220
reliability   220
repairability   220
style   220
product line   221
product mix   221
product life cycle (PLC)   223

fads   225
market penetration   227
market skimming   227
new-to-the-world product   228
upgrades or modifications to existing products   228
additions to existing product lines   228
reposition existing products   228
cost reduction   228
go-to-market mistake   231
stop-to-market mistake   231
business case analysis   233
innovation diffusion process   237

APPLICATION QUESTIONS

1. You are a marketing manager for Starbucks. Describe the following as it relates to the product experience at Starbucks: essential benefit, core product, and enhanced product. Now imagine you are the marketing manager for Aquafresh Extreme toothpaste. Describe the product experience in terms of essential benefit, core product, and enhanced product.

2. Choose two comparable phones from Samsung and Microsoft/Nokia and examine each product. How does the product form differ between the two products? How are they the same? Now consider the features of the two products. What features are unique to each phone? Which phone, overall, appeals to you most and why?

3. One of the most difficult characteristics of a product to define is style. You are the marketing manager for Cadillac; define the product style for an Escalade. Compare and contrast that with product style for a Chevrolet Tahoe (another large SUV built on the same platform as the Escalade).

connect

More application questions are available online.

4. You are the marketing manager for Coca-Cola products in the United States. Describe the product line for Coke-branded products and briefly describe how each product differs from the other products in the Coke brand product line.

5. Motorola is introducing a new phone that incorporates Internet surfing capability using new LTE technology, a GPS program, and other new features that will greatly expand the features available on a cell phone. Develop a marketing strategy for the launch of the new product.

MANAGEMENT DECISION CASE
Reaching Millennials through New Product Innovation at Campbell's Soup

What is a marketer to do when their whole product category is shrinking? That's the situation Campbell's Soup found itself in as many consumers decided that soup was no longer "*mmm mmm good.*"[53]

Campbell's Soup was a pioneer of mass food manufacturing, making "shelf-stable" (canned) goods a fixture in American pantries. But many of today's consumers prefer a different approach to eating—seasonal, fresh, and organic. This is particularly true for America's 80 million millennials, an important generation that Campbell's and other soup makers were not attracting to their traditional canned soup products. To reconnect with this market segment, new CEO Denise Morrison took the 125-year-old company in some bold new directions, using a combination of internally driven product innovation and acquisitions of food industry trailblazers.[54]

Job one was to understand what millennials want in food. For this research, Morrison sent Campbell's employees to cities known as hipster hubs—Austin, Texas; Portland, Oregon; London; and Paris—to learn about the preferences of these potential customers. This generation, they learned, is culturally diverse and globally connected. While they have college degrees, they also tend to be underemployed. This "dine-out" generation likes cuisines that were once considered exotic: Mexican, Indian, and Asian. Campbell's vice president of consumer insights summed it up: "They go through life hunting out and gathering different experiences. They sample foods in the same way they sample jobs." The Campbell's team didn't just ask customers what they wanted—they used a process of deep immersion, which involved executives eating meals with customers in their homes, looking in their pantries, and tagging along on trips to the supermarket.[55]

Campbell's also wanted to predict where food tastes would be headed in the future. For this task, the company interviewed chefs, nutritionists, and academics, but also experts of a different sort: designers, anthropologists, and futurists. Campbell's learned not only what consumers may soon be eating, but how they want to buy their food. Technologies such as augmented/virtual reality, artificial intelligence, and new kinds of currency will affect how food is purchased—both through mobile devices and brick-and-mortar retail.[56]

Acquisitions were one route Campbell's took to add to its product line. Garden Fresh Gourmet was a health-focused brand with a loyal following for its salsa and hummus. Now a Campbell's brand, it provides customers with gourmet soups in sizes to feed a whole family. Bolthouse Farms, a seller of fresh carrots and refrigerated beverages, brought additional expertise and customers. To reach millennial parents, Plum Organics was added, bringing with it a food line for babies and toddlers.[57]

These acquisitions helped address another finding of the research: the high priority placed on healthy, fresh food. Consumers were concerned about the levels of sodium and high fructose corn syrup in Campbell's traditional soups.[58] The trend toward a preference for organic food also influenced the company's innovation choices. Campbell's launched an internally developed product, Go Soups, a premium-priced line of soups focused on freshness and packaged not in cans, but in plastic pouches designed to convey that freshness.[59] But Campbell's has not kicked the can completely, offering its Well Yes! soups in a can, but without artificial ingredients. And Campbell's Souplicity line uses high-pressure processing, allowing the product to retain its flavor and color without the use of preservatives.[60]

This focus on health extends beyond products to education and a unique service offering. Campbell's now offers a website and app, whatsinmyfood.com, that allows consumers to see details about the ingredients, where the food is sourced, and how it's made.[61] Even more revolutionary is its acquisition of Habit, a start-up providing personalized diet recommendations. Customers send an at-home nutrition test kit to a certified lab and then receive a personalized diet along with coaching from a nutritionist, all based on the consumer's lifestyle, physiology, and health goals.[62]

For a company accustomed to a few innovations each year, the new pace of product development is breathtaking—in one year, they planned to introduce 200 new products.[63] Not all are hits: a kit to make soup in Keurig coffeemakers was abandoned due to disappointing sales.[64] However, to keep pace with the changing priorities of millennials and all its customers, Campbell's will likely have to keep up this aggressive rate of innovation, using additional acquisitions and continuous R&D to roll out more products and services.

Questions for Consideration

1. In what category of the product life cycle are Campbell's soup products? Can a company's products be in one stage of the PLC while the industry category is in another?

2. Beyond product innovation, what other parts of the Campbell's marketing mix could be adjusted to try to get millennials to grab their soup spoons?

3. Campbell's expanded its offerings through both its own R&D and by acquiring other companies and their products. What are the pros and cons of these two options? Which should be Campbell's focus going forward?

4. Since consumer research shows a clear preference among millennials for foods other than soup, should Campbell's slowly abandon soup in favor of other alternatives or continue to try to reinvigorate the soup product line?

MARKETING PLAN EXERCISE

ACTIVITY 8: Define the Product Strategy

In this chapter we looked at the essential element in the marketing mix—the product. Developing an effective marketing plan begins with an understanding of your product, its role in the company's overall business strategy, and, more specifically, where it fits in the company's product mix. Additionally, it is important to establish a new product development process that ensures a new product pipeline of potentially successful new products. Your assignment in this chapter includes the following activities:

1. Define the product to include:
   a. Value proposition.
   b. Characteristics.
   c. Nature of product (consumer versus business product, and what type of product it represents).

2. Identify the product's position in the product line (if offered with other similar products) and, more broadly, the company's overall product mix. Address the following:
   a. How would this product differ from other products in the product line (if appropriate)?
   b. What price point would this product target and is there any conflict with existing products?
   c. How does the marketing message differ for this product from other products in the product line?

ACTIVITY 9: New Product Development

In this chapter we looked at the essential element in the marketing mix—the product. Developing an effective marketing plan begins with an understanding of your product, its role in the company's overall business strategy, and, more specifically, where it fits in the company's product mix. Additionally, it is important to establish a new product development process that ensures a new product pipeline of potentially successful new products. Marketing plan activities in this section include the following:

1. Define a new product development process for next-generation products. While the product may be new, it is important to have a plan in place for next-generation models.

   a. Do you want to expand existing products into new markets?

   b. Define expected features that will likely be added over the next 36 months and a timeline for introduction.

2. Does the company want to be known as innovative with regard to new product development?

3. Chart the diffusion of the company's product into the market. Define each of the groups in the diffusion.

NOTES

1. Kupluthai Pungkanon, "Nothing Like a Nespresso," *Sunday Nation,* April 30, 2017, http://www.nationmultimedia.com /news/life/living_health/30313686.

2. Albert M. Muniz Jr. and Hope Jensen Schau, "Religiosity in the Abandoned Apple Newton Brand Community," *Journal of Consumer Research* 31, no. 4 (2005), pp. 737–48; and Hope Jensen Schau and Albert Muniz, "A Tale of Tales: The Apple Newton Narratives," *Journal of Strategic Marketing* 14, no. 1 (2006), pp. 19–28.

3. Hollister Jeans, www.hollisterco.com, January 2014.

4. Jack Neff, "Tide's Washday Miracle: Not Doing Laundry," *Advertising Age* 78, no. 45 (2007), p. 12.

5. Andreas B. Eisingerich and Tobias Kretschmer, "In E-Commerce, More Is More," *Harvard Business Review* 86, no. 3 (2008), pp. 20–35.

6. Lance A. Bettencourt and Anthony W. Ulwick, "The Customer-Centered Innovation Map," *Harvard Business Review* 86, no. 5 (2008), p. 109.

7. Stephen L. Vargo and Robert F. Lusch, "From Goods Go Service(s): Divergences and Convergences of Logics," *Industrial Marketing Management* 37, no. 3 (2008), pp. 254–68.

8. Preyas S. Desai, Oded Koenigsberg, and Devarat Purohit, "The Role of Production Lead Time and Demand Uncertainty in Marketing Durable Goods," *Management Science* 53, no. 1 (2007), pp. 150–59.

9. Benjamin Zhang, "Check Out Delta's New Canadian Airliner That's Trying to Challenge Boeing and Airbus," *Business Insider,* January 2, 2017, http://www.businessinsider.com /delta-bombardier-series-cs100-2016-12/#bombardier -offers-two-version-of-the-c-series-a-130-seat-cs300-and-a -smaller-108-seat-cs100-1.

10. Marc Abrahams, "A Pointed Lesson about Product Features," *Harvard Business Review* 84, no. 3 (2006), pp. 21–23.

11. Priceline, priceline.com, May 2017.

12. Ben Levisohn, "Keep That Rolex Ticking," *BusinessWeek,* March 24, 2008, no. 4076, p. 21; and Stacy Meichtry, "How Timex Plans to Upgrade Its Image," *Wall Street Journal,* June 21, 2007, p. B6.

13. Djoko Setijono and Jens J. Dahlgaard, "The Value of Quality Improvements," *International Journal of Quality and Reliability Management* 25, no. 3 (2008), pp. 292–306; and Gavriel Melirovich, "Quality of Design and Quality of Conformance: Contingency and Synergistic Approaches," *Total Quality Management and Business Excellence* 17, no. 2 (2008), pp. 205–20.

14. Rajeev K. Goel, "Uncertain Innovation with Uncertain Product Durability," *Applied Economics Letters* 13, no. 13 (2006), pp. 829–42.

15. Kamalini Ramdas and Taylor Randall, "Does Component Sharing Help or Hurt Reliability? An Empirical Study in the Automotive Industry," *Management Science* 54, no. 5 (2008), pp. 922–39; and Niranjan Pati and Dayr Reis, "The Quality Learning Curve: An Approach to Predicting Quality Improvement in Manufacturing and Services," *Journal of Global Business Issues* 1, no. 2 (2007), pp. 129–41.

16. Emily Matchar, "The Fight for the "Right to Repair," *Smithsonian.com,* July 13, 2016, http://www.smithsonianmag .com/innovation/fight-right-repair-180959764/.

17. Christian Wardlaw, "Exclusive Report: GM Slices Free OnStar Trial Period in 2017 Buick, Chevrolet, and GMC Models," *New York Daily News,* February 13, 2017, http:// www.nydailynews.com/autos/news/gm-reduces-free -onstar-trial-period-article-1.2970954.

18. Ravinda Chitturi, Rajagopal Raghunathan, and Vijar Mahajan, "Delight by Design: The Role of Hedonic versus Utilitarian Benefits," *Journal of Marketing* 72, no. 3 (2008), pp. 48–61.

19. Penelope Green, "While You Were Out, the Post-it Went Home," *New York Times,* June 28, 2007, p. F1.

20. Sarah Halzack, "The Soup Business Has Grown Cold. Inside Campbell's Plan to Turn Up the Heat," *Washington Post,* February 3, 2017, https://www.washingtonpost.com/news /business/wp/2017/02/03/the-soup-business-has-grown -cold-inside-campbells-plan-to-turn-up-the-heat/?utm_term =.3a246cbe5abc.

21. Muhammad A. Noor, Rick Rabiser, and Paul Grunbacher, "Agile Product Line Planning: A Collaborative Approach and a Case Study," *Journal of Systems and Software* 81, no. 6 (2008), pp. 868–81.

22. Peter N. Golder and Gerald J. Tellis, "Growing, Growing, Gone: Cascades, Diffusion, and Turning Points in the Product Life Cycle," *Marketing Science* 23, no. 2 (2004), pp. 207–21.

23. Jack Stewart, "With the Model 3 Coming, Tesla Grapples with Quality Control," *Wired,* May 4, 2017, https://www.wired .com/2017/05/tesla-quality/.

24. Kate Niederhoffer, Rob Mooth, David Wiesenfeld, and Jonathon Gordon, "The Origin and Impact of CPG New Product

Buzz: Emerging Trends and Implications," *Journal of Advertising* 47, no. 4 (2007), pp. 420–36.

25. "New-to-the-World-Products." *Google Shopping,* n.d., https://www.google.com/search?q=new-to-the-world+products&rlz=1C1EJFA_enUS726US726&source=univ&tbm=shop&tbo=u&sa=X&ved=0ahUKEwiUlr_OoNrTAhWJeSYKHbXFAKIQsxgIJw; and "Project Jacquard," *Google ATAP,* n.d., https://atap.google.com/jacquard/, May 2017.

26. "New-to-the-World-Products," *Google Shopping,* n.d., https://www.google.com/search?q=new-to-the-world+products&rlz=1C1EJFA_enUS726US726&source=univ&tbm=shop&tbo=u&sa=X&ved=0ahUKEwiUlr_OoNrTAhWJeSYKHbXFAKIQsxgIJw; and "Project Jacquard," *Google ATAP,* n.d., https://atap.google.com/jacquard/, May 2017.

27. Kenneth J. Petersen, Robert B. Handfield, and Gary L. Ragatz, "Supplier Integration into New Product Development: Coordinating Product, Process and Supply Chain Design," *Journal of Operations Management* 23, no. 3/4 (2003), pp. 371–89.

28. Anjali Athavaley and Se Young Lee, "Samsung Launches Galaxy S8 and Dreams of Recovery from Note 7," *Reuters,* March 30, 2017, http://www.reuters.com/article/us-samsung-elec-smartphones-idUSKBN17027R.

29. Cornelia Droge, Roger Calantone, and Nukhet Harmancioglu, "New Product Success: Is It Really Controllable by Managers in Highly Turbulent Environments?" *Journal of Production Innovation Management* 25, no. 3 (2008), pp. 272–90.

30. "Eclipse 500 Wins Export Approvals," *Flight International* 173, no. 5137 (2008), p. 12; and Bruce Nussbuam, "The Best Product Design of 2007," *BusinessWeek,* no. 4044 (2007), p. 52.

31. Rajesh Sethi and Zafar Iqbal, "State Gate Controls, Learning Failure, and Adverse Effect on Novel New Products," *Journal of Marketing* 72, no. 1 (2008), pp. 118–32.

32. "Johns Hopkins, Under Armour Announce Personal Fitness Partnership," *Johns Hopkins University Hub,* January 5, 2017, https://hub.jhu.edu/2017/01/05/hopkins-under-armour-personal-fitness/.

33. John Saunders, Veronica Wong, Chris Stagg, and Mariadel Mar Souza Fontana, "How Screening Criteria Change during Brand Management," *Journal of Product and Brand Management* 14, no. 4/5 (2005), pp. 239–50.

34. "Apple Prototypes: 5 Products We Never Saw," *Applegazette,* June 20, 2008, www.applegazette.com/mac.

35. Raul O. Chao and Stylianon Kavadias, "A Theoretical Framework for Managing the New Product Development Portfolio: When and How to Use Strategic Buckets," *Management Science* 54, no. 5 (2008), pp. 907–22.

36. Dean Richard Prebble, Gerritt Anton De Waal, and Cristiaan de Groot, "Applying Multiple Perspectives to the Design of a Commercialization Process," *R&D Management* 38, no. 3 (2008), pp. 311–27.

37. Karan Girotra, Christian Terwiesch, and Karl T. Ulrich, "Valuing R&D Projects in a Portfolio: Evidence from the Pharmaceutical Industry," *Management Science* 53, no. 9 (2007), pp. 1452–66.

38. Lenny H. Pattikawa, Ernst Verwaal, and Harry R. Commandeur, "Understanding New Product Project Performance," *European Journal of Marketing* 40, no. 11/12 (2006), pp. 1178–93.

39. Nukhel Armancioglu, Regina C. McNally, Roger J. Calantone, and Serdar S. Durmusoglu, "Your New Product Development (NPD) Is Only as Good as Your Process: An Exploratory Analysis of New NPD Process Design and Implementation," *R&D Management* 37, no. 95 (2007), pp. 399–415.

40. Glen L. Urban and John R. Hauser, "Listening In to Find and Explore New Combinations of Customer Needs," *Journal of Marketing* 68, no. 2 (2004), pp. 72–90.

41. Stefan Thomke and Donald Reinertsen, "Six Myths of Product Development," *Harvard Business Review,* May 2012, https://hbr.org/2012/05/six-myths-of-product-development.

42. B. Sorescu and Jelena Spanjol, "Innovation's Effect on Firm Value and Risk: Insights from Consumer Packaged Goods," *Journal of Marketing* 72, no. 2 (2008), pp. 114–31.

43. J. Brock Smith and Mark Colgate, "Customer Value Creation: A Practical Framework," *Journal of Marketing Theory and Practice* 15, no. 1 (2007), pp. 7–24.

44. Sanjiv Erat and Stylianos Kavadias, "Sequential Testing of Product Designs: Implications for Learning," *Management Science* 54, no. 5 (2008), pp. 956–69.

45. Wei-Lun Chang, "A Typology of Co-Branding Strategy: Position and Classification," *Journal of the Academy of Business* 12, no. 92 (2008), pp. 220–27.

46. Sharan Jagpal, Kamel Jedidi, and M. Jamil, "A Multibrand Concept Testing Methodology for New Product Strategy," *Journal of Product Innovation Management* 24, no. 1 (2007), pp. 34–51.

47. Destan Kandemir, Roger Calantone, and Rosanna Garcia, "An Exploration of Organizational Factors in New Product Development Success," *Journal of Business and Industrial Marketing* 21, no. 5 (2006), pp. 300–18.

48. Keith Shaw, "Netgear Doubles Down on Orbi Wireless Gear," *Network World,* March 28, 2017, http://www.networkworld.com/article/3185444/mobile-wireless/netgear-doubles-down-on-orbi-wireless-gear.html.

49. Henrik Sjodin, "Upsetting Brand Extensions: An Enquiry into Current Customer Inclination to Spread Negative Word of Mouth," *Journal of Brand Management* 15, no. 4 (2008), pp. 258–62; and Niederhoffer et al., "The Origin and Impact of CPG New Product Buzz."

50. Christophe Van Den Butte and Yogesh V. Joshi, "New Product Diffusion with Influentials and Imitators," *Marketing Science* 26, no. 3 (2007), pp. 400–24.

51. Kapil Bawa and Robert Shoemaker, "The Effects of Free Sample Promotions on Incremental Brand Sales," *Marketing Science* 23, no. 3 (2004), pp. 345–64.

52. Morris Kalliny and Angela Hausman, "The Impact of Cultural and Religious Values on Consumer's Adoption of Innovation," *Journal of the Academy of Marketing Studies* 11, no. 1 (2007), pp. 125–37; and Stacy L. Wood and C. Page Moreau, "From Fear to Loathing? How Emotion Influences the Evaluation and Early Use of Innovations," *Journal of Marketing* 70, no. 3 (July 2006), pp. 44–60.

53. Sarah Halzack, "The Soup Business Has Grown Cold. Inside Campbell's Plan to Turn Up the Heat," *Washington Post,* February 3, 2017, https://www.washingtonpost.com/news/business/wp/2017/02/03/the-soup-business-has-grown-cold-inside-campbells-plan-to-turn-up-the-heat/?utm_term=.6401befc68d7.

54. Halzack, "The Soup Business Has Grown Cold"; and Avi Dan, "Soup's On at Campbell's as It Reinvents Itself with Innovations and Acquisitions," *Forbes.com,* June 3, 2013, https://www.forbes.com/sites/avidan/2013/06/03/soups-on-at-campbells-as-it-reinvents-itself-with-innovations-and-acquisitions/#7c7db77740bf.

55. J. Goudreau, "Kicking the Can," *Forbes* 190, no. 11 (2012), pp. 46–51, 2012; Dan, "Soup's On at Campbell's."

56. Don Seiffert, "Campbell Soup CEO Makes Three Predictions about the Future of Food," *Boston Business Journal,* April 12, 2017, http://www.bizjournals.com/boston/news/2017/04/12/campbell-soup-ceo-makes-three-predictions-about.html.

57. Halzack, "The Soup Business Has Grown Cold"; and Aaron Hurst, "How Denise Morrison Took Processed Food Icon Campbell's on a Fresh Food Buying Spree," *FastCompany.com,* March 2, 2017, https://www.fastcompany.com/3068634/the-purposeful-ceo/how-denise-morrison-took-processed-food-icon-campbells-on-a-fresh-food-bu.

58. Jennifer Bissell, "Campbell Soup Aims to Recapture Wholesome Image," *Financial Times,* February 22, 2017, https://www.ft.com/content/92a108c2-e95c-11e6-967b-c88452263daf.

59. Goudreau, "Kicking the Can."

60. Halzack, "The Soup Business Has Grown Cold."

61. "How Campbell Soup and Panera See Shifting Consumer Tastes." *Wall Street Journal,* October 16, 2016, https://www.wsj.com/articles/how-campbell-soup-and-panera-see-shifting-consumer-tastes-1476670500.

62. Seiffert, "Campbell Soup CEO Makes Three Predictions"; Bissell, "Campbell Soup Aims to Recapture Wholesome Image."

63. Dan, "Soup's On at Campbell's"; Campbell's Soup Company, "Campbell to Launch More Than 200 New Products in Fiscal 2015 to Meet Evolving Consumer Preferences," *Campbell's Soup Company,* July 21, 2014, https://www.campbellsoupcompany.com/newsroom/press-releases/campbell-to-launch-more-than-200-new-products-in-fiscal-2015-to-meet-evolving-consumer-preferences/.

64. Carolyn Heneghan, "Why Campbell Discontinued Its K-Cup Soups Line," *FoodDive.com,* May 18, 2016, http://www.fooddive.com/news/why-campbell-discontinued-its-k-cup-soups-line/419401/.

CHAPTER 9

Build the Brand

LEARNING OBJECTIVES

LO 9-1 Recognize the essential elements in a brand.

LO 9-2 Learn the importance of brand equity in product strategy.

LO 9-3 Explain the role of packaging and labeling as critical brand elements.

LO 9-4 Define the responsibility of warranties and service agreements in building consumer confidence.

BRAND: THE FUNDAMENTAL CHARACTER OF A PRODUCT

Why does someone purchase an $89 Tommy Hilfiger Polo shirt instead of a $12 Walmart pullover polo shirt? In part, the quality is better, but something else is also driving the purchase—a complex relationship between the individual purchasing the shirt and the brand Tommy Hilfiger. Why do Tommy Hilfiger and other manufacturers such as Lacoste and Under Armour prominently display their logo on merchandise? Because people who buy those products want others to know who manufactured the shirt, jacket, or pants. Equally important, the manufacturers want everyone to see the logo. Both customers and manufacturers realize the importance of the brand.

If asked, you could probably identify the logo for Tommy Hilfiger, but how would you define the brand? Exhibit 9.1 highlights some of the different ways Tommy Hilfiger translates his brand into products and services. A **brand,** as defined by the American Marketing Association, is "a name, term, design, symbol, or any other feature that identifies one seller's goods or services as distinct from those of other sellers." While the Hilfiger flag is a recognizable symbol of Tommy Hilfiger products, customers and noncustomers assign a much deeper meaning to the brand.[1] In this chapter we'll focus on branding and critical elements in the branding process to learn more about this essential product building block. First we will discuss the many roles of a brand, including those assigned by customer, company, and competition as well as potential problems for a brand. Next, we'll examine an important concept—brand equity—which is used to frame the relationship of the brand to the customer. In addition, we examine four branding strategies. Finally, two other key elements of a customer's overall perception of a brand are examined: packaging and labeling as well as warranties and service agreements.

The importance of branding is not limited to consumer products. Business-to-business customers also consider brands when making purchase decisions. As we will see in this chapter, brands are important for customers and companies, which is why marketing managers are vitally interested in learning as much as possible about their customers' brand perceptions when developing effective branding strategies.

Brands Play Many Roles

Brands take on different roles for customers, manufacturers, even competitors. No other single product element conveys more information about the company. **Brand strategy** is an integral part of the product development process because companies know that successful new products result from a well-conceived branding strategy. At the same time, established products are defined, in large measure, by their brand, and companies work very hard to protect this critical asset. Let's examine brand roles.

Customer Brand Roles Whether the customer is a consumer or another business, brands have three primary roles. First, the brand conveys information about the product. Without any additional data, customers construct expectations about quality, service, even features based on the brand. Netflix is a leader in online digital media content, and the brand is recognized around the world for its ease of use and variety of choices. More recently it has become known for its original content with shows like *House of Cards*. Despite being one of the more expensive options, the brand conveys a strong image of quality to many of its customers.

Brands also educate the customer about the product. People assign meaning to their product experiences by brand and, over time, make judgments about which brands are best at meeting their needs and which are not. As a result, product evaluations and purchase decisions become less formidable as the customer relies on the cumulative brand experience to simplify the purchase process.[2] The thought process works something like this: "I have had great product experiences with Brand X in the past. I will purchase Brand X again, making this purchase decision easier and faster." In essence, the customer's "brand education" helps make the purchase decision with less effort. For many, home repair is daunting, so hardware retailers like Lowe's provide as much information as possible to reduce anxiety

EXHIBIT 9.1 | The Tommy Hilfiger Brand

Source: Tommy Hilfiger Licensing, LLC

about the process. Indeed, Lowe's has worked hard to develop a reputation for making the home repair process easy for everyone.

A third brand role is to help reassure the customer in the purchase decision.[3] For many years there was a phrase in IT: "No one ever got fired for buying IBM." IBM's reputation and market dominance in the large computer and network server market meant that even if the product did not meet performance expectations, the customer felt more secure and less anxious about choosing IBM equipment. Older, established brands like Lysol provide a sense of security and reduce concerns about product quality (see Exhibit 9.2).

Company Brand Roles Brands also perform important roles for the brand's sponsor (manufacturer, distributor, or retailer). They offer legal protection for the product through a trademark. By protecting the brand, the company is able to defend essential product elements such as its features, patentable ideas in manufacturing or product design, and packaging.[4] A second critical role is that brands offer an effective and efficient methodology for categorizing products.[5] Samsung has thousands of products across many product categories and branding helps keep track of those products.

Competitor Brand Roles Market-leading brands provide competitors with a benchmark against which to compete. In industries with strong market-leading brands, competitors design and build products targeted specifically at the market leader. In these situations, the competitor leverages its product strength against the market-leading brand's perceived weakness. In the highly competitive smartphone market everyone is familiar with global brands like Samsung and Apple. However, there are a number of competitors working to get noticed in the marketplace. Companies like Huawei and LG compare their phones to the market leaders (like Samsung) to highlight additional features they provide, often at a lower price.

The Boundaries of Branding

While branding can have a strong effect on the product experience, it is not all-powerful. A good branding strategy will not overcome a poorly designed product that fails to deliver on the value proposition.[6] Too frequently companies put a good brand on a bad product, which often leads to erosion of the brand's value. Years before the iPhone there was BlackBerry, the smartphone leader in the early 2000s. Unfortunately, the company was not able to keep up with innovations in the smartphone market such as touch screen technology (BlackBerrys had buttons). While highly regarded in its time, the product, company, and brand were overwhelmed by their competitors and changing customer preferences. A brand must also be protected. Counterfeit products or illegal activities conducted under the name of another company's brand can do significant damage to the brand.[7]

Finally, there must be real, identifiable, and meaningful differences among products. If all products are perceived to be equal, then it is more difficult to create a **brand identity,** which is a summary of unique qualities attributed to the brand.[8] Commodities are difficult to brand because customers often fail to perceive a difference among products. Major oil companies such as ExxonMobil, Shell, and BP want to differentiate their gasoline from competitors' but find it difficult because most people do not perceive a difference. Despite all their efforts, companies still find it difficult to overcome perceptions about a brand.

BRAND EQUITY—OWNING A BRAND

Equity is about ownership and value. For example, people often think of their homes when they consider the term *equity.* Home equity is the difference between the price of the home (asset) and the mortgage (liability). The larger the difference between the value of the property and the mortgage loan value, the more equity is accrued to the homeowner.

In a very real sense the same is true of brand equity. Every brand has positives—for example, Mercedes-Benz has a reputation for high-quality cars—and negatives—Mercedes also has a reputation for being expensive. The greater the perceived difference between the positives and negatives, the more a customer will develop equity in the brand. When customers take "ownership" of a brand, they make an "investment" that often extends beyond a financial obligation and includes emotional and psychological attachment. Then the company can realize a number of benefits, which we discuss in the next section; however, if the company does a poor job of managing the brand, such as lowering the product quality, those same customers may become negative. As a marketing manager, you want to learn about the brand equity of your product to better understand the relationship of your product to target markets and create more effective marketing strategies.[9]

Defining Brand Equity

Brand equity can be defined as "a set of assets (and liabilities) linked to a brand's name and symbol that adds to (or subtracts from) the value provided by a product or service to a firm or that firm's customers." This definition, developed by David Aaker, can be broken into five dimensions:[10]

- **Brand awareness:** The most basic form of brand equity is simply being aware of the brand. Awareness is the foundation of all other brand relationships. It signals a familiarity and *potential* commitment to the brand.
- **Brand loyalty:** This is the strongest form of brand equity and reflects a commitment to repeat purchases. Loyal customers are reassured by the brand and are often

EXHIBIT 9.2 | Consumer Brand Roles

Convey image and information: Netflix

Educate the customer: Lowe's

Help reassure the customer

Sources: (Netflix): ©Grzegorz Knec/Alamy Stock Photo; (Lowe's): ©Jonathan Weiss/Shutterstock; and (Lysol): ©Editorial Image, LLC.

LO 9-2

Learn the importance of brand equity in product strategy.

ambassadors to new customers. Loyal customers enable a company to reduce marketing costs, leverage trade relationships, and speak to competitive threats with greater success.

- **Perceived quality:** Brands convey a perception of quality that is either positive or negative. Companies use a positive perceived quality to differentiate the product and create higher price points. Rolex watches have been able to sustain a price premium long into their life cycle because of the perceived quality in design and performance of the product.

- **Brand association:** Customers develop a number of emotional, psychological, and performance associations with a brand. In many cases, these associations become a primary purchase driver, particularly with brand-loyal users. Dell has a reputation as a mass-market computer company with reasonably good-quality products but poor customer service. As a result, competitors, such as Hewlett-Packard, have been able to create market opportunities by associating their brand with higher levels of product support and customer service.

- **Brand assets:** Brands possess other assets such as trademarks and patents that represent a significant competitive advantage. Google is very protective of its search algorithm intellectual property, which, in the view of the company, gives the company a significant advantage over other search engines.

Let's consider the implications of these dimensions for marketing managers. First, moving customers from brand awareness to loyalty requires a thorough understanding of the target market and a successful marketing strategy. This is accomplished by developing a strong value offering and then communicating that to the target market. This is an essential element of the marketing manager's job.[11] Second, as we discussed in Chapter 6, customers develop perceptions about a product and associate it with attitudes and even emotions that are encompassed in a product's brand equity. By learning how customers view competitors' as well as their own brand, managers seek to affect people's perceptions and attitudes about their product.[12] Finally, managers protect their brands because they represent a vital asset for the company. They are vigilant about how they are portrayed in the marketplace, particularly by competitors.

Both the customers and the company have a stake in the brand's success. People do not want to purchase a brand if there is a question about quality, performance, or some other dimension of the product experience. They seek to maximize the benefits of the purchase and minimize the disadvantages. At the same time, companies understand every brand has liabilities that must be overcome to enhance the customer's perceived equity in the product. As a result, marketing managers constantly battle to increase brand equity or the customer's perception that the product's positive elements are greater than the negative elements. Brands do have real value and represent a significant company asset.[13] Exhibit 9.3 lists the most valuable brands in the world as measured by Brand Z. Note the value of these brands runs into the billions of dollars and changes are based on a number of things including changes in company strategy, brand success or failure, competitive pressures, and consumer acceptance.

Coca-Cola has created one of the most powerful global brands and its logo, displayed on a Coke truck in India, is recognized around the world.

©Erica Simone Leeds

Benefits of Brand Equity

Building brand equity takes time and money. Given the necessary commitment of resources required to build brand equity, it is reasonable to question whether it is worth the investment. High brand equity delivers a number of benefits to the customers and manufacturers, retailers, and distributors or brand sponsors who control the brand. Three benefits are perceived quality, brand connections, and brand loyalty. Let's consider each of these benefits

EXHIBIT 9.3 | The Most Valuable Brands in the World

	Category	Brand	Brand value 2016 $Mil	Brand contribution	Brand value % change 2016 vs. 2015	Rank change
1	Technology	Google	229,198	4	32%	1
2	Technology	(Apple)	228,460	4	–8%	–1
3	Technology	Microsoft	121,824	3	5%	0
4	Telecom Providers	at&t	107,387	3	20%	2
5	Technology	f	102,551	4	44%	7
6	Payments	VISA	100,800	4	10%	–1
7	Retail	amazon	98,988	3	–59%	7
8	Telecom Providers	verizon√	93,220	3	8%	–1
9	Fast Food	(McDonald's)	88,654	4	9%	0
10	Technology	IBM	86,206	4	–8%	–6

Source: Brand Z, *Top 100 Most Valuable Global Brands 2016,* April 29, 2017. Photos: (Google, Microsoft, Facebook, VISA, Amazon, Verizon, and IBM): ©rvlsoft/Shutterstock; (Apple): ©tanuha2001/Shutterstock; (AT&T): ©Peter Probst/Alamy Stock Photo; and (McDonald's): ©Rose Carson/Shutterstock.

from two perspectives, the customer and the company managing the brand or the brand sponsor. Many of these benefits are difficult to quantify but dramatically affect the success or failure of the brand.

Perceived Quality

Customers   All things being equal (value proposition, product features), the *branded product gives customers a reason to buy.* This is a big advantage over unbranded products because customers will infer a level of quality from the branded product that facilitates their purchase decision.[14]

Brand Sponsor The perceived quality of a brand provides three distinct benefits to the company. First, the perception of a brand's quality enables companies to extend the product range. Ford Motor continues to maintain a strong brand, which has been an important factor in building consumer interest and confidence in the Fusion Hybrid, Ford's answer to the challenge of Prius's domination of the hybrid market. Second, the perception of quality can lead to a price premium opportunity.[15] P&G and other consumer products companies, for instance, enjoy consistently higher prices (and margins) than generic and other locally branded products in the same category. Finally, the perception of quality is an excellent differentiator in the market. For example, Ray-Ban was among the first to successfully brand sunglasses. Its branding strategy positions the sunglasses in the high-quality, premium-priced segment of the market and has been successful for more than 65 years.

Linking Benefit to Strategy Successful marketing strategy builds quality into the entire customer experience—product, service, and any interaction with the company. As companies extend their product lines, they must ensure the customer's brand experience remains positive; put simply, get it right before you introduce new products and services.[16] Quality can create a price premium, but managers understand that to validate that price premium they must constantly validate the value proposition for the customer and answer the customer question, "what makes this product different?"[17]

Brand Connections

Customers Two primary customer advantages result from brand associations. First, customers process, store, and retrieve product information by brand, which is a big advantage for strong brands. People are more likely to connect information with a brand they know rather than sort through information on unfamiliar brands. For example, consumers generally don't consider checking accounts from all banks; rather, they consider the branded product such as Bank of America's checking or another brand they know. A second benefit is that strong brands generate a more positive attitude toward the product.[18] Customers generally have more upbeat thoughts about a powerful brand than a weak brand or generic product. Cisco network servers are an industry leader with an excellent reputation supported by IT professionals, who use a wide range of other manufacturers.

Brand Sponsor When customers identify with a brand and then transfer that loyalty to the product, it creates an additional barrier to entry for new brands,[19] particularly for smaller firms that lack brand recognition. The default choice for network servers is Cisco in many corporate IT departments because executives have heard of Cisco even if they are not familiar with the product itself, thus making it harder for other servers to enter the market.

Linking Benefit to Strategy Because of customer brand connections, marketing managers generally want to extend the brand to new products. However, extending a brand needs to fit the target market's perception of the brand. When Toyota, Honda, and Nissan created luxury cars, they realized the need to create a new brand because the target markets would be less willing to accept their current brands in a luxury automobile. It is also important for strong brands to reinforce their market presence because it helps maintain a barrier to entry.

Brand Loyalty

Customers Brand-loyal customers do not spend as much time searching for new information and, as a result, generally spend less time in the purchase decision process.[20] Motorcycles have experienced a high degree of brand loyalty among the major competitors such as BMW, Honda, and Harley-Davidson. It is not unusual to find owners across all three brands who are driving their third or fourth motorcycle.

Brand Sponsor Loyalty to the brand offers four distinct benefits that represent real market advantages to the brand sponsor. A well-executed branding strategy helps reduce long-term marketing costs, giving the brand sponsor more flexibility in the marketing budgets. While Starbucks spends several hundred million dollars on advertising around the world every year, its advertising budget is much smaller than its competitors'. The Starbucks brand is so well known that the company doesn't need to spend much money raising brand awareness. Branded products give sponsors additional channel leverage.[21] Walmart's ability to extract lower prices from suppliers is legendary, but companies understand the importance of having their products in the world's largest retailer. Brand-loyal customers are vocal and tell others about their experiences, which attracts new customers. Disney has a loyal base of guests who visit the parks every year and become excellent ambassadors for the company. The company offers loyal users specific benefits to cultivate continued loyalty and encourage them to bring new guests. Finally, brand-loyal customers are forgiving, which enables companies to respond to a negative experience. Frequent guests to the Disney parks are not shy about voicing their opinions about everything from rides to the cleanliness of the parks. This creates a sense of ownership (equity) and loyalty.

Linking Benefit to Strategy Because of customer loyalty, marketing managers with a strong brand have greater flexibility in their marketing budgets. For example, Rolls Royce spends very little on paid advertising because customers already have brand equity. At the same time, Intel, which makes a product most people never see, spends a great deal of money building its brand, and now people ask for "Intel Inside." Marketing managers know that loyal customers are great advocates for a brand. As a result, blogs and other online communities have become excellent tools for marketers to reinforce the brand's message.[22]

BRANDING DECISIONS

Branding is a complex concept that brings together all the elements of a product into a single, focused customer idea. As a result, the branding decision is among the most important in marketing. Four basic strategic decisions in defining a brand are (1) stand-alone or family branding, (2) national or store branding, (3) licensing, and (4) co-branding.

Stand-Alone or Family Branding

Does the brand stand alone or exist as part of a brand family? Each choice has advantages and disadvantages. **Stand-alone brands** separate the company from the brand, which insulates the company if there is a problem with the brand. But stand-alone brands are expensive to create and maintain as there is little or no synergy between company brands. **Family branding** advantages and disadvantages are just the opposite. There is synergy among members of a brand family, but a negative event with one product often leads to negative publicity for the entire brand family.[23]

Unilever, a worldwide leader in consumer products, follows a stand-alone brand strategy in its personal care division with brands that operate independently of each other (AXE, Dove, Lifebuoy, Lux, Ponds, Rexona, Sunsilk, Signal, and Vaseline) (see Exhibit 9.4). Kraft Heinz, on the other hand, uses a family branding strategy with all products introduced under the Heinz brand (ketchup and other condiments).

Companies also use branding to extend a line. For example, Microsoft extends its Windows OS platform to a broad range of machines including mobile devices, laptops, and desktops. Each new extension of the Windows OS connects the customer back to the brand and provides a seamless experience across devices.[24] Also, a company can use its brand to expand into new product categories, known as a **category extension**.[25] Patagonia uses its strong brand to expand into new product categories such as food and liquor. Exhibit 9.5 illustrates product extensions through brand, line, and category.

Yet another option is combining family brands with a more distinct individual product brand. Many companies follow a variation of this strategy. American Express introduced the One card that incorporates the American Express brand as well as its own stand-alone brand One.

National or Store Branding

Another decision is whether the product should adopt a national or store brand strategy. Large consumer products companies such as Procter & Gamble create **national brands**

EXHIBIT 9.4 | Sample of Branding Decisions

Unilever

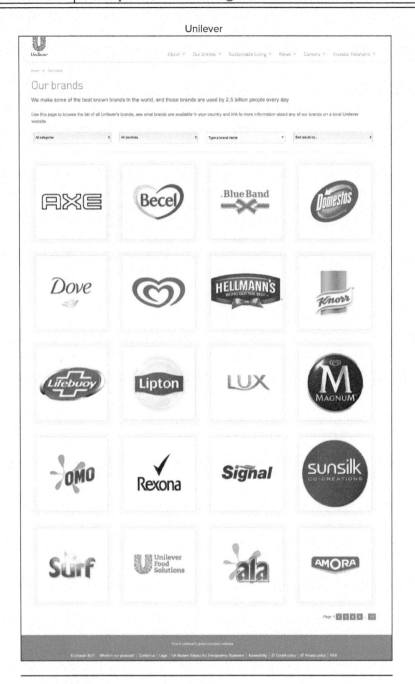

Kraft Heinz

Sources: Unilever; and The Kraft Heinz Company.

EXHIBIT 9.5 | Brand, Line, and Category Extensions

Brand Extension: Dove Men+Care adding bar soaps and deodorant

Line Extension: Windows OS to multiple devices

Category Extension: Patagonia

Sources: (Dove Men+ Care and Patagonia): Editorial Image, LLC; and (Windows OS): Microsoft.

that are sold around the country under the same brand. Gillette Fusion, Crest toothpaste, and many others are national brands that can be found anywhere. National brands enable manufacturers to leverage marketing resources by creating efficiencies in marketing communications and distribution.[26] In addition, national brands generally have a higher perceived quality and, as a result, enjoy a price premium. However, developing a national brand is costly and lower-priced store brands are strong competitors in many product categories.[27]

An alternative to creating a national brand is a **store brand.** Many large retailers create a store brand to market their own products. For example, Target has a number of store brands including "Up & Up," which includes a broad range of household commodities (including everything from contact solution to laundry detergent to paper plates). Often contracting with the large manufacturers such as Procter & Gamble, retailers are able to compete directly with national brands by offering lower prices.

Licensing

Companies can also choose to extend their brand by **licensing**—offering other manufacturers the right to use the brand in exchange for a set fee or percentage of sales. There is very little risk to the brand sponsor, and licensing can generate incremental revenue. In addition, it can extend the brand and build more brand associations among new users, creating additional benefits.[28] The brand sponsor does need to monitor the licensees to ensure product quality and proper use of the brand. Finally, license partners should fit the company's overall marketing strategy for the brand.[29] Among the best followers of the license strategy are movies, which license their brand (the movie) to a wide range of companies (restaurants, toy manufacturers, and others). *Rogue One: A Star Wars Story,* while not part of the main Star Wars story line, still did well at the box office, with over $1 billion in global box office revenue, but license agreements still keep making money for the franchise. Not only did Disney sell merchandise, it had licensing agreements with Nissan, General Mills, Gillette, Duracell, and Verizon, which continue to generate revenue long after the movie's release.

Co-Branding

Frequently a company discovers advantages to linking its products with other products inside the company or externally with products from other companies, called **co-branding.** Co-branding joins two or more well-known brands in a common product or takes two brands and markets them in partnership. One advantage of co-branding is the opportunity to leverage the strengths of each brand to increase sales beyond what they could do independently. In addition, it may open each product up to new markets as well as lower costs by sharing marketing communications expenses.[30]

There are also several potential disadvantages. First, companies that co-brand externally give up some measure of control over their brand; by joining brands, each company sacrifices some control to market the co-branded product. If one of the brands encounters a problem, for example, a quality issue, it can have a negative effect on the co-branded product. Another potential disadvantage is overexposure; a successful product does not want too many co-branded relationships because it can dilute the brand's image.[31]

Successful co-branding relationships work best when both brands come together as equals that make sense in the marketplace. Costco and Visa joined together to offer a Costco Visa card that allows users to earn rebates on their purchases at Costco while expanding the reach of Visa to Costco members. Critical decisions in the process revolve around resource commitments, which company is spending what, and what other resources are asked of each company. In addition, it is important for each company in the relationship to understand the performance objectives and expected benefits of each partner.

Generally, co-branding involves one of four relationships. The first is a joint venture between two companies; for example, American Express uses this model frequently, partnering with a variety of third-party financial institutions that issue the Amex-branded cards and are responsible for customer service and billing, but the credit card company supplies the transaction processing and merchant network. A second type of co-branding affiliation happens when a company combines two of its own products. Procter & Gamble combined its Crest toothpaste and Scope mouthwash to create Crest + Scope Outlast—a toothpaste that combines teeth cleaning properties with a "fresh breath feeling." A third type of co-branding relationship involves bringing multiple companies together to form a new branded product. For instance, Moxy Hotels is a joint venture effort from Marriott Hotels and Inter IKEA, the parent company of Swedish furniture company IKEA. The JV will be Marriot's first line of budget hotels in Europe, and is designed specifically to appeal to millennials.

PACKAGING AND LABELING: ESSENTIAL BRAND ELEMENTS

The product package and label must perform several critical roles in support of the brand. As a result, marketers, product developers, and package design specialists are involved in package design early in product development. Then, as product updates occur, the package is reconfigured to accommodate product modifications.

LO 9-3

Explain the role of packaging and labeling as critical brand elements.

Package Objectives

Protect Above all, the package must protect the product. The challenge is defining how much protection is necessary and cost-effective. In some cases, as in a can of Coke, the package is a significant component of the product's overall cost so there is concern about any increases in package cost. However, the can of Coke must be strong enough to hold the carbonated beverage under variations in temperature and other use conditions. Additionally, Coca-Cola must consider a variety of package materials (plastic, metal), sizes, and shapes (regular can, Coke's classic "contour" design), and it must design each to operate more or less the same under a variety of situations (see Exhibit 9.6).

Protecting customers from unauthorized access to the product is also part of package design. Prescription bottles and most over-the-counter medicines are required to be tamper-proof and child-proof to protect customers. Package safety seals provide a layer of security and verification to the customer that the product has not been altered before purchase. Finally, a growing concern is product theft, particularly in the retail store.[32] As a result, the package design should include anti-theft methodology, such as bar coding or magnetic stripes, that discourages shoplifting.

Communicate Packages communicate a great deal of information about the product. Some of that information is designed as marketing communications. At the point of sale, the package is the last marketing communication the customer will see before the purchase. Consequently, packaging plays a critical role in the company's overall marketing communications strategy, particularly for consumer products. Coke's distinctive contour bottle design (pictured in Exhibit 9.6) is so unique the package can be identified in the dark. Additionally, packaging offers the brand sponsor the opportunity to present the trademark, logo, and other relevant information in an appealing and persuasive manner. As the customer stands in front of a shelf full of products in a store, the marketer wants the brand to be clearly visible to the buyer. This means packaging must be designed to easily communicate critical brand messages quickly through color or design cues.[33] The familiar Coke swirl logo is among the most recognized brand symbols in the world and is easily identified on a store shelf or in a vending machine.

Unique package design can create a distinctive competitive advantage. Coke's contour bottle is an important component of Coke's overall brand image. Its distinctive package

---

EXHIBIT 9.6 | Coke Bottle Designs Over the Years

Source: The Coca-Cola Company

EXHIBIT 9.7 | Innovative Package Designs

Source: Water in a Box

Water in a Box is a water product that seeks to use packaging that's better for the environment. The paperboard packaging attempts to emphasize the purity of the product. It is made of 100 percent renewable and sustainable material.

Source: Festina

Festina Watches are expensive watches. To demonstrate that the watches hold up to their waterproof promise, they are packaged in bags with distilled water at their point of sale.

Source: Nike, Inc.

The Nike Air packaging was a shift from the traditional cardboard box typically used for shoes. It helped to demonstrate the cushioning of the brand, and it conveyed the illusion of floating.

EXHIBIT 9.8 | Nerf Puts Smiling Kids on Their Packaging

©Editorial Image, LLC

design increases brand awareness at the point of sale where the customer makes the final purchase decision (see Exhibit 9.7).

Promote Usage Package design also encourages product use. It does this in several ways. First, packages frequently show the product being used by a happy customer (Nerf shows kids using and enjoying its products on many of its boxes), which supports the overall marketing message (see Exhibit 9.8). This connects the product to the target customer. Second, in many cases, packages visually demonstrate a product. In Exhibit 9.8, the boy is shown using the Nerf Alpha Hawk, and the product itself is clearly visible in the package. Third, marketers and package designers make extensive use of blister packs (products encased in clear plastic) and other package designs to visibly present and protect the product. When buying a SanDisk Cruzer flash drive, it is much easier to visualize using it when you can see the product and have key features highlighted on the package.

Effective Packaging

Effective packaging accomplishes the objectives noted above in a persuasive, interesting, and visually appealing manner consistent with the target market's expectations. Materials, shape, colors, graphics, indeed all the design elements are used to create an aesthetically appealing package for the customer.

Aesthetics Color plays a significant role in package design, indeed, in the entire branding strategy.[34] It is no accident that Coke's packaging has red as the dominant color (red connotes active and energetic) while Pepsi uses blue (fresh and relaxed). The colors reflect the brand and are carried through in the package design. Exhibit 9.9 relates the aesthetics of color to package design.

A visually appealing package, however, is not enough. It must be directed at the target audience to be successful. In most retail environments, a package has very little time to connect with the customer at the point of purchase. As a result, designs that are appropriate, interesting, and persuasive to the target market are critical.

Harmonizes with All Marketing Mix Elements A successful product package coordinates with all other marketing mix elements and is an extension of the product's

---

EXHIBIT 9.9 | The Meaning of Color in Package Design

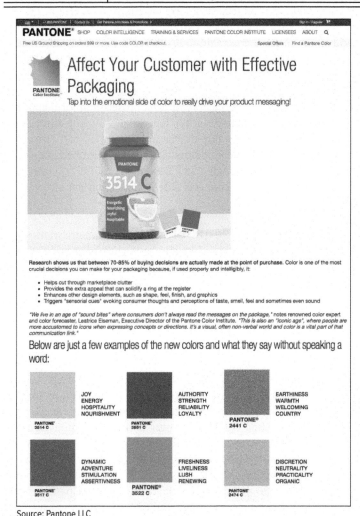

Source: Pantone LLC

Color plays an important role in package design. Each color conveys a different mood.

marketing strategy. At the point of purchase, the package reinforces marketing communications by connecting advertising images (logo, pictures on the package) to the customer. As a result, package designers frequently work closely with advertising and other marketing communications specialists to orchestrate an integrated message and look throughout the marketing communications process. Canon professional digital cameras are packaged in a box dominated by a picture of the camera. The boxes stand alone as a promotional tool that includes the logo, camera model number, and picture. In addition, the package design and logo are coordinated with other collateral marketing literature as well as the website.

Labeling

The package label is an important and valuable location. Often there is not enough space to accommodate all the information relevant parties would like to include on the label. Consider, for example, that government agencies require certain information on almost every label while company attorneys want disclaimers to limit product liability. Also, marketing managers want promotional messages and brand information, while product managers would like product use instructions.

Legal Requirements Labels must meet federal, state, even local rules and regulations. The Food and Drug Administration (FDA) requires all processed-food companies to provide detailed nutritional information clearly identifying calories, fats, carbohydrates, and other information. Other products must have warnings of a certain size that are easily read and understood by the customer.[35] Hazardous materials such as cleaning products, pesticides, and many other items require 14 different pieces of information be included on the label. It is easy to understand why space on the label is at such a premium.

Consumer advocacy groups and government agencies evaluate labels to identify misleading or mislabeled products, and there is a long history of legal prosecution for inappropriate, unethical, even illegal product labeling. In 1914, the federal government, through the Federal Trade Commission, first ruled misleading or blatantly phony labels were illegal and represented unfair competition. Since then, additional legislation has been passed by the federal government such as the Fair Packaging and Labeling Act (1967). States have also passed legislation, which, in most cases, supports federal legislation but also extends specific rules and policies.

Consumer Requirements Consumers want to use products out of the box and package labeling is the most convenient place for initial use instructions. Additionally, product precautions, simple assembly information, and appropriate age for product use may also be included on the package. Essentially, any information the consumer needs to make a product choice, particularly at the point of purchase, needs to be on the package.

Marketing Requirements Since package labeling represents the last marketing opportunity before the purchase decision, as much label space as possible is allocated to marketing communications. Brand, logo, product image, and other relevant marketing messages take up the dominant space on the label. On a box of Procter & Gamble's Bounce fabric softener sheets, the brand name "Bounce" is approximately 50 percent of the space on the front panel and the rest of the space is a bright color (orange) with clean, fresh clothes hanging on the line and a green field. P&G uses the entire front panel of the box to support the marketing efforts of the brand (see Exhibit 9.10).

EXHIBIT 9.10 | **Bounce Fabric Softener Packaging**

©Editorial Image, LLC

WARRANTIES AND SERVICE AGREEMENTS: BUILDING CUSTOMER CONFIDENCE

Part of the customer's overall perception of a brand is the seller's commitment to the product. This commitment is most clearly articulated in the product's warranties and service agreements.[36] As part of the purchase contract with the customer, manufacturers are required by law to state the reasonable expectations for product performance. If the product does not meet those reasonable performance expectations, the customer has the legal right to return the product to the appropriate location for repair, replacement, or refund.

LO 9-4

Define the responsibility of warranties and service agreements in building consumer confidence.

The two kinds of warranties are general and specific. **General warranties** make broad promises about product performance and customer satisfaction. These warranties are generally open to customers returning the product for a broad range of reasons beyond specific product performance problems. Many companies have adopted lenient policies that allow a product return without even asking the customer for a reason. Others require a reason, although there is often a great deal of latitude in what is an acceptable justification. **Specific warranties,** on the other hand, offer explicit product performance promises related to components of the product. Automobile warranties are specific warranties covering various components of the product with different warranties. The warranty for tires is by the tire manufacturer while warranties for the power train (engine, drive system) are generally different from those for the rest of the automobile.

Warranties Help Define the Brand

The manufacturer's promise of performance helps define the brand for the customer. Victorinox, maker of the famous Swiss Army knife, states its warranty as follows: "Swiss Army Brands, Inc., warrants its Victorinox Original Swiss Army Knives to be free from defects in material and workmanship for the entire life of the knife." Swiss Army knives have the reputation of being among the best knives in the world, and the company's warranty supports that perception. A company willing to stand behind its product for life provides a lot of reassurance to the customer. In addition, there is an implied quality perception about a product warranted for life.

Cost versus Benefit Honoring a warranty incurs costs. At one level, the company must be competitive and offer warranties consistent with the industry. However, companies constantly evaluate their warranties (length of time, return/replacement/refund policies, nature of product performance) to consider whether the benefits of the warranty exceed the costs.[37] This is particularly true when companies offer warranties above the industry average. For years, luxury carmakers such as Lexus, Mercedes-Benz, BMW, Audi, and others offered warranties (four years or 50,000 miles bumper to bumper) beyond those provided by other manufacturers (GM, Ford, and Chrysler, which offered three years or 36,000 miles). Offering longer warranties helped validate the perception of a luxury, quality automobile manufacturer. Recently, however, BMW has quietly reduced its warranty coverage by eliminating some free scheduled maintenance because the costs were too high. At the same time, Hyundai and others have expanded their warranties to build consumer confidence in their cars. They realize that extending the period of warranty coverage demonstrates they are making better cars in a very tangible way.

Convey a Message to the Customer Warranties convey a powerful message to the customer about perceived product quality and manufacturer commitment to customer satisfaction. Particularly with expensive products or purchase decisions in which the customer has anxiety, the warranty can play a significant role in the final product choice. As a result, companies focus a lot of time not only creating the warranty but also considering how best to communicate it to the customer. John Deere, one of the world's leading agricultural manufacturers, continues to use a tag line even after many years, because it says a great deal about the product and the company. The promise of John Deere products is understood in the simple phrase "Nothing Runs Like a Deere." With most products, however, companies take a lower profile and build warranty statements into the overall marketing communications strategy and product information.[38]

SUMMARY

An essential element in any product is its brand. The brand conveys a great deal of information about the product and the customer experience. Powerful brands enjoy benefits in the market that other products do not. As a result, companies carefully consider a product's branding strategy in creating an overall marketing plan. Packaging and labeling are also critical brand elements that convey a lot about the product to the customer. Finally, customers attach great importance to the sellers' commitment to the products as conveyed in the product's warranties and service agreements.

KEY TERMS

brand   247
brand strategy   247
brand identity   249
brand equity   249
brand awareness   249
brand loyalty   249

perceived quality   250
brand association   250
brand assets   250
stand-alone brands   253
family branding   253
category extension   253

national brands   253
store brand   256
licensing   256
co-branding   256
general warranties   261
specific warranties   261

APPLICATION QUESTIONS

connect

More application questions are available online.

1. You are the product manager for Ralph Lauren's Polo shirts. What specific information are you trying to convey in the brand's iconic polo pony logo? For example, what does the Polo brand say about quality, features, and style relative to the Tommy Hilfiger and Lacoste brands?

2. Johnson & Johnson has been able to establish strong brand equity for its line of baby products. What benefits does J&J have because of its brand equity for these products?

3. You have been asked by Coca-Cola's product manager to present the arguments for and against extending the Coke brand to a new cola drink. What would be the arguments for and against extending the Coke brand to a new cola drink?

4. SanDisk is introducing a new line of flash drives to complement its existing products, and you are responsible for creating the package design. What key information and other creative elements would you include on the package?

MANAGEMENT DECISION CASE
Virgin Group Brand Extensions: Lots of Hits and a Few Misses

One of the most valuable aspects of a strong brand is its ability to be extended to new products in the category and even into completely new categories. This capability allows companies to take advantage of the strong brand equity that has been built through good customer experiences with the brand's products and the many marketing activities that have helped build the brand's image. Most companies tread carefully into new product or category territory, but the Virgin Group is a corporation known for its bold moves in extending its brand with new companies and products marketed around the world. Its successes and failures provide insights for marketers using a brand extension strategy to increase brand equity and company revenues.

Virgin's flamboyant founder, Sir Richard Branson, has become well known as an adventurer, playboy, and the brand's chief cheerleader. He named his new enterprise "Virgin" to represent his lack of business experience in his early days.[39] His first major venture was his independent record label, Virgin Records, in 1972. Signing music superstars Phil Collins, Janet Jackson, and the Rolling Stones propelled the company's growth and eventually led to the opening of the Virgin Records Megastore in London in 1976, and later in major cities around the world.[40]

During the high-flying years of the record business, Virgin decided to fly high in a more literal way. Virgin Atlantic focused on more comfortable air travel for transatlantic passengers; it was the first airline to offer individual TV screens with a choice of channels—even in economy class. This superior service caught the attention of customers, but also of its major competitor, British Airways, whose employees used underhanded techniques to poach Virgin Atlantic customers.[41] The Virgin airline business soon expanded to other parts of the world with Virgin Australia and Virgin America.[42]

Branson next observed that many young people found expensive monthly cell phone charges too high for their budgets. Virgin Mobile was born, offering a pay-as-you-go approach so teenagers wouldn't have to be locked into yearlong contracts. The youth-oriented marketing offered features designed to make cell phones more playful and fun, such as Rescue Rings (a feature allowing you to save yourself from a bad blind date), wake-up calls, and ringtones using the latest hit songs.[43]

There have been a few other businesses, too: Virgin Media, Virgin Active (health clubs), Virgin Books, Virgin Cosmetics, Virgin Games, Virgin Radio, Virgin Wines, Virgin Vodka, Virgin Hotels, Virgin Vacation, Virgin Trains—these plus more, for a total of about 400 companies in all.[44] If it seems that the sky is the limit for Virgin's ambitions, think again. Virgin Galactic is currently testing spacecraft that will take passengers on a joyride into space. So far, 700 people have either paid their full fare of $250,000 or a deposit of $20,000 to hold their spot, including renowned physicist Stephen Hawking.[45]

But with such a large number of brand extensions, not all could be hits. Virgin Cola fizzled because it was not different enough from Coca-Cola. The company's website for buying and selling cars (Virgin Cars, of course) failed, Branson said, due to a "wrong angle" and because the business was not focused on sustainability. VirginStudent .com tried to beat MySpace and Facebook to the social media game, but didn't gain traction. Virgin Pulse followed the Apple iPod's lead, but did it with a much larger portable music player that never took off. Despite (or perhaps because of) a launch that included founder Branson dressed in a wedding gown, Virgin Bride was also a bust.[46] However, even these failures served to build the Virgin brand.

Each time Virgin took on a major brand (like Coca-Cola) a tremendous amount of media coverage was generated and Branson's image as a risk-taker was reinforced.[47]

Although the list of Virgin businesses represents a diverse group of industries, they share two common attributes: an unconventional approach to marketing and flying in the face of ordinary customer service.[48] Perhaps the most important common denominator is Sir Richard Branson himself. Although many modern executives have been visible parts of their company's marketing messaging, few can match the promotional energy of Branson. In addition to a Virgin bride, he also dressed as a female flight attendant and a Zulu warrior (to promote a new South African flight route). To take a shot at Coca-Cola, he drove a tank down New York City's Fifth Avenue and "fired a missile" at the famous Coca-Cola sign on Times Square. Bolstering his image as an adventurous risk-taker, he attempted to circumnavigate the globe in a hot air balloon.[49] Having a mere mortal personifying the brand comes with risks. "Every day that Richard gets older the issue of the Virgin brand becomes a bigger one because so much of it is tied to him," according to an executive at brand consultancy Interbrand.[50]

For now, the Virgin Group brand is strong, with brand recognition of 99 percent in the UK, 96 percent in the United States, and 97 percent in Australia and South Africa, and with annual sales of $24 billion.[51] After 50 years and 400 businesses opened (and many closed), the "virgin" name may no longer fit its founder. Whether this breathtaking pace of brand extension can continue will be closely watched by brand strategists and by fans of the Virgin Group and its flashy founder.

Questions for Consideration

1. When founder Richard Branson is no longer at the helm (and in the news), do you believe Virgin will be able to continue its forays into radically different brand extensions? What strategies can the Virgin Group employ to ensure continued brand success after Branson is out of the picture? Should those strategies be implemented now or after the founder's departure?

2. In this chapter, you learned about Aaker's five dimensions of brand equity. Assess the Virgin brand on the basis of these dimensions. With these dimensions in mind, what steps could the Virgin Group take to increase brand equity even further?

3. Is the Virgin experience with brand extensions an anomaly, or are there lessons that could be applied to any brand wanting to expand this way?

MARKETING PLAN EXERCISE

ACTIVITY 10: Define the Branding Strategy

As we have learned in this chapter, building a strong brand is critical to a product's long-term success. At the same time, it is important to understand how a product's position in its life cycle influences marketing mix decisions. Specific activities include:

1. Create a package design for the product. Specifically, the design should include necessary legal statements, marketing communications, and other information considered important for the package.

2. Develop a warranty for the product. What elements are specifically covered in the warranty? Does the warranty meet, equal, or fail to meet market expectations and competitor warranties?

3. Create a branding strategy to include
   a. National/store branding.
   b. Stand-alone/family branding.
   c. Possible licensing considerations.
   d. Co-branding opportunities.

NOTES

1. "Tommy Hilfiger: A Culture of Innovation," *Business of Fashion*, April 25, 2017, https://www.businessoffashion.com/articles/news-analysis/tommy-hilfiger-a-culture-of-innovation.

2. Arch G. Woodside, Suresh Sood, and Kenneth E. Miller, "When Consumers and Brands Talk: Storytelling Theory and Research in Psychology and Marketing," *Psychology & Marketing* 25, no. 2 (2008), pp. 97–111.

3. Sebastian Molinillo, Arnold Japutra, Bang Nguyen, and Cheng-Hao Steve Chen, "Responsible Brands vs. Active Brands? An Examination of Brand Personality on Brand Awareness, Brand Trust, and Brand Loyalty," *Marketing Intelligence & Planning,* 35, no. 2 (2017), pp. 166–79, doi: 10.1108/MIP-04-2016-0064.

4. William Kingston, "Trademark Registration Is Not a Right," *Journal of Macromarketing* 26, no. 1 (2006), pp. 17–26.

5. Vasileios Davvetas and Adamantios Diamantopoulos, "How Product Category Shapes Preferences Toward Global and Local Brands: A Schema Theory Perspective." *Journal of International Marketing* 24, no. 4 (2016), pp. 61–81.

6. Pamela Miles Homer, "Perceived Quality and Image: When All Is Not 'Rosy,' " *Journal of Business Research* 61, no. 6 (2008), pp. 715–30.

7. Davidson Heath and Chris Mace, "What's a Brand Worth? Trademark Protection, Profits and Product Quality," *SSRN,* March 17, 2017, https://ssrn.com/abstract=2798473.

8. Bing Jing, "Product Differentiation Under Imperfect Information: When Does Offering a Lower Quality Pay?" *Quantitative Marketing and Economics* 5, no. 1 (2007), pp. 35–62.

9. Zeynep Gürhan-Canli, Ceren Hayran, and Gulen Sarial-Abi, "Customer-Based Brand Equity in a Technologically Fast-Paced, Connected and Constrained Environment," *AMS Review* 6, no. 1 (2016), pp. 23–32. doi: 10.1007/s13162-016-0079-y.

10. David Aaker, *Managing Brand Equity* (New York: Free Press, 1991).

11. Saikat Banerjee, "Strategic Brand-Culture Fit: A Conceptual Framework for Brand Management," *Journal of Brand Management* 15, no. 5 (2008), pp. 312–22.

12. "The New Brand Landscape," *Marketing Health Services* 28, no. 1 (2008), p. 14; and Helen Stride and Stephen Lee, "No Logo? No Way, Branding in the Non-Profit Sector," *Journal of Marketing Management* 23, no. 1/2 (2007), pp. 107–22.

13. Hui-Ming Deanna Wang and Sanjit Sengupta, "Stakeholder Relationships, Brand Equity, Firm Performance: A Resource-Based Perspective," *Journal of Business Research* 69, no. 12 (December 2016), pp. 5561–68.

14. B. Ramaseshan and Hsiu-Yuan Tsao, "Moderating Effects of the Brand Concept on the Relationship Between Brand Personality and Perceived Quality," *Journal of Brand Management* 14, no. 6 (2007), pp. 458–67; and Joel Espejel, Carmina Fandos, and Carlos Flavian, "The Role of Intrinsic and Extrinsic Quality Attributes on Consumer Behavior for Traditional Food Products," *Managing Service Quality* 17, no. 6 (2007), pp. 681–99.

15. Rob Beintema, "Plugged in with the Ford C-Max Energi," *Wheels.ca,* April 7, 2017, http://www.wheels.ca/car-reviews/plugged-in-with-the-ford-c-max-energi/.

16. Wai Jin (Thomas) Lee, Aron O'Cass, and Phyra Sok, "Unpacking Brand Management Superiority: Examining the Interplay of Brand Management Capability, Brand Orientation and Formalisation," *European Journal of Marketing* 51, no. 1 (2017), pp. 177–99, doi: 10.1108/EJM-09-2015-0698.

17. Marc Fisher and Alexander Himme, "The Financial Brand Value Chain: How Brand Investments Contribute to the Financial Health of Firms," *International Journal of Research in Marketing* 34, no. 1 (March 2017), pp. 137–53.

18. Eric Viardot, "Branding in B2B: The Value of Consumer Goods Brands in Industrial Markets," *Journal of Business & Industrial Marketing* 32, no. 3 (2017), pp. 337–46, doi: 10.1108/JBIM-11-2014-0225.

19. Sungwook Min, Namwoon Kim, and Ge Zhan, "The Impact of Market Size on New Market Entry: A Contingency Approach," *European Journal of Marketing* 51, no. 1 (2017), pp. 2–22, doi: 10.1108/EJM-12-2013-0696

20. Rong Huang and Emine Sarigollu, "Assessing Satisfaction with Core and Secondary Attributes," *Journal of Business Research* 61, no. 9 (2008), pp. 942–59.

21. Suraksah Gupta, Susan Grant, and T. C. Melewar, "The Expanding Role of Intangible Assets of the Brand," *Management Decision* 46, no. 6 (2008), pp. 948–61.

22. Brad D. Carlson, Tracy A. Suter, and Tom J. Brown, "Social versus Psychological Brand Community: The Role of Psychological Sense of Brand Community," *Journal of Business Research* 61, no. 4 (2008), pp. 284–301.

23. Jing Lei, Niraj Dawar, and Jos Lemmink, "Negative Spillover in Brand Portfolios: Exploring the Antecedents of Asymmetric Effects," *Journal of Marketing* 72, no. 3 (May 2008), pp. 111–29.

24. Satish Nambisan and Priya Nambisan, "How to Profit from a Better 'Virtual Customer Environment,'" *MIT Sloan Management Review* 49, no. 3 (2008), pp. 53–70.

25. Graham Ferguson, Kong Cheen Lau, and Ian Phau, "Brand Personality as a Direct Cause of Brand Extension Success: Does Self-Monitoring Matter?" *Journal of Consumer Marketing* 33, no. 5 (2016), pp. 343–53, doi: 10.1108/JCM-04-2014-0954.

26. N. Amrouche, G. Martin-Herran, and G. Zaccour, "Pricing and Advertising of Private and National Brands in a Dynamic Marketing Channel," *Journal of Optimization Theory and Applications* 137, no. 3 (2008), pp. 465–84.

27. Tsung-Chi Liu and Chung-Yu Want, "Factors Affecting Attitudes toward Private Labels and Promoted Brands," *Journal of Marketing Management* 24, no. 3/4 (2008), pp. 283–99; and Kyong-Nan Kwon, Mi-Hee Lee, and Yoo Jin Kin, "The Effect of Perceived Product Characteristics on Private Brand Purchases," *Journal of Consumer Marketing* 25, no. 2 (2008), pp. 105–22.

28. Najam Saqib and Rajesh V. Manchanda, "Consumers' Evaluations of Co-Branded Products; The Licensing Effect," *Journal of Product and Brand Management* 17, no. 2 (2008), pp. 73–89.

29. Klaus-Peter Wiedmann and Dirk Ludewig, "How Risky Are Brand Licensing Strategies in View of Customer Perceptions and Reactions?" *Journal of General Management* 33, no. 3 (2008), pp. 31–50.

30. Alokparna Basu Monga and Loraine Lau-Gesk, "Blending Co-Brand Personalities: An Examination of the Complex Self," *Journal of Marketing Research* 44, no. 3 (2007), pp. 389–402.

31. Wei-Lun Chang, "A Typology of Co-Branding Strategy: Position and Classification," *Journal of the American Academy of Business* 12, no. 2 (March 2008), pp. 220–27.

32. Bo Rundh, "The Role of Packaging within Marketing and Value Creation," *British Food Journal* 118, no. 10 (2016), pp. 2491–2511, doi: 10.1108/BFJ-10-2015-0390.

33. Ulrich R. Orth and Keven Malkewitz, "Holistic Package Design and Consumer Brand Impressions," *Journal of Marketing* 72, no. 3 (2008), pp. 64–81.

34. Marina Puzakova, Hyokjin Kwak, Suresh Ramanathan, and Joseph F. Rocereto, "Painting Your Point: The Role of Color in Firms' Strategic Responses to Product Failures via Advertising and Marketing Communications," *Journal of Advertising* 45, no. 4 (2016), pp. 365–76.

35. Eric F. Shaver and Curt C. Braun, "Caution: How to Develop an Effective Product Warning," *Risk Management* 55, no. 6 (2008), pp. 46–52.

36. Yu Ying, Fengjie Jing, Bang Nguyen, and Junsong Chen, "As Time Goes By . . . Maintaining Longitudinal Satisfaction: A Perspective of Hedonic Adaptation," *Journal of Services Marketing* 30, no. 1 (2016), pp. 63–74, doi: 10.1108/JSM-05-2014-0160.

37. D. N. P. Murthy, O. Solem, and T. Roren, "Product Warranty Logistics: Issues and Challenges," *European Journal of Operational Research* 156, no. 1 (2004), pp. 110–25.

38. Shallendra Pratap Jain, Rebecca J. Slotegraaf, and Charles D. Lindsey, "Towards Dimensionalizing Warranty Information: The Role of Consumer Costs of Warranty Information," *Journal of Consumer Psychology* 17, no. 1 (2007), pp. 70–88.

39. Alan Deutschman, "The Gonzo Way of Branding," *FastCompany.com,* October 1, 2004, https://www.fastcompany.com/51052/gonzo-way-branding.

40. Judy Mottl, "Virgin's Branson Talks Retail Fails, Retail Success and What Makes for a Rewarding Customer Experience," *CustomerExperience.com,* February 7, 2017, https://www.retailcustomerexperience.com/articles/virgins-branson-talks-retail-fails-retail-success-and-what-makes-for-a-rewarding-customer-experience/; Fastco Studios, "Virgin Group's Brand Evolution: A Rookie in Business No More," *FastCompany.com,* August 12, 2016, https://www.fastcompany.com/3062766/virgin-groups-brand-evolution-a-rookie-in-business-no-more; and "Virgin Megastore. Seriously Fun," *Virgin Group,* https://www.virgin.com/company/virgin-megastore, accessed April 24, 2017.

41. "Why Did Richard Branson Start an Airline?" *Virgin Group,* https://www.virgin.com/travel/why-did-richard-branson-start-an-airline, accessed April 24, 2017; Catherine Clifford, "Why Richard Branson Had Tears Streaming Down His Face When He Sold Virgin Records for a Billion Dollars," *CNBC.com,* February 6, 2017, http://www.cnbc.com/2017/02/06/richard-branson-wept-when-he-sold-virgin-records-for-a-billion-dollars.html.

42. Fastco, "Virgin Group's Brand Evolution: A Rookie in Business No More."

43. Deutschman, "The Gonzo Way of Branding."

44. "Find a Virgin Company," *Virgin Group,* https://www.virgin.com/virgingroup/content/about-us, accessed May 6, 2017; Mottl, "Virgin's Branson Talks Retail Fails."

45. Elizabeth Howell, "Stephen Hawking to Visit Space Aboard Virgin Galactic," *Seeker.com,* March 20, 2017, https://www.seeker.com/stephen-hawking-to-visit-space-aboard-virgin-galactic-2322034945.html.

46. Anna Hensel, "7 Failures That Helped Richard Branson Become a Multibillionaire," *Inc.com,* https://www.inc.com/anna-hensel/ss/failures-that-turned-richard-branson-into-billionaire.html, accessed April 24, 2017.

47. Deutschman, "The Gonzo Way of Branding."

48. "Smart Brand Extension Allows Virgin to Keep Up Appearances," *The Guardian,* https://www.theguardian.com/media-network/media-network-blog/2014/oct/23/virgin-success-brand-extension-easygroup, accessed April 24, 2017.

49. "This Is Why Richard Branson's Best Publicity Stunts Smash It," *DealWithTheMedia.com,* http://dealwiththemedia.com/case-study/richard-bransons-best-publicity-stunts/, accessed April 24, 2017.

50. Sarah Gordon, "Virgin Group: Brand It Like Branson," *Financial Times,* November 5, 2014, https://www.ft.com/content/4d4fb05e-64cd-11e4-bb43-00144feabdc0.

51. "About Us," *Virgin Group,* https://www.virgin.com/virgingroup/content/about-us, accessed April 24, 2017.

CHAPTER 10

Service as the Core Offering

LEARNING OBJECTIVES

LO 10-1 Understand why service is a key source of potential differentiation.

LO 10-2 Explain the characteristics that set services apart from physical goods.

LO 10-3 Explain the service-profit chain and how it guides marketing management decisions about service.

LO 10-4 Describe the continuum from pure goods to pure services.

LO 10-5 Discuss the elements of service quality and gap analysis.

LO 10-6 Measure service quality through use of SERVQUAL.

LO 10-7 Understand service blueprinting and how it aids marketing managers.

WHY SERVICE IS IMPORTANT

LO 10-1

Understand why service is a key source of potential differentiation.

There's no debate that today we operate in an economy that is increasingly focused on intangible offerings—services—instead of just physical goods. A **service** is a product in the sense that it represents a bundle of benefits that can satisfy customer wants and needs, yet it does so without physical form. As such, the value a customer realizes from purchasing a service is not based on its physical attributes, but rather on some other effect the service has on him or her in fulfilling needs and wants. And differences in the quality of a service can be profound; just think for a moment about the best and worst experiences you've had with a server in a restaurant. Even if the food itself is good, it is the service aspect of a meal out that everyone remembers most. All the data suggest that we now live in a predominantly **service economy**. More than 80 percent of jobs in the United States are service-related. Compare that to 55 percent of jobs in 1970. The Bureau of Labor Statistics expects service jobs to account for *all* new domestic job growth for the foreseeable future, partly because the number of jobs outside the service sector is actually declining. Jobs represented in the **service sector** of the economy include such important categories as intellectual property, consulting, hospitality, travel, law, health care, education, technology, telecommunications, and entertainment—all high-growth job categories. In terms of U.S. gross domestic product, services account for more than 75 percent and that number is growing. The long-term shift from goods-producing to service-producing employment is expected to continue. Service-providing industries are expected to see continued growth over the next 10 years, while goods-producing industries will see overall job loss. In today's workplace everyone is involved in service in some way; everyone has customers either outside or inside the firm, or both.

Changing U.S. demographics represent a major driver for why the service sector is thriving. For example, as baby boomers retire and spend their discretionary income on travel and entertainment, firms in those industries will prosper. As the baby boomers continue to age, health services will begin to predominate their spending. In the meantime, the fixation of Generation Y and millennials toward all things technological will continue to drive impressive growth in gaming, music, computing, cellular phone, and other technological industries.

Service as a Differentiator

In Chapter 7, we mentioned that service leadership and personnel leadership are two important sources of differentiation for a company. Recall that differentiation means communicating and delivering value in different ways to different customer groups. Presumably these groups are segments that show the most promise for return on marketing investment. As a marketing manager, a significant challenge with using differentiation as a core market strategy is that competitors are constantly coming to market with new differentiators that trump the efficacy of the current ones.

In his book *On Great Service,* Leonard Berry, a leading expert in the field of services marketing, advocates that a focus on service and on enabling employees to effectively deliver service can be one differentiator that is hard for the competition to replicate. Many firms are reluctant to invest in great service, largely because it takes time and patience before a return on the investment may be noticeable. But Berry's point is that although the payback might take time, once a firm is able to deliver great service as a core differentiator, it is much more likely to provide a sustainable competitive advantage than are most other sources of differentiation.[1]

SERVICE IS THE DOMINANT LOGIC OF MARKETING

For more than a hundred years it was believed that a company's purpose was to manufacture and distribute products that were then purchased by customers. The organization's value and competitive advantage were embedded in the product, maximum control and efficiency was achieved through product standardization, and products could be produced away from the market and then inventoried and distributed to markets as needed.

Singapore Airlines provides a spacious seat with attentive flight attendants as a way to differentiate itself as a premium provider of air travel.

Source: Singapore Airlines

Today's global economies are driven, however, by a new logic that considers service and the customer experience to be the principal rationality in marketing. Articulated as **service-dominant logic** more than a decade ago, and widely researched since then, there are a number of principles that guide the development of this new view of marketing.[2] However, let's consider three basic axioms that help support this new logic:

1. *Service is the fundamental basis of exchange.* Remember that historically, goods or products were the basis of exchange. In the new logic, service (defined as unique skills and competencies offered by the company) is the basis of exchange. Put simply, customers don't buy a car (product)—they buy the company's ability to add value through a defined set of benefits. For example, a customer who may be concerned about safety will evaluate the company in terms of how well it builds safety into its cars. The more a company knows about safety and is able to build it into the customer's car experience, the more favorable that customer will evaluate the company.

2. *Value is co-created by multiple parties, including the company and the customer.* The customer is an integral, even essential, part of creating value in the experience. To continue the car example, every customer interacts with the car in a different way, creating a unique value experience for that individual. His or her interaction can be initiated by the company's marketing efforts (for example, the website could highlight key features), influenced by the salesperson pointing out certain functional or aesthetic elements of the car, and directed by the car's layout and physical characteristics. In the end, however, the customer creates a unique experience by interacting with the company's marketing efforts and product in his or her own way.

3. *Value is defined by the customer.* Customers receive value from their experience, not from the company. The "bundle" of benefits that create value are different for each customer, making it important to understand the unique buying trends of specific customers in addition to broad customer behavior trends. So, while target markets may define the BMW product experience based on the driving experience or new technologies, individual customers can and do have very different definitions of the value delivered by BMW. It is clear that service-dominant logic puts even more emphasis on data analytics and the ability to learn about individual customers in addition to broad markets.[3]

The service-dominant logic of marketing has radically altered the focus of the marketing manager, who must now ask the question, "Just what is it we are marketing?" Put another way, the marketing manager must identify what the product is and where the value comes from. Since the customer is now central to value creation, a "customer-centric" approach that aligns people, processes, systems, and other resources to best serve customers is fundamental to a successful marketing strategy.

The remainder of this chapter is devoted to providing insights for effectively capitalizing on the service opportunities associated with a company's value offering. First, unique characteristics of services are described that set services apart from physical goods for marketing managers. Second, the concept of the service profit chain is discussed. Third, service attributes are discussed along with a continuum of products from pure goods to pure services. Fourth, the concept of service quality is presented along with its measurement and uses by management. Finally, blueprinting is discussed as a way for a marketing manager to map out the overall delivery system for a business.

CHARACTERISTICS OF SERVICES

Services possess several distinct characteristics different from physical goods. As illustrated in Exhibit 10.1, these are intangibility, inseparability, variability, and perishability. We'll discuss each one and its impact on customers and marketing.

Intangibility

A service cannot be experienced through the physical senses. It cannot be seen, heard, tasted, felt, or smelled by a customer. This property represents the **intangibility** of services versus goods; goods can easily be experienced through the senses. A State Farm Insurance agent issues a policy for an automobile. Yes, the customer will receive a written policy document. But the policy itself is not the product in the sense of a physical good such as a box of cereal or a bottle of shampoo. Instead, the product is the sense of financial security the insurance policy provides to the customer. It is the confidence that if something dire happens to the car, State Farm will fix it or replace it.

EXHIBIT 10.1 | **Characteristics of Services**

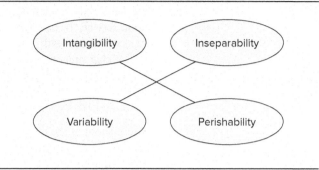

So how do customers draw conclusions about a brand such as State Farm if they can't actually try the product before purchase? This is one of the challenges of intangibles. Strong branding can be an important way to make a service seem more tangible. Service firms such as State Farm use strong imagery to send out signals about their products, increase trust, and ease customer uncertainty about what is being purchased. Ever see the ads saying, "Like a good neighbor, State Farm is there"? This phrase and the accompanying visual images provide cues about the dependability of the service, replacing to an extent the ability customers have to try physical products in advance of purchase. When it comes to making purchase decisions about services, customers draw conclusions from what tangibles they can experience—things like the company's people, website, marketing communications, office ambience, and pricing. In a service setting, the importance and impact of marketing are heightened considerably because in many cases there's little else tangible for the customer to experience before purchase.[4]

Sometimes it is possible to enhance tangibility of a service through a bit of customer trial. For example, MBA programs often encourage prospective students to come to open houses or visit classes to gain a sense of how the school they are considering approaches teaching and learning. Vacation ownership companies such as Hilton Grand Vacations Club and Marriott Vacation Club actively solicit guests for tours of their facilities while they are visiting an area to allow them to experience a taste of what the location is like as a regular vacation destination. And advertising agencies make portfolios of past work available to prospective clients as a sampling of the firm's creative capabilities.[5]

Inseparability

Even with the best efforts at enhancing a service's tangibility, a customer still can't really experience it until it is actually consumed. This characteristic represents the **inseparability** of a service—it is produced and consumed at the same time and cannot be separated from its provider. With physical goods, the familiar process is production, storage, sale, and then consumption. But with services, first the service is sold and then it is produced and consumed at the same time. Perhaps it is more accurate to think of a service as being *performed* rather than produced.[6] In a theatrical play or an orchestral concert, many individuals have a part in the performance. Similarly, the quality of a service encounter is determined in part by the interaction of the players. Most elegant restaurants structure their customer encounters as elaborate productions involving servers, the wine steward, the maître d', the chef, and, of course, the table of diners. Benihana restaurants take the concept of service as drama to truly new heights of customer involvement and excitement—the company's tag line is "an experience at every table."

The inseparability of performance and consumption of services heightens the role of the human service providers in the customer's experience. It also leads to opportunities for considerable customization in delivering the service. Finicky customers in the hair stylist's chair can coax just the right cut. Want two scoops of cinnamon ice cream instead of one on that apple tort? Just ask the server.

In the financial services industry, for example, customization of services is prominent. As the need for physical bank branches diminishes with the growth in online banking, banks are faced with the challenge of maintaining a strong customer connection and providing good service. To provide greater customization options, customers can "create" their own bank web page with information specifically targeted to their needs. At the same time, online chat support is ready to provide real-time, specific help when needed.[7]

Variability

An offshoot of the inseparability issue, **variability** of a service means that because it can't be separated from the provider, a service's quality can only be as good as that of the provider him-/herself.[8] Ritz-Carlton, Nordstrom, Disney, and Southwest Airlines have become iconic firms in their industries largely by focusing on their people—hiring, training, keeping, and promoting the very best people they can get. Legendary Southwest Chairman Herb Kelleher built a business in part around ensuring that his people were *different* from typical airline employees—more engaged, fun, and fiercely loyal to the company.[9] The same can be said for the other firms above. Focusing on employees as a source of differentiation in marketing is usually a smart move, mainly because so many firms just can't seem to pull it off very well. The point is to remove much of the variability of customers' experiences with your service and instead provide a more dependable level of quality. Go into any Nordstrom and work with any of Nordstrom's sales associates and you will very likely experience the same high level of satisfaction with the service. The same is true for Ritz-Carlton, and any of the great service organizations.[10]

Goods, in general, tend to be much more standardized than services because, once a firm has invested in continuous process improvement and quality control in its manufacturing operations, products flow off the line with very little variation. With services, continual investment in training, retraining, and good management of people is required if variability is to be consistently low. It is in this area where the disciplines of marketing, operations, leadership, and human resource management probably have their closest intersection. What makes Ritz-Carlton great? A quick answer is: its people. But what makes its people great? World-class operations, leadership, and HR practices. And the net effect for Ritz-Carlton is that its branding and market positioning are largely defined by its wonderful people and the way they handle each customer as a valued guest. For service firms, great marketing cannot take place without a strong overarching culture that values employees.

Perishability

If you schedule an appointment for a routine physical with your physician and then simply don't show up, the doctor loses the revenue from that time slot. That's **perishability**—the fact that a service can't be stored or saved up for future use.[11] Perishability is a major potential problem for service providers, and explains why, under the circumstances above, many physicians have a policy of charging the patient for the missed appointment. Ever wonder why an airline won't issue a refund or let you change your super-low-fare ticket after the door closes and the plane leaves without you? It's because the value of that empty seat—its ability to generate incremental revenue for the airline—dropped to zero when the door closed and the plane backed away from the gate.

Fluctuating demand is related to perishability of services.[12] Consider rental car firms such as Hertz, Avis, and the like in a city such as Orlando, which brings in both tourists and conventions. If demand were relatively constant, the rental car companies could keep the same basic inventory on the lot at all times. However, in the case of both individual vacationers and conventioneers, demand for cars varies considerably by season, and for the latter is driven by the size of the convention. The worst scenario is for the city to attract a huge convention and for the rental firms not to have sufficient cars available. No cars, no revenue for Hertz and Avis. Not to mention, the convention organizers would likely think twice before scheduling their event in Orlando again.

Because demand for most goods tends to be more stable and because they can generally be stored for use after purchase, this critical issue of synchronizing supply and demand is easier to deal with for goods than for services. Hertz and Avis don't want to maintain huge extra inventories of vehicles in off-peak periods; hence they might use price incentives to promote more rentals during those times. Or they might literally move cars around—pulling in massive numbers of extra vehicles from other nearby markets such as Miami or Tampa to take care of high-demand periods. One thing they know for sure is that if there are no cars on the lot, any opportunity for revenue perishes.

THE SERVICE-PROFIT CHAIN

In a now-famous *Harvard Business Review* article and follow-up book, James Heskett and his colleagues proposed a formalization of linkages between employee and customer aspects of service delivery called the **service-profit chain**. Because of the inseparability and variability of services, employees play a critical role in their level of success. The service-profit chain, which is portrayed in Exhibit 10.2, is designed to help managers better understand the key linkages in a service delivery system that drive customer loyalty, revenue growth, and higher profits.

LO 10-3

Explain the service-profit chain and how it guides marketing management decisions about service.

Internal Service Quality

This aspect of the service-profit chain includes elements of workplace design, job design, employee selection and development processes, employee rewards and recognition approaches, and availability of effective tools for use by employees in serving customers.

EXHIBIT 10.2 | The Service-Profit Chain

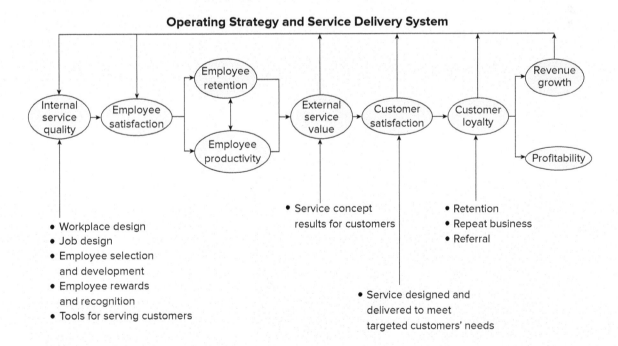

Source: Heskett, James L., Thomas O. Jones, Gary W. Loveman, W. Earl Sasser Jr, Leonard A. Schlesinger, "Putting the Service-Profit Chain to Work," *Harvard Business Review*, March/April 1994.

Considerable evidence exists that **internal marketing**, treating employees as customers and developing systems and benefits that satisfy their needs, is an essential element of internal service quality. Firms practicing internal service quality are **customer-centric**—they place the customer at the center of everything that takes place both inside and outside the firm. Firms that are customer-centric exhibit a high degree of customer orientation, which means they do the following:

1. Instill an organization-wide focus on understanding customers' requirements.
2. Generate an understanding of the marketplace and disseminate that knowledge to everyone in the firm.
3. Align system capabilities internally so that the organization can respond effectively with innovative, competitively differentiated, satisfaction-generating goods and services.

In the context of internal service quality, it is assumed that a firm's culture, business philosophy, strategy, structure, and processes will be aligned in order to create, communicate, and deliver value to customers. Finally, a focus on internal service quality implies that employees hold a **customer mind-set**, meaning that employees believe that understanding and satisfying customers, whether internal or external to the firm, is central to doing their job well.[13]

Satisfied, Productive, and Loyal Employees

Great service doesn't happen without great people. A big part of making the service-profit chain work is creating an environment in which all employees can be successful. Internal marketing is an integral element of this, and Caesars Entertainment is a great example of a firm that almost obsessively focuses on facilitating the success of its people, regardless of their position, and especially if they are in direct contact with customers. It's not surprising Caesars has such a zest for internal marketing and enablement of employee success. Gary Loveman, one of the original authors of the service-profit chain concept, went on to become chairman, CEO, and president. During his tenure, the company became the most successful hotelier/casino in Las Vegas and continues to expand elsewhere as well. Caesars' stable of brands includes Caesars Palace, Bally's, Paris, Rio, Flamingo, Harrah's, and others.[14] Caesars' focus on employees and great customer service continues under the current CEO. The company wins awards for both employee loyalty and guest service, with a large staff dedicated to ensuring a satisfied guest experience even when the guest loses at the gaming tables.

To be executed effectively, internal marketing must include the following critical elements: competing for talent, offering an overall vision, training and developing people, stressing teamwork, modeling desired behaviors by managers, enabling employees to make their own decisions, measuring and rewarding great service performance, and knowing and reacting to employees' needs. Perhaps most important of all, employees must have a deep understanding of the brand and must be able to consistently articulate a clear, concise message to customers that reflects the firm's service strategy and branding.[15] At Caesars, the CEO points with pride to the fact that everyone in the firm understands and can articulate its branding and values.

Michael Phelps as a symbol for Under Armour adds a strong sense of pride to the company and its products. It also captures the attention of prospective customers.

Source: Under Armour®, Inc.

Greater Service Value for External Customers

There is strong evidence that attention to internal service quality and to employee satisfaction, productivity, and retention results in stronger value to external customers of a service. Remember that when the concept of value was introduced in Chapter 1 we discussed it as the ratio of what a customer gives versus what he or she gets in return from a purchase. Importantly, the customer inputs are not just financial—customers give up time, convenience, and other opportunities in making a purchase choice. Customers set their expectations for the value they hope to derive from a service based largely on the evidence provided by the marketer before the purchase. A fundamental rule in marketing is to not set customer expectations so high that they cannot be effectively met on a consistent basis.[16] This is because it is always better to underpromise and overdeliver than the reverse scenario. This concept is often called **customer expectations management**.

When the Oklahoma City Thunder were founded, the owners understood the importance of personalizing the fan base. So they invested in a CRM system, which they continue to update and improve. The Thunder wanted to be the most fan-focused team in all of sports (not just the NBA), and they are able to target specific fans with special promotions based on their analysis of spending patterns and fan interest. The NBA even created an award for teams that exhibit excellence in delivering great guest experience and named it after the senior vice president of guest relations at the Oklahoma City Thunder.[17]

Customer Satisfaction and Loyalty

In the service-profit chain, meeting or exceeding customer expectations leads to customer satisfaction, since the service was designed and delivered in a manner that added value. A strong correlation exists between satisfied and loyal customers. Loyalty sparks high **customer retention**—low propensity to consider switching to other providers—as well as repeat business, referrals, and **customer advocacy**, a willingness and ability on the part of a customer to participate in communicating the brand message to others within his or her sphere of influence.[18] Why do customers consider switching from one service provider to another? Reasons run the gamut from low utility to various forms of service failure to concerns about a firm's practices. A summary of causes of switching behavior is presented in Exhibit 10.3.

EXHIBIT 10.3 | Causes of Switching Behavior

Pricing
- High price
- Price increases
- Unfair pricing
- Deceptive pricing

Inconvenience
- Location/hours
- Wait for appointment
- Wait for service

Core Service Failure
- Service mistakes
- Billing errors
- Service catastrophe

Service Encounter Failures
- Uncaring
- Impolite
- Unresponsive
- Unknowledgeable

Response to Service Failure
- Negative response
- No response
- Reluctant response

Competition
- Found better service

Ethical Problems
- Cheating
- Hard sell
- Safety concerns
- Conflict of interest

Involuntary switching
- Customer moved
- Provider closed

Source: Keaveney, Susan M., "Customer Switching Behavior in Service Industries: An Exploratory Study," *Journal of Marketing*, pp. 71–82, April 1995.

EXHIBIT 10.4 | Focus on the Most Satisfied Customers

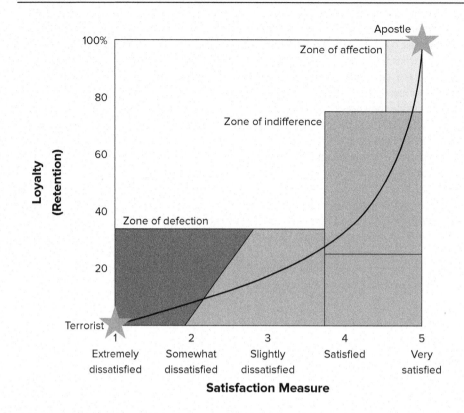

Source: Heskett, James L., Thomas O. Jones, Gary W. Loveman, W. Earl Sasser Jr, Leonard A. Schlesinger, "Putting the Service-Profit Chain to Work," *Harvard Business Review,* March/April 1994.

Caesars Entertainment understands the strong linkage between high customer satisfaction and loyalty and invests heavily in its most highly satisfied customers to ensure their loyalty and advocacy. Exhibit 10.4 portrays this relationship.

CRM and database marketing are key tools that allow Caesars Entertainment, as well as any firm interested in increasing satisfaction and loyalty and improving retention, to use the concepts in Exhibit 10.4 to focus on serving the most profitable customers. For the various Caesars casino brands, this approach manifests itself through the Total Rewards loyalty program. Caesars has found that its ROI for customers in the "Zone of Affection" is considerably higher than in the other zones ("Indifference" and "Defection"). Very satisfied customer "apostles" are the ones that Caesars wants to develop to the fullest extent to keep them coming back and spending money in its hotels and casinos. Research indicates that, although investing in indifferent customers to improve their satisfaction may yield some returns, only when customers reach the "Zone of Affection" do they truly maximize their profitability to the brand.

Revenue and Profit Growth

In the context of Exhibit 10.4, customers that are "satisfied" and "very satisfied" are identified through Caesars' Total Rewards loyalty program cards, which they use at hotel check-in, in slot machines, and at all gaming tables. They truly are the apple of the eye of Caesars' employees while they are on the property, and more broadly they represent the total focus of Caesars' marketing efforts—largely through direct marketing approaches with customized offers. Like slots? You'll get an invitation to a slot tournament. Poker's your thing? Look for an invitation to a poker tournament. It's not that Caesars is disinterested in or doesn't want the money of the other customers, but it has learned from its research that customers in the

"Zone of Affection" spend considerably more money and provide a substantially greater return on customer investment than others.[19]

Caesars embraces customer satisfaction measurement and it segments markets based on satisfaction score groups. The ultimate Caesars customer is the "apostle"–highly satisfied, fiercely loyal, a frequent Caesars guest who serves as a strong advocate for the Caesars experience to friends and acquaintances. For the service-profit chain to provide insight for marketing managers into how to best develop and execute service strategies, a variety of metrics must be in place with measures taken continually. In fact, all aspects of the chain–from internal service quality to employee issues to value to satisfaction and loyalty to financial performance–must be quantified and used for marketing management decision making. Chapter 5 provides a detailed treatment of marketing metrics, and many of the measures developed and exemplified in that chapter relate directly to executing the service-profit chain.

SERVICE ATTRIBUTES

So far we've looked at why service is at the core of firm success, identified characteristics of services, and gained an understanding of the linkages in the service-profit chain. We're now ready to gain a better understanding of how services fit within the broader context of different types of offerings. A useful way to approach answering this question is through consideration of a continuum of goods and services that range from easy to evaluate to difficult to evaluate based on three major types of attributes relevant to any offering: search attributes, experience attributes, and credence attributes. Exhibit 10.5 illustrates exemplar goods and services across a continuum of these attributes.

Search Attributes

Depending on the type of offering, consumers may engage in a search for various alternative products to find the one that most closely meets their decision criteria for purchase. With physical goods, such comparison is usually relatively simple as there are many **search attributes**, which are aspects of an offering that are physically observable before

EXHIBIT 10.5 | **Continuum of Evaluation for Different Types of Offerings**

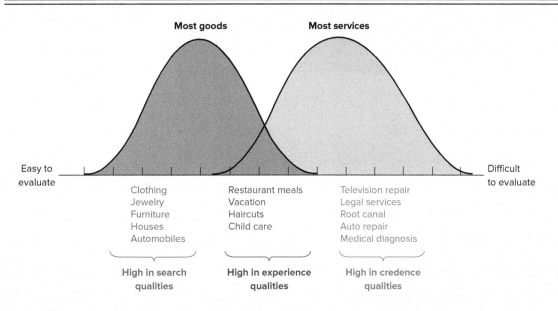

Source: Zeithami, Valarie A., "How Consumer Evaluation Processes Differ between Goods and Services," in *Marketing of Services,* James H. Donnelly and William R. George, eds., American Marketing Association, 1991.

consumption. For example, a shopper can compare the picture quality, price, and warranty of several high-definition televisions right on the Best Buy showroom floor. Because of the intangibility aspect of services, however, it is much more difficult to do such direct comparisons during a search process. Try comparing the performance of one mutual fund over another; the exercise gives new meaning to the old phrase "comparing apples and oranges." The bottom line is that services are low in search qualities because it is difficult to evaluate many aspects of them before purchase. Usually the customer doesn't truly know how the service performs until *after* the sale—that's the inseparability aspect of services.[20]

Experience Attributes

Experience attributes are aspects of an offering that can be evaluated only during or after consumption. Many services fit this category, including restaurants, vacations, haircuts, and child care. They tend to have both tangible and intangible aspects; for example, a dining-out experience includes a physical good, the meal, as well as the service portion. Based on the level to which customer expectations were met, a decision will be made about whether or not to repeat the purchase another time.[21]

Credence Attributes

In many cases, a customer cannot make a reasonable evaluation of the quality of a service even after use. Services such as television repair, legal services, dentistry, auto repair, and medical services require specialized training to deliver. The customer may only know the desired end state—a car that runs or a pretty new crown molar. To assess these **credence attributes** would require customers to have expertise not generally shared by the public. As such, many providers of services in this category rely on professional certifications or degrees to convey a level of trust to the purchaser. Thus, services at this end of the continuum are often referred to as **professional services**—providers such as doctors, lawyers, accountants, even plumbers. They typically have industry or trade groups that self-regulate the quality of their services and serve as a clearinghouse for information and referrals.

One interesting professional service for consideration is higher education. College business courses are high in credence attributes because of the difficulty in evaluating their real impact until much later, often after a student is able to apply knowledge and skills gained to a particular job situation. The perennial question in business education is, "Who is the customer?" One approach frames the companies that hire a business school's students as the primary customer, which would seem to imply the students are a product of the business school rather than its customers. Employing a marketing metaphor, this approach puts the professor in the role of product development and branding—positioning the student for success in the marketplace. This overall approach may be appropriate because business education is high in credence attributes. Understandably, however, all students want to be treated as "customers" too.

May we suggest a **hands on** *approach to stress management?*

A touch of indulgence is just what you need. With 40 treatment rooms, a private 4,000 square-foot heated outdoor lap pool, a Carita salon, a boutique, and a café, the Spa at the Ritz-Carlton, Orlando, Grande Lakes offers a blissful array of relaxing and rejuvenating options, all in one exquisite space.

Call us today to book your spa escape—407/393-4200.

THE RITZ-CARLTON®

Ritz-Carlton presents imagery and a tag line that are clearly reflective of a service heavy in experience attributes.

Source: The Ritz-Carlton Hotel Company, L.L.C.

Importance of Understanding Service Attributes

Because services tend to exhibit high experience and credence attributes, marketing strategies must be developed that consider the implications of these characteristics. As we've discussed, service customers tend to take their cues on what to purchase from whatever evidence they can gather to make up for the lack of ability to try the service beforehand. Word-of-mouth referrals, physical cues such as the ambience of the physical location, functionality of the website, and professionalism of the employees operate as a surrogate for trial. Because of the higher risk involved in purchasing a service versus a good, once a customer begins to have a positive experience with a service provider and build a relationship with the firm, customer loyalty to services tends to be greater than loyalty to goods. Of course, the flip side of that for the marketing manager is that if your competitor offers great service and people as a key differentiator, and you can't match it, it can be very difficult to get customers to switch to or even try a new provider.[22]

SERVICE QUALITY

Earlier we mentioned the importance of managing customer expectations—the notion that underpromising and overdelivering is powerful because it contributes to a high level of customer satisfaction. Exceeding customer expectations is often referred to as **customer delight**, which has been shown to correlate highly with loyalty and high return on customer investment.[23] Firms practicing great service often build in **delightful surprises** for their customers as part of their service experience—the warm chocolate chip cookie you get at Doubletree on every stay was originally conceived as a delightful surprise, a fairly inexpensive way to make a memorable impact on weary travelers. Although Doubletree patrons have now come to expect their cookie, this little extra has become a part of the firm's branding and image, and customer surveys regularly indicate it is one of the most-loved aspects of the Doubletree experience.

Just what is service quality? In many respects, **service quality** represents a formalization of the measurement of customer expectations of a service compared to perceptions of actual service performance. The playing field for service quality is the **service encounter**, which is the period during which a customer interacts in any way with a service provider. This can be in person, by phone, or through other electronic means. While much of the actual service delivery might occur behind the curtain—consider the tax preparer who works on your IRS return or the travel agent who spends hours pulling together your extreme sport trip to Reykjavík—customer evaluations of a service tend to be based on the behaviors of the service provider and the accompanying physical surroundings during the service encounter itself. This is why the face-to-face time between customer and service provider is often called the **moment of truth**. Most customer judgments take place at that moment.[24]

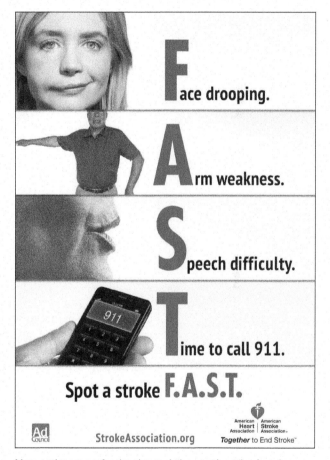

More and more professional associations such as the American Heart and American Stroke Associations are marketing themselves and providing value-added information to end-user consumers.

Source: American Heart Association, Inc.

Gap Analysis

Review the Gap Model of Service Quality, presented in Exhibit 10.6. The basis of the **gap model** is the identification and measurement of differences in five key areas of the service delivery process. Notice how the model is divided by a horizontal line, with the area below the line representing the provider side of the service encounter and the area above the line representing the customer side. For marketing managers, ongoing

LO 10-5

Discuss the elements of service quality and gap analysis.

EXHIBIT 10.6 | Gap Model of Service Quality

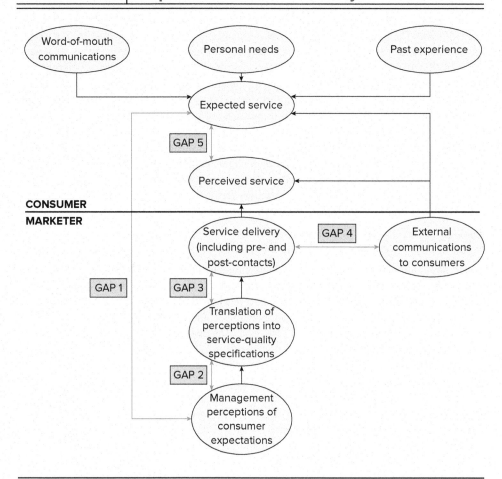

Source: A. Parasuraman, Valarie A. Zeithaml, and Leonard L. Berry, "A Conceptual Model of Service Quality and Its Implications for Future Research," *Journal of Marketing*, Fall 1985, pp. 41–50.

use of the gap model to identify emerging problems in service delivery is an important way to ensure service quality.

Let's take a closer look at each of the gaps. To illustrate the power of the analysis, we will develop a threaded example involving Outback Steakhouse, one of the restaurant brands owned and operated by Bloomin' Brands, Inc. of Tampa, Florida. Their other brands include Carrabba's Italian Grill, Bonefish Grill, and Fleming's Prime Steakhouse & Wine Bar. From a surface viewpoint, most people might assume that the founders of Outback—the original restaurant was in Tampa, Florida—built their differentiation primarily on the Australian theme and hearty portions at moderate prices. However, that is only part of their original success formula. From the beginning, Outback's founders relied heavily on its service delivery system to set it apart from other mid-priced, family-style restaurants. Their success is undeniable, with Outback units consistently leading their segment of the industry in customer turns per table, revenue and profit per square foot, and the all-important metrics of customer satisfaction. Using a service-profit chain approach to the business, Outback's founders focused strongly on its people, assuring that every store manager is a proprietor/owner of the business. Servers, even college students, tend to stay much longer than the industry average due to higher tips generated by more rapid table turnover.[25]

Gap 1: Management's Perceptions of Customer Service Expectations versus Actual Customer Expectations of Service

In Chapter 4 you learned about the importance of ongoing, well-executed market research to provide input for marketing management decision making. Gap 1 is where a lack of the right customer data can wreak havoc on service delivery. Unfortunately, firms all too often make unfounded assumptions about customers' wants and needs and translate them into product offerings. Then management is surprised when new products fail or customers begin to switch to other providers.

Outback Steakhouse was an early leader in providing convenient phone-ahead curbside service for customer pickup. Although it varies by location, some stores do as much as 15 to 20 percent of their revenue in customer takeout. This is especially profitable because it requires little extra server labor to fill these pickup orders. How did Outback know to add this new service? Not surprisingly, it was through market research that showed customers were increasingly disappointed with traditional fast-food drive-throughs and were willing to pay more for a quality, convenient meal they could enjoy at home. Convenience and time utility are two major drivers of busy young professional families today, which just happens to be Outback's primary target market.[26]

Gap 2: Management's Perceptions of Customer Service Expectations versus the Actual Service Quality Specifications Developed

In Gap 2, management may or may not accurately perceive actual customer expectations of service, but regardless builds an aspect of the service delivery system that does not meet customer wants and needs. A perfect example of this would be if Outback had designed its curbside carryout system differently. Customers grabbing takeout after work do not want to park, get out of the car, and go into the restaurant to pick up the food. Almost all of Outback's competitors originally designed takeout that way. By designing the system as a curbside pickup in front of the store, Outback not only accurately met customer expectations of service but also designed service delivery specifications to match.

Gap 3: Actual Service Quality Specifications versus Actual Service Delivery

Interestingly, unlike the previous two gaps, this one has no element of perception—this gap strictly asks whether the service is provided in the manner intended. As such, when there is a negative gap at Gap 3, it nearly always points to management and employees simply not getting the job done. This could be due to vague performance standards, poor training, or ineffective monitoring by management.

Like many firms, Outback uses teamwork to enhance its service delivery system. Ever notice that more than one person makes contact with you at your table, asks how you are doing, brings food or drink, and so forth? To make the curbside pickup system work like clockwork, employees from the phone order-taker to the cooks to the car-runner must be in sync. If cars back up, employees are trained to go down the line to make contact, provide estimated remaining wait times, and even handle payment so that when the food does come out the customer can immediately depart. You may wait a while to get your table at an Outback restaurant on a peak evening (if it's a nice night, you can sit outside and sip a beverage), but once you're seated the restaurant has aggressive standards for wait times for getting your meal at the table. When these wait times are significantly exceeded, the employees are trained to apologize, not offer lame excuses, and then offer something extra like a free dessert or a coupon for a free Bloomin' Onion next time.

This process is called **service recovery** and is actually a very strategic aspect of marketing management. Much research in services marketing has shown that **service failure**, when properly handled through service recovery, does not necessarily impact customer satisfaction, loyalty, or retention unless service failures become habitual.[27] All firms employing service as a marketing strategy must plan ahead for the eventuality of service failures and train employees to properly execute service recovery.

Sometimes a service failure can be quite severe. A good example occurred in April 2017, when members of the flight and ground crews for United Airlines Flight 3411 allowed local police to forcibly remove a passenger from the flight by dragging him down the aisle. Video of the event was soon posted to YouTube and the Internet exploded with condemnation. Calling it an "involuntary de-boarding situation," United compounded the problem by initially blaming the passenger—CEO Oscar Munoz called the passenger "belligerent" and uncooperative. The reaction to the event was profoundly negative and widespread, with United's stock dropping more than 6 percent the day after the events were reported and many people saying they would never fly United Airlines again.

Is service recovery even possible given the magnitude of the service failure that United Airlines experienced on that flight? After realizing its initial reaction was inappropriate, the company—and more specifically, the CEO—sent out a letter to members of United's frequent flyer program (see Exhibit 10.7). In the letter, Mr. Munoz apologized for the incident and acknowledged that "our corporate policies were placed ahead of our shared values." In addition, the company announced 10 changes it would make to the way it conducts business, including reducing the amount of overbooking (a key issue in the incident) and increasing the amount of passenger compensation for voluntary denied boarding to $10,000. Unfortunately for United, the incident was only one of several service failures, as the airline continues to be in the middle of the pack in terms of on-time arrivals and lost luggage. So, while United Airlines' business model may not have suffered, its reputation certainly was damaged as a result of the incident.

Gap 4: Actual Service Delivery versus What the Firm Communicates It Delivers

This gap fundamentally represents customer expectations management through marketing communications. Part Five of this book will familiarize you with different ways to communicate the value offering to customers. The messages the marketing manager puts out through various communication vehicles are in large measure what sets the expectations for the customer. Thus, deceptive advertising, overly zealous sales pitches, and coupon promotions backed by too little stock to handle demand all create a negative gap at Gap 4. In the case of Outback's curbside pickup, although it has done some advertising over the years, most of Outback's media ads focus more on special occasions and the fun theme of the restaurant. Because much of Outback's product is the experience provided the diner inside the restaurant, it has allowed the pickup business to grow more through word of mouth and in-store signage. Outback has not set any unrealistic expectations about its curbside takeout via its marketing communications.

Gap 5: Perceived Service by Customers versus Actual Customer Expectations of Service

Finally, Gap 5 represents the core issue of expectations versus perceptions and is the only gap that occurs exclusively in the customer's space. This is the gap between the service a customer expects to receive and the customer's perceptions of the level of service actually received. The score for this gap, which can be positive or negative, is the manifestation of a firm's customer expectations management strategy and the efficacy of its service delivery system.[28] For Outback Steakhouse, as well as most other firms, these scores are a direct flow-through into customer satisfaction measurement. Occasionally after eating at Outback, you might get a special receipt that has a toll-free number to call at Outback to answer a brief telephone questionnaire about your service encounter. Outback might offer some free food for completing the survey by providing you with an activation number. Almost always such survey research efforts are aimed at measuring importance scores (how important various aspects of a service are to the customer) versus actual performance scores (how well did we do on delivering against these service aspects during your last service encounter with us).

To provide an example of Gap 5 in practice, Exhibit 10.8 lists 14 hypothetical attributes that a restaurant like Outback might consider for analysis in terms of customer perceptions of their importance. Then, Exhibit 10.9 portrays a matrix based on a hypothetical analysis of importance perceptions versus performance perceptions for those 14 attributes, showing areas where the restaurant can invest in service improvement, areas where it needs to simply keep up the current service, areas of low priority for attention, and areas where too much emphasis is being placed on service aspects. One other analysis could be easily added—comparative matrices for several of Outback's closest competitors so the chain can easily see how well the competition is doing in delivering against the same attributes. Such analytical approaches are invaluable in allowing marketing managers to know how to best invest in service quality.

UNITED

MileagePlus # XXXXX

Dear Mr. Honig,

Each flight you take with us represents an important promise we make to you, our customer. It's not simply that we make sure you reach your destination safely and on time, but also that you will be treated with the highest level of service and the deepest sense of dignity and respect.

Earlier this month, we broke that trust when a passenger was forcibly removed from one of our planes. We can never say we are sorry enough for what occurred, but we also know meaningful actions will speak louder than words.

For the past several weeks, we have been urgently working to answer two questions: How did this happen, and how can we do our best to ensure this never happens again?

It happened because our corporate policies were placed ahead of our shared values. Our procedures got in the way of our employees doing what they know is right.

Fixing that problem starts now with changing how we fly, serve and respect our customers. This is a turning point for all of us here at United - and as CEO, it's my responsibility to make sure that we learn from this experience and redouble our efforts to put our customers at the center of everything we do.

That's why we announced that we will no longer ask law enforcement to remove customers from a flight and customers will not be required to give up their seat once on board - except in matters of safety or security.

We also know that despite our best efforts, when things don't go the way they should, we need to be there for you to make things right. There are several new ways we're going to do just that.

We will increase incentives for voluntary rebooking up to $10,000 and will be eliminating the red tape on permanently lost bags with a new "no-questions-asked" $1,500 reimbursement policy. We will also be rolling out a new app for our employees that will enable them to provide on-the-spot goodwill gestures in the form of miles, travel credit and other amenities when your experience with us misses the mark. You can learn more about these commitments and many other changes at hub.united.com.

While these actions are important, I have found myself reflecting more broadly on the role we play and the responsibilities we have to you and the communities we serve.

I believe we must go further in redefining what United's corporate citizenship looks like in our society. If our chief good as a company is only getting you to and from your destination, that would show a lack of moral imagination on our part. You can and ought to expect more from us, and we intend to live up to those higher expectations in the way we embody social responsibility and civic leadership everywhere we operate. I hope you will see that pledge express itself in our actions going forward, of which these initial, though important, changes are merely a first step.

Our goal should be nothing less than to make you truly proud to say, "I fly United."

Ultimately, the measure of our success is your satisfaction and the past several weeks have moved us to go further than ever before in elevating your experience with us. I know our 87,000 employees have taken this message to heart, and they are as energized as ever to fulfill our promise to serve you better with each flight and earn the trust you've given us.

We are working harder than ever for the privilege to serve you and I know we will be stronger, better and the customer-focused airline you expect and deserve.

With Great Gratitude,

Oscar

Oscar Munoz
CEO
United Airlines

EXHIBIT 10.8 | Example Attributes

1. Healthy food options.	12. Accommodating hours of operation.
2. Convenient locations.	13. Children's play area.
3. Quick to-go pickup outside.	14. Innovative new menu items.
4. Clean restrooms.	Customers would likely be surveyed on
5. Variety of menu items.	the attributes with questions such as the
6. Friendly and courteous staff.	following, using an appropriate rating
7. Children's food choices.	scale:
8. Fun ambience.	
9. Accurate order fulfillment.	Rate the importance of each attribute to
10. Speed of service.	your decision to dine at _____ restaurant.
11. Senior discounts.	Rate how well _____ restaurant
	provides each attribute.

EXHIBIT 10.9 | Importance–Performance Analysis Matrix

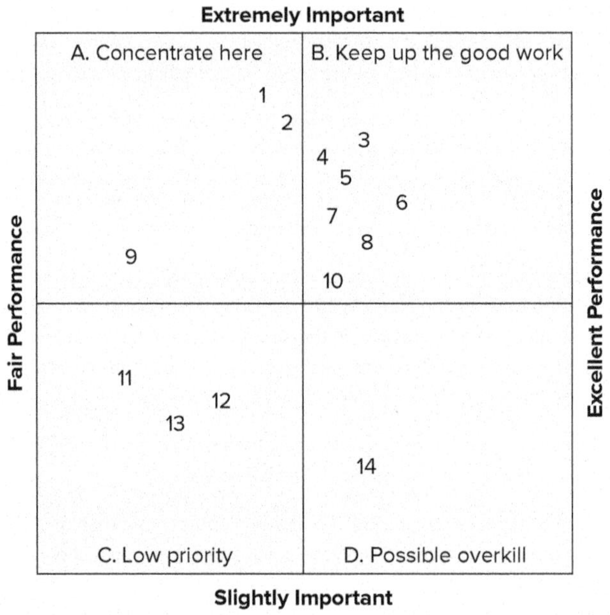

SERVQUAL: A Multiple-Item Scale to Measure Service Quality

LO 10-6

Measure service quality through use of SERVQUAL.

Marketers didn't separate out services for separate study from goods until the early 1980s. The movement toward a focus on service as a core differentiator was driven, in part, by a team of professors: Leonard Berry, Valarie Zeithaml, and A. Parasuraman. Much of their work resulted in the gap analysis approach described in the prior section.[29] But another important aspect of their research was determining what service quality really means from the perspective of customers. Their work uncovered five **dimensions of service quality**, illustrated by Exhibit 10.10 and described below.

Tangibles Tangibles are the physical evidence of a service or the observable aspects that help customers form advance opinions about the service despite its general intangibility.

Examples of tangibles include appearance of service providers, website, marketing communications materials, and the ambience and look of the office or retail store. Such tangibles send cues to the customer about the quality of the service.

Reliability Reliability is the ability to provide service dependably and accurately and thus to deliver what was promised. Reliability means performing the service right the first time and every time. Research has consistently demonstrated that reliability tends to be one of the most important aspects of service quality.

Responsiveness Responsiveness is the willingness and ability to provide prompt service and to respond quickly to customer requests. Customers often complain about a lack of responsiveness on the part of service providers. Service providers exhibit poor responsiveness when they create difficulty making contact, exhibit poor follow-up, make excuses for poor service, and generally act as though they are doing the customer a favor.

Assurance Assurance is the knowledge and courtesy of employees, and the ability to convey trust and build a customer's confidence in the quality of the service. Service providers often provide assurance primarily through their own competence in the job.

Empathy Empathy is the caring and individual attention a service provider gives to customers. Empathy means considering things from the customer's point of view.

The SERVQUAL Instrument

Parasuraman, Zeithaml, and Berry developed a measurement instrument called **SERVQUAL** to reflect these five dimensions.[30] The scale has been applied in tens of thousands of service settings across all types of industries. It can be adapted to most any application in which the marketing manager wishes to gain customer input about the importance and performance of a firm against the five dimensions of service quality. Companies track SERVQUAL scores over time to understand how their service quality is tracking so that marketing managers can create approaches to improve areas as needed.[31] Exhibit 10.11 provides a generic version of the SERVQUAL scale.

EXHIBIT 10.10 | **Dimensions of Service Quality**

EXHIBIT 10.11 | **Generic SERVQUAL Instrument for XYZ Company**

Please circle the number that best corresponds with your view related to XYZ.

1. XYZ has modern-looking equipment.

Strongly disagree			Neither agree nor disagree			Strongly agree
1	2	3	4	5	6	7

2. The physical facilities at XYZ are visually appealing.

1	2	3	4	5	6	7

3. Employees at XYZ appear professionally dressed.

1	2	3	4	5	6	7

(cont.)

EXHIBIT 10.11 | **Generic SERVQUAL Instrument for XYZ Company** *(cont.)*

4. Materials associated with XYZ (website, promotional brochures, service tracking documents, invoices, etc.) are visually appealing.

    1   2   3   4   5   6   7

5. When employees at XYZ promise to do something by a certain time, they do so.

    1   2   3   4   5   6   7

6. When a customer has a problem, employees at XYZ show a sincere interest in solving it.

    1   2   3   4   5   6   7

7. XYZ employees perform the service right the first time.

    1   2   3   4   5   6   7

8. XYZ employees provide their services at the time they promise to do so.

    1   2   3   4   5   6   7

9. XYZ insists on error-free records.

    1   2   3   4   5   6   7

10. Employees at XYZ tell you exactly when services will be performed.

    1   2   3   4   5   6   7

11. Employees at XYZ give prompt service to you.

    1   2   3   4   5   6   7

12. Employees at XYZ are always willing to help you.

    1   2   3   4   5   6   7

13. Employees at XYZ are never too busy to respond to your requests.

    1   2   3   4   5   6   7

14. The behavior of employees at XYZ instills confidence in you.

    1   2   3   4   5   6   7

15. You feel safe in your transactions with XYZ.

    1   2   3   4   5   6   7

16. Employees at XYZ are consistently courteous to you.

    1   2   3   4   5   6   7

17. Employees at XYZ have the knowledge to answer your questions.

    1   2   3   4   5   6   7

18. XYZ employees give you individual attention.

    1   2   3   4   5   6   7

19. XYZ has operating hours convenient to all its customers.

    1   2   3   4   5   6   7

20. XYZ has employees who give you personal attention.

    1   2   3   4   5   6   7

21. XYZ employees have your best interests at heart.

    1   2   3   4   5   6   7

22. XYZ employees understand your needs.

    1   2   3   4   5   6   7

Key to the instrument by SERVQUAL dimension: Tangibles = Questions 1–4; Reliability = Questions 5–9; Responsiveness = Questions 10–13; Assurance = Questions 14–17; Empathy = Questions 18–22.

SERVICE BLUEPRINTS

Earlier in the chapter, you read that from its inception Outback Steakhouse conceived of its service delivery system as an important source of differentiation in its positioning against other mid-priced family restaurants. How does a marketing manager conceive of such a system, lay it out, and then implement it so that everyone in the firm can follow it and play their part? The answer is through **service blueprints**, which borrows concepts from manufacturing and operations management to actually map out (likely through the use of computer software) a complete pictorial design and flow chart of all the activities from the first customer contact to the actual delivery of the service.

A simple example of a service blueprint for a floral delivery service is mapped out in Exhibit 10.12.

Note in tracking through the floral delivery service blueprint that activities are divided between those above the **line of visibility** (or those activities directly involving the customer that the customer sees) and those below the line of visibility to the customer (in this case, backstage operations and processing activities). The "moments of truth" we discussed earlier occur above the line of visibility.

A service blueprint is invaluable as a tool for marketing managers, especially for service encounters that are more complex than floral delivery, restaurants, and the like. First, the mere creation of the document serves to uncover potential bottlenecks in the service delivery system before it goes operational. Second, it represents a tremendous training device for employees involved in service delivery. Especially in a teamwork environment such as Outback Steakhouse where servers, cooks, and bartenders are so dependent on each other's performance to maximize the customer's positive experience overall, familiarizing each person involved in service delivery with exactly how his or her role fits into the entire system helps everyone take on a customer mind-set—even employees who ordinarily don't directly interface with the external customers such as the cooks.[32] Finally, using a service blueprint provides managers with an important way to integrate service topics into the performance evaluation process for all employees. Smart firms that rely on service for differentiation such as Outback, Ritz-Carlton, and Southwest Airlines provide incentives to their people who consistently contribute to the delivery of great service.

LO 10-7

Understand service blueprinting and how it aids marketing managers.

EXHIBIT 10.12 | **Service Blueprint for Floral Delivery**

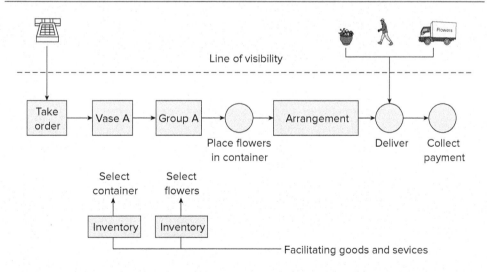

SUMMARY

In today's competitive marketplace, service is an important source of differentiation. But services have unique characteristics that must be understood as well as attributes that make services quite different from goods. An important concept for marketing managers to master is the service-profit chain, which provides a framework for linking elements of the service delivery system that drive customer loyalty, revenue growth, and higher profits. Key tools for establishing and measuring effective service include gap analysis, SERVQUAL, and service blueprints.

KEY TERMS

service   267
service economy   267
service sector   267
service dominant
  logic   268
intangibility   269
inseparability   269
variability   270
perishability   270
fluctuating
  demand   270
service-profit chain   271
internal marketing   272
customer-centric   272

customer mind-set   272
customer expectations
  management   273
customer retention   273
customer advocacy   273
search attributes   275
experience attributes   276
credence attributes   276
professional services   276
customer delight   277
delightful surprises   277
service quality   277
service encounter   277
moment of truth   277

gap model   277
service recovery   279
service failure   279
dimensions of
  service quality   282
tangibles   282
reliability   283
responsiveness   283
assurance   283
empathy   283
SERVQUAL   283
service blueprints   285
line of visibility   285

APPLICATION QUESTIONS

connect

More application questions are available online.

1. Marketing managers must be cognizant of the unique characteristics of services: intangibility, inseparability, variability, and perishability.

   a. How does each of these characteristics potentially impact the development and execution of marketing plans?

   b. What might a manager do to mitigate any negative consequences of each characteristic on the delivery of his or her firm's service?

   c. Come up with an example of a service encounter you have had as a customer (either in the B2C or B2B market) in which each of these characteristics came into play in how the service was delivered.

2. The service-profit chain guides managers toward understanding and facilitating successful linkages in the service delivery system to drive loyalty, revenue growth, and higher profits.

   a. What functional areas of a firm must a marketing manager effectively interface with to implement a service-profit chain approach?

   b. What potential impediments do you foresee in implementing the service-profit chain in an organization? How might these impediments best be overcome?

   c. What do you believe are the key advantages in implementing a service-profit chain approach?

3. Review Exhibit 10.5 and the accompanying discussion on search, experience, and credence attributes of offerings.

   a. Why are the types of offerings on the far right side of the continuum—professional services—difficult for customers to evaluate?

b. What challenges does this difficulty create for marketing managers in professional services firms? Why?

4. Review the Gap Model of Service Quality (Exhibit 10.6). Consider each of the five gaps where customer expectations might not be met. Select a firm of your choice and for each potential gap list specific actions that the firm could take to improve the likelihood that customer expectations will be met on a regular basis.

5. Consider the five dimensions of service quality: tangibles, reliability, responsiveness, assurance, and empathy.

a. Identify a recent service encounter you have experienced as a customer (either B2C or B2B) that you would classify as a generally bad experience. In what ways specifically did each of the five service quality dimensions contribute to your perceptions of poor service? Be as specific with your examples as you can. What could the service provider have done to improve each of the relevant dimensions and thus improve your experience?

b. Repeat the above process but instead of a bad service experience this time identify a generally good service experience. For each relevant dimension, specifically what did the service provider do really well? Did you experience any delightful surprise? If so, what?

MANAGEMENT DECISION CASE
Amazon Dash: More Than Just a Dash of Service

Imagine you just walked into your local Target. What do you see? We're betting that you picture the aisles of goods for sale. This might lead you to believe that retail stores are mostly in the business of providing products. However, retailers rarely manufacture the goods they sell—in fact, they're actually in the business of service.

Most retailers rely on repeat business and referrals to earn their profits, and therefore need to maintain high levels of service. The American Consumer Satisfaction Index (ACSI) has been tracking U.S. consumer satisfaction across different retail segments since the 1990s. A quick review of the ACSI consumer satisfaction scores shows higher satisfaction for all types of retail stores, including supermarkets, specialty retail, and department stores, over other industries such as banks or cable companies. But the leading edge of customer satisfaction with retail is Internet retail, and its star is Amazon.com.[33]

Amazon.com (Amazon), founded in 1994 by Jeff Bezos, has grown into the world's largest Internet retailer, capturing nearly three-quarters of all online commerce in 2016. It has nearly 125 million customers, half of whom subscribe to Amazon Prime, which provides free two-day shipping along with access to a large catalog of streaming music, movies, and TV shows.[34] Many companies have a difficult time justifying the cost of providing top-notch service, but Bezos actually planned for it, budgeting a loss for Amazon's first five years. It ended up taking seven years for Amazon to see its first profit! But as Leonard Berry once said, if a firm is able to deliver great service as its core differentiator, it can likely create a sustainable competitive advantage, and Amazon has done just that. Amazon's investments and relentless customer focus have created innovations that align to the key service attributes of search, credence, and experience.

In the search attribute, which applies to Amazon due to the large number of products it sells, Amazon has invested heavily in algorithms that recommend and suggest products for each individual customer. Amazon is so focused on correctly understanding the customer that Bezos sees a future where a customer coming to Amazon's home page finds "one product, the one you are about to buy."[35]

While the credence attribute typically applies to services where special skills are required, it applies to Amazon because it sells products online, where customers cannot rely on the usual clues as to product quality. To address this issue, Amazon allows customers to share their opinions (positive and negative) about both Amazon's service and the products it sells. This provides potential buyers a consensus of the post-purchase evaluations of other customers. (In fact, Amazon was one of the first Internet retailers to establish this type of review system!)

Finally, in the experience attribute, Amazon designs its service to give customers as much control as possible, allowing them to create the experience that meets their specific needs. Through personalized settings and features, customers can "tell" Amazon exactly what they want to experience when they place an order. For example, Amazon's customer can preselect the delivery speed, destination, and payment method, and then order simply with "One-Click," a technology that Amazon patented. The customer can just as easily override these settings for a single order. In addition, when ordering items that need to be installed, Amazon allows customers to order a professional installer at the same time the product order is placed. And that's just for ordering via their website.

Although it may sound like Amazon has done enough to stay at the head of the pack, it continues to innovate in ways beyond web-based ordering. A recent service innovation, the Amazon Dash, allows customers to immediately place an order for a specific item from any location in their home—all with the push of one button. The Dash is a consumer goods offering that combines a replenishment service with two different physical devices, the Dash Button and the Dash Wand. The main device, the Dash Button, is a small, single-purpose button that is predefined for a specific product and can be placed where that product is used. For example, the Dash Button for Tide detergent can be hung or mounted in your laundry room, and pushing the Dash Button automatically reorders Tide. To setup a Dash, the customer orders the button for the desired product type from Amazon and pairs it to his or her Amazon account.

The Dash Button is part of a complete platform, combining physical devices, software linked to the devices, and Amazon's fulfillment capabilities. Hundreds of Dash Buttons, each for a different product, are available. And thousands of products are accessible as part of the Amazon Dash subscription service. In addition, Amazon offers the Dash Wand, which allows customers to say an item's name (or scan a barcode) to quickly create a shopping list. And while the Dash is designed for consumable consumer goods, Amazon's Echo and Dot products (voice-activated "assistants") can help customers place orders from a listing of hundreds of thousands of Amazon Prime–eligible products.

Amazon's customer-centric actions emanate from the top; Bezos has said, "If you're competitor-focused, you have to wait until there is a competitor doing something. Being customer-focused allows you to be more pioneering."[36] And, to emphasize the point, Bezos periodically brings an empty chair into meetings, telling employees the chair represents the most important person in the room: the customer.[37]

Questions for Consideration

1. Leonard Berry suggests that companies delivering great service as a differentiator may create a sustainable competitive advantage. Using Amazon as an example, what problems might some companies face in trying to create that advantage?

2. Amazon invests in predictive algorithms to assist its customers in finding products they may be interested in. What are some concerns Amazon should look out for as it improves its search and recommendation tools?

3. Amazon Prime, briefly mentioned in the case, is a subscription service that gives members free two-day shipping on hundreds of thousands of products, as well as many other features such as access to music, movies, TV shows, book sharing, and more. In the United States, Prime membership is $100 per year. What effect do you think Prime membership has on customer loyalty and switching costs?

MARKETING PLAN EXERCISE

ACTIVITY 11: Differentiating via Service Quality

In your marketing plan, consider how you might effectively use service as a source of differentiation for your offering(s). As you learned in this chapter, to successfully accomplish this, you must be sensitive to nuances of services versus goods and also be able to ensure that the people and processes in your firm are able to properly support the service.

1. Evaluate the opportunity to utilize service as an important differentiator.

2. Employ a service-profit chain approach to identify people and operational aspects of your plan to support service differentiation.

3. Develop specific action plans and metrics in support of your service differentiation approach.

NOTES

1. Leonard L. Berry, *On Great Service: A Framework for Action* (New York: The Free Press, 1995).

2. Stephen L. Vargo and Robert F. Lusch, "Evolving to a New Dominant Login for Marketing," *Journal of Marketing,* 68, no. 1 (January 2004), pp. 1–17; Stephen L. Vargo and Robert F. Lusch, "Service-Dominant Logic: Continuing the Evolution," *Academy of Marketing Science Journal,* 36, no. 1 (2008), pp. 1–10; and Stephen L. Vargo and Robert F. Lusch, "Institutions and Axioms: An Extension and Update of Service Dominant Logic," *Journal of the Academy of Marketing Science,* 44 no. 1, (2016), pp. 5–23.

3. Brian A. Zinser and Gary J. Brunswick, "The Evolution of Service-Dominant Logic and Its Impact on Marketing Theory and Practice: A Review," *Academy of Marketing Studies Journal,* 20 no. 2, (2016), pp 120–36.

4. Michael K. Brady, Brian L. Bourdeau, and Julia Heskel, "The Importance of Brand Cues in Intangible Service Industries: An Application to Investment Services," *Journal of Services Marketing* 19, no. 6/7 (2005), pp. 401–11.

5. Harvir S. Bansal, Shirley F. Taylor, and Yannik St. James, "'Migrating' to New Service Providers: Toward a Unifying Framework of Customers' Switching Behaviors," *Journal of the Academy of Marketing Science* 33, no. 1 (Winter 2005), pp. 96–116.

6. Jeremy J. Sierra and Shaun McQuitty, "Service Providers and Customers: Social Exchange Theory and Service Loyalty," *Journal of Services Marketing* 19, no. 6/7 (2005), pp. 392–401.

7. Dylan Baddour, "Branches Dwindle as Bank Customers Spend More Time Online," *Houston Chronicle,* May 4, 2017, http://www.houstonchronicle.com/business/article/Branches-dwindle-as-bank-customers-spend-more-11121129.php.

8. Christian Homburg, Wayne D. Hoyer, and Martin Fassnacht, "Service Orientation of a Retailer's Business Strategy: Dimensions, Antecedents, and Performance Outcomes," *Journal of Marketing* 66, no. 4 (October 2002), pp. 86–102; and Medhi Mourali, Michael Laroche, and Frank Pons, "Individualistic Orientation and Customer Susceptibility to Interpersonal Influence," *Journal of Services Marketing* 19, no. 3 (2005), pp. 164–74.

9. Conor Shine, "New Southwest President, Ready for Airline's Takeoff, Says Your Bags Will Still Fly Free," *Dallas News,* May 3, 2017, https://www.dallasnews.com/business/southwest-airlines/2017/05/03/new-southwest-president-plotting-next-chapter-airlines-growth-bags-will-still-fly-free.

10. Ram Sharma, "Top 10 Companies with the Best Customer Service," *Trendintopmost.com,* February 2017, http://www.trendingtopmost.com/worlds-popular-list-top-10/2017-2018-2019-2020-2021/highest-selling-brands-products-companies-reviews/companies-with-the-best-customer-service/.

11. Rajshekhar G. Javalgi, Thomas W. Whipple, Amit K. Ghosh, and Robert B. Young, "Market Orientation, Strategic Flexibility, and Performance: Implications for Services Providers," *Journal of Services Marketing* 19, no. 4 (2005), pp. 212–22.

12. Kenneth J. Klassen and Thomas R. Rohleder, "Combining Operations and Marketing to Manage Capacity and Demand in Services," *Service Industries Journal* 21, no. 2 (April 2001), pp. 1–30.

13. D. Todd Donovan, Tom J. Brown, and John C. Mowen, "Internal Benefits of Service-Worker Customer Orientation: Job Satisfaction, Commitment, and Organizational Citizenship Behaviors," *Journal of Marketing* 68, no. 1 (January 2004), pp. 128–46.

14. Jim Tierney, "Caesars Entertainment Hits Jackpot at Loyalty 360 Awards," Loyalty360, May 4, 2017, https://www.loyalty360.org/content-gallery/daily-news/caesars-entertainment-hits-jackpot-at-loyalty360-a.

15. Ceridwyn King and Debra Grace, "Exploring the Role of Employees in the Delivery of the Brand: A Case Study Approach," *Qualitative Market Research* 8, no. 3 (2005), pp. 277–96.

16. Deepak Sirdeshmukh, Jagdip Singh, and Barry Sabol, "Customer Trust, Value, and Loyalty in Relational Exchanges," *Journal of Marketing* 66, no. 1 (January 2002), pp. 15–38.

17. Jason Gumpert, "NBA Team Reboots Customer Engagement with Microsoft Dynamics CRM Upgrade, Data Management Refresh," *MSDynamicsWorld,* April 25, 2016, https://msdynamicsworld.com/story/nba-team-rethinks-customer-engagement-microsoft-dynamics-crm-upgrade-data-management-refresh; "NBA Announces Pete Winemiller Guest Experience Innovation Award," *ABS-CBN Sports,* March 24, 2017, http://sports.abs-cbn.com/nba/news/2017/03/24/nba-announces-guest-experience-innovation-award-23692.

18. Lawrence A. Crosby and Brian Lunde, "Loyalty Linkage," *Marketing Management* 16, no. 3 (May/June 2007), p. 12; and James H. McAlexander, John W. Schouten, and Harold F. Koening, "Building Brand Community," *Journal of Marketing* 66, no. 1 (January 2002), pp. 38–55.

19. Sudhir N. Kale and Peter Klugsberger, "Reaping Rewards," *Marketing Management* 16, no. 4 (July/August 2007), p. 14.

20. Anita Goyal, "Consumer Perceptions towards the Purchase of Credit Cards," *Journal of Service Research* 6 (July 2006), pp. 179–91.

21. Minakshi Trivedi, Michael S. Morgan, and Kalpesh Kaushik Desai, "Consumer's Value for Informational Role of Agent in Service Industry," *Journal of Services Marketing* 22, no. 2 (2008), pp. 149–59.

22. Frances X. Frei, "The Four Things a Service Business Must Get Right," *Harvard Business Review* 86, no. 4 (April 2008), pp. 70–80.

23. Kevin M. McNeilly and Terri Feldman Barr, "I Love My Accountants—They're Wonderful: Understanding Customer Delight in the Professional Services Arena," *Journal of Services Marketing* 20, no. 3 (2006), pp. 152–59.

24. Kenneth R. Evans, Simona Stan, and Lynn Murray, "The Customer Socialization Paradox: The Mixed Effects of Communicating Customer Role Expectations," *Journal of Services Marketing* 22, no. 3 (2008), pp. 213–23; and Amy K. Smith and Ruth N. Bolton, "The Effect of Customers' Emotional Responses to Service Failures on Their Recovery Effort Evaluations and Satisfaction Judgments," *Journal of the Academy of Marketing Science* 30, no. 1 (Winter 2002), pp. 5–23.

25. Chris T. Sullivan, "A Stake in the Business," *Harvard Business Review* 83, no. 9 (September 2005), p. 57.

26. "Takeout Trend," *BusinessWeek,* August 24, 2007, www.businessweek.com/mediacenter/video/businessweektv/f3dcbeb754a244fb3ad7082bfe62af0362e7d167.html?chan=search.

27. "Is Customer Delight a Viable Goal?" *Businessline,* March 23, 2007, p. 1.

28. Teck H. Ho and Yu-Sheng Zheng, "Setting Customer Expectation in Service Delivery: An Integrated Marketing-Operations Perspective," *Management Science* 50, no. 4 (April 2004), pp. 479–89.

29. A. Parasuraman, Valarie A. Zeithaml, and Leonard L. Berry, "A Conceptual Model of Service Quality and Its Implications for Future Research," *Journal of Marketing, Fall* 1985, pp. 41–50.

30. A. Parasuraman, Leonard L. Barry, and Valarie A. Zeithaml, "SERVQUAL: A Multiple-Item Scale for Measuring Consumer Perceptions of Service Quality," *Journal of Retailing* 64, no. 1 (1988), pp. 12–40; and A. Parasuraman, Leonard L. Barry, and Valarie A. Zeithaml, "Refinement and Reassessment of the SERVQUAL Scale," *Journal of Retailing* 67, no. 4 (1991), pp. 420–50.

31. A. Parasuraman, Leonard L. Berry, and Valarie A. Zeithaml, "Perceived Service Quality as a Customer-Based Performance Measure: An Empirical Examination of Organizational Barriers Using an Extended Service Quality Model," *Human Resource Management* 30, no. 3 (Fall 1991), pp. 335–42.

32. Pao-Tiao Chuang, "Combining Service Blueprint and FMEA for Service Design," *Service Industries Journal* 27, no. 2 (March 2007), pp. 91–105.

33. Alice Fornell, "ACSI: Retailers Improve Customer Satisfaction amid Store Closings," *ACSI,* February 28, 2017, http://www.theacsi.org/news-and-resources/press-releases/press-2017/press-release-retail-2016.

34. Arthur Zaczkiewicz, "Amazon, Wal-Mart Lead Top 25 e-Commerce Retail List," *Women's Wear Daily,* March 7, 2016, http://wwd.com/business-news/financial/amazon-walmart-top-ecommerce-retailers-10383750; and Eugene Kim, "Amazon Just Shared New Numbers That Give a Clue about How Many Prime Members It Has," *Business Insider,* February 13, 2017, http://www.businessinsider.com/amazon-gives-clue-number-of-prime-users-2017-2.

35. Tomasz Karwatka, "Omnichannel Customer Experience," *SlideShare,* February 4, 2016, https://www.slideshare.net/divanteltd/omnichannel-customer-experience.

36. David LaGesse, "America's Best Leaders: Jeff Bezos, Amazon.com CEO," *U.S. News & World Report,* November 19, 2008, https://www.usnews.com/news/best-leaders/articles/2008/11/19/americas-best-leaders-jeff-bezos-amazoncom-ceo.

37. George Anders, "Inside Amazon's Idea Machine: How Bezos Decodes Customers," *Forbes,* April 4, 2012, https://www.forbes.com/sites/georgeanders/2012/04/04/inside-amazon/#d0ee24d61998.

PART FOUR

Price and Deliver the Value Offering

CHAPTER 11

Manage Pricing Decisions

LEARNING OBJECTIVES

LO 11-1   Understand the integral role of price as a core component of value.

LO 11-2   Explore different pricing objectives and related strategies.

LO 11-3   Identify pricing tactics.

LO 11-4   Describe approaches to setting the exact price.

LO 11-5   Determine discounts and allowances to offer to channel members.

LO 11-6   Understand how to execute price changes.

LO 11-7   Examine legal considerations in pricing.

PRICE IS A CORE COMPONENT OF VALUE

You have learned that *value* is a ratio of the bundle of benefits a customer receives from an offering compared to the costs incurred by the customer in acquiring that bundle of benefits. From the customer's perspective, many but not all of those costs are reflected within the price paid for the offering. There are other types of costs, such as time invested in the purchase process or the opportunity costs of choosing one offering over another. But for most purchasers, regardless of whether the setting is B2C or B2B, the vast majority of costs are associated with the purchase price. As such, price—or, more specifically, the customer's *perception* of the offering's pricing—is a key determinant of perceived value. When customers exhibit strongly held beliefs that a firm's offerings provide high value, they are much more likely to remain loyal to the firm and its brands as well as actively tell others about their favorable experiences. Thus, marketing managers must take pricing decisions very seriously.[1]

LO 11-1

Understand the integral role of price as a core component of value.

From a marketing planning and strategy perspective, Michael Porter has consistently advocated that firms that are able to compete based on some extraordinary efficiency in one or more internal processes bring to the market a competitive advantage based on **cost leadership**. And although firms competing on cost leadership will likely also engage in one of Porter's other competitive strategies (differentiation or focus/niche), their core cost advantages translate directly to an edge over their competitors, based on much more flexibility in their pricing strategies as well as their ability to translate some of the cost savings to the bottom line.[2]

For example, Southwest Airlines is widely regarded as a cost leader in its industry, which becomes a critical factor when jet fuel prices go up. Southwest's internal process efficiencies stem from several important sources. First, it flies mostly the same type of plane—various series of the Boeing 737. This makes the maintenance process much more efficient than carriers whose fleet includes multiple types of aircraft. Second, Southwest has a very simple process of booking passengers and does not offer assigned seats. Finally, it only has one class of cabin service and does not serve meals, mostly opting for nuts and pretzels instead. These and other internal efficiencies translate into a cost structure second to none in the industry.

But what does such cost leadership mean for Southwest's pricing decision making? A knee-jerk response might be to simply lower fares to match the level of cost advantage. That might increase sales volume, but it also might start a price war with other airlines that have cost advantages (JetBlue, for instance). A more strategic approach—and the approach Southwest actually uses—is to translate part of its cost advantage into a more transparent, mileage-driven pricing structure for customers but at the same time take a portion of the cost advantage to increase the firm's profit margins, partly to reward shareholders and partly to reinvest for the firm's growth.

Most importantly, Southwest's pricing model not only contributes to its financial performance but also is an integral part of its overall value proposition and provides a valuable lesson for the way a marketing manager should approach pricing decisions—that is, pricing decisions cannot be made in a vacuum but rather must consider the whole of the firm's offering, especially the concurrent decisions the firm is making about branding and products, service approaches, supply chain, and marketing communication. For the marketing manager, pricing is much more than an economic break-even point or a cost-plus accounting calculation. Price is a critical component that plays into a customer's assessment of the value afforded by a firm and its offerings. As such, managerial decisions about pricing should be undertaken methodically and always with a focus on how price impacts the all-important cost-versus-bundle-of-benefits assessment that equates to customer perceived value.[3]

The rest of this chapter details the important pricing decision-making process from a marketing manager's perspective: establish pricing objectives and related strategies; select pricing tactics; set the exact price; determine channel discounts and allowances; execute price

EXHIBIT 11.1 | **Elements of Pricing Decisions**

changes; and understand legal considerations in pricing. Exhibit 11.1 portrays these elements of pricing decisions.

Establish Pricing Objectives
and Related Strategies

↓

Select Pricing
Tactics

↓

Set the Exact
Price

↓

Determine Channel
Discounts and Allowances

↓

Execute Price
Changes

↓

Understand Legal
Considerations in
Pricing

Explore different pricing
objectives and related
strategies.

ESTABLISH PRICING OBJECTIVES AND RELATED STRATEGIES

As illustrated in the Southwest Airlines example, pricing objectives are but one component leading to an overall value proposition. However, a product's price tends to be so visible and definitive that customers often have trouble moving past price to consider other critical benefits the product affords. This characteristic puts pressure on marketing managers to establish pricing objectives that best reflect and enhance the value proposition, while at the same time achieving the firm's financial objectives. Striking a balance between these two forces sometimes makes pricing an especially challenging part of marketing.[4]

Pricing objectives are the desired or expected result associated with a pricing strategy. Pricing objectives must be consistent with other marketing-related objectives (positioning, branding, etc.) as well as with the firm's overall objectives (including financial objectives) for doing business.[5] Exhibit 11.2 portrays several of the most common pricing objectives, along with their related strategies.

The decision of which pricing objective or objectives to establish is driven by many interrelated factors. As you learn about each of the approaches, keep in mind that most firms attempt to balance a range of issues through their pricing objectives, including internal organization-level goals, internal capabilities, and a host of external market and competitive factors. Dunkin' Donuts' pricing objective is a competitor-based approach (more on that later), and its pricing strategy is based on its positioning relative to rivals McDonald's and Starbucks in the breakfast market. Rather than engage in a price war with McDonald's, Dunkin' Donuts has tried to close the gap between itself and Starbucks. Although Dunkin' Donuts makes more money on breakfast sales overall than Starbucks, its average customer check is much lower. Additionally, Panera Bread and Starbucks have seen an impressive sales boost due to their loyalty programs that offer deals to customers after a certain amount of money has been spent. But not to be left behind, Dunkin' Donuts has its own loyalty program called DD Perks that gives you free beverages when you sign up, on your birthday, and with every 200 points earned. Members can use the associated app to call ahead and speed past the line. And to keep things really interesting, DD Perks serves up surprises every month for members, including offers and discounts on favorite items, points with every purchase, and other extra treats and goodies. Fortunately for Dunkin' Donuts, to date McDonald's does not feature a consumer loyalty program.[6]

Penetration Pricing

Market share is the percentage of total category sales accounted for by a firm. When a firm's objective is to gain as much market share as possible, a likely pricing strategy is **penetration pricing**, sometimes also referred to as pricing for maximum marketing share. In markets where customers are sensitive to price and where internal efficiencies lead to cost advantages allowing for acceptable margins even with aggressive pricing, a penetration objective can create a powerful barrier to market entry for other firms, thus protecting market share.

Sometimes penetration pricing is used as part of a new-product introduction. In both the B2C and B2B markets, it is common for prices to be set low initially to ward off competition and then for prices to creep up over time.[7] Such pricing is built into the product's budget over the life cycle of the item. Recall from Chapter 8 that as a product progresses through the product life cycle, margins tend to be at their highest during the maturity stage. This is partly because weaker competitors tend to drop out due to penetration pricing earlier in the cycle (introduction and growth stages), which creates the potential for remaining firms to decrease spending and raise prices during the maturity stage.

Be careful with a penetration pricing strategy. Because price is a cue for developing customer perceptions of product quality, the value proposition may be reduced if a low price belies the product's actual quality attributes.[8] An axiom in marketing is that customers always find it more palatable when a firm reduces a price than when it raises a price, and a corollary to the axiom is that once a price has been changed (one way or the other), changing it back creates confusion about positioning and brand image.

When Pringles was introduced by P&G years ago, its vacuum-packed tube and less greasy product created a sensation (Pringles are now marketed by Kellogg). Not to be usurped by this upstart, more recently the number-one snack producer Frito-Lay launched its Lay's Stax, a chip nearly the same as Pringles' curve-shaped chips. To make sure people tried them, at the initial product launch Stax cans were priced super-low at 69 cents—a penetration pricing strategy. Gradually, the can has risen to above a dollar. Putting Stax's pricing strategy even more clearly into perspective, today Lay's Stax sell for approximately 22 cents per ounce, while Pringles sell for about 29 cents per ounce, revealing that post-penetration Frito-Lay wanted Stax positioned lower in price than its closest competitor.[9]

Price Skimming

A strategy of **price skimming** addresses the objective of entering a market at a relatively high price point. In proposing price skimming, the marketing manager usually is convinced that a strong price–quality relationship exists for the product. This might be done to lend prestige to a brand, or skimming is sometimes used in a new-product introduction by a firm with a first-mover advantage to skim early sales while the product has a high level of panache and exclusivity in the marketplace.[10]

Major developers of gaming consoles, including Nintendo, Microsoft, and Sony, always introduce a new platform with the objective of price skimming. Flat-panel televisions all started with very high price points and have gradually inched pricing downward as more and more customers began to purchase. Pharmaceutical companies justify very high introductory prices for new medications based on a necessity to recoup exorbitant R&D costs associated with their industry. Those same drugs steadily decline in price as more advanced competitive drugs come along, and, when patent protection runs out, the price drops precipitously as generic versions of the drug flood the market.

Regardless of the motivation for a price skimming strategy, as with penetration pricing, when multiple-year budgets are developed, marketing managers must consider the likelihood of competitive entry and adjust pricing projections accordingly. An initial pricing objective of skimming will require modification over time based in part on the rate of adoption and diffusion by consumers.

In general, skimming can be an appropriate pricing objective within the context of a focus (niche) strategy. By definition,

EXHIBIT 11.2 | **Pricing Objectives and Related Strategies**

Objective: Market share maximization
Strategy: Penetration pricing
Objective: Market entry at the highest possible initial price
Strategy: Price skimming
Objective: Profit maximization
Strategy: Target ROI
Objective: Benchmark the competition
Strategy: Competitor-based pricing
Objective: Communicate positioning through price
Strategy: Value pricing

You gamers know that when a new generation of a gaming console is introduced the price starts high and then typically declines over time—that's price skimming!

©Joseph Branston/T3 Magazine via Getty Images.

such an approach positions a product for appeal to a limited (narrow) customer group or submarket of a larger market. Because niche market players typically attract fewer and less-aggressive competitors than those employing differentiation strategies within the larger market, a focus strategy can usually support higher prices and the potential for skimming can be extended. The ability to use price skimming declines precipitously, however, if the product migrates from a niche position to that of a differentiated product within the larger market.[11]

Profit Maximization and Target ROI

Pricing objectives very frequently are designed for profit maximization, which necessitates a **target return on investment (ROI)** pricing strategy. Here, a bottom-line profit is established first and then pricing is set to achieve the target. Although this approach sounds straightforward, it actually brings up an important reason pricing is best cast within the purview of marketing instead of under the sole control of accountants or financial managers in a firm. When pricing decisions on a given product are made strictly to bolster gross margins, bottom-line profits, or ROI without regard to the short- and long-term impacts of the pricing strategy on other important market- and customer-related elements of success, the product becomes strategically vulnerable. Marketing managers are in the best position to take into account the competitor, customer, and brand image impact of pricing approaches.[12]

Still, in preparing product budgets and forecasts, marketing managers are expected to pay close attention to their organization's financial objectives. During the research that leads to a decision to introduce a new product or modify an existing one, one key variable of interest is whether the market will bear a price point that enhances the firm's overall financial performance. Often, **price elasticity of demand**—the measure of customers' price sensitivity estimated by dividing relative changes in quantity sold by relative changes in price—becomes central to whether a product can even be viably introduced within the context of a firm's financial objectives.[13] The basic price elasticity (e) equation is portrayed below:

$$e = \frac{\% \text{ change inquantity demanded}}{\% \text{ change in price}}$$

Unfortunately, price sensitivity is notoriously one of the most difficult issues to determine through market research. Sometimes, historical records or secondary data can provide evidence of pricing's impact on sales volume. When primary research methods are used to ask customers about pricing—whether through survey, focus group, experiments, or other methodology—they most often place the respondents into a hypothetical "what if" mode of thinking in which they are asked to predict how one price or the other might impact their decision to buy. This is a very difficult assertion for a person to make and can lead to bad data and ultimately poor pricing decisions. Importantly, in many instances, much of a customer's reaction to pricing is more psychological or emotional in nature than rational and logical.[14]

Finally, the idea of pricing based on purely economic models and solely for profit maximization raises important ethical concerns, especially in cases where essential products are in short supply. The latest wonder drugs, building materials after a major disaster, and new technologies needed for emerging markets are but three examples in which pricing for pure profit motive can damage both a firm's image and ultimately its relationships with customers. Mylan, a pharmaceutical company, jumped onto the radar screens of many people due to its pricing strategy for the EpiPen, which has been widely interpreted by consumers and consumer advocates as unethical. An EpiPen is a potentially life-saving allergy-reaction injector that was selling for $100 for a two-pack in 2009. But by 2016, the price of a two-pack had spiked to a whopping $608—a six-fold price increase!—giving the impression that Mylan thought it could demand the high price until the expected arrival of a generic version of the drug. Recently, though, CVS announced that it will sell a new, generic two-pack for about $110 before potential discounts.[15]

Competitor-Based Pricing

Gaining a thorough understanding of competitors' marketing practices is a key element of successful marketing planning and execution. A competitor's price is one of the most visible elements of its marketing strategy, and you can often infer the pricing objective by carefully analyzing historical and current pricing patterns. Based on such analysis, a firm may develop **competitor-based pricing** strategies. This approach might lead the marketing manager to decide to price at some market average price, or perhaps above or below it in the context of penetration or skimming objectives.

The logic of competitor-based pricing is quite rational unless (1) it is the *only* approach considered when making the ultimate pricing decisions or (2) it leads to exaggerated extremes in pricing such that on the high end a firm's products do not project customer value or on the low end price wars ensue. A **price war** occurs when a company purposefully makes pricing decisions to undercut one or more competitors and gain sales and net market share.[16] Such was the case in the early 1990s when Sears embarked on a short-lived "low-price" strategy to compete with Walmart on certain high-profile goods, sparking a major price war. Sears management, concerned at the time about losing the Gen X market to Walmart and other discounters, fired the first salvo by publicly announcing a list of items on which it would not be undersold. One of these items, branded disposable diapers such as Pampers and Luvs, led the way in Sears' ads nationwide at prices well below cost.

Unfortunately for Sears, management grossly underestimated the power of Walmart to thwart such competitive threats. First, Walmart's chairman went public in the press by reiterating that Walmart was the true low-price king in retailing (the company's tagline at the time was "Always Low Prices") and assuring customers Walmart would match any advertised Sears price. Then, within days and in market after market, Walmart took to the newspapers with full-page ads discounting diapers to ridiculous levels never before seen, thus negating Sears' approach. This price war was short-lived and forced Sears to immediately rethink its pricing strategy.

Stability Pricing A potentially more productive strategy related to competitor-based pricing is **stability pricing**, in which a firm attempts to find a neutral *set point* for price that is neither low enough to raise the ire of competition nor high enough to put the value proposition at risk with customers. Many factors go into selecting a specific product's stability price point. In markets where customers typically witness rapidly changing prices, stability pricing can provide a source of competitive advantage.[17] Southwest Airlines employs a stability pricing strategy by displaying only five or six fares to a particular destination, with price points based on when the ticket is purchased and the days of the week the customer will be traveling. Unlike most other domestic carriers, Southwest actually bases prices more on the distance of the trip and is less tied to load-maximization formulas in which a fare can change minute by minute depending on ticket sales. The airline's stability pricing approach has proved highly popular with customers, and it's been successful for the firm as its seat occupancy rate continues to be among the highest in the industry.

Value Pricing

Firms that have an objective of utilizing pricing to communicate positioning use a **value pricing** strategy. Value pricing overtly attempts to consider the role of price as it reflects the bundle of benefits sought by the customer. Because value is in the eyes of the beholder, affected by his or her perceptions of the offering coupled with the operative needs and wants, pricing decisions are strongly driven by the sources of differential advantage a product can realistically deliver. Effectively communicating a product's differential advantages is

Metro PCS sends a strong value pricing signal with its $30 unlimited data, talk, text.

Source: T-Mobile USA, Inc.

at the heart of positioning strategy, and exposure to these elements spurs the customer to develop perceptions of value and a subsequent understanding of the value proposition.[18]

Value pricing is complex and overarches the other pricing objectives discussed so far. Through value pricing, a marketing manager seeks to ensure that the offering meets or exceeds the customer's expectations—that is, when he or she does the mental arithmetic that calculates whether the investment in the offering is likely to provide sufficient benefits to justify the cost. Put another way, value pricing considers the whole deliverable and its possible sources of differential advantage—image, service, product quality, personnel, innovation, and many others—the whole gamut of elements that create customer benefit. For instance, Toyotas and Hondas cost more to purchase initially than other comparable vehicles, but they last longer, require fewer repairs, are more fuel-efficient, and hold their resale value much better; overall, they have a lower lifetime cost of ownership.

From this assessment, the marketing manager makes a pricing decision that best reflects the product's capacity to be perceived as a good customer value. This high-impact decision helps frame customers' reactions and their relationship with the product and the company. Not surprisingly, Toyota and Honda drivers tend to be very brand loyal, with a very high repeat purchase rate, and many multiple-car families of one or the other.

Would a firm ever benefit from pricing without regard to value? This is an intriguing question that can best be illustrated through the example of a positioning map like the one in Chapter 7. Exhibit 11.3 provides a positioning map with price on one axis and quality on the other. In this instance, we're using the term *quality* rather generically to simply denote a range of differential advantages that might comprise the perceived bundle of benefits for the offering.

Notice in Exhibit 11.3 that a diagonal range of feasible positioning options exists based on matching price to the benefits achieved. For most products, as long as the customer perceives the ratio of price and benefit to be at least at equilibrium, perceptions of value will likely be favorable. Thus, a poorer-quality product offset by a super-low price can be perceived as a good value just as a higher-quality product at a high price can be.

The key lesson marketing managers should draw about value pricing goes back to a key point about managing customer expectations in Chapter 10: Overpromising and underdelivering is one of the quickest ways to create poor value perceptions and thus alienate customers. Marketers will do well to not overpromise benefits, but rather should communicate and deliver a realistic level of benefits for a price.[19]

But what happens when one strays off the favorable diagonal of price/benefit harmony? In the lower-right quadrant—high quality/low price—a penetration strategy might be in play. Or perhaps a firm is taking advantage of its cost leadership by offering a somewhat reduced price. However, over the long run, reducing price too much based on either of these pricing strategies can unnecessarily damage both margins and brand image. Penetration is usually intended to be a temporary strategy, giving the product a chance to gain a strong foothold in

EXHIBIT 11.3 | Generic Price–Quality Positioning Map

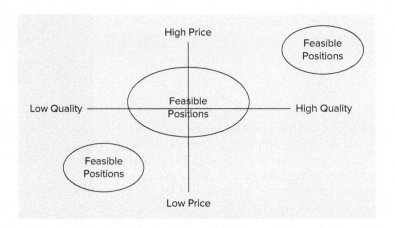

market share while warding off competition for a time. Michael Porter has long advocated that cost leadership based on value chain efficiencies should not be translated wholesale to low prices—the reason the approach is called *cost* leadership, not *price* leadership. Successful cost leaders tend to offer a somewhat lower price in the marketplace, but they also translate a substantial portion of their efficiencies to margin, thus enhancing the long-term growth and performance of the firm. Bottom line, it may be all right to play in the bottom-right quadrant temporarily in the case of penetration or to creep slightly into that quadrant over the long haul with a properly executed cost leadership approach.

Clearly, operating in the upper-left (high price/low benefits) quadrant can be problematic. Some firms utilize price skimming strategies, especially on product introductions, even when all the bugs have yet to be worked out of the product. New technology products are notorious for having surprises in quality, functionality, and reliability crop up soon after introduction. When this happens, it can be extremely damaging to the value proposition and to the brand. In such cases, from an ethical perspective, one could question the firm's intent. Did the company rush a product to market to beat an impending entry by competition, pricing it high due to first-mover advantage, all the while knowing that serious quality problems existed? Firms and brands that continually attempt to operate in the high-price/low-benefits quadrant do not survive over the long run as customer trust is damaged. Unfortunately, some highly unscrupulous companies perpetuate their operations in this quadrant by constantly changing company name, location, and brand names. Stories of customer rip-offs are particularly prolific in the service sector (from construction to financial services to health care) because in this sector the offering is inextricably linked to the provider and it's difficult to assess quality until after the service is rendered.

Opening 2 million unauthorized accounts in the retail segment of business to meet sales quotas, and charging the fake accounts service fees, are the colossally unbecoming actions that likely will leave their mark indefinitely on Wells Fargo's reputation. The firm reached a $110 million settlement to help make things right for their customers by paying back out-of-pocket losses resulting from the unauthorized accounts. Shortly after the debacle, credit card applications were down 43 percent and new checking account openings were down 40 percent from the prior year. Only time will tell how this massive rip-off will affect Wells Fargo's viability with customers over the long haul.[20]

SELECT PRICING TACTICS

Once management establishes the overall pricing objectives and strategies, it's time to develop and execute the pricing tactics in the marketplace that will operationalize the strategies. Exhibit 11.4 summarizes tactical pricing approaches.

LO 11-3

Identify pricing tactics.

As with establishing pricing strategies, for a variety of reasons firms frequently rely on combinations of pricing tactics in the marketplace rather than putting all their eggs in one basket. As you read about each approach, don't think of it as a stand-alone strategy but instead consider how it might work in tandem with other approaches that a marketing manager might decide to employ.

EXHIBIT 11.4 | Tactical Pricing Approaches

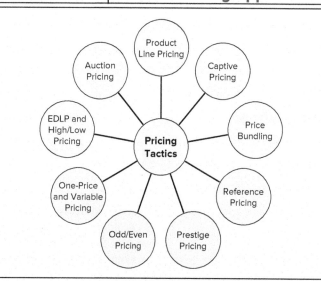

Product Line Pricing

As you have learned, firms rarely market single products. Most products are part of an overall product line of related offerings, and this is true whether the product is in the B2C or B2B marketplace, or in the realm of goods or service. **Product line pricing** (or **price lining**) affords the marketing manager an opportunity to develop a rational pricing strategy across a complete line of related items. As a customer is evaluating the choices

EXHIBIT 11.5 | Product Line Pricing by Room Type at the Fairmont Kea Lani on Maui

Room Type	Description of View	Price
Fairmont	Neighborhood side streets and landscaping	$ 669
Fairmont Mountainside	Majestic Haleakala and sunrise	$ 719
Fairmont Garden View	Tropical gardens and landscaping	$ 759
Partial Ocean View	Partial or angled view from outside the suite on lanai	$ 839
Poolside	Upper lagoon pool and garden	$ 839
Ocean View	Superb ocean and sunset views from lanai	$ 909
Deluxe Ocean View	Best ocean and sunset views	$ 999
Kilohana Signature	Spectacular panoramic ocean and sunset views	$1,269

Source: Fairmont Kea Lani. www.fairmont.com/kea-lani-maui, accessed May 22, 2017, for reservation dates in August 2017.

available within a firm's product line, the **price points** established for the various items in the line need to make sense and reflect the differences in benefits offered as the customer moves up and down the product line.

Consider the different types of rooms offered by a resort hotel on Maui. At top properties such as the Fairmont Kea Lani in Wailea, even a room on a lower floor with a limited view might easily run well over $600 per night during peak season. Exhibit 11.5 shows the array of room types and prices across the product line—the different grades of guest room.

In price lining, the escalation of product prices up the product line has to consider factors such as real cost differences among the various features offered, customer assessments of the value added by the increasing level of benefits, and prices competitors are charging for similar products. Price lining can greatly simplify a customer's purchase decision making by clearly defining a smorgasbord of offerings based on different bundles of benefits at different prices. Regardless of the product category, customers often approach a purchase with some preconceived range of price acceptability in mind, and product line pricing helps guide them toward the best purchase match to their needs while facilitating easy comparison among offerings.[21]

The venerable Ford Mustang has been a popular cultural icon for over 50 years. It's still a stunning pony car with muscular lines at a relatively affordable price. Auto manufacturers often use price lining, and the Mustang is no exception. For example, the 2017 Ford Mustang Fastback started with a base model that could be upgraded to premium and Ecoboost versions, and the V6 engine could be upgraded to a V8 (which is a staple of the Mustang GTs). What was the base MSRP, you might ask? Base was a very reasonable $25,185. But Ford would much prefer you stack on the extras—a top-of-the-line 2017 Shelby GT350R Mustang had a stout MSRP of $63,645! But the "secret sauce" of the Mustang family is that no matter which model you price yourself up to, each car still has that distinctive "Mustang look."[22]

Price lining can occur at a level much broader in scope than individual products. For example, Marriott has branded its entire family of accommodations based on different value propositions, supported by clearly delineated pricing strategies. Its offerings include Ritz-Carlton and JW Marriott for the most discriminating patron, Marriott and Renaissance at the next level of full service, and an array of differentially positioned brands such as Courtyard, Residence Inn, SpringHill Suites, Fairfield Inn, and TownePlace Suites.

Mariott's acquisition of Starwood Hotels brings even more variety of brands with different pricing strategies into their portfolio of offerings. Marriott clearly communicates the differences and value in each of these brands, partly by how each is priced in relation to the others. By now you should have a strong sense of how strategically important price is within the marketing mix as a cue for the customer's perceptions of value.[23]

Captive Pricing

Captive pricing, sometimes called **complementary pricing**, entails gaining a commitment from a customer to a basic product or system that requires continual purchase of peripherals to operate.[24] What is the most *profitable* part of Hewlett-Packard's office products business: printers or ink cartridges? It's the cartridges. And although other sources for replacement cartridges exist for HP machines, the company does a great job of convincing users that only genuine HP cartridges can be depended on for high-quality performance.

Like HP in printers, Gillette built its business in razors by hooking customers on the latest and greatest new multi-blade system through every type of promotion possible, from Super Bowl ads to free samples. Gillette counts on the fact that we will go back time and again to repurchase the replacement blades that carry the real margins the company is after. However, captive pricing strategies are not guaranteed to be successful! HP faces serious challenges by other providers and recyclers, while Gillette is trying to stave off competition from Dollar Shave Club and other lower-priced, convenience-oriented, direct-delivery competitors.

Captive pricing is just as common in the service sector, where it is sometimes called two-part pricing. Any firm that charges a monthly access fee, membership, retainer fee, or service charge and then bills by the specific service provided is using this pricing approach.

Buy 2 ink cartridges, get 1 black ink free.

FREE Black Ink Cartridge

Buy a set of HP Original Black and Tri-Color Ink Cartridges and get another HP Original Black Ink Cartridge for free*

HP certainly wants to encourage its printer owners to use genuine HP replacement ink cartridges. This special pricing encourages multiple cartridge purchases all at once.

Source: HP Development Company, L.P.

Price Bundling

When customers are given the opportunity to purchase a package deal at a reduced price compared to what the individual components of the package would cost separately, the firm is using a **price bundling** strategy.[25] Cable television providers want you to buy the full gamut of entertainment products from them, and the more you add to your bundle—digital television, premium channels, downloadable movies, local and long-distance phone service, cellular service, gaming, high-speed Internet—the better the deal becomes compared to the total of the individual prices of each piece of the bundle.

Price bundling is commonly used by television providers to sell cable subscriptions. However, streaming services and smaller bundle options are threatening the traditional large subscription bundle business. Amazon, Google's YouTube, and Hulu continue to negotiate the rights to stream live television over the Internet in an innovative approach that will offer consumers TV on demand in smaller bundle options at lower costs. These smaller bundles provide viewers with more limited, specialized channel options at a lower price. YouTube's "Unplugged" streaming TV service, for example, offers a "skinny bundle" that features TV's most popular channels for $30 to $40 a month. In an era when Americans are paying all-time-high cable subscription fees, these slimmer streaming bundles cut monthly cable fees almost in half—a benefit appreciated especially by millennials.[26]

A potential dark side to price bundling is that, in some industries, it can become unclear just what the regular, or unbundled, price is for a given component of a package. The cable/telecommunications industry is regulated to the point that this is less an issue, but in unregulated industries, unscrupulous firms sometimes set artificially high prices for the sake of pushing customers into buying a package. Later in the chapter we will review several of the most important legal considerations related to pricing.

Beyond legalities, ethical issues sometimes arise with regard to price bundling. For example, car shoppers often find every car on the lot within a given model has many of the same features automatically bundled as add-ons. How many of those features would you buy if you had a choice? The extra features being bundled typically carry much larger margins than the margin on the core vehicle itself. If you special order a car without the bundle, chances are you will be waiting months for it to be delivered to the lot—*if* the dealer will even order it for you.

Reference Pricing

As in price bundling, it can be useful for customers to have some type of comparative price when considering a product purchase. Such a comparison is referred to as **reference pricing** and, in the case of price bundling, the reference price is the total price of the components of the bundle if purchased separately versus the bundled price. The savings would be expected to stimulate purchase of the bundle so long as the perceived value realized is sufficient.

Reference pricing is implemented in a number of ways. Sometimes a product catalog might show a manufacturer's suggested list price next to the actual price the product is offered for in the catalog. In retail stores, in any given product category a private-label product (say, the Walgreens brand for instance) is often purposely displayed on a shelf right next to its national brand equivalent. The retailer hopes the savings realized by the direct price comparison of a bottle of Walgreens' mint mouthwash versus the bottle of Scope next to it will be enough to stimulate purchase. Reference pricing is very heavily used in B2B price lists, often reflecting price level differences depending on how many items are purchased or reflecting the amount saved by a firm's special "contract rate" with a vendor versus what a noncontract rate would be.

Clearly, reference pricing can create a powerful psychological impact on a customer by virtue of the savings (real or imagined) demonstrated by the comparison. Ever have a salesperson tell you that a price increase is imminent and if you don't purchase today you'll pay more tomorrow? Customer hedging behaviors against pricing uncertainty are driven by referencing projected prices in the future. And, of course, a sale or promotional price provides a strong reference point and, if the comparative difference is great enough, shoppers flock to the store as if going into battle to take advantage of temporary price reductions while they are in effect.[27]

Prestige Pricing

As mentioned earlier, one rationale for establishing a price skimming objective is **prestige pricing**—lending prestige to a product or brand by virtue of a price relatively higher than the competition. With prestige pricing, some of the traditional price/demand curves cannot properly predict sales or market response because it violates the common assumption that increasing price decreases volume. From the perspective of financial returns, prestige pricing is a phenomenal approach because, everything else being equal, commanding a premium price reflects directly on margins and bottom line.[28]

Prestige pricing plays on psychological principles that attach quality attributions to higher-priced goods—a typical response to some higher-priced products is that they must be better than their competitors; otherwise the price would be lower. When the Norwegian glacier water Voss entered the U.S. market in the 2000s, it entered with a prestige pricing strategy that helped create a whole new category of ultra-premium bottled waters. Order Voss in a chic restaurant and you can expect to pay a double-digit price per bottle. What's the value proposition that would support such a high price? The exclusivity of distribution, unique cylinder shape of the bottle, and exotic glacial imagery all combine so that a premium price actually enhances the customer's feelings of experiencing something really special (yes, water can be an experiential purchase). Promotion of Voss water has included numerous product placements showing celebrities and others among the rich and famous partaking of the brand. Had Voss entered the market without such a prestige pricing strategy, it is highly unlikely it would have achieved the buzz and early cult status it did.

Prestige pricing is crucial in the luxury goods market, where elite prices and limited availability are key factors that attract customers. Handbag and accessories companies Coach and Michael Kors (MK) both experienced the consequences for brand image of selling handbags at discounted rates at department stores. As it became easier and less expensive to purchase price-discounted Coach and MK handbags at multiple outlets, many of their high-end customers no longer desired to be associated with the brand and began carrying other, more chic handbags. Some high-end retailers began to react to this shift in target market as well—Nordstrom even dropped some MK lines due to perceptions of lower quality. In response, Coach and MK recognized this market problem and have pulled many of the lines back away from department stores, requested exclusion from department store coupons, reduced inventory to reestablish their brands as true luxury, and moved back toward a true prestige pricing approach once again.[29]

Coach is working hard to maintain the level of exclusivity of its brand necessary to successfully utilize a prestige pricing approach.
Source: Coach, Inc.

Odd/Even Pricing

Odd pricing simply means that the price is not expressed in whole dollars, while **even pricing** is a whole-dollar amount ($1.99 versus $2.00, for example). Odd pricing originally came about before the advent of sales taxes and widespread credit card use to bolster cash register security and reduce theft. That is, if a customer brings a $5.00 item to a clerk and presents a $5.00 bill for payment, it was believed that the temptation would be greater for the clerk to simply pocket the bill and not record the sale. It was reasoned that if the clerk had to make change—say a nickel if the item were priced at $4.95—the likelihood was higher that the sale would actually be rung into the cash register.[30]

Now, the rationale for odd pricing is very different and it is often regarded as a key element of **psychological pricing**, or creating a perception about price merely from the image the numbers provide the customer. Studies indicate that at certain important price breaks—$9.99 versus $10.00, $99.95 versus $100.00, and so on—customers mentally process the price as significantly lower because of the reduced digit count in the price point.[31] However, odd pricing can backfire if misapplied. For example, it seems acceptable for a bottle of Voss to be prestige priced at $12.95 instead of $13.00, but a physician, management consultant, or CPA wouldn't want to charge a client $195 instead of simply $200 for services rendered.

One-Price Strategy and Variable Pricing

An ethnocentric aspect of the U.S. marketplace is the nearly total reliance by marketers on a **one-price strategy** with end-user consumers. That is, except for temporary price reductions for promotional or clearance purposes, the price marked on a good is what it typically sells for. The Snicker bar at the convenience store is $1.25 regardless of whether you are a schoolchild or corporate CEO, and the clerk doesn't want to bargain with you about the price. A one-price strategy makes planning and forecasting infinitely easier than the alternative approach, **variable pricing**, which is found in many other countries and cultures but is relatively rare in the United States. With variable pricing, customers are allowed—even encouraged—to haggle about prices. Ultimately, *the* price is whatever the buyer and seller agree to—a marked price is nothing more than a starting point for negotiation. Variable pricing is traditional in the United States with a few consumer goods—cars, boats, houses, and the like. But it is the pervasive way of doing business with all sorts of products across large parts of the globe.

In the U.S. service sector, variable pricing is much more common. It is also more common in B2B in general versus B2C. When variable pricing is used in the United States, in some cases it carries legal limitations. Many pricing laws have been enacted specifically to protect both channel purchasers and end-user consumers from a variety of unfair pricing practices.

Everyday Low Pricing (EDLP) and High/Low Pricing

The rise of Walmart as one of the world's largest corporations brought the concept of **everyday low pricing (EDLP)** to the forefront of global consumer consciousness. EDLP is not an option just for retailers; it's an important strategic choice for nearly any firm. The fundamental philosophy behind EDLP is to reduce investment in promotion and transfer part of the savings to lower price. Thus, firms practicing an EDLP strategy typically report substantially reduced promotional expenditures on their financial statements. They instead rely much more on generating buzz in the market about the EDLP to create and maintain customer traffic and sales volume. EDLP, when successfully implemented, has a strong advantage of reducing ups and downs in customer traffic, thus making forecasting more accurate.

The antithesis to EDLP is a **high/low pricing** strategy, in which firms rely on periodic heavy *promotional pricing,* primarily communicated through advertising and sales promotion, to build traffic and sales volume. The promotional investment is offset by somewhat higher everyday prices. Why would a firm elect high/low pricing instead of EDLP? Usually, the firm has little choice because of what competitors are doing. It takes a long time for any product or service provider to convince the market that it has EDLP. Most often, firms use various elements of promotion to build sales of new products, shore up sales of declining products, or combat competitors' promotional activity in the same marketplace. Some industries truly are over the top in employing high/low pricing strategies—airlines, auto dealerships, and personal computers are a few that run so many price promotions that customers are conditioned to wait and rarely purchase a product at full price. When high/low pricing reaches this fevered pitch in an industry, it almost always hurts the bottom line of all firms.[32]

Walmart has historically used its EDLP strategy to grow the business and expand its market. Recently Walmart is shifting emphasis from giant supercenters to stores with smaller footprints. As such, the launch and growth of Walmart Neighborhood Market continues to pose a real threat to traditional supermarket competitors like Kroger, Publix, and H-E-B, and even to a degree to niche players like Whole Foods and Trader Joe's. Walmart Neighborhood Markets are smaller stores that are more plentiful and more centrally located within communities than Walmart's traditional supercenters. These markets focus more on the customer experience—especially convenience—and feature an increased array of specialized and fresh foods, offering locally grown produce and organic food items at much more attractive prices than their specialty food competitors. This new Walmart formula combining EDLP and shopper convenience is proving to be a powerful competitive win for the world's largest retailer.[33]

Auction Pricing

Auctions have been around for centuries. In an auction, in which individuals competitively bid against each other and the purchase goes to the high bidder, the market truly sets the price (although some minimum bid amount is often established by the seller). As a strategy, **auction pricing** has gained in prominence as Internet commerce has come of age. Of course, the most famous example of auction pricing is eBay, but there are numerous others. Whereas in the past prices at auction were wholly dependent on the level of demand represented by a fairly small number of people either physically gathered at the auction location or connected through traditional telecommunication, today the Internet provides a vast electronic playing field for customers to participate in the auction on a real-time basis.

This phenomenon has resulted in a marketplace in which auction prices can be considerably more reflective of the real value of an offering versus other static price purchase environments. Besides standard auction approaches (buyers bid for a seller's offering), online **reverse auctions** are now very common in which sellers bid prices to capture a buyer's business. Priceline.com is a prominent example of a reverse auction firm that serves as a clearinghouse for extra capacity from hotels and rental car firms.[34]

SET THE EXACT PRICE

To set an exact price for an offering, be it a good or service, marketing managers should consider several calculations to arrive at the optimal price. We will discuss four methods here that are frequently used: cost-plus pricing/markup on cost, markup on sales price, average-cost pricing, and target return pricing.

LO 11-4

Describe approaches to setting the exact price.

Cost-Plus Pricing/Markup on Cost

Cost-plus pricing is really just a general heuristic that builds a price by adding a standardized markup on top of costs for an offering, hence the term **markup on cost**.[35] First, an estimate of costs involved must be developed. In accounting courses, you learn that determining costs is no easy task. For example, many different types of costs can be considered, including fixed and variable costs, direct costs and indirect costs, and shared or overhead costs, which might be allocated to the offering on some prorated basis. Nevertheless, once a cost has been established, cost-plus pricing requires the predetermination of some standardized markup percentage that is to be applied based on company guidelines. Often, managers will receive a list of standard markup amounts by product line. Easy pricing decision making is the advantage of cost-plus pricing, but for most firms it is too simplistic.

Consider the following example. Assume the firm desires a standard markup of 50 percent over cost. Thus:

$$\text{Cost} = \$ \ 7.00$$
$$\text{Markup on cost} \ (.50 \times \$7.00) = + \$ \ 3.50$$
$$\text{Price} = \$10.50$$

Markup on Sales Price

In determining markup, one approach is to use the sales price as a basis. Consider the following example:

$$\text{Sales price} = \$12.00$$
$$\text{Cost} = \$ \ 7.00$$
$$\text{Markup} = \$ \ 5.00$$

The markup percentage is $\$5.00 \div \$12.00 = 41.7$ percent. That is, the $5.00 markup is 41.7 percent of the sales price. In most applications, when a marketing manager simply refers to "markup," he or she is referring to this calculation—**markup on sales price**, which uses the sales price as a basis for calculating the markup percentage. This is because most important items on financial reports (gross sales, revenue, etc.) are sales, not cost, figures.[36]

All else being equal, calculating a markup on cost makes the markup appear higher than a markup on price even though the dollar figures are identical. For the above example, the markup on cost is $\$5.00 \div \$7.00 = 71.4$ percent, which seems more attractive than the 41.7 percent we calculated above. Sometimes marketers will refer to "100 percent markup," usually meaning they are simply doubling the cost to establish a price.

Average-Cost Pricing

Often pricing decisions are made by identifying all costs associated with an offering to come up with what the average cost of a single unit might be.[37] The basic formula for **average-cost pricing** is:

$$\text{All costs} \div \text{Total number of units} = \text{Average cost of a single unit}$$

To make this calculation requires predicting how much of the offering will be demanded. Assuming total costs of $100,000 and forecasted total number of units of 250, the average cost of a single unit is:

$$\$100,000 \div 250 = \$400$$

One can then add a profit margin to the total cost figures to calculate a likely price for a unit of the offering:

$$\$100{,}000 \text{ total cost} + \$25{,}000 \text{ profit margin} = \$125{,}000$$

Thus, the average price of a single unit based on the above profit margin is:

$$\$125{,}000 \div 250 \text{ units} = \$500$$

Caution is warranted in employing average-cost pricing, as it is always possible that the quantity demanded will not match the marketing manager's forecast. Let's assume that instead of 250, the actual number of units in the above example turns out to be only 200. Revenue would drop to $100,000, but total costs would not drop proportionately because many of the costs are incurred regardless of sales volume. This example vividly illustrates the point made earlier in the chapter that it is unwise to base pricing decisions on costs alone. Market and customer factors must also be carefully considered in establishing a price.

Target Return Pricing

To better take into account the differential impact of fixed and variable costs, marketing managers can use **target return pricing**. First, a few definitions are in order. Fixed costs are incurred over time, regardless of volume. Variable costs fluctuate with volume. And total costs are simply the sum of the fixed and variable costs.[38] To use target return pricing, one must first calculate total fixed costs. Second, a target return must be established. Let's assume that total fixed costs are $250,000 and the target return is set at $50,000 for a total of $300,000.

Next, a demand forecast must be made. If demand is forecast at 1,500 units:

$$(\text{Fixed costs} + \text{Target return}) \div \text{Units} = (\$250{,}000 + \$50{,}000) \div 1{,}500 = \$200 \text{ per unit}$$

Suppose the variable costs per unit are $50. This results in a price per unit of:

$$\$200 + \$50 = \$250$$

As with average-cost pricing, the effectiveness of target return pricing is highly dependent on the accuracy of the forecast. In the example above, if customer demand comes in at 1,000 units instead of 1,500, at a price of $250 the marketing manager will experience a $50 per unit loss!

DETERMINE CHANNEL DISCOUNTS AND ALLOWANCES

Discounts are direct, immediate reductions in price provided to purchasers. **Allowances** remit monies to purchasers after the fact. In general, in B2B transactions, marketing managers must be cognizant of several types of discount and allowance approaches that essentially amount to price adjustments for channel buyers. While the pricing discounts and purchasing allowances mentioned in this section primarily pertain to B2B, in some instances, end-user consumers may be offered some of the same price adjustments.

Sellers offer discounts and allowances for a variety of reasons. Paying a bill early, purchasing a certain quantity, purchasing seasonal products during the off-season, and experiencing an overstock on certain products are common rationales for offering various discounts and allowances. At its essence, the approach hopes to impact purchaser behavior in directions that benefit the selling firm by sweetening the buying organization's terms of sale.

Cash Discounts

Sellers offer **cash discounts** to elicit quicker payment of invoices. The rational purchaser weighs the discount offered for early payment versus the value of keeping the money until it is due. Ideally, the cash discount results in financial advantage for both parties. Cash discounts are stated in a typical format such as 2%/10, Net/40, which translates to the buyer receiving 2 percent off the total bill if payment is received within 10 days of the invoice date, but after that point there is no discount and the whole invoice is due within 40 days of the invoice date.

Trade Discounts

Trade discounts, also sometimes called functional discounts, provide an incentive to a channel member for performing some function in the channel that benefits the seller. Examples include stocking a seller's product or performing a service related to that product, such as installation or repair, within the channel. Trade discounts are normally expressed as a percentage off the invoice price.

Walmart is a master at taking advantage of all types of channel discounts and allowances. Doing so results in lower costs and helps keep their retail prices low for consumers.

© Patrick T. Fallon/Bloomberg via Getty Images

Quantity Discounts

Quantity discounts are taken off an invoice price based on different levels of product purchased. Quantity discounts may be offered on an order-by-order basis, in which case they are noncumulative, or they may be offered on a cumulative basis over time as an incentive to promote customer loyalty. From a legal standpoint, it is essential that quantity discounts are offered to all customers on an equally proportionate basis so that small buyers as well as large buyers follow the same rules for qualification. The later section on legal considerations in pricing extends the discussion about fairness in pricing practices.[39]

Seasonal Discounts

Firms often purchase seasonal products many months before the season begins. For example, a retailer might purchase a winter apparel line at a trade show a year before its season, accept delivery in August, begin displaying it in September, yet cold weather may not hit until November or December. To accommodate such lengthy sales processes, firms offer **seasonal discounts**, which reward the purchaser for shifting part of the inventory storage function away from the manufacturer.[40] Seasonal discounts are often expressed as greatly extended invoice due dates. In the winter clothes line example, terms of 2%/120, Net 145 would not be unusual.

Promotional Allowances

Within a given channel, sellers often want purchasers to help execute their promotional strategies. A consumer products marketer like P&G, for example, depends heavily on wholesalers, distributors, and retailers to promote its brands. When a retailer runs an ad for a P&G brand such as Crest toothpaste, it is nearly always in response to **promotional allowances** provided by the manufacturer. Ordinarily, upon proof of performance of the promotion, the retailer will receive a check back from the manufacturer to compensate for part of the promotional costs. The allowance might be calculated as a percentage of the invoice for Crest purchased from P&G or it might be a fixed dollar figure per dozen or per case.[41]

Geographic Aspects of Pricing

A variety of geographically driven pricing options are common within a channel. Among those most used are FOB pricing, uniform delivered pricing, and zone pricing.

FOB Pricing The initials **FOB** stand for free on board, meaning that title transfer and freight paid on the goods being shipped are based on the FOB location. For example, FOB-origin or FOB-factory pricing indicates that the purchaser pays freight charges and takes title the moment the goods are placed on the truck or other transportation vehicle. The greater the distance between shipper and customer, the higher the freight charges to the customer. In contrast, FOB-destination indicates that until the goods arrive at the purchaser's location, title doesn't change hands and freight charges are the responsibility of the seller.[42]

Uniform Delivered Pricing Many direct-to-consumer marketers such as Amazon and Lands' End practice **uniform delivered pricing**, in which the same delivery fee is charged to customers regardless of geographic location within the 48 contiguous states.[43] Pricing rates are quoted for other locations, and expedited delivery is generally available for a higher fee.

Zone Pricing In a **zone pricing** approach, shippers set up geographic pricing zones based on the distance from the shipping location. The parcel post system of the U.S. Postal Service is set up this way.[44] Rates are calculated for the various combinations of sending and receiving zones.

EXECUTE PRICE CHANGES

LO 11-6

Understand how to execute price changes.

Over time, price changes are inevitable. A marketing manager may want to raise or lower a price for competitive or other reasons, or competitors may make price changes that require a considered pricing response from your own firm. Among the marketing mix variables, price is the easiest and quickest to alter, so sometimes firms overrely on price changes to stimulate additional sales or gain market share. You've already seen that establishing pricing objectives and strategies and implementing pricing tactics are complex and entail important managerial decisions. It is important to also recall that in the overall scope of marketing planning and strategy, pricing does not take place in a vacuum. That is, a change in an offering's price—either up or down—can dramatically impact the effectiveness of the overall marketing mix variables in reflecting your offering's positioning in the eyes of customers.

It is important for marketing managers to conduct appropriate market research in advance of major price changes to try to determine the likely impact of a price change on customer perceptions of the offering and likelihood to purchase. Both qualitative research approaches, such as focus groups, and quantitative approaches, such as surveys and experiments, can be designed to determine the degree to which an anticipated price change might influence customer response. Ideally, price changes upward will reflect the **just noticeable difference (JND)** in a price, which is the amount of price increase that can be taken without affecting customer demand.

If a potential upward price change is being driven by pressure on margins, creative marketers often look for ways to save margin without increasing price. Over the years, candy manufacturers have been severely affected by swings in the price of sugar. As the sugar price has gone up, a good portion of the profit margin of a candy bar has been preserved by simply reducing the size of the bar. Today's chocolate lovers would be amazed at seeing how much larger a Snickers bar was in 1970 versus today. At the same time, the basic bar size has shrunk multiple times during that period, including the most recent 10 percent reduction (and concurrent 30-calorie reduction) in early 2013. While the price of a bar has also risen dramatically during the same period (an average of four times the 1970 price), the price increase would have been even more dramatic without the reduction in ounces.

In addition to reducing the offering in terms of size or quantity, other nonprice approaches to mitigating the pressure to maintain margins include altering or reducing discounts and allowances, unbundling some services or features from the original offering, increasing minimum order quantities, or simply reducing product quality. However, marketing managers should be cautious when they begin to consider altering the product itself to retain margins; customer response to such tinkering might be negative.

A worst-case scenario occurs when a firm takes a price decrease on an offering to stimulate volume and grow share, only to have one or more competitors immediately and aggressively jump in to meet or beat the price decrease, resulting in a price war. Price wars are the quickest way to destroy margins and bottom-line profit. The old marketing adage "We'll price our product lower but make it up on volume" doesn't work when competitive price pressure forces prices below cost!

Assume that you, as a marketing manager, just found out that a competitor has taken a price increase or decrease. You must evaluate the change and select the appropriate response for your product line. The basic principles and cautions about competing on price are the same, regardless of whether your firm or a competitor fires the first shot. If your firm is the market leader, you may find that competitors tend to create similar but somewhat inferior offerings at attractive prices in an attempt to knock you off as leader.

When formulating a response to a competitor's price reduction, remember to consider your offering from the perspective of its overall value proposition to customers and not be too quick to react in kind with a price decrease. In the case of a competitor's price increase, perhaps based on escalating costs or margin pressure, analysis may reveal the increase is an opportunity to both gain a price advantage and perhaps increase your volume and share, especially if you are a cost leader and can maintain desired margins at your current price. Or you may simply wish to take a concurrent price increase and enjoy the related margin enhancement. Remember, a cost leadership strategy does not necessarily imply price leadership; rather, the best cost leader firms take a portion of their cost leadership to margin and perhaps a portion to price advantage.

UNDERSTAND LEGAL CONSIDERATIONS IN PRICING

In the process of setting pricing objectives and developing and implementing pricing strategies and tactics, marketing managers must be aware that some aspects of pricing decision making can be very sensitive legally. Laws at the national, state, and local levels are in place that impact a firm's pricing practices. Federal legislation includes the Sherman Antitrust Act (1890), Clayton Act (1914), Robinson-Patman Act (1936), and Consumer Goods Pricing Act (1975). The Federal Trade Commission (FTC) actively monitors and enforces federal pricing laws. Several of the more important legal considerations in pricing and their associated regulatory bases are discussed below.

Price-Fixing

Companies that collude to set prices at a mutually beneficial high level are engaged in **price-fixing**. When competitors are involved in the collusion, horizontal price-fixing occurs.[45] The Sherman Act forbids horizontal price-fixing, which could result in overall higher prices for consumers since various competitors are all pricing the same to maximize their profits.

When independent members of a channel (for example, manufacturers, distributors, and retailers) collude to establish a minimum retail price, referred to as retail price maintenance, vertical price-fixing occurs. Vertical price-fixing is illegal under the Consumer Goods Pricing Act, and for good reason. Vertical price-fixing ensures everybody in the channel is satisfied with their "cut" of the profits, but the profit boost is achieved by increased prices to consumers.

Price Discrimination

Price discrimination occurs when a seller offers different prices to different customers without a substantive basis, such that competition is reduced. The Robinson-Patman Act explicitly prohibits giving, inducing, or receiving discriminatory prices except under certain specific conditions such as situations where proof exists that the costs of selling to one customer are higher than to another (such as making distributions to remote locations) or when temporary, defensive price reductions are necessary to meet competition in a specific local area.[46]

Deceptive Pricing

Knowingly stating prices in a manner that gives a false impression to customers is **deceptive pricing**. Deceptive pricing practices are monitored and enforced by the FTC. Deceptive pricing may take several forms. Sometimes, firms will set artificially high reference prices for merchandise just before a promotion so that an advertised sale price will look much more attractive to customers.[47] Or a seller may advertise an item at an unbelievably low price to lure customers into a store, and once the customer arrives refuse to sell the advertised item and instead push a similar item with a much higher price and higher margin. When this occurs and it can be demonstrated that a seller had no true intent to actually make the lower-priced item available for sale, the practice is called **bait and switch** and is illegal. Finally, the ubiquitous reliance of retailers on scanner-based pricing has opened a plethora of stealth pricing fraud schemes, perpetrated by dishonest retailers who label an item on the shelf sign at a lower price than it is actually priced within the scanner database. For certain, some of the scanner errors result from mistakes and not fraud, but the non-transparent nature of scanner pricing puts a burden on the customer to return to the days of "buyer beware."

Predatory Pricing

A strategy to intentionally sell below cost to push a competitor out of a market, then raise prices to new highs, is called predatory pricing. Predatory pricing is illegal but prosecuting it can be very tricky because intent must be proved. Other plausible explanations exist for drastic price reductions including inventory overstocks, so proving that predatory pricing has occurred is difficult.

Fair Trade and Minimum Markup Laws

Fair trade laws were popular in the past because they allowed manufacturers to establish artificially high prices by limiting the ability of wholesalers and retailers to offer reduced or discounted prices. Fair trade laws varied greatly from state to state, depending largely on how strong the independent retailer and wholesaler lobby was in a particular locale. These laws protected mom-and-pop operators from the price discounting by chain stores.[48]

Closely associated with fair trade laws are **minimum markup laws**, which require a certain percentage markup be applied to products. In one extreme case in the 1970s, the State of Oklahoma took legal action against Target Corporation to force the discounter to obey Oklahoma's minimum markup law that prohibited advertising a wide variety of merchandise for less than a 6 percent profit. This effectively shut down Target's ability to advertise **loss leader products**, items (typically paper towels, toilet paper, toothpaste, and the like) sacrificed at prices below cost to attract shoppers to the store.[49] Target fought back by creating special versions of its famous full-color Sunday advertising inserts for Oklahoma shoppers that showed in very large type the nationally advertised sales price accompanied by a disclaimer clearly showing a much higher "in Oklahoma" price. In effect, the ads told Oklahomans they couldn't get the same prices as the rest of the country, and it didn't take long for Oklahoma consumers to come to their senses and realize that the state's fair pricing law might protect small retailers, but it hurt everyday shoppers. In 1975, the federal Consumer Goods Pricing Act repealed all state fair trade laws and minimum markup laws.

SUMMARY

Clearly, price is a critical element in an offering's perceived value. Marketing managers must establish clear pricing objectives and related strategies, supported by well-executed pricing tactics. In setting the exact price, it is best to compare several approaches before making a decision. Several channel discounts and allowances are available that can impact purchaser behavior in ways that benefit the selling firm. Price changes are inevitable and marketing managers must anticipate customer and competitor responses. Finally, marketing managers must be sensitive to legal ramifications of certain pricing practices.

KEY TERMS

APPLICATION QUESTIONS

1. Why might penetration pricing potentially negatively impact brand image and product positioning in the long run? Given this risk, why would a marketing manager use penetration pricing? Identify a brand (other than the examples in the chapter) that you believe is engaged in penetration pricing.

connect

More application questions are available online.

2. Pricing against competitors is common. Yet the approach carries some significant problems.

   a. What are the advantages of competitor-based pricing?

   b. What are the risks of using competitor-based pricing exclusive of other approaches?

   c. Identify a few industries in which taking competitor-based pricing into account might be especially beneficial when developing an overall pricing strategy. What caused you to select the industries you did?

3. Review Exhibit 11.3 on price-quality positioning, along with the accompanying discussion.

   a. Consider the low quality/high price quadrant. Identify a brand (other than the examples in the chapter) that you believe currently resides in this quadrant. How is it able to command a high price? Do you believe the pricing strategy is sustainable for that brand? Why or why not?

    b. Consider the high quality/low price quadrant. Identify a brand (other than the examples in the chapter) that you believe currently resides in this quadrant. In your opinion, why has the brand undertaken this pricing strategy? Do you believe there are risks to the brand in remaining too long in that quadrant? Why or why not?

4. Select any three of the pricing tactics identified in the chapter. For *each* tactic:

    a. Identify a brand (other than the examples in the chapter) that you believe is currently employing that tactic.

    b. Provide evidence to support the use of that tactic.

    c. Is the use of the tactic effective? Why or why not?

    d. What factors might cause a need to abandon this tactic in favor of another?

5. Assume that you are a marketing manager for Pantene shampoo and conditioner, two of P&G's star products, and that several of P&G's competitors have recently begun to cut prices to retailers and also to offer more aggressive channel allowances to boost sales and market share.

    a. What options do you have as a response to the competitive price declines?

    b. What are the risks associated with each of the options?

    c. Assuming Pantene is the market leader in its category, what response to the price cuts do you recommend?

MANAGEMENT DECISION CASE
Surge Pricing: But Is It a Surge of Customer Value?

Would you be willing to pay a higher price for a good or service just because demand is high? Actually, you may already be doing so more often than you think. When demand is up, consumers pay higher prices for airline seats, hotel rooms, electricity (in some cities), theater tickets, and even newly minted and (seemingly scarce) iPhones. Some of these prices, such as those for airline seats, react quickly to changes in demand, changing even within minutes as bookings occur. Other prices shift over a longer period, as in price skimming or penetration pricing strategies you read about in the chapter. Of note, and as often commented on by the press and on social media, is a demand-based pricing strategy that is referred to as "surge pricing," that is, pricing flexibly based on real-time market demand. One company that's received a lot of attention for its implementation of surge pricing is the ride-sharing firm Uber.

Uber currently completes about 40 million rides globally per month (that's about 54,000 rides per hour).[50] A key aspect of its business model is the fact that drivers are not considered employees of Uber, but rather independent contractors. This means that Uber cannot mandate specific hours a driver must work, and hence it's entirely possible there might be a shortage of passenger capacity available when a particular rider wants to take a trip. To manage this,

Uber has two forms of pricing: The first and more traditional approach bases a fare on variables such as route, traffic conditions, and number of riders. Most conventional taxis use this approach—after all, it makes sense to a customer that a 40-mile ride to the airport costs more than a ride to the supermarket 3 miles away. The value proposition to the customer of those two scenarios is clear. But the customer value proposition behind surge pricing is not so self-evident!

Uber makes the switch to surge pricing at times of high demand. (For the record, Disney does the same thing at its theme parks, so don't get the idea that surge pricing is evil.) As Uber explains it, "Fares may increase to make sure those who need a ride can get one. Surge rates are charged as a multiplier of X. For example, a rider in a surging area may see and accept a surge multiplier of 1.3x or 2.1x."[51] Breaking down the math simply, a surge multiplier of 2x on a fare that is normally $10 would mean the new fare is now $20, or twice as much.

If customers were perfect economists, they would understand and accept that when the supply of drivers is down it's reasonable for prices to go up as the customer is vying for a scarcer resource. But alas, many riders feel that Uber's implementation of surge pricing is a form of price gouging.[52] Perhaps it is the uncertainty and unpredictability of it—Uber's surge pricing can kick in suddenly and frequently (up to 20 times an hour), and the multiplier does not have a known cap (there have been cases of local fares that were more than $300).[53] This price variability makes it difficult for customers with some flexibility to decide when to request a ride, as they're unsure if waiting a few minutes will result in a lower or higher price.[54] Further exacerbating the issue is the fact that Uber has marketed the value of surge pricing almost exclusively to drivers, and not to riders. Professor Utpal Dholakia, a pricing expert at Rice University, suggests that Uber should instead be explaining the benefit of surge pricing to the customer, and that even the name "surge pricing" is focused on the driver side of the transaction rather than its riders.[55] Put another way, it's hard for the customer to think of surge pricing as adding value to them when it seems focused only on the upside to Uber of the supply/demand relationship.

In the end, for marketing managers the concept of surge pricing is really not that new and is certainly not limited to just Uber (we've already mentioned that Disney uses it). In fact, even automated surge pricing has been tested in the past, with Coke deploying vending machines specially outfitted with thermometers in the price display to investigate the potential for raising the price of the soda as the temperature went up.[56] Electronic shelf labels that would allow retail stores to change prices automatically based on stock and demand are already available, if not widely implemented.[57] And some upscale restaurants have taken to selling prepaid meal tickets, with higher prices during peak dining times. Believe it or not, even the city of Chicago is getting into the act, as it is installing surge-priced parking meters near Wrigley Field to capture more revenue during games.

So despite the negative attention Uber received for its surge pricing—which as we now understand may be more attributable to its implementation and communication with customers than the practice of surge pricing per se—it's clearly a valid pricing strategy that we'll all as customers likely experience more commonly in the future.

Questions for Consideration

1. While many consumers don't like Uber's surge pricing, it can't easily be claimed that it is price-fixing (as it is not coordinated with competitors such as Lyft), price discrimination (as all customers in a surge area are subject to the same price increase), or deceptive pricing (Uber is nothing if not obvious about the price increase). Thus, despite the negative reactions, surge pricing is legal. Do you agree that it should be legal? Build a strong case either way, depending on your feelings about surge pricing.

2. What adjustments and improvements to the implementation and communication with customers about Uber's surge pricing strategy do you suggest in order to help those customers better understand the value proposition and improve acceptance? How might you explain surge pricing to consumers so the benefit they receive from it is better understood?

3. If surge pricing were found to be illegal, do you think prices for Uber's service would rise in general? Why or why not?

MARKETING PLAN EXERCISE

ACTIVITY 12: Price Your Offering

As you learned in this chapter, your approach to pricing is an integral aspect of positioning your offering. Price sends a signal to customers about the offering's quality and other characteristics. At the same time, effective pricing ensures margins and profits needed for continued success.

1. Review the options for pricing objectives and strategies and establish an appropriate set for your offering.

2. Review the various available pricing tactics and select a mix of tactics that you believe is most appropriate for your offering.

3. Consider the methods of establishing an exact price presented in the chapter. Use these approaches to develop a comparative set for review. Select a final price for the offering.

4. What channel discounts and allowances will you provide on your offering?

NOTES

1. Richard G. Netemeyer, Balaji Krishnan, Chris Pullig, and Guangping Wang, "Developing and Validating Measures of Facets of Customer-Based Brand Equity," *Journal of Business Research* 57, no. 2 (February 2004), pp. 209–24.

2. Richard J. Speed, "Oh Mr. Porter! A Re-Appraisal of Competitive Strategy," *Marketing Intelligence & Planning* 7, no. 5/6 (1989), pp. 8–11.

3. Roy W. Ralston, "The Effects of Customer Service, Branding, and Price on the Perceived Value of Local Telephone Service," *Journal of Business Research* 56, no. 3 (March 2003), pp. 201–13.

4. Kent B. Monroe, "Pricing Practices That Endanger Profits," *Marketing Management* 10, no. 3 (September/October 2001), pp. 42–46.

5. George J. Avlonitis and Kostis A. Indounas, "Pricing Objectives and Pricing Methods in the Services Sector," *Journal of Services Marketing* 19, no. 1 (2005), pp. 47–57.

6. T. Gara, "Your Donut Loyalty Will Soon Be Rewarded," *The Wall Street Journal,* January 31, 2013, http://blogs.wsj.com /corporate-intelligence/2013/01/31/your-donut-loyalty-will -soon-be-rewarded/; and https://www.dunkindonuts.com/en /dd-perks.

7. Yikuan Lee and Gina Colarelli O'Connor, "New Product Launch Strategy for Network Effects Products," *Journal of the Academy of Marketing Science* 31, no. 3 (Summer 2003), pp. 241–55.

8. Angel F. Villarejo-Ramos and Manuel J. Sanchez-Franco, "The Impact of Marketing Communication and Price Promotion on Brand Equity," *Journal of Brand Management* 12, no. 6 (August 2005), pp. 431–44.

9. Neil Kokemuller, "Penetration Pricing Examples," *Azcentral,* http://yourbusiness.azcentral.com/penetration-pricing -examples-13162.html; "Lay's Stax," *Walmart,* https://www .walmart.com/search/searchng.do?search_query=lay%27s+ stax&ic=16_0&Find=Find&search_constraint=0;and"Pringles Original Potato Crisps," Walmart, https://www.walmart.com /ip/PRINGLES-CRISPS-ORIGINAL-6.8OZ/136119600 ?wmlspartner=wlpa&selectedSellerId=0&adid=22222 222227075684943&wmlspartner=wmtlabs&wl0=&wl1 =g&wl2=c&wl3=188286056570&wl4=pla-291896542270&wl5 =9011778&wl6=&wl7=&wl8=&wl9=pla&wl10=8175035&wl11 =online&wl12=136119600&wl13=&veh=sem.

10. Ana Garrido-Rubio and Yolanda Polo-Redondo, "Tactical Launch Decisions: Influence on Innovation Success/Failure," *Journal of Product and Brand Management* 14, no. 1 (2005), pp. 29–38.

11. Ioana Popescu and Yaozhong Wu, "Dynamic Pricing Strategies with Reference Effects," *Operations Research* 55, no. 3 (May/June 2007), pp. 413–32.

12. Mark Burton and Steve Haggett, "Rocket PLAN," *Marketing Management* 16, no. 5 (September/October 2007), p. 32.

13. Tulin Erdem, Michael P. Keane, and Baohong Sun, "The Impact of Advertising on Consumer Price Sensitivity in Experience Goods Markets," *Quantitative Marketing and Economics* 6, no. 2 (June 2008), pp. 139–76.

14. Harun Ahmet Kuyumcu, "Emerging Trends in Scientific Pricing," *Journal of Revenue and Pricing Management* 6, no. 4 (December 2007), pp. 293–99.

15. Daniel Kozarich, "Mylan's EpiPen Pricing Crossed Ethical Boundaries," *Fortune,* September 27, 2016, http://fortune .com/2016/09/27/mylan-epipen-heather-bresch/; Nathan Bomey, "CVS Targets EpiPen with Cheaper Generic Version," *USAToday,* January 12, 2017, https://www.usatoday .com/story/money/2017/01/12/cvs-health-mylan-epipen-injector -impax-adrenaclick-donald-trump/96479776/.

16. Tridib Mazumdar, S. P. Raj, and Indrajit Sinha, "Reference Price Research: Review and Propositions," *Journal of Marketing* 69, no. 4 (October 2005), pp. 84–102; and Xueming Luo, Aric Rindfleisch, and David K. Tse, "Working with Rivals: The Impact of Competitor Alliances on Financial Performance," *Journal of Marketing Research* 44, no. 1 (February 2007), pp. 73–83.

17. Marc Vanhuele and Xavier Dreze, "Measuring the Price Knowledge Shoppers Bring to the Store," *Journal of Marketing* 66, no. 4 (October 2002), pp. 72–85.

18. Kusum Ailawadi, Donald R. Lehmann, and Scott A. Neslin, "Market Response to a Major Policy Change in the Marketing Mix: Learning from Procter & Gamble's Value Pricing Strategy," *Journal of Marketing* 65, no. 1 (January 2001), pp. 44–61.

19. Stephan Zielke and Thomas Dobbelstein, "Customers' Willingness to Purchase New Store Brands," *Journal of Product and Brand Management* 16, no. 2 (2007), pp. 112–21.

20. Matt Egan, "Wells Fargo Customers in $110 Million Settlement over Fake Accounts," *CNN Money,* March 29, 2017, http://money.cnn.com/2017/03/29/investing/wells-fargo -settles-fake-account-lawsuit-110-million/; and Michael Corkery, "Wells Fargo Struggling in Aftermath of Fraud Scandal," *New York Times,* January 13, 2017, https://www.nytimes .com/2017/01/13/business/dealbook/wells-fargo-earnings -report.html?_r=0.

21. Michaela Draganska and Dipak C. Jain, "Consumer Preferences and Product-Line Pricing Strategies: An Empirical Analysis," *Marketing Science* 25, no. 2 (March/April 2006), pp. 164–75.

22. Jordan Golson, "The Mustang at 50: Inside the Evolution of an American Icon," *Wired,* April 17, 2014, https://www.wired .com/2014/04/ford-mustang-50th-anniversary/; and "2017 Mustang," *Ford,* http://shop.ford.com/build/mustang/?gnav =vhpnav#/chooseyourpath/Config%5B%7CFord%7C Mustang%7C2017%7C1%7C1.%7C900A.P8J...COU.SLB.~YZKAA .SHB.LESS.%5D.

23. Baba Shiv, Ziv Carmon, and Dan Ariely, "Placebo Effects of Marketing Actions: Consumers May Get What They Pay For," *Journal of Marketing Research* 42, no. 4 (November 2005), pp. 383–93.

24. Michael Levy, Dhruv Grewal, Praveen K. Kopalle, and James D. Hess, "Emerging Trends in Retail Pricing Practice: Implications for Research," *Journal of Retailing* 80, no. 3 (2004), pp. 13–21.

25. Chris Janiszewski and Marcus Cunha Jr., "The Influence of Price Discount Framing on the Evaluation of a Product Bundle," *Journal of Consumer Research* 30, no. 4 (March 2004), pp. 534–46.

26. "The Future of Television: Cutting the Cord," *Economist,* June 16, 2016, http://www.economist.com/news /business/21702177-television-last-having-its-digital-revolution -moment-cutting-cord; Steve Kovach, and "YouTube's Cable-Killing Live-TV Streaming Service Is Coming This Week," *Business Insider,* February 28, 2017, http://www .businessinsider.com/youtube-unplugged-streaming-tv -service-tuesday-2017-2.

27. Daniel J. Howard and Roger A. Kerin, "Broadening the Scope of Reference Price Advertising Research: A Field Study of Consumer Shopping Involvement," *Journal of Marketing* 70, no. 4 (October 2006), pp. 185–204.

28. James McClure and Erdogan Kumcu, "Promotions and Product Pricing: Parsimony versus Veblenesque Demand," *Journal of Economic Behavior & Organization* 65, no. 1 (January 2008), pp. 105–17.

29. "Michael Kors Has a Coach Problem," *Investopedia*, May 26, 2016, http://www.investopedia.com/stock-analysis/052616/michael-kors-has-coach-problem-coh-kors-jwn-m.aspx?ad=dirN&qo=serpSearchTopBox&qsrc=1&o=40186; and Sarah Halzack, "It's About to Get a Lot Harder to Get a Discounted Coach or Michael Kors Handbag," *Washington Post*, August 10, 2016, https://www.washingtonpost.com/news/business/wp/2016/08/10/its-about-to-get-a-lot-harder-to-get-a-discounted-coach-or-michael-kors-handbag/?utm_term=.66f809d1cff5.

30. Robert M. Schindler and Alan R. Wiman, "Effects of Odd Pricing on Price Recall," *Journal of Business Research* 19, no. 3 (November 1989), pp. 165–77.

31. John Huston and Nipoli Kamdar, "$9.99: Can 'Just-Below' Pricing Be Reconciled with Rationality?" *Eastern Economic Journal* 22, no. 2 (Spring 1996), pp. 137–45.

32. Kathleen Seiders and Glenn B. Voss, "From Price to Purchase," *Marketing Management* 13, no. 6 (November/December 2004), pp. 38–43.

33. Hayley Peterson, "What It's Like inside Wal-Mart's New Marketplace That's a Threat to Whole Foods and Trader Joe's," *Business Insider*, July 4, 2015, http://www.businessinsider.com/inside-walmarts-neighborhood-markets-2015-7; and Doug McMillon, "Why Walmart Is Positioned to Win the Future of Retail," *Walmart Blog*, October 14, 2015, http://blog.walmart.com/business/20160115/doug-mcmillon-answers-questions-about-sharpened-focus-on-stores.

34. Christian Terwiesch, Sergei Savin, and Il-Horn Hann, "Online Haggling at a Name-Your-Own-Price Retailer: Theory and Application," *Management Science* 51, no. 3 (March 2005), pp. 339–52.

35. Chris Guilding, Colin Drury, and Mike Tayles, "An Empirical Investigation of the Importance of Cost-Plus Pricing," *Managerial Auditing Journal* 20, no. 2 (2005), pp. 125–37.

36. J. Isaac Brannon, "The Effects of Resale Price Maintenance Laws on Petrol Prices and Station Attrition: Empirical Evidence from Wisconsin," *Applied Economics* 35, no. 3 (February 2003), pp. 343–49.

37. Chuan He and Yuxin Chen, "Managing e-Marketplace: A Strategic Analysis of Nonprice Advertising," *Management Science* 25, no. 2 (March/April 2006), pp. 175–87.

38. Ben Vinod, "Retail Revenue Management and the New Paradigm of Merchandise Optimisation," *Journal of Revenue and Pricing Management* 3, no. 4 (January 2005), pp. 358–68.

39. George J. Avlonitis and Kostis A. Indounas, "Pricing Practices of Service Organizations," *Journal of Services Marketing* 20, no. 5 (2006), pp. 346–57.

40. Keith S. Coulter, "Decreasing Price Sensitivity Involving Physical Product Inventory: A Yield Management Application," *Journal of Product and Brand Management* 10, no. 4/5 (2001), pp. 301–17.

41. Kusum L. Ailawadi and Bari Harlam, "An Empirical Analysis of the Determinants of Retail Margins: The Role of Store-Brand Share," *Journal of Marketing* 68, no. 1 (January 2004), pp. 147–65.

42. Fred S. McChesney and William F. Shughart II, "Delivered Pricing in Theory and Policy Practice," *Antitrust Bulletin* 52, no. 2 (Summer 2007), pp. 205–28.

43. Hiroshi Ohta, Yan-Shu Lin, and Masa K. Naito, "Spatial Perfect Competition: A Uniform Delivered Pricing Model," *Pacific Economic Review* 10, no. 4 (December 2005), pp. 407–20.

44. Pradeep K. Chintagunta, Jean-Pierre Dube, and Vishal Singh, "Balancing Profitability and Customer Welfare in a Supermarket Chain," *Quantitative Marketing and Economics* 1, no. 1 (March 2003), pp. 111–46.

45. John M. Connor, "Forensic Economics: An Introduction with Special Emphasis on Price Fixing," *Journal of Competition Law & Economics* 4, no. 1 (March 2008), pp. 21–59.

46. Siva Viswanathan, Jason Kuruzovich, Sanjay Gosain, and Ritu Agarwal, "Online Infomediaries and Price Discrimination: Evidence from the Automotive Retailing Sector," *Journal of Marketing* 71, no. 3 (July 2007), pp. 89–107.

47. Allan J. Kimmel, "Deception in Marketing Research and Practice: An Introduction," *Psychology & Marketing* 18, no. 7 (July 2001), pp. 657–61.

48. Jules Stuyck, Evelyne Terryn, and Tom van Dyck, "Confidence through Fairness? The New Directive on Unfair Business-to-Consumer Commercial Practices in the Internal Market," *Common Market Law Review* 43, no. 1 (February 2006), pp. 107–52.

49. Patrick DeGraba, "The Loss Leader Is a Turkey: Targeted Discounts from Multi-Product Competitors," *International Journal of Industrial Organization* 24, no. 3 (May 2006), pp. 613–28.

50. "Uber Cities," *Uber*, May 9, 2017, https://uberestimator.com/cities; and Kia Kokalitcheva, "Uber Now Has 40 Million Monthly Riders Worldwide," *Fortune*, October 19, 2016, http://fortune.com/2016/10/20/uber-app-riders/.

51. "What Is Surge?" *Uber*, 2016, https://help.uber.com/h/e9375d5e-917b-4bc5-8142-23b89a440eec.

52. Annie Lowrey, "Is Uber's Surge-Pricing an Example of High-Tech Gouging?" *New York Times*, January 10, 2014, https://www.nytimes.com/2014/01/12/magazine/is-ubers-surge-pricing-an-example-of-high-tech-gouging.html?_r=0.

53. Steve Kovach, "Uber Did Its Best to Warn You about New Year's Eve Surge Pricing, but Everyone Complained Anyway," *Business Insider*, January 1, 2014, http://www.businessinsider.com/uber-new-years-eve-surge-pricing-2014-1.

54. Nicholas Diakopoulos, "How Uber Surge Pricing Really Works," *Washington Post*, April 17, 2015, https://www.washingtonpost.com/news/wonk/wp/2015/04/17/how-uber-surge-pricing-really-works/?utm_term=.896a547414e5.

55. Utpal M. Dholakia, "Everyone Hates Uber's Surge Pricing—Here's How to Fix It," *Harvard Business Review*, December 21, 2015, https://hbr.org/2015/12/everyone-hates-ubers-surge-pricing-heres-how-to-fix-it.

56. Constance L. Hays, "Variable-Price Coke Machine Being Tested," *New York Times*, October 28, 1999, http://www.nytimes.com/1999/10/28/business/variable-price-coke-machine-being-tested.html.

57. John Byrne, "Emanuel's Wrigleyville 'Surge Pricing' for Parking Could Be Just the Beginning," *Chicago Tribune*, March 24, 2017, http://www.chicagotribune.com/news/local/politics/ct-wrigley-field-surge-pricing-emanuel-met-20170323-story.html; and Robins Kaplan, "Dynamic Pricing: Is 'Surge' Pricing Coming to Retail?" *JD Supra*, April 13, 2017, https://www.jdsupra.com/legalnews/dynamic-pricing-is-surge-pricing-coming-60868/.

CHAPTER 12

Manage Marketing Channels, Logistics, and Supply Chain

LEARNING OBJECTIVES

LO 12-1 Define a value network and how organizations operate within this approach.

LO 12-2 Identify various types of intermediaries and distribution channels.

LO 12-3 Understand the impact of intermediary contributions via physical distribution functions, transaction and communication functions, and facilitating functions.

LO 12-4 Explain the different types of vertical marketing systems.

LO 12-5 Utilize suitable criteria to select appropriate channel approaches.

LO 12-6 Identify the logistics aspects of supply chain management.

LO 12-7 Understand the role of retailing and e-commerce in delivering the value offering to the customer.

THE VALUE CHAIN AND VALUE NETWORKS

The concept of the value chain, which was introduced in Chapter 3, is worth revisiting at this point. The value chain portrays a synthesis of primary and support activities utilized by an organization to design, produce, market, deliver, and support its products (see Exhibit 12.1).

EXHIBIT 12.1 │ **Porter's Generic Value Chain**

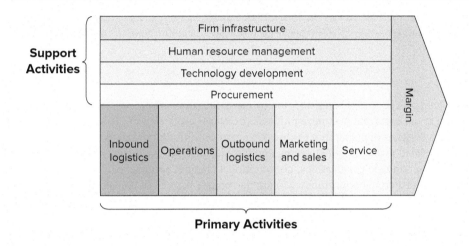

Source: Porter, Michael, E., *Competitive Advantage: Creating and Sustaining Superior Performance.* New York, NY: Simon & Schuster, 1998.

Several of the value chain activities are directly relevant to what you will read about in this chapter, including inbound and outbound logistics, operations issues, and procurement. A **supply chain** represents all organizations involved in supplying a firm, the members of its channels of distribution, and its end-user consumers and business users. The goal is coordination of these value-adding flows among the entities in a way that maximizes overall value delivered and profit realized.[1] The management of this process is called **supply chain management**. Emblematic of the central role that channel and supply chain issues play in forming the value proposition of modern firms, it is telling that today more and more marketing managers are turning to elements of the "place P" within the 4Ps of the marketing mix for sources of differential competitive advantage.[2] How value is added by successfully managing a firm's channels and the supply chain is the central topic of this chapter.

At the broadest level, a firm might view itself as an integral part of a **value network**, which may be thought of as an overarching system of formal and informal relationships within which the firm participates to procure, transform and enhance, and ultimately supply its offerings in final form within a market space. Value networks are fluid and complex. They are composed of potentially numerous firms with which a company interacts vertically within its channel of distribution and horizontally across other firms whose contributions are essential to getting the right offering to the right customers. A value network perspective is a macro-level

Yes, FedEx delivers packages—but it also prides itself on being a provider of integrated supply chain solutions to businesses of all kinds.

Source: FedEx

EXHIBIT 12.2 | Elements of a Value Network

- The overarching process focus is on value co-creation.
- A shared vision exists within the network with a common aim of fostering value co-creation.
- Value co-creation is viewed as emanating from the expertise and competencies of all parties within the network.

- Network and team *relationships* are key elements in the co-creation of the value.
- This value is viewed as *network value.*
- Relationship conflicts are viewed as potential barriers to the creation of network value and a process for conflict co-management is essential.

Source: Stephen L. Vargo and Robert F. Lusch, "Evolving to a New Dominant Logic for Marketing," *Journal of Marketing* 68 (January 2004), pp. 1–17.

strategic approach that is being adopted by many firms in part because of the intense competition to cut costs and maximize process efficiencies every step of the way to market. The approach suggests opportunities for breaking outside of traditional thinking that marketing is encapsulated *within* an organization, and instead suggests looking for such opportunities as alliances, strategic partnerships, nontraditional channel approaches, episodic collaborations, and outsourcing opportunities to provide unique sources of competitive edge.[3]

At its core, a value network exists to co-create value. The aim is **value co-creation** by the participating suppliers, customers, and other stakeholders in which the members of the network combine capabilities according to their expertise and the competencies required from the situation.[4] The key elements of a value network are portrayed in Exhibit 12.2.

Based on the concept of value networks, a whole new breed of organization is arising called a **network organization**, or **virtual organization**, because it eliminates many in-house business functions and activities in favor of focusing only on those aspects for which it is best equipped to add value.[5] Such approaches are often pursued to provide quicker market response and to free resources to focus on the firm's core deliverables. Network firms usually formalize contracts with suppliers, distributors, and other important partners to contribute the aspects of the value chain those entities do best, then draw on their own internal capabilities to focus on core internal sources of value. Some network organizations operate much like a shell in which most or all of the actual manufacturing, distribution, operations, and maybe even R&D and marketing execution are outsourced to efficient experts.[6]

The now infamous Chipotle Mexican Grills restaurants' food illness outbreaks a few years back evidenced the critical role that supply chain management plays in a company's success. In 2015, Chipotle experienced numerous food-borne illness outbreaks within its restaurants, including salmonella, *E. coli*, and norovirus, that infected scores of customers in Chipotle restaurants across the United States. Chipotle built huge brand loyalty among millennials through its "build-your-own" menu layout as well as its commitment to ethical food standards. However, since the food-borne illness outbreaks, some have argued that these very standards, which contributed to Chipotle's success, are also responsible for Chipotle's supply chain breakdowns, which compromised the integrity of its food—the very thing Chipotle champions. Due to its farm-raised, hormone-free meat policy, Chipotle has had difficulty finding sufficient numbers of sustainable suppliers who meet their standards. At times, this has resulted in meat shortages for the restaurant chain. In essence, Chipotle's supply chain historically has been comprised of many small, local suppliers. The approach is great for sustainability but makes it considerably more challenging both to ensure food safety in the first place and to trace the origins of any food-borne illnesses that may manifest within its supply chain.[7]

In the future, more firms, and especially start-ups, entrepreneurial organizations, and those whose core products are in the critical introduction and growth phases, will opt for a network organization approach to take advantage of the value network concept. This prediction is based on a competitive need for firms to be **nimble** in all aspects of their operation— that is, to be in a position to be maximally flexible, adaptable, and speedy in response to the many key change drivers affecting business today such as rapidly shifting technology, discontinuous innovation, fickle consumer markets, and relentless market globalization.[8] Taking a value network approach frees up internal resources so a firm can be more nimble in addressing external uncontrollable opportunities and threats, thus yielding a potential competitive advantage over firms that have high costs associated with performing many of the value chain functions themselves. A network organization facilitates concentration on one's own distinctive competencies while efficiently gathering value from outside firms that are concentrating their efforts in their own areas of expertise within your value network.

Many organizations are beginning to consider their customers—both end users and within a channel—as important members of a value network. That is, firms cultivate customer involvement in various aspects of product and market development to enable customer advocacy, which is a willingness and ability on the part of a customer to participate in communicating the brand message to others within his or her sphere of influence. There are several potential value-adding ways to involve customers, in both B2B and B2C settings, including participation in ongoing research and customer advisory panels and provision of recognition, rewards, and delightful surprises for customers that participate in the relationship at a high level.

Overall, managing marketing channels and the supply chain is a fruitful area of concentration for marketing managers because of its potential to enhance the value of the firm's goods and services in a variety of ways. As you read further about the various specific components of the "place P" in the marketing mix, keep in mind that in today's business environments, the boundaries of just *how* these value-adding activities are delivered and *by whom* within the value network is a very open opportunity. As we have learned, these decisions are made with the knowledge that intelligent investment in the primary and support activities within the value chain should positively enhance profit margin through more efficient and effective firm performance.

CHANNELS AND INTERMEDIARIES

A **channel of distribution** consists of interdependent entities that are aligned for the purpose of transferring possession of a product from producer to consumer or business user. Put another way, a channel is a system of interdependent relationships among a set of organizations that facilitates the exchange process.[9] Most channels are not direct from producer to consumer. Instead, they contain a variety of **intermediaries**, formerly called middlemen, that play a role in the exchange process between producer and consumer.[10] A wide variety of types of intermediaries exist, and they usually fall within two principal categories: **merchant intermediaries**, who take title to the product, and **agent intermediaries**, who do not take title to the product.[11] Agent intermediaries perform a variety of physical distribution, transaction and communication, and facilitating functions that make exchange possible. Exhibit 12.3 provides further insight about major types of intermediaries.

On the surface, intermediaries may seem unnecessary. Wouldn't it be much more efficient for all channels to be direct from producer to consumer? Put another way: Why don't manufacturers just distribute directly to consumers instead of through Amazon and other intermediaries? The answer goes back to what we learned in Chapter 3 about the different types of utilities—form, time, place, and ownership. Sometimes you might hear a phrase such as, "We save you money by cutting out the middleman!" But, in reality, cutting out intermediaries is not a guarantee of saving consumers money. In the long run, channel intermediaries tend to continue to participate in a channel only as long as their value added to the channel supports their inclusion. If an intermediary of any of the types shown in Exhibit 12.3 doesn't carry its weight, the channel structure eventually will change

The majority of L.L. Bean's sales are through its online and catalog direct channels. But they also have a channel intermediary in the form of their own retail stores and outlets.
©Andre Jenny/Alamy Stock Photo

EXHIBIT 12.3 | Major Types of Intermediaries

MIDDLEMAN: Independent business entity that links producers and end-user consumers or organizational buyers.

MERCHANT MIDDLEMAN: Middleman that buys goods outright, taking title to them.

AGENT: Business entity that negotiates purchases, sales, or both but does not take title to the goods involved.

MANUFACTURERS' AGENT: Agent that usually operates on an extended contract, often sells within an exclusive territory, handles noncompeting but related lines of goods, and has limited authority to price and create terms of sale.

DISTRIBUTOR: Wholesale middleman, found especially when selective or exclusive distribution is common and strong promotional support is needed. Sometimes used synonymously for a wholesaler.

WHOLESALER: Entity primarily engaged in buying, taking title to, storing (usually), and physically handling goods in large quantities. Wholesalers resell the goods (usually in smaller quantities) to retailers or to organizational buyers.

JOBBER: Middleman that buys from manufacturers and sells to retailers. This intermediary is sometimes called a "rack jobber" to connote the service of stocking racks or shelves with merchandise.

FACILITATING AGENT: Entity that assists in the performance of distribution tasks other than buying, selling, and transferring title (examples include trucking companies, warehouses, importers, etc.).

RETAILER: Entity primarily engaged in selling to end-user consumers.

Source: Bennett, Peter D., ed. *Dictionary of Marketing Terms.* Chicago, IL: American Marketing Association, 1995.

accordingly to maximize efficiencies across the utilities. Thus, channel members add their value by bridging gaps in form, time, place, and ownership that naturally exist between producers and consumers.

Exhibits 12.4 and 12.5 illustrate examples within two distinct channel situations: one with end-user consumers as the final element in the channel and one ending with an organizational buyer in which the product is used within the business. The exhibits call attention to the fact that channels are distinguishable based on the number of intermediaries

EXHIBIT 12.4 | End-User Consumer Channels

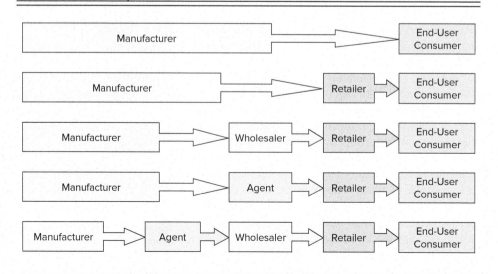

EXHIBIT 12.5 | Organizational Channels

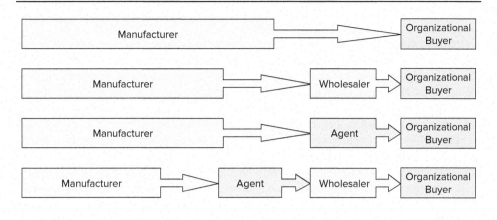

they contain—the more intermediaries that are involved, the longer the channel. A **direct channel**, portrayed as the first example in each exhibit, has no intermediaries and operates strictly from producer to end-user consumer or business user. An **indirect channel** contains one or more intermediary levels, as represented by all the other examples within each exhibit.[12]

FUNCTIONS OF CHANNEL INTERMEDIARIES

Channel intermediaries enhance utilities by providing a wide array of specific functions. Their contributions can be classified into physical distribution functions, transaction and communication functions, and facilitating functions.

Physical Distribution Functions

One function of channel intermediaries is **physical distribution**, or **logistics**, which is the integrated process of moving input materials to the producer, in-process inventory through the firm, and finished goods out of the firm through the channel of distribution. Let's examine how channel intermediaries contribute to the physical distribution function in five key ways: breaking bulk, accumulating bulk and sorting, creating assortments, reducing transactions, and transportation and storage.

Breaking Bulk In many industries, such as consumer health products, when finished goods come off a firm's production line, the manufacturer packages the individual pieces into large cartons for shipping into the channel of distribution. This is a convenient way for manufacturers to ship out the product. In physical distribution, shipping a "gross" of any product represents 12 dozen (144). But consumers shopping in a drugstore, whether a national chain such as Walgreens or an independent pharmacy in your hometown, don't need to see 144 units of a shampoo or deodorant on a store shelf. The function of **breaking bulk** occurs within a channel to better match quantities needed to space constraints and inventory turnover requirements.[13] Importantly, like most channel functions, breaking bulk could be performed by different types of intermediaries, in the case of Walgreens by the retailer's own warehouse and in the case of the local pharmacy by a drug wholesaler such as McKesson.

Accumulating Bulk and Sorting In some industries, rather than breaking bulk, the intermediaries perform a process of **accumulating bulk**—that is, they take in product from multiple sources and transform it, often through **sorting** it into different classifications for sales through the channel.[14] Eggs, for example, might come into a processing house from individual farm operators for sorting by grade and size, then to be packaged and sent on their way to retailers.

Creating Assortments Intermediaries engage in **creating assortments** when they accumulate products from several sources and then make those products available down the channel as a convenient assortment for consumers.[15] Assume for a moment you are looking for a new HD smart TV. With no channel intermediaries you would have to review the entire line of HD smart TVs from each manufacturer to truly understand the different product features offered across their product lines. But walk into Best Buy or go to the retailer's website and an assortment across those manufacturers is already waiting for your review, selected by Best Buy's expert buying staff based on features and value. Most consumers appreciate the convenience associated with having an assortment of choices available for review. Shoppers love Costco, and Costco uses economies of scale to purchase its inventory in bulk at lower prices, allowing them to accumulate assortments and then subsequently resell the items—in smaller bulk chunks—to customers at low prices. The corporation's business model is remarkably successful, and it has proven resilient even against retail giant and industry disrupter Amazon. Through its warehouse membership model, Costco has become a multi-billion-dollar global retailer that now operates in eight countries.[16]

Reducing Transactions We've already seen how the introduction of even one intermediary into a channel can contribute to greatly **reducing transactions** necessary to complete an exchange. While it might seem counterintuitive to those who are not studying marketing management, channels with intermediaries actually tend to save end-user consumers money over what most direct producer to consumer distribution approaches would cost, given the same product.[17] Manufacturers' costs would skyrocket if they held the responsibility for interfacing with and delivering product to every one of their end users. Consider that conveniently located retailers save consumers a lot of money by reducing travel costs versus buying directly from a manufacturer. As mentioned earlier, in the long run, channel intermediaries remain in the channel only as long as they are adding efficiencies, reducing costs, and adding value within that channel.

Transportation and Storage Relatively few producers operate their own transportation networks or provide warehousing facilities. Producers make money by pushing finished goods out the door and into the channel of distribution. As such, **transportation and storage** functions are among the most commonly provided channel intermediary activities. In the publishing industry, Amazon.com and other online booksellers play an invaluable role for both publishers and consumers by ensuring that sufficient inventories of the right books are available for shipping across a variety of transportation choices, from UPS ground to next-day air depending on the urgency of the order.

Transaction and Communication Functions

Another category of intermediary contribution within a channel is the performance of transaction and communication functions. These functions include:

- *Selling.* Often, intermediaries provide a sales force to represent a manufacturer's product line. This could take the form of manufacturers' representatives, or brokers, that represent a product line down the channel. Alternatively, the salespeople might work for a wholesaler or retailer.[18]
- *Buying.* Both wholesalers and retailers perform an important function by evaluating products and ultimately simplifying purchase decisions by creating assortments.[19]
- *Marketing communications.* Intermediaries frequently receive incentives from manufacturers to participate in helping promote products in the channel.[20] When a Target ad features Tide laundry detergent, it's a safe bet that Target has received a promotional allowance from P&G to feature the brand. Likewise, that shelf tag in

your neighborhood pharmacy featuring a special price on Tums very likely was placed there by the pharmacy's wholesaler as part of a promotion by GlaxoSmithKline, its producer.

Facilitating Functions

In a channel, **facilitating functions** performed by intermediaries include a variety of activities that help fulfill completed transactions and also maintain the viability of the channel relationships. These include:

- *Financing.* Without readily available credit at various stages in the distribution process, many channels could not operate. In any given channel, when credit is required by one channel member, it may be facilitated by another channel member such as a producer, wholesaler, or retailer, depending on the situation. Alternatively, credit may be facilitated by outside sources such as banks and credit card providers.[21]

- *Market research.* Because intermediaries are closer to end-user consumers and business users than manufacturers, they are in an ideal position to gather information about the market and consumer trends. Collecting and sharing market and competitive information helps members of the channel continue to offer the right product mix at the right prices.[22] Between Internet tracking and smartphone technology, data are being collected on consumers 24/7. Your smartphone offers a conduit for collecting valuable insights on your geographic location, Internet browsing history, health information, and product preferences to omnipresent companies like Google and Facebook, as well as cellular service providers like Verizon and AT&T. As you read in Chapter 5, this constant, instantaneous collection of consumer data facilitated the rise of Big Data and has greatly heightened the importance of data analytics to marketing managers. Although this trend has raised security concerns, some companies such as Fitbit have strategically leveraged the opportunity to generate consumer interest in collecting and analyzing personal data. Through its wearable technology, Fitbit collects data on a host of wearers' daily activities such as steps taken, calories burned, and more. The company then uses the data not only to improve its products but also to inform its users as part of its personal training services.[23]

- *Risk-taking.* A big part of how an intermediary can add value is by reducing the risk of others in the channel. Any of the major physical distribution functions described above that are assumed by a channel member come with potential risks and liabilities.[24] For example, accumulating bulk in perishable goods comes with a risk of spoilage if customer demand estimates are inaccurately high. Also, when product liability lawsuits are filed, the defendants named are nearly always anyone within the distribution channel that played a part in getting the product to market.

- *Other services.* Services performed by intermediaries run a gamut of activities such as training others in the channel on how to display or sell the products, performing repair and maintenance of products after a sale, and providing customized software for inventory management, accounting and billing, and other operational processes. ADP is one of the largest global providers of business processing and cloud-based human capital management solutions. Serving over 650,000 clients in over 110 countries, ADP provides services such as payroll processing, human resources management, and benefits administration so that clients can allocate time and resources to focus on their core business instead of investing in internal specialty operations.[25]

DISINTERMEDIATION AND E-CHANNELS

Driven largely by the advent of electronic commerce and online marketing, **disintermediation**, or the shortening or collapsing of marketing channels due to the elimination of one or more intermediaries, is common in the electronic channel. In the early days of e-commerce, many entrepreneurs rushed to market with a website to sell their favorite products. This dot-com boom quickly turned to a bust, however, in part because many of these new-age marketers didn't understand the basics of distribution channels. Simply opening a website that features a product is one thing, but it's another thing entirely to invest in the infrastructure and capabilities needed to consistently fulfill orders in a timely and accurate manner. Most postmortems on the cause of the dot-com bust point to poor channel and supply chain practices as the No. 1 reason so many of those initial e-marketers failed. That is, customer expectations were peaked by the novelty and convenience of buying online only to be dashed by delays and errors in product fulfillment after the sale.[26]

Today, electronic commerce has settled into a more rational position as one of several approaches within marketing management for distributing and promoting goods and services. E-marketers are much more savvy about how they set up and manage their channels and realize that disintermediation may not improve aggregate channel performance. The trend toward more stability in online shopping was facilitated in large measure by the entry of firms such as UPS and FedEx into the market of providing a broad range of integrated supply chain solutions.

Recently, many e-commerce (and other) firms are finding that handing over one or more of their core internal functions, such as most or all of their supply chain activities, to other (third-party) companies that are experts in those areas allows the firm to better focus on its core business. This approach, which is referred to as **outsourcing** or **third-party logistics (3PL)**, is attractive for many firms whose own core competencies do not include these elements. The trend has opened up opportunities for firms such as UPS and FedEx, as well as a host of other smaller firms, to change their business focus from mere shippers into broad-based logistics consultancies that handle all aspects of clients' supply chain functions.[27]

Amazon offers intermediary services to aspiring entrepreneurs and business start-ups through its Fulfilled by Amazon (FBA) services. By adopting the FBA business model, small businesses can advertise and sell their products through Amazon, and Amazon stores and ships the inventory and handles the distribution and fulfillment logistics. In addition, Amazon provides customer support and Prime shipping eligibility for FBA products. The FBA business model allows individual sellers and small businesses to utilize the existing infrastructure, capabilities, and consumer base of a large company.[28]

VERTICAL MARKETING SYSTEMS

LO 12-4

Explain the different types of vertical marketing systems.

Whereas standard marketing channels are comprised of independent entities, a **vertical marketing system (VMS)** consists of vertically aligned networks behaving and performing as a unified system.[29] A VMS can be set up in three different ways: corporate systems, contractual systems, and administered systems. At its essence, in a VMS a channel member (1) owns the others, (2) has contracts with them, or (3) simply forces cooperation through sheer clout within the channel.

Corporate Systems

In **corporate VMS**, a channel member has invested in backward or forward **vertical integration** by buying a controlling interest in other intermediaries. In the Midwest, the Braum's chain started in the 1930s as a family dairy farm in Kansas. Over time, the Braum family acquired almost every aspect of its distribution channel—milk processing, other product manufacturing, transportation, warehousing, and the Braum's stores. An owned, or corporate, VMS such as that practiced by Braum's creates a powerful competitive advantage in the marketplace due to cost and process efficiencies realized when a channel is strictly controlled by one entity.

Contractual Systems

A **contractual VMS** consists of otherwise independent entities that are bound together legally through contractual agreement. The most famous example of this arrangement is a **franchise organization**, which is designed to create a contractual relationship between a franchisor that grants the franchise and the franchisee, or the independent entity entering into an agreement to perform at the standards required by the franchisor.[30] *Entrepreneur* magazine reports that franchising remains the highest-potential start-up and growth mechanism for small-business owners, and it's an effective way to expand a distribution channel quickly and efficiently. Subway, the world's largest franchise system, has over 44,000 outlets in over 100 countries.

Another common contractual VMS is the **retailer cooperative**, or co-op. In this era of chain stores, independent retailers across a variety of product categories have banded together to gain cost and operating economies of scale in the channel. Associated Wholesale Grocers (AWG) is the largest co-op food wholesaler to independently owned supermarkets in the United States, with more than 3,500 stores in 35 states. Through enhanced buying and distribution power, AWG-serviced stores can better compete with supermarket chains than if the stores were buying separately.[31] A variation on this concept is the **wholesaler cooperative**, such as Ace Hardware, in which retailers contract for varying degrees of exclusive dealings with a particular wholesaler.[32]

Administered Systems

In an **administered VMS**, the sheer size and power of one of the channel members place it in a position of channel control. The lead player in such situations may be referred to as the **channel captain** or **channel leader**, signifying its ability to control many aspects of that channel's operations.[33] For decades, P&G was the channel captain in every channel in which it was a member based on the clout of its extensive stable of No. 1 brands. It became notorious for dictating terms of sale, limiting quantities of promotional goods to intermediaries, and steamrolling uncooperative wholesalers and retailers into submission. But the rise of giant retailers—Walmart, in particular—shifted the power in the channel and forced P&G to become more customer-compliant.

It is possible that an administered VMS can be more formally structured through strategic alliances and partnership agreements among channel members that agree to work in mutual cooperation. P&G and Walmart have a long-standing strategic alliance that includes connectivity of inventory, billing systems, and market research. The result is improved inventory management, more efficient invoice processing, and product development that better serves the consumer marketplace. Approaches such as this are often referred to as **partner relationship management (PRM) strategies**. The goal of PRM is to share resources, especially knowledge-based resources, to effect optimally profitable relationships between two channel members.[34]

CHANNEL BEHAVIOR: CONFLICT AND POWER

The very nature of channels, especially traditional channels composed of independent entities, fosters differences in channel power among members. **Channel power** is the degree to which any member of a marketing channel can exercise influence over the other members of the channel. As we saw with the administered VMS, power can directly influence the relationships within the channel. Ultimately, **channel conflict** can occur in which channel members experience disagreements and their relationship can become strained or fall apart. Unresolved channel conflict not only can result in an uncooperative and inefficient channel, but it also can ultimately impact end-user consumers through inferior products, spotty inventory, and higher prices.

Danskin sells activewear through thousands of retail outlets, not the least of which are Amazon and Danskin's own online presence. But when the company first decided to launch its website, it was very mindful of potential channel conflict. Thus, the company initially offered only plus-sized products on the web so that it would not compete directly with the retail stores. When Danskin's retail customers did not show resistance to the website, the company slowly expanded its online presence, adding regular-sized apparel and more fashion styles. To avoid competing with its retail customers on price, Danskin's online merchandise was offered at the manufacturer's suggested retail price. But recently as various online channels have become

EXHIBIT 12.6 | Sources of Channel Power

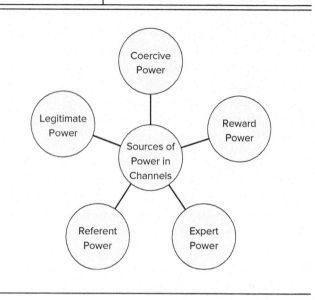

ubiquitous, they've become more aggressive on their websites—for example, offering a Memorial Weekend sale in 2017 with every item 25 percent off.[35]

French and Raven have identified five important sources of power that are relevant in a channel setting. Those power sources are illustrated in Exhibit 12.6 and explained below.

- *Coercive power.* **Coercive power** involves an explicit or implicit threat that a channel captain will invoke negative consequences on a channel member if it does not comply with the leader's request or expectations. Walmart has exceedingly tight standards for how shippers must schedule delivery appointments at a Walmart distribution center. If the truck misses the appointment by even a few minutes, the error results in punitive financial consequences for the vendor. If the problem becomes repetitive, a vendor will be placed on probation as an approved source.

- *Reward power.* Despite Walmart's ability to coerce, few vendors will turn up their nose at potential business from the retailing giant just because they can be difficult to work with. Naturally, the motivating force is Walmart's huge **reward power** in the form of writing big orders.

- *Expert power.* Often, channel members adopt an approach of utilizing their unique competencies to influence others in the channel. **Expert power** might take the form of sharing important product knowledge, such as a representative from Clinique setting up a demonstration for cosmetic consultants in a Nordstrom store to stimulate sales expertise. Or it might involve sharing of information such as Kroger Supermarkets providing consumer preference data to Frito-Lay to get it to produce a special flavor of chips for a specific geographic area that Kroger serves.

- *Referent power.* When a channel member is respected, admired, or revered based on one or more attributes, that member enjoys **referent power** within the channel. Only the best of the best brands can rely on this power source. In frozen foods, Stouffer's (a unit of Nestlé) commands a level of respect well above the competition because of its outstanding quality standards, successful marketing and branding strategies, and cooperativeness with retailers. When frozen-food sections of supermarkets are reset to accommodate new-product entries and remove discontinued items, Stouffer reps are often trusted to help store clerks reset the shelves, and in many instances Stouffer's is given prime display space in the freezer case.

- *Legitimate power.* **Legitimate power** results from contracts such as franchise agreements or other formal agreements. When McDonald's requires franchisees that want to participate in the latest iteration of their famous Monopoly scratch-off game to sign an agreement as to how the game will be promoted and administered in the store, it is exercising legitimate power to control misuse of the promotional activity.[36]

SELECTING CHANNEL APPROACHES

LO 12-5

Utilize suitable criteria to select appropriate channel approaches.

Given the plethora of choices of channel intermediaries and channel structures that we've reviewed, marketing managers have a lot to consider when designing or selecting the channel approach that will best meet their needs. When marketing planning, a good channel decision can be one of the most important within the entire planning process and can lead to market advantage over competitors. Among the issues for consideration are:

1. What is the level of distribution intensity sought within the channel?
2. How much control and adaptability are required over the channel and its activities?
3. What are the priority channel functions that require investment?

Distribution Intensity

Distribution intensity refers to the number of intermediaries involved in distributing the product. Distribution strategies can be intensive, selective, or exclusive.

Intensive Distribution When the objective is to obtain maximum product exposure throughout the channel, an **intensive distribution** strategy is designed to saturate every possible intermediary and especially retailers. Intensive distribution is typically associated with low-cost **convenience goods. Impulse goods** are also appropriate for intensive distribution, as their sales rely on the consumer seeing the product, feeling an immediate want, and being able to purchase now.

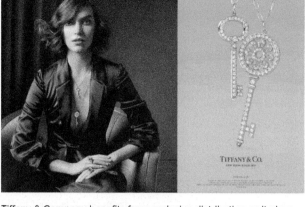

Tiffany & Company benefits from exclusive distribution as it plays up the luxurious benefits of its products.

Source: T&CO

Chobani uses intensive distribution to sell its yogurt throughout the United States, Australia, Asia, and Latin America.[37] Chobani founder Hamdi Ulukaya describes the company's journey as beginning "in 2005 in a hundred-year-old, shuttered manufacturing plant in Central New York [state], where we spent more than 540 tireless days and nights perfecting the recipe for our authentic strained Greek Yogurt."[38] The company's first distributor was a small grocer in Long Island, New York, in 2007. Within three years, Chobani had become the No. 1–selling Greek yogurt in the United States.[39] Chobani products are now distributed by virtually every major grocer across the United States as well as by convenience stores such as Wawa and 7-Eleven, and online platforms such as Amazon Fresh, Fresh Direct, and Instacart.[40] In 2017, Chobani launched a food incubator program for food industry entrepreneurs where selected start-ups showcase products to potential investors, distributors, and customers upon completion of the program.[41]

Selective Distribution Shopping goods, goods for which a consumer may engage in a limited search, are candidates for **selective distribution**. Examples of goods that fit this approach include most appliances, midrange fashion apparel, and home furnishings. A selective distribution strategy may require that intermediaries provide a modicum of customer service during the sale and, depending on the type of good, follow-up service after the sale. Intermediary reputation, especially of the retailers, can be an asset in selective distribution. For example, selecting a retailer whose brand connection enhances and is compatible with the product is essential. Distributing a Kenneth Cole watch or accessory at either Walgreens or Tiffany & Company is not a good fit, but gaining distribution in Dillard's and Macy's makes a lot of sense.

Exclusive Distribution When a manufacturer opts for **exclusive distribution** in a channel, it is often part of an overall positioning strategy built on prestige, scarcity, and premium pricing. In Chapter 11, you read about Voss water's highly successful entry into the ultra-premium bottled water market. Voss's prestige was greatly enhanced by a distribution strategy that involved only one wholesale distributor per state, which had to be a liquor, wine, and spirits wholesaler with relationships already built among the exclusive restaurants and hotels that Voss was targeting. Exclusive distribution also often arises because a significant personal selling effort is required with the consumer before product purchase. Products that possess complex or unique properties that only a one-to-one in-person interaction with a customer can explain are often best served by intermediaries with specialized sales capabilities.[42]

Channel Control and Adaptability

Review of the types of intermediaries in Exhibit 12.3 and channel examples in Exhibits 12.4 and 12.5 reveals a variety of options that can lead to more or less control and adaptability over the channel. Hiring an in-house sales force, investing in a fleet of trucks, building a warehouse facility, pursuing a corporate VMS through vertical integration, and engaging in a contractual VMS with other intermediaries each would increase a firm's control of the channel but at the same time limit its flexibility to change if the competition and other external forces require it. Other options such as brokers, manufacturer's agents, and common carriers have the opposite effect in that a firm's influence and control in the channel are minimized but great flexibility is attained to dramatically and quickly alter aspects of the channel if needed.

In deciding on the right balance between control and flexibility in a channel, marketing managers must consider the type of products involved, cost issues among the various options, strength of belief in the accuracy of the sales forecast, and likelihood that major changes will occur in the customer or competitive marketplace that would necessitate restructuring the channel. Often, customers drive the ultimate choice a marketing manager makes about a channel, as flexibility or control differentially impact the value proposition from one customer to the next.

Prioritization of Channel Functions—Push versus Pull Strategy

The third aspect of channel decisions by marketing managers relates to what channel functions are most important to the success of the particular products. In large measure, this decision is framed by whether the general approach is a push strategy or a pull strategy. A **push strategy** means that much of the intensive promotional activities take place from the manufacturer downward through the channel of distribution. Think of this approach as an investment by the manufacturer in intermediaries so that they will have a maximal incentive to stock, promote, sell, and ship the firm's products. Push strategies usually are supported by heavy allowance payments to intermediaries for helping accomplish the manufacturer's goals. Examples include funding an extra incentive to a wholesale drug salesperson for pushing a particular medication to an independent pharmacy, or paying a **slotting allowance** or **shelf fee** to secure distribution in an intermediary's inventory listing and warehouse or onto a retail shelf.[43]

In contrast, a manufacturer employing a **pull straegy** focuses much of its promotional investment on the end-user consumer. In this case, heavy advertising in mass media, direct marketing, couponing, and other direct-to-consumer promotion are expected to create demand from intermediaries from the bottom of the channel upward. A pull strategy doesn't mean a manufacturer wouldn't engage in any channel incentives, but rather that the incentives would likely be greatly reduced versus a push strategy.[44]

Obviously, a number of important marketing management decisions about channel structure and types of intermediaries to best utilize are influenced by the degree to which the channel intermediaries are relied on to help create and support demand. The degree of push versus pull used is fundamental in framing the channel structure and relationships that are likely to optimize a product's success.

LOGISTICS ASPECTS OF SUPPLY CHAIN MANAGEMENT

LO 12-6

Identify the logistics aspects of supply chain management.

Physical distribution, or logistics, is the integrated process of moving input materials to the producer, in-process inventory through the firm, and finished goods out of the firm through the channel of distribution. Traditionally, logistics was thought of as an internal flow going one direction—**outbound logistics**. That is, it was thought that logistics started with production and ended with receipt of the finished good by the end-user consumer or business user. From a supply chain perspective, logistics professionals today tend to take a more holistic view of physical distribution. Thus, along with outbound logistics, it is important to consider **inbound logistics**—sourcing materials and knowledge inputs from external suppliers to the point at which production begins.

Today, the concept of reverse logistics must also be taken into account. **Reverse logistics** deals with how to get goods back to a manufacturer or intermediary after purchase.

Product returns result for many reasons including spoilage and breakage, excess inventory, customer dissatisfaction, and overstocks.[45] In particular, online sellers in both the B2C and B2B space recognize that an inherent aspect of electronic commerce is the increased likelihood of product return. Returns are higher in this channel in large part because of the inability to physically examine the merchandise before purchase. Smart online sellers build return allowances—either free, with shipping charges, or with a restocking fee—into their pricing model. To do this, the seller must work out an efficient and customer-friendly procedure for how merchandise is to be returned. In many cases, the selling firm partners with one logistics company to handle the reverse logistics. For example, Zappos partners with UPS and the USPS and provides its customers the convenience of printing a free return label online at the Zappos website.

Several logistics aspects of supply chain management require close attention by marketing managers. These are order processing, warehousing and materials handling, inventory management, and transportation.

Order Processing

Receiving and properly processing customer orders is a critical step in getting product moving through the supply chain. It is also a point at which mistakes can easily occur, and when a mistake occurs in the order, it usually carries through the whole fulfillment system. If the item ordered is in stock, outbound processing from inventory occurs. If the item is not in stock, referred to as a **stock-out**, then inbound replenishment processes are triggered.

Fortunately, in many modern organizations, order processing has become highly mechanized. Sophisticated and integrated **enterprise resource planning (ERP) systems** now manage much of the logistics and other processes for many firms. ERP is a software application designed to integrate information related to logistics processes throughout the organization. Once data are entered, they are automatically linked through internal systems and become available for use with all relevant decisions that rely on the ERP information. ERP enables employees throughout the system, whether in sales, billing, customer service, or some other group, to take ownership of their piece of the supply chain and to accurately communicate order status both to the customer and among themselves.[46]

Warehousing and Materials Handling

In an ideal supply chain, materials of all kinds are handled as few times as possible. Any warehouse needs to be designed so that after goods are received and checked in, they move directly to their designated storage locations. Efficient, orderly, clean, and well-marked warehouses enhance the flow of goods.

Decisions must be made about the optimal size for a warehouse, how many warehouses to have, and where they should be located to minimize transportation costs. The last point is especially important if the warehouse serves as a distribution center in which functions such as breaking and accumulating bulk occur for ultimate reshipping to customers.

Inventory Management

To ensure that inventories of both raw materials and finished goods are sufficient to meet customer demand without undue delay, firms utilize sophisticated **just-in-time (JIT) inventory control systems**. A JIT system's goal is to balance the double-edged sword of potentially having too many goods on hand and creating unnecessary warehousing costs, with the

Logistics issues are critical in shipping food products such as produce. Exposure to too much heat or cold can ruin the inventory in transit.
©Cultura Limited/SuperStock

EXHIBIT 12.7 | Comparative Attributes across Different Transportation Modes

Low Cost	Speed	Reliability of Delivery	Flexibility of Delivery	Reputation for Delivering Undamaged Goods
1. Pipeline	1. Air	1. Pipeline	1. Motor	1. Pipeline
2. Water	2. Motor	2. Air	2. Rail	2. Water
3. Rail	3. Rail	3. Motor	3. Air	3. Air
4. Motor	4. Pipeline	4. Rail	4. Water	4. Motor
5. Air	5. Water	5. Water	5. Pipeline	5. Rail

Note: Numbers indicate relative ranking based on general trade-offs of cost versus other attributes of each mode.

chance of having so little inventory in stock that stock-outs occur, requiring expensive rush production and express delivery situations.[47]

PRM arrangements often open up their collective IT systems for data sharing toward more reliable JIT inventory management. Walmart's legendary capability of real-time analysis and data transmission to vendors about inventories at any store or distribution center location has created a substantial competitive advantage over many other retailers. In any industry, customers expect product to be in stock and available, and when it's not they quickly become prone to switching to competitors. One component of ERP systems is usually **materials requirement planning (MRP)**. MRP guides overall management of the inbound materials from suppliers to facilitate minimal production delays.[48]

Transportation

With the cost of fuel today, it is not unusual for transportation costs to run as much as 10 percent of the cost of goods sold. Effective transportation management is one way that many firms keep a lid on costs while also optimizing delivery options for customers. Exhibit 12.7 provides a comparison of several transportation options on a variety of criteria such as dependability, cost, speed, and suitable products. The decision about which one or what mix of these transportation options to choose will have a major impact on a firm's bottom line.

LEGAL ISSUES IN SUPPLY CHAIN MANAGEMENT

As with pricing practices, a variety of laws impact the decision making about channels and logistics. Among others, the Sherman Antitrust Act (1890), Clayton Act (1914), and Federal Trade Commission Act (1914) provide much of the basis for legislation impacting supply chains. Three key legal issues related to distribution are exclusive dealing, exclusive territories, and tying contracts.

Exclusive Dealing

When a supplier creates a restrictive agreement that prohibits intermediaries that handle its product from selling competing firms' products, **exclusive dealing** has occurred. Whether a particular arrangement is legal depends on whether it interferes with the intermediary's right to act independently or the rights of competitors to succeed—that is, is competition lessened by the arrangement? Exclusive dealing lessens competition if it (1) accounts for substantial market share, (2) involves a substantial dollar amount, and (3) involves a big supplier and smaller intermediary, which sets up a case for coercion.

For example, the Federal Trade Commission (FTC) reached a settlement with Transitions Optical on charges of illegally maintaining a monopoly by engaging in exclusive dealing in the photochromic lens distribution chain. Photochromic treatments are applied to eyeglass lenses, and treated lenses darken when exposed to UV light. It was alleged that the company illegally maintained its monopoly by engaging in exclusive dealing at nearly every level of the photochromic lens distribution chain and that Transitions' exclusionary tactics locked out rivals from approximately 85 percent of the lens caster market, and partially or completely locked out rivals from up to 40 percent or more of the retail and wholesale lab market. Essentially, they accomplished this by using exclusive agreements that restricted retail and wholesale parties' ability to sell competing lens. Under the FTC consent order, Transitions agreed to stop all exclusive dealing practices that pose a threat to competition, making it easier for competitors to enter.[49]

Exclusive dealing may be legal if the parties show exclusivity is essential for strategic reasons, such as to maintain product image. High-fashion brands often engage in exclusive dealing with retailers so that their image is not sullied by being merchandised in the store next to step-down labels. Also, if limited production capacity on the part of the supplier legitimately restricts its sales capabilities, exclusive dealing may also be legal. In this case, the point of the exclusive deal is to try to ensure the limited quantities of product have the best possible chance of being "sold through" to end users.[50]

Exclusive Territories

An **exclusive territory** protects an intermediary from having to compete with others selling a producer's goods. Can a producer always grant an intermediary an exclusive territory for sales purposes? Not necessarily. For this practice to be legal, it would have to be demonstrated that the exclusivity doesn't violate any statutes on restriction of competition. This issue often manifests itself in the context of suppliers limiting the number of retail outlets within a certain geographic area. One possible defense of exclusive territories might be that the costs of a new store (restaurant, retailer, dealer, etc.) entering the market are so great that the nature of the market and risks involved demand an opportunity for exclusivity.[51]

Years ago, health and nutrition retailer GNC famously and very publicly faced class action lawsuits after the firm opened company-owned stores near its franchised locations and lowered prices. Inevitably, franchised locations lost customers and some went out of business. The highly visible and brand-damaging lawsuits included charges of territory violations and unfair competition. Ultimately, a multimillion dollar settlement was reached designed to enhance GNC's franchising system and customer service.[52]

Tying Contracts

If a seller requires an intermediary to purchase a supplementary product to qualify to purchase the primary product the intermediary wishes to buy, a **tying contract** is in place. Example: "You can buy my printer, but to do so you *must* sign a contract to buy my ink"—thus, the products are "tied together" as terms of sale. Tying contracts are illegal, but historically it has often been difficult to prove in a court of law whether an agreement is or isn't a tying contract.[53] In a classic example, prior to going out of business, Kodak had become embroiled in a legal battle after unlawfully tying the sale of service for Kodak copying machines to the sale of parts. Independent service organizations contended that Kodak restricted their access to replacement parts for Kodak machines, thus effectively shutting them out of the service business. Effectively, customers were left to either buy service directly from Kodak or service the machines themselves.[54]

RETAILING AND ELECTRONIC COMMERCE

LO 12-7

Understand the role of retailing and e-commerce in delivering the value offering to the customer.

You have learned that retailers are one form of channel intermediary. In this section we will focus a bit more on them as they tend to be the type of intermediary that most people encounter most frequently. **Retailing** is any business activity that creates value in the delivery of goods and services to consumers for their personal, nonbusiness consumption

Most people know Walmart is the world's largest retailer, but the world's second-largest retailer—Carrefour, based in France—is also very powerful with thousands of different retail formats around the world.
©Kevin Foy/Alamy Stock Photo

and is an essential component of the supply chain. As we discussed earlier in the chapter, an efficient, effective supply chain moves materials from manufacturer to consumer. Retailing, in whatever form, is the point of contact in the supply chain with the consumer of the product. Put another way, retailing in its various forms represents a very important point of customer interface.

In our highly interconnected world where customers interface with manufacturers directly and through social media, much traditional brick-and-mortar retailing is migrating online, either through manufacturer websites or via Amazon and similar broad-based online providers. To be sure, in many cases online shopping is putting a serious dent in in-store purchases. **Electronic commerce (e-commerce)** refers to any action using electronic media to communicate with customers; facilitate the inventory, exchange, and distribution of goods and services; or make payments. It is the fastest-growing customer interface and has fundamentally changed the way companies and customers interact.

Electronic commerce has created new business opportunities and enabled existing business models to be more efficient. Less than a decade ago, for many retailers e-commerce was basically just a secondary channel to their traditional store operations. Today, that's changed and an effective e-commerce strategy is central to most firms' marketing strategy. E-commerce is relevant in both the B2B and B2C space.

Business-to-Consumer Electronic Commerce

Electronic retailing (e-retailing or **e-tailing)** is the communication and sale of products or services to consumers over the Internet. E-retailing is by far the fastest-growing retail format, with growth of upwards of 10 percent per year.[55] A recent study by Pew Research indicates that nearly 80 percent of Americans do at least some shopping on the Internet, with 43 percent shopping weekly or a few times a month. When this question was first asked by Pew in 2000, just 22 percent of respondents said they'd ever made a purchase online![56]

E-retailing offers even the smallest entrepreneur the opportunity to open a shop on the Internet. However, although many small and mid-size companies utilize e-retailing, the vast majority of e-retail sales and Internet traffic is dominated by all sorts of famous names that started in brick-and-mortar retailing of their products or services. Companies such as Walmart, Best Buy, Merrill Lynch, and many others offer products and services as well as extensive customer support online. Today, most of these companies coordinate a sophisticated brick (store, physical location) and click (online) strategy that links the retail formats. **Omnichannel retailing** uses a variety of channels in a customer's shopping experience, including research before a purchase. Such channels include physical stores, online stores, mobile stores, mobile app stores, telephone sales, and any other method of transacting with a customer.

The greatest success in e-retailing has been in products where convenience and price are key drivers in the purchase decision. People do enjoy shopping at Barnes & Noble, but they also appreciate the convenience of shopping online for books. Companies such as e-Trade and traditional financial organizations such as Merrill Lynch are successful offering low-cost trading options and other services online. As consumers become more comfortable evaluating products and making purchase decisions online, they expand their electronic shopping experience. And of course the 800-pound gorilla of e-retailing—Amazon—continues to set the bar for variety and convenience in the customer interface.

Advantages of E-Retailing

Extensive Selection No other channel offers the breadth and depth of selection. From information search to purchase, the Internet gives consumers greater access to more choices and different product options. In the time it takes someone to drive to Barnes & Noble and find a book, it is possible to visit the Barnes & Noble website, order the book (probably at a lower price), and have it shipped for next-day delivery (or visit Amazon for increasing access to same-day delivery!).[57]

Online retailers like eBay have moved into mobile apps for easier customer access.

© dennizn/Shutterstock

Considerable Information Available for Product Research and Evaluation The Internet dramatically expands consumers' knowledge, offering an almost unlimited number of websites that research, evaluate, and recommend products and services. From retailers (Best Buy in electronics) to independent testing organizations (CNet in technology), consumers can find information on anything.[58] For example, if a consumer wants to find out more about a 1958 John Deere 420T tractor, all he or she has to do is visit www.antiquetractors.com. If a consumer wants a 1935 Whittall Bird of Paradise rug, he or she can simply check out eBay. Additionally, many sites offer additional tools such as side-by-side product comparisons, video product reviews, or three-dimensional interactive product displays that educate consumers in an entertaining and visually informative manner.

Build Product Communities The Internet brings together groups of individuals with a shared interest to create virtual communities. These communities share information, ideas, and product information. Babycenter.com offers parents a one-stop source for information about babies, children, and parenting. These sites are an excellent communication channel for companies marketing products to relevant target markets. One example is Babycenter.com, a part of the Johnson & Johnson family of companies. It serves as a popular online community where parents connect on a variety of topics.[59]

Individualized Customer Experience The Internet allows a great deal of personalization for both the consumer and the company. Consumers can get one-on-one interaction from a customer service representative and create their own web content based on personal preferences. At the same time, companies can tailor messages and web content by analyzing consumer web history. The end result is a more customized, personal experience for the consumer.

Disadvantages of E-Retailing
Despite clear advantages to e-retailing, it does have several drawbacks.

- ***Easier for Customers to Walk Away*** The customer is in total control of the web experience and has the opportunity to walk away at any time. In sharp contrast to a personal-selling situation or even a retail store, the customer can simply click to another site. This puts additional pressure on the website to attract and then hold on to visitors. In evaluating a website, one of the key measures is its "stickiness," which refers to the amount of time visitors remain at the site. A good website not only attracts a lot of visitors, but it also gets them to remain and explore the site. Chapter 13 provides some ideas on using digital and social media marketing in ways that increase customer stickiness.

- ***Reduced Ability to Sell Features and Benefits*** Websites incorporate sophisticated tools to display and highlight critical features and benefits. However, unless the customer initiates additional contact via web live chat, phone, or e-mail, it can prove challenging to engage the customer to answer questions or deal with objections.

- ***Security of Personal Data*** Over the past several years, numerous highly publicized data security breaches have occurred involving e-retailers (as well as retail stores). While companies work hard to make their websites secure and keep personal data such as credit card numbers private, many consumers still have concerns about the security of their data. These concerns lead some consumers to limit their electronic purchases.[60]

B2B E-commerce

Although the Internet has reshaped the way businesses and consumers interact, it also plays a significant role in B2B customer interface. Forrester estimates that B2B e-commerce will top $1.1 trillion and will account for over 12 percent of all B2B sales in the United States by 2020. For perspective, they predict the B2C e-commerce market to reach about $480 billion by that time. (Yes, you read it correctly, B2B e-commerce will be valued at over double that of B2C.) Just like B2C firms, B2B providers are investing heavily in delivering excellent omnichannel customer experiences.[61]

Many companies now require their vendors to do business online. Disney suppliers become part of Disney's EDI (electronic data interchange) network and process orders via the Internet. This requires an initial investment of thousands of dollars to get the infrastructure (hardware and software) to connect with Disney. As mentioned earlier in the chapter, Walmart, a pioneer in the application of technology into business processes, directly connects its large suppliers such as P&G with its IT network so that stock replenishment is fast and seamlessly accurate.

The Internet has also increased the efficiency of B2B relationships through dedicated B2B sites that facilitate the exchange of products and services. This has made many markets, such as the wholesale distribution of electricity, more efficient as buyers and sellers get together quickly. Known as **market makers**, these sites (such as Lendingtree.com for mortgage and other loans) bring buyers and sellers together.[62]

Customer communities are, as the name suggests, websites (often gated) where customers come to engage with other customers, the sponsoring firm, and others in the ecosystem to share ideas and collaborate on topics of mutual interest. Today, there are many such communities including firms such as Adobe, Cisco, Oracle, and Spiceworks (for IT pros and tech vendors), among many others. As has been a theme throughout this chapter, the key goal of such communities is to enhance the experience of the customer.[63]

SUMMARY

Channel and supply chain decisions are central to creating a firm's value proposition. Competitive advantage can be gained through effective and efficient channel management, physical distribution, and logistics. Vertical marketing systems and partner relationship management strategies add attractive levels of integration among channel members. The aim of such value networks is value co-creation by the participating suppliers, customers, and other stakeholders in which the members of the network combine capabilities according to their expertise and the competencies required from the situation.

Retailers are the type of channel intermediary that most people encounter most frequently. Technology has dramatically changed how, where, and when consumers choose to interact with retailers. Although the growth of B2C e-retailing has certainly been impressive, B2B e-commerce actually has grown even faster and now accounts for considerably more revenue than B2C.

KEY TERMS

APPLICATION QUESTIONS

1. Consider the concept of value co-creation.
   a. In your own words, explain the concept of value co-creation.
   b. What are some specific ways value can be co-created?

More application questions are available online.

c. Provide an example of a specific value network you believe results in a high level of value co-creation.

d. Provide an example of a specific firm or firms that could benefit by establishing a value network and engaging in value co-creation. In what ways would this approach be an improvement over their existing business approach?

2. The chapter discusses the importance of being "nimble" in all aspects of a firm's operation—that is, to be in a position to be maximally flexible, adaptable, and speedy in response to change.

a. Identify two firms in two different industries that you believe exhibit a nimble nature in their operations.

b. What specific evidence leads you to believe these firms are nimble, especially in their channel and supply chain activities?

3. Consider the issue of disintermediation in electronic channels.

a. Do you believe that *all* channels will disintermediate down to simple direct channels over time? Why or why not?

b. Does your opinion change if the question is asked only about B2C channels? Only for B2B channels? Why?

4. Consider this statement: "It's important in business today for all firms to work to cut out the middleman. Intermediaries represent costs that can be saved by finding ways to cut them out of the system. Down-channel buyers always benefit when this happens." Do you agree with this statement? Why or why not? Be specific in arguing your point based on what you learned in the chapter.

5. Exhorting firms to develop networks and alliances for purposes of value co-creation sounds like a good idea. However, is there a point at which such approaches can be taken too far (a) from a legal perspective, (b) from an ethical perspective, and (c) from a strategic perspective? Explain your viewpoint.

6. Consider your school's e-commerce capabilities.

a. From a student's perspective, what e-commerce functions are available on your campus website (for example, class registration, payment, delivery of course materials)?

b. How would you rate the website's ease of use for the functions you identified?

c. What functions does the campus website perform well and what functions does it perform poorly? Explain.

d. What e-commerce functions do you think should be added to the website's capabilities that are not currently offered?

MANAGEMENT DECISION CASE
Restoration Hardware—Using the Brick-and-Mortar Store as a "3D Catalog"

The Internet has been a major disruptive force in modern retailing, helping bring about the demise of numerous familiar stores in your local mall: The Limited, American Apparel, Wet Seal, Aeropostale, and Pacific Sunwear, to name a few.[64] Even stalwart Macy's has closed at least 100 of its stores.[65] While most retailers have rushed to embrace e-retailing as their future, interestingly Restoration Hardware (or RH, as it likes to be called) is not ready to write an obituary for its brick-and-mortar presence.[66]

To the contrary, it is utilizing an array of rather "traditional" retail marketing approaches, including one that may seem to some like a relic of retailing's past.

RH is a luxury brand offering home furnishings, lighting, décor, bathware, and a variety of other products clearly targeted to an upper-income clientele.[67] Visit its stores and you can pick up a nice linen couch for $7,000 or perhaps a crystal chandelier for $9,000.[68] You can also find a selection of decorative drawer pulls, faux fur throws, and even some affordable plush toys for under $50.[69] RH has decreased its total number of stores, but then has "doubled down" on the remaining ones by renovating them into big, beautiful galleries located in renovated historic buildings. These 45,000-square-foot stores are filled with natural light and include cafés where you can enjoy a latte or a Bellini cocktail while you contemplate just which French steamer trunk you want to purchase.[70] One store even has a wine cellar![71] And of course, child care will also be provided (we would expect nothing less in such a rarefied retail environment).[72]

Particularly fascinating about RH is how it views its retail spaces—not as stores, but rather as galleries or showrooms, where customers can get inspiration and style guidance.[73] CEO Gary Friedman's vision is to "reinvent physical retail" with these elaborate new stores and a broader set of services. RH's emphasis on the service experience puts it in a league with retailers like Apple, where customers get to see, touch, and try out all the latest Apple products.[74] According to one retail consultant, these new RH showrooms serve as a kind of "giant 3D real-time catalog."[75]

And RH knows a thing or two about catalogs. It is famous (some would say infamous) for its annual catalogs called Source Books. One year, it sent out a shrink-wrapped set of 13 different books weighing in at a reported 17 pounds and 3,000 pages.[76] These are not your grandpa's Sears catalogs—rather, they are more like fashion magazines, with high-quality photography throughout. Rather than timing the mailing of these catalogs with seasons, RH gives customers the whole source book of products all at once so that it can be referenced throughout the entire year.[77]

In another break from tradition, the chain is implementing a loyalty card with a blanket discount for members and no regular promotional sales. The RH Grey Card costs $100 per year, but provides members with a 25 percent savings on all full-priced purchases (there are still clearance sales).[78] Ninety percent of RH revenue now comes from Grey Card members, and since its implementation RH has seen growth in the average order size. The company also expects margins to grow due to deferred memberships and renewals from the program's current members. It also expects additional new members to join every year.[79]

But perhaps RH's most striking departure from current "mainstream" retail strategic thinking is the lack of priority they place on Internet sales, which is near heresy in today's market where e-commerce rules. Although approximately 37 percent of its business comes via the web, CEO Friedman insists that RH's business is "not about the Internet."[80] Rather than competing with other retailers through websites (where it is difficult to differentiate by size and quality), RH leverages its extravagant physical retail spaces (and its stylish source books) to strategically differentiate its brand in the marketplace. Friedman sums up his feelings about Internet-obsessed retailers as follows: "Make no mistake, many retailers find themselves in a race to the bottom, a race we at RH have chosen not to join." Recent RH sales numbers show an increase in "same store sales," but not as great as in past years.[81] So it remains to be seen whether the firm's contrarian approach is one that will have long-term positive profit impact, and also whether any other retailers will embrace a similar swim upstream from convention to lure customers away from their laptops and smartphones and back into brick-and-mortar stores.

Questions for Consideration

1. RH's CEO believes that the Internet is limited in its ability to facilitate differentiation among retailers. Do you agree? Which retailers do a particularly effective job at presenting their products through their websites?

2. Does the RH strategy work only for high-end/prestige products or are there elements of its approach that would be appropriate for retailers at all price levels? Choose one of your favorite retailers and discuss how that company could best apply the approach that RH is using.

3. Is it environmentally responsible for RH to produce and distribute such large paper catalogs? Are there ways it could mitigate the environmental impact of this program? How could it best deal with the likely negative reaction from "green" customers?

4. What are some other novel ways that retailers could define the role of their brick-and-mortar stores to optimize their effectiveness in contributing to increasing firm revenues and profits?

ACTIVITY 13: Establish Distribution Channels for Your Offering

Selecting the most appropriate channels of distribution for your offering and then working out the overall best approach to establishing and operating your supply chain is a critical element of your marketing plan.

1. Define and describe the value network within which you will operate. Develop an approach to ensure that your supply chain operation is a nimble as possible.

2. Decide what type of channel configuration is optimal for you and what intermediaries should be part of the channel.

3. Select what physical distribution functions you will accomplish in-house and how these will be set up. Then select what physical distribution functions you will outsource and to whom.

4. Identify what aspects of e-channels you must address.

5. Decide:

   a. What level of distribution intensity you seek within each channel.

   b. How much control and adaptability are required over the channel and its activities.

   c. The priority channel functions that require investment.

6. Develop your plans for the following logistics functions:

   a. Order processing.

   b. Warehousing and materials handling.

   c. Inventory management.

   d. Transportation.

NOTES

1. Aksel I. Rokkan, Jan B. Heide, and Kenneth H. Wathne, "Specific Investments in Marketing Relationships: Expropriation and Bonding Effects," *Journal of Marketing Research* 40, no. 2 (May 2003), pp. 210–24.

2. Sjoerd Schaafsma and Joerg Hofstetter, "Raising the Game to a New Level," *ECR Journal: International Commerce Review* 5, no. 1 (Summer 2005), pp. 66–69.

3. Lee G. Cooper, "Strategic Marketing Planning for Radically New Products," *Journal of Marketing* 64, no. 1 (January 2000), pp. 1–16.

4. Bernard Cova and Robert Salle, "Marketing Solutions in Accordance with the S-D Logic: Co-Creating Value with Customer Network Actors," *Industrial Marketing Management* 37, no. 3 (May 2008), pp. 270–77.

5. Jennifer Rowley, "Synergy and Strategy in E-Business," *Marketing Intelligence & Planning* 20, no. 4/5 (2002), pp. 215–22.

6. Ravi S. Achrol and Michael J. Etzel, "The Structure of Reseller Goals and Performance in Marketing Channels," *Journal of the Academy of Marketing Science* 31, no. 2 (Spring 2003), pp. 146–63.

7. Craig Giammona and Leslie Patton, "Chipotle's Biggest Strength Is Suddenly Its Biggest Weakness," *Bloomberg*, December 8, 2015, https://www.bloomberg.com/news/articles/2015-12-08/chipotle-s-greatest-strength-is-now-its-greatest -weakness-too; Mindy Weinstein, "A Trillion-Dollar Demographic: 10 Brands That Got Millennial Marketing Right," *Search Engine Journal*, July 23, 2015, https://www.searchengine journal.com/trillion-dollar-demographic-10-brands-got -millennial-marketing-right/135969/; Kevin O'Marah, "Chipotle Lessons: Supply Chain Visibility and Higher Prices," *Forbes*, December 16, 2015, https://www.forbes.com/sites /kevinomarah/2015/12/16/chipotle-lessons-supply-chain -visibility-and-higher-prices/#2f842cd3332b; Hayley Peterson, "Chipotle Has 4 Problems That Are Threatening Its Growth," *Business Insider*, October 20, 2015, http://www .businessinsider.com/chipotle-has-4-challenges-threatening -business-2015-10; and James Surowiecki, "Can Chipotle Recover from Food Poisoning?" *New Yorker*, December 10, 2015, http://www.newyorker.com/business/currency/can -chipotle-recover-from-food-poisoning.

8. "Tie Your Own Bow Tie: How to Make Smart Product Management Decisions," *Strategic Direction* 23, no. 5 (2007), pp. 5–8.

9. Stephen Keysuk Kim, "Relational Behaviors in Marketing Channel Relationships: Transaction Cost Implications," *Journal of Business Research* 60, no. 11 (November 2007), pp. 1125–34.

10. Junhong Chu, Pradeep K. Chintagunta, and Naufel J. Vilcassim, "Assessing the Economic Value of Distribution Channels: An Application to the Personal Computer Industry," *Journal of Marketing Research* 44, no. 1 (February 2007), pp. 29–41.

11. Daniel C. Bello and Nicholas C. Williamson, "The American Export Trading Company: Designing a New International Marketing Institution," *Journal of Marketing* 49, no. 4 (Fall 1985), pp. 60–69.

12. Alberto Sa Vinhas and Erin Anderson, "How Potential Conflict Drives Channel Structure (Direct and Indirect) Channels," *Journal of Marketing Research* 42, no. 4 (November 2005), pp. 507–15.

13. Michael Ketzenberg, Richard Metters, and Vicente Vargas, "Quantifying the Benefits of Breaking Bulk in Retail Operations," *International Journal of Production Economics* 80, no. 3 (December 2002), pp. 249–63.

14. E. Bashkansky, S. Dror, R. Ravid, and P. Grabov, "Effectiveness of Product Quality Classifier," *Quality Engineering* 19, no. 3 (July 2007), p. 235.

15. Jason M. Carpenter, "Demographics and Patronage Motives of Supercenter Shoppers in the United States," *International Journal of Retail & Distribution Management* 36, no. 1 (2008), pp. 5–16.

16. Kate Taylor, "Costco Is Beating Walmart and Amazon with the 'Best Business Model' in Retail," *Business Insider*, February 22, 2016, http://www.businessinsider.com/why -costcos-business-model-is-so-great-2016-2; and "About Us." *Cosco*, n.d., https://www.costco.com/about.html.

17. Devon S. Johnson and Sundar Bharadwaj, "Digitization of Selling Activity and Sales Force Performance: An Empirical Investigation," *Journal of the Academy of Marketing Science* 33, no. 1 (Winter 2005), pp. 3–18; and Xueming Luo and Naveen Donthu, "The Role of Cyber-Intermediaries: A Framework Based on Transaction Cost Analysis, Agency, Relationship Marketing, and Social Exchange Theories," *Journal of Business & Industrial Marketing* 22, no. 7 (2007), pp. 452–58.

18. Joseph Pancras and K. Sudhir, "Optimal Marketing Strategies for a Customer Data Intermediary," *Journal of Marketing Research* 44, no. 4 (November 2007), pp. 452–58.

19. Virpi Havila, Jan Johanson, and Peter Thilenius, "International Business-Relationship Triads," *International Marketing Review* 21, no. 2 (2004), pp. 172–86.

20. Kevin Lane Keller, "Building Customer-Based Brand Equity," *Marketing Management* 10, no. 2 (July/ August 2001), pp. 14–19.

21. Phillip Bond, "Bank and Nonbank Financial Intermediation," *Journal of Finance* 59, no. 6 (December 2004), pp. 2489–530.

22. Pancras and Sudhir, "Optimal Marketing Strategies for a Customer Data Intermediary."

23. Jason Kint, "Facebook, Google and Now Verizon Are Accelerating Their Tracking Efforts Despite Consumers' Privacy Concerns," *Recode*, November 21, 2016, https://www.recode .net/2016/11/21/13692250/verizon-competing-facebook-google -isp-tracking-consumers-personal-data; FB, "Fitbit—Leveraging Consumers' Obsession with Data," *Harvard Business School Digital Initiative*, November 21, 2015, https://digit.hbs.org /submission/fitbit-leveraging-consumers-obsession-with-data/; and "Our Technology," *Fitbit*, n.d., https://www.fitbit.com /technology.

24. Amal R. Karunaratna and Lester W. Johnson, "Initiating and Maintaining Export Channel Intermediary Relationships," *Journal of International Marketing* 5, no. 2 (1997), pp. 11–32.

25. "Who We Are," *ADP*, n.d., https://www.adp.com/who-we-are .aspx; and "Working with ADP," *ADP*, n.d., https://www.adp.com /who-we-are/corporate-social-responsibility/working-with-adp .aspx.

26. Bert Rosenbloom, "The Wholesaler's Role in the Marketing Channel: Disintermediation vs. Reintermediation," *International Review of Retail, Distribution, and Consumer Research* 17, no. 4 (September 2007), pp. 327–39.

27. Kenneth K. Boyer and G. Tomas M. Hult, "Extending the Supply Chain: Integrating Operations and Marketing in the Online Grocery Industry," *Journal of Operations Management* 23, no. 6 (September 2005), pp. 642–61; and Thomas L. Friedman, *The World Is Flat 3.0: A Brief History of the Twenty-First Century* (New York: Picador, 2007).

28. "Help Boost Your Sales with Amazon's World-Class Fulfillment," *Amazon*, n.d., https://services.amazon.com/fulfillment-by-amazon /how-it-works.htm; and Thomas Smale, "Guide to Starting a Fulfillment by Amazon Business," *Entrepreneur*, September 14, 2016, https://www.entrepreneur.com/article/282277.

29. Achrol and Etzel, "The Structure of Reseller Goals and Performance in Marketing Channels."

30. Gilles Corriveau and Robert D. Tamilla, "Comparing Transactional Forms in Administered, Contractual, and Corporate Systems in Grocery Distribution," *Journal of Business Research* 55, no. 9 (September 2002), pp. 771–73.

31. L. Lynn Judd and Bobby C. Vaught, "Three Differential Variables and Their Relation to Retail Strategy and Profitability," *Journal of the Academy of Marketing Science* 16, no. 3/4 (Fall 1988), pp. 30–37.

32. Tim Burkink, "Cooperative and Voluntary Wholesale Groups: Channel Coordination and Interim Knowledge Transfer," *Supply Chain Management* 7, no. 2 (2002), pp. 60–70.

33. Corriveau and Tamilla, "Comparing Transactional Forms in Administered, Contractual, and Corporate Systems in Grocery Distribution."

34. Nancy Nix, Robert Lusch, Zach Zacharia, and Wesley Bridges, "Competent Collaborations," *Marketing Management* 17, no. 2 (March/April 2008), p. 18.

35. www.Danskin.com, accessed May 29, 2017.

36. John R. P. French and Bertram Raven, *The Bases of Social Power* (Ann Arbor: University of Michigan Press, 1959).

37. Michael Gonda, "Chobani Announces Major Expansion of World's Largest Yogurt Manufacturing Plant in Twin Falls, Idaho," *PR Newswire*, March 17, 2016, http://www.prnewswire .com/news-releases/chobani-announces-major-expansion-of -worlds-largest-yogurt-manufacturing-plant-in-twin-falls-idaho -300237539.html.

38. Hamdi Ulukaya, "Founder's Note," *Chobani*, 2013, http://www .chobani.com/core/wp-content/uploads/2013/04/Chobani -Media-Kit-2013.pdf.

39. "The Chobani Story," *Chobani*, 2013, http://www.chobani.com /core/wp-content/uploads/2013/04/Chobani-Media-Kit-2013.pdf.

40. "Chobani Product Locator," *Chobani*, n.d., http://www.chobani.com /core/wp-content/uploads/2013/04/Chobani-Media-Kit-2013.pdf.

41. Emily Rella, "Chobani Mentors Six Startups to Nearly $3M in Revenue, Showcases in 'Expo West,'" *AOL*, March 28, 2017, https:// www.aol.com/article/finance/2017/03/28/chobani-mentors -six-startups-to-nearly-3m-in-revenue-showcases/22016030/.

42. Boonghee Yoo, Naveen Donthu, and Sungho Lee, "An Examination of Selected Marketing Mix Elements and Brand Equity," *Journal of the Academy of Marketing Science* 28, no. 2 (Spring 2000), pp. 195–211.

43. P. Rajan Varadarajan, Satish Jayachandran, and J. Chris White, "Strategic Interdependence in Organizations: Deconglomeration and Marketing Strategy," *Journal of Marketing* 65, no. 1 (January 2001), pp. 15–28.

44. Frederick E. Webster Jr., "Understanding the Relationships among Brands, Consumers, and Resellers," *Journal of the Academy of Marketing Science* 28, no. 1 (Winter 2000), pp. 17–23.

45. Vaidyanathan Jayaraman and Yadong Luo, "Creating Competitive Advantages through New Value Creation: A Reverse Logistics Perspective," *Academy of Management Perspectives* 21, no. 2 (May 2007), pp. 56–73.

46. Stanley C. Gardiner, Joe B. Hanna, and Michael S. LaTour, "ERP and the Reengineering of Industrial Marketing Processes: A Prescriptive Overview for the New-Age Marketing Manager," *Industrial Marketing Management* 31, no. 4 (July 2002), pp. 357–65.

47. Dale G. Sauers, "Evaluating Just-In-Time Projects from a More Focused Framework," *Quality Process* 34, no. 1 (January 2001), p. 160.

48. Alan D. Smith, "Effective Supplier Selection and Management Issues in Modern Manufacturing and Marketing Service Environments," *Services Marketing Quarterly* 29, no. 2 (2007), pp. 45–65.

49. "FTC Reaches Settlement with Transitions on Alleged Antitrust Violations," *Review of Optometry*, March 4, 2010, https://www.reviewofoptometry.com/article/ftc-reaches-settlement-with-transitions-on-alleged-antitrust-violations.

50. Richard J. Gilbert, "Exclusive Dealing, Preferential Dealing, and Dynamic Efficiency," *Review of Industrial Organization* 16, no. 2 (2000), pp. 167–84.

51. Howard P. Marvel and Stephen McCafferty, "Comparing Vertical Restraints," *Journal of Economics and Business* 48, no. 5 (December 1996), pp. 473–86.

52. Devlin Smith, "Exclusively Yours: Having a Protected Territory Is a Good Thing, Right?" *Entrepreneur*, October 22, 2001, https://www.entrepreneur.com/article/45520.

53. Alan J. Meese, "Tying Meets the New Institutional Economics: Farewell to the Chimera of Forcing," *University of Pennsylvania Law Review* 146, no. 1 (November 1997), pp. 1–98.

54. Linda Greenhouse, "Kodak Dealt a Setback in Antitrust Case Ruling," *New York Times*, June 9, 1992, http://www.nytimes.com/1992/06/09/business/kodak-dealt-a-setback-in-antitrust-case-ruling.html.

55. Andrew Soergel, "As Online Sales Boom, Is Brick-and-Mortar on the Way Out?" *U.S. News & World Report*, December 20, 2016, https://www.usnews.com/news/articles/2016-12-20/with-online-sales-booming-is-brick-and-mortar-on-the-way-out.

56. Aaron Smith and Monica Anderson, "Online Shopping and E-Commerce," *Pew Research Center: Internet and Technology*, December 19, 2016, http://www.pewinternet.org/2016/12/19/online-shopping-and-e-commerce/.

57. Pearl Pu, Li Chen, and Pratyush Kumar, "Evaluating Product Search and Recommender Systems for E-Commerce Environments," *Electronic Commerce Research* 8, no. 1/2 (2008), pp. 1–28.

58. Andreas B. Eisingerich and Tobia Kretschmer, "In E-Commerce, More Is More," *Harvard Business Review* 86, no. 3 (2008), pp. 20–38; and Amanda Spink and Bernard J. Jansen, "Trends in Searching for Commerce Related Information on Web-Search Engines," *Journal of Electronic Commerce Research* 9, no. 2 (2008), pp. 154–60.

59. Christy M. K. Cheung, Matthew K. O. Lee, and Neil Rabjohn, "The Impact of Electronic Word-of-Mouth: The Adoption of Online Opinions in Online Customer Communities," *Internet Research* 18, no. 3 (2008), pp. 229–41; and Dina Mayzlin, "Promotional Chat on the Internet," *Marketing Science* 25, no. 2 (2006), pp. 155–65.

60. Kyosti Pennanen, Tarja Tiainen, and Harri T. Luomala, "A Qualitative Exploration of a Consumer's Value Based e-Trust Building Process: A Framework Development," *Qualitative Market Research* 10, no. 1 (2007), pp. 28–42.

61. Louis Columbus, "Predicting the Future of B2B E-Commerce," *Forbes*, September 12, 2016, https://www.forbes.com/sites/louiscolumbus/2016/09/12/predicting-the-future-of-b2b-e-commerce/#24ea39de1eb9.

62. Myonung Soo Kim and Jae Hyeon Ahn, "Comparison of Trust Sources of an Online Market Maker in the E-Marketplace: Buyer's and Seller's Perspectives," *Journal of Computer Information Systems* 47, no. 1 (2006), pp. 84–95.

63. Vanessa DiMauro, "Big List 2.0: The Top Online Customer Communities 2014," *Leader Networks*, September 8, 2014, http://www.leadernetworks.com/2014/09/big-list-of-b2b-communities.html.

64. Deloitte, "Retail Industry Undergoing Massive Disruption," *Sponsored Content from Deloitte appearing in Wall Street Journal/CIO Journal*, http://deloitte.wsj.com/cio/2015/11/04/retail-industry-undergoing-massive-disruption/, accessed May 9, 2017.

65. Marcia Layton Turner, "Is Brick-And-Mortar Obsolete?" *Forbes*, January 31, 2017, https://www.forbes.com/sites/marciaturner/2017/01/31/is-brick-and-mortar-obsolete/#3bf5f83d37ce.

66. Turner, "Is Brick-and-Mortar Obsolete?"

67. "About Us," *Restoration Hardware*, https://www.restorationhardware.com/company-info/about-us.jsp, accessed May 9, 2017.

68. Sarah Halzack, "Restoration Hardware Is Betting That Americans Want Even More $7,000 Couches," *Washington Post*, June 16, 2015, https://www.washingtonpost.com/news/business/wp/2015/06/16/restoration-hardware-is-betting-that-americans-want-even-more-7000-couches/?utm_term=.ddf9c9b30831.

69. "Search Results," *Restoration Hardware*, https://www.restorationhardware.com/search/results.jsp?N=1012606503&Ntt=Pulls, accessed May 9, 2017; "Search Results," *Restoration Hardware*, https://www.restorationhardware.com/catalog/category/products.jsp?categoryId=cat2850001, accessed May 9, 2017; and "Search Results," *Restoration Hardware*, https://www.rhbabyandchild.com/search/results.jsp?N=3931888126&Ntt=Plush+Toys, accessed May 9, 2017.

70. Maxwell Ryan, "Why The Huge Catalog? And How Restoration Hardware Is Becoming the Ikea of Luxury Furnishings," *Apartment Therapy*, May 19, 2014, http://www.apartmenttherapy.com/why-the-huge-catalog-and-how-restoration-hardware-is-becoming-the-ikea-of-luxury-furnishings-203731.

71. Kathleen Kusek, "Does Restoration Hardware Deserve More Credit?" *Forbes*, June 14, 2016, https://www.forbes.com/sites/kathleenkusek/2016/06/14/does-restoration-hardware-deserve-more-credit/#2e812715e0f6.

72. Ryan, "Why The Huge Catalog?"

73. Turner, "Is Brick-And-Mortar Obsolete?"

74. Kusek, "Does Restoration Hardware Deserve More Credit?"; and Turner, "Is Brick-And-Mortar Obsolete?"

75. Turner, "Is Brick-And-Mortar Obsolete?"

76. Will Burns, "Restoration Hardware Direct-Mail Piece Sounds an Environmental Thud," *Forbes*, June 19, 2014, https://www.forbes.com/sites/willburns/2014/06/19/restoration-hardware-direct-mail-piece-sounds-an-environmental-thud/#7f85eb82f4f8.

77. Maxwell Ryan, "Why The Huge Catalog?"

78. "Membership," *Restoration Hardware*, https://www.restorationhardware.com/membership.jsp, accessed May 9, 2017.

79. Tom Ryan, "Is Restoration Hardware's Membership Program Flawed?" *Retail Wire*, December 16, 2016, http://www.retailwire.com/discussion/is-restoration-hardwares-membership-program-flawed/.

80. Sarah Halzack, "Restoration Hardware Is Having a Bad Week," *Chicago Tribune*, June 10, 2016, http://www.chicagotribune.com/business/ct-restoration-hardware-problems-20160610-story.html.

81. Halzack, "Restoration Hardware Is Having a Bad Week."

PART FIVE

Communicate the Value Offering

CHAPTER 13

Promotion Essentials: Digital and Social Media Marketing

LEARNING OBJECTIVES

LO 13-1 Understand promotion and identify the elements of the promotion mix.

LO 13-2 Explain the hierarchy of effects (AIDA) model and its usefulness to promotional strategy.

LO 13-3 Discuss the role and key types of digital marketing in communicating value to customers.

LO 13-4 Identify the key types of social media and their benefits to marketers in communicating value to customers.

ESSENTIALS OF PROMOTION

Marketing managers communicate with customers through promotion. **Promotion** involves communication with customers or potential customers designed to inform, persuade, or remind. Exhibit 13.1 identifies and defines five key promotional elements, and these elements make up the **promotion mix** used by marketing managers: **digital and social media marketing, advertising, sales promotion, public relations (PR),** and **personal selling**.

The promotion mix is vital to marketing planning. The development of **promotion mix strategies**, or simply *promotional strategies,* involves decisions about which combination of elements in the promotion mix is likely to best communicate the offering to the marketplace.

Entertainment companies like Cirque du Soleil recognize the importance of a strong promotion mix strategy. Here they present a beautiful and engaging website for their immersive touring show "OVO."

Source: Cirque du Soleil

EXHIBIT 13.1 | Definitions of Elements of the Promotion Mix

Promotion Mix Element	Definition
Digital and Social Media Marketing	Promotion through the use of digital technologies such as desktops, laptops, tablets, and smartphones that does not involve a salesperson. Often called *interactive marketing*, this approach enables customers to connect with a company directly in a two-way exchange.
Advertising	Paid form of relatively less personal marketing communications, often through a mass medium to one or more target markets. Example media include television, radio, magazines, newspapers, and outdoors.
Sales Promotion	Provides an inducement for an end-user consumer to buy your product or for a salesperson or someone else in the channel to sell it. Designed to augment other forms of promotion; rarely used alone. Example sales promotion tools for customers are coupons, rebates, and sweepstakes. Inducements for salespeople or channel members often involve special monies or prizes for pushing a particular offering.
Public Relations (PR)	Systematic approach to influencing attitudes, opinions, and behaviors of customers and others. Often executed through publicity, which is an unpaid and relatively less personal form of promotion, usually through news stories and mentions at public events.
Personal Selling	One-to-one personal communication with a customer by a salesperson, either in person or through other means.

EXHIBIT 13.2 | Capabilities of Promotion

Goal One: To Inform
- Indicate features when introducing new products or making product modifications
- Provide explanation of product functionality
- Articulate what a company and its brands stand for in order to develop a clear image
- Discuss various uses and applications for the product

Goal Two: To Persuade
- Impact customer perceptions of a product, especially in comparison to competitor's products
- Get customers to try a product, hopefully resulting in a more permanent switch from a competitor
- Influence customers to purchase right now due to some strong benefit or need
- Drive customers to seek more information online or through a salesperson

Goal Three: To Remind
- Maintain a customer relationship with a brand
- Provide impetus for purchase based on some impending event

The mix is designed to achieve an acceptable ROI for the marketer, given the product and target markets involved. For ongoing planning purposes, much of marketing communications operates on a campaign-to-campaign basis. A **promotional campaign** for a particular product or product line tracks the effectiveness and efficiency of promotional strategies as it allocates expenditures to a specific creative execution over a given time period.

Sometimes several media vehicles are used within one campaign. Nike+ is a built-in app in the iPhone, iPod, and iPod nano that allows you to pair a Nike+ Sensor to track your workouts. To promote the product, the firms combine multiple promotion mix elements that collectively provide more usage information, foster a sense of customer community, and of course allow for purchase of more related products! The purpose of the TV commercial is to drive traffic to the website.[1]

Earlier we defined promotion as the means by which various forms of communication are used to *inform*, *persuade*, or *remind* potential customers. Exhibit 13.2 summarizes these essential capabilities of promotion and some examples of how each might be deployed by marketing managers.

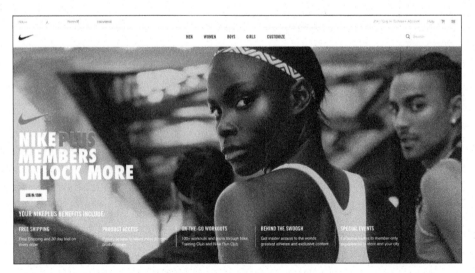

Nike+ members benefit from a variety of promotions designed to add value to their experience.

Source: Nike, Inc.

The Marketing Manager's Role in Promotional Strategy

The field of promotion is very broad and requires a good understanding in many distinct areas to execute effectively. As a part of the marketing field, the area of promotion tends more than any other to be heavily outsourced. Creative companies such as advertising and PR agencies have the focus and expertise to add substantial value to the execution of a marketer's promotional planning. And because of the unique nature of personal selling, most firms set up the sales organization as a separate entity from marketing, or they outsource it in the form of external distributors or brokers that represent a company's offerings to customers within the channel. But the proliferation of outsourcing of marketing communications and separation of sales from marketing do not absolve the marketing manager from the need to understand the basics of promotion so that the agency's contributions, as well as those of the sales force, can be properly integrated into the marketing planning process.

The seven major elements of the marketing manager's role in managing promotion are identified in Exhibit 13.3 as follows: identify targets for promotion, establish goals for promotion, select the promotion mix, develop the message, select media for use in promotion, prepare the promotion budget, and establish measures of results.

What kinds of decisions are involved in developing and executing a promotion mix strategy? Consider Exhibit 13.4, which compares the impact of marketing management factors in an advertising/sales promotion focused promotional approach with those of a personal selling focused approach. As you can see, a gamut of critical issues from buyer information needs to purchase size to the configuration of the marketing mix elements all influence the decision about where to invest promotional budget dollars. In fact, in many marketing planning situations, the promotional budget is the lion's share of the overall marketing budget—typically surpassing packaging, distribution, and other marketing elements by a wide margin.

EXHIBIT 13.3 | Elements of the Marketing Manager's Role in Promotional Strategy

Identify Targets for Promotion

↓

Establish Goals for Promotion

↓

Select the Promotion Mix

↓

Develop the Message

↓

Select Media for Use in Promotion

↓

Prepare Promotion Budget

↓

Establish Measures of Results

EXHIBIT 13.4 | Illustrative Factors Influencing Promotion Mix Strategy

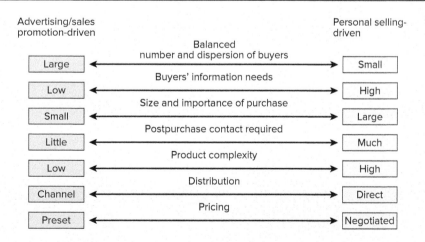

Source: Cravens, David R., and Piercy, Nigel F. *Strategic Marketing,* New York, NY: McGraw-Hill Education, 2013.

EXHIBIT 13.5 | Selected Pros and Cons of Individual Promotion Mix Elements

Promotion Mix Element	Pros	Cons
Digital and Social Media Marketing	• Message customization without high costs of personal selling • Strong relationship building, especially when customer can control the interaction	• Spam and other unwanted correspondence when targeting is poorly executed • Reliance on CRM and database marketing requires constant updating
Advertising	• Many media choices • Efficiently reaches large numbers of customers • Great creative flexibility	• Shotgun approach reaches many outside the target • Oversaturation of ads lessens impact • High production costs
Sales Promotion	• Stimulates purchase directly through incentive to buy • Serves as an effective accompaniment to other promotion forms	• Can lead customers to continually wait for the next coupon, rebate, etc. • Brand may be impacted by price-cutting image
Public Relations	• Unpaid communication seen as more credible than paid forms • Association of offering with quality media outlet enhances brand	• Low control of how the message turns out • Highly labor intensive cost of mounting PR campaigns
Personal Selling	• Strong two-way communication of ideas • Directly eases customer confusion and persuades purchase	• Very expensive cost per customer contact • Salesperson may go "off message" from brand to secure the sale

The allocation of the promotional marketing budget across the various elements of the promotion mix is a complex decision. Each promotional form has its own individual pros and cons, as Exhibit 13.5 shows. Within the promotion mix concept, it is the integration of the elements—not just each individual element—and the resulting synergies of the branding message that make the strongest sustainable impact on customers.

Push and Pull Strategies

Two fundamental approaches to promotional strategy utilized by marketing managers are *push* and *pull* strategies. These are depicted in Exhibit 13.6. The specific promotion mix elements selected for investment will vary depending on the relative degree of push or pull desired.

EXHIBIT 13.6 | Push and Pull Promotional Strategies

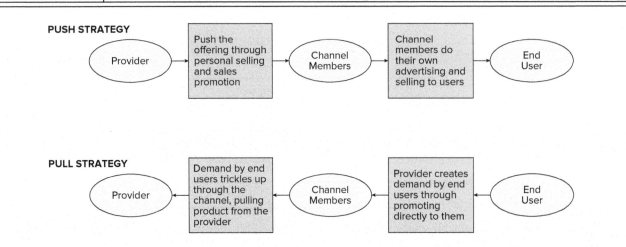

In a **push strategy**, the focus is on the channel of distribution, and in getting the offering into the channel. Members of the channel are targeted for promotion and are depended on to then push the offering into the hands of end users. A push strategy typically relies on a combination of personal selling and sales promotion directed toward channel members.[2] In a **pull strategy**, the focus shifts to stimulating demand for an offering directly from the end user. Advertising, consumer-directed sales promotion, PR, or direct and interactive marketing can be combined in various ways to target end users, creating demand that results in the channel making an offering available for purchase. In practice, push and pull strategies are rarely used mutually exclusively.[3] Rather, a promotional strategy is developed that strikes the best balance of investment of promotional funds in both push and pull strategies that make sense for the product and market involved.

Internal Marketing

A final critical aspect is **internal marketing**, which is the application of marketing concepts and strategies inside an organization. A great deal of research has shown that if members of an organization aren't knowledgeable about its offerings, don't understand who the customers are, and can't effectively articulate the branding message, successful marketing management is very difficult. The firm's employees are potentially its best and most trusted brand and message ambassadors. Properly armed, they can articulate what the firm and its offerings stand for in ways that nobody else can.[4]

Great brand marketers today pay a lot of attention to ensuring that *everybody* in the firm has pride of ownership in its brand, products, and services. From Southwest Airlines to Starbucks to Nordstrom to Ritz-Carlton, companies that do great marketing are placing a high priority on enabling each and every employee to communicate the marketing message. Most firms that are successful in internal marketing enlist the help of the human resources department to communicate the brand messages to all employees, beginning with employee orientation programs and continuing when new products are introduced or new markets are entered.

HIERARCHY OF EFFECTS (AIDA) MODEL

In developing and executing promotional strategy, it is important that marketing managers remember that customers pass through purchase decision processes in three steps: cognitive (learn), affective (feel), and behavioral (do). Various models support our understanding by illustrating these stages as a *hierarchy of effects* in the context of customer response to marketing communications. Here we illustrate one popular version of such models, the **AIDA model**, so named because the effects (or steps) build in this order: Attention (or Awareness), Interest, Desire, and Action. The attention stage correlates to the cognitive step of buyer decision making, the interest and desire stages to the affective step, and the action stage to the behavioral step.[5] Exhibit 13.7 portrays the AIDA model.

LO 13-2

Explain the hierarchy of effects (AIDA) model and its usefulness to promotional strategy.

Where target customers fit on the model is critically important to effective selection and execution of the promotion mix. As in the general communication model, various mixes of messages and media are required to ensure that the different targets are likely to decode and process the communication successfully. Below are tips for maximizing success in promoting across the stages of the AIDA model. Exhibit 13.8 suggests the general appropriateness of applying each of the promotion mix elements in coordination with each stage of the hierarchy of effects of the targets.

Attention

If target customers are essentially unaware of an offering, most of the investment in communication must be in raising awareness and gaining their attention. Depending on the situation, this may involve developing the customer's awareness for a whole new set of customer needs and wants as well as revealing that your product exists to address those needs and wants. In the initial

EXHIBIT 13.7 | **AIDA Model**

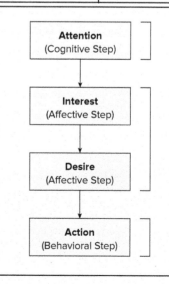

EXHIBIT 13.8 | General Suggestions for Applying Promotion Mix Elements at AIDA Stages

Promotion Mix Element	Attention Stage	Interest Stage	Desire Stage	Action Stage
Digital and Social Media Marketing	↑↑↑	↑↑↑	↑↑↑	↑↑↑
Advertising	↑↑↑	↑↑↑	↑↑	↑↑
Sales Promotion	↑↑	↑↑	↑↑↑	↑↑↑
Public Relations	↑↑↑	↑↑↑	↑↑	↑
Personal Selling	↑	↑	↑↑↑	↑↑↑

↑ = Generally least appropriate for use
↑↑↑ = Generally most appropriate for use

introduction of the Prius, Toyota put much effort into building awareness of the emerging need for hybrid cars and also into educating potential customers about what a hybrid car actually is. Essentially, the automaker created a product category from scratch, and for a while there was little return on the promotional investment. However, when gas prices began to soar and environmental issues became more prominent, Prius was in a prime position to become the leader in its product category, gaining a first-mover advantage and making it difficult for competitors to catch up. Now, every major car manufacturer is jumping into the category.

Gaining attention and building initial awareness can be a daunting task for marketers. Tremendous expenditures may be required to establish a foothold with customers, especially when a brand is relatively unknown or a product category is in its infancy. Chapter 6 covered different categories of adopters depending on how willing a potential customer is to try and buy a new product. At the attention stage of the AIDA model, marketing managers hope to use promotions to gain awareness of their offering with the innovators and early adopters. If marketers can influence these groups to purchase, innovators and early adopters can get others to jump on the bandwagon.

In many cases, gaining attention requires investment in mass appeal forms of promotion, especially advertising and PR. When ultra-premium Voss Artesian Water from Norway was introduced in the United States, marketers relied heavily on PR to create awareness, connecting the water to celebrities and gaining product placements in movies and in magazines sold in outlets frequented by the target customers.

Drink it
irresponsibly
artesian water from Norway

Ultra-premium Voss Artesian Water from Norway relied on heavy PR to create initial awareness when it was first introduced in the United States.

Source: Voss

Interest

To translate customer attention into interest requires persuasive communication. For more technical or complicated products, this means beginning to inform customers more specifically about what a product offering can do for *them*— how it helps fulfill needs and wants. To stimulate interest, the promotion must begin to touch a customer's hot buttons.

For example, generating awareness about the next-generation iPhone is not a problem for Apple—the buildup in the media is always gargantuan for months before the initial product introduction. But what would stimulate a person to move beyond inevitable awareness to interest in possibly purchasing? Apple masterfully uses its early promotion to cleverly point out new features and convince customers that any ordinary cell phone simply would not do. Interest is piqued by the communication of all the new bells and whistles that make your old iPhone "obsolete," and also by the imagery suggesting that each new iPhone is something really different.

Desire

Moving from interest to desire means that a customer has to move past a *need* and begin to really *want* that specific product. Promotion feeds desire through strong persuasive communication. At this stage, salespeople and customized direct and interactive marketing enter the promotion mix. Messages are altered to influence customers to feel that they simply can't do without the item. The innovators and early adopters show off their purchases to holdouts, and the ball is rolling.

Such is certainly the case with first-week purchasers of next-generation iPhones. Many people undoubtedly let their friends and co-workers see and touch their prized possession—sharing the experience of its functionality and form. Apple wisely drives the momentum through targeted promotions of all kinds, inviting potential customers into Apple stores so that salespeople can fully demonstrate the broad spectrum of product virtues. The interest stage of the hierarchy is generally where the emotional part of buyer decision making peaks, and much of the promotional message is centered on creating positive feelings for the brand and product.

Action

The action stage is the purchase itself. To stimulate ultimate purchase, marketers often rely on salespeople, accompanied by some form of sales promotion, to close the sale. The reason sales organizations put so much emphasis on training salespeople in closing techniques is that they are seen as the final stimulant to purchase. And sometimes sales promotion alone can stimulate purchase. For the customer, it can be a coupon, rebate, or other special extra to push them over the edge to buy.

Growing evidence suggests that millennials respond differently to promotional strategies than prior generations. These differences may be attributable to the hierarchy of effects they go through in making purchase decisions. Previous generations, which have been the focus of marketing for years (i.e., Gen X and older), did not grow up with the same level of information availability and access as the younger groups. As a result, marketers have traditionally been placed in the pivotal role of outbound information providers for these customers, largely through traditional promotional elements. This is true not only in the B2C marketplace, but also in B2B markets where organizational buyers have traditionally relied heavily on their salespeople for information about products and markets. Millennials have experienced a very different set of circumstances related to information. With today's web-based communications, they are accustomed to doing their own research on products, developing their own opinions, and then taking action with less influence from traditional promotional approaches (including salespeople).

This is not to say that the role of the marketing manager in developing promotional strategy is less important when it comes to the younger generation. Rather, the caution is that the response of younger generations to different promotional approaches is not the same as that of previous generations. They are much less likely to want to be "sold to," are generally disinterested in mass advertising, and tend to place high value on objective information for decision making, likely from sources outside of traditional promotion. For example, communication going on in social media, blogs, message boards, chat rooms, and other forms of virtual communities carry much more weight than other communication forms. Although in some ways these qualities make marketing to the younger generations different than to previous generations, be assured that their unique attitudes toward marketing also create important opportunities for marketers. For example, millennials are generally very tuned in to brands, thus affording an opportunity for marketing managers to smartly integrate branding into promotional themes.

In doing marketing planning in the 21st century, the marketing manager who addresses these preferences among the important younger generational markets will gain a competitive edge over marketers that attempt to capture this business through more traditional promotion forms.

THE ROLE OF DIGITAL MARKETING IN COMMUNICATING VALUE

LO 13-3

Discuss the role and key types of digital marketing in communicating value to customers.

The Internet has redefined the relationship between organizations and customers. As access to the Internet has grown and a wide range of Internet access points has proliferated, digital marketing has become a critical component of promotional strategy. Today some would say it is *the* most critical component. **Digital marketing** refers to the marketing of value offerings through the use of digital technologies (for example, desktops, laptops, tablets, and smartphones). Digital technologies have enabled individuals to access vast amounts of information almost instantaneously and have revolutionized the way organizations connect and communicate with their customers. An important aspect is that now customers have a great deal of control over when, where, and how they want to interact with marketers through digital media to gather information on products and services. This transformation presents a challenge to organizations, which now must determine how to expand digital access to information on their products and services in the most effective way. In both B2C and B2B markets, digital marketing is an essential element in an overall promotional strategy, thus becoming a key element in the promotion mix used by marketing managers to communicate the value offering.

The data collection capabilities facilitated by digital technologies enable marketing managers to gain access to information on customers at a breadth and depth never before possible, and at reasonable cost. These data can be collected either through interactions a firm creates or engages in with a customer, or via interactions that customers have with each other without direct firm involvement. As customers increasingly search for information, make transactions, and communicate through digital channels, an increasing amount of data will become available, enabling marketers to gain a more holistic view of individuals (recall our discussion of Big Data back in Chapter 5). Thus, for marketing managers one important aspect of a digital presence is the benefits it can provide in the form of enhanced information gathering and feedback.[6] This yields greater capability to apply key metrics to measure the effectiveness of specific marketing actions—for example, the percentage of customers who redeemed an online purchase discount code delivered through e-mail, or the average proportion of additional items that were included in the resulting online purchase.

Advances in digital technologies have opened the door to a broad array of potential means for marketers to interact with customers online, as illustrated by Exhibit 13.9. An important objective is to get the right information into the right hands at the right time in order to maximize desirable marketing outcomes. Options available to marketing managers for information dissemination can be classified as owned media, paid media, and earned media.[7] Exhibit 13.10 provides some examples and characteristics of these three types of digital media. **Paid media** refers to marketing communication channels requiring that the marketer pay someone else for customer access. In digital marketing, access to paid media can generally be purchased on a per-unit basis. Common pricing models include **cost per impression**, in which the marketing manager pays a set amount each time a customer is exposed to the promotion and **cost per click**, in which the marketing manager pays a set amount each time a customer clicks on a link. **Owned media** refers to marketing communication channels that the marketer's organization has complete control over. The content created on an organization's website is an example of owned media.

EXHIBIT 13.9 | **Examples of Digital Options for Marketing Information Sharing**

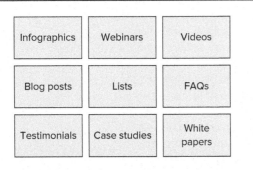

Infographics	Webinars	Videos
Blog posts	Lists	FAQs
Testimonials	Case studies	White papers

EXHIBIT 13.10 | Examples and Characteristics of Paid Media, Owned Media, and Earned Media

	Examples	Advantages	Potential Issues
Paid Media	• Display ads • Search ads • Native ads • Social network ads	• Speed • Flexibility • Targeting capabilities • Scalability • Control • Measurability	• Difficulty standing out • Declining response rates • Potential credibility issues
Owned Media	• Firm's website (mobile and non-mobile) • E-mail • Firm's blog • Firm's social media account	• Longevity • Flexibility • Ability to speak to niche audiences in depth	• Potential credibility issues • Potentially substantial development effort required • Desired results may be achieved over longer time horizons
Earned Media	• Social media shares • User reviews of products • Mentions of an organization on a third party's website or blog	• Credibility • Potential cost efficiencies • Transparency	• Lack of control • Communications and conversations may be negative • Value can be difficult to measure

Earned media is a bit different, as it refers to the case where either a customer or a commercial entity (such as a news media organization) chooses to act as a marketing communication channel for the dissemination of information associated with the marketer's organization at no cost. An example is when a customer shares a link to a blog post about a new product's launch on a social network because he or she is excited about the new product. Later on in this chapter there's a section specific to social media, and there we will discuss factors that motivate earned media and its benefits to marketers. For now, let's discuss various paid media and owned media options.

Digital Advertising

Digital advertising is the creation and execution of an advertisement via any form of digital media. Like other digital marketing efforts, digital advertising benefits from the richness of data that is generated by the customer's exposure to the ad, which in turn allows for a more granular review of the ad's performance. This measurement capability is especially clear when a digital ad drives a customer to take a specific action on a website that has a clear monetary value, such as when an ad contains a promotional offer to purchase a product at a discounted rate and clicking on it leads to a page where the offer can be redeemed and the purchase made. The ad's value in generating sales can be directly measured by how many customers were exposed to the ad and how many of those exposed customers redeemed the offer. Unlike most non-digital types of advertising, with this approach the promotional strategy can be adjusted quickly if the data indicate that the current message isn't working well.

Another key benefit of digital advertising is its ability to distribute different information to different segments of customers of varying sizes with greater flexibility. Because some digital communication channels such as social networking platforms and search engines are designed so that what is displayed on their pages can be custom-adjusted for a given viewer at relatively minimal cost, the marketer is afforded great flexibility in the communication. Ad messaging can be adjusted based on predetermined factors such as how many customers the marketing manager wishes to deliver the communication to or specific characteristics possessed by a customer (for example, customer demographics or the use of a specific search term). The result is that the marketing manager has greater confidence that the advertising expenditure is going toward targeting the desired customer. Contrast this level of confidence with that of a marketing manager placing an ad in a print magazine that boasts a substantial number of readers fitting the desired target market. Of course, the readership also contains a substantial (probably by a large majority) number of readers who are not a very good fit for the ad message. A magazine's advertising rates are typically based on its full readership base, yet the marketing manager is stuck communicating to many who will not find value in the message. And, adding insult to injury, it is much more difficult to gauge impact from print versus digital media via marketing metrics.

The above example isn't a bash on print advertising—rather, it is a reminder that marketers need to carefully think through what investments of their promotion budget are the best ROI for their offering. There are contexts where digital advertising may be a more appropriate choice versus more traditional advertising, as well as contexts where the opposite holds true. The customer whom the marketer is attempting to reach, the cost of reaching that customer through a given form of media, and the specific communication forms available through that media generally determine whether digital or other advertising is the more suitable choice and which of the potential options within each will produce the most desirable outcome.

Display Ads Digital ads that are displayed on a given page within a website that clearly demarcates the ad from the webpage's primary content (what the customer navigated to that page for) are called **display ads.** Display ads can take on multiple forms, including banner ads and interstitials. **Banner ads** are boxes embedded into a website that can contain graphics, text, or video elements as well as an embedded hyperlink to take the viewer to a webpage intended to facilitate subsequent interactions between the viewer and the advertiser. The sophistication of banner ads has increased over time, with the inclusion of greater interactive capabilities and richer media experiences. An interesting historical tidbit is that the original banner ad that was distributed in 1994 was a simple image with some graphical and textual elements contained within it. In its first four months, 44 percent of those exposed to it succumbed to temptation and clicked on it. Today's surfers are more wary—the average for a banner ad today is clicks by only four people for every 10,000 who are exposed to it![8] **Interstitials** are full-page ads that are delivered before the viewer is directed to the intended webpage visit. Interstitials tend to be very visually appealing, with graphical elements that capitalize on the substantial real estate they inherently hold.

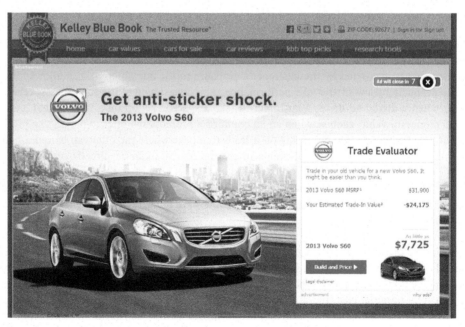

This Volvo ad is an interstitial ad on the Kelley Blue Book website.

Source: Kelley Blue Book Co.®, Inc./Volvo Car Corporation

EXHIBIT 13.11 | Example of Retargeting Process Flow

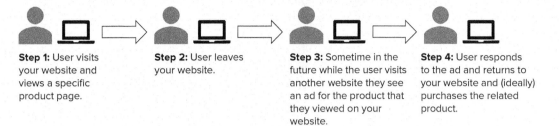

Step 1: User visits your website and views a specific product page.

Step 2: User leaves your website.

Step 3: Sometime in the future while the user visits another website they see an ad for the product that they viewed on your website.

Step 4: User responds to the ad and returns to your website and (ideally) purchases the related product.

Display ads can be placed on specific websites in which an ad is expected to be more relevant based on the assumed interests, characteristics, or preferences of visitors to the website. Banner ads can also be distributed to customers based on specific past behaviors online. For example, a method known as **retargeting** displays ads for a given product on different websites (not associated with the product) only after a customer has visited the website for the related product. The presumption is that this customer has a higher level of interest in the product, so the retargeting of display ads is more likely to result in a positive outcome (an inquiry or sale) for the advertiser of the product. Exhibit 13.11 provides an example of how the process of retargeting works.

Search Ads Another effective digital ad option is **search ads,** which are displayed with the results produced by search engines, typically at the top of or along a column to the side of the search results on a webpage. For example, Googling for "Orlando hotels" most likely will bring up at the top of the page search ads for Expedia, Hotels.com, Trip Advisor, and Kayak (all flagged by Google as "Ad") before you ever get to specific hotel websites in the area.

As with most types of digital advertising, a key component of a search ad is the inclusion of a hyperlink to the advertiser's webpage. Aside from the widespread use of search engines which provides marketers with the ability to reach a substantial proportion of the population through access to the results they display, search advertising also offers marketers the unique capability to target customers with ads based on the potential relationship between the specific information that a customer is interested in obtaining from the search and the information that can be obtained by engaging with the ad that appears. The way it works is that a marketer will bid on a specific keyword, which can be a combination of words and phrases, in order to have a text ad placed in the displayed results of a search that matches the keyword(s) that the marketer successfully bid on. Search ads can be priced on a cost-per-click, cost-per-impression, or cost-per-conversion basis—the latter being a desirable and trackable action such as a sale. Also, it is highly useful that the advertising firm is able to determine how many click-throughs or relevant interactions they are interested in paying for based on budget and related factors.[9]

Importantly, the contents of a customer's keyword search can offer key insights into both the information sought and the customer's stage in the buying process.[10] For example, a marketing manager may be more interested in purchasing search ads associated with a keyword that suggests that a customer is at one stage or another in the buying decision process. The message about the offering can be appropriately customized for a particular customer's stage in the process. In the case of cars, a customer who uses a keyword such as "deals on new cars" is probably more receptive to a search ad from any of the car dealers in the locale as compared to a customer who searches for "upcoming specials on Ford F-150s," who likely will be most receptive to an ad from the local Ford dealer (or who may just go directly to the relevant page on the dealer's website that is probably already displayed in the normal search results). In the case of this example, it is probably reasonable to believe that the keyword "deals on new cars" will carry a greater cost than the keyword "upcoming specials on Ford F-150s" due to the greater competition expected when bidding on the former versus the latter phrase.

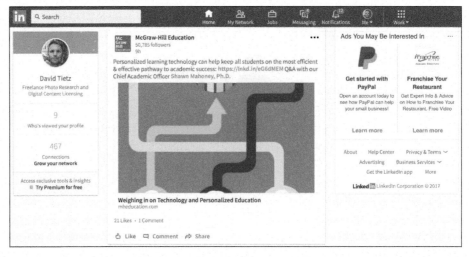

Notice the social network ads on the right in the LinkedIn page above. Such ads take advantage of a captive audience of viewers who hopefully will have a high likelihood of attracting click-through to provide more details about the offer.

Source: LinkedIn

Social Network Ads Digital ads displayed on various forms of social media are called **social network ads**. Distributed through a wide range of social networking platforms such as Facebook, Twitter, and LinkedIn, these can vary considerably in their format, placement, and style. Some forms of social network ads are designed to resemble and function in a manner similar to the different ways that users on the particular platform communicate with each other, while other forms resemble and function similarly to our earlier discussion of display ads.

Later in this chapter we will look in greater detail at the topic of social media (extending beyond just social networks) and its relevance to marketing managers. For now, it is important to know that social networking platforms can offer marketers the ability to reach very specific segments of customers based on criteria that could not easily be achieved through other digital or more traditional promotional channels. Users share a wide range of information on social networking platforms and engage in a wide range of interactions. Examples of customer information that is readily accessible to marketers through different social networking platforms include current and permanent location, demographic characteristics, purchase behaviors, general interests, and relationships with people, brands, and organizations. Obviously, this information can be gathered and used for reaching specific segments of customers and for crafting more personalized marketing communications.

Native Ads Digital ads that are designed to fit the format and style of content that is offered through the website on which the ad is being displayed are called **native ads**. In the case of online publications, native ads tend to be articles or posts that cover a topic of interest to the readership. The content of a native ad tends not to include any type of heavy sales pitch for a marketer's offering; instead, it will typically cover a topic that has some logical connection to the marketer's organization, and potentially one of their specific products or services. Most organizations that offer native advertising options on their websites or platforms take specific steps to ensure that viewers of the related ads understand that the content came from and was paid for by another organization. While increased recognition by viewers of some content as a native ad may have a negative influence on their evaluations of the content, it also helps avoid the risk that viewers will feel that the host provider of native advertising options is deceiving them.[11]

E-Mail

Although e-mail has been with us for over 20 years, it still offers marketers many advantages as a promotion tool. First, e-mail is a communication channel that the marketer has control over because it is owned media. Second, it can be targeted and customized to the individual. Third, it is immediate, so organizations can offer coupons or other sales promotions quickly and expect and monitor the results. Fourth, it allows for additional personalization as individuals can opt for specific messaging that increases the likelihood it will be read. Fifth, it produces a rich amount of data on how individuals interact with an e-mail. Examples include if and when they open the e-mail, specific links clicked on within the e-mail, subsequent customer actions on the organization's website, and if and when the e-mail is forwarded by one person to another person.

Despite all these potential advantages, e-mail does have a substantial downside as a digital marketing tool. The 800-pound gorilla is that, just like unsolicited direct mail sent through the post office, e-mail can easily be dumped without even opening the message. Most people are inundated with e-mail today and incorporate spam filters and other tools to limit the e-mails they receive. And the millennial and post-millennial generations look on e-mail as old hat, preferring to correspond by text or social media platforms. Bottom line, e-mail works best when it is part of a broader marketing communications strategy that includes a good mix of modalities to communicate with the target audience. In the current era of multimedia channels with customers and firms that over-rely or even rely solely on e-mail for promotional messaging risk coming up short on results.

Organizational Website

An organization's website is the primary point of connection with the online customer and arguably the most critical form of owned media for an organization. Customers visit a website to get information, ask questions, register complaints, develop a sense of community with other users, and hopefully ultimately make a purchase. As a result, a website must do a number of things well. Performing the traditional role of a retail storefront, an organization's website needs to convey the value proposition to anyone who visits. Effective sites are able to draw new potential customers inside to check out the products and services therein. At the same time, the website must service existing customers by providing access to customer service and information in an easy manner.

From a *technical* standpoint, a landing page is any page on a website that a user is directed to by clicking on a hyperlink. However, in the context of our present discussion on digital marketing a **landing page** is a distinct type of page on an organization's website designed for the sole purpose of getting a customer to take an action that increases the expected value of the customer to the organization. All of the marketing communications options discussed so far commonly contain a hyperlink pointing to a landing page that is intended to serve just such a specific purpose, such as enabling an immediate transaction, providing additional information about an offering, and capturing personal information (including contact information) from a customer so that the marketer can better customize subsequent communications. For example, a customer interested in exploring the possibility of obtaining an MBA degree online might begin the journey by clicking on an intriguing digital ad provided by a university. The ad takes the customer to a landing page where some initial information on the program is provided, along with a prompt to submit some personal information through an e-form, with the promise of prompt recontact with additional information by a university admissions officer.

Dimensions of Website Interface Customer website interface is often defined by 7 Cs: context, content, community, customization, communication, and commerce. Exhibit 13.12 illustrates the 7 Cs for the popular and very successful Zappos website.

Context Context refers to the overall layout, design, and aesthetic appeal of the site. Broadband and high-speed Internet has led to more graphics, video, and

Kingsley Judd Wine Investments is an example of an effective landing page designed for lead generation.

Source: Kingsley Judd

EXHIBIT 13.12 | **7 Cs of Customer Website Interface at Zappos**

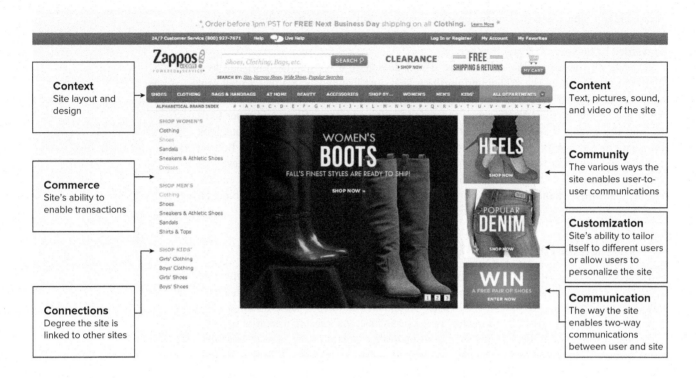

Source: Zappos.com, Inc

interesting design features that make a website more appealing. The perennial challenge for the web designer is balancing the aesthetic appeal of high graphic content with the download time for graphics and other complex visual elements. The look and feel of the site must be consistent with the organization or product's overall brand image. For example, visit the Zappos website and then go to Lucky Brand website to see how different organizations approach the layout and design of a website.

Content In the past, organizations put their existing print materials (catalogs, for example) on the website, and there was little in the way of original web content. Today, organizations' websites incorporate a great deal of web-specific content. Organizations such as Costco and Target have a specific web strategy that displays products not available in stores, and many organizations such as The Gap offer web-exclusive deals on products. Text, photos, videos, charts, and graphics are all part of web content.

Community A key advantage of web-based communication is the opportunity to create a community of users or visitors to the site. Blogs and organizational bulletin boards encourage a sense of community that enhances customers' experiences with the product and selling firm. In many cases, rather than selling firms, it is third parties such as Kelley Blue Book (an auto industry site) that operate the most powerful online communities. These communities bring users (or car owners in the case of Kelley Blue Book) together to discuss a variety of topics. They provide solutions (generated by members of the community) to problems, discuss the advantages and disadvantages of product features, and encourage people interested in the product to connect with each other and with the selling firms.

Customization The ability to create a unique individual experience with an organization website adds great value to the customer interface, because nowadays online customers appreciate and expect customization of their website experiences. Simple customization includes the ability to turn off the sound from the site and reduce the graphic interface (html versus flash sites). More customized sites enable customers to choose content and context. ESPN, for example, allows each user of the site to customize the homepage to display relevant information in a side column about a given user's favorite teams, including upcoming games, scores, and stories.

Communication Websites allow organizations to communicate with customers in three key ways. First, organizations communicate to customers and visitors to the website one on one through the Contact feature or e-mail. Second, customers and interested visitors communicate directly with the organization through customer service requests. Finally, organizations use instant messaging for customer service requests and sales inquiries (ever have one of those pop-up boxes that says "I'm here—do you need help?"). They're like convenient little salespeople who often can generate quite a lot of business.

Connection The web allows for communication among many sources. Information sites such as Edmunds.com (automobiles) and CNET.com (electronics) offer a lot of information at the site but also allow users to access relevant manufacturer and retailer websites when a customer needs more information or wishes to make a purchase. This easy, seamless connectivity greatly expands the usefulness of the site for customers.

WWF employs a simple, yet effective, call to action on its website.
Source: World Wildlife Fund

Commerce The number of products purchased online has grown dramatically in both B2C and B2B markets. Web designers know that creating a simple, easy-to-understand, and secure purchase experience is essential for success in online commerce. Given the proliferation of theft of credit card numbers electronically, customers are correctly concerned with a provider's level of online purchase security. Today, the website *must* be able to legitimately assure customers that their data are secure.

Microsites In addition to an organization's primary website, they may also create smaller, more focused sites that deal with specific topics such as new product introductions or targeted products. The smaller, more focused websites within such a portfolio are called **microsites.** For example, Audi, Mercedes-Benz, and Sony create smaller sites to highlight certain products. In another application, banks create microsites to help customers work through specific issues such as home financing (value of current home, links to real estate sites like Zillow) or information about cars (reviews, getting a loan).

Blogs As noted previously, *content* is one of the seven key dimensions of web interface. One of the ways that an organization can communicate with potential customers and continue to communicate with current customers is through the development of a blog (a word that truncates the words "web" and "log"). An organization's **blog** serves as a repository of content they create to provide information of interest to customers in the form of blog posts, which can be one or more paragraphs in length and written to stand on their own or be thematically connected to other posts. A blog can either be developed as a stand-alone website or integrated into an organization's primary website. Blog posts can contain information specific to the organization (such as information on a new product) or they can provide information on a relevant topic that customers are interested in learning more about. In the B2B space, organizations such as Salesforce and Hubspot have incorporated blogs into their websites which contain posts written both by employee experts and industry thought leaders with the objective of providing valuable information to marketing and sales professionals (and, of course, influencing them to adopt their products).

Search Engine Optimization (SEO)

As mentioned in our discussion of search ads, search engines play an important role in how customers search for and gather information. **Search engine optimization (SEO)** comprises the set of different actions that can be undertaken by an organization to positively influence the placement of their digital assets (vis-à-vis their websites) in relevant search engine results. For many organizations, being able to be displayed near the top of organic search results (searches that are not paid for) is of high value because it increases the likelihood of being found by potential customers and further strengthening relationships with existing customers. The old adage that you want to be on the first page of a list of search results is absolutely true! Most, if not all, of the digital communication options we've discussed so far have implications for an organization's SEO efforts. This is because, in a fairly simplified sense, search engines attempt to provide users with web results viewed to be the best fit for their specific searches based both on the relevance and the reputation of the source that pours into the output results.[12] A benefit of having a website displayed toward the top of the results is that customers tend to view it as a more credible source, resulting in additional benefits to an organization and its brand beyond just a greater likelihood that the customer will click on the link.[13] A *well-integrated* digital communication strategy can help improve an organization's SEO performance by ensuring that their paid, earned, and owned media efforts all provide value to current customers, potential customers, and other stakeholders in a consistently relevant manner.

Mobile Marketing

Today, for a massive number of customers, it's all about the handheld device. Mobile communication devices have accelerated in sophisticated capabilities and are literally an omnipresent part of the daily lives of many customers (some might call it an obsession). Hence, **mobile marketing**, or the marketing of value offerings through a mobile communication device, is a central aspect of digital marketing strategies.

Before we proceed, it is worth reinforcing that when we refer to mobile communication devices we are *primarily* talking about smartphones and tablets. Their extreme portability and ubiquitous nature provides marketers with many advantages, including the fact that both time-sensitive and location-sensitive communications can be most effectively delivered to customers through them. Some estimates suggest that the average adult in the United States spends almost three hours per day on a mobile device, and this is *increasing.*[14] Because of the characteristic differences in how mobile devices are both designed by manufacturers and used by customers, we need to point out how marketing communications are designed and executed on them differently than their non-mobile counterparts.

Ads and Website Experiences Designed for Mobile Devices Differences in how information is displayed and interacted with on mobile devices create both opportunities and challenges for how marketing managers communicate with customers. For example, a smartphone's relatively smaller screen size and touch-based interface means that certain aspects of websites or ads designed may be viewed and interacted with differently than they would be on other media. Obviously, a navigational element on a website that would require a user to hover a mouse to view its contents would not be suitable on a smartphone. So organizations tend to either construct separate mobile-friendly websites, or alternatively to include within their main websites responsive design elements that contain the ability to make adjustments (reorientation and resizing of sections of the site, touch-friendly interfaces, and the like) based on the type of device that is being used to view it. For marketing managers, clearly these same considerations are important when developing ads that will be offered exclusively on mobile devices or across both mobile and non-mobile media types.

Customers are massively engaging in making purchases with mobile devices. **M-commerce**, sales generated from a mobile device, is a rapidly growing component of the customer mobile experience. Given the process complexities involved in purchasing a product or service online, it is critical that marketing

Gatwick Airport in the London area offers great consistency in style and messaging to users accessing their site via either computer or mobile device.

Source: Gatwick Airport Limited

managers have a lead seat at the table with IT and operations to ensure that their organization's websites are designed to make the shopping experience on different customer interface modalities as seamless as possible. Think of it this way: Customers who become frustrated with the process of making a purchase on their mobile device may drop out of the purchase process and instead seek out a competitor's more user-friendly site instead, or they may slog through the painful purchase but vow never to come back.

Location-Based Targeting Mobile devices accommodate tracking of an individual's location at a level of precision that is not possible with most other types of devices. **Geolocation marketing** is the use of geographic data to drive marketing messaging and other marketing management decisions. In mobile marketing, this capability has several potential applications. One such application is that it can be used to provide promotional offers from an organization to customers when they are near one of the organization's storefronts. Or promotions can be offered to individuals when they are not near the location but have been in or near the store recently, as a way to get the customer's attention to go back. For example, Whole Foods has used geolocation marketing to deliver ads to smartphones both when customers were near its own locations or when they were near the locations of competitors. Ads were primarily served on weekends when "out and about" customers were more likely to have plans to shop for groceries. People exposed to these ads responded to them at a rate about triple the industry average.[15] Also, promotional offers for specific products can be offered to customers in-store as they shop in order to drive product sales that otherwise might not have been part of their shopping basket.[16] For these types of applications, best practice in marketing dictates that customers willingly opt in in advance. In addition to transparency, as with all things digital marketing, customer privacy and security issues must be paramount for marketing managers when deploying geolocation marketing.

Another opportunistic application of geolocation marketing is enhancement of specific services where knowledge of a customer's location and improved timing of service delivery can increase customer satisfaction. For example, enabling a restaurant customer to order, pay for a food or beverage item, and receive an estimated time that the item will be ready from a nearby location via smartphone provides increased convenience for the customer, who is able to save time by showing up right when the item is ready. Previous technological limitations to consistently executing such a real-time service approach are being overcome, and one can imagine many uses for this approach by savvy marketers determined to tap into the convenience-seeking customer.

Text Messaging Text messaging (also referred to as short message service or SMS) is certainly a popular form of communication and ideally suited for marketing messaging when a shorter format is feasible and appropriate. Text messaging can be effectively used for instantly redeemable promotional offers, contest voting, sweepstakes participation, informational alerts, and many other real-time offers. SMS campaigns are inherently simple to develop and execute, and can serve as a particularly effective communication medium for reaching a younger segment of the market for whom e-mail is not a first or primary choice for correspondence.[17] Despite the potential advantages of SMS, it is important for organizations to make sure that customers are given the choice to opt in to text message communications and also have an easy and transparent means of opting out at any point in time. The delivery of unsolicited text messages or difficulty in getting off of a text messaging list can badly damage an organization's image and even potentially result in legal ramifications (remember that text messages go to *phone numbers,* which may be on do not call lists).[18] And even in the case where a customer does opt in to text messaging of promotions, the delivery of a high frequency of messages can be perceived as intrusive and damage the brand and customer relationship. In sum, it is important for marketing managers to monitor and understand how effective their SMS communications are and when they border on being excessive.

Branded Mobile Apps and In-App Based Ads Mobile apps offer marketers another robust digital mobile marketing approach to promoting their offerings to customers. **Branded mobile apps** display the brand's name and logo prominently throughout the various screens and features within the app. These apps, which are a type of owned media, can be an effective means of communicating with customers because they offer numerous valuable functions and benefits that cause the customer to willingly decide to make the effort to do the download (many are free, of course). An app can positively influence how the customer views the brand and stimulate purchase and loyalty.[19]

In addition, a variety of other types of mobile apps (for example, mobile game apps, social media apps, and nonbranded productivity apps) offer opportunities for marketing managers to communicate with customers through ads that feature a mix of text, image, and video elements. Ads displayed within such mobile apps are called **in-app ads**, and these have become an increasingly important option within the marketer's digital tool kit. Their popularity is driven by the overall growth of app usage on mobile devices. Basically, all of the advantages and capabilities we have discussed in relation to digital marketing and mobile marketing are available for marketing managers to leverage within the context of in-app ads.

MANAGING SOCIAL MEDIA MARKETING: NOW THE CUSTOMER IS INVOLVED IN THE DIALOGUE

LO 13-4

Identify the key types of social media and their benefits to marketers in communicating value to customers.

Perhaps no change has had a greater impact on how organizations communicate with customers than the exponential growth of social media. Evidence of social media's widespread use and adoption is supported by research finding that more than half of adults within the United States use two or more social networking sites.[20] The ability for people to come together online has moved the conversation about an organization and its offerings away from the organization as initiator and into the hands of the public. Customers speak directly to each other about the good and bad of their product and service experiences. Organizations can monitor, participate, and respond, but they *cannot control* this external dialogue, thus creating both opportunities and threats for organizations as they look to first understand the impact of social media on their business and then to develop effective marketing strategies to manage it. When done well, an organization's social media presence can reinforce existing marketing messaging as well as give them a more community-focused, tech-savvy presence. In addition, the immediacy of social media actually works to "force" marketers to stay connected to their customers 24/7. On the flip side, an ineffective or poorly executed social media strategy can immediately damage an organization's image and spill over to reduce the effectiveness of other marketing communications.

Communications about an organization that are distributed through social media can fit into all three of the classifications of marketing communications discussed earlier in the chapter—paid media, earned media, and owned media. Because of the "social" aspect of social media, an organization can benefit from the generation of earned media by customers who are passionate about the organization's brands, products, or services, with the potential for these communications to reach huge audiences at little or no cost to the marketing budget. Within social media platforms, marketers typically seek to create communications that customers will find informative, entertaining, or hopefully both, with the potential added benefit that some members of the audience will act to spread the communication to an even larger audience (a topic we will discuss in greater detail later in this chapter). In addition, the interactive nature of social media platforms allows marketers to identify conversations about a brand and join into those conversations. Put another way, rather than simply "talking at" customers, as is the case with some other marketing communications, social media marketing fosters a more salient two-way relationship in real time.

Types of Social Media

The key forms of social media most relevant to marketers are social networks and viral marketing, product/service review sites, and online brand communities.

Social Networks As the name implies, **social networks** are about connecting people through friendships, mutual interest, or some other characteristics. The concept of a social network goes back to the 1800s, when it referred to a collection of people who developed a relationship based on some unifying element. A modern interpretation of the term refers to groups of people connected through technology. Today, there are hundreds of social networks that vary widely in the interests catered to and the ways that users communicate and interact within the network. Given the sheer number of social networking platforms available to customers, it is generally not feasible (or desirable) for even the largest organizations to maintain an effective digital presence across them all. Thus, identifying the particular social networks that an organization's customers tend to interact with most helps determine where a marketing manager can best invest promotional budget.

As mentioned previously, each social network tends to possess unique characteristics of how users communicate on the network. So the content developed and communication strategy employed typically is different for the marketer on each network. For example, a strategy focused on sharing short videos on one platform and sharing still images on another platform is common. These varying ways of media sharing across networks give marketers a chance to spread their creative wings and have some fun reflecting brand personalities through different approaches such as making a funny comment about a specific current event as it is happening on one platform, while sharing an amusing meme on another. A well-orchestrated mix of actions on social media has positive benefits for brand image and reinforces customer relationship quality with the brand.[21]

To get a better sense of some of the more distinctive characteristics and capabilities of social networks and their implications for marketers, let's examine four of the more popular social networking platforms: Facebook, Twitter, Snapchat, and LinkedIn.

Facebook Active users at present: over 1.5 billion and growing. Facebook currently is the largest social networking platform in the world. It was originally started as a site for college students to connect with each other, but Facebook has grown to include a broad

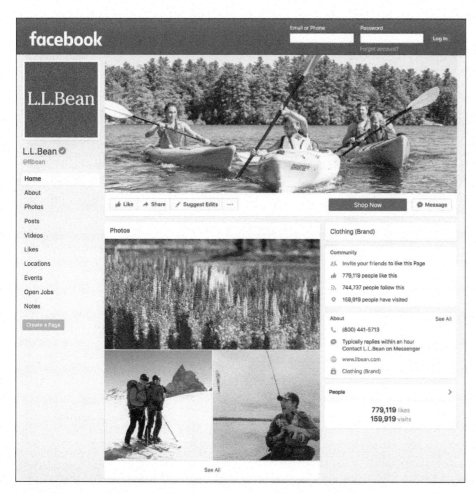

L.L. Bean has a strong presence on Facebook, a smart approach that contributes to their overall success in the marketplace.

Source: L.L. Bean/Facebook

base of different users, from grandparents to kids, large organizations to small entrepreneurs. For marketers, Facebook represents one of the best opportunities to engage a social network, as its open access and broad appeal can translate to a large number of Facebook friends. Some organizations such as L.L. Bean, with over 700,000 followers, have embraced Facebook with a strategy designed to offer unique photos, videos, and tips related to experiences in the outdoors. Other organizations such as Apple take a more conservative approach, with minimal presence on Facebook. One of the challenges for organizations is the never-ending need for currency and immediacy of postings on social network sites. Creating a Facebook page may not have budget implications in and of itself, but making it continually interesting and, more importantly, giving people a reason to come back requires a significant ongoing commitment. In addition, as individuals post comments, the company must dedicate resources to make sure that the folks posting "feel the love" of being connected in a two-way dialogue with the organization.

Twitter Active users at present: over 300 million and growing. Twitter features the creation and dissemination of short-form communications (tweets). Users on Twitter can post photos, videos, and text. One of the hallmark characteristics of Twitter is its limited number of characters per given tweet. This parameter creates some interesting dynamics for the nature of interactions between customers and marketers, as marketers learn how best to maximize the value of this platform for communications.[22] Twitter clearly presents an opportunity to engage in discussions with customers and disseminate or respond to news related to the brand. Note, though, that a hallmark of Twitter is the user expectation of very quick and timely response to questions or comments. Organizations such as JetBlue use Twitter to deliver customer service excellence by closely monitoring and responding to basically every tweet that is sent its way. If a bunch of passengers are stuck on a delayed plane on the tarmac at JFK airport, you can bet that one or more will tweet, and you can count on JetBlue to respond probably before the plane finally takes off. More broadly, Twitter activity can offer marketers

JetBlue embraces Twitter as a key way to stay on top of customer sentiments and trends.

Source: JetBlue Airways/Twitter

valuable insights into customer experiences with products and services as well as capture their feelings about organizations and their brands.

Snapchat Active users at present: over 200 million and growing. Snapchat offers users the capability to share photos and videos, but with limits on the number of views and length of time of views. This temporary nature of the content on Snapchat provides a certain level of appeal to users that arguably resonates most with a younger demographic. While many social networks may have user-age distributions that skew toward the younger side, Snapchat boasts that about 60 percent of its users are between the ages of 13 and 24.[23] Snapchat also features the use of filters, which are visual effects that alter a user's face in different, oftentimes amusing ways. Organizations can even work with Snapchat to develop sponsored filters to promote specific products or brands. For example, Gatorade worked with Snapchat to create a Super Bowl filter where users could create videos that showcased a floating Gatorade cooler being dumped on their heads (as a takeoff from the iconic "Gatorade bath" that the players on a sports teams that just won a championship typically give their coach). The fleeting nature of content shared on Snapchat likely also encourages customers to be more honest in their posts, and marketers that take a similar approach to providing brand-related content that comes across as more honest and less polished can see substantial benefits from this platform.

LinkedIn Active users at present: over 400 million and growing. Targeted toward working professionals, LinkedIn offers some distinct advantages in terms of a professional calling card. Key features include the ability to create a contact network of people that allows for offering introductions, staying in touch, reading and sharing content relevant to a professional audience (such as industry news, opinions on how a profession is changing, and tips on job hunting), and gaining access to resources for developing or enhancing professional skills. People opt in to an individual's contact network by being asked to join and responding affirmatively. Organizations are making extensive use of LinkedIn for recruiting. The amount of information individuals place on LinkedIn about their professional background and industry affiliations make it an especially valuable tool for recruiters looking for great candidates for a job opening. For jobs that have especially technical or unique requirements, LinkedIn's search capabilities allow recruiters to identify a set of potential individuals to whom to promote a job opportunity, folks who very closely match the job requirements. Not surprisingly, salespeople are prolific users of LinkedIn to smoke out prospects or to find influencers of purchase decisions in target firms. The good news about LinkedIn for marketing managers is its strong focus on B2B, allowing for communication of goods and services relevant to B2B users.

Viral Marketing The immediacy and personalization of social networks (and actually the web itself) sets the stage for viral marketing, sometimes also called buzz marketing. **Viral marketing** is simply a marketing phenomenon that facilitates and encourages people to pass along a marketing message.[24] The concept is called "viral" because the process of exposure to a message mimics the process of passing a virus or disease from one person to another. It's the process of creating a video clip, image, message, e-book, or some other content in an effort to have it passed on by individuals within a social network or by word of mouth. Marketing managers have understood for decades how valuable strong word of mouth can be to product success. The rapid growth of social networking on the Internet and today's laser-targeting capabilities in marketing combine to make it possible to create marketing communication campaigns that simulate an in-person, word-of-mouth, one-to-one approach online.

Important considerations for viral marketing include the characteristics of the social networks (that is, how members communicate and what they value) to be used and the relationship characteristics (such as the strength and number of relationships) of those networks. Finding the right combination of these elements hopefully yields appropriate conditions for a successful **seeding strategy**, which entails initiating a viral marketing approach to specific customers or groups of customers who then further stimulate the internal dynamics of the target market, thus resulting in the diffusion process (spread of the virus). A seeding strategy benefits from including both individuals who can spread a message effectively

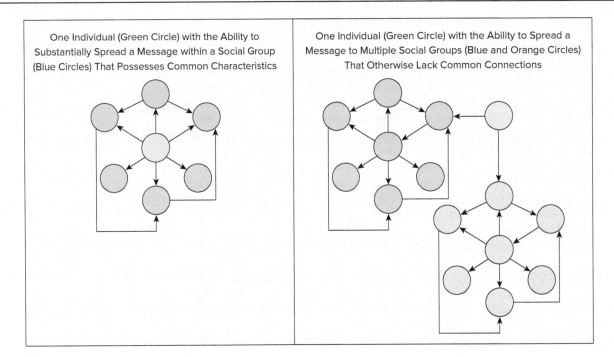

One Individual (Green Circle) with the Ability to Substantially Spread a Message within a Social Group (Blue Circles) That Possesses Common Characteristics

One Individual (Green Circle) with the Ability to Spread a Message to Multiple Social Groups (Blue and Orange Circles) That Otherwise Lack Common Connections

within one or several large social groups that share common characteristics, as well as individuals who can spread a message across a set of social groups that don't otherwise share many connections in common.[25] Exhibit 13.13 provides a graphical depiction of these two types of beneficial approaches to seeding strategy.

Effective viral marketing approaches and content typically capture the attention of people in a unique way, speak to their interests and needs, and connect recipients to an experience that is enriched when shared with others. Dove Beauty Bar's "Real Beauty Sketches" campaign was an uplifting example of effective viral marketing. The video featured sketches of women produced by an FBI-trained forensic artist. The artist created the sketches based on each woman's *description* of her own appearance, along with separate sketches of the same women based on a stranger's description. The drawings based on the strangers' accounts were more closely aligned with reality and also generally more flattering than those self-described by the women. The message of the videos was clear and resonated with a large audience, evidenced by the more than 114 million views and close to 4 million shares generated in the first month.[26] Was it inherently obvious in advance to Dove's marketing managers that their approach would be a viral hit? Unlikely, as viral marketing is as much or more of an art than a science, and marketers often have difficulty predicting what actions and conditions will result in a big viral marketing hit with the public!

Viral marketing has practical advantages for marketing managers. First, the "birds of a feather" aspect of viral marketing works to one's advantage since the group targeted by a seeding strategy most often possesses common bonds, and thus content shared with by a social network member with other members may be viewed as more relevant, credible, and trustworthy than the same content received directly from the marketer. Second, marketing budget efficiencies can be obtained when viral marketing is done successfully. Think of viral marketing as one of the most potent types of earned media, in that it enables the spread of a marketing communication to potentially large audiences through the activation of individual users as marketing communication channels. In some cases, audience size reached through a viral marketing effort could be equivalent to what might have been obtained through the purchase of a television advertising spot requiring a substantial chunk of marketing budget.

Product and Service Review Sites Product and service review sites offer the opportunity for customers to provide feedback on their experience with the organization and its offering, and also provide an information repository for customers to search of information before purchase. Because of these customer uses, marketers must continually monitor review sites that are relevant for their offerings. Examples of some well-known product and service review sites include the following:

- *CNET* is one of the most popular sites for individuals interested in consumer technology and electronics. The site posts professional product reviews across a wide range of products and also encourages users to post their own feedback.
- *Urbanspoon* is a user-generated review site of local restaurants. Urbanspoon creates a local community of users (supported by professional critical reviews from local media), with restaurant reviews posted by location, price, cuisine, and features.
- *Consumersearch* acts as an aggregator of reviews across a wide range of products—everything from home and garden to automotive. The site includes Consumersearch's own reviews of many products, and also posts reviews from other sources as well as customer reviews from Amazon.

Consider the results of a recent study finding that about 70 percent of Americans consult either a user review site or an independent review site (with equal likelihood) before making a purchase.[27] This trend makes it makes it imperative that marketers develop and execute a consistent strategy for staying on top of postings on product and service review sites relevant to their offerings. Such monitoring allows marketing managers to track and learn from customers' experiences and identify opportunities to both take remedial actions with customers and make modifications in offerings as appropriate. Post-purchase, marketers can run into potential reputational and ethical issues if they go too far in trying to influence ratings and reviews on these websites. It's not unusual for marketers to offer financial incentives or other customer benefits in exchange for users posting ratings and reviews on various sites after purchase. The implicit assumption is that incentivized participants will be more inclined to provide positive ratings and reviews. These types of influence approaches must be undertaken with extreme care, lest the customer feel manipulated by the organization. In more overt cases, an organization may use paid (sponsored) web bloggers to post ratings and reviews in a positive light in an attempt to stack the deck more favorably on the review site. Review sites themselves must be diligent in working to screen out such unscrupulous activity, as it ruins the credibility of the site. For the organization sponsoring such fake posts, the risk is high that exposure will do irreparable damage to the brand and customer trust in the organization.

Online Brand Communities In recent years marketing managers have led their organizations to understand the potential of creating their own **online brand communities**, where customers can engage in meaningful interaction right on the organization's own website rather than at independent sites. For such an owned media review site to be attractive and effective, naturally it must be perceived as "honest," meaning that the organization must not selectively delete negative posts; rather, it must allow participants to share a wide range of views. Online brand communities, whether hosted by an organization or by an independent third party, can have substantial value for an organization in terms of useful feedback for the design and marketing of its offerings.[28] Probably not too surprisingly, Apple is one organization that has embraced the online brand community strategy, with thousands of communities built around their products and end-user consumers. These forums offer important product support, deal with product and service concerns, and build a strong sense of community among Apple users.

Interactions among online brand community members can deliver major benefits to the host organization in different forms. For example, cost savings can be achieved when customers are able to answer each other's questions related to technical difficulties and the like, rather than contacting customer service. Another benefit occurs when the host organization learns from the online community dialogue ways to better educate its customers on product or service usage after the sale. Also, aesthetically, online brand communities can make a customer's experience with offerings more enjoyable through the sharing and comparing of ideas and war stories among users, building a greater bond with the brand. When user-generated content is developed and loaded onto the online brand community by customers, it brings the customer directly into the process of communicating the value offering, which no doubt increases customer satisfaction, loyalty, and pride of association with the brand and organization.

Sony's PlayStation Community is aimed at engaging and entertaining customers. It offers users of different PlayStation products and services the opportunity to ask questions and to engage in conversations about different systems, services, and games. In addition, users can upload in-game images and videos directly onto specific forums within the online community so they can share interesting aspects of the different games they are currently playing with other members of the community. Sony also allows selected outside brands to share content through the platform to further enhance its value to PlayStation users.

Assessing the Value of Social Media Marketing

Assessing the value of social media marketing efforts can be a real challenge for marketing managers, especially in terms that other organizational stakeholders are willing to accept as important to performance. This is especially the case when social media efforts do not drive easily tractable types of customer behaviors that are clearly and directly linked to a specific product purchase (thus de facto linked to the broader revenue and financial performance of the organization). For example, it is not at all uncommon for C-suite executives to question the value of the number of "likes" or "followers" that are being generated by a given social media marketing campaign. As discussed in Chapter 5, nowadays greater analytic capabilities are making it easier for marketers to demonstrate the value derived from various digital marketing efforts, including social media marketing. Marketing managers need to redouble efforts to firm up the linkages between investments in marketing via social media platforms and important ROI-based organizational outcomes.

One way to approach this challenge is for marketing managers to take full advantage of the data collection capabilities inherent in interacting with customers through social media and other digital marketing approaches. Marketing has a strong story to tell the C-suite about the value of customer insights to a wide range of strategic organizational decisions, from product design and modification to supply chain approaches to branding and marketing approaches and more. Mindful of the value of their data to organizations for insight-based decision making, many social networks understand the importance of providing advanced analytic capabilities within their own platforms to organizations that are keen to understand the ROI of their social media efforts. All that being said, it is nonetheless still important to be able to set realistic expectations for upper management ahead of time about what a given social media marketing effort is intended to accomplish, exactly how the related objectives will be measured and controlled for, and what specifically those measurable outcomes will mean for the organization's success (especially if their value is not inherently self-evident).

SUMMARY

Developing promotional strategies is an integral part of marketing. A firm's investment in promotion often involves a substantial amount of money. Marketing managers utilize a promotion mix in developing promotional strategies that includes elements of digital and social media marketing, advertising, sales promotion, public relations (PR), and personal selling. These promotion mix elements all have advantages and disadvantages; the goal is to align the right tool with the right objective.

In recent years, digital marketing has emerged as a key component of promotional strategy. Widespread adoption of digital technologies has a significant impact on how marketing managers communicate with current and potential customers in both B2C and B2B markets. The resulting data collection capabilities provide marketers with the ability to better understand the personal characteristics and behaviors of individual customers and gather more in-depth feedback on the efficacy of digital marketing efforts almost instantaneously. Marketing managers have access to a wide variety of digital communication options including paid media, owned media, and earned media. In addition, the proliferation of mobile devices provides substantial new opportunities but also comes with important considerations such as the ability to use location information to target individuals with promotions in real time and the need to tailor specific promotions and other types of digital experiences to the unique design features and interactive characteristics of a mobile device.

Clearly, social media has revolutionized the way customers interact with each other and with organizations interested in marketing to them. Social media has the capability to be a powerful generator of earned media for savvy marketers who understand how current and potential customers interact via the many diverse social media platforms in common use today. The interactive nature of social media requires marketers to both listen to and engage users, increasingly turning away from old-style marketing that is reliant on "talking at" customers. Three main forms of social media tend to have the most impact for marketers: social networks, product/service review sites, and online brand communities. There's no doubt that today that the capability to engage current and potential customers effectively on social media is mission critical. As such, it is also very important that marketing managers effectively measure, analyze, and communicate the value of social media marketing strategies internally within their firms to others who might otherwise be wary or skeptical of the ROI of investing in this robust promotion mix element.

KEY TERMS

promotion   343

promotion mix   343

digital and social media marketing   343

advertising   343

sales promotion   343

public relations (PR)   343

personal selling   343

promotion mix strategies   343

promotional campaign   344

push strategy   347

pull strategy   347

internal marketing   347

AIDA model   347

digital marketing   350

paid media   350

cost per impression   350

cost per click   350

owned media   350

earned media   351

digital advertising   351

display ads   352

banner ads   352

interstitials   352

retargeting   353

search ads   353

social network ads   354

native ads   354

landing page   355

microsites   357

APPLICATION QUESTIONS

1. The chapter discusses the role of the marketing manager in promotional strategy (Exhibit 13.3 and accompanying discussion). The trend today in both large and small firms is for much of the promotion function to be outsourced.

    a. Comment on this outsourcing trend. What are the major reasons for the trend? What are the pros and cons? What is your personal view about outsourcing all or part of promotion?

    b. Assume you are a marketing manager for a firm that outsources promotion to a creative agency. In what ways does this arrangement impact your job? In particular, concentrate on how it impacts your marketing planning (being mindful that promotion planning is a key element of marketing planning). How would you interact with the agency as a manager representing your firm (assume you have responsibility for the agency relationship with your company)? That is, what are the key things you should do to ensure a productive relationship?

2. Consider a major purchase you have made recently. Review the AIDA model (Exhibits 13.7 and 13.8) and accompanying discussion.

    a. Think back on the process that led up to your purchase and reconstruct the types of promotion that you experienced during each stage of the AIDA model. Which of the promotional forms was most effective in your situation, and why?

    b. As you reconstruct this purchase experience and the promotional messages you received during it, what other promotion mix elements that you did *not* experience at the time might have been effective in convincing you to make the purchase? At what stage of the AIDA model would they have been helpful, and in what ways do you believe they might have impacted your decision process?

3. Select a B2C company that you are familiar with, along with a product sold by that company. Identify a particular consumer target market. Imagine you have been tasked with developing a paid media strategy for the related product to that target.

    a. Pick two of the digital ad options listed in the chapter. Explain the concept for each of the two digital ads (they can be the same or different) and identify the content (text, imagery, video, and other elements) of each digital ad and explain why the related concept and content will be an effective match for communicating to your selected consumer segment. In doing so, be sure to explain how you would use the capabilities associated with each chosen ad option to effectively target the associated consumer segment.

    b. For each of the two selected digital ad options, specify the pricing model that you believe is most appropriate for the type of ad (that is, cost-per-impression or cost-per-click). If the pricing models discussed in the chapter do not seem to be appropriate for the ad option selected, then explain why not and propose an alternative pricing model (that is, what do you suggest is more appropriate in terms of compensation between the advertiser and the communication channel).

4. Consider the concept of a landing page and its use in assisting the completion of specific desirable actions as well as its relationship with other forms of digital marketing communication. Identify one landing page associated with a display ad as well as one landing page associated with a search ad where the user is required to submit some information on the landing page. In your response, make sure to identify the company that each landing page is associated with.

    a. What makes the ad tied to each landing page effective or ineffective in motivating an individual to click on it?

    b. Do the ad and the landing page seem well integrated together? If yes, what visual, textual, and other elements support the connection between the ad and the related landing page?

    c. Put yourself in the shoes of someone who has a legitimate need for the products or services offered by the organization responsible for each ad and associated landing page. Does the landing page do an effective job of motivating the user to fill out the related form? Are there any particular aspects of the page that serve as potential motivators or detractors for completing the form?

5. Select a specific branded product associated with a company and assume you are the marketing manager in charge of mobile marketing strategy for the product.

    a. Come up with a simple concept for a branded mobile app and explain how the specific purpose of the app (or functionality provided by it) fits thematically with your branded product and how it will help create value for customers.

    b. Identify a specific mobile app or game (not associated with the brand) that would be a good fit for the distribution of in-app ads. Explain what characteristics of the app make it a good fit based on what is known (or assumed) about your branded product's target market.

6. You are the marketing manager for the Tesla Model 3 and have been tasked with developing an effective social media strategy. Review the discussion of social media and consider the following:

    a. Develop a concept for an online brand community for Tesla Model 3 enthusiasts. Outline the specific features that the brand community will have as well as the value of the specific features to the community members and to Tesla.

    b. Identify specific social networking platforms that you would use in the development of a social media strategy for Tesla, explain the reasons why you would use each of the selected platforms, identify the specific ways that you would use each one, and list the specific outcomes that you would use to determine the effectiveness of your overall social media strategy across those platforms.

MANAGEMENT DECISION CASE
How Oreo Uses Social Media to Market Milk's Favorite Cookie

For many Oreo lovers, the question is not *whether* to eat them, but *how* to eat them—twist and lick or just eat them whole. For the record, about 50 percent of Oreo lovers eat their cookies whole and 50 percent are "pull-aparters," but men eat them whole more often than do women. Several years ago the marketing team at Kraft, the company that produced Oreos at the time, was dealing with weightier matters: how to move the popular brand "from old school advertiser to new-age content creator."[29]

First introduced in 1912, the Oreo grew to be the most popular cookie in the world, with a roughly 5 percent share of worldwide cookie sales—three times more than any other cookie.[30] However, Oreo's senior marketing managers at Kraft came to the realization that for decades Oreo had been approaching their promotions in a formulaic and repetitive manner. Advertising stories had been limited to those that could be told in the kitchen, "staring down the barrel of a glass of milk." And the overall approach was very self-focused—as their CMO put it, "We loved to look in the mirror . . . the power of looking out the window was that we said this brand can behave in and drive culture." With this revelation, social media became the vehicle for opening that window and reaching out to the broader consumer culture—with some carefully orchestrated programs and one serendipitous opportunity seized.[31]

To coordinate with its 100th anniversary, Oreo launched the *Daily Twist,* in which for 100 days its famous cookie was cast on Facebook in a series of cultural moments and stories tied to trending news. For its first promotion under this approach, a controversial rainbow-filled Oreo was created for Gay Pride week.[32] Later, a red cookie with tire tracks celebrated the Mars Rover landing. Then the king of cookies delivered an Oreo made to look like the king of rock and roll—Elvis—on his birthday.[33] But the most successful post was one featuring an Oreo designed to look like the famous Tokyo Ueno Zoo panda Shin-Shin in celebration of the birth of a new baby panda, which reached almost 4.5 million views.[34]

Pulling off these daily messages required some real marketing acrobatics by Oreo's advertising agency. After checking the news each day, the team would mock up four options judged to be the most culturally interesting. Within hours, one of these would get approved by the client, the legal department, and the corporate communications department, and then it was released to the world on Facebook. It is noteworthy that in "the old days" it could take more than *three months* to get a proposed traditional ad fully through the approval process.[35]

The agility developed during this social media campaign paid off when opportunity came knocking a few months later. For the first time ever, the power went out at the New Orleans Superdome during the biggest sports (and marketing) event of the year—the Super Bowl. While the Ravens and 49ers took an unplanned time out, the Oreo social media team jumped into action.[36] Within a few minutes, Oreo sent out a tweet that said "Power out? No Problem. You Can Still Dunk in the Dark."[37] Without spending a cent on expensive Super Bowl advertising, Oreo managed to reach a massive group of hungry (and bored) football fans with "The Tweet Heard around the World."[38] Truly a marketing tour de force!

In its *Wonderfilled* campaign, the team used clever animated videos to show how some of the darker characters in our memories (like a vampire or the Big Bad Wolf) can be made more cheerful with the help of America's favorite cookie.[39] These videos were delivered via traditional TV advertising but also on YouTube, Facebook, and Twitter.[40] Oreo also executed a mobile app called *Twist, Lick, Dunk* that was the number one "advergame" in 15 countries and not only promoted the brand but actually made money for the company—about $100,000—from virtual Oreo cookies sold and from in-app advertising.[41]

Social media has been important to Oreo not only for its reach and low cost, but also because so many of us are glued to our smartphones at the very moment when we could be encouraged to consider buying an Oreo snack. In the past, the time spent waiting in line to pay at the grocery store was prime time for a visual suggestion for an impulse purchase—gum, candy, or a sleeve of delicious Oreos displayed on a rack right in front of us. However, in today's connected world, we are more likely to be looking at Facebook and Twitter on our smartphones while waiting rather than at the racks full of "suggestions." So to recapture shoppers' attention, Oreo regularly sends a clever and entertaining suggestion for satisfying that sweet tooth using those same social media tools.[42]

Oreo's efforts to become more social media savvy have paid off. Today, Oreo's Facebook community numbers more than 42 million in 200 countries, which incredibly puts it among the top 10 Facebook brand pages in the world.[43] In the year in which the *Wonderfilled* campaign was launched, Oreo's North American business saw double-digit growth. Although many other marketing efforts, including product innovation, were also executed, there is little doubt that "looking out the window" and engaging with the culture made a difference in Oreo's phenomenal success.[44]

Questions for Consideration

1. How should Oreo's success in social engagement be evaluated? What metrics would be most useful? Consider both the usage-specific metrics that a social media provider might supply as well as outcome-based measures. What are the pros and cons of relying on one of these types of measures versus the other?

2. While growing their social media presence, Oreo continues to advertise in traditional media. Why is it important to ensure that messages are consistent among platforms? What specific tactics could be used to ensure this consistency?

3. Although most of Oreo's social media efforts are directed toward adults, many Oreo lovers are children. To what degree should Oreo also have a focus on marketing directly to children? What are the risks and ethical considerations of such an approach? Are there approaches to marketing Oreos to children that would stand up to ethical scrutiny? (Hint: Among other issues, consider the trend toward childhood obesity.)

MARKETING PLAN EXERCISE

ACTIVITY 14: Promote Your Offering

The promotion plan is an integral part of any marketing plan, and often carries a significant portion of the marketing budget. Develop the following elements for promoting your offering:

1. Review the promotion mix elements and begin to develop goals for promotion and a promotional strategy utilizing the elements of the mix that are most appropriate for your offering.

2. Link the promotional strategy to PLC stages as well as the stages your customers will go through on the AIDA model.

3. Decide how you intend to manage promotion for the offering. Decide on outsourced elements versus elements that will be handled in-house. Establish a structure and process for promotion management.

NOTES

1. Bob Garfield, "The Post Advertising Age," *Advertising Age,* March 26, 2007.

2. P. Rajan Varadarajan, Satish Jayachandran, and J. Chris White, "Strategic Interdependence in Organizations: Deconglomeration and Marketing Strategy," *Journal of Marketing* 65, no. 1 (January 2001), pp. 15–28.

3. Frederick E. Webster Jr., "Understanding the Relationships among Brands, Consumers, and Resellers," *Journal of the Academy of Marketing Science* 28, no. 1 (Winter 2000), pp. 17–23.

4. Emim Babakus, Ugar Yavas, Osman M. Karatepe, and Turgay Avci, "The Effect of Management Commitment to Service Quality on Employees' Affective and Performance Outcomes," *Journal of the Academy of Marketing Science* 31, no. 3 (Summer 2003), pp. 272–86.

5. Yu-Shan Lin and Jun-Ying Huang, "Internet Blogs as a Tourism Marketing Medium: A Case Study," *Journal of Business Research* 59, no. 10/11 (October 2006), pp. 1201–05.

6. Maria Teresa Pinheiro and José Manuel Cristóvão Veríssimo, "Digital Marketing and Social Media: Why Bother?" *Business Horizons* 57, no. 6 (2014), pp. 703–8.

7. Sean Corcoran, "Defining Earned, Owned, and Paid Media," *Forrester,* December 16, 2009, http://blogs.forrester.com /interactive_marketing/2009/12/defining-earned-owned -and-paid-media.html.

8. Joe McCambley, "The First Ever Banner Ad: Why Did It Work So Well?" *The Guardian,* December 12, 2013, https://www .theguardian.com/media-network/media-network-blog/2013 /dec/12/first-ever-banner-ad-advertising.

9. "Understanding Bidding Basics," https://support.google .com/adwords/answer/2459326.

10. Oliver J. Rutz, Michael Trusov, and Randolph E. Bucklin, "Modeling Indirect Effects of Paid Search Advertising: Which Keywords Lead to More Future Visits," *Marketing Science* 30, no. 4 (2011), pp. 646–65.

11. Bartosz W. Woldjynski and Nathaniel J. Evans, "Going Native: Effects of Disclosure Position and Language on the Recognition and Evaluation of Online Native Advertising," *Journal of Advertising* 45, no. 2 (2015), pp. 157–68.

12. Arvind Rangaswamy, C. Lee Giles, and Silvija Seres, "A Strategic Perspective on Search Engines: Thought Candies for Practitioners and Researchers," *Journal of Interactive Marketing* 23, no. 1 (2009), pp. 49–60.

13. Ron Berman and Zsolt Katona, "The Role of Search Engine Optimization in Search Marketing," *Marketing Science* 32, no. 4 (2013), pp. 644–51.

14. Dave Chaffey, "Digesting Mary Meeker's 2015 Internet Trends Analysis," *Smart Insights,* June 11, 2015, http://www .smartinsights.com/internet-marketing-statistics/insights -from-kpcb-us-and-global-internet-trends-2015-report/.

15. "Whole Foods Market Partners with Thinknear to Drive Store Visits," *Thinknear,* http://www.thinknear.com/wp-content /uploads/2015/06/Case-Study-Whole-Foods-Thinknear.pdf.

16. Dhruv Grewal, Yakov Bart, Martin Spann, and Peter Pal Zubcsek, "Mobile Advertising: A Framework and Research Agenda," *Journal of Interactive Marketing* 34, no. 2 (2016), pp. 3–14.

17. Venkatesh Shankar and Sridhar Balasubramanian, "Mobile Marketing: A Synthesis and Prognosis," *Journal of Interactive Marketing* 23, no. 2 (2009), pp. 118–29.

18. Graham Winfrey, "8 Best Practices for Text Message Marketing," *Inc.,* August 20, 2014, http://www.inc.com /graham-winfrey/8-text-message-marketing-best-practices .html.

19. Steve Bellman, Robert F. Potter, Shiree Treleaven-Hassard, Jennifer A. Robinson, and Duane Varan, "The Effectiveness of Branded Mobile Phone Apps," *Journal of Interactive Marketing* 25, no. 4 (2011), pp. 191–200.

20. Shannon Greenwood, Andrew Perrin, and Maeve Duggan, "Social Media Update 2016," *Pew Internet,* November 11, 2016, http://www.pewinternet.org/2016/11/11/social-media -update-2016/.

21. Simon Hudson, Li Huang, Martin S. Roth, and Thomas J. Madden, "The Influence of Social Media Interactions on Consumer–Brand Relationships: A Three-Country Study of Brand Perceptions and Marketing Behaviors," *International Journal of Research in Marketing* 33, no. 1 (2016), pp. 27–41.

22. Andrew N. Smith, Eileen Fischer, and Chen Yongjian, "How Does Brand-Related User-Generated Content Differ across YouTube, Facebook, and Twitter?" *Journal of Interactive Marketing* 26, no. 2 (2012), pp. 102–13.

23. Giselle Abramovich, "15 Mind-Blowing Stats about Snapchat," *CMO,* August 19, 2016, http://www.cmo.com/features /articles/2016/8/15/15-mind-blowing-stats-about-snapchat .html#gs.6YUw9s4.

24. http://www.ama.org.

25. Oliver Hinz, Bernd Skiera, Christian Barrot, and Jan U. Becker, "Seeding Strategies for Viral Marketing: An Empirical Comparison," *Journal of Marketing* 75, no. 6 (2011), pp. 55–71.

26. Jason Ankeny, "How These 10 Marketing Campaigns Became Viral Hits," *Entrepreneur,* April 23, 2014, https:// www.entrepreneur.com/article/233207.

27. "Seven in 10 Americans Seek Out Opinions before Making Purchases," *Mintel,* June 3, 2015, http://www.mintel.com /press-centre/social-and-lifestyle/seven-in-10-americans -seek-out-opinions-before-making-purchases

28. Mavis T. Adjei, Stephanie M. Noble, and Charles H. Noble, "The Influence of C2C Communications in Online Brand Communities on Customer Purchase Behavior," *Journal of the Academy of Marketing Science* 38, no. 5 (2010), pp. 634–53.

29. Danielle Sacks, "The Story of Oreo: How an Old Cookie Became a Modern Marketing Personality," *Fast Company,* October 23, 2014, https://www.fastcompany.com/3037068 /the-story-of-oreo-how-an-old-cookie-became-a-modern -marketing-personality.

30. Roberto A. Ferdman, "Why Oreos Might as Well Exist in Their Own Cookie Stratosphere," *Washington Post,* July 7, 2015, https://www.washingtonpost.com/news/wonk/wp/2015 /07/07/why-oreos-might-as-well-exist-in-their-own-cookie -stratosphere/?utm_term=.51815f9cd7f4.

31. Sacks, "The Story of Oreo."

32. Sacks, "The Story of Oreo."

33. Ann-Christine Diaz, "Oreo's 100-Day 'Daily Twist' Campaign Puts Cookie in Conversation," *Advertising Age,* September 10, 2012, http://adage.com/article/digital/oreo-s-daily-twist -campaign-puts-cookie-conversation/237104/.

34. Dan Milano, "Oreo's 'Daily Twist' on Social Marketing," *ABC News,* October 2, 2012, http://abcnews.go.com/blogs /business/2012/10/oreos-daily-twist-on-social-marketing -ends-in-grand-style/.

35. Sacks, "The Story of Oreo."

36. Jeff Briggs, "Super Bowl 2013 Start Time and Location for Ravens vs. 49ers," *SBNation,* January 24, 2013, http://dc .sbnation.com/2013/1/24/3907878/2013-super-bowl-start-time.

37. Sacks, "The Story of Oreo."

38. Brian Sheehan, "How Oreo Stayed Relevant for 100 Years," *Adweek,* July 17, 2015, http://www.adweek.com/digital /how-oreo-stayed-relevant-for-100-years/.

39. Ann-Christine Diaz, "Oreo's New 'Wonderfilled' Campaign Wants to Sap the Cynicism Out of Your Day," *Advertising Age,* May 14, 2013, http://adage.com/article/behind-the-work/ oreo-s-wonderfilled-campaign-sap-cynicism-day/241459/.

40. "Wonderfilled," *Bēhance,* https://www.behance.net/gallery /36260905/Oreo-Wonderfilled-Animation-Social-Media, accessed May 9, 2017.

41. Sacks, "The Story of Oreo"; "Twist, Lick, Dunk, 5," *Advertolog,* http://www.advertolog.com/oreo/casestudy/twist-lick-dunk -5-18597405/, accessed May 9, 2017.

42. Sacks, "The Story of Oreo."

43. "2017 Fact Sheet," *Mondelez International,* http://www .mondelezinternational.com/~/media/MondelezCorporate /Uploads/downloads/OREO_Fact_Sheet.pdf, accessed May 9, 2017.

44. Sacks, "The Story of Oreo."

CHAPTER 14

Promotion Essentials: Legacy Approaches

LEARNING OBJECTIVES

LO 14-1   Understand the key types of advertising and the role of the creative agency.

LO 14-2   Identify various approaches to sales promotion and how each might be used.

LO 14-3   Describe the activities and aims of public relations.

LO 14-4   Understand the role of personal selling in marketing communications.

LO 14-5   Learn the process of relationship selling.

LO 14-6   Understand the major job responsibilities of sales management.

In this chapter we explore critical marketing communication tools that we refer to as "legacy approaches" to promotion. We like the term legacy because it denotes a heritage of tools that still carry great value for marketing managers, but are distinct from the digital and social media marketing approaches that comprise much of the focus of Chapter 13. Some of these legacy approaches tend to be directed toward broad or mass markets–advertising, sales promotion, and public relations PR–while personal selling tends to be one-on-one. In the introductory section of Chapter 13 that defines and compares each element of the promotion mix, you read that advertising is a paid form of relatively less personal marketing communications, often through a mass medium to one or more target markets. For much of the general public, advertising is synonymous with marketing because advertising is a very visible side of marketing–not surprising, since advertising is one of the dominant forms of marketing communication.

Beyond advertising, marketers have additional promotional tools–sales promotion and PR–to facilitate communication with their broad target markets. Recall from Chapter 13 that sales promotion provides an inducement for an end-user consumer to buy your product or for a salesperson or someone else in the channel to sell it. It is rarely used as the sole promotional method; instead it usually augments other forms of promotion. And PR is a systematic approach to influencing attitudes, opinions, and behaviors of customers and others. PR is often executed through publicity, which is an unpaid and relatively less personal form of marketing communications, usually through news stories and mentions at public events.

Let's first take a look at each of these three approaches to marketing communications to broad markets in greater detail. Then, later in the chapter, we will turn attention to personal selling as a more laser-focused element of the promotion mix.

ADVERTISING

To most of the general public, advertising is synonymous with marketing. Advertising is what most people see as the visible side of marketing–of course, this is due in part to the large amount of money spent on advertising. According to MAGNA (IPG Mediabrands research company), global spending on advertising is over $500 billion dollars per year. However, this figure comes with an important caveat: these numbers only track more traditional forms of advertising that are considered "measured media"–magazine, TV, radio, outdoor, and display advertising on the Internet. Not included are so-called unmeasured media such as Internet paid search and social media.

Who are the largest advertisers in the world? The list includes many companies you recognize such as P&G, Unilever, L'Oréal, and Volkswagen. It is noteworthy that the largest global advertisers operate primarily in the consumer marketplace. Advertising is ubiquitous

LO 14-1

Understand the key types of advertising and the role of the creative agency.

EXHIBIT 14.1 | The World's Most Effective Advertisers

Rank	Advertiser	Points
1	Procter & Gamble	594.3
2	Unilever	477.5
3	Coca-Cola Company	454.9
4	Heineken	287.6
5	PepsiCo	231.1
6	McDonald's	207.7
7	Volkswagen Group	207.2
8	Mondelez International	193.5
9	Tata Group	177.5
10	Luxottica	151.0

Source: Vizard, Sarah, "P&G Overtakes Unilever to Top List of Most Effective Global Advertisers," *Marketing Week*, March 1, 2016.

promotion, and because it is so visible and seemingly easily understood, many turn to advertising as their promotion mix element of first choice. However, for the advertiser a more important question is: How effective is the company's advertising? Exhibit 14.1 highlights a research firm's analysis of the most effective advertisers in the world. It should come as no surprise that the largest advertisers are also among the most effective. It is also interesting to note, however, that companies like Heineken can still be very effective despite spending much less (about $400 million each year) than the largest advertisers like P&G (which spent $7 billion on global advertising in 2016).

There is a danger in overrelying on advertising to the exclusion of other promotional choices. Customers can quickly and easily become bored with any given advertising campaign, a concept referred to as **advertising wearout**. This phenomenon necessitates a constant creation of new ads with new or adjusted themes, resulting in a constant churn of messages.[1] For several years Apple ran a series of ads around the "Mac vs. PC" theme. The campaign featured two actors who represented Mac (cool computers that work) versus PC (computers that were complicated and didn't always work). While the campaign was hugely successful, the company eventually stopped the ads because they were no longer perceived as original or effective in conveying the brand message for Apple's Mac computers. The need for constant renewal of ads is great for advertising agencies, which get paid to create them, but incredibly expensive for marketing managers.

Another problem with advertising is that beyond a certain ad spending level, diminishing returns tend to set in. That is, market share stops growing—or even begins to decline—despite continued spending. This effect is known as the **advertising response function** and leads marketing managers to rely more heavily on advertising early in the product life cycle (PLC), as well as to focus on it during target customers' initial stages of the AIDA model that we presented in Chapter 13.[2] Spending higher dollars, in this case on advertising, on the promotional goals of *informing* and *persuading* is likely to pay back at a higher level than spending equal dollars on the promotional goal of *reminding*.

Despite these challenges, advertising is not only a potentially highly effective promotional vehicle (when applied properly), but it is also a part of the very fabric of the U.S. culture and, increasingly, of the global culture. The craze associated with the annual Super Bowl advertisements is a testament to the power of advertising to excite the masses.

Types of Advertising

There are two major types of advertising: institutional advertising and product advertising. The choice of which approach to use depends on the promotional goals and the situation.

Institutional Advertising The goal of **institutional advertising** is to promote an industry, company, family of brands, or other issues broader than a specific product. Institutional advertising is often used to inform or remind, but to a lesser degree to persuade. Earlier you read about the concept of corporate identity in the context of the sender of communication.[3] Many customers pay a great deal of attention to the organization behind an advertising message, how socially responsible the company is, and what values for which it stands. Institutional advertising can help build and enhance a corporate brand or family brand. For instance, P&G runs institutional ads about a charitable cause it supports—the Special Olympics. Certain families of P&G brands (Crest, Pampers, etc.) generally are featured as well. Such an approach helps build the corporate identity of P&G and can enhance its brands through positive association.

Sometimes entire industries will run institutional advertising. For example, the trade organization for cotton, Cotton Incorporated, introduced a new campaign called "Leave Comfort to Clothes" to reinforce people's connection with the fabric, cotton. Famous for its "Cotton, the fabric of our lives" campaign, industries like cotton search for messages that help connect customers to their products, a bit like the famous "Intel Inside" branding on computers.[4] Consider these additional examples of industry-sponsored institutional advertising, manifest through catchy taglines:

- The incredible edible egg.
- Pork, the other white meat.
- Beef, it's what's for dinner.

Institutional advertising is a particularly smart strategy during the early phases of the PLC and AIDA model in that it can enhance feelings of trust in potential customers with a message that is broader than just "buy me." Institutional advertising is also often employed when a company or industry has a PR problem to dig out from. Recall from Chapter 10 that when United Airlines experienced a significant customer service issue in 2017 the airline started a massive service recovery effort that included a letter from the CEO and institutional advertising to reinforce the airline's commitment to better service for its passengers.

Doritos does a great job of product advertising by showing its products surrounded by distinct imagery and bold tag lines.

Source: Frito-Lay North America, Inc.

Product Advertising The vast majority of advertising is **product advertising**, designed to increase purchase of a specific offering (good or service). Three principal types of product advertising are available: pioneering advertising, competitive advertising, and comparative advertising. The decision as to which to employ often depends on the stage of the PLC.

Pioneering advertising stimulates primary demand. Hence, it tends to be used during the introductory and early growth stages of the PLC when it is important to gain purchase by innovators and early adopters. From an AIDA model perspective, pioneering advertising seeks to gain awareness and initial interest. Marketing managers introducing new products almost always focus advertising on this form, letting potential customers know what the product is and how it is used. The appeal is usually more rational than emotional.[5]

Marketing managers employ **competitive advertising** to build sales of a specific brand. Here, the appeal often shifts to more emotion and the goal is persuasion as well as providing information. Building a positive customer attitude toward the brand is a key component of competitive advertising, and this approach is heavily used during the growth and early maturity stages of the PLC. Triggering the desire and action stages of the AIDA model is a focus of the message.[6]

In **comparative advertising**, two or more brands are directly compared against each other on certain attributes.[7] Comparative advertising is common during the maturity stage of the PLC, as attempts at shaking out weaker competitors are generally part of a marketing strategy. Obviously, a key to successfully employing this approach is having one or more legitimate claims about your brand that put it in a favorable position against the competition. For example, Samsung has done a great job of whittling away at Apple's market share in the smartphone category through its strong comparative approach to touting the advantages of its Galaxy line over the iPhone.

Comparative advertising works especially well when you are not No. 1 in a product category because you can put the market leader on the defensive. The cellular provider T-Mobile has made significant market share gains in the United States by aggressively lowering data plan rates. The company's success prompted major competitors like Verizon and AT&T to lower their rates to offset T-Mobile's success. However, it is a very risky advertising approach when you *are* the top brand. Customers may perceive that you are on the defensive, when in reality you are not. The psychology of a top brand stooping to comparisons with a lower brand usually does not make sense. Most experts recommend avoiding comparative advertising if your brand is the leader.

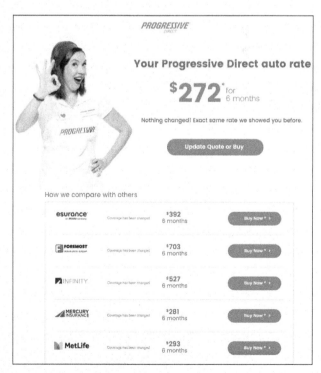

This comparative ad by Progressive Insurance takes on competitors by directly comparing insurance rates.

Source: Progressive Casualty Insurance Company

Advertising Execution and Media Types

In selecting which types of advertising media to employ, the marketing manager must consider reach and frequency. **Reach** measures the percentage of individuals in a defined target market that are exposed to an ad during a specified time period. **Frequency** measures the average number of times a person in the target market is exposed to the message. Obviously, the greater the reach and the higher the frequency, the more expensive the overall advertising campaign will be. As you might imagine, because advertising budgets are not unlimited, trade-offs are usually required in balancing reach and frequency within budgetary constraints. Goals are generally set and budgeted based on a desired level of reach and frequency. During the course of a campaign, the marketing manager may intentionally vary the reach and frequency. For example, the intensity of the campaign might start heavily to gain initial exposure, then be reduced to stave off advertising wearout.

Advertising execution is the way an advertisement communicates the information and image. A variety of different types of advertising execution are available. In Chapter 13 you learned about three general types of promotional appeals: rational, emotional, and moral. Think of the different approaches to advertising execution as the creative operationalization of these different types of appeal. Exhibit 14.2 presents several of the more common advertising execution approaches.

Seven broad categories of advertising media are available: television, radio, newspapers, magazines, outdoor (billboard, bus and train signs, etc.), direct mail, and the Internet. Each of these media types has a variety of pros and cons that must be considered by marketing managers in deciding how to allocate advertising dollars. Exhibit 14.3 summarizes some of the more important issues when making media choices.

The Energizer Bunny is a long-standing "spokesperson" for the company's line of batteries.

Source: Energizer Brands, LLC

EXHIBIT 14.2 | Common Approaches to Advertising Execution

Slice of Life	Portrays regular people in everyday settings. The college student doing laundry with Tide in the Laundromat.
Humor	Gains attention and interest through humorous portrayal. Budweiser's famous frogs are not soon forgotten.
Mood/Affect	Sets a positive tone around the offering. Sandals Resorts provides visual images to back the theme of "Luxury Included."
Research-Based	Often used in comparative ads, a brand provides scientific evidence of its superiority. L'Oréal Youth Code products message the science behind their development.
Demonstration	Physically shows how the product works. Bounty paper towels are regularly shown on TV ads as having superior absorbency.
Musical	Uses music or a specific song to connect directly to a brand or product. Jingles may not be as pervasive as in the past, but Subway has immortalized the "five dollar footlong" to music.
Endorser	Connects a celebrity, actor posing as an authority figure (with appropriate disclaimer), company officer, or everyday consumer with the product to sanction and support its use, such as LeBron James for Nike.
Lifestyle	Portrays ways a product will connect with a target customer's lifestyle; Dodge Ram pickup trucks navigating through the back roads of America.
Fantasy Creation	Offers a fantasy look at how it might be if a customer purchases the product; Taco Bell's "Live Más" ads.
Animation and Animal	An animated character or an animal is featured in the ads, sometimes as a spokesperson; the GEICO Gecko.

EXHIBIT 14.3 | Pros and Cons of Key Advertising Media

Type of Media	Pros	Cons
Television	• Combines multimedia • Appeals to multiple senses • Works for both mass coverage and selected markets • Infomercial option	• Impressions are fleeting • Short shelf life • Din (clutter) of competing ads • TiVo effect—cutting out ads • High cost
Radio	• Quick placement and high message immediacy • Easy selectivity by market and station programming • Low cost • Geographic flexibility	• Audio only • Short shelf life • Din of competing ads
Newspapers	• Flexible • Timely • Highly credible medium	• Short shelf life • Big city and national papers can be very costly • Poor reproduction quality, especially in color • Low pass-along rate
Magazines	• Many titles; high geographic, demographic, and lifestyle selectivity • Good reproduction quality and color • High pass-along rate	• Long lead time for ad placement due to production • Final location of ad within the publication often cannot be guaranteed
Outdoor	• Repeat exposure in heavy traffic areas • Relatively low cost • Fewer competing ads • Easy geographic targeting	• Space and structure limit creative execution • Sometimes requires longer-than-desired commitments to a location • Public discontent over environmental clutter
Direct Mail	• High audience selectivity • Creates feel of one-to-one marketing • Flexible	• Overuse and "junk mail" image • Too many competing ads • Relatively high cost
Online and Social Media	• Interactive capabilities • Flexible • Timely • Low cost per exposure	• Reader in control of exposure (click-through) • Spam • Variations in connectivity speed and computers • Privacy concerns

In reviewing the pros and cons of each of the major media choices, it becomes apparent that decisions on media selection always involve trade-offs. One issue inherent to most media forms is some degree of **clutter**—the level of competing messages on that medium. Clutter is sometimes described in the context of the overall din of advertising, meaning that consumers are bombarded by so many messages that they become confused or have difficulty distinguishing what ad goes with what brand. Rising above the din is an overarching goal in media selection and creative execution of the message.

The Role of the Creative Agency

Advertising and PR are among the most outsourced functions in marketing, and with good reason. Most organizations naturally focus on their own product or service expertise; thus, developing sufficient internal expertise in the creative side of promotion would be extremely costly and could reduce their focus on their core business. For many marketing managers, the relationship with their firm's creative agency is an important part of the job. Agencies vary, with some being specialized firms that focus on an industry or on a particular area of promotion, such as print media or product placement. Others are full-service shops that manage all aspects of their clients' marketing communications. Today, the trend is toward more full-service creative agencies and even toward integration of marketing planning and branding services with traditional agency tasks. Almost always a client is billed an hourly rate, plus the costs of media purchases.

Over the past several years, another major trend has been the development of strategic partnerships between creative agencies and full-service web builders. For many marketers, the website is the core of their marketing communications strategy. Often a new-product introduction or rebranding initiative focuses largely on the website, with print and other media types used primarily to drive customers to the web. Some of the very largest agencies have even established their own comprehensive web operations and are able to perform a full gamut of web services for clients including website building and maintenance, hosting, management of direct e-mail correspondence with customers, and management of the client's overall CRM system.

It is likely that the importance of the outsourced full-service marketing agency will continue to grow into the next decade. As marketing itself becomes more strategic within organizations, more and more of the tactical or programmatic aspects of marketing that were formerly handled in-house will be outsourced. In such a scenario, the importance of the marketing manager role is heightened, as that individual will be the front-line person in a firm that is charged with managing all aspects of the outsourced agency relationship.

SALES PROMOTION

LO 14-2

Identify various approaches to sales promotion and how each might be used.

Sales promotion was defined in Chapter 13 as a promotion mix element that provides an inducement for an end-user consumer to buy a product or for a salesperson or someone else in the channel to sell it. Sales promotion is designed to augment other forms of promotion and is rarely used alone. This is because sales promotion initiatives rely on other media forms such as advertising and direct or interactive marketing as a communication vehicle. Think of sales promotion as prompting a "buy now" response; that is, it is squarely aimed at the action (behavior) stage of the AIDA model.

Sales promotion can be aimed directly at end-user consumers, or it can be targeted to members of a channel on which a firm relies to sell product. In the latter case, sales promotion is an important element of a push strategy. One additional potential target for sales promotion is a firm's own sales force. Bonus payments, prizes, trips, and other incentives to induce a salesperson to push one product over another are forms of internal sales promotion. Let's look at sales promotion to consumers and to channel members.

In this sales promotion, Domino's offers a number of "specials" to customers based on what and how many items they wish to purchase.

Source: Domino's Pizza

Sales Promotion to Consumers

When a firm is looking to gain product trial, spike distribution, shore up sagging quarterly sales, or rekindle interest in a waning brand, sales promotion can be an appropriate choice for investment of promotional dollars. Exhibit 14.4 summarizes nine popular consumer sales promotion approaches.

As with most promotional elements, marketing managers rarely select only one form of consumer sales promotion for execution. Many of the sales promotion options complement each other and all are potentially complementary of the overall promotion mix. One potential downside

EXHIBIT 14.4 | Consumer Sales Promotion Options

Sales Promotion Approach	Description	Comments	Example
Product sampling	A physical sample of the product is given to consumers.	Excellent for inducing trial. Sample can be received by mail or in a store.	Gillette sends out a free razor to induce switching from an older model.
Coupons	An instant price reduction at point of sale, available in print media, online, or in-store.	Coupon usage is generally down among consumers. Still a good inducement to "buy now."	Inside the free razor from Gillette is a coupon for $1.00 off the purchase of a pack of blades.
Rebates	A price reduction for purchase of a specific product during a specific time period.	Possibly instant at point of sale, but more frequently requires submission and delay in processing.	Samsung offers a rebate for its televisions purchased at Best Buy.
Contests and sweepstakes	Appeal to consumers' sense of fun and luck. May suggest a purchase but legally must be offered without a purchase requirement.	Contests require some element of skill beyond mere chance. Sweepstakes are pure chance.	McDonald's famous Monopoly game—the more you eat, the more you play (and vice versa!).
Premiums	Another product offered free for purchasing the brand targeted in the promotion.	Gives the customer a bonus for purchase. Products may be complementary or unrelated.	Burger King offers the latest movie hero toy with purchase of a meal.
Multiple-purchase offers	Incentive to buy more of the brand at a special price.	Typically "buy 2, get 1 free" or similar.	Centrum Vitamin offer—buy a bottle of 100, get an extra mini-bottle of 20.
Point-of-purchase materials	Displays set up in a retail store to support advertising and remind customers to purchase.	Especially good at driving purchase toward a featured brand in a product category at the store aisle.	Dr. Scholl's FootMapping Center kiosk at Walgreens.
Product placements	Having product images appear in movies, on television, or in photographs in print media.	Strong connections with the show or story, as well as to any associated celebrities.	Apple products often appear in popular movies and TV shows.
Loyalty programs	Accumulate points for doing business with a company. Designed to strengthen long-term customer relationships and reduce switching.	Especially popular among the airline and hospitality industry. Credit card providers often facilitate.	American Airlines AAdvantage program, facilitated by Citi and MasterCard.

to sales promotion is a tendency by some firms and industries to overrely on sales promotion to bring in sales on a regular basis. This occurs because of sales promotion's power to elicit an actual purchase. Consider the proliferation of rebates on new-car purchases. Car manufacturers essentially "train" car shoppers not to look for a new vehicle unless a rebate is being offered. Ultimately, if sales promotion becomes institutionalized in such a manner, firms simply build in a hefty cushion into the "everyday" price of the product, thus negating any real benefit to the customer of the promotion. Overuse of sales promotion is not a good promotional strategy and can lead to a general cheapening of brand image and distrust by customers.

Sales Promotion to Channel Members

Several sales promotion approaches are available for use with members of a firm's channel of distribution. Typically, these channel members would be distributors, brokers, agents, and other forms of middlemen. The purpose is to stimulate them to push your product, resulting in more sales in the channel and ultimately to end users.

Trade shows can be a very fruitful form of sales promotion. A **trade show** is an industry- or company-sponsored event in which booths are set up for the dissemination of information about offerings to members of a channel. Sometimes actual sales occur at a trade show, but often the primary purpose is promotion to attendees. Sales leads are obtained and passed along to the firm's sales organization for follow-up after the trade show.[8]

Another form of sales promotion to a channel is **cooperative advertising and promotion**. In cooperative advertising, a manufacturer provides special incentive money to channel members for certain performances such as running advertisements for one of the manufacturer's brands or doing product demonstrations with potential customers. The idea of cooperative advertising and promotion is that the manufacturer shares promotional expenses with channel members in the process of marketing to end-user consumers.[9]

Sometimes money is made available for a channel member in the form of a special payment for selling certain products, making a large order, or other specific performance. This form of channel-focused sales promotion is called an **allowance**. In addition, as with the consumer market, contests and displays with point-of-purchase materials are also frequently used as sales promotion approaches in the channel.[10]

PUBLIC RELATIONS (PR)

LO 14-3

Describe the activities and aims of public relations.

In Chapter 13 we defined public relations (PR) as a systematic approach to influencing attitudes, opinions, and behaviors of customers and others. PR is often executed through **publicity**, which is an unpaid and relatively less personal form of marketing communications, usually through news stories and mentions at public events.[11]

PR is a specialized field. Usually, undergraduate and graduate marketing programs do not include training in PR. Many PR professionals receive specialized training in communication, and outstanding PR people are highly sought after. Some firms have in-house PR departments, while others outsource much or all of the PR function to external agencies. Major responsibilities of a PR department might include any of the following activities:

- Gaining product publicity and buzz.
- Securing event sponsorships (for the company and its brands).
- Managing a crisis.
- Managing and writing news stories.
- Facilitating community affairs.
- Managing relationships with members of the local, national, and global media (media relations).
- Serving as organizational spokesperson.
- Educating consumers.
- Lobbying and governmental affairs.
- Handling investor relations.

However, few PR departments perform all of these functions; some of the above functions are often spread across other areas of a firm, such as investor relations to the finance department and lobbying and governmental affairs to the legal department.

We'll focus on the three core functions of PR that are most closely aligned with the role of the marketing manager: gaining product publicity and buzz, securing event sponsorships, and crisis management.

Gaining Product Publicity and Buzz

Especially when it comes to new product offerings, gaining publicity in news outlets and other public forums can provide a major boost to sales. During the introductory phase of the PLC, communication of information is a central promotional goal. The most credible and trusted information sources for potential customers are those that write or tell about a product for free. Newspaper and magazine articles, web postings and blogs, social marketing websites, news stories on television and radio—all of these forms of communication can be cultivated through an active PR program. Many new products have benefited from the initial awareness generated by a well-placed story in a publication or on a website frequented by targeted customers.

Although the media employed are free, by no means is the process of securing the story placements free. In fact, PR can account for a great deal of money in a promotion budget due to the work hours required to constantly be writing stories and cultivating media outlets. But the payoff on that investment can be substantial due to the buzz generated among everyday consumers about a brand. **Buzz**, or word-of-mouth communication, is consumer-to-consumer communication generated about a brand in the marketplace. The impact of buzz is not limited to current customers or even potential customers. When buzz about a brand hits the marketplace, and especially when it sweeps through social media, it can quickly become a cultural phenomenon. With an estimated 50 million users, and 8 billion resulting "connections," Tinder has become a one-stop shop for finding romantic prospects and is a major threat to traditional online dating sites. Tinder shies away from traditional media outlets, opting to rely on word-of-mouth, even from the onset. When the app was first released, Tinder hired college campus representatives to host events that required downloading and using the Tinder app to generate brand advocacy.[12]

Securing Event Sponsorships

Event sponsorships, having your brand and company associated with events in the sports, music, arts, and other entertainment communities, can add tremendous brand equity and also provide substantial exposure with the right target customers. Event sponsorships have become a mainstay of promotional strategy. A huge success story for marketers in event sponsorship is NASCAR, which appeals to millions of loyal and passionate racing fans. Consumers transfer the loyalty and passion about NASCAR directly to the brands represented by the sponsorships. No wonder NASCAR cars are referred to as "speeding billboards."[13]

Closely related to event sponsorship is issue sponsorship, in which a firm and its brands connect with a cause or issue that is especially important to its customers. Ever since the movie *Super Size Me* railed on McDonald's unhealthy menu items, the venerable chain has been under fire for not taking a lead in nutrition education. In recent years the company has taken a significant stand against obesity by introducing healthier meal options, such as salads, and providing nutritional information right on the menu boards. Sure, you can still eat your burger and fries there, but at least consumers can now compare those calories with the counts of several less-fattening items now available. Like publicity, the right sponsorships can generate positive buzz in the marketplace that enhances brand image.

Crisis Management

Crisis management is a planned, coordinated approach for disseminating information during times of emergency and for handling the effects of unfavorable publicity.[14] In 2017, several airlines encountered significant crises. United Airlines had to

The heart of an Olympian is always performing

And so are we.
2000 payments are made through our system each and every second, so we're ready whenever you need us.

Visa always on.

VISA | ◯◯◯
worldwide sponsor

One of the world's biggest sponsorship opportunities is the Olympics.
Source: Visa

deal with a passenger being dragged off an airplane (which we discussed in more detail in Chapter 10), British Airways had to manage a massive computer malfunction that impacted the airline for several days, and American Airlines had to handle an incident in which a mother had a stroller taken from her while boarding the plane and carrying her infant. In much the same way as earlier incidents, video of the American Airlines incident quickly showed up on a number of media sites, presenting American Airlines in an unfavorable light. In the video the passenger is clearly upset, and the American Airlines flight attendant comes across as argumentative and uncaring. However, American chose to handle the incident proactively by posting an apology on the company's website within minutes. In addition, the airline dealt with the woman's concerns quickly, respectfully, and compassionately. The result was that while the airline was "technically" correct in refusing to allow the woman to put the stroller in the overhead compartment, the reality of the situation required a different solution that focused on the passenger's needs. All firms should have a crisis management plan in place for contingencies that are relevant to their industry and customers.

PERSONAL SELLING—THE MOST PERSONAL FORM OF COMMUNICATION

LO 14-4

Understand the role of personal selling in marketing communications.

Interactive communications enable companies to create a conversation with their customers. As we discussed in Chapter 13, these tools offer some powerful advantages over traditional marketing communications, while still connecting to broader marketing communication strategies. Advertising, sales promotion, and public relations are essential marketing communication tools, but unidirectional for the most part. In other words, the company communicates with the customer, but the customer has limited ability to provide feedback. Companies know how important it is to communicate directly with the customer and, in turn, receive direct feedback from the customer. Effective marketing communications therefore incorporates personal communication elements. Companies like GAP combine traditional marketing communication tools like advertising with more personal communication, using social media and personal selling (in their stores) to foster a stronger relationship with their customers.

Brands like GAP are expected to maintain constant contact with customers through social media and other web services anywhere in the world.

Source: Gap Inc.

With the average cost of a sales call exceeding $500 and the Internet's interactive capabilities, some people have predicted the decline of personal selling as an effective marketing communications tool. However, this has not been the case. While there is no question that selling is among the most expensive forms of marketing communication, personal selling offers three distinct advantages over other marketing communications methods:

- *Immediate feedback to the customer.* Customers don't want to wait for information. They demand accurate information quickly, putting pressure on companies for immediate, personal communication with a salesperson or customer service representative.[15]

- *Ability to tailor the message to the customer.* No other marketing communication method does a better job of creating personal, unique customer messages in real time. Salespeople generate distinctive sales messages that directly address customer problems and concerns.[16]

- *Enhance the personal relationship between company and customer.* Salespeople and the personal selling function are the single most effective approach for establishing and enhancing the personal relationship between company and customer. In particular, business-to-business (B2B) customers appreciate the efficiency of the Internet and other communication tools but expect a personal relationship with their suppliers. There is no substitute for a salesperson working with the customer one-on-one to solve problems.[17]

Activities in Personal Selling

Personal selling is a two-way communication process between salesperson and buyer with the goal of securing, building, and maintaining long-term relationships with profitable customers. To be successful in this process, salespeople need a variety of skills that change all the time. Research suggests salespeople today are expected to be more skilled, available, and better communicators than ever before. Four basic selling activities composed of dozens of individual tasks define the salesperson's job: communicate, sell, build customer relationships, and manage information. The challenge for many companies is defining the correct mix of activities and then adapting the activities as the selling environment changes.[18] Exhibit 14.5 identifies the four major selling activities and specific tasks associated with each activity.

Communicate Effective communication is an essential selling activity. As the point of contact between customer and company, a salesperson must communicate effectively with both. With the customer, the salesperson needs good verbal communication skills to present the sales message. Equally important are good presentation skills and tools that incorporate technology (PowerPoint, social media) into the sales presentation. Finally, customers expect near constant access to the company so the salesperson must also have mobile communications skills.[19]

Communication with the company is also important. As discussed in Chapter 3, salespeople represent an excellent source of market information; they are familiar with customers and their needs. Customer feedback is also an excellent source of new-product ideas. Finally, field salespeople frequently find out about competitor or marketplace changes before anyone else in the company. All this information needs to be collected, analyzed, and disseminated to appropriate marketing managers.

EXHIBIT 14.5 | Matrix of Selling Activities

	Communicate	Sell	Build Customer Relationships	Manage Information
Technology	1. E-mail 2. Make telephone calls/leave voice-mail messages	1. Script sales pitch 2. Create customer-specific content 3. Provide relevant technology to customer	1. Create useful company web page content 2. Develop good team skills inside the company	1. Develop database management skills to manage customer database
Nontechnology	1. Enhance language and overall communication skills 2. Develop effective presentation skills	1. Learn relationship-selling skills 2. Conduct research on customer's business 3. Define and sell value-added services to customer 4. Follow up after customer contact 5. Identify and target key customer accounts 6. Listen effectively	1. Develop strong supplier alliances 2. Build rapport with all members of the customer's buying center 3. Network inside the company and throughout the customer's business 4. Build trust 5. Coordinate customer relationships inside the company	1. Develop time management skills 2. Organize information flow to maximize effectiveness and reduce irrelevant data

Sell Selling requires a specific, complex set of tasks to reach the point where the customer agrees to purchase the product. From customer research early in the process through the sales presentation and customer support after purchase, the sales process is difficult.[20]

Build Customer Relationships Customers demand a close, strategic relationship with suppliers, and, as the primary point of contact with the company, salespeople are expected to build and support the customer relationship. This means spending time with the customer, developing excellent customer relationship management skills, and ultimately building trust with a customer.[21]

Information Management Salespeople today must be excellent information managers, collecting information from a variety of sources (their own company, customers, competitors, and independent information sources), determining what is relevant, and then presenting it to the customer. For example, managing the flow of customer information inside the company to ensure the right people get the right information at the right time takes time and follow-up. Often, information is collected from customers and other external sources such as transportation companies to facilitate an order inside the company. Customers will have preferred shipping times that need to be coordinated with transportation companies to ensure on-time arrival. At the same time, being sensitive to customer security concerns means controlling access to information.[22]

Sales in B2C versus B2B Markets

In terms of sheer numbers, most salespeople are employed in various kinds of retail selling, or B2C. These jobs involve selling products to end users for their personal use. Examples of these types of sales positions are direct sellers such as Mary Kay and Tupperware, residential real estate agents, and retail store salespeople. However, salespeople in B2B markets do much more relationship selling.

Some personal characteristics and sales activities are similar across both B2C and B2B markets. Good interpersonal and communication skills, excellent knowledge of the products being sold, and an ability to discover customer needs and solve their problems are characteristics common to both sales environments. Similarly, managers must recruit and train appropriate people no matter what the sales job, provide them with objectives that match the firm's overall marketing program, then supervise, motivate, and finally evaluate their performance.[23]

But B2C and B2B selling also differ in some important ways. Many of the goods and services sold by B2B salespeople are more expensive and technically complex than those in B2C. In addition, B2B customers tend to be larger and engage in extensive decision-making processes involving many people.

Though we typically think of business-to-consumer salespeople in retailing, a great deal more selling occurs between businesses.
©Blend Images/Getty Images

Classifying Sales Positions

While retail selling employs more people, personal selling plays a more important and strategic purpose in business-to-business markets. Because of the important strategic function of personal selling in B2B markets, our discussion of sales positions will focus on various sales positions in this arena. There are many different types of sales jobs that require a variety of specific and unique skills. However, no matter what the job title, the salesperson's primary responsibility is to increase business from current and potential customers by providing a good value proposition to customers and effectively dealing with their concerns. The four major types of sales positions are trade servicer, missionary seller, technical seller, and solutions seller.

Trade Servicer **Trade servicers** are the group of resellers such as retailers or distributors with whom the sales force does business. Their primary responsibility is to increase business from current or potential customers by providing them with merchandising and promotional assistance. For example, the P&G salesperson selling soap products to individual store managers in a large grocery chain is an example of a trade servicer.

Anheuser-Busch uses missionary selling to get its Budweiser beer into stores.
©Fred de Novelle/Photononstop/Getty Images

Missionary Seller **Missionary salespeople** often do not take orders from customers directly but persuade customers to buy their firm's product from distributors or other suppliers. Anheuser-Busch does missionary selling when its salespeople call on bar owners and encourage them to order a particular brand of beer from the local distributor. One of the best examples of missionary salespeople is a pharmaceutical rep, or detailer, who calls on doctors as a representative of the pharmaceutical manufacturers. When Sanofi and Regeneron Pharmaceuticals introduced Kevzara, a top-selling drug for treating rheumatoid arthritis, its salespeople communicated with physicians to alert them of the efficacy of the product, explain its advantages over other drugs, and influence them to prescribe it to their patients. Keep in mind that the Sanofi salesperson does not "sell" any product directly to the patient.[24]

Technical Seller An example of **technical selling** is the sales engineer from General Electric who calls on Boeing to sell the GE90 jet engine to be used in Boeing 777 aircraft. The trend is for most technical selling to be done in cross-functional teams. The complexity of many of the products and associated services involved in technical selling makes it difficult for any one salesperson to master all aspects of the sale. Cross-functional teams often include someone who is technically competent in the product (an engineer), a customer service specialist, a financial analyst, and an account manager responsible for maintaining the customer-company relationship.

Solution Seller More and more customers look for strategic partners who provide comprehensive solutions to their business problems. **Key account salespeople**, those responsible for managing large accounts, are skilled in developing complex solutions to a particular customer problem.[25] In addition, in industries such as information technology, customers look to suppliers for wide-ranging solutions from IT infrastructure design to defining product specifications, to purchase and installation of equipment or software, and support after the sale. A Cisco Systems or IBM salesperson, for example, needs to know not only a great deal about hardware and software but also the customer's business in order to develop a solution to the customer's IT problems.

The Personal Selling Process

Because personal selling is so important in establishing and maintaining customer relationships, particularly in B2B markets, many companies create a separate personal selling function that operates independently from the rest of marketing. As a result, marketing managers often do not have salespeople reporting directly to them. However, marketing managers need to understand the personal selling process for two reasons. First, in companies where salespeople play an important role, personal selling is the single most critical connection to the customer. From selling to customer service, salespeople are often the customer's primary contact point with the company. Marketing managers need a clear understanding of the selling process because it has such a profound effect on the customer relationship. Second, a number of marketing activities such as customer service and marketing communications will be affected by the personal selling function. Understanding the selling process helps marketing managers better plan a marketing communications strategy and coordinate other marketing activities such as customer service.

> **LO 14-5**
> Learn the process of relationship selling.

Exhibit 14.6 shows the six stages in the personal selling process. Although the selling process involves only a few steps, the specific activities involved at each step vary greatly depending on the type of sales position and the firm's overall customer relationship strategy.

EXHIBIT 14.6 | The Personal Selling Process

| Prospect for Customers | → | Open the Relationship | → | Qualify the Prospect | → | Make the Sales Presentation | → | Handle Customer Objections | → | Follow-Up with Customers |

Marketing managers must ensure that a firm's sales program incorporates sufficient policies to guide each salesperson while at the same time coordinating the selling effort with the firm's marketing and relationship strategy. B2C and B2B salespeople use the same selling process, although how the process works varies greatly between the two environments. For example, B2C salespeople generally do not actively prospect for customers, since the customer is visiting the store, or follow up with the customer after the sale.

Prospect for Customers Prospecting is critical because recruiting new customers is an essential element in a company's growth strategy. Marketing managers encourage salespeople to use a variety of sources to identify prospects, including trade association and industry directories, other customers and suppliers, and referrals from company marketing efforts.

Telemarketing and other direct marketing efforts, which we will discuss in the next section, are also used to generate prospective customers. **Outbound telemarketing** involves calling potential customers at their home or office, either to make a sales call via telephone or to set up an appointment for a field salesperson. **Inbound telemarketing**, where prospective customers call a toll-free number for more information, is also used to identify and qualify prospects. When prospects call for more information, a telemarketing representative determines the extent of interest and assesses the prospect qualifications, then passes the contact information on to the appropriate salesperson. The Internet has the ability to generate potential new customer leads, and a number of companies have dedicated teams to manage their Internet lead generation and customer inquiries. In addition, many companies, particularly those selling complex products, provide technical product information to customers. Salespeople, assigned in some firms specifically for Internet customers, follow up on legitimate inquiries with a traditional sales call. Hubspot is a software service company that allows its users (companies) to use its inbound marketing techniques to build up businesses, which is great news for smaller companies that don't have the marketing budgets of larger companies. Not only does Hubspot offer inbound marketing techniques, but it practices what it preaches, using inbound marketing techniques to attract new customers with great success.[26]

In coordinating the marketing effort, marketing managers must understand how much emphasis salespeople give to prospecting for new customers versus calling on existing customers. The appropriate policy depends on the selling and customer relationship strategy of the company, the nature of the product, and the firm's customers. Working with sales managers, the marketing manager considers the right mix of activities for the salesperson. For example, firms that have established customer relationships or products that require substantial service after the sale like Epic Healthcare encourage salespeople to devote most of their effort to servicing existing customers.[27]

Open the Relationship In the initial approach to the prospective customer, the sales representative should try to determine who has the greatest influence or authority in the purchase. For example, when the firm's product is inexpensive and purchased routinely, salespeople are frequently instructed to deal with the purchasing department. At the other end of the continuum, the sales effort for complex, technical products generally requires an extensive program: calling on influencers and decision makers in various departments and different managerial levels. When the purchase involves people across the customer's organization, the sales staff often works in teams.

Qualify the Prospect Before salespeople spend much time trying to establish a relationship with the prospective account, it is important to qualify the prospect to determine if the company is a legitimate potential customer. The process involves answering five questions:

- Does the prospect have a need for the company's products?
- Can the prospect derive added value from the product in ways that the company can deliver?

- Can the salesperson effectively contact, communicate, and work with the prospect over an extended time period (the time it takes to complete the sale and follow up after the sale)?
- Does the prospect have the financial ability and authority to make the sale?
- Will the account be profitable for the company?

Sales Presentation The **sales presentation** is the delivery of information relevant to meet the customer's needs and is the heart of the selling process. It is the process salespeople use to transition customers from interest in the product to purchase of the product.

Sales presentations are an important element of personal selling.

©monkeybusinessimages/Getty Images

Communicating the sales message is the number one priority of the presentation. The stereotype of a sales presentation is a salesperson talking in front of a customer or group of customers. In reality, sales presentations are carefully choreographed interactions in which the salesperson tries to discern the customer's real needs while at the same time providing critical information in a persuasive way so the customer appreciates the benefits and advantages of the product. Remember, the goal is not simply to make the sale but to create a strong value proposition that will lead to a mutually beneficial long-term relationship.[28]

Setting goals and objectives is the first step in communicating. Ultimately, the goal of the presentation is to secure a purchase commitment from the customer. However, the salesperson does not just walk in asking for the purchase order. Successful salespeople understand that the purchase order does not come until customers believe the company's products offer the best solution to their needs. In defining the goal, salespeople consider where the customer is in the buying process and have a clear understanding of the customer relationship.[29] New customers, for example, generally need more information about company products, policies, and procedures than existing customers. Based on an analysis of these factors, salespeople identify at least one of five principal goals for the presentation. At some point, however, the goal of the presentation will be to obtain customer action.

- Educate the customer by providing enough knowledge about the company's products.
- Get the customer's attention.
- Build interest for the company's products.
- Nurture the customer's desire and conviction to purchase.
- Obtain a customer commitment to action (purchase).

Characteristics of a Great Sales Presentation How would you respond if someone asked you, "What makes a great sales presentation?" Many people can give examples of a bad presentation, such as not listening to the customer, but not the characteristics of a great sales presentation.[30] Perhaps an even more important question is, "Does a great sales presentation make a difference?" Consider this example: what started as a Maine lobster food truck now has 20 franchised trucks in 13 cities across the United States and an e-commerce platform. The company, Cousins Maine Lobster, flourished after it appeared on Shark Tank, a television show where entrepreneurs present their businesses in hopes of securing funds from a shark.[31] In Cousins Maine Lobster's episode, the cousins made a deal with Barbara Corcoran, a successful businesswoman. Corcoran credited the cousins' sales presentation as what secured the deal because they answered objections and questions flawlessly, and were very clear.[32] The cousins' extensive preparation of their sales presentation paid off hugely for their small business.[33] Exhibit 14.7 identifies the four characteristics of a great presentation.

Handle Objections—Negotiating Win-Win Solutions Casual observation may suggest there are many different customer concerns; however, when you look closely, customer anxieties fall into four areas. Customers often mask true concerns with general problems, but successful salespeople know how to identify and clarify true objections.[34] Exhibit 14.8 identifies common customer concerns.

EXHIBIT 14.7 | Characteristics of a Great Sales Presentation

Characteristic	Answers the Customer Question
Explains the value proposition	What is the value-added of the product?
Asserts the advantages and benefits of the product	What are the advantages and benefits of the product?
Enhances the customer's knowledge of the company, product, and services	What are the key points I should know about this company, product, and services?
Creates a memorable experience	What should I remember about this presentation?

Source: Johnston, Mark W., and Marshall, Greg W. *Contemporary Selling.* London, UK: Routledge Publishing, 2013.

EXHIBIT 14.8 | Common Customer Concerns

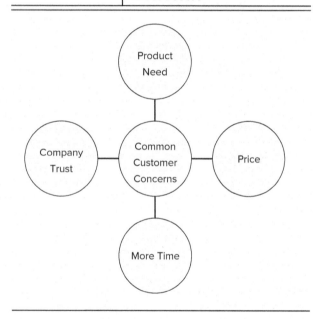

Product Need The customer may not be convinced there is a need for the product. The customer's perspective can be summarized as, "We've always done it one way; why should we start something new now?" Key to the answer is a well-conceived value proposition that explains clearly how the product will benefit the customer and how it will be better than the existing solution.[35] It is important to remember that customers are generally not risk takers.

A much more common concern is whether the customer views the salesperson's product as a better solution than existing options. The customer is already familiar with the current products and change means learning a new product. Careful preparation is critical in dealing with questions about competitors, which is why salespeople spend a great deal of time learning about competitors' products. Cisco has developed an excellent reputation with its customers. It is leveraging that reputation with a sophisticated line of teleconferencing products. Business customers have confidence in Cisco, which translates into business opportunities.

Company Trust Personal selling is based a great deal on mutual trust between the buyer and the seller. As we discussed, most customers already have a supplier, and while they may not be totally satisfied, they are familiar with it. For example, they know the process for resolving a problem (who to call, expected wait times, costs, etc.). If the customer is unaware of the company, a common concern is the company's ability to deliver what is needed, when it's needed, and where it's needed.[36] This is a legitimate concern as the customer puts the company at risk by choosing the salesperson's company as the supplier. In other situations, customers may not object to the salesperson's company but are happy with their existing supplier. When a company trusts a supplier, the relationship can be beneficial to both parties. Accenture, a leading global business services firm, has had 98 out of its top 100 customers on the books for at least 10 years.[37] Accenture was named the 2017 World's Most Ethical Company, an award given to a company that, among other qualities, makes trust part of its corporate DNA—it's an award Accenture has earned for the past 10 years consecutively. Integrity is part of Accenture's core values and is defined as inspiring trust by following through on its word.[38]

More Time One of the most common customer objections is, "I need more time to consider the proposal." Certainly, concern about making a purchase decision too quickly is legitimate; however, the most likely scenario is that the value proposition has not been sufficiently developed.

Price Salespeople consistently report that price is the most common customer apprehension. In many cases, the customer has legitimate objections about the price of a product. Nevertheless, the price objection usually means the customer has not accepted the value proposition. In essence, if the customer does not perceive that the product benefits exceed the price, there will be no sale. The salesperson is left with two options: lower the price until it is below the product's perceived benefits or raise the perceived benefits until they exceed the price.[39]

Close the Sale Closing the sale is obtaining commitment from the customer to make the purchase. The close is not a discrete event but rather a nonlinear process that begins with the approach to the customer. Research suggests salespeople make four critical mistakes in closing. First, a negative attitude about the customer or situation can affect the sales presentation and customer relationship. Second, the failure to conduct an effective pre-approach shows a lack of preparation that turns off customers. Third, too much talking and not enough listening demonstrates a lack of interest in finding out the customer's real needs. Fourth, using a "one size fits all" approach indicates the salesperson lacks creativity and is unwilling to focus on the customer's unique situation.[40]

Follow-Up after the Sale One of the most critical aspects to the selling process is not what happens before the purchase decision but what happens after, the **follow-up**. Salespeople often rely on support people inside the company to help in post-sales service. Customer service personnel, product service call centers, technicians, and others are part of the follow-up process. But no matter who else has contact with the customer, the customer will hold the primary salesperson most responsible for the level and quality of service and support after the sale.

Customers expect three activities after the purchase decision: (1) delivery, installation, and initial service of the product: (2) any training needed to operate the equipment correctly: and (3) the effective and efficient disposition of appropriate customer problems that arise from the product purchase. Not meeting those expectations is a primary reason for customer complaints.[41] Any following purchase decisions are based to a large extent on the customer's experience with the product and the company. Douglas McIntyre, the editor of *24/7 Wall Street*, publishes an annual Customer Service Hall of Fame.[42] The results each year are republished by major news sources such as *USA Today* and *CNN Money*. Amazon, Chick-fil-A, and Marriott consistently rank among the top five customer service companies, and Amazon has taken first place for the past seven consecutive years. It is no coincidence that these companies are consistently ranked as leaders in the industries due, in part, to maintaining a strong customer service culture.[43]

Organizing the Sales Force

Since salespeople work closely with many departments inside the company, marketing managers have a real interest in working with sales managers to organize the sales force to maximize the efficiency and effectiveness of not only the sales force but also everyone in the company who interacts with the customer. The best sales structures are based on the company's objectives and strategies. In addition, as the firm's environment, objectives, or marketing strategy changes, its sales force must be flexible enough to change as well.[44]

Company Sales Force or Independent Agents Maintaining a sales force is expensive, and companies are constantly assessing the most practical method to reach customers. One option is to use independent agents instead of company salespeople. It is not unusual for a company, such as IBM, to use both company salespeople and independent agents. Using independent sales agents is referred to as **outsourcing the sales force**.

The decision to use independent agents or a company sales force involves four factors:

- *Economic:* The costs and expected revenue associated with maintaining a sales force are analyzed and weighed against outsourcing to independent agents.
- *Control:* A critical factor is the amount of control senior management believes is necessary for the sales function. A company sales force offers complete control in key

areas such as recruiting, training, and compensation. On the other hand, independent agents operate without direct company management supervision.

- *Transaction costs:* Finding a good replacement for a poor-performing independent sales agent can be difficult, and once one is found, it is often months before the new agent learns enough about the product and its applications to be effective in the sales job. **Transaction cost analysis (TCA)** states that when substantial transaction-specific assets are necessary to sell a manufacturer's product, the cost of using and administering independent agents is likely higher than the cost of hiring and managing a company's sales force.[45]

- *Strategic flexibility:* In general, a vertically integrated distribution system incorporating a company sales force is less flexible than outsourcing. Independent agents can be added or dismissed at short notice, especially if no specialized assets are needed to sell the product. Furthermore, it is not necessary to sign a long-term contract with independent agents. Firms facing uncertain and rapidly changing competitive or market environments and industries characterized by shifting technology or short product life cycles often use independent agents to preserve flexibility in the distribution channel.

Geographic Orientation The simplest and most common method of organizing a company sales force is geographic orientation, as illustrated in Exhibit 14.9. Individual salespeople are assigned to separate geographic territories. In this type of organization, each salesperson is responsible for performing all the sales activities in a given territory. The geographic sales organization has several advantages. First, and most importantly, it tends to have the lowest cost because (1) there is only one salesperson in each territory, (2) territories tend to be smaller than other organizational structures so travel time and expenses are minimized, and (3) fewer managerial levels are required for coordination so sales administration and overhead expenses are lower. Second, the simplicity of the geographical structure minimizes customer confusion because each customer is called on by one salesperson. The major disadvantage is that it does not encourage or support any division or specialization of labor. Each salesperson is expected to be good at many things (various customer needs, product applications and specifications).

Product Organization Some companies have a separate sales force for each product or product category (see Exhibit 14.10). The primary advantage of a product organization is that individual salespeople can develop familiarity with the technical attributes, applications, and most effective selling methods associated with a single product. Also, there tends to be a closer relationship between sales and engineering, product development, and manufacturing when salespeople focus on one product or product category. Finally, this structure enables greater control in the allocation of selling effort across various products. Management can then adjust sales assets based on the needs of individual products. The major disadvantage

EXHIBIT 14.9 | Example of Geographic Organization

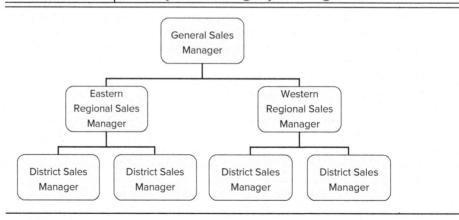

Source: Johnston, Mark W., and Marshall, Greg W. *Sales Force Management* (12th ed.). London, UK: Routledge Publishing, 2016.

EXHIBIT 14.10 | Example of Product Orientation

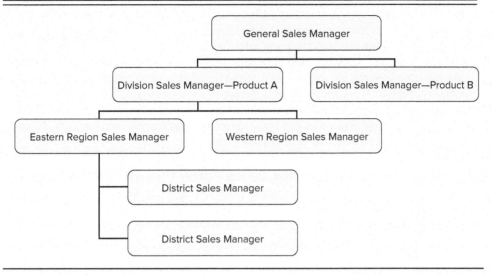

Source: Johnston, Mark W., and Marshall, Greg W. *Sales Force Management* (12th ed.). London, UK: Routledge Publishing, 2016.

is the duplication of effort with salespeople across different products assigned to the same geographic territory. This generally leads to higher sales costs.

Customer Type or Market Segmentation It has become increasingly popular for organizations to structure their sales force by customer type, as IBM did when it created separate sales teams to call on small and large business customers. Organizing by customer type is a natural extension of creating value for the customer and reflects a market segmentation strategy (see Exhibit 14.11). When salespeople specialize in calling on a particular type of customer, they gain a better understanding of those customers' needs and requirements. They can be trained to use different selling approaches for different markets and to implement specialized marketing and promotional programs.[46]

A related advantage is that as salespeople become familiar with the customers' specific needs, they are more likely to discover ideas for new products and marketing approaches that will appeal to those customers. The disadvantage, as with product organization, is that sales costs are higher as a result of having multiple salespeople operating in the same geographic area. In addition, when customers have different departments operating in different industries, two or more salespeople from the same company may be calling on the same customer.

EXHIBIT 14.11 | Example of Customer Orientation

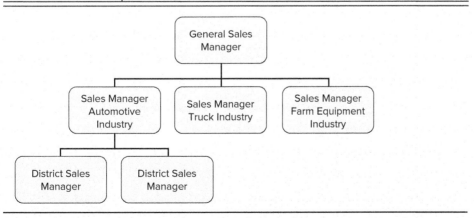

Source: Johnston, Mark W., and Marshall, Greg W. *Sales Force Management* (12th ed.). London, UK: Routledge Publishing, 2016.

Managing the Sales Force

LO 14-6

Understand the major job responsibilities of sales management.

Sales and marketing work together to deliver value to the customer and achieve company objectives. While primary responsibility for managing a sales force generally falls to sales managers, integrating the marketing and sales function requires a coordinated effort with marketing managers. Understanding how salespeople are managed helps marketing managers better understand the selling function and coordinate sales with the rest of the marketing department. The sales function is unique in the organization and requires talented management to maximize its efficiency and effectiveness. Managing a sales force involves five primary responsibilities: salesperson performance, recruitment and selection, training, compensation and rewards, and performance evaluation.

Performance: Motivating the Sales Force Understanding sales agents' performance is important to sales managers because almost everything they as managers do influences sales performance one way or another. For example, how the manager selects staff members and the kind of training they receive affect their own aptitude and skills. The compensation program and the way it is administered influence motivation and overall sales performance.

It helps to understand what people want and expect from their jobs. Gen Yers entered the workforce with a different set of rules than their baby boomer parents. While still focused on high performance and high-paying jobs, they also look for positions that are fun and exciting. In essence, they are not just looking for a job but an opportunity to both enjoy their job and be well rewarded in the process. Gen Yers place a higher priority on finding the right life-work balance, so the 60-hour workweek does not appeal to them, but working remotely and with flexible schedules does.[47] For marketing managers this means developing positions that offer a broader range of experiences (for example, increased travel and opportunities for faster and more frequent promotions).

As presented in Exhibit 14.12, salesperson performance is a function of five factors: (1) role perceptions, (2) aptitude, (3) skill level, (4) motivation, and (5) personal, organizational, and environmental factors.

Role Perceptions. The role of a salesperson is the set of activities or behaviors he or she must perform on the job. This role is largely defined through the expectations, demands, and pressure communicated to the salesperson by role partners. These partners include people inside as well as outside the company with a vested interest in how a salesperson performs the job—top management, the salesperson's sales manager,

EXHIBIT 14.12 | **Model of Salesperson Performance**

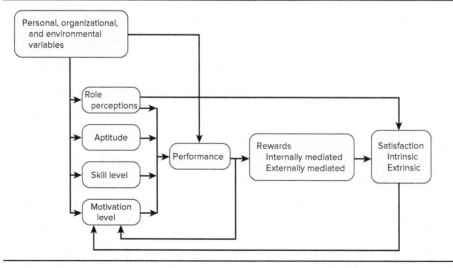

Source: Johnston, Mark W., and Marshall, Greg W. *Sales Force Management* (12th ed.). London, UK: Routledge Publishing, 2016.

customers, and family members. How salespeople perceive their roles has significant consequences that affect job satisfaction and motivation, which, in turn, have the potential to increase sales force turnover and hurt performance.[48]

Sales Aptitude: Are Good Salespeople Born or Made? Sales ability has historically been considered a function of (1) physical factors such as age and physical attractiveness, (2) aptitude factors such as verbal skills and sales expertise, and (3) personality characteristics such as empathy. However, there is no proof these measures, by themselves, affect sales performance. As a result, most managers believe the things a company does to train and develop its salespeople are the most important determinants of success.

Sales Skill Levels. **Sales skill levels** are the individual's learned proficiency at performing necessary sales tasks. They include such learned abilities as interpersonal skills, leadership, technical knowledge, and presentation skills. The relative importance of each of these skills and the need for other skills depend on the selling situation.[49]

Motivation. **Motivation** is how much the salesperson wants to expend effort on each activity or task associated with the sales job. Sales managers constantly try to find the optimal mix of motivation elements that direct salespeople to perform sales activities. Companies often use motivators such as remote workdays and flexible work schedules to inspire employees. Global security and aerospace company Lockheed Martin offers 9-80 and 4-10 flexible work schedules and telecommuting options to employees at most of its locations across the United States and around the world. Such options are designed to promote productivity and motivate employees through workplace flexibility.[50] As you would expect, motivational factors that work well with one person may not motivate another. For example, an autocratic managerial style may work with a midcareer salesperson but have a profoundly negative effect on a senior salesperson. In addition, a number of motivational factors are not directly under the sales manager's control, such as personal family issues or general economic conditions.[51]

Organizational, Environmental, and Personal Factors. Organizational factors include the company marketing budget, current market share for the company's products, and the degree of sales management supervision. Personal and organizational variables such as job experience, the manager's interaction style, and performance feedback influence the amount of role conflict and ambiguity salespeople perceive.[52] In addition, the desire for job-related rewards (such as higher pay or promotion) differs with age, education, family size, career stage, and organizational climate.

Rewards. A company bestows a variety of rewards on any given level of performance. There are two types of rewards—extrinsic and intrinsic. **Extrinsic rewards** are those controlled and given by people other than the salesperson such as managers and customers. They include pay, financial incentives, security, recognition, and promotion. **Intrinsic rewards** are those salespeople primarily attain for themselves and include feelings of accomplishment, personal growth, and self-worth.[53]

Satisfaction. Salesperson job satisfaction refers to all the characteristics of the job individuals find rewarding, fulfilling, and satisfying—or frustrating and unsatisfying. Satisfaction is a complex job attitude, and salespeople can be satisfied or dissatisfied with many different aspects of the job.[54]

Recruiting and Selecting Salespeople Hiring the people who best fit the job and organization is important to long-term success, so there is a great deal of focus on recruiting and selecting qualified salespeople. The recruitment and selection process has three steps: (1) analyze the job and determine selection criteria, (2) find and attract a pool of applicants, and (3) develop and apply selection procedures to evaluate applicants.

Firms can easily be up against competitors and other industries for the best candidates. As a result, companies develop a well-coordinated recruiting strategy that, contrary to popular belief, does not seek to maximize the number of applicants. Having too many recruits overloads the selection process. The true objective of a successful recruiting strategy is to identify a few exceptionally qualified recruits.[55]

EXHIBIT 14.13 | Sales Training Topics

Source: Johnston, Mark W., and Marshall, Greg W. *Sales Force Management* (12th ed.). London, UK: Routledge Publishing, 2016.

Training Sales managers work with marketing managers to identify training objectives that integrate the needs of the salesperson with corporate marketing objectives. These objectives typically include (1) improved customer relationships, (2) increased productivity, (3) improved morale, (4) lower turnover, and (5) improved selling skills. The challenge for sales managers is measuring the effectiveness of sales training.[56]

Sales training most often involves one or more of the seven topics listed in Exhibit 14.13, ranging from product knowledge to very specialized topics such as communication and customer relationship building. The key for sales managers is fitting the sales training content to the needs of the individual salespeople.

Johnson & Johnson incorporates several online tools to help train employees. Its online "e-university" provides a variety of learning experiences for employees. In addition, personalized learning and development programs deliver specific training based on the individual's own career goals. Some of the topics included are management fundamentals, negotiation skills, and mentoring essentials. Once they have completed the learning and development program, certain employees are allowed to take additional course work in a leadership development program. Ultimately J&J wants to develop the full potential of salespeople and other employees to maximize their performance opportunities.[57]

Compensation and Rewards The total financial compensation paid to salespeople has several components designed to achieve different objectives. A **salary** is a fixed sum of money paid at regular intervals. Most firms that pay a salary also offer *incentives* or *incentive pay* to encourage better performance. **Incentives** are generally commissions tied to sales volume or profitability, or bonuses for meeting or exceeding specific performance targets (for example, meeting quotas for a particular product). Such incentives direct salespeople's efforts toward specific strategic objectives during the year, as well as offer additional rewards for top performers. A **commission** is payment based on short-term results, usually a salesperson's dollar or unit sales volume. Since there is a direct link between sales volume and the amount of commission received, commission payments are useful for increasing salespeople's sales efforts.[58] Exhibit 14.14 summarizes the components and objectives of financial compensation plans.

In addition to financial compensation, sales management (and management across the company) incorporates a range of **nonfinancial incentives**. Most sales managers consider promotional opportunities second only to financial incentives as effective sales force motivators. This is particularly true for young, well-educated salespeople who tend to view their sales position as a stepping-stone to a senior management position.

Evaluating Salesperson Performance Monitoring sales activity and evaluating salesperson performance are fundamental issues. Salespeople should be evaluated solely on those elements of the sales process they control. To do this, a company develops objective and subjective measures that distinguish between controllable and noncontrollable factors.[59] For example, companies, for the most part, understand that the overall economic environment is not within the salesperson's control; however, direct sales to a customer are quite clearly in the salesperson's control. This means that if sales are declining because the economy is not doing well, the salesperson should not be penalized; however, if sales are declining because the salesperson is not meeting the customer's needs, then he or she should be held accountable. For many Chick-fil-A restaurant employees, high performance

EXHIBIT 14.14 | Components and Objectives of Financial Compensation Plans

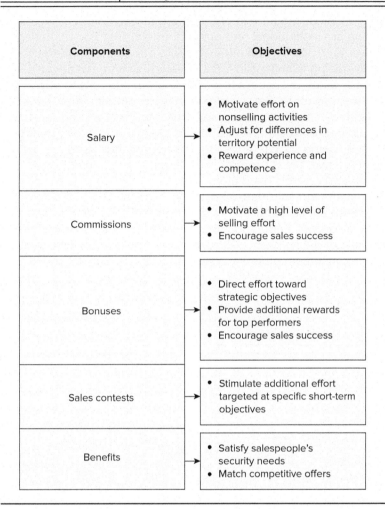

Components	Objectives
Salary	• Motivate effort on nonselling activities • Adjust for differences in territory potential • Reward experience and competence
Commissions	• Motivate a high level of selling effort • Encourage sales success
Bonuses	• Direct effort toward strategic objectives • Provide additional rewards for top performers • Encourage sales success
Sales contests	• Stimulate additional effort targeted at specific short-term objectives
Benefits	• Satisfy salespeople's security needs • Match competitive offers

Source: Johnston, Mark W., and Marshall, Greg W. *Sales Force Management* (12th ed.). London, UK: Routledge Publishing, 2016.

evaluations and low food waste records equate to free food, an often-overlooked but highly effective motivator for young teen and college-aged employees. At many Chick-fil-A locations, employees are rewarded with discounts on food (ranging from percentages off to free) depending on food waste quantities for the month. Such reward systems encourage efficiency and discourage kitchen staff from wasting food, a problem that generates significant costs for restaurants.[60]

SUMMARY

Advertising is a paid form of relatively less personal marketing communications, often through a mass medium to one or more target markets. Two major forms of advertising are institutional and product advertising. For marketing managers, creative agencies play an important role due to the proliferation of outsourcing of advertising initiatives in firms. A variety of types of advertising media are available—a key to success is knowing when and how to apply each type of those approaches. Sales promotion is a promotion mix element that provides an inducement for an end-user consumer to buy a product or for a salesperson or someone else in the channel to sell it. Thus, sales promotion is relevant in both B2C and B2B settings, but the approaches used are quite different between the two. Sales promotion is designed to augment other forms of promotion and is rarely used alone. Public relations (PR) is a systematic approach to influencing attitudes, opinions, and behaviors of customers and others. PR is often executed through publicity, which is an unpaid and relatively less personal form of marketing communications, usually through news stories and mentions at public events. Buzz, or word-of-mouth communication, is the consumer-to-consumer communication generated about a brand in the marketplace. Finally, the most important personal communication tool is personal selling. Personal selling is a unique company function, and managing the sales force presents several unique challenges.

KEY TERMS

advertising wearout   376
advertising response function   376
institutional advertising   376
product advertising   377
pioneering advertising   377
competitive advertising   377
comparative advertising   377
reach   378
frequency   378
advertising execution   378
clutter   379
trade show   382
cooperative advertising
  and promotion   382

allowance   382
publicity   382
buzz   383
event sponsorships   383
crisis management   383
personal selling   385
trade servicers   387
missionary salespeople   387
technical selling   387
key account salespeople   387
outbound telemarketing   388
inbound telemarketing   388
sales presentation   389

closing the sale   391
follow-up   391
outsourcing the sales force   391
transaction cost analysis
  (TCA)   392
sales skill levels   395
motivation   395
extrinsic rewards   395
intrinsic rewards   395
salary   396
incentives   396
commission   396
nonfinancial incentives   396

APPLICATION QUESTIONS

More application questions are available online.

1. Consider the concept of advertising wearout.
   a. What is advertising wearout?
   b. What do you think are some causes of wearout?
   c. Come up with as many ads as you can that, for you, are "worn out." Can you recall how long each ad interested you before wearout began to set in?

2. You are the vice president of sales for a $30 million manufacturer of home building materials. The company employs 50 salespeople around the country to market the company's products to hardware stores and major building contractors. The CEO believes the company needs to cut costs and wants to

reduce the sales force by 50 percent. You have been asked to come in and explain why that is a bad long-term strategy for the company. Discuss why salespeople are critical to the success of the company.

3. Review the Common Approaches to Advertising Execution (Exhibit 14.2) and Pros and Cons of Key Advertising Media (Exhibit 14.3). Review some ads in any three of the seven different types of media identified, watching for examples of the different execution approaches.

   a. Make notes about the ads you reviewed and the different types of media execution you witnessed. Which ads do you think were the most effective? Why?

   b. For the same ads, based on the chapter's list of pros and cons for each, identify specific examples of ads for which one or more of the pros and cons apply.

   c. Share your findings with another student or with the class.

4. Exhibit 14.4 presents some of the most common consumer sales promotion approaches. Select any three of the approaches and think of a purchase you have made in response to each. How important was the availability of the sales promotion to your ultimate decision to buy?

   a. Crisis management is a very important function of any type of organization including for-profit firms, nonprofits, governmental entities, and others. Identify an example of an organization that faced a crisis of some type that was highly publicized. This could be a product recall that challenged a firm, a management or financial scandal, a natural disaster faced by a governmental body or charitable agency, or any other such issue.

   b. How did the organization address the crisis? What specifically did they do once it was evident a crisis was afoot?

   c. Give your opinion of how they handled the crisis. What would you recommend that they could have done better?

MANAGEMENT DECISION CASE
Intel Uses Storytelling to "Let the Inside Out"

Many users of personal computers are very familiar with the little stickers that appear on the keyboard, reminding you that your device has "Intel Inside." For years, tech giant Intel's marketing was centered on telling us that its technology was the secret sauce inside the gadgets we've come to depend upon. And that marketing has worked: its five-note chime tune is probably clearly imprinted upon your memory (can you hear it?). While Intel's chips are best known for their role in personal computing, today the company has moved far beyond the microprocessor and PC into other areas. The brand, however, was still stuck in this limited role in the minds of consumers.[61]

Intel's marketing team decided that it was time to change the image of the brand. The goal was to "Let the inside out" and highlight the exciting work that their chips allow people to do.[62] To accomplish that goal, Intel executed a major advertising campaign that used the power of storytelling to make the

invisible nature of the Intel technology visible.[63] And to create those stories, Intel used a new and different approach that might seem strange for a company trying to move away from the concept of "inside."

To introduce its new persona, Intel produced an ad called "Intel Amazing," showing the things in American life that the processors from Intel make possible. This included movie maker DreamWorks Animation, NASA missions, and prosthetic hands. Other stories show how Intel technology helps young innovators in different parts of the world. Jessica Orji of Lagos, Nigeria, participated in Intel's #SheWillConnect program, learning how to grow her hairdressing business. The Intel XDK coding language was featured in the story of Caroline Wambui, a 16-year-old from Nairobi, Kenya. She and fellow classmates used the programming language to create an organ donor app.[64] Another video shows a woman in India who used the Intel Edison to help her epileptic son. The

Edison is a minicomputer the size of a postage stamp, and was used in the creation of a glove that can detect oncoming epileptic episodes.[65]

The advertising team recognized that Intel was not getting credit for its role in major cultural events that were centered around technology: the space shuttle, the Hubble Space Telescope—even Stephen Hawkings's computer. This new approach was important for reaching the next generation of Intel customers. As Intel's vice president and global creative director, Teresa Herd, put it: "Kids today don't care about what's inside—they care about what they get to do with it."[66]

Popular culture became part of the strategy in a real-time display of Intel technology at the Grammy Awards show. Using its video-projection technology, Intel merged performer Lady Gaga's face with that of the late David Bowie in a special tribute performance. The Intel magic helped create "digital skin" that changed Gaga's "makeup" and created a digital spider that appeared to dart across her face![67] This was not only a live event promotion (viewed by 25 million), but later was incorporated into an ad for television. The campaign accompanying the event worked, generating more than 120 news stories. It also drove a 122 percent "brand lift" among millennials, evaluating their view of Intel as an innovative brand.[68]

Ironically, one of the keys to "getting the inside out" was moving responsibility for much of the creation of the advertising *inside* Intel. Like many major corporations, Intel depended heavily on outside advertising agencies to create its campaigns. For this change in direction, the CMO felt it was important to have Intel's own employees driving the creative process. This provided Intel with efficiencies and cost savings, but it also provided something more. The 90-person team has a major advantage over an outside agency: they have visibility and access to current projects and those planned for the future. Intel still uses outside agencies, and the internal team works collaboratively with those groups. But with special access to the creative minds at Intel, Herd says that this inside team can go to the business side of Intel and ask, "All right, what do you have now?"[69]

Intel's advertising and its approach to managing its creation has paid off, changing the brand's image from a microchip manufacturer to a technology innovator used by icons such as Lady Gaga and football's Tom Brady.[70] Between advertising, related event marketing, and other initiatives, Intel generated nearly *60 billion* media impressions in a single year.[71] Brand consultant Millward Brown moved the company up from the 86th position to 51st in its Brand Z list—a good indication that the brand is growing in value and that the marketing efforts to reposition the brand are working.[72] And the next time you see an Intel sticker on a computer or other gadget, you may notice a visible result of this changing personality for the brand: Instead of "Intel Inside," the new labels carry the tag line "Experience what's inside."[73]

Questions for Consideration

1. What was the issue with Intel's old branding? Was this just change for change's sake? Why might it be important for Intel's future business success to promote a new brand image?

2. Intel uses both its new internal creative team and outside advertising agencies. What are the pros and cons of using an internally staffed creative advertising team? What activities that an ad agency performs might be more efficiently handled by an outside group?

3. Intel shows its storytelling ads on both TV and via the Internet. Is TV still a viable media choice for tech companies like Intel, or should it migrate all these ads to the Internet? If it uses both types of media, how can it use a coordinated communications approach to optimize its advertising spend?

MARKETING PLAN EXERCISE

ACTIVITY 15: Building the Promotional Elements

Building on Activity 14 in the last chapter, continue to build your promotion plan as an integral part of your marketing plan.

1. What approaches to advertising will you take? Select and justify the media types to be used and discuss how you will execute each.

2. Make a decision on whether some forms of sales promotion will be part of your promotion plan to consumers and/or channel members. If so, select the sales promotion approaches you will employ and justify each.

3. Develop your PR plan.

4. Decide how you intend to manage promotion for the offering. Decide on outsourced elements versus elements that will be handled in-house. Establish a structure and process for promotion management.

ACTIVITY 16: Building the Interpersonal Relationship

A critical component of your company's marketing communications is the interpersonal connection to the customer. Developing an effective interpersonal communications strategy is essential and can include (1) sales force, (2) website, and (3) direct marketing. In this exercise, you will create an interpersonal communications strategy as part of the overall marketing communications plan. The following tasks are part of the strategy:

1. Review the overall marketing communications plan and determine the role of interpersonal marketing communications in communicating with target customers.

2. If personal selling is part of the marketing communications plan, create a sales strategy to include nature of sales force (company sales force or external sales team), sales structure, hiring/recruiting policies, and compensation program.

3. Determine the level of direct marketing for the company. Specifically, define the role of direct marketing in the overall marketing communications plan. Next, identify specific objectives for the direct marketing effort. Finally, create a direct marketing campaign and follow-up plan.

NOTES

1. Margaret Henderson Blair, "An Empirical Investigation of Advertising Wearin and Wearout," *Journal of Advertising Research* 40, no. 6 (November/December 2000), pp. 95–100.

2. John R. Hauser and Steven M. Shugan, "Defensive Marketing Strategies," *Marketing Science* 27, no. 1 (January/February 2008), pp. 88–112.

3. Janas Sinclair and Tracy Irani, "Advocacy Advertising for Biotechnology," *Journal of Advertising* 34, no. 3 (Fall 2005), pp. 59–63.

4. Jim Steadman, "Cotton Inc. Launches New Consumer Ad Campaign," *Cotton Grower*, June 2017, http://www.cottongrower.com/marketing/promotion/cotton-inc-launches-new-consumer-ad-campaign.

5. Glen L. Urban, Theresa Carter, Steven Gaskin, and Zofia Mucha, "Market Share Rewards to Pioneering Brands: An Empirical Analysis and Strategic Implications," *Management Science* 32, no. 6 (June 1986), pp. 645–59.

6. Peter J. Danaher, André Bonfrer, and Sanjay Dhar, "The Effect of Competitive Advertising Interference on Sales for Packaged Goods," *Journal of Marketing Research* 45, no. 2 (April 2008), pp. 211–25.

7. Chingching Chang, "The Relative Effectiveness of Comparative and Noncomparative Advertising: Evidence for Gender Differences in Information Processing Strategies," *Journal of Advertising* 36, no. 1 (Spring 2007), pp. 21–35.

8. Li Ling-yee, "The Effects of Firm Resources on Trade Show Performance: How Do Trade Show Marketing Processes Matter?," *Journal of Business & Industrial Marketing* 23, no. 1 (2008), pp. 35–47.

9. Salma Karray and Georges Zaccour, "Could Co-op Advertising Be a Manufacturer's Counterstrategy to Store Brands?," *Journal of Business Research* 59, no. 9 (September 2006), pp. 1008–15.

10. Sang Yong Kim and Richard Staelin, "Manufacturer Allowances and Retailer Pass-through Rates in a Competitive Environment," *Marketing Science* 18, no. 1 (1999), pp. 59–77.

11. Hyun Seung Jin, Jaebeom Suh, and D. Todd Donavan, "Salient Effects of Publicity in Advertised Brand Recall and Recognition: The List-Strength Paradigm," *Journal of Advertising* 37, no. 1 (Spring 2008), pp. 45–57.

12. Kenny Kline, "6 Companies That Prove the Power of Word-of-Mouth Marketing," *Huffington Post*, March 20, 2017, http://www.huffingtonpost.com/entry/6-companies-that-prove-the-power-of-word-of-mouth-marketing_us_58d09600e4b0e0d348b3474a.

13. "Win Sunday, Sell Monday," *LoganRacing.com*, www.loganracing.com/Marketing/NASCAR_General.html, accessed June 10, 2008.

14. Joseph Eric Massey and John P. Larsen, "Qualitative Research—Case Studies—Crisis Management in Real Time: How to Successfully Plan for and Respond to a Crisis," *Journal of Promotion Management* 12, no. 3/4 (2006), pp. 63–97.

15. D. Mayer and H. M Greenberg, "What Makes a Good Salesperson," *Harvard Business Review* 84, no. 7/8 (2006), pp. 164–79.

16. M. C. Johlke, "Sales Presentation Skills and Salesperson Job Performance," *Journal of Business and Industrial Marketing* 21, no. 5, pp. 311–29.

17. Chia-Chi Chang, "When Service Fails: The Role of the Salesperson and the Customer," *Psychology & Marketing* 23,

no. 3 (2006), pp. 203–18; and J. T. Johnson, H. C. Barksdale Jr., and J. S. Boles, "The Strategic Role of the Salesperson in Reducing Customer Defection in Business Relationships," *Journal of Personal Selling and Sales Management* 21, no. 2, pp. 123–35.

18. R. G. McFarland, G. N. Challagalla, and T. A. Shervani, "Influence Tactics for Effective Adaptive Selling," *Journal of Marketing* 70, no. 4 (2006), pp. 103–17.

19. D. T. Norris, "Sales Communication in a Mobile World: Using the Latest Technology and Retaining the Personal Touch," *Business Communication Quarterly* 70, no. 4 (2007), pp. 492–510.

20. P. Declos, R. Luzardo, and Y. H. Mirza, "Refocusing the Sales Force to Cross-Sell," *The McKinsey Quarterly* 1 (2008), pp. 13–15; and R. M. Peterson and G. H. Lucas, "What Buyers Want Most from Salespeople: A View from the Senior Level," *Business Horizons* 44, no. 5 (2001), pp. 39–45.

21. R. W. Palmatier, L. K. Scheer, and Jan-Benedict E. M. Steenkamp, "Customer Loyalty to Whom? Managing the Benefits and Risks of Salesperson-Owned Loyalty," *Journal of Marketing Research* 44, no. 2 (2007), pp. 185–201.

22. S. S. Liu and L. B. Comer, "Salespeople as Information Gatherers: Associated Success Factors," *Industrial Marketing Management* 36, no. 5 (2007), pp. 565–79; and L. Robinson Jr., G. W. Marshall, and M. B. Stamps, "An Empirical Investigation of Technology Acceptance in a Field Sales Force Setting," *Industrial Marketing Management* 34, no. 4 (2005), pp. 407–22.

23. J. N. Sheth and A. Sharma, "The Impact of the Product to Service Shift in Industrial Markets and the Evolution of the Sales Organization," *Industrial Marketing Management* 37, no. 3 (2008), pp. 260–77; and P. Kriendler and G. Rajguru, "What B2B Customers Really Expect," *Harvard Business Review* 84, no. 40 (2006), pp. 22–37.

24. "Sanofi, Regeneron RA Drug Kevzara Win FDA approval," *Genetic Engineering and Biotechnology News*, May 23, 2017, http://www.genengnews.com/gen-news-highlights/sanofi-regeneron-ra-drug-kevzara-wins-fda-approval/81254387.

25. P. Guenzi, C. Pardo, and L. Georges, "Relational Selling Strategy and Key Account Managers' Relational Behaviors: An Exploratory Study," *Industrial Marketing Management* 36, no. 1 (2007), pp. 121–38.

26. K. Alspach, "Prospecting for New Customers: Hubspot," *Boston Business Journal*, December 14, 2011, www.bizjournals.com/boston/blog/startups/2011/12/hubspot-amazon-personalization-marketing.html; and C. Sichtmann, "An Analysis of Antecedents and Consequences of Trust in Corporate Brand," *European Journal of Marketing* 41, no. 9/10 (2007), pp. 999–1115.

27. D. Ledingham, M. Kovac, and H. L. Smith, "The New Science of Sales Force Productivity," *Harvard Business Review* 84, no. 9 (2006), pp. 124–40.

28. L. Hershey, "The Role of Sales Presentations in Developing Customer Relationships," *Services Marketing Quarterly* 26, no. 3 (2005), pp. 41–59.

29. J. Rossman, "Value Selling at Cisco," *Marketing Management* 13, no. 2 (2004), pp. 16–23.

30. M. C. Johlke, "Sales Presentation Skills and Salesperson Job Performance," *Journal of Business and Industrial Marketing* 21, no. 5 (2006), pp. 311–28.

31. "About," *Cousins Maine Lobster*, n.d., https://www.cousinsmainelobster.com/the-cousins/.

32. Richard Feloni, "The 18 Best 'Shark Tank' Pitches of All Time," *Business Insider*, September 17, 2015, http://www.businessinsider.com/the-18-best-shark-tank-pitches-ever-2015-9/#beatbox-beverages-season-6-1.

33. "About."

34. K. S. Campbell, L. Davis, and L. Skinner, "Rapport Management during the Exploration Phase of the Salesperson Customer Relationship," *Journal of Personal Selling & Sales Management* 26, no. 4 (2006), pp. 359–72.

35. J. Braselton and B. Blair, "Cementing Relationships," *Marketing Management* 16, no. 3 (2007), pp. 14–29.

36. J. E. Swan, M. R. Bowers, and L. D. Richardson, "Customer Trust in the Salesperson: An Integrative Review of Meta Analysis of the Empirical Literature," *Journal of Business Research* 44, no. 2 (1999), pp. 93–108; and J. L. M. Tam and Y. J. Wong, "Interactive Selling: A Dynamic Framework for Services," *Journal of Services Marketing* 15, no. 4/5 (2001), pp. 379–95.

37. "About Accenture," *Accenture*, June 2017, https://www.accenture.com/us-en/company.

38. "Accenture Code of Business Ethics," *Accenture*, June 2017, https://www.accenture.com/us-en/company-ethics-code.

39. T. Nagle and J. Hogan, "Is Your Sales Force a Barrier to More Profitable Pricing . . . or Is It You?" *Business Strategy Series* 8, no. 5 (2007), pp. 365–79.

40. J. J. Belonax Jr., S. J. Newell, and R. E. Plank, "The Role of Purchase Importance on Buyer Perceptions of the Trust and Expertise Components of Supplier and Salesperson Credibility in Business to Business Relationships," *Journal of Personal Selling & Sales Management* 27, no. 3 (2007), pp. 247–60; T. V. Bonoma, "Major Sales: Who Really Does the Buying?" *Harvard Business Review* 84, no. 7/8 (2006), pp. 172–90; and E. C. Bursk, "Low Pressure Selling," *Harvard Business Review* 84, no. 7/8 (2006), pp. 150–69.

41. G. A. Wyner, "The Customer," *Marketing Management* 14, no. 1 (2005), pp. 8–10.

42. Thomas Frohlich, Samuel Stebbins, and Evan Comen, "24/7 Wall St.'s Customer Service Hall of Fame." *USA Today*, August 27, 2016, https://www.usatoday.com/story/money/business/2016/08/27/customer-service-hall-fame/87657894/.

43. *24/7 Wall Street*, n.d., http://247wallst.com/?s=hall+of+fame&x=0&y=0, June 2017.

44. A. A. Zoltners, P. Sinha, and S. E. Lorimer, "Match Your Sales Force Structure to Your Business Life Cycle," *Harvard Business Review* 84, no. 7/8 (2006), pp. 80–97.

45. E. Anderson, "The Salesperson as Outside Agent or Employee: A Transaction Cost Analysis," *Marketing Science* 27, no. 1 (2001), pp. 70–86.

46. E. Waaser, M. Dahneke, M. Pekkarinen, and M. Weissel, "How You Slice It: Smarter Segmentation of Your Sales Force," *Harvard Business Review* 82, no. 3 (2004), pp. 105–22.

47. K. Weinmann, "Generation Y Isn't Impressed with Your Pension Plan and Doesn't Have Time for Your Hiring Process," *Business Insider*, December 6, 2011, http://articles.businessinsider.com/2011-12-06/strategy/30480497_1_millennials-social-media-generation; and M. Goldsmith, "Getting to Know Gen Why," *BusinessWeek*, February 28, 2008, www.businessweek.com/print/managing/content/feb2008/ca20080226_921853.htm.

48. C. F. Miao and K. R. Evans, "The Impact of Salesperson Motivation on Role Perceptions and Job Performance: A Cognitive and Affective Perspective," *Journal of Personal Selling & Sales Management* 27, no. 1 (2007), pp. 89–103.

49. W. J. Verbeke, F. D. Belschak, A. B. Bakker, and B. Dietz, "When Intelligence Is (Dys)Functional Achieving Sales Performance," *Journal of Marketing* 72, no. 4 (2008), pp. 44–57.

50. "Lockheed Martin," *Glassdoor*, June 2017, https://www.glassdoor.com/Reviews/Lockheed-Martin-9-80-schedule-Reviews-EI_IE404.0,15_KH16,29.htm; "Employees," *Lockheed Martin*, June 2017, http://www.lockheedmartin.com/us/employees.html; and "Missiles and Fire Control," *Lockheed Martin*, 2012, http://www.lockheedmartin.com/content/dam/lockheed/data/mfc/photo/baldrige/mfc-baldrige-app.pdf.

51. F. Jaramillo and J. P. Mulki, "Sales Effort: The Intertwined Roles of the Leader, Customers, and the Salesperson," *Journal of Personal Selling & Sales Management* 28, no. 1 (2008), pp. 37–51; and C. F. Miao, K. R. Evans, and Z. Shaoming, "The Role of Salesperson Motivation in Sales Control Systems—Intrinsic and Extrinsic Motivation Revisited," *Journal of Business Research* 60, no. 5 (2007), pp. 417–32.

52. C. Muir, "Relationship Building and Sales Success: Are Climate and Leadership Key?" *Academy of Management Perspectives* 21, no. 1 (2007), pp. 71–89; and K. LeMeunier-FitzHugh and N. F. Piercy, "Does Collaboration between Sales and Marketing Affect Business Performance?" *Journal of Personal Selling & Sales Management* 27, no. 3 (2007), pp. 207–20.

53. D. H. Lee, "The Moderating Effect of Salesperson Reward Orientation on the Relative Effectiveness of Alternative Compensation Plans, "*Journal of Business Research* 43, no. 2 (1998), pp. 63–78.

54. G. R. Franke and J. E. Park, "Salesperson Adaptive Selling Behavior and Customer Orientation: A Meta-Analysis," *Journal of Marketing Research* 43, no. 4 (2006), pp. 34–50; and C. E. Pettijohn, L. S. Pettijohn, and A. J. Taylor, "Does Salesperson Perception of the Importance of Sales Skills Improve Sales Performance, Customer Orientation, Job Satisfaction, and Organizational Commitment, and Reduce Turnover?" *Journal of Personal Selling & Sales Management* 27, no. 1 (2007), p. 75.

55. R. Y. Darmon, "Controlling Sales Force Turnover Costs through Optimal Recruiting Training Policies," *European Journal of Operational Research* 154, no. 10 (2004), pp. 291–308; and P. T. Adidam, "Causes and Consequences of High Turnover by Sales Professionals," *Journal of American Academy of Business* 10, no. 1 (2006), pp. 137–42.

56. J. M. Ricks Jr., J. A. Williams, and W. A. Weeks, "Sales Trainer Roles, Competencies, Skills, and Behaviors: A Case Study," *Industrial Marketing Management* 37, no. 5 (2008), pp. 593–610; and M. P. Leach and A. H. Liu, "Investigating Interrelationships among Sales Training Methods," *Journal of Personal Selling & Sales Management* 23, no. 4 (2003), pp. 327–40.

57. Johnson & Johnson e-University website, December 26, 2011, www.jnjmedical.com.au/benefits/personal-development#euniversity; and A. McConnon, "The Name of the Game Is Work," *BusinessWeek,* August 13, 2007, www.businessweek.com/innovate/content/august2007/id20070813_467743.htm.

58. T. B. Jopez, C. D. Hopkins, and M. A. Raymond, "Reward Preferences of Salespeople: How Do Commissions Rate?" *Journal of Personal Selling & Sales Management* 26, no. 4 (2006), pp. 381–87; and S. N. Ramaswami and J. Singh, "Antecedents and Consequences of Merit Pay Fairness for Industrial Salespeople," *Journal of Marketing* 67, no. 4 (2003), pp. 46–60.

59. R. Y. Darmon and X. C. Martin, "A New Conceptual Framework of Sales Force Control Systems," *Journal of Personal Selling & Sales Management* 31, no. 3 (Summer 2011), pp. 297–310.

60. Personal interviews with staff members at multiple Central Florida Chick-fil-A locations, April 2017.

61. Marty Swant, "Intel's CMO Showed the World How a Tech Company Can Sing, Dance and Send Rockets into Space," *Adweek*, October 24, 2016, http://www.adweek.com/brand-marketing/intels-cmo-showed-world-how-tech-company-can-sing-dance-and-send-rockets-space-174197/.

62. Jeff Beer, "Why Intel Is Betting Big on Bringing Creative Advertising Inside," *Fast Company*, May 2, 2016, https://www.fastcompany.com/3059435/why-intel-is-betting-big-on-bringing-creative-advertising-inside; and Swant, "Intel's CMO Showed the World How a Tech Company Can Sing."

63. Swant, "Intel's CMO Showed the World How a Tech Company Can Sing."

64. Swant, "Intel's CMO Showed the World How a Tech Company Can Sing."

65. Rob Walker, "Intel Tells Stories That Go beyond Chips," *New York Times*, June 26, 2016, https://www.nytimes.com/2016/06/27/business/media/intel-tells-stories-that-go-beyond-chips.html?_r=0.

66. George Siefo, "With New Campaign, Intel Focuses on Its 'Amazing Human Experiences,'" *Advertising Age*, January 19, 2016, http://adage.com/article/cmo-strategy/intel-spent-a-year-campaign/302188/.

67. Walker, "Intel Tells Stories That Go Beyond Chips."

68. Swant, "Intel's CMO Showed the World How a Tech Company Can Sing."

69. Walker, "Intel Tells Stories That Go Beyond Chips"; and Adrianne Pasquarelli, "2017 In-House Agency of the Year: Intel's Agency Inside," *Advertising Age*, http://adage.com/article/special-report-agency-alist-2017/intel-2017-house-agency-year/307608/, accessed May 7, 2017.

70. Pasquarelli, "2017 In-House Agency of the Year."

71. Swant, "Intel's CMO Showed the World How a Tech Company Can Sing."

72. Pasquarelli, "2017 In-House Agency of the Year."

73. Walker, "Intel Tells Stories That Go Beyond Chips."

GLOSSARY

A

acceleration effect When small changes in consumer demand lead to considerable shifts in business product demand.

accumulating bulk A function performed by intermediaries that involves taking product from multiple sources and sorting it into different classifications for sales through the channel.

action plans The implementation element of a marketing plan that discusses issues such as timing, persons responsible, and resources necessary.

adaptive selling Being able to adjust the sales style from one sales situation to another in real time based on customer feedback.

additions to existing product lines An extension to an existing product that has already been developed and introduced to the market.

administered vertical marketing system (VMS) When the channel control of a vertical marketing system is determined by the size and power of one of its channel members.

advantages The particular product/service characteristic that helps meet the customer's needs.

advertising Paid form of relatively less personal marketing communications often through a mass medium to one or more target markets.

advertising execution The way an advertisement communicates the information and image.

advertising response function An effect in which, beyond a certain ad spending level, diminishing returns tend to set in.

advertising wearout When customers become bored with an existing advertising campaign.

agent intermediaries Intermediaries who do not take title to the product during the exchange process.

AIDA model A model designed to illustrate the hierarchy of effects in the context of customer response to marketing communications. It states that the effects build in this order: Attention (or Awareness), Interest, Desire, and Action.

allowances A remittance of monies to the consumer after the purchase of the product.

all-you-can-afford method Method of promotional budgeting that sets the promotional budget as whatever funds are left over after everything else that's considered a necessity is paid for.

ASEAN Founded in 1967, it is the most important Asian market zone and includes 10 countries running the entire length of the Pacific Rim (Brunei Darussalam, Indonesia, Malaysia, Philippines, Cambodia, Laos, Myanmar, Singapore, Thailand, and Vietnam).

aspirational purchases Products bought outside the individual's social standing.

assortment The number of different product items within a product category.

attitude Learned predisposition to respond to an object or class of objects in a consistently favorable or unfavorable way.

attitude-based choice A product choice that relies on an individual's beliefs and values to direct his or her assessment.

attribute-based choice A product choice based on the premise that product choices are made by comparing brands across a defined set of attributes.

auction pricing A pricing tactic in which individuals competitively bid against each other and the purchase goes to the highest bidder.

average-cost pricing A pricing decision made by identifying all costs associated with an offering to come up with what the average cost of a single unit might be.

awareness set A reduced set of possible alternatives a consumer considers after eliminating available options based on gathered information and personal preference.

B

backward integration When a firm merges operations back up the supply chain away from the consumer.

bait and switch When a seller advertises a low price but has no intent to actually make the lower-priced item available for sale.

banner ads Internet advertisements that are small boxes containing graphics and text, and have a hyperlink embedded in them.

basket of global advertising themes Global advertising strategy in which distinct ads built around several marketing messages are created that local marketers can select from to best fit their specific market situation.

behavioral data Information about when, what, and how often customers purchase products and services as well as other customer "touches."

behavioral segmentation Dividing consumer groups based on similarities in benefits sought or product usage patterns.

benefits The advantageous outcome from the advantage found in a product feature.

Boston Consulting Group (BCG) Growth-Share Matrix A popular approach for in-firm portfolio analysis that categorizes business units' level of contribution to the overall firm based on two factors: market growth rate and competitive position.

brand A name, term, sign, symbol, or design, or a combination of these elements, intended to identify the goods or services of one seller or groups of sellers and to differentiate them from those of competitors.

brand assets Other assets brands possess such as trademarks and patents that represent a significant competitive advantage.

brand association When customers develop a number of emotional, psychological, and performance associations with a brand. These associations become a primary purchase driver, particularly with brand loyal users.

brand awareness The most basic form of brand equity is simply being aware of the brand. Awareness is the foundation of all other brand relationships.

brand equity A set of assets and liabilities linked to a brand's name and symbol that adds to or subtracts from the value provided by a product or service to a firm or that firm's customers.

brand extensions A firm's use of knowledge of an existing brand when introducing a new product.

brand identity A summary of unique qualities attributed to a brand.

brand loyalty The strongest form of brand equity, reflecting a commitment to repeat purchases.

brand strategy The unique elements of a brand that define the products sold by a firm.

breadth of merchandise The number of different product categories offered by a retailer.

breaking bulk A shipping method used by manufacturers to better match quantities needed in terms of the space constraints and inventory turnover requirements of their buyers.

B2B (business-to-business) markets Markets in which a firm's customers are other firms, characterized by few but large customers, personal relationships, complex buying processes, less price-sensitive demand.

business case analysis An overall evaluation of a product that usually assesses the product's probability of success.

buying center A number of individuals with a stake in a purchase decision who manage the purchase decision process and ultimately make the decision.

buying decision Decisions made throughout the purchase decision process that vary widely and are based on factors such as nature of the purchase, number of people involved in the decision, understanding of the product being purchased, and time frame for the decision.

buzz Word-of-mouth communication generated about a brand in the marketplace.

C

capital equipment A firm's significant, long-term investments in critical equipment or technology necessary for its manufacturing and production activities.

capital goods Major purchases in support of significant business functions.

captive pricing (complementary pricing) A pricing tactic of gaining a commitment from a customer to a basic product or system that requires continual purchase of peripherals to operate.

cash discounts A percentage discount off invoice to elicit quicker payment by the customer.

catalog retailer A retailer that offers merchandise in the form of a printed or online catalog.

category extensions When a firm uses its brand to expand into new product categories.

causal research Descriptive research designed to identify associations between variables.

census A comprehensive record of each individual in the population.

change conflict A customer's reluctance to choose change by selecting a company's product.

channel captain (channel leader) The lead player in an administered vertical marketing system (VMS).

channel conflict Disagreements among channel members that can result in their relationship becoming strained or even falling apart.

channel of distribution A system of interdependent relationships among a set of organizations that facilitates the exchange process.

channel or medium The conduit by which an encoded message travels.

channel power The degree to which any member of a marketing channel can exercise influence over the other members of the channel.

closed-ended questions Question format that encourages respondents to provide specific responses.

closing the sale Obtaining commitment from the customer to make the purchase.

clutter The level of competing messages on a particular medium.

co-branding The joining of two or more well-known brands in a common product or taking two brands and marketing them in partnership.

coercive power An explicit or implicit threat that a channel captain will invoke negative consequences on a channel member if it does not comply with the leader's request or expectations.

cognitive learning Active learning that involves mental processes that acquire information to work through problems and manage life situations.

commission Payment based on short-term results; usually a salesperson's dollar or unit sales volume.

communication The process of exchanging information and conveying meaning from one party to another.

community A group of intended visitors to the website.

comparative advertising Advertising in which two or more brands are directly compared against each other on certain attributes.

comparative-parity method Method of promotional budgeting that focuses on comparing promotion expenditures across all key competitors in the market to determine a budget number.

competitive advertising Advertising intended to build sales of a specific brand through shifting emotional appeal, persuasion, and providing information.

competitive scenario analysis Analyzing competitors using various scenarios to predict competitor behavior.

competitive strategy An organization-wide strategy designed to increase a firm's performance within the marketplace in terms of its competitors.

competitor-based pricing A pricing strategy in which a firm decides to price at some market average price in context with prices of competitors.

competitor orientation A reactive marketing strategy that uses competitor analysis as its primary driver.

complete set The very large set of possible alternatives a consumer considers during the initial search for information.

concentrated target marketing (focus or niche strategy) The target marketing approach that involves targeting a large portion of a small market.

conditioning The creation of a psychological association between two stimuli.

conformance A product's ability to deliver on features and performance characteristics promised in marketing communications.

consideration (evoked) set A refined list that encompasses the strongest options an individual considers in a purchase decision once he or she has obtained additional information and carried out an evaluation.

consumer marketing The practice of marketing toward large groups of like-minded customers.

content The materials that are included on the website.

context The overall layout, design, and aesthetic appeal of a website.

contingency planning Also called scenario planning, a planning approach that requires the establishment of different planning options depending on the expected case, best case, or worst case.

contractual agreements Enduring, nonequity relationships with another company that allow a company to expand its participation in a foreign market.

contractual VMS The binding of otherwise independent entities in the vertical marketing system legally through contractual agreements.

controls Elements put in place to ensure progress is being made in the implementation of a marketing plan. Controls must be in place from the outset of the planning process to specify the timing, procedure, and persons responsible for systematically monitoring.

convenience goods Frequently purchased, relatively low-cost products that customers have little interest in seeking new information about or considering other product options.

cooperative advertising and promotion When a manufacturer provides special incentive money to channel members for certain promotional performance.

core competencies The activities a firm can do exceedingly well.

core product The physical, tangible elements that make up a product's essential benefit.

corporate identity Consumers' perceptions of a corporation that influences their attitudes and responses toward products or services offered by it.

corporate-level strategic plan An umbrella plan for the overall direction of the corporation developed above the strategic business unit (SBU) level.

corporate vertical marketing system (VMS) The investment of a channel member in backward or forward vertical integration by buying controlling interests in other intermediaries.

cost-based price An international pricing strategy in which the firm considers cost plus markup to arrive at a final price.

cost leadership A marketing strategy in which a firm utilizes its core cost advantages to gain an advantage over competitors due to flexibility in pricing strategies as well as its ability to translate cost savings to the bottom line.

cost-plus pricing Building a price by adding standardized markup on top of the costs associated with the offering.

cost reduction A specific method for introducing lower-cost products that frequently focuses on value-oriented product price points in the product mix.

country-of-origin effect The influence of the country of manufacture, assembly, or design on a customer's positive or negative perception of a product.

creating assortments The process of accumulating products from several sources to then make those products available down the channel as a convenient assortment for consumers.

credence attributes Aspects of an offering for which customers cannot make a reasonable evaluation, even after use.

crisis management A planned, coordinated approach for disseminating information during times of emergency and for handling the effects of unfavorable publicity.

cultural values Principles shared by a society that assert positive ideals.

culture A system of values, beliefs, and morals shared by a particular group of people that permeates over time.

customer advocacy A willingness and ability on the part of a customer to participate in communicating the brand message to others within his or her sphere of influence.

customer benefit Some type of utility that a company and its products (and services) provide its customers.

customer-centric Placing the customer at the core of the enterprise and focusing on investments in customers over the long term.

customer communities Websites where customers come and share stories about their vendor experiences.

customer delight The exceeding of customer expectations.

customer expectations management The process of making sure the firm does not set customer expectations so high that they cannot be effectively met on a consistent basis.

customer loyalty A customer's commitment to a company and its products and brands for the long run.

customer marketing The practice of marketing that focuses on developing relationships with individuals.

customer mind-set An individual's belief that understanding and satisfying customers, whether internal or external to the organization, is central to the proper execution of his or her job.

customer orientation Placing the customer at the core of all aspects of the enterprise.

customer relationship management (CRM) A comprehensive business model for increasing revenues and profits by focusing on customers.

customer retention Low propensity among a firm's customer base to consider switching to other providers.

customer satisfaction The level of liking an individual harbors for an offering.

customer touchpoints Where the selling firm touches the customer in some way, thus allowing for information about him or her to be collected.

customization The degree to which the website creates a unique individual experience for each visitor.

customized (one-to-one) marketing A marketing strategy that involves directing energy and resources into establishing a learning relationship with each customer to increase the firm's customer knowledge.

D

data collection Distributing a survey to its respondents, recording the respondents' responses, and making the data available for analysis.

data mining A sophisticated analytical approach to using the massive amounts of data accumulated through a firm's CRM system to develop segments and microsegments of customers for purposes of either market research or development of market segmentation strategies.

data warehouse A compilation of customer data generated through touchpoints that can be transformed into useful information for marketing management decision making and marketing planning.

database marketing Direct marketing involving the utilization of the data generated through CRM practices to create lists of customer prospects who are then contacted individually by various means of marketing communication.

deceptive pricing Knowingly stating prices in a manner that gives a false impression to customers.

decider An individual within the buying center who ultimately makes the purchase decision.

decision-making authority An issue that arises when companies grow internationally and lines of authority become longer and more complicated, resulting in difficulty in defining decision-making protocols.

decoding process When a receiver interprets the meaning of the message's symbols as encoded by the sender.

degree of affiliation The amount of interpersonal contact an individual has with the reference group.

degree of centralization The degree to which decisions are made at the firm's home office.

delightful surprises Built-in extras in service delivery not expected by the customer.

Delphi technique A subjective method of forecasting that is done iteratively, employing repeated measurement and controlled anonymous feedback instead of direct confrontation and debate among those preparing the forecast.

demographic segmentation Dividing consumer groups based on a variety of readily measurable descriptive factors about the group.

demographics The characteristics of human populations and population segments, especially when used to identify consumer markets.

depth of merchandise The number of different product items within a product category.

derived demand Demand that originates from the demand for consumer products in business-to-business (B-to-B) marketing.

descriptive research Research designed to explain or illustrate some phenomenon.

desirability The extent and direction of the emotional connection an individual wishes to have with a particular group.

developed economies Specific economies that have fueled world economic growth for much of the 20th century, including Western Europe, the United States, and Japan.

differentiation Communicating and delivering value in different ways to different customer groups.

dimensions of service quality The five aspects of a service that make up its total quality, including tangibles, reliability, responsiveness, assurance, and empathy.

direct and interactive marketing Personal communication with a customer by means other than a salesperson.

direct channel A channel that has no intermediaries and operates strictly from producer to end-user consumer or business user.

direct competitors Competing firms that produce products considered very close substitutes for those of other firms' current products and services.

direct foreign investment A strategic alliance with long-term implications in which a company moves manufacturing or operations into a foreign market.

direct marketing An interactive marketing system that uses one or more advertising media to effect a measurable response and/or transaction at any location.

direct selling A form of non-store retailing that involves independent businesspeople contacting consumers directly to demonstrate and sell products or services in convenient locations.

discounts Direct, immediate reductions in price provided to purchasers.

disintermediation The shortening or collapsing of marketing channels due to the elimination of one or more intermediaries.

display ads Ads put out by companies for advertising on the Internet that include banner ads and interstitials.

distinctive competencies A firm's core competencies that are superior to those of their competitors.

distribution intensity The number of intermediaries involved in distributing the product.

distributor Represents the company and often many others in foreign markets.

diversification strategies Strategies designed to seize on opportunities to serve new markets with new products.

dumping A global pricing issue that refers to the practice of charging less than their actual costs or less than the product's price in the firm's home markets.

durability The length of product usage.

durable product Products with a comparatively long product life that are often expensive.

E

early adopter A consumer who is a product opinion leader who seeks out new products consistent with his or her personal self-image.

early majority Consumers who are product watchers who want to be convinced of the product's claims and value proposition before making a commitment to it.

e-commerce The degree to which the website allows direct purchase of products and services.

electronic commerce (e-commerce) Any action that uses electronic media to communicate with customers; facilitate the inventory, exchange, and distribution of goods and services; or facilitate payment.

electronic data interchange (EDI) Sophisticated programs that link a customer with its suppliers to manage inventories and automatically replenish supplies.

electronic retailing (e-retailing or e-tailing) The communication and sale of products or services to consumers over the Internet.

e-mail Mail communications delivered by electronic device.

emerging markets Growing economies that have developed over the last 25 years that are projected to contribute toward 75 percent of world economic growth over the next 20 years.

emotional appeal Promotional appeal that plays on human nature using a variety of human emotions and aspirations in developing promotional messages.

emotional choice A product choice based more on emotional attitudes about a product rather than rational thought.

encoding process The process in communication in which the sender translates an idea to be communicated into a symbolic message in preparation for transmittal to a receiver.

end-user purchase A category of products purchased by manufacturers that represents the equipment, supplies, and services needed to keep their business operational.

enhanced product Additional features, designs, or innovations that extend beyond the core product to exceed customer expectations.

enterprise resource planning (ERP) system A software application designed to integrate information related to logistics processes throughout the organization.

e-procurement The process of online business purchasing.

essential benefit The fundamental need met by a product.

European Union A successful regional marketing zone founded more than 50 years ago by six European countries (Belgium, France, Italy, Luxembourg, The Netherlands, and West Germany) with the Treaty of Rome and that now includes 28 countries.

even pricing A pricing tactic in which the price is expressed in whole-dollar increments.

event sponsorship Having your brand and company associated with events in the sports, music, arts, and other entertainment communities.

everyday low pricing (EDLP) A pricing tactic that entails relatively low, constant prices and minimal spending on promotional efforts.

exchange The giving up of something of value for something desired.

exclusive dealing When a supplier creates a restrictive agreement that prohibits intermediaries that handle its product from selling competing firms' products.

exclusive distribution Distribution strategy built on prestige, scarcity, and premium pricing in which a producer only distributes its products to one or very few vendors.

exclusive territory The protection of an intermediary from having to compete with others selling a producer's goods.

experience attributes Aspects of an offering that can be evaluated only during or after consumption.

expert power A channel member's utilization of its unique competencies and knowledge to influence others in the channel.

exploratory research Research geared toward discovery that can either answer the research question or identify other research variables for further study. It is generally the first step in the marketing research process.

exporter International market specialist that helps companies by acting as the export marketing department.

exporting The most common method for entering foreign markets, it offers firms the ability to penetrate foreign markets with minimal investment and very little risk.

extensive information search When a consumer makes a purchase decision based on a thorough process of investigation and research.

external information sources Additional information an individual seeks from outside sources when internal information is not sufficient to make a purchase decision.

extrinsic rewards Rewards controlled and given by people other than the salesperson such as a manager and customers.

F

FAB A selling approach designed to make the company's products more relevant for customers by explaining the product's features, advantages, and benefits.

facilitating functions Activities that help fulfill completed transactions and also maintain the viability of the channel relationships.

fad Products that come and go quickly, often reaching only a limited number of individuals but creating a lot of buzz in the marketplace.

fair trade laws Laws designed to allow manufacturers to establish artificially high prices by limiting the ability of wholesalers and retailers to offer reduced or discounted prices.

family A group of two or more people living together and related by birth, marriage, or adoption.

family branding The creation of brands that have synergy between them in terms of the overall company brand.

family life cycle The changes in life stage that transform an individual's buying habits.

feature Any product attribute or performance characteristic.

feedback loop Two-way communication in which a receiver can communicate reactions back to the sender.

firing a customer The shifting of investment of resources from a less attractive customer to more profitable ones.

first-mover advantage When a firm introduces a new market offering, thus defining the scope of the competitive marketplace.

fluctuating demand When the level of consumer demand is not constant, having serious implications related to the perishability of services.

FOB (free on board) Determination of title transfer and freight payment based on shipping location.

focus group A qualitative research method that consists of a meeting (either in person or increasingly online) of 6 to 10 people that is moderated by a professional who carefully moves the conversation through a defined agenda in an unstructured, open format.

follow-up A company's actions after the customer has decided to purchase the product.

food retailer Any retailer that includes food as a part of its breadth of merchandise.

form The physical elements of a product, such as size, shape, and color.

formalization The formal establishment of a firm's structure, processes and tools, and managerial knowledge and commitment to support its culture.

forward integration When a firm moves its operations more toward the end user.

franchise organization A contractual relationship between a franchisor, who is the grantor of the franchise, and the franchisee, who is the independent entity entering into an agreement to perform at the standards required by the franchisor.

franchising A contractual agreement in which a firm provides a contracted company in a foreign market with a bundle of products, systems, services, and management expertise in return for local market knowledge, financial consideration, and local management experience.

frequency The average number of times a person in the target market is exposed to the message.

functional-level plans Plans for each business function that makes up one of the firm's strategic business units (SBUs). These include core business functions within each SBU such as operations, marketing, and finance, as well as other pertinent operational areas.

G

gap model A visual tool used in the measurement of service quality that identifies and measures the differences between consumer and marketer perceptions of a provided service.

gatekeeper An individual who controls access to information and relevant individuals in the buying center.

GE business screen A popular approach for in-firm portfolio analysis that categorizes business units' level of contribution to the overall firm based on two factors: business position and market attractiveness.

gender roles Behaviors regarded as proper for men and women in a particular society.

general warranties Broad promises about product performance and customer satisfaction.

generic strategy An overall directional strategy at the business level.

geographic regions An international organizational structure that divides international markets by geography, building autonomous regional organizations that perform business functions in the geographic areas.

geographic segmentation Dividing consumer groups based on physical location.

geolocation marketing The use of geographic data to drive marketing messaging and other marketing decisions.

global marketing themes Global advertising strategy in which a basic template is used for global ads that allows for slight modifications depending on local markets.

global marketing with local content Global advertising strategy in which a firm keeps the same global marketing theme as the home market but adapts it with local content.

global product lines Products that are sold across country borders.

goals General statements of what the firm wishes to accomplish in support of the mission and vision.

go-to-market mistake When a company fails to stop a bad product idea from moving into product development.

government Local, state, and federal entities that have unique and frequently challenging purchasing practices for manufacturing firms.

gray market A global pricing issue that references the unauthorized diversion of branded products into global markets.

growth phase A stage of the product life cycle marked by rapid expansion as competitors come into the market and customers learn, understand, and begin to adopt the product.

H

harvesting A product strategy that involves a measured but consistent investment reduction in a product.

high-involvement learning The learning process in which an individual is stimulated to acquire new information.

high mass consumption An economy characterized by rising income levels, creating a large population with discretionary income, which results in consumers that demand higher levels of service and more durable goods.

high/low pricing A pricing strategy in which the retailer offers frequent discounts, primarily through sales promotions, to stated regular prices.

household life cycle (HLC) A structured set of chronological activities a particular household follows over time.

I

impulse goods Goods whose sales rely on the consumer seeing the product, feeling an immediate want, and being able to purchase now.

inbound logistics The process of sourcing materials and knowledge inputs from external suppliers to the point at which production begins.

inbound telemarketing When a prospective customer contacts a company for more information.

incentives Generally commissions tied to sales volume or profitability, or bonuses for meeting or exceeding specific performance targets.

in-depth interview A qualitative research method that consists of an unstructured (or loosely structured) interview with an individual who has been chosen based on some characteristic of interest, often a demographic attribute.

indirect channel A channel that contains one or more intermediary levels.

indirect competitors Competing firms that offer products that may be substituted based on the customer's need and choice options.

inelastic demand When changes in demand are not significantly affected by changes in price.

influencer An individual, either inside or outside the organization, with relevant expertise in a particular area who provides information used by the buying center in making a final buying decision.

information search The process consumers use to gather information to make a purchase decision.

initiator The individual who starts the buying decision process.

innovation diffusion process How long it takes a product to move from first purchase to last purchase (the last set of users to adopt the product).

innovator A consumer who is a product enthusiast who is among the first to try and master a new product.

inseparability The characteristic of a service in which it is produced and consumed at the same time and cannot be separated from its provider.

institutional advertising Advertising that promotes industry, company, family of brands, or some other issues broader than a specific product.

institutions Nongovernmental organizations driven by the delivery of service to the target constituency, rather than by profits.

instrumental performance The actual performance features of the product in terms of what it was promised to do.

intangibility The characteristic of a service in which it cannot be experienced through the physical senses of the consumer.

integrated marketing communications (IMC) A strategic approach to communicating the brand and company message to targeted customers in ways that are clear, concise, and consistent and yet are customizable as needed to maximize the impact on a particular audience.

intensive distribution A distribution strategy designed to saturate every possible intermediary, especially retailers.

interactive marketing An Internet-driven relationship between companies, their brands, and customers. Interactive marketing enables customers to control information flow and encourages customer-company interaction as well as a higher level of customer service.

intermediaries Organizations that play a role in the exchange process between producers and consumers.

internal information sources All information stored in memory and accessed by the individual regarding a purchase decision.

internal marketing The treating of employees as customers and developing systems and benefits that satisfy their needs to promote internal service quality.

international joint ventures A strategic alliance formed by legal entities, consisting of a partnership of two or more participating companies that share management duties and a defined management structure in which every partner holds an equity position.

interstitials Graphic, visually interesting Internet advertisements that move across the web page.

intrinsic rewards Those rewards salespeople primarily attain for themselves; they include feelings of accomplishment, personal growth, and self-worth.

involvement A significant outcome of an individual's motivation that mediates the product choice decision. It is activated by three elements: background and psychological profile, aspirational focus, and the environment at the time of purchase decision.

J

joint venture A partnership of two or more participating companies that differs from other strategic alliances in that (1) management duties are shared and a management structure is defined; (2) other corporations or legal entities, not individuals, formed the venture; and (3) every partner holds an equity position.

jury of executive opinion Subjective method of forecasting that relies on a formal or informal poll of key executives within the firm to gain their assessment of sales potential.

just-in-time (JIT) inventory control system An inventory management system designed to balance levels of overstock and stock-out in an effort to reduce warehousing costs.

just noticeable difference (JND) The amount of price increase that can be taken without impacting customer demand.

K

key account salespeople Salespeople responsible for the firm's largest customers.

L

laggard A consumer who is a product avoider and evades adoption until there is no other product choice.

language An established system of ideas and phonetics shared by members of a particular culture that serves as their primary communication tool.

late majority Consumers who are product followers and are price sensitive, are risk averse, and generally prefer products with fewer features.

learning Any change in the content or organization of long-term memory or behavior.

legitimate power A channel member's ability to influence other members based on contracts or other formal agreements.

licensing When a firm offers other manufacturers the right to use its brand in exchange for a set fee or percentage of sales.

lifestyle An individual's perspective on life that manifests itself in activities, interests, and opinions.

lifetime value of a customer The measurement of important business success factors related to long-term relationships with customers.

limited information search When a consumer makes a purchase decision based on incomplete information and/or lack of personal knowledge.

line extensions Introducing a new product to an existing product line.

line of visibility The separation between activities customers see and those they do not see in the process of service delivery.

local market ad generation Global marketing strategy in which a firm allows local marketers to create local ads that do not necessarily coordinate with its global marketing messages.

local market conditions price An international pricing strategy in which the firm assigns a price based on local market conditions with minimal consideration for the actual cost of putting the product into the market.

long-term memory Enduring memory storage that can remain with an individual for years or even a lifetime.

loss leader products Products sacrificed at prices below costs in an effort to attract shoppers to the retail location.

low-involvement learning The learning process in which an individual is not prompted to value new information, characterized by little or no interest in learning about a new product offering.

low-price guarantee policy A pricing strategy used by retailers that guarantees consumers the lowest price for any given product by matching the sales price of competitors.

loyalty programs Programs that reinforce the customer's benefits of purchasing at the retailer.

M

macroeconomics The study of economic activity in terms of broad measures of output and input as well as the interaction among various sectors of an entire economy.

management research deliverable The definition of what management wants to do with marketing research.

market creation Approaches that drive the market toward fulfilling a whole new set of needs that customers did not realize was possible or feasible before.

market deterioration The third and final phase of the maturity stage of the product life cycle in which the market starts to lose customers and competitors begin to feel the pressure of overcapacity in the market.

market development strategies Strategies designed to allow for expansion of the firm's product line into heretofore untapped markets, often internationally.

market-driven strategic planning The process at the corporate or strategic business unit (SBU) level of a firm that acts to marshal the various resource and functional areas toward a central purpose around the customer.

market expansion When a firm that operates in closely related markets expands into new markets to compete more directly.

market information system (MIS) A continuing process of identifying, collecting, analyzing, accumulating, and dispensing critical information to marketing decision makers.

market makers Websites that bring buyers and sellers together.

market mavens Individuals who have information about many kinds of products, places to shop, and other facets of markets, and initiate discussions with consumers and respond to requests from consumers for market information.

market orientation The implementation of the marketing concept, based on an understanding of customers and competitors.

market penetration strategies Strategies designed to involve investing against existing customers to gain additional usage of existing products.

market research The methodical identification, collection, analysis, and distribution of data related to discovering and then solving marketing problems or opportunities and enhancing good decision making.

market segmentation Dividing a market into meaningful smaller markets or submarkets based on common characteristics.

market share The percentage of total category sales accounted for by a firm.

market space A powerful new communication channel that encourages customer-company interaction and a higher level of customer service.

market stability The second phase of the maturity stage of the product life cycle in which a product experiences no market growth as the market reaches saturation.

market test Objective method of forecasting that involves placing a product in several representative geographic areas to see how well it performs and then projecting that experience to the market as a whole.

marketing The activity, set of institutions, and processes for creating, communicating, delivering, and exchanging offerings that have value for customers, clients, partners, and society at large.

Marketing (big M) The dimension of marketing that focuses on external forces that affect the organization and serves as the driver of business strategy.

marketing (little m) The dimension of marketing that focuses on the functional or operational level of the organization.

marketing audit A systematic review of the current state of marketing within an organization.

marketing concept Business philosophy that emphasizes an organization-wide customer orientation with the objective of achieving long-run profits.

marketing control The process of measuring marketing results and adjusting the firm's marketing plan as needed.

marketing dashboard A comprehensive system of metrics and information uniquely relevant to the role of the marketing manager in a particular organization. Dashboards provide managers with up-to-the-minute information necessary to run their operation.

marketing intelligence The collecting, analyzing, and storing of data from the macro environment on a continuous basis.

marketing management The leading and managing of the facets of marketing to improve individual, unit, and organizational performance.

marketing metrics Tools and processes designed to identify, track, evaluate, and provide key benchmarks for improvement of marketing activities.

marketing mix (4Ps of marketing) Product, price, place, and promotion—the fundamental elements that comprise the marketer's tool kit that can be developed in unique combinations to set the product or brand apart from the competition.

marketing plan The resulting document that records the marketing planning process in a useful framework.

marketing planning The ongoing process of developing and implementing market-driven strategies for an organization.

marketing's stakeholders Any person or entity inside or outside a firm with whom marketing interacts, impacts, and is impacted by.

markup on cost The addition to the price of an offering after costs have been considered.

markup on sales price Using the sales price as a basis for calculating the markup percentage.

mass customization Combining flexible manufacturing with flexible marketing to greatly enhance customer choice.

mass marketing The classic style of consumer marketing in which a firm views all consumers as equal reactors to a firm's marketing strategies.

materials Natural or agricultural products that become part of the final product.

materials, repairs, operational (MRO) Products used in everyday business operations that are not typically considered to be a significant expense for the firm.

materials requirement planning (MRP) The overall management of the inbound materials from suppliers to facilitate minimal production delays.

matrix structure An international organizational structure that encourages regional autonomy among organizations while building product competence in key areas around the world.

maturity An economy that, through private and public investments, has reached the point where it seeks to maintain its growth rates.

maturity stage A stage of the product life cycle in which a product is in the transition from high growth to relative sales decline. There are three phases in the maturity stage: relative market expansion, market stability, and market deterioration.

m-commerce Sales generated by a mobile device.

mechanical observation A variation of observational data that uses a device to chronicle activity.

memory Where people store all past learning events.

merchandise category An assortment of items considered substitutes for each other.

merchant intermediaries Intermediaries who take title to the product during the exchange process.

MERCOSUR Inaugurated in 1995, it is the most powerful market zone in South America and includes the major economies of South America: Argentina, Bolivia, Brazil, Chile, Paraguay, and Uruguay.

message transmission Placing a communication into some channel or medium so that it can make its way to the intended receiver.

microeconomics The study of individual economic activity.

microsite A more focused site from a company's primary site that addresses specific topics such as new product introductions or targeted products within a large product.

minimal information search When a consumer makes a purchase decision based on very little information or investigation.

minimum markup laws Laws that require retailers to apply a certain percentage of markup to their products for sale.

mission statement The verbal articulation of an organization's purpose, or reason for existence.

missionary salespeople Salespeople who do not take orders from customers directly but persuade customers to buy their firm's product from distributors or other suppliers.

modifications to existing products Creating newer, better, faster versions of existing products that target, for the most part, existing customers.

modified rebuy A buying decision in which a customer is familiar with the product and supplier in a purchase decision but is looking for additional information because of one or more of three circumstances: the supplier has performed poorly, new products have come into the market, or the customer believes it is time for a change.

moment of truth The face-to-face time between customer and service provider.

monopolistic competition When there are many companies offering unique products in different market segments.

monopoly When a market is controlled by a single company offering one set of products.

moral appeal Promotional appeal that strikes a chord with a target customer's sense of right and wrong.

motivation The stimulating power that induces and then directs an individual's behavior.

MRO supplies (maintenance, repair, operating) The everyday items that a company needs to keep running.

multiattribute model A model that measures an individual's attitudes toward an object by evaluating it on several important attributes.

N

NAFTA (North American Free Trade Agreement) Created to eliminate tariffs between Canada, Mexico, and the United States, and which stands as the single largest economic alliance today.

national brands Products created, manufactured, and marketed by a company and sold to retailers around the country and the world.

network organization (virtual organization) Organization that eliminates many in-house business functions and activities in favor of focusing only on those aspects for which it is best equipped to add value.

new purchase A buying decision in which the purchase of a product or service by a customer is for the first time.

new-to-the-world product A product that has not been available before or bears little resemblance to an existing product.

nimble Being in a position to be maximally flexible, adaptable, and speedy in response to the many key change drivers affecting business.

noise The distortion or interference that can occur at any stage of a communication process.

nondurable product Products that are usually consumed in a few uses and, in general, are of low cost to the consumer.

nonfinancial incentives Sales force motivators beyond financial compensation.

nonprobability sampling The selection of individuals for statistical research in which the probability of everyone in the population being included in the sample is not identified.

non-store retailer A retailer that uses alternative methods to reach the customer that do not require a physical location.

nonverbal communication The means of communicating through facial expressions, eye behavior, gestures, posture, and any other body language.

North American Industrial Classification System (NAICS) A system developed by the United States, Canada, and Mexico that classifies companies on the basis of their primary output to define and segment business markets.

O

objective forecasting methods Forecasting methods that rely primarily on sophisticated quantitative (empirical) analytical approaches.

objective-and-task method Method of promotional budgeting that takes an investment approach in that goals are set for the upcoming year and then promotional dollars are budgeted to support the achievement of those goals.

objectives Specific, measurable, and potentially attainable milestones necessary for a firm to achieve its goals.

observational data The documentation of behavioral patterns among the population of interest.

odd pricing A pricing tactic in which the price is not expressed in whole dollar increments.

offering A product or service that delivers value to satisfy a need or want.

oligopoly When a market is controlled by more than one company in an industry that is either standardized or differentiated.

one-price strategy A pricing tactic in which the price marked on a good is what it typically sells for.

one-to-one marketing Directing energy and resources into establishing a learning relationship with each customer and connecting that knowledge with the firm's production and service capabilities to fulfill that customer's needs in as customary a manner as possible.

one world price An international pricing strategy in which the firm assigns one price for its products in every global market.

online database Data stored on a server that is accessed remotely over the Internet or some other telecommunications network.

open-ended questions Question format that encourages respondents to be expressive and offers them the opportunity to provide more detailed, qualitative responses.

opinion leaders Individuals with expertise in certain products or technologies who classify, explain, and then bestow information to a broader audience.

organizational factors Organization-wide beliefs and attitudes that factor into a purchase decision.

organizational learning The analysis and refinement phase of the CRM process that is based on customer response to the firm's implementation strategies and programs.

original equipment manufacturer (OEM) Manufacturing firms that sell products that are used as integral manufacturing components by their customer companies.

out supplier A company that is not on a firm's list of approved suppliers.

outbound logistics The process of a product's movement from production by the manufacturer to purchase by the end-user consumer.

outbound telemarketing Calling potential customers at their home or office, either to make a sales call via telephone or to set up an appointment for a field salesperson.

outsourcing (third-party logistics, 3PL) Handing over one or more of its core internal functions, such as most or all of its supply chain activities, to other (third-party) companies that are experts in those areas allows the firm to better focus on its core business.

outsourcing the sales force Using independent sales agents to sell a company's products.

P

partner relationship management (PRM) strategies A strategic alliance that includes connectivity of inventory, billing systems, and market research among marketing channel members.

parts Equipment that is either fully assembled or in smaller pieces that will be assembled in larger components and then used in the production process.

penetration pricing A pricing strategy in which a firm's objective is to gain as much market share as possible.

perceived quality The conveyed perception of quality of a brand that is either positive or negative.

percent-of-sales method Method of promotional budgeting that allocates funding for promotional activities to certain products as a function of their forecasted sales revenues.

perception A system to select, organize, and interpret information to create a useful, informative picture of the world.

perceptual maps A visual tool used in positioning that allows for comparing attributes to gauge consumer perceptions of each competitor's delivery against those attributes.

perishability The characteristic of a product or service in which it cannot be stored or saved for future use.

personal factors The needs, desires, and objectives of those involved in a purchase decision.

personal selling A two-way communication process between salesperson and buyer with the goal of securing, building, and maintaining long-term relationships with profitable customers.

personality An individual's set of unique personal qualities that produce distinctive responses across similar situations.

physical distribution (logistics) The integrated process of moving input materials to the producer, in-process inventory through the firm, and finished goods out of the firm through the channel of distribution.

pioneering advertising Advertising intended to stimulate primary demand, typically during the introductory or early growth stages of an offering.

portfolio analysis A tool used in strategic planning for multibusiness corporations that views SBUs, and sometimes even product lines, as a series of investments from which it expects maximization of returns.

positioning The communication of sources of value to customers so they can easily make the connection between their needs and wants and what the product has to offer.

post-purchase dissonance A feeling of doubt or anxiety following a recent purchase, generally associated with high-involvement, large purchases.

preferred state An individual's desires that reflect how he or she would like to feel or live in the present time.

prestige pricing A pricing tactic that lends prestige to a product or brand by virtue of a price relatively higher than the competition.

price bundling A pricing tactic in which customers are given the opportunity to purchase a package deal at a reduced price compared to what the individual components of the package would cost separately.

price elasticity of demand The measure of customers' price sensitivity, estimated by dividing relative changes in quantity sold by relative changes in price.

price-fixing When companies collude to set prices at a mutually beneficial high level.

price points Prices established to convey the differences in benefits offered as the customer moves up and down the product line.

price skimming A pricing strategy in which a firm enters a market at a relatively high price point, usually in an effort to create a strong price-quality relationship for the product.

price war When a company purposefully makes pricing decisions to undercut one or more competitors and gain sales and net market share.

pricing objectives The desired or expected results associated with a pricing strategy that is consistent with other marketing-related objectives.

primary data Data collected specifically for a particular research question.

primary group A reference group an individual has frequent contact with.

primary target markets Market segments that clearly have the best chance of meeting ROI goals and the other attractiveness factors.

private-label brands Products managed and marketed by retailers, also known as store or house brands.

probability sampling The specific protocol used to identify and select individuals from the population in which each population element has a known nonzero chance of being selected.

product advertising Advertising designed to increase purchase of a specific offering.

product choice The end result of evaluating product alternatives in the purchase decision process.

product deletion Discontinuing the production of a product.

product demand Demand within business markets affected by three critical dimensions: derived demand, fluctuating demand, and inelastic demand.

product development strategies Strategies designed to recognize the opportunity to invest in new products that will increase usage from the current customer base.

product expansion When a firm leverages its existing expertise (technical product experience or supply chain) to create new products for existing or new markets.

product life cycle (PLC) The life of a product that includes four stages: introduction, growth, maturity, and decline.

product line A group of products linked through usage, customer profile, price points, and distribution channels or needs satisfaction.

product line pricing (price lining) A pricing tactic in which a firm affords the marketing manager an opportunity to develop a rational pricing approach across a complete line of related items.

product mix The combination of all the products offered by a firm.

production orientation The maximization of production capacity through improvements in products and production activities without much regard for what is going on in the marketplace.

professional services Services that require specialized training and certification that are typically self-regulated by industry or trade groups.

profitability analysis A thorough analysis that accounts for all costs associated with bringing a product to market to determine short- and long-term product profitability.

promotion Various forms of communication to inform, persuade, or remind.

promotion mix The elements of promotion, including advertising, sales promotion, public relations (PR), personal selling, direct marketing, and interactive marketing.

promotion mix strategies Decisions about which combination of elements in the promotion mix is likely to best communicate the offering to the marketplace and achieve an acceptable ROI for the marketer.

promotional allowances Sales promotions initiated by the manufacturer and carried out by the retailer, who is then compensated by the manufacturer.

promotional appeal The connection an offering establishes with customers; includes rational appeals, emotional appeals, and moral appeals.

promotional campaign Promotional expenditures to a particular creative execution aimed at a particular product or product line during a specified time period.

psychographic segmentation Dividing consumer groups based on variables such as personality and AIOs: activities, interests, and opinions.

psychological pricing Creating a perception about price merely from the image the numbers provide the customer.

public relations (PR) Systematic approach to influencing attitudes, opinions, and behaviors of customers and others.

publicity An unpaid and relatively less personal form of marketing communications, usually through news stories and mentions at public events.

puffery Relatively minor embellishments of product claims to bolster the persuasive message.

pull strategy Promotional and distribution strategy in which the focus is on stimulating demand for an offering directly from the end user.

pure competition When there are many companies offering essentially the same product in the market.

push strategy Promotional and distribution strategy in which the focus is on stimulating demand within the channel of distribution.

Q

qualitative research Less structured research not meant to be used for statistical analysis that can employ methods such as surveys and interviews to collect data.

quantitative research Research used to develop a measured understanding using statistical analysis to assess and quantify the results.

quantity discounts Discounts taken off an invoice price based on different levels of product purchased.

R

rational appeal Promotional appeal that centers on the benefits an offering can provide to a customer.

reach The percentage of individuals in a defined target market that are exposed to an ad during a specific time period.

real state An individual's perceived reality of present time.

receiver The individual who is the target of the communication.

reducing transactions The process of lowering the number of purchasing transactions carried out by a firm by utilizing the services of intermediaries.

reference group A group of individuals whose beliefs, attitudes, and behavior influence (positively or negatively) the beliefs, attitudes, and behavior of an individual.

reference pricing A pricing strategy in which a firm gives customers comparative prices when considering purchase of a product so they are not viewing a price in isolation from prices of other choices.

referent power A channel member's ability to influence other members based on respect, admiration, or reverence.

regional market zones A group of countries that create formal relationships for mutual economic benefit through lower tariffs and reduced trade barriers.

relationship orientation Investing in keeping and cultivating profitable current customers instead of constantly having to invest in gaining new ones.

relationship-based enterprise A firm that strives to facilitate long-term, win-win relationships between buyers and sellers.

relative market expansion The first phase in the maturity stage of the product life cycle in which product category sales continue to grow but at a rate significantly less than in the growth stage.

reliability The percentage of time a product works without failure or stoppage.

repairability The ease of fixing a problem with a product.

repeat purchase A function of total demand that considers the number of products purchased by the same customer.

replacement purchase A function of total demand that considers the number of products purchased to replace existing products that have either become obsolete or malfunctioned.

reposition existing products A "new" product approach that targets new markets with existing products.

repositioning Using the marketing mix approach to change present consumer perceptions of a firm's product or service.

request for proposal (RFP) The document distributed to potential vendors that outlines an organization's product or service needs. It serves as a starting point from which vendors put together their product solution.

research design A framework for a study that directs the identification of a problem and collection and analysis of data.

research problem The definition of what information is needed to help management in a particular situation.

resellers Companies that buy products and then resell them to other businesses or consumers for a profit.

retail positioning The retailer's brand image in the consumer's mind.

retail target market The group of consumers targeted by a retailer.

retailer cooperative (co-op) The binding of retailers across a variety of product categories to gain cost and operating economies of scale in the channel.

retailer experience The overall experience a consumer has shopping at a retail location or online.

retailing Any business activity that creates value in the delivery of goods and services to consumers for their personal, nonbusiness consumption and is an essential component of the supply chain.

return on customer investment (ROCI) A calculation that estimates the projected financial returns from a customer. It is a useful strategic tool for deciding which customers deserve what levels of investment of various resources.

return on marketing investment (ROMI) What impact an investment in marketing has on a firm's success, especially financially.

reverse auctions When sellers bid prices to buyers and the purchase typically goes to the lowest bidder.

reverse logistics The process of moving goods back to the manufacturer or intermediary after purchase.

reward power A channel member's ability to coerce vendors by offering them incentives.

S

salary A fixed sum of money paid at regular intervals.

sales contests Short-term incentive programs designed to motivate salespeople to accomplish specific sales objectives.

sales experience The level of ease a consumer experiences in purchasing and returning merchandise at a retailer.

sales force composite Subjective method of forecasting that relies on the opinion of each member of the field sales staff.

sales orientation The increase of sales and consequently production capacity utilization by having salespeople "push" product into the hands of customers.

sales presentation The delivery of information relevant to meet the customer's needs.

sales promotion An inducement for an end-user consumer to buy a product or for a salesperson or someone else in the channel to sell it.

sales skill levels The individual's learned proficiency at performing necessary sales tasks.

sample A subgroup of the population selected for participation in research.

SBU-level strategic plan Planning that occurs within each of the firm's strategic business units (SBUs) designed to meet individual performance requirements and contribute satisfactorily to the overall corporate plan.

search ads Paid advertisements featured in Internet search engine results based on analysis of keywords entered in the search field.

search attributes Aspects of an offering that are physically observable before consumption.

seasonal discounts Discounts that reward the purchaser for shifting part of the inventory storage function away from the manufacturer.

SEC 10-K report A document filed with the Securities and Exchange Commission (SEC) that reports detailed information about a firm's operations and strategies.

secondary data Data collected for some other purpose than the problem currently being considered.

secondary group A reference group with which an individual has limited contact.

secondary target markets Market segments that have reasonable potential but for one reason or another are not best suited for development immediately.

seeding strategy A viral marketing approach to specific customers or groups of customers who then further stimulate the internal dynamics of the target market, thus resulting in the diffusion process (spread of the virus).

selective awareness A psychological tool an individual uses to help focus on what is relevant and eliminate what is not relevant.

selective distortion The process in which an individual can misunderstand information or make it fit existing beliefs.

selective distribution A distribution strategy in which goods are distributed only to a limited number of intermediaries.

selective perception Different meanings assigned to the same message by different receivers that are based on an array of individual differences.

selective retention The process of placing in one's memory only those stimuli that support existing beliefs and attitudes about a product or brand.

sender The source of the message in communication.

service A product that represents a bundle of benefits that can satisfy customer wants and needs without having physical form.

service blueprints Complete pictorial designs and flow charts of all of a service's activities from the first customer contact to the actual delivery of the service.

service dominant logic The logic that considers service and the customer experience to be the principal rationality of marketing.

service economy An economy that is predominantly comprised of service-related jobs.

service encounter The time period during which a customer interacts in any way with a service provider.

service failure When a service fails to meet the quality level promised by the provider.

service-profit chain The formalization of linkages between employee and customer aspects of service delivery.

service quality The formalization of the measurement of customer expectations of a service compared to perceptions of actual service performance.

service recovery The restoring of service quality to a level at or above the customer's expectations following a service failure.

service sector The portion of an economy that is comprised of service-related jobs.

SERVQUAL A measurement instrument designed to reflect the five dimensions of service quality.

shopping experience The consumer's holistic experience while looking for and evaluating products during the purchase decision process.

shopping goods Products that require consumers to do research and compare across product dimensions like color, size, features, and price.

short-term memory The information an individual recalls at the present time. Sometimes referred to as working memory.

showrooming Consumers going into a store and taking advantage of a product demonstration and the expertise of the salesperson and then buying the product from an online retailer at a lower price.

situation analysis An analysis of the macro- and micro-level environment within which a firm's marketing plan is being developed.

SKU (stock-keeping unit) Unique identification numbers used in tracking products through a distribution system, inventory management, and pricing.

slotting allowance (shelf fee) Extra incentives paid to wholesalers or retailers by the manufacturer for placing a particular product into inventory.

social class A ranking of individuals into harmonized groups based on demographic characteristics such as age, education, income, and occupation.

societal marketing The concept that, at the broadest level, members of society at large can be viewed as a stakeholder for marketing.

sorting The process of classifying products for sale through different channels.

specialty goods Unique products in which consumers' purchase decision is based on a defining characteristic.

specific warranties Explicit product performance promises related to components of the product.

sponsorships Spaces sold on high-traffic websites that enable companies to subsidize some section of the web page on the site.

stability pricing A pricing strategy in which a firm attempts to find a neutral set point for price that is neither low enough to raise the ire of competition nor high enough to put the value proposition at risk with customers.

stand-alone brands Brands created to be separate from a company brand that can insulate the company if there is a problem with the brand.

stock-out When an item is not in stock.

stop-to-market mistake When a product that is a good idea is prematurely eliminated during the screening process and ultimately never introduced to the market.

store brands Brands created by retailers for sale only in their store locations.

straight rebuy A buying decision that requires little evaluation because the products are purchased on a consistent, regular basis.

strategic alliances A market entry strategy designed to spread the risk of foreign investment among its partners. Examples of strategic alliances would be international joint ventures or direct foreign investment.

strategic marketing The long-term, firm-level commitment to investing in marketing—supported at the highest organization level—for the purpose of enhancing organizational performance.

strategic type Firms of a particular strategic type have a common strategic orientation and a similar combination of structure, culture, and processes consistent with that strategy. Four strategic types are prospectors, analyzers, defenders, and reactors—depending on a firm's approach to the competitive marketplace.

strategic vision Often included within a firm's mission statement, it is a discussion of what the company would like to become in the future.

strategy A comprehensive plan stating how the organization will achieve its mission and objectives.

style The look and feel of a product.

subculture A group within a culture that shares similar cultural artifacts created by differences in ethnicity, religion, race, or geography.

subjective forecasting methods Forecasting methods that do not rely primarily on sophisticated quantitative (empirical) analytical approaches.

supplier choice Selecting between multiple suppliers offering similar product configurations by examining their qualifications.

supply chain A complex logistics network characterized by high levels of coordination and integration among its members.

supply chain management The process of managing the aspects of the supply chain.

survey A quantitative research method that employs structured questionnaires given to a sample group of individuals representing the population of interest and intended to solicit specific responses to explicit questions.

sustainability The practicing of business that meets humanity's needs without harming future generations.

sustainable competitive advantage The resulting advantage a firm has when it invests in distinctive competencies.

SWOT analysis A convenient framework used to summarize key findings from a firm's situational analysis into a matrix of strengths, weaknesses, opportunities, and threats.

symbolic performance The image-building aspects of the product in terms of how it makes the consumer feel after purchase.

T

tactical marketing Marketing activities that take place at the functional or operational level of a firm.

tangibility The physical aspects of a product.

target marketing Evaluating market segments and making a decision about which among them shows the most promise for development.

target return on investment (ROI) A pricing strategy in which a bottom-line profit is established first and then pricing is set to achieve that target.

target return pricing A pricing decision made by considering fixed and variable costs and then demand forecasting to determine the price per unit.

technical selling Selling that requires a salesperson to have technical understanding of the product or service.

television home shopping A form of non-store retailing that involves showcasing products on a television network that can be ordered by the consumer.

tertiary target markets Market segments that may develop emerging attractiveness for investment in the future but that do not appear attractive at present.

time-series analysis Objective method of forecasting that relies on the analysis of historical data to develop a prediction for the future.

total demand The cumulative demand for a product over a given time period.

trade discounts An incentive to a channel member for performing some function in the channel that benefits the seller.

trade servicer Resellers such as retailers or distributors with whom the sales force does business.

trade show An industry- or company-sponsored event in which booths are set up for the dissemination of information about offerings to members of a channel.

traditional society A society dependent on agriculture as the primary driver of the economy; these economies lack the capabilities to industrialize and have high rates of illiteracy, which hinders advances in technology.

transaction cost analysis (TCA) A tool that measures the cost of using different types of selling agents.

transfer pricing The cost companies charge internally to move products between subsidiaries or divisions.

transportation and storage Commonly provided intermediary functions for producers that do not perform these functions themselves.

tying contract A formal requirement by the seller of an intermediary to purchase a supplementary product to qualify to purchase the primary product the intermediary wishes to buy.

U

undifferentiated target marketing (mass market) The broadest approach to target marketing that involves offering a product or service that can be perceived as valuable to a very generalized group of consumers.

uniform delivered pricing When the same delivery fee is charged to customers regardless of geographic location within a set area.

unsought goods Products that consumers do not seek out and often would rather not purchase at all.

users Actual customers of a product or service who have a great deal of input at various stages of the buying decision process but are typically not decision makers.

user expectations Subjective method of forecasting that relies on answers from customers regarding their expected consumption or purchase of a product.

utility The want-satisfying power of a good or service. There are four types of utility: form utility, time utility, place utility, and ownership utility.

V

VALS™ A proprietary psychographic instrument developed by Strategic Business Insights (SBI) that divides U.S. adults into groups based on their primary motivation and resources. The acronym VALS™ was originally derived from "values and lifestyles."

value A ratio of the bundle of benefits a customer receives from an offering compared to the costs incurred by the customer in acquiring that bundle of benefits.

value chain The synthesis of activities within a firm involved in designing, producing, marketing, delivering, and supporting its products or services.

value co-creation The combining of capabilities among members of a value network to create value.

value-creating activities Activities within a firm's value chain that act to increase the value of its products and services for its customers. These can take the form of either primary activities or support activities.

value network An overarching system of formal and informal relationships within which the firm participates to procure, transform, and enhance, and ultimately supply its offerings in final form within a market space.

value pricing A pricing strategy in which a firm attempts to take into account the role of price as it reflects the bundle of benefits sought by the customer.

value proposition The whole bundle of benefits a company promises to deliver to the customer, not just the benefits of the product itself.

variability The characteristic of a service in which its service quality can only be as good as that of its provider.

variable pricing A pricing tactic in which customers are allowed or encouraged to haggle about prices.

variety The number of different product categories offered by a retailer.

vending machine retailing The selling of merchandise or services that are stored in a machine, then dispensed to the consumer when the payment has been made.

vendor reliability A vendor's ability to meet contractual obligations including delivery time and service schedules.

vertical marketing system (VMS) Vertically aligned networks behaving and performing as a unified system.

viral marketing Entertaining and informative messaging created by a firm intended to be passed among individuals and delivered through online and other media channels.

W

wholesaler cooperative When retailers contract for varying degrees of exclusive dealings with a particular wholesaler.

workload method A method for determining the correct size of a company's sales force based on the premise that all salespeople should undertake an equal amount of work.

Z

zero-based budgeting An investment approach in that marketing goals and objectives are set for the upcoming year and then budget dollars are secured to support the achievement of those goals and objectives.

zone pricing When shippers set up geographic pricing zones based on the distance from the shipping location.

COMPANY INDEX

NAME INDEX

Golson, Jordan, 314
Gonda, Michael, 339
Gong, James J., 181
Goode, Caroline, 182
Goodstein, Ronald C., 208
Goodwin, Ross, 78
Goolsby, Jerry R., 78, 119, 138
Gorchels, Linda, 137
Gordon, Jonathon, 242
Gordon, Sarah, 265
Gosain, Sanjay, 315
Goudreau, J., 243, 244
Goyal, Anita, 289
Grabov, P., 339
Grace, Debra, 289
Graham, John, 39
Grant, John, 20
Grant, Susan, 265
Green, David, 181
Green, Penelope, 242
Greenberg, H. M., 401
Greenhouse, Linda, 340
Greenwood, Shannon, 372
Grewal, Dhruv, 21, 314, 372
Grewal, Rajdeep, 78
Griffith, David A., 51
Griin, B., 113
Gruber, V., 51
Gruca, Thomas S., 22
Grunbacher, Paul, 242
Guenzi, P., 402
Guilding, Chris, 315
Gumpert, Jason, 289
Gupta, Pola B., 20
Gupta, Suraksah, 265
Gürhan-Canli, Zeynep, 264
Gustafsson, Anders, 77, 137, 208
Gutierrez-Cilian, Jesus, 208

H

Haggett, Steve, 314
Haider, Murtaza, 138
Hair, Joe F., Jr., 138
Halzack, Sarah, 242, 243, 244, 315, 340
Handfield, Robert B., 243
Hanlon, Patrick, 78
Hanlon, Zachary, 183
Hann, Il-Horn, 315
Hanna, Joe B., 340
Hansen, Havard, 183
Hansotia, Behram, 139
Hanssens, Dominique M., 139
Harlam, Bari, 315
Harmal, Bari, 77
Harmancioglu, Nukhet, 243
Harris, James Edwin, 209
Hartley, Steven W., 224
Harvey, Michael G., 51
Hauser, John R., 243, 401
Hausman, Angela, 243
Havila, Virpi, 339
Hawking, Stephen, 263, 400
Hays, Constance L., 315
He, Chuan, 315
Heath, Davidson, 264
Heide, Jan B., 338
Heitmeyer, J., 181
Henderson, Naomi R., 113
Heneghan, Carolyn, 244

Hensel, Anna, 265
Hensgen, Tobin, 78
Herd, Teresa, 400
Herndon, Neil, 51
Herrman, Andreas, 77
Hershey, L., 402
Heskel, Julia, 289
Heskett, James L., 271, 274
Hess, James D., 314
Hesseldahl, Arik, 208
Hill, C. Jeanne, 51
Hill, Logan, 210
Himme, Alexander, 264
Hinz, Oliver, 372
Ho, Shu Hsun, 51
Ho, Teck H., 289
Hofstetter, Joerg, 338
Hogan, J., 402
Holmlund, Maria, 183
Homburg, Christian, 289
Homer, Pamela Miles, 264
Hong, Paul, 182
Hoornweg, Daniel, 96
Hopkins, Christopher D., 208, 403
Horner, Pamela Miles, 181
Houston, Mark B., 78
Howard, Daniel J., 314
Howell, Elizabeth, 265
Hoyer, Wayne D., 21, 289
Hoyt, Jennifer, 50
Hozier, George C., Jr., 113
Hsieh, Yi-Ting, 182
Huang, Jen-Hung, 51
Huang, Jun-Ying, 371
Huang, Li, 372
Huang, Rong, 265
Huber, Frank, 77
Hudson, Simon, 372
Huff, Sid L., 138
Hult, G. Tomas M., 51, 77, 182, 339
Hunger, J. David, 64, 70, 77, 78, 210
Hupfer, Maureen E., 181
Huston, John, 315
Hutt, Michael D., 78

I

Iezzio, Teresa, 79
Im, Subin, 208, 210
Indounas, Kostis A., 314, 315
Ingenbleek, Paul, 51, 112
Inglis, Robert, 78
Iqbal, Zafar, 243
Irani, Tracy, 401

J

Jackson, Janet, 263
Jagadish, H. V., 138
Jagpal, Sharan, 243
Jain, Chaman L., 78
Jain, Dipak C., 314
Jain, Shallendra Pratap, 265
Jamil, M., 243
Janiszewski, Chris, 182, 314
Jansen, Bernard J., 340
Japutra, Arnold, 264
Jaramillo, F., 403
Javalgi, Rajshekhar G., 289
Jaworski, Bernie, 21

Jayachandran, Satish, 78, 339, 371
Jayaraman, Vaidyanathan, 339
Jedidi, Kamel, 243
Jeuland, Abel P., 51
Jin, Hyun Seung, 401
Jing, Bing, 264
Jocumsen, Graham, 113
Johanson, Jan, 339
Johlke, M. C., 401, 402
Johnson, Devon S., 339
Johnson, James P., 182
Johnson, Julie T., 182, 402
Johnson, Lester W., 339
Johnson, Michael D., 77, 208
Johnston, Mark W., 21, 182, 390, 392, 393, 394, 396, 397
Johnston, Wesley J., 138, 183, 208
Jones, Riley, 77
Jones, Thomas O., 271, 274
Joo, Mingyu, 138
Jopez, T. B., 403
Joshi, Yogesh V., 243
Judd, L. Lynn, 339

K

Kale, Sudhir N., 208, 289
Kalliny, Morris, 243
Kalra, Ajay, 208
Kamakura, Wagner A., 51, 182, 209
Kambewa, Emma, 51
Kamdar, Nipoli, 315
Kandemir, Destan, 243
Kandil, Magda, 51
Kang, Wooseong, 51
Kannan, P. K., 113, 138
Kapferer, Jean-Noel, 182
Karatepe, Osman M., 371
Karray, Salma, 401
Karunaratna, Amal R., 339
Karwatka, Tomasz, 290
Katona, Zsolt, 372
Katsikeas, Constantine S., 183
Kavadias, Stylianos, 243
Keane, Michael P., 314
Keaveney, Susan M., 273
Keh, Hean Tat, 112
Keliner, Peter, 113
Kell, John, 22
Kelleher, Herb, 270
Keller, Kevin Lane, 339
Kennedy, Karen Norman, 78, 119, 138
Kerin, Roger A., 224, 314
Ketchen, David J., Jr., 182
Ketzenberg, Michael, 339
Khan, M. Sajid, 183
Kilgore, Patricia, 138
Kim, Eugene, 290
Kim, MinChung, 139
Kim, Myonung Soo, 340
Kim, Namwoon, 208, 265
Kim, Sang Yong, 401
Kim, Stephen Keysuk, 338
Kimmel, Allan J., 315
Kin, Yoo Jin, 265
King, Ceridwyn, 289
King, Stephen F., 137
Kingston, William, 264
Kint, Jason, 339
Kiridena, Senevi, 183

SUBJECT INDEX